W9-AGE-415

Fodor's

AUSTRIA

13th Edition

Where to Stay and Eat
for All Budgets

Must-See Sights
and Local Secrets

Ratings You Can Trust

Fodor's Travel Publications   New York, Toronto, London, Sydney, Auckland
www.fodors.com

FODOR'S AUSTRIA

Editors: Caroline Trefler, Mark Sullivan

Editorial Contributors: Uli Ehrhardt, Joyce Eisenberg, Diane Naar-Elphee, Karin Hanta, Daniela Lettner, Jess Moss, Giambattista Pace, Horst Ernst Reischenböck

Production Editor: Carrie Parker

Maps & Illustrations: David Lindroth, *cartographer;* Bob Blake, Rebecca Baer, *map editors;* William Wu, *information graphics*

Design: Fabrizio La Rocca, *creative director;* Guido Caroti, Siobhan O'Hare, *art directors;* Tina Malaney, Chie Ushio, Ann McBride, Jessica Walsh, *designers;* Melanie Marin, *senior picture editor*

Cover Photo (Marionettes, Salzburg): J-C. & D. Pratt/Photononstop

Production Manager: Angela L. McLean

13th Edition

ISBN 978-1-4000-0817-9

ISSN 0071-6340

SPECIAL SALES

This book is available at special discounts for bulk purchases for sales promotions or premiums. Special editions, including personalized covers, excerpts of existing books, and corporate imprints, can be created in large quantities for special needs. For more information, write to Special Markets/Premium Sales, 1745 Broadway, MD 6-2, New York, New York 10019, or e-mail specialmarkets@randomhouse.com.

AN IMPORTANT TIP & AN INVITATION

Although all prices, opening times, and other details in this book are based on information supplied to us at press time, changes occur all the time in the travel world, and Fodor's cannot accept responsibility for facts that become outdated or for inadvertent errors or omissions. So **always confirm information when it matters,** especially if you're making a detour to visit a specific place. Your experiences—positive and negative—matter to us. If we have missed or misstated something, **please write to us.** We follow up on all suggestions. Contact the Austria editor at editors@fodors.com or c/o Fodor's at 1745 Broadway, New York, NY 10019.

PRINTED IN THE UNITED STATES OF AMERICA

10 9 8 7 6 5 4 3 2 1

Be a Fodor's Correspondent

Your opinion matters. It matters to us. It matters to your fellow Fodor's travelers, too. And we'd like to hear it. In fact, we need to hear it.

When you share your experiences and opinions, you become an active member of the Fodor's community. That means we'll not only use your feedback to make our books better, but we'll publish your names and comments whenever possible. Throughout our guides, look for "Word of Mouth," excerpts of your unvarnished feedback.

Here's how you can help improve Fodor's for all of us.

Tell us when we're right. We rely on local writers to give you an insider's perspective. But our writers and staff editors—who are the best in the business—depend on you. Your positive feedback is a vote to renew our recommendations for the next edition.

Tell us when we're wrong. We're proud that we update most of our guides every year. But we're not perfect. Things change. Hotels cut services. Museums change hours. Charming cafés lose charm. If our writer didn't quite capture the essence of a place, tell us how you'd do it differently. If any of our descriptions are inaccurate or inadequate, we'll incorporate your changes in the next edition and will correct factual errors at fodors.com immediately.

Tell us what to include. You probably have had fantastic travel experiences that aren't yet in Fodor's. Why not share them with a community of like-minded travelers? Maybe you chanced upon a beach or bistro or B&B that you don't want to keep to yourself. Tell us why we should include it. And share your discoveries and experiences with everyone directly at fodors.com. Your input may lead us to add a new listing or highlight a place we cover with a "Highly Recommended" star or with our highest rating, "Fodor's Choice."

Give us your opinion instantly at our feedback center at www.fodors.com/feedback. You may also e-mail editors@fodors.com with the subject line "Austria Editor." Or send your nominations, comments, and complaints by mail to Austria Editor, Fodor's, 1745 Broadway, New York, NY 10019.

You and travelers like you are the heart of the Fodor's community. Make our community richer by sharing your experiences. Be a Fodor's correspondent.

Gute Reise!

Tim Jarrell, Publisher

CONTENTS

ABOUT
THIS BOOK

Our Ratings

Sometimes you find terrific travel experiences and sometimes they just find you. But usually the burden is on you to select the right combination of experiences. That's where our ratings come in.

As travelers we've all discovered a place so wonderful that its worthiness is obvious. And sometimes that place is so unique that superlatives don't do it justice: you just have to be there to know. These sights, properties, and experiences get our highest rating, **Fodor's Choice**, indicated by orange stars throughout this book.

Black stars highlight sights and properties we deem **Highly Recommended**, places that our writers, editors, and readers praise again and again for consistency and excellence.

By default, there's another category: any place we include in this book is by definition worth your time, unless we say otherwise. And we will.

Disagree with any of our choices? Care to nominate a place or suggest that we rate one higher? Visit our feedback center at www.fodors.com/feedback.

Budget Well

Hotel and restaurant price categories from ¢ to $$$$ are defined in the opening pages of each chapter. For attractions, we always give standard adult admission fees; reductions are usually available for children, students, and senior citizens. Want to pay with plastic? **AE, D, DC, MC, V** following restaurant and hotel listings indicate whether American Express, Discover, Diners Club, MasterCard, and Visa are accepted.

Restaurants

Unless we state otherwise, restaurants are open for lunch and dinner daily. We mention dress only when there's a specific requirement and reservations only when they're essential or not accepted—it's always best to book ahead.

Hotels

Hotels have private bath, phone, TV, and air-conditioning and operate on the European Plan (aka EP, meaning without meals), unless we specify that they use the Continental Plan (CP, with a continental breakfast), Breakfast Plan (BP, with a full breakfast), or Modified American Plan (MAP, with breakfast and dinner) or are all-inclusive (AI, including all meals and most activities). We always

list facilities but not whether you'll be charged an extra fee to use them, so when pricing accommodations, find out what's included.

Many Listings

★ Fodor's Choice
★ Highly recommended
✉ Physical address
✛ Directions
🏛 Mailing address
☎ Telephone
🖷 Fax
⊕ On the Web
✎ E-mail
🎫 Admission fee
🕓 Open/closed times
Ⓤ Metro stations
💳 Credit cards

Hotels & Restaurants

🏨 Hotel
🛏 Number of rooms
⟋ Facilities
🍴 Meal plans
✕ Restaurant
⟋ Reservations
╲ Smoking
🆒 BYOB
✕🏨 Hotel with restaurant that warrants a visit

Outdoors

⛳ Golf
⛺ Camping

Other

🕓 Family-friendly
⇨ See also
✉ Branch address
☞ Take note

WHEN TO GO

Austria has two main tourist seasons. The weather usually turns glorious around Easter and holds until about mid-October, sometimes later. Because much of the country remains "undiscovered," you will usually find crowds only in the major cities and resorts. May and early June, September, and October are the most pleasant months for travel; there is less demand for restaurant tables, and hotel prices tend to be lower. A foreign invasion takes place between Christmas and New Year's Day and over the long Easter weekend, and hotel rooms in Vienna are then at a premium.

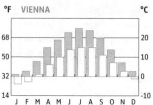

Climate
Austria has four distinct seasons, all fairly mild. But because of altitudes and the Alpine divide, temperatures and dampness vary considerably from one part of the country to another; for example, northern Austria's winter is often overcast and dreary, while the southern half of the country basks in sunshine. The eastern part of the country, especially Vienna and the areas near the Czech border, can become bitterly cold in winter. The *Föhn* is a wind that makes the country as a whole go haywire. It comes from the south, is warm, and announces itself by clear air, blue skies, and long wisps of cloud. Whatever the reason, the Alpine people (all the way to Vienna) begin acting up; some become obnoxiously aggressive, others depressive, many people have headaches, and (allegedly) accident rates rise. The Föhn breaks with clouds and rain.

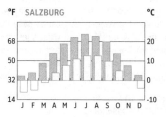

WHAT'S WHERE

1 Vienna. Vienna mixes old-word charm with elements of a modern metropolis. The city's neighborhoods offer a journey thick with history and architecture, and the famous coffeehouses are havens for an age-old coffee-drinking ritual.

2 Vienna Environs. Vienna is surrounded with enticing options such as hiking in the Vienna Woods—the Wiener-wald—on the city's outskirts and sipping the famous white wine in Gumpoldskirchen, a tiny village south of Vienna.

3 Eastern Austria. Eastern Austria offers a wonderful contrast of simple, exceptionally charming pleasures. Burgenland is a region of castle-capped hills, fields of grain, and vineyards, while Graz, the capital of Styria, is the country's second-largest city.

4 The Danube Valley. The famously blue Danube courses through Austria past medieval abbeys, fanciful Baroque monasteries, verdant pastures, and compact riverside villages. A convenient base is Linz, Austria's third-largest city, and probably its most underrated.

5 Salzburg. Salzburg is an elegant city with a rich musical heritage that also draws visitors for its museums and architecture, the Trapp family history, old-fashioned cafés, and glorious fountains.

6 Salzkammergut. The Salzkammergut stretches across three states—from Salzburg through Styria to Upper Austria—and includes Austria's Lake District. Hallstatt is touted as one of the world's prettiest lakeside villages.

7 Carinthia. Carinthia is the country's sunniest (and southernmost) province. Here you'll find the Austrian Riviera, a blend of mountains, valleys, and placid blue-green lakes with lovely resorts.

8 Eastern Alps. Panoramic little towns, spas, and an array of sports highlight this section of Austria. No road in Europe matches the Grossglockner High Alpine Highway, the most spectacular pass through the Alps.

9 Innsbruck & Tirol. The Tirol is a region graced with cosmopolitan cities and monuments, but with the glorious Alps playing the stellar role, Nature steals every scene.

10 Vorarlberg. Tops on all Vorarlberg visitors' lists are the fresh air of the Bregenz Music Festivale; the Bregenzerwald—forests of Wagnerian romanticism; and its powdery skiing regions.

CZECH REPUBLIC

Waidhofen

Gmünd
Zwettl
Horn
Poysdorf

LOWER AUSTRIA
(NIEDERÖSTERREICH)

Schärding
Freistadt
Krems
Stockerau

Linz
4

Eferding
Enns
Melk
St. Pölten
Vienna
1

Ried
Wels
Danube (Donau)
A1
A21
Mödling
Danube
Hainburg

UPPER AUSTRIA
(OBERÖSTERREICH)
Steyr
Scheibbs
Baden
Bruck

Vöcklabruck
6
Gmunden
Wiener
Neustadt
Neusiedler
See

A1
5
St. Wolfgang
Mariazell
Neunkirchen
Eisenstadt

Bad Ischl
Bad Aussee
Enns
Mürzzuschlag
2

Bischofshofen
Liezen
Kapfenberg
BURGENLAND
3

Radstadt
Leoben
Bruck a. d. Mur
Hártberg

St. Johann
A10
Knittelfeld
Judenburg
STYRIA
(STEIERMARK)
Fürstenfeld

CARINTHIA
(KÄRNTEN)
Graz
Feldbach
HUNGARY

Spittal
7
St. Veit
Bad
Gleichenberg
Bad
Radkersburg

Feldkirchen
A2
Mura

Drau
Villach
Klagenfurt
Drava

SLOVENIA

QUINTESSENTIAL AUSTRIA

The Viennese Coffeehouse

Twice the Ottoman armies stood at the gates of Vienna (in the 16th and 17th centuries), and twice they were turned back after long, bitter sieges. Although the Turks never captured the city, they left a lasting legacy: the art of preparing and consuming coffee. Emotions about coffee tend to run high throughout Austria: ask anyone on the street where you can get a good cup of coffee or homemade *Apfelstrudel*, and you're likely to get a lengthy and passionate exposition on why you must try a certain coffeehouse. Many Austrians spend a good part of the day sitting over a single cup of coffee in their favorite coffeehouse while reading the newspaper, discussing business or politics, or just catching up on the local gossip. As any Austrian will tell you, many of the world's great cultural moments had their genesis in coffeehouse discussions in Vienna. You'll hear about where Leo Trotsky regularly played chess while working out the subtleties of Communist theory (at Café Central), where Gustav Klimt and Egon Schiele worked out their ideas for modern art (Café Museum), and where Sigmund Freud spent Wednesday evenings laying the foundation for modern psychoanalytic theory (Kaffeehaus Korb). Although more and more generic Italian espresso bars and even Starbuck's coffee shops (gasp!) are cropping up in urban areas, these fulfill another purpose entirely and cannot begin to compete with the role the traditional Viennese coffeehouse has in defining Austrian identity.

The Outdoors

"Land der Berge, Land am Strome" ("Land of mountains, land on the river") is the first verse of the Austrian national anthem, and it sums up what Austrians treasure most about their country: the breathtaking and diverse landscapes.

If you want to get a sense of contemporary Austrian culture and indulge in some of its pleasures, start by familiarizing yourself with the rituals of daily life. These are a few highlights—things you can take part in with relative ease.

Austrians take every opportunity they can to get out and enjoy their natural surroundings. The mania for the outdoors transcends all age groups. Ten year olds, determined to follow in the footsteps of great Austrian skiers like Hermann Maier, will overtake you on the ski slope. And on a warm summer day when you finally reach that mountain hut in an Alpine meadow near the peak, out of breath after a five-hour hike, you'll find a score of 70 year olds who beat you there, occupying the best spots and enjoying glasses of schnapps and beer on the sunny terrace.

Music

Austrians are serious about their music. Cities and towns vie to put their special venue or music festival in the limelight. Top of the bill is of course Vienna, with the Vienna State Opera and the Vienna Philharmonic Orchestra. But even the Viennese are prepared to make the seven-hour journey to Bregenz, where elaborate opera productions on a giant stage overlooking Lake Constance occur every summer. Summer evenings in the Alps can often be quite chilly and wet, but music-hungry Austrians will brave even a downpour, sitting on heavy blankets and wearing parkas. Other events, such as the annual Salzburg festival, provide the perfect backdrop for society-conscious Austrians who gather in their most opulent evening attire to admire each other (and to hear good music, too). Such spectacles, however, are more the exception than the rule. Many Viennese, dressed only in jeans and a pullover, will go several times a week to the opera. They won't pay the high price for a seat but instead pay a few euros for a spot in the standing room (where they know the acoustics are better anyway).

IF YOU LIKE

Wine

Although not as well known as regional varieties in France and Italy, Austrian wines, particularly whites, are now recognized by wine experts around the world for their excellent quality. The center of wine production in Austria is found in northern and eastern Lower Austria, in Burgenland, in Styria, and on the hilly terraces overlooking Vienna. Whites account for nearly 70% of production, but the quality of Austrian reds continues to improve. The most popular white variety is grüner veltliner, followed by riesling, sauvignon blanc, and pinot blanc (often labeled as weissburgunder). The major red varieties are zweigelt and blaufränkisch. Wines to look for include:

- **Wieninger.** Some of the best wine in the Vienna region comes from this winery—and at reasonable prices. Look for sauvignon blanc and grüner veltliner, but also a very complex chardonnay.

- **Bründlmayer.** This house in Kamptal in Lower Austria produces some of Austria's most acclaimed whites, especially grüner veltliner and riesling.

- **Umathum.** Austrian reds are drawing more and more attention from the wine press, including those produced in south Burgenland at this winery known for its full-bodied pinot noirs and a very interesting St. Laurent.

Skiing

Austria is synonymous with great skiing. Aside from world-class runs, the close proximity of the many ski areas to one another and an excellent infrastructure make moving around from one place to another quick and easy. The action is concentrated on the big ski regions of the Arlberg, Tirol, and Land Salzburg for good reason—here, many individual ski areas span and connect multiple mountains and valleys, and they are linked together with common ski passes. The question, then, is where to begin? The answer depends on what you're looking to do. Posh resorts such as Lech am Arlberg and Kitzbühel are popular with the society crowd—and usually come with the price to fit. Nearby villages, however, are often much less expensive, and their lifts serve the same large ski domain.

Here are some classics to get you started:

- **Lech am Arlberg and St. Anton am Arlberg.** Exclusive, and a paradise for purists.

- **Kitzbühel, Tirol.** The elegant resort in the heart of Tirol has well-groomed pistes.

- **Sölden, Tirol.** The snow conditions are excellent, and so are the spa facilities.

Castles, Palaces & Abbeys

It seems that if you travel a few miles in any direction in Austria, you are confronted with a fairy-tale castle, an ostentatious palace, or an ornate Baroque abbey. It's easy to be overwhelmed by all of the architectural splendor, the fanciful decorations, and the often impossibly intricate mythical lore attached to these sites. The secret to overcoming the "not-another-castle" syndrome is to take your time at each, and not to limit yourself to the site alone.

Discover how rewarding it can be to leave the palace grounds or castle walls and to explore the surroundings, whether a city, small village, or mountainside. Around the corner might be a lovely chapel, a spectacular view, or an excellent local restaurant that, because it is somewhat off the beaten path and perhaps not (yet) in any guidebook, is yours alone to appreciate.

- **Schönbrunn Palace, Vienna.** You could spend an entire day here (and still not see all the rooms in the palace), or choose from several shorter tours of one of Austria's premier attractions, the palace built by Empress Maria Theresa.

- **Melk, Lower Austria.** Perched on a hill overlooking the Danube and the Wachau, the giant abbey of Melk features imposing architecture, lovely gardens, and one of Europe's most resplendent Baroque libraries.

- **Fortress Hohensalzburg, Salzburg.** The medieval fortress, central Europe's largest, towers over Salzburg and offers lavish state rooms, a collection of medieval art, a late-Gothic chapel, and magnificent views over the entire region.

Biking

Over the last decade or so, Austria has invested a lot in the construction and maintenance of thousands of kilometers of cycle routes along its rivers and through its lush valleys. The close proximity of many sites of interest means that cycling is often the best means of leisurely exploration. Many hotels now provide bikes to their guests for a nominal fee, or your hotel can direct you to a nearby bike-rental shop. You will need a Radkarte (a map with the local bike routes), available at hotels or at the local tourist office. Here are some of the best routes that combine cultural attractions with stimulating landscapes:

- **The Wachau, Lower Austria.** The Donauradweg—or Danube bike route— follows the Danube all the way from Passau to Vienna. The Wachau is not far from Vienna, and it offers one of the most beautiful landscapes along Austria's stretch of the Danube. Very well-maintained bike paths take you past the abbey of Melk and through the charming wine-making towns of Spitz, Weissenkirchen, and Krems. The best time to go is spring, when the apricot trees are in glorious blossom, or in early fall, when grapes hang ripe and heavy on the vines of the terraced slopes.

- **Mozart Radweg, Salzburg.** The Mozart Route is a circuit around Salzburg, the city where the great musician was born. Leaving Salzburg the route passes through stations associated with Mozart's life and work, and continues on through the Salzburger Seenland, an arrestingly beautiful landscape of mountain lakes, castles, and small villages.

GREAT ITINERARIES

VIENNA TO VORARLBERG

This itinerary travels the country from end to end, hitting the heights and seeing the sights—all in a one-week to 10-day trip.

Days 1–3: Vienna

Austria's glorious past is evident everywhere, but especially where this tour begins, in Vienna. Get to know the city by trolley with a sightseeing tour of the Ringstrasse. Take in the Kunsthistoriches Museum (the incredible detail of the famous Brueghel paintings could keep you fascinated for hours), walk along Kärntnerstrasse to magnificent St. Stephen's Cathedral, and spend an afternoon in one of the city's cozy coffeehouses. Devote a half day to Schönbrunn Palace, and set aside an evening for a visit to a jovial *Heurige* wine tavern. ⇨ *Chapter 1: Vienna.*

Day 4: Danube River from Vienna to Linz

To zoom from Vienna to Linz by autobahn would be to miss out on one of Austria's most treasured sights, the blue Danube. To tour some quaint wine villages, follow the "Austrian Romantic Road" (Route 3), along the north bank of the river, instead of the speedier A1 autobahn. Cross to the south side of the Danube to the breathtaking Baroque abbey at Melk, and along the way visit the 1,000-year-old town of Krems and picture-perfect Dürnstein, in the heart of the Wachau wine region. ⇨ *Chapter 4: The Danube Valley.*

Days 5 & 6: Linz

Fast-forward into Austria's future with a stop in progressive Linz, the country's third-largest city. Linz is a busy port on the Danube and an important center for trade and business. Techno geeks will enjoy the Ars Electronica Center; others can wander the beautifully restored medieval courtyards of the Altstadt (Old Town). For great views, ride the city's Pöstlingbergbahn, the world's steepest mountain railway, or opt for a Danube steamer cruise to Enns. ⇨ *Chapter 4: The Danube Valley.*

Days 7 & 8: Salzkammergut

For Austria in all its Hollywood splendor, head to the idyllic Salzkammergut, better known as the Lake District, where *The Sound of Music* was filmed. The town of Bad Ischl—famous for its operetta festival and pastries—makes a good base. Travel south to Ebensee on Route 145 toward Hallstatt, one of Austria's most photographed lakeside villages. Return to Bad Ischl, then head west to St. Wolfgang and St. Gilgen for swimming and sailing. ⇨ *Chapter 6: Salzkammergut.*

Days 9 & 10: Salzburg

This is a city made for pedestrians, with an abundance of churches, palaces, mansions, and—as befits the birthplace of Mozart—music festivals. Stroll through the old city center with its wrought-iron shop signs, tour the medieval Fortress Hohensalzburg, and relax in the Mirabell Gardens (where the von Trapp children "Do-Re-Mi"-ed). Children of all ages will adore the famed Marionettentheater. ⇨ *Chapter 5: Salzburg.*

Days 11 & 12: Innsbruck & Tirol

Tour Innsbruck's treasures—including the famous Golden Roof mansion and the Hofburg—but do as the Tiroleans do and spend time reveling in the high-mountain majesty. After all, Innsbruck is the only major city in the Alps. For a splendid panorama, take the Hungerburgbahn (cable railway) to the Hafelekar, high above the Inn Valley. For a trip through the quaint villages around Innsbruck, ride the Stubaitalbahn, a charming old-time train, to Neustift, or head by bus to the Stubai Glacier for year-round skiing. ⇨ *Chapter 9: Innsbruck & Tirol.*

Days 13 & 14: Bregenz

Taking the Arlberg Pass (or the much more scenic Silvretta High Alpine Highway), head to the city of Bregenz, capital of Vorarlberg. Bregenz owes its character as much to neighboring Switzerland and Germany as to Austria, and is most appealing in summer, when sun-worshippers crowd the shores of Lake Constance to enjoy an opera festival set on the world's largest outdoor floating stage. Take a lake excursion and explore Bregenz's medieval Oberstadt (Upper Town). ⇨ *Chapter 10: Vorarlberg.*

TIPS

❶ There is frequent train service between the major cities in this itinerary. Side trips into the countryside are possible by bus or train. Trains leave every half hour from the Westbahnhof in Vienna, arriving in Linz in about two hours. From Linz it is 2½ hours to the Salzburg Hauptbahnhof and another two hours to the Innsbruck terminal, then another 2½ hours to Bregenz.

❷ For a more romantic kickoff, travel by a DDSG/Blue Danube Schiffahrt riverboat from Vienna to Linz (departs from Vienna daily at 7 AM).

GREAT ITINERARIES

MOUNTAIN MAGIC

This is a trip where Alpine glory is all around you: meadows and forests set against a backdrop of towering craggy peaks, and gentle wooded rambles that lead to clear mountain lakes and storybook castles. Let go of your worries and let the natural beauty of the countryside work its magic.

Days 1 & 2: Bad Ischl/St. Wolfgang

The villages and lakes of the Salzkammergut region extend south from Salzburg like a string of pearls. Base yourself in Bad Ischl, a first-class spa in the heart of the Lake District. From there, head 16 km (10 mi) west to St. Wolfgang, one of the most photo-friendly villages in Austria. For the most scenic surroundings, park in nearby Strobl and hop one of the lake ferries to the pedestrian-only village, where you can relax with a coffee on the terrace of the famous Weisses Rössl (White Horse Inn), marvel at the 16th-century Michael Pacher altarpiece in the parish church, and take the railway up the 5,800-foot Schafberg peak for gasp-inducing vistas. ⇨ *Chapter 6: Salzkammergut.*

Day 3: Hallstatt

Set on fjordlike Hallstätter See, this jewel is an optical illusion perched between water and mountain—a tight grouping of terraced fishermen's cottages and churches offering, at first glance, no apparent reason why it doesn't tumble into the lake. On a sunny day the views of the lake and village, considered the oldest settlement in Austria, are spectacular, and on a misty morning they are even more so. Consider a canoe outing, or tour the Hallstatt salt mine, the oldest in the world. ⇨ *Chapter 6: Salzkammergut.*

Day 4: Werfen

Take in the birds-of-prey show at the formidable Burg Hohenwerfen castle, built in the 11th century, tour the Eisriesenwelt ("World of the Ice Giants")—the largest collection of ice caves in Europe—and cap the day with dinner at Obauer, one of Austria's finest restaurants. ⇨ *Chapter 8: Eastern Alps.*

Day 5: Zell am See

Some 50 km (30 mi) from Werfen, the charming lake resort of Zell am See is nestled under the 6,000-foot Schmittenhöhe mountain. Ride the cable car from the center of town for a bird's-eye view, then take the narrow-gauge Pinzgauer railroad through the Salzach river valley to famous Krimmler Falls. ⇨ *Chapter 8: Eastern Alps.*

Day 6: Heiligenblut

Head skyward over the dizzying Hochglockner High Alpine Highway (open May–October) to one of Austria's loveliest villages, Heiligenblut, which fans out across the upper Möll Valley with fabulous views of the Grossglockner, at 12,470 feet the highest mountain in Austria. ⇨ *Chapter 8: Eastern Alps.*

Day 7: Kitzbühel/Going

Travel to the glamorous resort town of Kitzbühel for a bit of window-shopping and celebrity-spotting, then continue to Going, Ellmau, and Söll along Route 312. These villages have superb restaurants and hotels, but the real reason to overnight here is to admire the view of the rugged "Wild Emperor," one of the most beautiful mountains in the Alps. ⇨ *Chapter 9: Innsbruck & Tirol.*

Days 8 & 9: Rattenberg/Alpbach

In these two charming villages you might think you've been transported back in time, if it weren't for all the tourists roaming the ancient streets. Rattenberg has colorful medieval facades, famous glassware, and a delightful Inn River promenade, and the narrow, flower-bedecked streets of tiny Alpbach are set within one of Tirol's most bucolic valleys. Take the Wiedersbergerhorn gondola to the top of the mountain for a panorama, then hike back to town. End your trip in Innsbruck, 32 km (20 mi) west. ⇨ *Chapter 9: Innsbruck & Tirol.*

TIPS

Although it is much simpler to travel this route by car, it can also be undertaken using public transportation (note that many trains do not run on Sunday). Trains link Salzburg, Bad Ischl, and Hallstatt; travel to St. Wolfgang by post bus. From Hallstatt, hop the train to Bad Aussee and on to Irdning, where you may have to change trains to Bischofshofen before reaching Zell am See. Travel to and from Heiligenblut by bus. Trains will take you to Kitzbühel but not to Going, so bus it from Kitz, and then continue by bus to the train station in Wörgl, which is on the main line to Innsbruck. This line includes a stop in Rattenberg, but the bus is the only way to get to Alpbach.

Vienna

WORD OF MOUTH

"We walked through the Hofburg complex, admiring the architecture, and bought tickets for the Schatzkammer (Imperial Treasury). The visit inside was well worth it. Excellent collection of cloaks and dresses of kings of a bygone era. The jewels were jaw-dropping: a 2680 carat emerald, a 450 carat aquamarine! . . . Then we walked to Hotel Sacher to have their famed Sacher Torte. It looked as beautiful as it tasted. Delicious."

—indiancouple

Updated by
Diane Naar-
Elphee

ONE OF THE GREAT CAPITALS of Europe, Vienna was for centuries the main stamping grounds for the Habsburg rulers of the Austro-Hungarian Empire. The empire is long gone, but many reminders of the city's imperial heyday remain, carefully preserved by the tradition-loving Viennese. When it comes to the arts, the glories of the past are particularly evergreen, thanks to the cultural legacy created by the many artistic geniuses nourished here.

From the late 18th century on, Vienna's culture—particularly its music—was famous throughout Europe. Haydn, Mozart, Beethoven, Schubert, Brahms, Strauss, Mahler, and Bruckner all lived in the city, composing glorious music still played in concert halls all over the world. And at the tail end of the 19th century the city's artists and architects—Gustav Klimt, Egon Schiele, Oskar Kokoschka, Josef Hoffmann, Otto Wagner, and Adolf Loos ("Form follows function") among them—brought about an unprecedented artistic revolution, one that swept away the past and set the stage for the radically experimental art of the 20th century. Innovation can still be seen in the city's contemporary arts-and-crafts galleries—even in the glinting, Space Needle-like object that hovers over the north end of Vienna—actually the city's waste incinerator, designed by the late, great artist Friedensreich Hundertwasser.

At the close of World War I the Austro-Hungarian Empire was dismembered, and Vienna lost its cherished status as the seat of imperial power. Its influence was much reduced, and its population began to decline (unlike that of Europe's other great cities), falling from around 2 million to the current 1.8 million. Today, however, the city's future looks brighter, for with the collapse of the Iron Curtain, Vienna regained its traditional status as one of the main hubs of Central Europe.

When Vienna was founded as a Roman military encampment around AD 100, the walled garrison was not built on the Danube's main stream. The wide, present-day Danube did not take shape until the late 19th century, when, to prevent flooding, its various branches were rerouted and merged.

The Romans maintained their camp for some 300 years (the emperor Marcus Aurelius is thought to have died in Vindobona, as it was called, in 180), not abandoning the site until around 400. The settlement survived the Roman withdrawal, however, and by the 13th century development was sufficient to require new city walls to the south. According to legend, the walls were financed by the English: in 1192 the local duke kidnapped England's King Richard I (the Lion-Hearted), en route home from the Third Crusade, and held him prisoner upriver in Dürnstein for several months then turned him over to the Austrian king after two years, until he was expensively ransomed by his mother, Eleanor of Aquitaine.

Vienna's third set of walls dates from 1544, when the existing walls were improved and extended. The new fortifications were built by the Habsburg dynasty, which ruled the Austro-Hungarian Empire for an astonishing 640 years, beginning with Rudolf I in 1273 and ending with Karl I in 1918. These walls stood until 1857, when Emperor Franz Josef decreed that they finally be demolished and replaced by the series of boulevards that make up the tree-lined Ringstrasse.

During medieval times the city's growth was relatively slow, and its heyday as a European capital did not begin until 1683, after a huge force of invading Turks laid siege to the city for a two-month period before being routed by an army of Habsburg allies. Among the supplies that the fleeing Turks left behind were sacks filled with coffee beans, and it was these beans, so the story goes, that gave a local entrepreneur the idea of opening the first public coffeehouse; they remain a Viennese institution to this day.

The passing of the Turkish threat encouraged a Viennese building boom in the Baroque style, the architectural choice of the day. Flamboyant, triumphant, joyous, and extravagantly ostentatious, the new art form—imported from Italy—transformed the city into a vast theater over the course of the 17th and 18th centuries. Life became a dream—the gorgeous dream of the Baroque, with its gilt madonnas and cherubs; its soaring, twisted columns; its painted heavens on ceilings; its graceful domes. In the early 19th century a reaction began to set in as middle-class industriousness and sober family values led the way to a new epoch characterized by the Biedermeier style. Then followed the Strauss era—that lighthearted period that conjures up imperial balls, "Wine, Women, and Song," heel clicking, and hand kissing. Today's visitors will find that each of these eras has left its mark on Vienna, making it a city filled with a special grace. It is this grace that gives Vienna the cohesive architectural character that sets the city so memorably apart from its great rivals—London, Paris, and Rome.

ORIENTATION & PLANNING

GETTING ORIENTED

The Medieval Heart of the 1st District. Time seems to stand still in this part of Vienna, where hidden architectural treasures await discovery down narrow lanes and cobbled streets. This is certainly one of the quieter parts of the city.

Baroque Gems & Cozy Cafes. Sip a *mélange* while admiring the rich facades of Viennese aristocrats' former palatial homes from a comfy café. Waiters, dressed as if they're off to a ball, serve coffee and cakes to the regulars.

From Michaelerplatz to the Graben: Vienna's Shop Window. Check out ancient Roman ruins and the glass-fronted shops showcasing the fashion world's most famous labels. Make sure you don't miss the ultimate in patisserie pleasures at Demel's.

The Hofburg: An Imperial City. The huge former Habsburg winter abode for seven centuries now houses many of the belongings that the family left behind. The Imperial Treasury advertises with the slogan "We don't have the emperors but we do have their jewels."

GREAT ITINERARIES

Like a well-bred grande dame, Vienna doesn't rush about, and neither should you. We suggest sauntering through its stately streets and marveling at its Baroque palaces, but don't forget to leave time to dream an afternoon away at a cozy *Kaffeehaus*.

IF YOU HAVE 3 DAYS

Begin with an organized sightseeing tour, which will describe the highlights. Plan to spend time at the **Stephansdom** ❶ and a full afternoon at **Schönbrunn Palace** ❽❾. Reserve the second day for art, tackling the **Kunsthistoriches Museum** ❸❾ after breakfast; then, for lunch and afternoon enjoyment head for the **MuseumsQuartier** ❸❽, which comprises several major modern art collections. If your tastes tend to the grand and royal, visit instead the Old Master drawings at the **Albertina Museum** ❻❶ and the **Belvedere Palace** ❹❻. Do as the Viennese do, and fill in any gaps with stops at cafés, reserving evenings for relaxing over music or wine. On the third day, head for the **Spanische Reitschule** ❻❼ and watch the Lipizzaners prance through morning training. While you're in the neighborhood, view the sparkling imperial jewels in the Imperial Treasury, the **Schatzkammer** ❼❷, and the glitzy **Silberkammer** ❻❾, the museum of court silver and tableware, and take in one of Vienna's most spectacular Baroque settings, the Grand Hall of the **Hofbibliothek** ❼❻. For a total contrast either spend the morning viewing the vegetables and vendors on **Naschmarkt** ❹❶ (the biggest and most attractive food market) and having lunch at one of the many eateries there (don't overlook the superb Jugendstil buildings on the north side of the market) and then grab a city bike and head out to the Prater amusement park in the afternoon for a ride on the giant Ferris wheel, then cycle along the Danube and end the day in a wine restaurant on the outskirts, perhaps in Stammersdorf, Sievering, or Nussdorf.

IF YOU HAVE 5 DAYS

Spend your first three days as outlined above. On your fourth day, get better acquainted with the 1st District—the heart of the city. Treasures here range from Roman ruins to the residences of Mozart and Beethoven, the **Mozarthaus** ❺❶ and the **Pasqualatihaus** ❷❺; then, slightly afield, the **Freud Haus** ❷❻ (in the 9th District) or the oddball **Hundertwasserhaus** (in the 3rd). Put it all in contemporary perspective with a tour of the **Staatsoper** ❻❹, the State Opera. On the fifth day, fill in some of the blanks by taking a walk to the **Secession Building** ❹❸ with Gustav Klimt's *Beethoven Frieze*. If you're still game for museums, head for any one of the less-usual offerings, such as the Jewish Museum, the Haus der Musik, or the Ephesus Museum in the **Hofburg,** or visit the city's historical museum, **Wien Museum Karlsplatz** ❹❺; by now, you'll have acquired a good concept of the city and its background, so the exhibits will make more sense. Cap the day by visiting the **Kaisergruft** ❻❷ under the Kapuzinerkirche to view the tombs of the Habsburgs responsible for so much of Vienna.

TOP REASONS TO GO

Ride the Ringstrasse. Hop on streetcar No. 1 or No. 2 and travel full circle along Vienna's best-known avenue. Those monumental buildings along it reflect the imperial splendor of yesteryear.

World of Music. Delight your eyes and ears with a night out at the State Opera or Musikverein to experience what secured Vienna the title "heart of the music world."

Kunst Historisches Museum. Enjoy the classic collection of fine art, including the best of Breughel, Titian, Rembrandt, and Rubens, at Austria's leading museum.

Schönbrunn Palace. Rococo romantics and Habsburg acolytes should step back in time and spend a half day experiencing the Habsburgs' former summer home.

An extended coffee break. Savor the true flavor of Vienna at some of its great café landmarks. Every afternoon around 4 the coffee-and-pastry ritual of *Kaffeejause* takes place from one end of the city to the other. For historical overtones, head for the Café Central or the opulent Café Landtmann, or elegant Café Sacher. Café Hawelka is the contrasting seat of the smoky art scene.

The Ringstrasse: Gems of the "Ring." For many Vienna visitors, this is the most beautiful avenue in the world; for others it's a colossal mismatch of a myriad of styles. See what you think, but whatever you do, don't miss this.

From St. Stephen's to the Opera House. As you saunter down Kärntner Strasse, the main thoroughfare, remember to peek at the side streets and squares. Wander down these narrow paths to step out of the noisy shopper's world into one of peace and quiet.

South of the Ring to the Belvedere. Crossing Schwarzenbergplatz past equestrian monuments and grand fountains, you'll walk through the beautiful gardens of Prince Eugene's residence. The palace interior is filled with works by such artists as Klimt, Kokoschka, and Schiele.

The Habsburgs' Schönbrunn Palace. Allow plenty of time for this petite version of Versailles, to be able to see the oldest zoo in the world, the huge, incredibly beautiful park and gardens, and an amazing maze. This is not the most frequently visited site in Austria for nothing.

PLANNING

WHEN TO GO

Vienna is warm and sunny in May and June, and in September and October; July and August can be hot and stormy, with temperatures reaching into the high 90s°F. From November through March winter can get cold, with snow falling in January and February; lows of 10°F are frequent.

Culturally, high season in Vienna is May, June, and September, when festivals, marathons, concerts, and operas are in full swing. The ball season December to February offers everyone a chance to brush up on his or her footwork and the many Christmas markets attract crowds from all over the world.

Many Viennese leave the city in July and August, so the city tones down some, though this is also when you might find discounted rates at hotels.

In Vienna the biggest **Christkindlmarkt** (Christmas Market) goes up in November in the plaza in front of the city's Rathaus (town hall); there are more than 20 smaller ones dotted around town (including outside Schönbrunn and the Belvedere Palace, in the Spittelberg Quarter on the Freyung square, and in front of Karlkirche on Karlsplatz).

The New Year opens in Vienna with the concert by the **Wiener Philhar-moniker Orchestra** (☎*01/505–6525* ⊕*www.musikverein.at*); reserve a year, or more, in advance. Those who can't get into the Philharmonic concert can try for one of the performances of the Johann Strauss operetta *Die Fledermaus* or another light delight in the **Volksoper** (☎*01/513–1513* ⊕*www.volksoper.at*) or at the intimate **Kammeroper** (☎*01/513–1513*). The New Year is marked by an array of balls, such as the **Kaiserball** (☎*01/587–3666–14* ⊕*www.kaiserball.at*), held in the elegant rooms of the Hofburg.

On January 6 children disguised as the Magi walk the streets, especially out in the country, knock on doors, sing a song and recite poems about coming from afar, and ask for a small donation.

Fasching (or Fasnacht, as it's called in the western part of the country), the Carnival period before Lent, in February, can become very wild, with huge processions of disguised figures, and occasional unwilling participation by spectators, who may even suffer (light) blows. In Vienna, which is comparatively quiet at this time, the ball season, which officially begins in November but gets into swing in late December or early January, lasts through Shrove Tuesday (Mardi Gras). The biggest society event is the **Opernball** (*Opera Ball*), held at the **Staatsoper** (☎*01/514–44–2606* ⊕*www.staatsoper.at*).

The **Wiener Festwochen** (⊕*www.festwochen.at*)—a festival of theater, music, films, and exhibitions—takes over Vienna from mid-May to mid-June.

September 1 marks the start of Vienna's **theater and music season.**

GETTING HERE & AROUND

BY AIR Vienna's airport is at Schwechat, about 19 km (12 mi) southeast of the city. Austrian Airlines flies into Schwechat from North America.

AIRPORT The *fastest* way into Vienna from Schwechat Airport is the sleek, dou-
TRANSFERS ble-decker **CAT, or City Airport Train.** From the airport to Wien–Mitte (the center of the city) takes only 16 minutes, and trains operate daily every 20 minutes between 5:30 AM and midnight. The cost is €8 one way and €15 round-trip. But the *cheapest* way to get into town from the airport is the **S7 train,** called the *Schnellbahn,* which shuttles twice an hour between the station beneath the airport and the Landstrasse/ Wien–Mitte (city center) and Wien–Nord (north Vienna) stations; the

fare is €3.40, and it takes about 35 minutes. Your ticket is also good for an immediate transfer to your destination within the city on street-car, bus, or U-Bahn.

Another cheap option is the **bus,** which has two separate lines. One line goes to Schwedenplatz/Postgasse (1st District, city center) every 30 minutes between 5 AM and 12:30 AM; traveling time is 20 minutes. The second line goes to the South and West train stations (Südbahnhof and Westbahnhof) in 20 and 35 minutes, respectively. Departure times are every 30 minutes from 5:30 AM to 11:10 PM. Fare is €6 one way, €11 round-trip.

If convenience is your priority, **Airport Driver** has private transfers to the airport; one-way is €29, but you must reserve 48 hours in advance by phone or online. For parties of four the minivan charge is €35. A regular taxi between the airport and the city center will charge between €33 and €37.

BY BOAT & FERRY — *For information about Danube River cruises,* ⇨ *Danube River Cruises in Chapter 4, the Danube Valley.* When you arrive in Vienna via the Danube, the Blue Danube Steamship Company/DDSG will leave you at Praterlände near Mexikoplatz. The Praterlände stop is a two-block taxi ride or walk from the Vorgartenstrasse U1/subway station, or you can take a taxi directly into town.

BY BUS — International long-distance bus services arrive either at the Südbahnhof (south railway station) on the Gürtel or at the large Erdbergstrasse bus station. Most postal (local) and railroad buses arrive at either a rail-way station or the Wien Mitte-Landstrasse Bahnhof located behind the Hotel Hilton on Stadtpark.

BY CAR — Vienna is 300 km (187 mi) east of Salzburg, 200 km (125 mi) north of Graz. Main routes leading into the city are the A1 Westautobahn from Germany, Salzburg, and Linz and the A2 Südautobahn from Graz and points south. Rental cars can be arranged at the airport or in town. Buch-binder is a local firm with particularly favorable rates and clean cars.

On highways from points south or west or from Vienna's airport, ZENTRUM signs clearly mark the route to the center of Vienna. From there, however, finding your way to your hotel is a challenge, because traffic planners have installed a devious scheme prohibiting through traffic in the city core (the 1st District). Traffic congestion within Vienna is not as bad as in some places, but driving to in-town destina-tions generally takes longer than public transportation does. In the city a car is a burden. Public transportation is always the better bet in the city—it's clean, reliable, and easy to use.

PARKING — The entire 1st through 9th districts, as well as the 20th and part of the 15th, are limited-parking zones and require that a *Parkschein,* a paid-parking chit available at most newsstands and tobacconists, be filled in and displayed on the dash during the day. At this writing, Parkscheine cost €0.80 for 30 minutes, €1.60 for one hour, €2.40 for 90 minutes and €3.20 for two hours. These are required from 8 AM until 10 PM but a maximum parking time of two hours is permitted. You can park for 10 minutes free of charge, but you must get a violet "gratis" sticker (check for one at a newsstand, tobacconist, or bank) to put in your windshield. You can also park free in the 1st District on Saturday from noon until Monday at 8 AM.

BY PUBLIC TRANSIT: BUS, TRAM & U-BAHN

When it comes to seeing the main historic sights, Vienna is a city to tackle on foot. With the exception of the Schönbrunn and Belvedere palaces and the Prater amusement park, most sights are concentrated in the center, the 1st District, much of which is a pedestrian zone. Happily, Vienna's subway system, called the U-Bahn, services the core of the inner city.

The main city-center subway stops in the 1st District are Stephansplatz, Karlsplatz, Herrengasse, Schottenring, and Schwedenplatz. Stephansplatz is the very heart of the city, at St. Stephen's cathedral, with exits to the Graben and Kärntnerstrasse. You can reach the amusement park of the Prater from Stephansplatz by taking the U1 to Praterstern. Near the southern edge of the Ringstrasse, the major Karlsplatz stop is right next to the Staatsoper, the pedestrian Kärntnerstrasse, and the Ringstrasse, with an easy connection to Belvedere Palace via the D Tram. You can also take the U4 from Karlsplatz to Schönbrunn Palace (Schönbrunn stop). Herrengasse is also in the city center, close to the Hofburg and Graben. Schottenring is on the Ringstrasse, offering quick tram connections or a short walk on foot to the Graben. Schwedenplatz is ideally situated for a 10-minute walk to St. Stephen's through some of Vienna's oldest streets. You can also take the U1 from Schwedenplatz to the Prater, getting off at Praterstern. Karlsplatz is serviced by the train lines U4, U2, U1, while U3 goes to Herrengasse and U2 to Stadion (the newly built station next to where the European Football Championship final was held in June 2008). In addition, there are handy U-Bahn stops along the rim of the city core, such as MuseumsQuartier, Stadtpark, Volkstheater, and Rathaus. You can also hop across the 1st District by using bus lines 1A, 2A, and 3A if you don't want to walk 10 minutes from one U-Bahn stop to another.

Vienna's public transportation system is fast, clean, safe, and easy to use. Get public transport maps at a tourist office or at the transport-information offices (*Wiener Verkehrsbetriebe*), underground at Karlsplatz, Stephansplatz, and Praterstern. You can transfer on the same ticket between subway, streetcar, bus, and long stretches of the fast suburban railway, or *Schnellbahn* (*S-Bahn*).

Five subway (*U-Bahn*) lines, whose stations are prominently marked with blue U signs, crisscross the city. Karlsplatz, Schwedenplatz, and Stephansplatz are the main transfer points between lines. The last subway (U4) runs at about 12:30 AM. Track the main lines of the U-Bahn system by their color codes on subway maps: U1 is red; U2, purple; U3, orange; U4, green; and U6, brown. Note that you have to open the subway door when the train stops, either by pushing a lighted button or pulling the door handle aside.

The first streetcars (*Strassenbahnen*) run from about 5:15 AM. From then on service is regular and reliable (barring gridlock on the streets), and most lines operate until about midnight. The most famous tram lines are No. 1, which travels the great Ringstrasse avenue clockwise, and No. 2, which travels it counterclockwise; each offers a cheap way to admire the glories of Vienna's 19th-century Ringstrasse monuments. Where streetcars don't run, buses—*Autobusse*—do; route maps and schedules are posted at each bus or subway stop and new electronic display boards at each stop show the minutes until the arrival of the next tube, bus, or tram.

Should you miss the last streetcar or bus, special night buses with an N designation operate at half-hour intervals over several key routes; the starting (and transfer) points are the Opera House and Schwedenplatz. These night-owl buses accept all normal tickets. There is no additional fare.

Tickets for public transportation are valid for all public transportation—buses, trams, and the subway. It's best to buy your ticket at a U-Bahn stop before boarding a bus or tram. Though there are ticket machines on trams and buses there is a surcharge of €0.50. Passengers can enter and exit buses and trams through any door. You'll need to punch your ticket before entering the boarding area at U-Bahn stops, but for buses and trams you punch it on board. Though Vienna's public transportation operates on the honor system, if you're caught without a ticket you'll pay a hefty fine.

Buy single tickets for €2.20 from dispensers on the streetcar or bus; you'll need exact change for the former. The ticket machines (labeled *VOR-Fahrkarten*) at subway stations give change and dispense 24-hour, 72-hour, and eight-day tickets, as well as single tickets. At Tabak-Trafik (cigarette shops–newsstands) or the underground Wiener Verkehrsbetriebe offices you can buy blocks or single tickets, each ticket good for one uninterrupted trip in the same general direction, with unlimited transfers. Or you can get a three-day ticket for €13.60, good on all lines for 72 hours from the time you validate the ticket; there's also a 24-hour ticket for €5.70. If you're staying longer, get an eight-day ticket (€27.20), which can be used on eight separate days or by any number of persons (up to eight) at any one time. A very cheap, less-well-known option is the *Wochenkarte* (week card). This ticket is valid for seven days, one calendar week (Monday to Sunday), includes unlimited travel, is transferable, and costs only €14. Prices, current at this writing, are subject to change. Children under six travel free on Vienna's public transport system; children under 15 travel free on Sunday, public holidays, and during Vienna school holidays. If you don't speak German, opt to purchase your tickets from a person at a Tabak or main U-Bahn station.

As with most transport systems in European cities, it is essential to validate, or punch, your ticket when you start your trip. You'll find the validation machines on all buses, trams, and at the entrance of each U-Bahn station—look for the blue box and slide your ticket into the machine until you hear a "punch." Public transportation is on the honor system, but if you're caught without a punched ticket the spot fine is €72. Tabak-Trafik Almassy is open every day from 8 AM to 7 PM, and has tickets as well as film and other items.

BY TAXI   Taxis in Vienna are relatively reasonable. The initial charge is €3.50 for as many as four people daytime, and about 5% more from 11 PM until 6 AM. Radio cabs ordered by phone have an initial charge of €6.50. They also may charge for each piece of luggage that must go into the trunk, and a charge is added for waiting beyond a reasonable limit. It's customary to round up the fare to cover the tip. You can flag a cab down in the street in Vienna, but it's easier to look for a taxi stand. Service is usually prompt, but when you hit rush hour, the weather is bad, or you need to keep to an exact schedule, call ahead and order a taxi for a specific time. If your destination is the airport, ask for a reduced-rate taxi. There are several companies that offer chauffeured limousines, which are listed below.

■ TIP➜ Taxi drivers may need to know which of the 23 districts you seek, as well as the street address. The district number is coded into the postal code with the second and third digits; thus A-1010 (the "01") is the 1st District, A-1030 is the 3rd, A-1110 is the 11th, and so on.

BY TRAIN   Trains from Germany, Switzerland, and western Austria arrive at the Westbahnhof (West Station), on Europaplatz, where Mariahilferstrasse crosses the Gürtel. If you're coming from Italy or Hungary, you'll generally arrive at the Südbahnhof (South Station). There are currently two stations for trains to and from Prague and Warsaw: Wien Nord (North Station) and Franz-Josef Bahnhof. Central train information has schedule information for train departures all over Austria. However, it's hard to find somebody who speaks English, so it's best to ask your hotel for help in calling. Note that massive construction work began 2008 at Westbahnhof, on a central railway station; expect detours and delays for at least the next three to four years.

TOURS

BUS TOURS   When you're pressed for time, a good way to see the highlights of Vienna is via a sightseeing bus tour, which gives you a once-over-lightly of the heart of the city and allows a closer look at Schönbrunn and Belvedere palaces. You can cover almost the same territory on your own by taking either streetcar 1 or 2 around the Ring and then walking through the heart of the city. For tours, there are a couple of reputable firms: Vienna Sightseeing Tours and Cityrama Sightseeing. Both run daily "get-acquainted" tours lasting about three hours (€35), including visits to the Schönbrunn and Belvedere palace grounds. The entrance fee and guided tour of Schönbrunn is included in the price, but not a guided tour of the Belvedere, just the grounds. Both firms offer a number of other tours as well (your hotel will have detailed programs) and provide hotel pickup for most tours. These tour operators also offer half-day trips outside the city. Check their offerings and compare packages and prices to be sure you get what you want.

You can tour at your own pace with Vienna Sightseeing's Hop On, Hop Off bus tour. There are 13 stops, and a day ticket purchased after 3 PM is valid for the whole next day, too. A running commentary describes the sights as you go along, and you can leave the tour at any of the stops and join again when you please. The short city tour costs

1

€13 and does a run around the major sites in about an hour. There is a two-hour tour for €16, but the day ticket for €20 allows far more freedom. All tickets can be purchased at hotels, directly at the stops, and on the bus. The first bus leaves the Opera stop at 10 AM and every half hour after until 6 PM.

FIAKER (HORSE CARRIAGE) TOURS
A *Fiaker,* or horse carriage, will trot you around to whatever destination you specify, but this is an expensive way to see the city. A short tour of the inner city takes about 20 minutes and costs €45; a longer one including the inner city and part of the Ringstrasse lasts about 40 minutes and costs €70, and an hour-long tour of the inner city and the whole Ringstrasse costs €95. The carriages accommodate four (five if someone sits next to the coachman). Starting points are Heldenplatz in front of the Hofburg, Stephansplatz beside the cathedral, and across from the Albertina, all in the 1st District. For longer trips, or any variation of the regular route, agree on the price first.

STREETCAR TOURS
From early May to early October, a 1929 vintage streetcar leaves Saturday at 11:30 AM and 1:30 PM and Sunday and holidays at 9:30, 11:30 AM, and 1:30 PM from the Otto Wagner Pavilion at Karlsplatz for a guided tour. For €16 (€14 if you have the Vienna-Card), you'll go around the Ring, out past the big Ferris wheel in the Prater, and past Schönbrunn and Belvedere palaces in the course of the two-hour trip. The old-timer trips are popular, so make your reservations at the transport-information office underground at Karlsplatz, weekdays 7 AM–6 PM, weekends and holidays 8:30–4. You must buy your ticket on the streetcar.

WALKING TOURS
Guided walking tours (in English) are a great way to see the city highlights. The city tourist office offers around 40 tour topics, ranging from "Unknown Underground Vienna" to "Hollywood in Vienna," "For Lovers of Music and Opera," "Old World Vienna–Off the Beaten Track," "Jewish Families and Their Past in Vienna," and many more. Vienna Walks and Talks offers informative walks through the old Jewish Quarter and a *Third Man* tour from the classic film starring Orson Welles, among other subjects. Tours take about 1½ hours, are held in any weather provided at least three people turn up, and cost €13, plus any entry fees. No reservations are needed for the city-sponsored tours. Get a full list of the guided-tour possibilities at the city information office. Ask for the monthly brochure "Walks in Vienna," which details the tours, days, times, and starting points. You can also arrange to have your own privately guided tour for €125 for a half day.

If you can, try to get a copy of Henriette Mandl's "Vienna Downtown Walking Tours" from a bookshop. The six tours take you through the highlights of central Vienna, with excellent commentary and some entertaining anecdotes that most of your Viennese acquaintances won't know. The booklet "Vienna from A–Z" (in English, €3.60; available at bookshops and city information offices) explains the numbered plaques attached to all major buildings.

VISITOR INFORMATION

The main center for information (walk-ins only) is the Vienna City Tourist Office, open daily 9–7 and centrally located between the Hofburg and Kärntnerstrasse.

Ask at tourist offices or your hotel about a Vienna-Card; costing €18.50, the card combines 72 hours' use of public transportation and more than 200 discounts listed in the 104-page Vienna-Card Coupon Book, which every Vienna-Card purchaser receives free of charge. The Vienna-Card is also available at all sales offices or information booths of the Vienna Transportation System (for example, Stephansplatz, Karlsplatz, Westbahnhof, Landstrasse/Wien-Mitte) or from outside Austria with credit card, call 0043–1–798–44–00–148.

ESSENTIALS

Airport Contacts **Airport Driver** (☎ *01/22822–0* ⊕ *www.airportdriver.at*). **Schwechat Airport** (*VIE* ☎ *01/7007–0 for flight information* ⊕ *www.viennaairport.com*).

Bus Contacts **Bus Station** (⊠ *Erdbergstrasse 200A*). **Wien-Mitte** (⊠ *Landstrasser Hauptstrasse 1b* ☎ *01/711–01*).

Car Rental Contacts **Buchbinder** (⊠ *Schlachthausgasse 38* ☎ *01/71750–0*).

Public Transporation Contacts **Tabak-Trafik Almassy** (⊠ *Stephansplatz 4, to right behind cathedral* ☎ *01/512–5909*). **VOR, or Vorverkaufsstellen der Wiener Linien** (☎ *7909/105* ⊕ *www.wienerlinien.at*).

Taxi Companies **Mazur** (☎ *01/604–2530*). **Taxi**(☎ *01/313–00*). **Wihup** (☎ *01/601–60*).

Train Contacts **Central train information** (☎ *05/1717*). **Franz-Josef Bahnhof** (⊠ *Julius-Tandler-Platz, 9th District/Alsergrund*). **Südbahnhof** (⊠ *Wiedner Gürtel 1, 4th District/Wieden*). **Westbahnhof** (⊠ *Westbahnhof, 15th District/Fünfhaus*). **Wien Nord** (⊠ *Praterstern, 2nd District/Leopoldstadt*).

Bus Tour Contacts **Cityrama Sightseeing** (⊠ *Börsegasse 1* ☎ *01/534–130* ⊕ *www.cityrama.at*). **Vienna Sightseeing Tours** (⊠ *Weyringergasse 28A* ☎ *01/712–4683–0* ⊕ *www.viennasightseeingtours.com*).

Streetcar Tour Contacts **Transport-information office** (☎ *01/7909–43426*).

Tourist Information **Vienna City Tourist Office** (⊠ *Am Albertinaplatz 1, 1st District* ☎ *01/24-555* 🖷 *01/216–84–92 or 01/24555–666*).

Walking Tour Contacts **City information office** (⊠ *Am Albertinaplatz 1*). **Vienna Guide Service** (⊠ *Werdertorgasse 9/2* ☎ *01/774–8901* ⊕ *www.wienguide.at*). **Vienna Walks and Talks** (⊠ *Werdertorgasse 9/2, 1st District* ☎ *01/774–8901* ⊕ *www.viennawalks.tix.at*).

EXPLORING VIENNA

Most of Vienna lies roughly within an arc of a circle with the straight line of the Danube Canal as its chord. The most prestigious address of city's 23 *Bezirke,* or districts, is its heart, the **Innere Stadt** ("Inner City"), or 1st District, bounded by the Ringstrasse (Ring). It's useful to note that the fabled 1st District holds the vast majority of sightseeing attractions and once encompassed the entire city. In 1857 Emperor Franz Josef decided to demolish the ancient wall surrounding the city to create the more cosmopolitan Ringstrasse, the multilane avenue that still encircles the expansive heart of Vienna. At that time several small villages bordering the inner city were given district numbers and incorporated into Vienna. Today the former villages go by their official district number, but they are sometimes referred to by their old village or neighborhood name, too.

The circular 1st District is bordered on its northeastern section by the Danube Canal and 2nd District, and clockwise from there along the Ringstrasse by the 3rd, 4th, 6th, 7th, 8th, and 9th districts. The 2nd District—Leopoldstadt—is home to the venerable Prater amusement park with its *Riesenrad* (Ferris wheel), as well as a huge park used for horseback riding and jogging. Along the southeastern edge of the 1st District is the 3rd District—Landstrasse—containing a number of embassies and the Belvedere Palace. Extending from its southern tip, the 4th District—Wieden—is firmly established as one of Vienna's hip areas, with trendy restaurants, art galleries, and shops, plus Vienna's biggest outdoor market, the Naschmarkt, which is lined with dazzling Jugendstil buildings.

The southwestern 6th District—Mariahilf—includes the biggest shopping street, Mariahilferstrasse, where small, old-fashioned shops compete with smart restaurants, movie theaters, bookstores, and department stores. Directly west of the 1st District is the 7th District—Neubau. Besides the celebrated Kunsthistorisches Museum and headline-making MuseumsQuartier, the 7th District also houses the charming Spittelberg quarter, its cobblestone streets lined with beautifully preserved 18th-century houses. Moving up the western side you come to the 8th District—Josefstadt—which is known for its theaters, good restaurants, and antiques shops. And completing the circle surrounding the Innere Stadt on its northwest side is the 9th District—Alsergrund—once Sigmund Freud's neighborhood and today a nice residential area with lots of outdoor restaurants, curio shops, and lovely early-20th-century apartment buildings.

The other districts—the 5th, and the 10th through the 23rd—form a concentric second circle around the 2nd through 9th districts. These are mainly suburbs and only a few hold sights of interest for tourists. The 11th District—Simmering—contains one of Vienna's architectural wonders, Gasometer, a former gasworks that has been remodeled into a housing and shopping complex. The 13th District—Hietzing—whose centerpiece is the fabulous Schönbrunn Palace, is also a coveted residential area, including the neighborhood Hütteldorf. The 19th District—Döbling—is Vienna's poshest neighborhood and also bears the nickname the "Noble District" because of all the embassy residences on its chestnut-tree-lined streets. The 19th District also incorporates several other neighborhoods within its borders, in particular, the wine villages of Grinzing, Sievering, Nussdorf, and Neustift am Walde. The 22nd District—Donaustadt—now headlines Donau City, a modern business and shopping complex that has grown around the United Nations center. The 22nd also has several grassy spots for bathing and sailboat watching along the Alte Donau (Old Danube).

It may be helpful to know the neighborhood names of other residential districts. These are: the 5th/Margareten; 10th/Favoriten; 12th/Meidling; 14th/Penzing; 15th/Fünfhaus; 16th/Ottakring; 17th/Hernals; 18th/Währing; 20th/Brigittenau; 21st/Floridsdorf; and 23rd/Liesing. For neighborhood site listings below—*except* the 1st District—both the district and neighborhood name will be given.

Vienna is a city to explore and discover on foot. The description of the city on the following pages is divided into eight areas: seven that explore the architectural riches of central Vienna and an eighth that describes Schönbrunn Palace and its gardens. Above all, *look up* as you tour Vienna: some of the most fascinating architectural and ornamental bits are on upper stories or atop the city's buildings.

Numbers in the text correspond to numbers in the margin and on the Exploring Vienna, Hofburg, and Schönbrunn Palace maps.

THE MEDIEVAL HEART OF THE 1ST DISTRICT

For more than eight centuries, the enormous bulk of the Stephansdom cathedral has remained the nucleus around which the city has grown. Vienna of the Middle Ages is encapsulated behind it, and you could easily spend half a day or more just prowling the narrow streets and passageways—Wollzeile, Bäckerstrasse, Blutgasse—typical remnants of an early era. Stephansplatz is the logical starting point from which to track down Vienna's past and present, as well as any acquaintance (natives believe that if you wait long enough at this intersection of eight streets you'll run into anyone you're searching for).

A GOOD WALK

Within a largely pedestrian zone, the **Stephansdom** ❶, the mighty cathedral, marks the point from which distances to and from Vienna are measured. From here wander up the Wollzeile, cutting through the narrow Essiggasse and right into the Bäckerstrasse, to the **Universitätskirche** ❸ or Jesuitenkirche, a lovely Jesuit church. Note the contrasting Academy of Science diagonally opposite (Beethoven premiered his "Battle Symphony"—today more commonly known as "Wellington's Victory"—in its Ceremonial Hall). Follow the Sonnenfelsgasse, ducking through one of the tiny alleys on the right to reach the Bäckerstrasse; turn right at Gutenbergplatz into the Köllnerhofgasse, right again into tiny Grashofgasse, and go through the gate into the surprising **Heiligenkreuzerhof** ❼, a peaceful oasis (unless a handicrafts market is taking place). Through the square, enter the **Schönlaterngasse** ❷ (Beautiful Lantern Street) to admire the house fronts—film companies at times block this street for picturesque shots—on your way to the **Dominikanerkirche** ❹, the Dominican church with its marvelous Baroque interior. Head east two blocks to that repository of Jugendstil treasures, the **Museum für Angewandte Kunst (MAK)** ❺, then head north along the Stubenring to enjoy the architectural contrast of the **Postsparkasse** ⑥ and former War Ministry, facing each other. Retrace your steps, following Postgasse into the Fleischmarkt to savor the inn **Griechenbeisl** ⑧. The extension of Fleischmarkt ends in a set of stairs leading up past the eccentric Kornhausel Tower. Up the stairs to the right on Ruprechtsplatz is the **Ruprechtskirche** ⑨, St. Rupert's Church, allegedly the city's oldest.

TIMING If you're pressed for time and happy with facades rather than what's behind them, this route could take half a day, but if you love to look inside and stop to ponder and explore the myriad narrow alleys, figure at least a day for this walk.

MAIN ATTRACTIONS

⑧ **Griechenbeisl** (*The "Greeks' Tavern"*). If you want to find a nook where
★ time seems to be holding its breath, head to the intersection of the Fleischmarkt (Meat Market) street and the hilly, cobblestoned, and tiny Griechengasse. Part of the city's oldest core, this street has a genuine medieval feel, thanks to Vienna's only surviving 14th-century watchtower, houses bearing statues of the Virgin Mary, and the enchanting scene that you encounter at the intersecting streets: an ivy-covered tavern, the Griechenbeisl, which has been in business for some 500 years, "*seit 1447.*" Half a millennium ago, this quarter was settled by Greek and Levantine traders (there are still many Near Eastern rug dealers here) and many of them made this tavern their "local." The wooden carving on the facade of the current restaurant commemorates Max Augustin—best known today from the song "Ach du lieber Augustin"—an itinerant musician who sang here during the plague of 1679. A favored Viennese figure, he managed to fall into a pit filled with plague victims but survived, presumably because he was so pickled in alcohol. In fact, this tavern introduced one of the great pilsner brews of the 19th century and everyone—from Schubert to Mark Twain, Wagner to Johann Strauss—came here to partake. Be sure to dine here to savor its low-vaulted rooms adorned with engravings, mounted antlers, and bric-a-brac; the Mark Twain Zimmer has a ceiling covered with autographs of the rich and famous dating back two centuries. Adjacent to the tavern is a Greek Orthodox Church partly designed by the most fashionable Neoclassical designer in Vienna, Theophil Hansen. (⇨ *Where to Eat*). ⊠ *Fleischmarkt 11, 1st District* ☎ *01/533–1941* ⊕ *www. griechenbeisl.at* Ⓤ *U1 or U4/Schwedenplatz.*

⑤ **Museum für Angewandte Kunst (MAK)** (*Museum of Applied Arts*). This
★ fascinating museum contains a large collection of Austrian furniture, porcelain, art objects, and priceless Oriental carpets. The Jugendstil display devoted to Josef Hoffman and his Secessionist followers at the Wiener Werkstätte is particularly fine. The museum also showcases changing exhibitions of contemporary works, and the museum shop sells furniture and other objects (including great bar accessories) designed by young local artists. ■TIP➔**Consider lunch or dinner at the revamped restaurant, bar, and lounge (Österreicher im MAK, open daily), run by one of Austria's best chefs, Helmut Österreicher.** ⊠ *Stubenring 5, 1st District* ☎ *01/711–36–0* ⊕ *www.mak.at* 🎟 *€7.90; free Sat.* ☉ *Tues. 10 ᴀᴍ–midnight; Wed.–Sun. 10–6* Ⓤ *U3/Stubentor.*

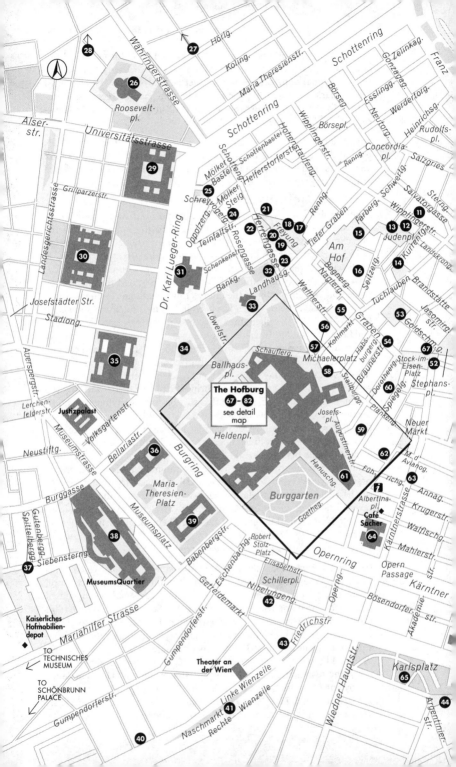

Exploring Vienna: The Historic Heart

KEY

ℹ️ Tourist Information

6 **Postsparkasse** (*Post Office Savings Bank*). The Post Office Savings Bank is one of modern architecture's greatest curiosities. It was designed in 1904 by Otto Wagner, whom many consider the father of 20th-century architecture. In his manifesto *Modern Architecture,* he condemned 19th-century revivalist architecture and pleaded for a modern style that honestly expressed modern building methods. Accordingly, the exterior walls of the Post Office Savings Bank are mostly flat and undecorated; visual interest is supplied merely by varying the pattern of the bolts used to hold the marble slabs in place on the wall surface during construction. Later architects embraced Wagner's beliefs wholeheartedly, although they used different, truly modern building materials: glass and concrete rather than marble. To see how Wagner carried his concepts over to interior design check out the building's new museum, which contains a permanent exhibition with over 200 photos, plans, models, and documents. ✉ *Georg-Coch-Platz 2, 1st District* ☎ *01/51400* ▨ *€5* ⊙ *Museum: Mon. and Thurs. 8:30–5:30, Tues., Wed., and Fri. 8:30–3, Sat. 8–5* Ⓤ *U1 or U4/Schwedenplatz, then Tram 1 or 2/Julius-Raab-Platz.*

OFF THE BEATEN PATH

Prater. You have to head northeast from the historic city center, across the Danube Canal along Praterstrasse, to find the Prater, the city's foremost amusement park. In 1766, to the dismay of the aristocracy, Emperor Josef II decreed that the vast expanse of imperial parklands known as the Prater would henceforth be open to the public. East of the inner city between the Danube Canal and the Danube proper, the Prater is a public park to this day, notable for its long promenade (the Hauptallee, more than 4½ km, or 3 mi, in length); its sports facilities (a golf course, a stadium, a racetrack, and a swimming pool, for starters); the landmark giant Ferris wheel (Riesenrad); the traditional, modern amusement-park rides; a number of less-innocent indoor, sex-oriented attractions; a planetarium; and a small but interesting museum devoted to the Prater's long history. If you look carefully, you can discover a handful of children's rides dating from the 1920s and '30s that survived the fire that consumed most of the Volksprater in 1945. The best-known attraction is the 200-foot Ferris wheel that figured so prominently in the 1949 film *The Third Man.* One of three built in Europe at the end of the last century (the others were in England and France but have long since been dismantled), the wheel was badly damaged during World War II but restored shortly thereafter. Its progress is slow and stately (a revolution takes 10 minutes), the views from its cars magnificent, particularly toward dusk. Try to eat at **Schweizerhaus** (✉ *Strasse des 1. Mai 116* ☎ *01/728–0152* ⊙ *Closed Nov.–Feb.*), which has been serving frosty mugs of beer, roast chicken, and *Stelze* (a huge hunk of crispy roast pork on the bone) for more than 100 years. The informal setting with wood-plank tables indoors or in the garden in summer adds to the fun. Credit cards are not accepted. ✉ *2nd District/Leopoldstadt* ▨ *Park free, Riesenrad €8* ⊙ *Mar., Apr., and Oct., daily 10–10; May–Sept., daily 9* AM–*midnight; Nov.–Feb., daily 10–8* Ⓤ *U1/Praterstern.*

⑨ Ruprechtskirche (*St. Ruprecht's Church*). Ruprechtsplatz, another of Vienna's time-warp backwaters, lies to the north of the Kornhäusel Tower. The church in the middle, Ruprechtskirche, is the city's oldest. According to legend it was founded in 740; the oldest part of the present structure (the lower half of the tower) dates from the 11th century. Set on the ancient ramparts overlooking the Danube Canal, it is serene and unpretentious. It's usually open afternoons and in evenings in summer for classical concerts. ⊠ *Ruprechtsplatz, 1st District* Ⓤ *U1 or U4/ Schwedenplatz*.

❷ Schönlaterngasse (*Street of the Beautiful Lantern*). Once part of Vienna's medieval Latin Quarter, Schönlaterngasse is the main artery of a historic neighborhood that has blossomed in recent years, thanks in part to government *Kulturschillinge*—or renovation loans. Streets are lined with beautiful Baroque town houses (often with colorfully painted facades), now distinctive showcases for art galleries, chic shops, and coffeehouses. At No. 5 you'll find a covered passage that leads to the historic **Heiligenkreuzerhof** courtyard. The quarter's most famous house is the **Basiliskenhaus** (*House of the Basilisk* ⊠ *Schönlaterngasse 7, 1st District*). According to legend, on June 26, 1212, a foul-smelling basilisk (half rooster, half toad, with a glance that could kill) took up residence in the courtyard well, poisoning the water. An enterprising apprentice dealt with the problem by climbing down the well armed with a mirror; when the basilisk saw its own reflection it turned to stone. The petrified creature can still be seen in a niche on the building's facade. Modern science accounts for the contamination with a more prosaic explanation: natural-gas seepage. Be sure to take a look in the house's miniature courtyard for a trip back to medieval Vienna (the house itself is private). The picturesque street is named for the ornate wrought-iron wall lantern at Schönlaterngasse 6. Just a few steps from the Basiliskenhaus, note the Baroque courtyard at Schönlaterngasse 8—one of the city's prettiest. A blacksmith's workshop, **Alte Schmiede** (*Old Smithy* ⊠ *Schönlaterngasse 9* Ⓤ *U1 or U3/Stephansplatz*), is now a museum.

❶ Stephansdom (*St. Stephen's Cathedral*). Vienna's soaring centerpiece,
★ this beloved cathedral enshrines the heart of the city—although when first built in 1144–47 it stood outside the city walls. Vienna can thank a period of hard times for the Catholic Church for the cathedral's distinctive silhouette. Originally the structure was to have had matching 445-foot-high spires, a standard design of the era, but funds ran out, and the north tower to this day remains a happy reminder of what gloriously is not. The lack of symmetry creates an imbalance that makes the cathedral instantly identifiable from its profile alone. The cathedral, like the Staatsoper and some other major buildings, was very heavily damaged in World War II but has risen from the fires of destruction like a phoenix.

It's difficult now to tell what was original and what parts of the walls and vaults were reconstructed. No matter: its history-rich atmosphere is dear to all Viennese. That noted, St. Stephen's has a fierce presence that is blatantly un-Viennese. It is a stylistic jumble ranging from 13th-century Romanesque to 15th-century Gothic. Like the exterior, St.

Stephen's interior lacks the soaring unity of Europe's greatest Gothic cathedrals, much of its decoration dating from the later Baroque era.

■ TIP→ **The wealth of decorative sculpture in St. Stephen's can be intimidating to the nonspecialist, so if you wish to explore the cathedral in detail, buy the admirably complete English-language description sold in the small room marked DOM SHOP.** One particularly masterly work should be seen by everyone: the stone pulpit attached to the second freestanding pier on the left of the central nave, carved by Anton Pilgram between 1510 and 1550. The delicacy of its decoration would in itself set the pulpit apart, but even more intriguing are its five sculpted figures. Carved around the outside of the pulpit proper are the four Church Fathers (from left to right: St. Augustine, St. Gregory, St. Jerome, and St. Ambrose), and each is given an individual personality so sharply etched as to suggest satire, perhaps of living models. There is no satire suggested by the fifth figure, however; below the pulpit's stairs Pilgram sculpted a fine self-portrait, showing himself peering out a half-open window. Note the toads, lizards, and other creatures climbing the spiral rail alongside the steps up to the pulpit. As you stroll through the aisles, remember that many notable events occurred here, including Mozart's marriage in 1782 and his funeral in December 1791. The funeral service was conducted in a small chapel beneath the Heidenturm, to the left of the cathedral's main doorway. The funeral bier on which his casket was placed stands in the Crucifix Chapel, which marks the entrance to the crypt and can be reached from outside the church. His body rested at a spot not far from the open-air pulpit—near the apse, at the other end of the cathedral—named after the monk St. John Capistrano who, in 1450, preached from it to rouse the people to fight the invading Turks. Continuing around the cathedral exterior, at the apse you'll find a centuries-old sculpted torso of the Man of Sorrows, known irreverently as Our Lord of the Toothache because of its agonized expression. Inside, nearly every corner has something to savor: the Marienchor (Virgin's Choir) has the Tomb of Rudolph IV, the Wiener Neustadt altar is a masterpiece of woodcarving; and the catacombs, where the internal organs of the Habsburgs rest.

The bird's-eye views from the cathedral's beloved **Alter Steffl** (Old Stephen Tower) will be a highlight for some. The south tower is 450 feet high and was built between 1359 and 1433. The climb up the 343 steps is rewarded with vistas that extend to the rising slopes of the Wienerwald. The north steeple houses the big Pummerin bell and a lookout terrace (access by elevator). For a special treat, take the 90-minute Saturday-evening tour including a roof walk. ⊠*Stephansplatz, 1st District* ☎*01/515–5237–67* ⊡*Guided tour €4.50; catacombs €4.50; stairs to south tower €3.50; elevator to Pummerin bell €4.50; Sat. tour €10* ⊙*Mon.–Sat. 6 AM–10 PM, Sun. 7 AM–10 PM. Guided tours in English daily Apr.–Oct. at 3:45; catacombs tour (minimum 5 people) Mon.–Sat. every half hr 10–11:30 and 1:30–4:30, Sun. every half hr 1:30–4:30; North Tower elevator to Pummerin bell, Apr.–Oct., daily 8:30–5:30; July and Aug., daily 8:30–6; Nov.–Mar., daily 8:30–5; evening tours June–Sept., Sat. at 7 pm* Ⓤ*U1 or U3/Stephansplatz.*

BIRD'S-EYE VIEW

A good way to introduce yourself to Vienna is from high above it. There's the terrace of the Upper Belvedere Palace or the Prater's Ferris wheel—but the city's preeminent panoramic lookout point is the observation platform of Vienna's mother cathedral, the Stephansdom. The young and agile will make it up the 343 steps of the south tower in 8 to 10 minutes; the slower paced will make it in closer to 20. There's also an elevator to the terrace of the north tower, which gives pretty much the same view. From atop, you can see that St. Stephen's is the veritable hub of the city's wheel. For an uplifting experience, join the Saturday-evening tour that takes place from June to September and includes a walk on the cathedral roof.

NEED A BREAK?

Zanoni & Zanoni (⊠*Am Lugeck 7, 1st District* ☎*01/512–7979*) near St. Stephen's, between Rotenturmstrasse and Bäckerstrasse, dishes up 25 or more flavors of smooth, Italian-style gelato, including mango, caramel, and chocolate chip. It's open 365 days a year and has tables, too.

❸ Universitätskirche (*Jesuit Church*). The east end of Bäckerstrasse is punctuated by Dr.-Ignaz-Seipel-Platz, named for the theology professor who was chancellor of Austria during the 1920s. On the north side is the Universitätskirche, or Jesuitenkirche, built around 1630. Its flamboyant Baroque interior contains a fine trompe-l'oeil ceiling fresco by Andrea Pozzo, the master of visual trickery, who was imported from Rome in 1702 for the job. You might hear a Mozart or Haydn mass sung here in Latin on many Sundays. ⊠*Dr.-Ignaz-Seipl-Platz, 1st District* ☎*01/512–5232-0* Ⓤ*U3 Stubentor/Dr.-Karl-Lueger-Platz.*

ALSO WORTH SEEING

❹ Dominikanerkirche (*Dominican Church*). The Postgasse, to the east of Schönlaterngasse, introduces an unexpected visitor from Rome: the Dominikanerkirche. Built in the 1630s, some 50 years before the Viennese Baroque building boom, its facade is modeled after any number of Roman churches of the 16th century. The interior illustrates why the Baroque style came to be considered the height of bad taste during the 19th century and still has many detractors today. "Sculpt 'til you drop" seems to have been the motto here, and the viewer's eye is given no respite. This sort of Roman architectural orgy never really gained a foothold in Vienna, and when the great Viennese architects did pull out all the decorative stops—Hildebrandt's interior at the Belvedere Palace, for instance—they did it in a very different style and with far greater success. ⊠*Postgasse 4, 1st District* ☎*01/512–7460-0* Ⓤ*U3/ Stubentor/Dr.-Karl-Lueger-Platz.*

❼ Heiligenkreuzerhof (*Holy Cross Court*). Amid the narrow streets and alleys behind the Stephansdom is this peaceful backwater, approximately a quarter mile from the cathedral. The beautiful Baroque court-yard has the distinct feeling of a retreat. ⊠*1st District* Ⓤ*U1 or U3/ Stephansplatz.*

NEED A BREAK? At last someone was wise enough to open up an eatery so weary wanderers could spend time appreciating the wonders of this Baroque court. The fare is as good a reason to come to **Hollmann Salon** as the tranquillity of the place. Smoke-free air pairs well organic ingredients used in the delicious, wallet-friendly, weekday three-course lunch for a mere €12. Actor-chef Hollmann also runs the nearby boutique hotel Hollmann Beletage. ⊠ *Grashofgasse 3/ Heiligenkreuzerhof, 1st District* ☏ *01/961–1960* ▭ *AE, DC, MC, V* ⊙ *Closed Sun.* Ⓤ *U1 or U4/Schwedenplatz.*

❿ Hoher Markt. This square was badly damaged during World War II, but the Anker Clock at the east end survived the artillery fire. The huge mechanical timepiece took six years (1911–17) to build and still attracts crowds at noon when the full panoply of mechanical figures representing Austrian historical personages parades by. The figures are identified on a plaque to the bottom left of the clock. The graceless buildings erected around the square since 1945 do little to show off the square's lovely Baroque centerpiece, the St. Joseph Fountain (por-traying the marriage of Joseph and Mary), designed in 1729 by Joseph Emanuel Fischer von Erlach, son of the great Johann Bernhard Fischer von Erlach. The Hoher Markt does harbor one wholly unexpected attraction, however: underground **Roman ruins** (⊠*Hoher Markt 3* ⊙*Tues.–Sun. 9–6* 🎫*€4* ⊠*1st District* Ⓤ*U1 or U4/Schwedenplatz*).

OFF THE BEATEN PATH **Hundertwasserhaus.** To see one of Vienna's most architecturally intrigu-ing buildings, travel eastward from Schwedenplatz or Julius-Raab-Platz along Radetzkystrasse to the junction of Kegelgasse and Löwengasse. Here you'll find the Hundertwasserhaus, a 50-apartment public-hous-ing complex designed by the late Austrian avant-garde artist Frieden-sreich Hundertwasser. The structure looks as though it was decorated by a crew of mischievous circus clowns wielding giant crayons. The building caused a sensation when it was erected in 1985 and still draws crowds of sightseers. ⊠*Löwengasse and Kegelgasse, 3rd District/Land-strasse* Ⓤ*U1 or U4/Schwedenplatz, then Tram N to Hetzgasse.*

Kunsthaus Wien. Near the Hundertwasserhaus is another Hundertwas-ser project, an art museum that mounts outstanding international exhibits in addition to showings of the colorful Hundertwasser works. Like the apartment complex nearby, the building itself is pure Hun-dertwasser, with irregular floors, windows with trees growing out of them, and sudden architectural surprises, a wholly appropriate set-ting for modern art. ⊠*Untere Weissgerberstrasse 13, 3rd District/ Landstrasse* ☏*01/712–0491–0* ⊕*www.kunsthauswien.com* 🎫*€9* ⊙*Daily 10–7* Ⓤ*U1 or U4/Schwedenplatz, then Tram N or O to Radetzkyplatz.*

NEED A
BREAK?

If you're ready for a coffee break, try the museum's Kunsthaus Café; if you need something more substantial, the *gasthaus* Wild on Radetzky Platz just around the corner (⇨ *Where to Eat*) is highly recommended.

Kriminal Museum (*Criminal Museum*). This might be the strangest museum in the city, and it's certainly the most macabre. The vast collection is entirely devoted to Viennese murders of the most gruesome kind, with the most grisly displays situated, appropriately, in the cellar. Murderers and their victims are depicted in photos and newspaper clippings, and many of the actual instruments used in the killings are displayed, axes seeming to be the most popular. The Criminal Museum is across the Danube Canal from Schwedenplatz, about a 15-minute walk from the Ruprechtskirche, the Hoher Markt, or the Heiligenkreuzerhof. ⊠ *Grosse Sperlgasse 24, 2nd District/Leopoldstadt* ☎ *01/214–4678* ⊡ *€5* ⊘ *Thurs.–Sun. 10–5* Ⓤ *Tram: From Schwedenplatz take Tram N along Taborstrasse to Obere Augartenstrasse.*

BAROQUE GEMS & COZY CAFÉS

As the city developed and expanded, new urban centers sprang up and were ornamented by government buildings and elegant town residences. Vienna was the heart of a vast empire, and nothing was spared to make the edifices as exuberant as possible, with utility often a secondary consideration. The best architects of the day were commissioned to create impressions as well as buildings, and they did their job well. That so much has survived is a testimony to the solidity both of the designs and of the structures on which the ornamentation has been overlaid.

Those not fortunate enough to afford town palaces were relegated to housing that was often confining and less than elegant, so the city's literati and its philosophers and artists took refuge in cafés, which in effect became combined salons and offices. To this day, cafés remain an important element of Viennese life. Many residents still have their *Stammtisch,* or regular table, at which they appear daily. Talk still prevails—but, increasingly, so do cell phones, BlackBerrys, and laptops.

A GOOD WALK
Start in the Wipplingerstrasse at the upper (west) end of Hoher Markt to find touches of both the imperial and the municipal Vienna. On the east side is the **Altes Rathaus** ⓫, which served as city hall until 1885; on the west is the **Bohemian Court Chancery** ⓬, once diplomatic headquarters for Bohemia's representation to the Habsburg court. Turn south into the short Fütterergasse to reach Judenplatz, in the Middle Ages the center of Judaism in Vienna and today site of the new **Judenplatz Museum** ⓭, landmarked by a memorial created by Rachel Whiteread, one of contemporary art's most important sculptors. Kurrentgasse leads south from the east end of Judenplatz; the beautifully restored 18th-century houses on its east side make this one of the most unpretentiously appealing streets in the city. At the end of Kurrentgasse is a clock-watcher's delight in the form of the **Uhrenmuseum** (Clock Museum) ⓮. Follow Parisergasse to Schulhof into the huge **Am Hof** ⓯

square, boasting the **Kirche am Hof** 🔟 and what must be the world's most elegant fire station. The square hosts an antiques and collectibles market on Thursday and Friday most of the year, plus other ad hoc events. Take the minuscule Irisgasse from Am Hof into Naglergasse, noting the mosaic Jugendstil facade on the pharmacy in Bognergasse, to your left. Around a bend in the narrow Naglergasse is the **Freyung,** an irregular square bounded on the south side by two stylish palaces, the **Palais Ferstel** 🔟, now a shopping arcade, and the elegantly restored **Palais Harrach** 🔟. The **Palais Daum-Kinsky** 🔟 at the beginning of Herrengasse is still partly a private residence. The north side of the Freyung is watched over by the **Schottenkirche** 🔟, established by Irish Benedictine monks; the complex also houses a small but worthwhile museum of the order's treasures. Follow Teinfaltstrasse from opposite the Schottenkirche, turning right into Schreyvogelgasse; at No. 8 is the **The Third Man Portal** 🔟. Climb the ramp on your right past the so-called Dreimäderlhaus at Schreyvogelgasse 10—note the ornate facade of this pre-Biedermeier patrician house—to reach Molker Bastei, where Beethoven lived in the **Pasqualatihaus** 🔟, now housing a museum commemorating the composer. Follow the ring south to Löwelstrasse, turning left into Bankgasse; then turn right into Abraham-a-Sancta-Clara-Gasse (the tiny street that runs off the Bankgasse) to Minoritenplatz and the **Minoritenkirche** 🔟, with its strangely hatless tower. Inside is a kitschy mosaic of the *Last Supper.* Landhausgasse will bring you to Herrengasse, and diagonally across the street, in the back corner of the Palais Ferstel, is the **Café Central** 🔟, one of Vienna's hangouts for the famous. Across the street from it is the **Palais Mollard** 🔟 and its collection of globes. As you go south on Herrengasse, on the left is the odd Hochhaus, a 20th-century building once renowned as Vienna's skyscraper. Opposite are elegant Baroque town palaces now used as museum and administration buildings by the province of Lower Austria.

TIMING   The distances in this walk are relatively short, and you could cover the route in 1½ hours or so. If you take time to linger in the museums and sample a coffee with whipped cream in the Café Central, though, you'll get a much better understanding of the contrasts between old and newer in the city. You could easily spend a day following this walk, if you were to take in all of the museums.

MAIN ATTRACTIONS

🔟 **Am Hof.** Am Hof is one of the city's oldest squares. In the Middle Ages the ruling Babenberg family built its castle on the site of No. 2; hence the name of the square, which means "at court." The grand residence hosted such luminaries as Barbarossa and Walter von der Vogelweide, the Minnesinger who stars in Wagner's *Tannhäuser.* The Baroque **Column of Our Lady** in the center dates from 1667, marking the Catholic victory over the Swedish Protestants in the Thirty Years' War (1618–48). The onetime **Civic Armory** at the northwest corner has been used as a fire station since 1685 (the high-spirited facade, with its Habsburg eagle, was "Baroqued" in 1731) and today houses the headquarters of Vienna's fire department. The complex includes a firefighting museum (open on Sunday mornings). Presiding over the east side of the square

1

is the noted Kirche Am Hof ("kirche" means church). In Bognergasse to the right of the church, around the corner from the imposing Bank Austria headquarters, is the **Engel Apotheke** (pharmacy) at No. 9 with a Jugendstil mosaic depicting winged women collecting the elixir of life in outstretched chalices. At the turn of the 20th century the inner city was dotted with storefronts decorated in a similar manner; today this is the sole survivor. Around the bend from the Naglergasse is the picturesque Freyung square. At No. 13 is the fairly stolid 17th-century **Palais Collalto**, famous as the setting for Mozart's first public engagement at the ripe age of six. This was but the first showing of the child prodigy in Vienna, for his father had him perform for three Viennese princes, four dukes, and five counts in the space of a few weeks. Having newly arrived from Salzburg, the child set Vienna on its ear, and he was showered with money and gifts, including some opulent children's clothes from Empress Maria Theresa. Next door is the Jesuit church where Leopold Mozart directed his son's *Father Dominicus Mass* (K. 66) in August 1773. Some years later Mozart's first child, Raimund Leopold, was baptized here. Sadly, the child died two months later. ✉*1st District* Ⓤ*U3/Herrengasse.*

㉓ Café Central. Part of the **Palais Ferstel** complex (⇨ *below*), the Café Central is one of Vienna's more famous cafés, its full authenticity blemished only by complete restoration in recent years. In its prime (before World War I), the café was "home" to some of the most famous literary figures of the day, who dined, socialized, worked, and even received mail here. The denizens of the Central favored political argument; indeed, their heated discussions became so well known that in October 1917, when Austria's foreign secretary was informed of the outbreak of the Russian Revolution, he dismissed the report with a facetious reference to a well-known local Marxist, the chess-loving (and presumably harmless) "Herr Bronstein from the Café Central." The remark was to become famous all over Austria, for Herr Bronstein had disappeared and was about to resurface in Russia bearing a new name: Leon Trotsky. Today things are a good deal more yuppified: the coffee now comes with a little chocolate biscuit and is overpriced, and the pianist is more likely to play Sinatra ballads than Strauss. But no matter how crowded the café may become, you can linger as long as you like over a single cup of coffee and a newspaper from the huge international selection provided. Across the street at Herrengasse 17 is the **Café Central Konditorei,** an excellent pastry and confectionery shop associated with the café. ✉*Herrengasse 14, 1st District* ☎*01/533–3763–26* ⊕*www.palaisevents. at* ▤*AE, DC, MC, V* Ⓤ*U3/Herrengasse.*

⑰ The Freyung. Naglergasse, at its curved end, flows into Heidenschuss, which in turn leads down a slight incline from Am Hof to one of Vienna's most prominent squares, the Freyung, meaning "freeing." The square was so named because for many centuries the monks at the adjacent Schottenhof had the privilege of offering sanctuary for three days. In the center of the square stands the allegorical **Austria Fountain** (1845), notable because its Bavarian designer, one Ludwig Schwanthaler, had the statues cast in Munich and then supposedly filled them with

Mozart, Mozart, Mozart!

The composer Wolfgang Amadeus Mozart (1756–91) crammed a prodigious number of compositions into his Vienna years (the last 10 of his life), along with the arrival of his six children and constantly changing Viennese addresses. It was in Vienna that many of his peaks were achieved, both personal and artistic. He wed his beloved Constanze Weber at St. Stephen's Cathedral in August 1782, and led the premieres of several of his greatest operas. But a knowledge of his troubled relations with his home city of Salzburg makes his Vienna sojourn an even more poignant one.

From the beginning of Wolfgang's precocious career, his father, frustrated in his own musical ambitions at the archbishopric in Salzburg, looked beyond the boundaries of the Austro-Hungarian empire to promote the boy's fame. At the age of six, his son caused a sensation in the royal courts of Europe with his skills as an instrumentalist and impromptu composer. As Mozart grew up, however, his virtuosity lost its power to amaze and he was forced to make his way as an "ordinary" musician, which then meant finding a position at court. Not much more successful in Salzburg than his father had been, he was never able to rise beyond the level of organist (allowing him, as he noted with sarcastic pride, to sit above the cooks at table), and, in disgust, he relocated to Vienna, where despite the popularity of his operas he was able to obtain only an unpaid appointment as assistant Kapellmeister at St. Stephen's mere months before his death. By then, patronage subscriptions had been taken up in Hungary and the Netherlands that would have paid him handsomely. But it was too late.

Whatever the truth about the theories still swirling around his untimely death, the fact remains that not only was he not given the state funeral he deserved, but he was buried in an unmarked grave (although most Viennese at that time were) after a hasty, sparsely attended funeral.

Only the flint-hearted can stand in Vienna's Währingerstrasse and look at the windows behind which Mozart wrote those last three symphonies in the incredibly short time of six weeks in the summer of 1788 and not be touched. For this was the time when the Mozart fortunes had slumped to their lowest. "If you, my best of friends, forsake me, I am unhappily and innocently lost with my poor sick wife and my child," he wrote. And if one is inclined to accuse Mozart's fellow countrymen of neglect, they would seem to have made up for it with a vengeance. The visitor to Vienna and Salzburg can hardly ignore the barrage of Mozart candies, wine, beer, coffee mugs, T-shirts, baseball caps—not to mention the gilt statues and all the other knickknacks. Mozart, always one to appreciate a joke, would surely see the irony in the belated veneration. Today the places he lived in or visited are all reverently marked by memorial plaques.

–Gary Dodson

cigars to be smuggled into Vienna for black-market sale. Around the sides of the square are some of Vienna's greatest patrician residences, including the Ferstel, Harrach, and Kinsky palaces. ⊠*At intersection of Am Hof and Herrengasse, 1st District* Ⓤ*U3/Herrengasse.*

⓭ Judenplatz Museum. In what was once the old Jewish ghetto, construction workers discovered the remains of a 13th-century synagogue while digging for a new parking garage. Simon Wiesenthal (a former Vienna resident) helped to turn it into a museum dedicated to the Austrian Jews who died in World War II. Marking the outside is a concrete cube whose faces are casts of library shelves, signifying Jewish love of learning, designed by Rachel Whiteread. Downstairs are three exhibition rooms devoted to medieval Jewish life and the synagogue excavations. Also in Judenplatz is a statue of the 18th-century playwright Gotthold Ephraim Lessing, erected after World War II. ⊠*Judenplatz 8, 1st District* ☎*01/535–0431* ⊕*www.jmw.at* ⊠*€4; combination ticket with Jewish Museum €10 (includes visit to the medieval synagogue)* ⊘*Sun.– Thurs. 10–6, Fri. 10–2.*

⓳ Palais Ferstel. At Freyung 2 stands the Palais Ferstel, not really a palace, but a commercial shop-and-office complex designed in 1856 and named for its architect, Heinrich Ferstel. The facade is Italianate, harking back in its 19th-century way to the Florentine palazzi of the early Renaissance. The interior is unashamedly eclectic: vaguely Romanesque in feel and Gothic in decoration, with here and there a bit of Renaissance or Baroque sculpted detail thrown in for good measure. Such eclecticism is sometimes dismissed as derivative, but here the architectural details are so respectfully and inventively combined that the interior is a pleasure to explore. The 19th-century stock-exchange rooms upstairs are now gloriously restored and used for conferences, concerts, and balls. ⊠*Freyung 2, 1st District* Ⓤ*U3/Herrengasse.*

⓲ Schottenhof. On the Freyung square and designed by Joseph Kornhäusel in a different style from his Fleischmarkt tower, the Schottenhof is a shaded courtyard. The facade typifies the change that came over Viennese architecture during the Biedermeier era (1815–48). The Viennese, according to the traditional view, were at the time so relieved to be rid of the upheavals of the Napoleonic Wars that they accepted without protest the iron-handed repression of Prince Metternich, chancellor of Austria, and retreated into a cozy and complacent domesticity. Restraint also ruled in architecture; Baroque license was rejected in favor of a new and historically "correct" style that was far more controlled and reserved. Kornhäusel led the way in establishing this trend in Vienna; his Schottenhof facade is all sober organization and frank repetition. But in its marriage of strong and delicate forces it still pulls off the great Viennese-waltz trick of successfully merging seemingly antithetical characteristics. ⊠*1st District* Ⓤ*U2/Schottentor.*

NEED A BREAK?

In summer, **Wienerwald** restaurant, in the delightful tree-shaded courtyard of the Schottenhof, open daily and ideal for relaxing over lunch or dinner with a glass of wine or frosty beer. The specialty here is chicken, prepared just about every possible way. Especially good is the spit-roasted *Knoblauch* (garlic) chicken. ⊠*Freyung 6, 1st District* ⊘*Daily* Ⓤ*U2/Schottentor.*

㉑ **Schottenkirche.** From 1758 to 1761 the noted Italian *vedutiste* (scene painter) Bernardo Bellotto did paintings of the Freyung square looking north toward the Schottenkirche; the pictures hang in the Kunsthistorisches Museum, and the similarity to the view you see more than two centuries later is arresting. In fact, a church has stood on the site of the Schottenkirche since 1177, when the monastery was established by Benedictine monks from Ireland—Scotia Minor, in Latin, hence the name "Scots Church." The present edifice dates from the mid-1600s, when it replaced its predecessor, which had collapsed because the architects of the time had built on weakened foundations. The interior, with its ornate ceiling and a decided surplus of cherubs and angels' faces, is in stark contrast to the plain exterior. The adjacent small **Museum im Schottenstift** includes the best of the monastery's artworks, including the celebrated Late Gothic high altar dating from about 1470. The winged altar is fascinating for its portrayal of the Holy Family in flight into Egypt—with the city of Vienna clearly identifiable in the background. ⊠*Freyung 6, 1st District* ☎*01/534–98–600* ⊕*www.schottenstift.at* 🗪*Church free, museum €5* ⊘*Museum Thurs.–Sat. 11–5* Ⓤ*U2/Schottentor.*

⑭ **Uhrenmuseum** (*Clock Museum*). At the far end of Kurrentgasse, which is lined with appealing 18th-century houses, is one of Vienna's most appealing museums: the Uhrenmuseum (enter to the right on the Schulhof side of the building). The museum's three floors display clocks and watches—more than 3,000 timepieces—dating from the 15th century to the present. The ruckus of bells and chimes pealing forth on any hour is impressive, but for the full cacophony try to be here at noon. ⊠*Schulhof 2, 1st District* ☎*01/533–2265* 🗪*€4, Sun. free* ⊘*Tues.–Sun. 10–6* Ⓤ*U1 or U3/Stephansplatz.*

ALSO WORTH SEEING

⑪ **Altes Rathaus** (*Old City Hall*). Opposite the Bohemian Chancery stands the Altes Rathaus, dating from the 14th century but displaying 18th-century Baroque motifs on its facade. The interior passageways and courtyards, which are open during the day, house a Gothic chapel (open at odd hours); a much-loved Baroque wall fountain (Georg Raphael Donner's **Andromeda Fountain** from 1741); and display cases exhibiting maps and photos illustrating the city's history. ⊠ *Wipplingerstrasse/Salvatorgasse 7, 1st District* Ⓤ*U1 or U4/Schwedenplatz.*

⑫ **Böhmischehofkanzlei** (*Bohemian Court Chancery*). This architectural jewel of the Inner City was built between 1708 and 1714 by Johann Bernhard Fischer von Erlach. He and his contemporary Johann Lukas von Hildebrandt were the reigning architectural geniuses of Baroque-era Vienna; they designed their churches and palaces during the building boom that followed the defeat of the Turks in 1683. Both had studied architecture in Rome, and both were deeply impressed by the work of the great Italian architect Francesco Borromini, who brought to his designs a freedom of invention that was looked upon with horror by most contemporary Romans. But for Fischer von Erlach and Hildebrandt, Borromini's ideas were a source of triumphant architectural inspiration, and when they returned to Vienna they produced between them many of the city's most beautiful buildings. Alas, narrow Wipplingerstrasse allows little more than an oblique view of this florid facade. The back side of the building, on Judenplatz, is less elaborate but gives a better idea of the design concept. The building first served as the offices of Bohemia's representatives to the Vienna-based monarchy, and still houses government offices today. ⊠ *Wipplingerstrasse 7, 1st District* Ⓤ*U1 or U4/Schwedenplatz.*

🄻 **Kirche Am Hof.** On the east side of the Am Hof square, the Kirche Am Hof, or Church of the Nine Choirs of Angels, is identified by its sprawling Baroque facade designed by Carlo Carlone in 1662. The somber interior lacks appeal, but the checkerboard marble floor may remind you of Dutch churches. ⊠ *Am Hof 1, 1st District* Ⓤ*U3/Herrengasse.*

🄵 **Minoritenkirche** (*Minorite Church*). Minoritenplatz is named after its centerpiece, the Minoritenkirche, a Gothic affair with a strange stump of a tower, built mostly in the 14th century. The front is brutally ugly, but the back is a wonderful, if predominantly 19th-century, surprise. The interior contains the city's most imposing piece of kitsch: a large mosaic reproduction of Leonardo da Vinci's *Last Supper,* commissioned by Napoléon in 1806 and later purchased by Emperor Francis I. ⊠ *Minoritenplatz 2A, 1st District* ☎ *01/533–4162* Ⓤ*U3/Herrengasse.*

🄼 **Palais Daum-Kinsky.** Just one of the architectural treasures that comprise the urban set piece of the Freyung, the Palais Kinsky is the square's best-known palace, and is one of the most sophisticated pieces of Baroque architecture in the whole city. It was built between 1713 and 1716 by Hildebrandt, and its only real competition comes a few yards farther on: the Greek-temple facade of the Schottenhof, which is at right angles to the Schottenkirche, up the street from the Kinsky Palace. The palace now houses Wiener Kunst Auktionen, a public auction business offering artworks and antiques. If there is an auction viewing, try to see the palace's spectacular 18th-century staircase, all marble goddesses and crowned with a trompe-l'oeil ceiling painted by Marcantonio Chiarini. ⊠ *Freyung 4, 1st District* ☎ *01/532–4200* ⊕ *www.imkinsky.com* ⊙ *Weekdays 10–6* Ⓤ*U3/Herrengasse.*

🄾 **Palais Harrach.** Next door to the Palais Ferstel is the Palais Harrach. Mozart and his sister Nannerl performed here, when they were children, for Count Ferdinand during their first visit to Vienna in 1762. The palace was altered after 1845 and severely damaged during World War II. Many of the state rooms have lost their historical luster, but the Marble Room, set with gilt boiseries, and the Red Gallery, topped with a spectacular ceiling painting, still provide grand settings for receptions. ⊠ *Freyung 3, 1st District* Ⓤ*U3/Herrengasse.*

🄿 **Palais Mollard.** Across the street from the Café Central, the beautifully renovated Palais Mollard has a rare collection of over 400 terrestrial and celestial globes on show on its second-floor museum—the only one of its kind in the world open to the public. The oldest globe is an earth globe dating from 1536, produced by Gemma Frisius, a Belgian doctor and cosmographer. On the ground floor is a small but fascinating exhibition of the history of Esperanto, including a film. ⊠*Herrengasse 9, 1st District* ☎*01/534–10* ⧄*€5* ⊙*Mon.–Wed., Fri., and Sat. 10–2, Thurs. 3–7* Ⓤ *U3/Herrengasse.*

㉕ **Pasqualatihaus.** Beethoven lived in the Pasqualatihaus while he was composing his only opera, *Fidelio,* as well as his Seventh Symphony and Fourth Piano Concerto. Today his apartment houses a small commemorative museum (in distressingly modern style). After navigating the narrow and twisting stairway, you might well ask how he maintained the jubilant spirit of the works he wrote there. Note particularly the prints that show what the window view out over the Mölker bastion was like when Beethoven lived here and the piano that dates from his era—one that was beefed-up to take the banging Beethoven made fashionable. This house is around the corner from the *Third Man* Portal. ⊠*8 Mölker Bastei, 1st District* ☎*01/535–8905* ⊕*www.wienmuseum. at* ⧄*€2, Sun. free* ⊙*Tues.–Sun. 10–1 and 2–6* Ⓤ*U2/Schottentor.*

㉔ ***Third Man* Portal.** The doorway at Schreyvogelgasse 8 (up the incline) was made famous in 1949 by the classic film *The Third Man* (⇨ *Close-up box, opposite).* It was here that Orson Welles, as the malevolently knowing Harry Lime, stood hiding in the dark, only to have his smiling face illuminated by a sudden light from the upper-story windows of the house across the alley. To get to this apartment building from the nearby and noted Schottenkirche, follow Teinfaltstrasse one block west to Schreyvogelgasse on the right. ⊠*1st District* Ⓤ*U2/Schottentor.*

FROM MICHAELERPLATZ TO THE GRABEN: VIENNA'S SHOPWINDOW

The compact area bounded roughly by the back side of the Hofburg palace complex, the Kohlmarkt, the Graben, and Kärntnerstrasse belongs to the oldest core of the city. Remains of the Roman city are just below the present-day surface. This was and still is the city's commercial heart, dense with shops and markets for various commodities; today, the Kohlmarkt and Graben in particular offer the choicest luxury shops, overflowing into the Graben end of Kärntnerstrasse. The area is marvelous for its visual treats, ranging from the squares and varied architecture to shopwindows. The evening view down Kohlmarkt from the Graben is an inspiring classic, with the night-lighted gilded dome of Michael's Gate into the palace complex as the glittering backdrop. Sights in this area range from the sacred—the Baroque Peterskirche—to the more profane pleasures of Demel, Vienna's beloved pastry shop, and the Modernist masterwork of the Looshaus.

A GOOD WALK

Start your walk through this fascinating quarter at **Michaelerplatz** 🏛, one of Vienna's most evocative squares, where the feel of the imperial city remains very strong; the buildings around the perimeter present a synopsis of the city's entire architectural history: medieval church

CLOSE UP

Tracking Down The *Third Man*

1

Nothing has done more to create the myth of postwar Vienna than Carol Reed's classic 1949 film *The Third Man*. The bombed-out ruins of this proud, imperial city created an indelible image of devastation and corruption in the war's aftermath. Vienna was then divided into four sectors, each commanded by one of the victorious armies—American, Russian, French, and British. But their attempts at rigid control could not prevent a thriving black market.

Reed's film version of the Graham Greene thriller features Vienna as a leading player, from the top of its Ferris wheel to the depth of its lowest sewers—"which run right into the Blue Danube." It was the first British film to be shot entirely on location.

Joseph Cotten plays Holly Martins, a pulp-fiction writer who comes to Vienna in search of his friend Harry Lime (Orson Welles). He makes the mistake of delving too deeply into Lime's affairs, even falling in love with his girlfriend, Anna Schmidt (Alida Valli), with fatal consequences.

Many of the sites where the film was shot are easily visited. Harry Lime appears for the first time nearly one hour into the film in the doorway of Anna's apartment building at No. 8 Schreyvogelgasse, around the corner from the Mölker-Bastei (a remnant of the old city wall). He then runs to Am Hof, a lovely square lined with Baroque town houses and churches, which appears much closer to Anna's neighborhood than it actually is.

The scene between Lime and Martins on the Ferris wheel was filmed on the Riesenrad at the Prater, the huge amusement park across the Danube Canal. While the two friends talk in the enclosed compartment, the wheel slowly makes a revolution, with all Vienna spread out below them.

In the memorable chase at the end of the movie, Lime is seen running through the damp sewers of Vienna, hotly pursued by the authorities. In reality, he would not have been able to use the sewer system as an escape route because the tunnels were too low and didn't connect between the different centers of the city. A more feasible, if less cinematic, possibility of escape was offered by the labyrinth of cellars that still connected many buildings in the city.

Lime's funeral is held at the Zentralfriedhof (Central Cemetery), reachable by the No. 71 streetcar. This is the final scene of the movie, where Anna Schmidt walks down the stark, wide avenue, refusing to acknowledge the wistful presence of Holly Martins.

After touring sewers and cemeteries, treat yourself to a stop at the Hotel Sacher, used for a scene in the beginning of the movie when Holly Martins is using the telephone in the lobby. The bar in the Sacher was a favorite hangout of director Carol Reed, who left a signed note to the bartender, saying: "To the creator of the best Bloody Marys in the whole world."

The film is screened on Tuesday, Friday, and Sunday in the Burg Kino, and a memorabilia museum open on Saturday is near the Naschmarkt.

–Bonnie Dodson

spire, Renaissance church facade, Baroque palace facade, 19th-century apartment house, and 20th-century bank. Opposite Michaelerkirche (St. Michael's Church) is the once-controversial **Looshaus** 🟤, considered a breakthrough in modern architecture (visitors are welcome to view the restored lobby). From Michaelerplatz, take the small passageway to the right of the church; in it on your right is a relief, dating from 1480, of Christ on the Mount of Olives. Follow the Stallburggasse through to Dorotheergasse, and turn right to discover the **Dorotheum** 🟤, the impressive auction house, the Viennese equivalent of Christie's or Sotheby's. On your right in the Dorotheergasse (toward the Graben) is the **Jewish Museum** 🟤, which includes a bookstore and café. On the left is the famous Café Hawelka, haunt to the contemporary art and literature crowd. Turn right in the Graben to come to **Stock-im-Eisen** 🟤; the famous nail-studded tree trunk is encased in the corner of the building. Opposite and impossible to overlook is the aggressive **Haas-Haus** 🟤, a new complex with an upscale restaurant and ground-floor shopping. Wander back through the **Graben** 🟤 for the full effect of this harmonious street and look up to see the ornamentation on the buildings. Pass the Pestsäule, or Plague Column, which shoots up from the middle of the Graben like a geyser of whipped cream. Just off to the north side is the **Peterskirche** 🟤, St. Peter's Church, a Baroque gem almost hidden by its surroundings. At the end of the Graben, turn left into the **Kohlmarkt** 🟤 for the classic view of the domed arch leading to the Hofburg, the imperial palace complex. Even if your feet aren't calling you a sit-down strike, finish up at **Demel** 🟤, at Kohlmarkt 14, for some of the best *Gebäck* (pastries) in the world.

TIMING   Inveterate shoppers, window or otherwise, will want to to see the elegant shops on this walk, which could easily take most of a day. If you're content with facades and general impressions, the exercise could be done in a bit over an hour, but it would be a shame to bypass the narrow side streets. In any case, look in at St. Michael's and consider the fascinating Dorotheum, itself easily worth an hour or more.

MAIN ATTRACTIONS

🟤 **Demel.** Vienna's best-known pastry shop, Demel offers a dizzying selection, so if you have a sweet tooth, a visit will be worth every euro. And Fodor'sChoice ★ in a city famous for its tortes, its almond-chocolate Senegaltorte takes the cake. Demel's shopwindows have some of the most mouthwatering and inventive displays in Austria. ⊠ *Kohlmarkt 14, 1st District* ☎ *01/535–1717–0* ⊕ *www.demel.at* Ⓤ *U1 or U3/Stephansplatz.*

🟤 **Dorotheum.** The narrow passageway just to the right of St. Michael's, with its large 15th-century relief depicting Christ on the Mount of Olives, leads into the Stallburggasse. The area is dotted with antiques stores, attracted by the presence of the Dorotheum, the famous Viennese auction house that began as a state-controlled pawnshop in 1707 and only recently privatized. Merchandise coming up for auction is on display at Dorotheergasse 17. The showrooms—packed with everything from carpets and pianos to cameras and jewelry and postage stamps—are well worth a visit. On the second floor the goods are not for auction but for immediate sale; the same goes for the terrific, mainly late-19th-to early-20th-century glass, wooden, and art objects in the glass-roofed court just opposite the reception area on the ground floor. ⊠ *Dorotheergasse 17, 1st District* ☎ *01/515–60–200* ⊕ *www.dorotheum. com* ⊙ *Weekdays 10–6, Sat. 9–5* Ⓤ *U1 or U3/Stephansplatz.*

🟤 **The Graben.** One of Vienna's major crossroads, the Graben, leading west from Stock-im-Eisen-Platz, is a street whose unusual width gives it the presence and weight of a city square. Its shape is due to the Romans, who dug the city's southwestern moat here (Graben literally means "moat" or "ditch") adjacent to the original city walls. The Graben's centerpiece is the effulgently Baroque **Pestsäule**, or Plague Column. Erected by Emperor Leopold I between 1687 and 1693 as thanks to God for delivering the city from a particularly virulent plague, today the representation looks more like a host of cherubs doing their best to cope with the icing of a wedding cake wilting under a hot sun. The Catholic Church has triumphed over Protestantism in Austria, and Protestants may be disappointed to learn that the foul figure of the Pest also stands for the heretic plunging away from the "true faith" into the depths of hell. ⊠ *Between Kärntnerstrasse and Kohlmarkt, 1st District* Ⓤ *U1 or U3/Stephansplatz.*

🟤 **Jewish Museum.** The former Eskeles Palace, once an elegant private residence, now houses the Jüdisches Museum der Stadt Wien. Permanent exhibits tell of the momentous role that Vienna-born Jews have played in realms from music to medicine, art to philosophy, both in Vienna—until abruptly halted in 1938—and in the world at large. Changing exhibits add contemporary touches. The museum complex includes a café and bookstore. ⊠ *Dorotheergasse 11, 1st District* ☎ *01/535–0431* 🎫 *€6.50 combination ticket with Judenplatz Museum; €10 (includes entry to the medieval synagogue)* ⊙ *Sun.–Fri. 10–6* Ⓤ *U1 or U3/Stephansplatz.*

🟤 **Kohlmarkt.** The Kohlmarkt, aside from its classic view of the domed entryway to the imperial palace complex of the Hofburg, is best known as Vienna's most elegant shopping street. All the big brand names are represented here; think Gucci, Louis Vuitton, Tiffany, Chanel, and Armani, to name a few. The shops, not the buildings, are remarkable, although there is an entertaining odd-couple pairing: No. 11 (early 18th century) and No. 9 (early 20th century). The mixture of architectural styles is similar to that of the Graben, but the general atmosphere is low-key, as if the street were consciously deferring to the showstopper dome at the west end. The composers Haydn and Chopin lived in houses on the street, and indeed, the Kohlmarkt lingers in the memory when flashier streets have faded. ⊠ *Between Graben and Michaelerplatz, 1st District* Ⓤ *U3/Herrengasse.*

🟤 **Looshaus.** In 1911 Adolf Loos, one of the founding fathers of 20th-century modern architecture, built the Looshaus on imposing Michaelerplatz, facing the Imperial Palace entrance. It was considered nothing less than an architectural declaration of war. After 200 years of Baroque and neo-Baroque exuberance, the first generation of 20th-century architects had had enough. Loos led the revolt against architectural tradition; *Ornament and Crime* was the title of his famous manifesto, in which he inveighed against the conventional architectural wisdom of the 19th century. Instead, he advocated buildings that were plain, honest, and functional. When he built the Looshaus for Goldman and Salatsch (men's clothiers) in 1911, the city was scandalized. Emperor Franz Josef, who lived across the road, was so offended that he ordered the curtains of his windows to remain permanently shut. Today the Looshaus has lost its power to shock, and the facade seems quite innocuous. The interior remains a breathtaking surprise; the building now houses a bank, and you can go inside to see the stylish chambers and staircase. ■TIP➔ **To really get up close and personal with Loos, head to the splendor of his Loos American Bar, about six blocks east at No. 10 Kärntnerdurchgang.** ⊠*Michaelerplatz 3, 1st District* Ⓤ*U3/Herrengasse.*

❺❽ **Michaelerplatz.** One of Vienna's most historic squares, this small plaza is now the site of an excavation revealing Roman plus 18th- and 19th-century layers of the past. The excavations are a latter-day distraction from the Michaelerplatz's most noted claim to fame—the eloquent entryway to the palace complex of the Hofburg.

Mozart's Requiem debuted in the **Michaelerkirche** on December 10, 1791. More people stop in today due a discovery American soldiers made in 1945, when they forced open the crypt doors, which had been sealed for 150 years. Found lying undisturbed for centuries were the mummified remains of former wealthy parishioners of the church—even the finery and buckled shoes worn at their burial had been preserved by the perfect temperatures contained within the crypt.

Ghoulish tours are offered throughout the year (from Easter to November 1, Monday–Saturday, at 11 and 1:30. For visits to the crypt during the rest of the year, phone 0650/533–80–03). The cost is €5. Bilingual (German and English) tours are given, in which visitors are led down into the shadowy gloom and through a labyrinth of passageways, pausing at several tombs (many of which are open so one can view the remains) for a brief explanation of the cause of death. ⊠*Between Hofburg Palace and Graben, 1st District* Ⓤ*U3/Herrengasse.*

❺❸ **Peterskirche** (*St. Peter's Church*). Considered the best example of church Baroque in Vienna—certainly the most theatrical—the Peterskirche was constructed between 1702 and 1708 by Lucas von Hildebrandt. According to legend, the original church on this site was founded in 792 by Charlemagne, a tale immortalized by the relief plaque on the right side of the church. The facade has angled towers, graceful turrets (said to have been inspired by the tents of the Turks during the siege of 1683), and an unusually fine entrance portal. Inside, the Baroque decoration is elaborate, with some fine touches (particularly the glass-crowned galleries high on the walls on either side of the altar and the amazing tableau of the martyrdom of St. John Nepomuk), but the lack of light and the years of accumulated dirt create a prevailing gloom, and the much-praised ceiling frescoes by J. M. Rottmayr are impossible to make out. ■TIP➔ **Just before Christmastime each year the basement crypt is filled with a display of nativity scenes.** The church is shoehorned into tiny Petersplatz, just off the Graben. ⊠*Petersplatz, 1st District* Ⓤ*U1 or U3/Stephansplatz.*

ALSO WORTH SEEING

㊅ **Haas-Haus.** Designed by Hans Hollein, one of Austria's best-known living architects, the Haas-Haus is one of Vienna's more controversial buildings. It's impossible to miss the modern lines of the glass-and-steel complex, which contrast sharply with the venerable walls of St. Stephen's, just across the way. ⊠*Stephansplatz 12, 1st District* Ⓤ*U1 or U3/Stephansplatz.*

EURO TOUR

The more important churches, such as Stephansdom, Peterskirche, Minoritenkirche, and Michaelerkirche, have coin-operated (€1–€2) tape machines that give an excellent commentary in English on each structure's history and architecture.

㊾ **Stock-im-Eisen.** In the southwest corner of Stock-im-Eisen-Platz, set into the building on the west side of Kärntnerstrasse, is one of the city's odder relics: the Stock-im-Eisen, or the "nail-studded stump." Chronicles first mention the Stock-im-Eisen in 1533, but it is probably far older, and for hundreds of years any apprentice metalsmith who came to Vienna to learn his trade hammered a nail into the tree trunk for good luck. During World War II, when there was talk of moving the relic to a museum in Munich, it mysteriously disappeared; it reappeared, perfectly preserved, after the threat of removal had passed. ⊠*Intersection of Kärntnerstrasse and Singerstrasse, 1st District* Ⓤ*U1 or U3/Stephansplatz.*

THE HOFBURG: AN IMPERIAL CITY

A walk through the Imperial Palace, called the Hofburg, brings you back to the days when Vienna was the capital of a mighty empire. You can still find in Viennese shops vintage postcards and prints that show the revered and bewhiskered Emperor Franz Josef leaving his Hofburg palace for a drive in his carriage. Today you can walk in his footsteps, gaze at the old tin bath the emperor kept under his simple iron bedstead, marvel at his bejeweled christening robe, and, along the way, feast your eyes on great works of art, impressive armor, and some of the finest Baroque interiors in Europe.

Until 1918 the Hofburg was the home of the Habsburgs, rulers of the Austro-Hungarian Empire. Now it is a vast smorgasbord of sightseeing attractions including the Imperial Apartments, two imperial treasuries, six museums, the National Library, and the famous Winter Riding School. One of the latest Hofburg attractions is a museum devoted to "Sisi," the beloved Empress Elisabeth, wife of Franz Josef, whose beauty was the talk of Europe and whose tragic assassination (the murder weapon is one of the various exhibits) was mourned by all. The entire complex takes a minimum of a full day to explore in detail. ■TIP→ If your time is limited (or if you want to save most of the interior sightseeing for a rainy day), omit the Imperial Apartments and all the museums mentioned below except the new museum of court silver and tableware, the Silberkammer, and probably the Schatzkammer. An excellent multilingual, full-color booklet, describing the palace in detail, is for sale at most ticket counters within the complex; it gives a complete list of attractions and maps out the palace's complicated ground plan and building history wing by wing.

Vienna took its imperial role seriously, as evidenced by the sprawling Hofburg complex, which is still today the seat of government. While the buildings cover a considerable area, the treasures lie within, discreet. Franz Josef was beneficent—witness the broad Ringstrasse he ordained and the panoply of museums and public buildings it hosts. With few exceptions (Vienna City Hall and the Votive Church), rooflines are on an even level, creating an ensemble effect that helps integrate the palace complex and its parks into the urban landscape without overwhelming it. Diplomats still bustle in and out of high-level international meetings along the elegant halls. Horse-drawn carriages still traverse the Ring and the roadway that cuts through the complex. Ignore the cars and tour buses, and you can easily imagine yourself in a Vienna of a hundred or more years ago.

Architecturally, the Hofburg—like St. Stephen's—is far from refined. It grew up over a period of 700 years (its earliest mention in court documents is from 1279, at the very beginning of Habsburg rule), and its spasmodic, haphazard growth kept it from attaining a unified identity. But many individual buildings are fine, and the National Library is a tour de force.

A GOOD WALK

The Hofburg palace complex is like a nest of boxes, courtyards opening off courtyards and wings (*Trakte*) spreading far and wide. First tackle **Josefsplatz** 74, the remarkable square that interrupts Augustinerstrasse, ornamented by the equestrian statue of Josef II. On your right to the north is the **Spanische Reitschule** 67, the Spanish Riding School—an emblem of Vienna known throughout the world—where the famous white horses reign. Across Reitschulgasse under the arches are the Imperial Stables. To the south stands the **Augustinerkirche** 75, St. Augustine's Church, where a total of 54 Habsburg rulers' hearts are preserved in urns. The grand main hall (*Prunksaal*) of the **Hofbibliothek** 76, the National Library, is one of the great Baroque treasures of Europe, a site not to be missed (enter from the southwest corner of Josefsplatz).

Under the Michaelerplatz dome is the entrance to the **Kaiserappartements** 68, which lack the elegance you might associate with royalty, but Franz Josef, the residing emperor from 1848 to 1916, was unostentatious in his personal life. Then go into the **In der Burg** 70 courtyard and look in at the elegant **Silberkammer** 69 museum of court silver and tableware. Then pass through the **Schweizertor** 71, the Swiss Gate, to the south off In der Burg, to reach the small Schweizer Hof courtyard with stairs leading to the **Hofburgkapelle** 72, the Imperial Chapel where the Vienna Boys' Choir makes its regular Sunday appearances. In a back corner of the courtyard, under the stairs, is the entrance to

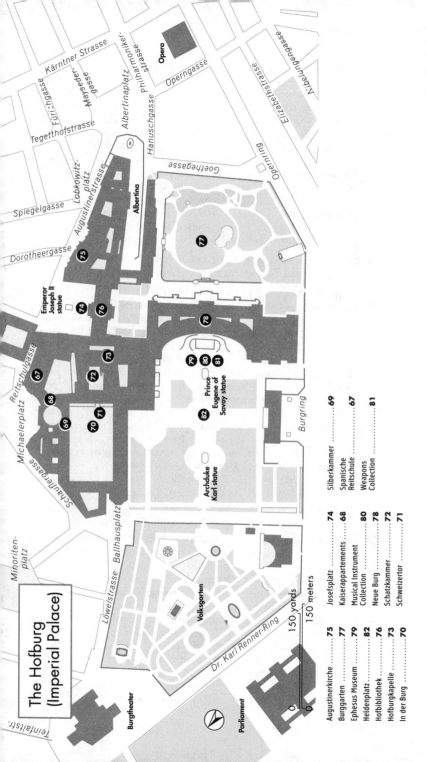

The Hofburg
(Imperial Palace)

0 _____ 150 meters
0 _____ 150 yards

the **Schatzkammer** (72), the Imperial Treasury, overflowing with jewels, robes, and royal trappings. From In der Burg, the roadway leads under the Leopold Wing of the complex into the vast park known as **Heldenplatz** (82), or Hero's Square. The heroes here are the equestrian statues of Archduke Karl and Prince Eugene of Savoy. The Hofburg wing to the south with its concave facade is the **Neue Burg** (78), the "new" section of the complex, now housing four specialized museums. Consider the **Ephesus Museum** (79), with Roman antiquities; the **Musical Instrument Collection** (80), where you also hear what you see; and the impressive **Weapons Collection** (81), with tons of steel armor. Ahead, the Burgtor gate separates the Hofburg complex from the Ringstrasse. The quiet oasis in back of the Neue Burg is the **Burggarten** (77), home to the magical **Schmetterlinghaus** (Butterfly House). Catch your breath and marvel that you've seen only a small part of the Hofburg—much of it houses the offices of the Austrian government and is not open to the public.

TIMING You could spend a day in the Hofburg complex. For most of the smaller museums, figure on anything from an hour upward.

MAIN ATTRACTIONS

(75) **Augustinerkirche** (*Augustinian Church*). Built during the 14th century and presenting the most unified Gothic interior in the city, the church is something of a fraud—the interior dates from the late 18th century, not the early 14th— though the view from the entrance doorway is stunning: a soaring harmony of vertical piers, ribbed vaults, and hanging chandeliers that makes Vienna's other Gothic interiors look earthbound by comparison. Note on the right the magnificent **Tomb of the Archduchess Maria-Christina,** sculpted by the great Antonio Canova in 1805 (his own tomb was to look just like this), with mourning figures (including that of her husband, who founded the Albertina) trooping into a pyramid. ■ TIP→ **The imposing Baroque organ sounds as heavenly as it looks, and the Sunday-morning high mass (frequently works by Mozart or Haydn) sung here at 11 AM can be the highlight of a trip.** To the right of the main altar in the small Loreto Chapel stand silver urns containing some 54 hearts of Habsburg rulers. This rather morbid sight is viewable after mass on Sunday or by appointment. ✉ *Josefsplatz, 1st District* ☎ *01/533–7099–0* Ⓤ *U3/Herrengasse.*

(77) **Burggarten.** The intimate Burggarten in back of the Neue Burg is a quiet oasis that includes a statue of a contemplative Franz Josef and an elegant statue of Mozart, moved here from the Albertinaplatz after the war, when the city's charred ruins were being rebuilt. Today the park is a favored time-out spot for the Viennese; an alluring backdrop is formed by the striking former greenhouses, now the gorgeous Palmenhaus restaurant and the **Schmetterlinghaus.** Enchantment awaits you at Vienna's unique Butterfly House. Inside are towering tropical trees, waterfalls, a butterfly nursery, and more than 150 species on display (usually 400 winged jewels are in residence). ✉ *Access from Opernring and Hanuschgasse/Goethegasse, 1st District* 🌐 *www.schmetterlinghaus.at* 💶 *€5.50* ⏲ *Apr.–Oct., weekdays 10–4:45, weekends 10–6:15; Nov.–Mar., daily 10–3:45* Ⓤ *U2/MuseumsQuartier; Tram: 1, 2, and D/Burgring.*

76 **Hofbibliothek** (*formerly Court, now National, Library*). This is one of the
Fodor'sChoice grandest Baroque libraries in the world, a cathedral of books. Its cen-
★ terpiece is the spectacular Prunksaal—the Grand Hall of the National
Library—which probably contains more book treasures than any com-
parable collection outside the Vatican. The main entrance to the ornate
reading room is in the left corner of Josefsplatz. Designed by Fischer
von Erlach the Elder just before his death in 1723 and completed by
his son, the Grand Hall is full-blown High Baroque, with trompe-l'oeil
ceiling frescoes by Daniel Gran. Usually twice a year, and lasting three
to six months, special exhibits highlight some of the finest and rarest
tomes, well documented in German and English. From 1782 Mozart
performed here regularly at the Sunday matinees of Baron Gottfried
van Swieten, who lived in a suite of rooms in the grand, palacelike
library. Four years later the baron founded the Society of Associated
Cavaliers, which set up oratorio performances with Mozart acting as
conductor. Across the street at Palais Palffy Mozart reportedly first
performed *The Marriage of Figaro* before a select, private audience
to see if it would pass the court censor. ⊠*Josefsplatz 1, 1st District*
☎*01/534–100* ⊕*www.onb.ac.at* ⊠*€7* ☉ *Tues., Wed., and Fri.–Sun.
10–6, Thurs. 10–9* Ⓤ*U3/Herrengasse.*

73 **Hofburgkapelle** (*Chapel of the Imperial Palace*). Fittingly, this is the main
venue for the beloved Vienna Boys' Choir (*Wiener Sängerknaben*),
since the group has its roots in the Hofmusikkapelle choir founded by
Emperor Maximilian I five centuries ago (Haydn and Schubert were
both participants as young boys). The choir sings mass here at 9:15 on
Sunday from mid-September to June (tickets, ranging in price from €5
to €29, are sold to hear the choir). Be aware that you *hear* the choir-
boys but don't see them: soprano and alto voices peal forth from a
gallery behind the seating area. In case you miss out on tickets to the
Sunday performance, note that just to the right of the chapel entrance
a door leads into a small foyer. Here a television screen shows the
whole mass for free. September through June, on Friday at 4 PM, the
boys also perform in the Musikverein/Brahmsaal. ⇨ *For ticket information, see Nightlife & the Arts, below.* ⊠*Hofburg, Schweizer Hof,
1st District* ☎*01/533–9927* ⊕*www.hofburgkapelle.at/ or www.wsk.
at* Ⓤ*U3/Herrengasse.*

70 **In der Burg.** This prominent courtyard of the Hofburg complex focuses
on a statue of Francis II and the noted **Schweizertor** gateway. Note
the **clock** on the far upper wall at the north end of the courtyard: it
tells time by a sundial, also gives the time mechanically, and even,
above the clock face, indicates the phase of the moon. ⊠*Hofburg, 1st
District* Ⓤ*U3/Herrengasse.*

74 **Josefsplatz.** Many consider this Vienna's loveliest courtyard and, indeed,
the beautifully restored imperial decor adorning the roof of the buildings forming Josefsplatz is one of the few visual demonstrations of Austria's onetime widespread power and influence. The square's namesake
is represented in the equestrian **statue of Emperor Joseph II** (1807) in
the center. ⊠*Herrengasse, 1st District* Ⓤ*U3/Herrengasse.*

68 **Kaiserappartements** (*Imperial Apartments*). From the spectacular portal gate of the Michaelertor—you can't miss the four gigantic statues of Hercules and his Labors—you climb the marble Kaiserstiege (Emperor's Staircase) to begin a tour of a long, repetitive suite of 18 conventionally luxurious state rooms. The red-and-gold decoration (19th-century imitation of 18th-century rococo) tries to look regal, but much like the empire itself in its latter days it's only going through the motions and ends up looking merely official. Still, these are the rooms where the ruling family of the Habsburg empire ate, slept, and dealt with family tragedy—in the emperor's study on January 30, 1889, Emperor Franz Josef was told about the tragic death of his only son, Crown Prince Rudolf, who had shot himself and his soulmate, 17-year-old Baroness Vetsera, at the hunting lodge at Mayerling. Among the few signs of life are Emperor Franz Josef's spartan, iron field bed, on which he slept every night, and his empress Elisabeth's wooden gymnastics equipment (obsessed with her looks, Sisi suffered from anorexia and was fanatically devoted to exercise). To commemorate the 150th wedding anniversary of this mismatched pair in 2004, a Sisi Museum was inaugurated, which is now part of the regular tour. Five rooms are given over to the myths and realities of this Princess Diana of the 19th century; exhibits are displayed in high style, with colored spotlights, painted murals, and many of her treasured possessions, including her jewels, the gown she wore the night before her marriage, her dressing gown, and the opulent court salon railroad car she used. There is also a death mask made after her assassination by an anarchist in Geneva in 1898, as well as the murder weapon that killed her: a short wooden-handled file. ⊠ *Hofburg, Schweizer Hof, 1st District* ⊕ *www.hofburg-wien. at* ☎ *01/533–7570* 🖾 *€9.90* ☉ *Sept.–June, daily 9–5; July and Aug., daily 9–5:30* Ⓤ *U3/Herrengasse.*

72 **Schatzkammer** (*Imperial Treasury*). The entrance to the Schatzkammer, with its 1,000 years of treasures, is tucked away at ground level behind the staircase to the Hofburgkapelle. The elegant display is a welcome antidote to the monotony of the Imperial Apartments, for the entire Treasury was completely renovated in 1983–87, and the crowns and relics and vestments fairly glow in their surroundings. Here you'll find such marvels as the Holy Lance—reputedly the lance that pierced Jesus's side—the Imperial Crown (a sacred symbol of sovereignty once stolen on Hitler's orders), and the Saber of Charlemagne. Don't miss the Burgundian Treasure, connected with that most romantic of medieval orders of chivalry, the Order of the Golden Fleece. ⊠ *Schweizer Hof, 1st District* ☎ *01/525240* 🖾 *€10* ☉ *Wed.–Mon. 10–6* Ⓤ *U3/Herrengasse.*

Fodor's Choice ★

69 **Silberkammer** (*Museum of Court Silver and Tableware*). The large courtyard on the far side of the Michaelertor rotunda is known as In der Burg; here on the west side is the entrance to the sparkling Silberkammer. Fascinating for its behind-the-scenes views of state banquets and other elegant affairs, there are more than forks and finger bowls here; stunning decorative pieces vie with glittering silver and gold for attention. Highlights include Emperor Franz Josef's vermeil banqueting service, the jardinière given to Empress Elisabeth by Queen Victoria, and gifts from Marie-Antoinette to her brother Josef II. The fully set tables give you a view of court life. ⊠*Hofburg, Michaelertrakt, 1st District* ☎*01/533–7570* ⌨*€9.90 including Kaiserappartements* ⊗*Sept.–June, daily 9–5; July and Aug., daily 9–5:30* Ⓤ*U3/Herrengasse.*

㊻ Spanische Reitschule (*Spanish Riding School*). Between Augustinerstrasse
★ and the Josefsplatz is the world-famous Spanish Riding School, a favorite for centuries, and no wonder: who can resist the sight of the stark-white Lipizzaner horses going through their masterful paces? For the last 300 years they have been perfecting their *haute école* riding demonstrations to the sound of Baroque music in a ballroom that seems to be a crystal-chandeliered stable. The interior of the riding school, the 1735 work of Fischer von Erlach the Younger, is itself an attraction—surely Europe's most elegant sports arena—and if the prancing horses begin to pall, move up to the top balcony and examine the ceiling. ■**TIP➔ Tickets to some performances must be ordered many weeks in advance.** Information offices have a brochure with the detailed schedule (performances are usually March–December, with the school closed July through mid-August). The new management under Elisabeth Gürtler (Hotel Sacher's owner) has brought about changes to performances; and, should you fall in love with one of the stallions, you can adopt it. Morning training sessions with music are held Tuesday–Saturday, 10–noon. Tickets are available at the visitor center, Michaelerplatz 1, Tuesday–Saturday (except holidays) 9–4, and at Josefsplatz, Gate 2 on the day of the morning exercise, 9–5. If you purchase your tickets through a ticket agency for a performance, it may add 22%–25% to the price of the ticket. Pick up reserved tickets at the office under the Michaelerplatz rotunda dome. ⊠*Michaelerplatz 1, Hofburg, 1st District* ☎*01/533–9031–0* ⊕*www.srs.at* ⌨*€35–€110, standing room €22–€28, morning training sessions €12* ⊗*Mar.–June and late Aug.– mid-Dec. Closed tour wks* Ⓤ*U3/Herrengasse.*

ALSO WORTH SEEING

㊼ Ephesus Museum. One of the museums in the Neue Burg, the Ephesus Museum contains exceptional Roman antiquities unearthed by Austrian archaeologists in Turkey at the turn of the century. ⊠*Hofburg, 1st District* ⌨*Combined ticket with Musical Instrument Collection and Weapons Collection €8* ⊗*Wed.–Mon. 10–6* Ⓤ*Tram: 1, 2, and D/Burgring.*

㊽ Heldenplatz. The long wing with the concave bay on the south side of the square, the Neue Burg, is the newest section here. The Neue Burg was never completed and so the Heldenplatz was left without a discernible shape, but the space is punctuated by two superb equestrian statues depicting Archduke Karl and Prince Eugene of Savoy. The older section on the north includes the offices of the federal president. ⊠*Hofburg, 1st District* Ⓤ*Tram: 1, 2, and D/Burgring.*

㊻ Musical Instrument Collection. This Neue Burg museum houses pianos that belonged to Brahms, Schumann, and Mahler. An acoustic guided tour allows you to hear the various instruments on headphones as you move from room to room. ⊠*Hofburg, 1st District Combined ticket with Ephesus Museum and Weapons Collection €8, more for special exhibits* ☉ *Wed.–Mon. 10–6* Ⓤ*U2/MuseumsQuartier.*

㉘ Neue Burg. The Neue Burg stands today as a symbol of architectural overconfidence. Designed for Emperor Franz Josef in 1869, this "new château" was part of a much larger scheme that was meant to make the Hofburg rival the Louvre, if not Versailles. The German architect Gottfried Semper planned a twin of the present Neue Burg on the opposite side of the Heldenplatz, with arches connecting the two with the other pair of twins on the Ringstrasse, the Kunsthistorisches Museum (Museum of Art History) and the Naturhistorisches Museum (Museum of Natural History). But World War I intervened, and with the empire's collapse the Neue Burg became the last in a long series of failed attempts to bring architectural order to the Hofburg. (From its main balcony, in March 1938, Adolf Hitler told a huge cheering crowd below of his plan for the new German empire, declaring that Vienna "is a pearl! I am going to put it into a setting of which it is worthy!") Today the Neue Burg houses four specialty museums: the **Ephesus Museum, Musical Instruments Collection, Ethnological Museum,** and **Weapons Collection.** For details on these museums, see separate listings, though the Ethnological Museum doesn't have much to recommend it. ⊠*Heldenplatz, 1st District* ☎*01/525240* Ⓤ*U2/MuseumsQuartier.*

㉗ Schweizertor *(Swiss Gate).* Dating from 1552 and decorated with some of the earliest classical motifs in the city, the Schweizertor leads from In der Burg through to the oldest section of the palace, a small courtyard known as the Schweizer Hof. The gateway is painted maroon, black, and gold; it gives a fine Renaissance flourish to its building facade. ⊠*Hofburg, Schweizertor, 1st District* Ⓤ*U3/Herrengasse.*

㉛ Weapons Collection. Rivaling the armory in Graz as one of the most extensive arms and armor collections in the world is this Neue Burg museum. Enter at the triumphal arch set into the middle of the curved portion of the facade. ⊠*Heldenplatz, 1st District* ☎*Combined ticket with Ephesus Museum and Musical Instrument Collection €8, more for special exhibits* ☉ *Wed.–Mon. 10–6* Ⓤ*U2/MuseumsQuartier.*

THE RINGSTRASSE: GEMS OF THE "RING"

Late in 1857 Emperor Franz Josef issued a decree announcing the most ambitious piece of urban redevelopment Vienna had ever seen. The inner city's centuries-old walls were to be torn down, and the *glacis*—the wide expanse of open field that acted as a protective buffer between inner city and suburbs—was to be filled in. In its place was to rise a wide, tree-lined, circular boulevard, upon which would stand an imposing collection of new buildings reflecting Vienna's status as the political, economic, and cultural heart of the Austro-Hungarian Empire. During the 50 years of building that followed, many factors combined to produce the Ringstrasse as it now stands, but the most important was the gradual rise of liberalism after the failed Revolution of 1848. By the latter half of the Ringstrasse era, support for constitutional government, democracy, and equality—all the concepts that liberalism traditionally equates with progress—was steadily increasing. As the Ringstrasse went up, it became the definitive symbol of this liberal progress; as Carl E. Schorske put it in his *Fin-de-Siècle Vienna,* it celebrated "the triumph of constitutional *Recht* (right) over imperial *Macht* (might), of secular culture over religious faith. Not palaces, garrisons, and churches, but centers of constitutional government and higher culture dominated the Ring."

As an ensemble, the collection is astonishing in its architectural presumption: it is nothing less than an attempt to assimilate and summarize the entire architectural history of Europe. The highest concentration of public building is found in the area around the Volksgarten. In and around the Ring ribbon you'll find an array of other unmissable gems: the quaint-now-trendy Spittelberg Quarter, Freud's apartment, and Vienna's new-old dazzler, the Liechtenstein "garden palace," home to princely Old Masters, including a fabled collection of paintings by Peter Paul Rubens.

A GOOD WALK

Is there a best way to explore the Ring? You can walk it from one end to the other—from where it begins at the Danube Canal to where it returns to the canal after its curving flight. Or, you can explore it whenever you happen to cross it on other missions. Although it is a pleasant sequence of boulevards, seeing its succession of rather pompous buildings all in one walk can be overpowering. You can obtain the best of both options by following this suggested itinerary, which leavens the bombast of the Ring with some of Vienna's most fascinating sights. If you want to do the highlights, plan on spending the morning at the Kunsthistorisches Museum, then take in the MuseumsQuartier (and lunch in the complex), followed by a leisurely afternoon spent at the Freud Haus, and a peek at the Rubens in the nearby Liechtenstein Museum.

Begin at the twin museums across the Ringstrasse from the Hofburg. To the west is the **Naturhistorisches Museum** 36; to the east, the **Kunsthistorisches Museum** 39, the art museum packed with world-famous treasures. Allow ample time for exploration here. Behind them is the **MuseumsQuartier** 38, a complex that includes several important modern-art collections, including the Leopold Collection of Austrian Art and the Museum Moderner Kunst. Farther west of the MuseumsQuartier is the compact and hip **Spittelberg Quarter** 37 of tiny streets between Burggasse and Siebensterngasse, often the site of handicraft and seasonal fairs. For more, and spectacular, evidence of handicraft of an earlier era, detour south to Mariahilferstrasse and the **Hofmobiliendepot,** the repository of much of the sumptuous furnishings of the old Habsburg palaces.

Heading back to the Ring, the **Volksgarten** 34 directly west of the Hofburg includes a café and rose garden among its attractions; look also for the lovely memorial to Franz Josef's wife, Empress Elisabeth, in the rear corner. Tackle the Ringstrasse buildings by the **Parlament** 35, the **Rathaus** 30(City Hall), the **Burgtheater** 31 on the inside of the Ring, then the **Universität** ㉙ (the main building of Vienna's university) beyond, again on the outside of the Ring. Next to the university stands the neo-Gothic **Votivkirche** ㉗. If you still have time and energy, walk farther along the Ring to discover the Börse at the corner of the Ring and Wipplingerstrasse. The outside end of Hohenstaufengasse leads into Liechtensteinstrasse, which will bring you to Berggasse. Turn right to reach No. 19, the **Freud Haus** ㉖, now a museum and research facility. Not far from Freud's apartment and just off the Liechtensteinstrasse on Fürstengasse, is the **Liechtenstein Museum** ㉘, home of the Prince of Liechtenstein's fabulous private art collection, housed in the family's summer palace.

TIMING   If you can, plan to visit Vienna's Louvre—the Kunsthistorisches Museum—early in the day before the crowds arrive, although the size of crowds depends greatly on whatever special shows the museum may be exhibiting. As for the main sights off the Ringstrasse, you could easily lump together visits to the Freud Apartment and the MuseumsQuartier, figuring on about a half day for the two combined. ■ TIP→ **Tram 1 and 2 go clockwise and counterclockwise, respectively, around the Ring.**

MAIN ATTRACTIONS

㉛ **Burgtheater** *(National Theater).* One of the most important theaters in the German-speaking world, the Burgtheater was built between 1874 and 1888 in the Italian Renaissance style, replacing the old court theater at Michaelerplatz. Emperor Franz Josef's mistress, Katherina Schratt, was once a star performer here, and famous Austrian and German actors still stride across this stage. The opulent interior, with its 60-foot relief *Worshippers of Bacchus* by Rudolf Wyer and foyer ceiling frescoes by Ernst and Gustav Klimt, makes it well worth a visit. *For information about performances here, ⇨ see Theater in Nightlife & the Arts, below.* ⊠ *Dr.-Karl-Lueger-Ring 2, 1st District* ☎ *01/514–4441–40* ⊡ *€5.50* ☉ *Guided tours daily at 3; in July and Aug. also Fri. and Sat. at 4, and Sun. at 11 and 4* Ⓤ *Tram: 1, 2, and D/Burgtheater, Rathaus.*

㉖ **Freud Haus.** Not far from the historic Hofburg district, beyond the Votivkirche at the Schottenring along the Ringstrasse, you can skip over several centuries and visit that outstanding symbol of 20th-century Vienna: Sigmund Freud's apartment at Berggasse 19 (Apartment 6, one flight up; ring the bell and push the door simultaneously); this was his residence from 1891 to 1938. The five-room collection of memorabilia is mostly a photographic record of Freud's life, with some documents, publications, and a portion of his collection of antiquities also on display. The waiting-room furniture is authentic, but the consulting room and study furniture (including the famous couch) can be seen only in photographs. ⊠ *Berggasse 19, 9th District/Alsergrund* ☎ *01/319–1596* ⊕ *www.freud-museum.at* ⊡ *€7, with guided tour €8* ☉ *Jan.–June and Oct.–Dec., daily 9–5; July–Sept., daily 9–6* Ⓤ *U2/Schottentor.*

㉟ **Kunsthistorisches Museum** *(Museum of Fine Art).* However short your
FodorsChoice   stay in Vienna, you'll want to visit one of the greatest art collections
★   in the world, that of the Kunsthistorisches Museum. This is no dry-as-dust museum illustrating the history of art, as its name implies. Rather

its collections of Old Master paintings reveal the royal taste and style of many members of the mighty House of Habsburg, who during the 16th and 17th centuries ruled over the greater part of the Western world. Today you can enjoy what this great ruling house assiduously (and in most cases, selectively) brought together through the centuries. The collection stands in the same class with those of the Louvre, the Prado, and the Vatican. It is most famous for the largest collection of paintings under one roof by the Netherlandish 16th-century master Pieter Brueghel the Elder—many art historians say that seeing his sublime *Hunters in the Snow* is worth a trip to Vienna. Brueghel's depictions of peasant scenes, often set in magnificent landscapes, dis-

> ### ART ON THURSDAY
>
> One of the best times to visit the Kunsthistorisches Museum is Thursday, when the museum caterer Gerstner sets out a sumptuous buffet dinner (€48, including museum entrance, but not including drinks) in the cupola rotunda. Just across from the seating area, take a leisurely stroll through the almost empty gallery chambers. Seating starts at 6:30 PM, and there's plenty of time between courses to take your fill of the finest art available. The museum galleries close at 9 PM, so make sure you get your fill of art beforehand. The buffet remains open until 10:30 PM.

till the poetry and magic of the 16th century as few other paintings do. Room RX (Room 10) is the Brueghel shrine—on its walls, in addition to *Hunters in the Snow* hang *Children's Games,* the *Tower of Babel,* the *Peasant Wedding,* the *Nest-Robber,* and eight other priceless canvases. There are also hundreds of other celebrated Old Master paintings here. Even a cursory description would run on for pages. The large-scale works concentrated in the main galleries shouldn't distract you from the equal share of masterworks in the more intimate side wings.

The Flemish wing also includes Rogier van der Weyden's *Crucifixion Triptych,* Holbein's *Portrait of Jane Seymour, Queen of England,* a fine series of Rembrandt portraits, and Vermeer's peerless *Allegory of the Art of Painting.* The grand style of the 17th century is represented by Rubens's towering altarpieces and his *Nude of Hélène Fourment.* In the Italian wing are works by Titian, including his *Portrait of Isabella d'Este,* whose fiercely intelligent eyes make you realize why she was the first lady of the Renaissance, and Giorgione's *The Three Philosophers,* an enigmatic composition in uniquely radiant Venetian coloring. A short list of other highlights includes Raphael's *Madonna in the Meadow,* Correggio's *Jupiter Embracing Io,* Parmigianino's *Cupid Cutting a Bow,* Guercino's *Return of the Prodigal Son,* and Caravaggio's *Madonna of the Rosary.* One level down is the remarkable, less-visited **Kunstkammer,** displaying priceless objects created for the Habsburg emperors. These include curiosities made of gold, silver, and crystal (including Cellini's famous salt cellar "La Saliera"), and more exotic materials, such as ivory, horn, and gemstones. In addition, there are rooms devoted to Egyptian antiquities, Greek and Roman art, sculpture (ranging from masterworks by Tilmann Riemenschneider to Italian Mannerist bronzes, which the Habsburgs collected by the roomful) and the decorative arts, and numerous other collections. When your feet are ready to call a sit-down strike, repair to a comfy armchair in the wonderful café on the museum's second floor. Set under a grand dome, adorned with paintings, sculpture, and framed by gilt-tipped black marble columns, this spot is run by Gerstner, the famed pastry shop. ⊠ *Maria-Theresien-Platz, 7th District/Neubau* ☎ *01/525240* ⊕ *www.khm.at* 🎫 *€10* ☾ *Tues.–Sun. 10–6, Thurs. until 9* PM Ⓤ *U2/ MuseumsQuartier, U2, or U3/Volkstheater.*

㊳ ★ ☾ MuseumsQuartier (*Museum Quarter*). New and old, past and present, Baroque and Modernism collide in this headline-making, vast culture center that opened in 2001. Claiming to be among the 10 largest of its kind in the world, the MuseumsQuartier—or MQ as many now call it—is housed in what was once the Imperial Court Stables, the 260-year-old Baroque complex designed by Fischer von Erlach, and is situated between the great Old Master treasures of the Kunsthistorisches Museum and the Spittelberg neighborhood, today one of Vienna's hippest enclaves. Where once 900 cavalry horses were housed, now thousands of artistic masterworks of the 20th and 21st centuries are exhibited, all in a complex that is architecturally an expert and subtle blending of historic and cutting-edge—the original structure (adorned with pastry-white stuccoed ceilings and rococo flourishes) was retained, while ultramodern wings were added to house five museums, most of which showcase modern art at its best.

The **Leopold Museum** (☎ *01/525–700* ⊕ *www.leopoldmuseum.org* 🎫 *€10 Mon., Wed., Fri.–Sun. 10–6, Thurs. 10–9*) comprises the holdings amassed by Rudolf and Elizabeth Leopold and contains one of the greatest collections of Egon Schiele in the world, as well as impressive works by Gustav Klimt and Oskar Kokoschka. Other artists worth noting are Josef Dobrowsky, Anton Faistauer, and Richard Gerstl. Emil Jakob Schindler's landscapes are well represented, as are those by Biedermeier artist Ferdinand Georg Waldmüller. Center stage is held by Schiele (1890–1918), who died young, along with his wife and young baby, in the Spanish flu pandemic of 1918. His colorful, appealing landscapes are here, but all eyes are invariably drawn to the artist's tortured depictions of nude mistresses, orgiastic self-portraits, and provocatively sexual couples, all elbows and organs. Adjacent, in a modernistic, dark-stone edifice, is **MUMOK, Museum moderner Kunst Stiftung Ludwig** (*Museum of Modern Art* ⊕ *www.mumok.at* 🎫 *€9* ☾ *Daily 10–6, Thurs. 10–9*), which houses the national collection of 20th-century art (once ensconced in the Palais Liechtenstein) on eight floors, mainly a bequest of Herr Ludwig, a billionaire industrialist who collected the cream 20th-century art. Top works here are of the American Pop Art school, but all the trends of the last century—Nouveau Réalisme, Radical Realism, and Hyperrealism of the '60s and '70s, Fluxus, Viennese Actionism, Conceptual Art and Minimal Art, Land Art and Arte Povera, as well as installation art vie for your attention. Names run from René Magritte and Max Ernst to Andy Warhol, Jackson Pollock, Cy Twombly, Nam June Paik, and the very latest superstars of contemporary art. Kids will make a beeline for Claes Oldenburg's walk-in sculpture in the shape of Mickey Mouse. Nearby, the **Kunsthalle** (⊕*www.kunsthallewien.at* ✆*€8.50* ⊙*Daily 10–7, Thurs. 10–10*) has gigantic halls used for temporary exhibitions of avant-avant-garde art. The **Architekturzentrum** (*Architecture Center* ⊕*www.azw.at* ✆*€7* ⊙*Daily 10–7*) holds, besides the permanent show of Austrian architecture in the 20th and 21st centuries, major exhibitions presenting the breadth of architecture history and visions of what is to come. A change of pace is offered by the **ZOOM Kinder Museum** (☎*01/524–7908* ⊕*www.kindermuseum.at* ✆ *€5; Zoom Ozean, child with one adult €4* ⊙*By reservation at least 24 hrs in advance*), which caters to children. In the ZOOM lab, kids ages 7 and up can experience the fine line between the real and virtual worlds, making screenplays come to life by becoming directors, sound technicians, authors, and actors. For the little ones there's the ZOOM Ozean (ocean), where kids and parents enter a play area inhabited by magical underwater creatures, featuring a ship with a captain's quarters and lighthouse. The **Quartier21** showcase up-and-coming artists and musicians in the huge Fischer von Erlach wing facing the Museumsplatz. Planned are artist studios that will be open to the public. The annual Wiener Festwochen (theater-arts festival) and the International Tanzwochen (dance festival) are held every year in the former Winter Riding Hall. Modern-art lovers will find it easy to spend at least an entire day at MuseumsQuartier, and with several cafés, restaurants, gift shops, and bookstores, won't even need to venture outside. ⊠*Museumsplatz 1–5, 7th District/Neubau* ☎*01/523–5881* ⊕*www.mqw.at* ✆*Combination ticket to museums €16–€25, depending on museums/exhibitions included* ⊙*Daily 24 hrs* ⓤ*U2 MuseumsQuartier/U2 or U3/Volkstheater.*

36 **Naturhistorisches Museum** (*Natural History Museum*). The palatial, archetypally "Ringstrasse" 19th-century museum complex just outside the Ring has two elements—to the east is the celebrated Kunsthistorisches Museum, to the west is the Naturhistorisches Museum, or Natural History Museum. This is the home of, among other artifacts, the Venus of Willendorf, a tiny statuette (actually, a replica—the original is in a vault) thought to be some 20,000 years old; this symbol of the Stone Age was originally unearthed in the Wachau Valley, not far from Melk. The reconstructed dinosaur skeletons draw the most attention. ⊠*Maria-Theresien-Platz, 7th District/Neubau* ☎*01/521–77–0* ✆*€8* ⊙*Wed. 9–9, Thurs.–Mon. 9–6:30* ⓤ*U2 or U3/Volkstheater.*

35 **Parlament.** This sprawling building reminiscent of an ancient Greek temple is the seat of Austria's elected representative assembly. An embracing, heroic ramp on either side of the main structure is lined with carved marble figures of ancient Greek and Roman historians. Its centerpiece is the **Pallas-Athene-Brunnen** (fountain), designed by Theophil Hansen, which is crowned by the goddess of wisdom and surrounded by water nymphs symbolizing the executive and legislative powers governing the country. ⊠*Dr. Karl-Renner-Ring 1, 1st District* ☎*01/401–110–2570* ⊕*www.parlament.gv.at* ✆*€4* ⊙*Tours mid-Sept.–mid-July, Mon.–Thurs. 11, 2, 3, and 4, Fri. 11, 1, 2, and 3*

The "Neue" City

One morning in 1911, Emperor Franz Josef, starting out on a morning drive from the Hofburg, opened his eyes in amazement as he beheld the defiantly plain Looshaus, constructed just opposite the Michaelerplatz entrance to the imperial palace. Never again, it was said, did the royal carriage use the route, so offensive was this Modernist building to His Imperial Highness. One can only imagine the Josefian reaction to the Haas-Haus, built in 1985 on Stephansplatz. Here, across from the Gothic cathedral of St. Stephen's, famed architect Hans Hollein designed a complex whose elegant curved surfaces and reflecting glass interact beautifully with its environment. The architecture proved an intelligent alternative to the demands of historicism on one hand and aggressive Modernism on the other.

This balancing act has always been a particular challenge in Vienna. For a few critics, the Gaudíesque eccentricities of the late Friedensreich Hundertwasser (besides the Kunsthaus museum he is also responsible for the multicolor, golden-globe-top central heating tower that has become almost as much a part of the skyline as St. Stephen's spire) did the trick. But for all their charm, they have now been overshadowed by the Viennese Modernism of today. By far the most exciting urban undertaking has to be the Spittelau Viaducts, just across from the Hundertwasser power plant. This revitalization plan for the Wiener Gürtel, perhaps Vienna's busiest thoroughfare, includes public-housing apartments, offices, and artists' studios that interact with the arched bays of the viaduct, a landmarked structure built by Otto Wagner. Responsible for the staggering three-part complex,

partly perched on stilts, is star architect Zaha Hadid. A pedestrian and bicycle bridge connects the whole project to the University of Business and the North Railway Station and the Danube Canal.

A discreet example of Vienna's new architecture is the vast Museums-Quartier. Hidden behind the Baroque facade of the former imperial stables, the design by Laurids and Manfred Ortner uses its enclosed space to set up a counterpoint between Fischer von Erlach's riding school and the imposing new structures built to house the Leopold Museum and the Modern Art Museum. From the first, old and new collide: to enter the complex's Halle E + G, you pass below the Emperor's Loge, whose double-headed imperial eagles now form a striking contrast to a silver-hue steel double staircase. Other important projects—notably the new underground Jewish history museum on Judenplatz (look for a stark cube memorial by English sculptor Rachel Whiteread); the Gasometer complex, a planned community recycled from the immense brick drums of 19th-century gasworks; the ellipse-shape Uniqa Tower on the Danube Canal designed by Heinz Neumann, and the ecologically responsible Donau City—are among the architectural highlights on tours now organized by the Architecture Center (AZW) of the Museums-Quartier; its maps and brochures can be used for self-guided tours.

–Gary Dodson

*(except when Parliament is in session); mid-July–mid-Sept., Mon.–Sat.
11, noon, 1, 2, 3, and 4* Ⓤ*Tram: 1, 2, or D/Stadiongasse, Parlament.*

㉚ **Rathaus** (*City Hall*). Designed by Friedrich Schmidt and resembling a
Gothic fantasy castle with its many spires and turrets, the Rathaus
was actually built between 1872 and 1883. The facade holds a lavish
display of standard-bearers brandishing the coats of arms of the city
of Vienna and the monarchy. Guided tours include the banqueting hall
and various committee rooms. A regally landscaped park graces the
front of the building, and is usually brimming with activity. In winter it
is the scene of the *Christkindlmarkt,* the most famous Christmas market in Vienna; in summer concerts are performed here. ✉*Rathausplatz
1, 1st District* ☎*01/5255–0* ✉*Free* ◷*Guided tours Mon., Wed., and
Fri., at 1. 5-person minimum* Ⓤ*Tram: 1, 2, or D/Rathaus.*

ALSO WORTH SEEING

<table><tr><td>OFF THE
BEATEN
PATH</td><td>

Hofmobiliendepot (Furniture Museum). In the days of the Habsburg
empire, palaces remained practically empty if the ruling family was
not in residence. Cavalcades laden with enough furniture to fill a pal-
ace would set out in anticipation of a change of scene, while another
caravan accompanied the royal party, carrying everything from travel-
ing thrones to velvet-lined portable toilets. Much of this furniture is
on display here, allowing a glimpse into everyday court life. The upper
floors contain re-created rooms from the Biedermeier to the Jugendstil
periods, and document the tradition of furniture making in Vienna.
Explanations are in German and English. ■TIP➔ A €22.50 combined
ticket includes the Furniture Museum, Imperial Apartments in the
Hofburg, the Silver Chamber (aka Silberkammer), and a grand tour of
Schönbrunn Palace with audio guide. Across the street from the Fur-
niture Museum is the fabulous restaurant Schon Schön (⇨ *Where to
Eat*). ✉*Mariahilferstrasse 88, entrance on Andreasgasse, 7th District/
Neubau* ☎*01/524–3357–0* ✉*€6.90* ◷*Tues.–Sun. 10–6* Ⓤ*U3 Zieg-
lergasse/follow signs to Otto-Bauer-Gasse/exit Andreasgasse.*

</td></tr></table>

㉘ **Liechtenstein Museum.** Palais Liechtenstein is home to the Prince of Liech-
★ tenstein's private art collection, an accumulation so vast only a tenth
of it is on display. Prince Karl I of Liechtenstein began collecting art
back in the 17th century, and each of his descendents added to the family treasure trove. The palace itself is a splendid example of Baroque
architecture. While this was built up on the then-outskirts of the city, a
mere "summer palace" was not grand enough for Prince Johann Adam
Andreas I, who had already erected five other Liechtenstein palaces,
including his family's gigantic Viennese winter palace on the Bankgasse.
He instead commissioned a full-blown town palace from plans drawn
up by Domenicio Martinelli. A Marble Hall, grand staircases, impressive stuccowork by Santino Bussi (who was paid with 40 buckets of
wine in addition to a tidy sum), and sumptuous ceiling frescoes by Marcantonio Franceschini and Andrea Pozzo made this a residence fitting
for one of the J. Paul Gettys of his day. Surrounding the palace was a
great swampland dubbed "Lichtenthal" when it was transformed into
a Baroque-style garden; today, it has been restored along the lines of an
English landscape park, but with Baroque statues and topiaries.

The pride of the museum is the Peter Paul Rubens Room, showcasing the Decius Mus cycle, which illustrates episodes from the life of the heroic ancient Roman consul who waged a war against the Latins. The grandest picture of the eight-painting cycle illustrates the death of the consul, and it is high drama, indeed: Decius Mus gazes up to heaven as he falls off his massive gray steed as a lance pierces his throat in the middle of a pitched battle. All these paintings were made as models for a tapestry series, which is why Rubens's panels are so enormous. There are other Rubens gems here, including one of his best children's portraits, that of his daughter, *Clara Serena Rubens*. It's easy to spend the greater part of a day here. Behind the palace is the exquisite landscaped park. ⊠*Fürstengasse 1, 9th District/Alsergrund* ☎*01/319–5767–0* ⊕*www.liechtensteinmuseum.at* ⚐*€10* ⊗*Fri.–Tues. 10–5* Ⓤ*Bus: 40A/ Bauernfeldplatz, Tram: D/Bauernfeldplatz.*

🔟 **Spittelberg Quarter.** The Spittelberg is like a slice of Old Vienna, a perfectly preserved little enclave that allows you to experience the 18th century by strolling along cobblestone pedestrian streets lined with pretty Baroque town houses. The quarter—one block northwest of Maria-Theresien-Platz off the Burggasse—offers a fair visual idea of the Vienna that existed outside the city walls a century ago. Most buildings have been replaced, but the engaging 18th-century survivors at Burggasse 11 and 13 are adorned with religious and secular decorative sculpture, the latter with a niche statue of St. Joseph, the former with cherubic work-and-play bas-reliefs. For several blocks around—walk down Gutenberggasse and back up Spittelberggasse—the 18th-century houses have been beautifully restored. The sequence from Spittelberggasse 5 to 19 is an especially fine array of Viennese plain and fancy. Around holidays, particularly Easter and Christmas, the Spittelberg quarter, known for arts and handicrafts, hosts seasonal markets offering unusual and interesting wares. Promenaders will also find art galleries and loads of restaurants. ⊠*Off Burggasse, 7th District/Spittelberg* Ⓤ*U2 or U3/Volkstheater.*

🔟 **Universität** (*University of Vienna*). After the one in Prague, Vienna's is the oldest university in the German-speaking world (founded in 1365, but this is not the original building). The main section of the university is a massive block in Italian Renaissance style designed by Heinrich Ferstel and built between 1873 and 1884. Thirty-eight statues representing important men of letters decorate the front of the building, while the rear, which encompasses the library (with nearly 2 million volumes), is adorned with *sgraffito*. ⊠*Dr.-Karl-Lueger-Ring/Universitätstrasse, 1st District* Ⓤ*U2/Schottentor.*

🔟 **Volksgarten.** Just opposite the Hofburg is a green oasis with a rose garden, a 19th-century Greek temple, and a rather wistful white-marble monument to Empress Elisabeth—Franz Josef's Bavarian wife, who died of a dagger wound inflicted by an Italian anarchist in Geneva in 1898. If not overrun with latter-day hippies, these can offer spots to sit for a few minutes while contemplating Vienna's most ambitious piece of 19th-century city planning: the Ringstrasse. ⊠*Volksgarten, 1st District* Ⓤ*Tram: 1, 2, or D/Rathausplatz, Burgtheater.*

27 **Votivkirche** (*Votive Church*). When Emperor Franz Josef was a young man, he was strolling along the Mölker Bastei, now one of the few remaining portions of the old wall that once surrounded the city, when he was taken unawares and stabbed in the neck by a Hungarian revolutionary. The assassination attempt was unsuccessful, and in gratitude for his survival Franz Josef's family ordered that a church be built exactly at the spot he was gazing at when he was struck down. The neo-Gothic church was built of gray limestone with two openwork turrets between 1856 and 1879. ✉ *Rooseveltplatz, 9th District/Alsergrund* ☎ *01/406–1192* ⊙ *Tours by prior arrangement* Ⓤ *U2/Schottentor.*

FROM ST. STEPHEN'S TO THE OPERA HOUSE

The cramped, ancient quarter behind St. Stephen's Cathedral offers a fascinating contrast to the luxurious expanses of the Ringstrasse and more recent parts of Vienna. This was—and still is—concentrated residential territory in the heart of the city. Mozart lived here; later, Prince Eugene and others built elegant town palaces as the smaller buildings were replaced. Streets—now mostly reserved for pedestrians—are narrow, and tiny alleyways abound. Facades open into courtyards that once housed carriages and horses. The magnificent State Opera shares with St. Stephen's the honor of being one of the city's most familiar and beloved landmarks.

A GOOD WALK

To pass through these streets is to take a short journey through history and art. In the process—as you visit former haunts of Mozart, kings, and emperors—you can get a clear sense of how Vienna's glittering Habsburg centuries unfolded. Start from St. Stephen's Cathedral by walking down Singerstrasse to Blutgasse and turn left into the **Blutgasse District** ❺⓿—a neighborhood redolent of the 18th century. At the north end, in Domgasse, is the **Mozarthaus** ❺❶, now a memorial museum, the house in which Wolfgang Amadeus Mozart lived when he wrote the opera *The Marriage of Figaro*. Follow Domgasse east to Grünangergasse, which will bring you to Franziskanerplatz and the Gothic-Renaissance Franziskanerkirche (Franciscan Church). Follow the ancient Ballgasse to Rauhensteingasse, turning left onto **Himmelpfortgasse** ❹❾—Gates of Heaven Street. Prince Eugene of Savoy had his town palace here at No. 8, now the **Finanzministerium** ❹❽, and lived here when he wasn't enjoying his other residence, the Belvedere Palace. Continue down Himmelpfortgasse to Seilerstätte to visit a museum devoted to the wonders of music, the **Haus der Musik** ❹❼. Then turn in to Annagasse with its beautiful houses, which brings you back to the main shopping street, **Kärntnerstrasse** ❻❸, where you can find everything from Austrian crystal to the latest fashions. Turn left, walking north two blocks, and take the short Donnergasse to reach **Neuer Markt** square and the Providence Fountain. At the southwest corner of the square is the **Kaisergruft** ❻❷ in the Kapuzinerkirche (Capuchin Church), the burial vault for rows of Habsburgs. Tegetthofstrasse south will bring you to Albertinaplatz, the square noted for the war memorial and the **Albertina Museum** ❻❶, one of the world's great collections of Old Master

A Hop Through Hip Vienna

Paris has the Latin Quarter, London has Notting Hill, and the bohemian district in Vienna is the **Freihaus** sector, Vienna's trendiest neighborhood.

Freihaus, in the 17th century, within what is now the 4th District (Wieden), provided free housing to the city's poor, hence its name "Freihaus" or Free House. Destroyed in the Turkish siege of 1683, the complex was rebuilt on a much larger scale, becoming arguably the largest housing project in Europe at the time. It was a city within a city, including shops and the old Theater auf der Wieden, in which Mozart's *The Magic Flute* premiered. A slow decline followed, spanning Franz Josef's reign from the mid-19th century to the early 20th century, with some of the area razed to the ground before World War I. During World War II, bombing raids practically finished it off.

But then in the late 1990s a group of savvy local merchants revitalized the area, opening funky art galleries, antiques shops, espresso bars, trendy restaurants, and fashion boutiques. Freihaus is small, stretching from Karlsplatz to Kettenbrückengasse, which encompasses part of the Naschmarkt, the city's largest open-air market. Two of the best streets are Operngasse and Schleifmühlgasse.

What do you do with four immense gasometers more than 100 years old? Turn them into a cool, urban complex combining living and shopping, that's what. Looming large on the Vienna horizon, the **Gasometer** (⊕ *www. gasometer.org*) has generated a lot of publicity. Just to give an idea of their size, Vienna's giant Ferris wheel (the Riesenrad) at the Prater Amusement Park would fit easily inside each one.

Top architects were hired to accomplish the sleek and modern interior renovations, creating more than 600 modern apartments and a huge shopping mall with movie theaters and restaurants. It's in Simmering, Vienna's 11th District, and is eight minutes from the heart of the city on the U3 subway.

A visit to Vienna during the summer months would not be complete without a few hours spent on the Donauinsel (Danube Island), more popularly known as the **Copa Kagrana.** ("Kagrana" is taken from the name of the nearby local area known as Kagran.) It was originally built as a safeguard against flooding, but now this 13-square-mi island is where the Viennese head for bicycling, skateboarding, jogging, swimming, or just a leisurely stroll and dinner by the water. There are dozens of stalls and restaurants, offering grilled steaks, fried chicken, or freshly caught fish to go along with a mug of ice-cold draft beer or Austrian wine. Every year, 2 million visitors converge on the island for three days in June for an admission-free summer festival, the Donaufest (⊕ *www.donauinselfest.at*). The Copa Kagrana can be reached by subway: either the U1 to Donauinsel or the U6 to Handelskai.

drawings and prints. The southeast side of the square is bounded by the **Staatsoper** ❻ the State Opera House; check for tour possibilities or, better, book tickets for *Rosenkavalier*. Celebrate with a regal time-out at the **Café Sacher.**

TIMING This route could take you a half day if you stop occasionally to survey the scene. The restyled Mozarthaus is worth a visit, and the Kaisergruft in the Kapuzinerkirche is impressive for its shadows of past glories, but there are crowds, and you may have to wait to get in; the best times are early morning and around lunchtime. Tours of the State Opera House take place in the afternoon; check the schedule posted outside one of the doors on the arcaded Kärntnerstrasse side. Figure about an hour each for the various visits and tours.

MAIN ATTRACTIONS

❻ **Albertina Museum.** This not-to-be-missed collection is home to some
★ of the greatest Old Master drawings in Vienna—including Dürer's iconic *Praying Hands* and beloved *Alpine Hare*. The core collection of nearly 65,000 drawings and almost a million prints was begun by the 18th-century Duke Albert of Saxony-Teschen. All the names are here, from Leonardo da Vinci, Michelangelo, Raphael, and Rembrandt on down. The mansion's early-19th-century salons—all gilt-boiserie and mirrors—provide a jewel-box setting. DO & CO Albertina, the excellent in-house restaurant with a patio long enough for an empress's promenade, offers splendid vistas of the historical center and the Burggarten—the perfect place to take a break for a meal *(⇨ Where to Eat)*. ✉*Augustinerstrasse 1, 1st District* ☎*01/534–830* ⊕*www.albertina.at* ☞*€9.50* ☉*Daily 10–6, Wed. 10–9* Ⓤ*U3/Herrengasse.*

❹ **Haus der Musik** (*House of Music*). You could spend an entire day at this
☾ ultra-high-tech museum housed on several floors of an early-19th-century palace near Schwarzenbergplatz. Pride of place goes to the rooms dedicated to each of the great Viennese composers—Haydn, Mozart, Beethoven, Strauss, and Mahler—complete with music samples and manuscripts. Other exhibits trace the evolution of sound (from primitive noises to the music of the masters) and illustrate the mechanics of the human ear (measure your own frequency threshold). There are also dozens of interactive computer games. You can even take a turn as conductor of the Vienna Philharmonic—the conductor's baton is hooked to a computer, which allows you to have full control over the computer-simulated orchestra. Cantino is the wonderful in-house restaurant with fabulous views of the city *(⇨ Where to Eat)*. ✉*Seilerstätte 30, 1st District* ☎*01/51648–51* ☞*€10* ☉*Daily 10–10* ♿*Restaurant* Ⓤ*U1, U2, or U4/Karlsplatz, then Tram D/Schwarzenbergplatz.*

NEED A BREAK? This landmark café is in one of the most charming squares in Vienna, between Himmelpfortgasse and Singerstrasse. The **Kleines Cafe** (✉*Franziskanerplatz 3, 1st District* ☎*01/330–9138*) is open daily for coffee, cocktails, and light snacks, and few places are more delightful to sit and relax on a warm afternoon or evening. In summer, tables are set up outside on the intimate cobblestone square where the only sounds are the tinkling fountain and the occasional chiming of bells from the ancient Franciscan monastery next door. If you have time, take a stroll up Ballgasse, the tiny 18th-century street opposite the café, it's very quaint and pleasant.

49 Himmelpfortgasse. The maze of tiny streets including Ballgasse, Rauhensteingasse, and Himmelpfortgasse (literally, "Gates of Heaven Street") conjures up the Vienna of the 19th century. The most impressive house on the street is the Ministry of Finance. The back side of the Steffl department store on Rauhensteingasse now marks the site of the house in which Mozart died in 1791. There's a commemorative plaque that once identified the street-side site together with a small memorial corner devoted to Mozart memorabilia that can be found on the sixth floor of the store. ⊠ *1st District* Ⓤ *U1 or U3/Stephansplatz.*

63 Kärntnerstrasse. Kärntnerstrasse remains Vienna's leading central shopping street, if much maligned. Too commercial, too crowded, too many tasteless signs, too much gaudy neon—so the complaints go. Nevertheless, when the daytime tourist crowds dissolve, the Viennese arrive regularly for their evening promenade, and it is easy to see why. Vulgar the street may be, but it is also alive and vital, with an energy that the more tasteful Graben and the impeccable Kohlmarkt lack. For the sightseer beginning to suffer from an excess of art history, classic buildings, and museums, a Kärntnerstrasse window-shopping respite will be welcome. ⊠ *1st District* Ⓤ *U1, U4/Karlsplatz, or U1, U3/Stephansplatz.*

51 Mozarthaus. This is Mozart's only still-existing abode in Vienna.
★ Equipped with an excellent audio guide and starting out on the third floor of the building, you can hear about Mozart's time in Vienna: where he lived and performed, who his friends and supporters were, his relationship to the Freemasons, and his passion for expensive attire and gambling—he spent more money on clothes than most royals at that time. The second floor deals with Mozart's operatic works. The first floor focuses on the 2½ years that Mozart lived here, when he wrote dozens of piano concertos, as well as *The Marriage of Figaro* and the six quartets dedicated to Joseph Haydn (who once called on Mozart here, saying to Leopold, Mozart's father, "your son is the greatest composer that I know in person or by name"). For two weeks in April 1787 Mozart taught a pupil who would become famous in his own right, the 16-year-old Beethoven. ■TIP➜ **Save on the entrance fee by purchasing a combined ticket for Mozarthaus Vienna and Haus der Musik for €15.** ⊠ *Domgasse 5, 1st District* ☎ *01/512–1791* ⊕ *www.mozarthaus vienna.at* 💲 *€9* ⊙ *Daily 10–8* Ⓤ *U1 or U3/Stephansplatz.*

64 Staatsoper (*State Opera House*). The Vienna Staatsoper on the Ring vies
★ with the cathedral for the honor of emotional heart of the city—it's a focus for Viennese life and one of the chief symbols of resurgence after World War II. Its directorship is one of the top jobs in Austria, almost as important as that of the president of the country, and one that comes in for even more public attention. The first of the Ringstrasse projects to be completed (in 1869), the opera house suffered disastrous bomb damage in the last days of World War II (only the outer walls, the front facade, and the main staircase area behind it survived). The

1

auditorium is plain when compared to the red-and-gold eruptions of London's Covent Garden or some of the Italian opera houses, but it has an elegant individuality that shows to best advantage when the stage and auditorium are turned into a ballroom for the great Opera Ball.

The construction of the Opera House is the stuff of legend. When the foundation was laid, the plans for the Opernring were not yet complete, and in the end the avenue turned out to be several feet higher than originally planned. As a result, the Opera House lacked the commanding prospect that its architects, Eduard van der Null and August Sicard von Sicardsburg, had intended, and even Emperor Franz Josef pronounced the building a bit low to the ground. For the sensitive van der Null (and here the story becomes a bit suspect), failing his beloved emperor was the last straw. In disgrace and despair, he committed suicide. Sicardsburg died of grief shortly thereafter. And the emperor, horrified at the deaths his innocuous remark had caused, limited all his future artistic pronouncements to a single immutable formula: *"Es war sehr schön, es hat mich sehr gefreut"* ("It was very nice, it pleased me very much").

Renovation could not avoid a postwar look, for the cost of fully restoring the 19th-century interior was prohibitive. The original design was followed in the 1945–55 reconstruction, meaning that sight lines from some of the front boxes are poor at best. These disappointments hardly detract from the fact that this is one of the world's half-dozen greatest opera houses, and experiencing a performance here can be the highlight of a trip to Vienna. Tours of the Opera House are given regularly, but starting times vary according to opera rehearsals; the current schedule is posted under the arcades on both sides of the building. Under the arcade on the Kärntnerstrasse side is an information office that also sells tickets to the main opera and the Volksoper. ⊠*Opernring 2, 1st District* ☎*01/514–44–2613* ⊕*www.staatsoper.at* ⊠*€5* ⊙*Tours year-round when there are no rehearsals, but call for times* ⓊU1, U2, or U4 Karlsplatz.*

ALSO WORTH SEEING

⑤⓪ Blutgasse District. The small block bounded by Singerstrasse, Grünangergasse, and Blutgasse is known as the Blutgasse District. Nobody knows for certain how the gruesome name—*Blut* is German for "blood"—originated, although one legend has it that Knights Templar were slaughtered here when their order was abolished in 1312, although in later years the narrow street was known in those pre-pavement days as Mud Lane. Today the block is a splendid example of city renovation and restoration, with cafés, small shops, and galleries tucked into the corners. You can look inside the courtyards to see the open galleries that connect various apartments on the upper floors, the finest example being at Blutgasse 3. At the corner of Singerstrasse sits the 18th-century **Neupauer-Breuner Palace,** with its monumental entranceway and delicate windows. Opposite, at Singerstrasse 17, is the **Rottal Palace,** attributed to Hildebrandt, with its wealth of classical wall motifs. For contrast, turn up the narrow Blutgasse, with its simple 18th-century facades. ⊠*1st District* ⓊU1 or U3/Stephansplatz.*

48 Finanzministerium (*Ministry of Finance*). The architectural jewel of Himmelpfortgasse, this imposing abode—designed by Fischer von Erlach in 1697 and later expanded by Hildebrandt—was originally the town palace of Prince Eugene of Savoy. The Baroque details here are among the most inventive and beautifully executed in the city; all the decorative motifs are so softly carved that they appear to have been freshly squeezed from a pastry tube. Such Baroque elegance may seem inappropriate for a finance ministry, but the contrast between place and purpose could hardly be more Viennese. ✉ *Himmelpfortgasse 8, 1st District* Ⓤ *U1 or U3/Stephansplatz.*

62 Kaisergruft (*Imperial Burial Vault*). In the basement of the Kapuzinerkirche, or Capuchin Church (on the southwest corner of the Neuer Markt), is one of the more intriguing sights in Vienna: the Kaisergruft, or Imperial Burial Vault. The crypts contain the partial remains of some 140 Habsburgs (most of the hearts are in the Augustinerkirche and the entrails in St. Stephen's) plus one non-Habsburg governess ("She was always with us in life," said Maria Theresa, "why not in death?"). Perhaps starting with their tombs is the wrong way to approach the Habsburgs in Vienna, but it does give you a chance to get their names in sequence, as they lie in rows, their pewter coffins ranging from the simplest explosions of funerary conceit—with decorations of skulls, snakes, and other morbid symbols—to the huge and distinguished tomb of Maria Theresa and her husband. Designed while the couple still lived, their monument shows the empress in bed with her husband—awaking to the Last Judgment as if it were just another weekday morning, while the remains of her son (the ascetic Josef II) lie in a simple copper casket at the foot of the bed as if he were the family dog. ✉ *Neuer Markt/Tegetthofstrasse 2, 1st District* ☎ *01/512–6853–12* 💶 *€4* ⊙ *Daily 10–6* Ⓤ *U1, U3/Stephansplatz or U1, U4/Karlsplatz.*

SOUTH OF THE RING TO THE BELVEDERE

City planning in the late 1800s and early 1900s was essential in managing the growth of the burgeoning imperial capital. The elegant Ringstrasse alone was not a sufficient showcase, and anyway, it focused on public rather than private buildings. The city fathers as well as private individuals commissioned the architect Otto Wagner to plan and undertake a series of projects. Not all of Wagner's concepts for Karlsplatz were realized, but enough remains to convey the impression of what might have been.

A GOOD WALK

The often overlooked **Akademie der bildenen Künste** 42, or Academy of Fine Arts, is an appropriate starting point for this walk, as it puts into perspective the artistic arguments taking place around the turn of the century. While the Academy represented the conservative viewpoint, a group of Modernist revolutionaries broke away and founded the Secessionist movement, with its culmination in the gold-crowned **Secession Building** 43. Now housing changing exhibits and Gustav Klimt's *Beethoven Frieze*, the museum stands close to the Academy: from it, take Makartgasse south one block. The **Naschmarkt** ❹ open food market starts diagonally south from the Secession; follow the rows of stalls southwest. Pay attention to the northwest side, the Linke Wienzeile, with the Theater an der Wien at the intersection with Millöckergasse (Beethoven premiered some of his finest works at this opera house–theater) and the **Otto Wagner Houses** ❹. Head back north through the Naschmarkt; at the top end, cross Wiedner Hauptstrasse, to your right, into the park complex that forms Karlsplatz, creating a frame for the **Karlskirche** ❹. Around **Karlsplatz** ❻, note the Technical University on the south side, and the Otto Wagner subway-station buildings on the north. Across Lothringer Strasse on the north side are the Künstlerhaus art exhibition hall and the Musikverein. The out-of-place and undistinguished modern building to the left of the Karlskirche houses the worthwhile **Wien Museum Karlsplatz** ❹. Cut through Symphonikerstrasse (a passageway through the modern complex) and take Brucknerstrasse to **Schwarzenbergplatz** ❻. The Jugendstil edifice on your left is the French Embassy; ahead is the Russian War Memorial. On a rise behind the memorial sits Palais Schwarzenberg, a jewel of a onetime summer palace and now a luxury hotel. Follow Prinz-Eugen-Strasse up to the entrance of the **Belvedere Palace** ❹ complex on your left. Besides the palace itself there are other structures and, off to the east side, a remarkable botanical garden. After viewing the palace and grounds you can exit the complex from the lower building, the Untere Belvedere, onto Rennweg, which will steer you back to Schwarzenbergplatz.

TIMING The first part of this walk, taking in the Academy of Fine Arts and the Secession, plus the Naschmarkt and Karlsplatz, can be accomplished in an easy half day. The Wien Museum Karlsplatz is good for a couple of hours, more if you understand some German. Give the Belvedere Palace and gardens as much time as you can. Organized tours breeze in and out of the grounds—without so much as a glance at the outstanding art museum—in a half hour or so, not even scratching the surface here. If you can, budget up to a half day here, but plan to arrive fairly early in the morning or afternoon before the busloads descend. Bus tourists aren't taken to the Lower Belvedere, so you'll have that to yourself.

MAIN ATTRACTIONS

OFF THE
BEATEN
PATH

Am Steinhof Church. Otto Wagner's most exalted piece of Jugendstil architecture lies in the suburbs to the west: the Am Steinhof Church, designed in 1904 during his Secessionist phase. You can reach the church by taking the U4 subway line, which is adjacent to the Otto Wagner Houses. On the grounds of the Vienna City Psychiatric Hospital, Wagner's design unites functional details (rounded edges on the pews to prevent injury to the patients and a slightly sloped tile floor to facilitate cleaning) with a soaring, airy dome and glittering Jugendstil decoration (stained glass by Koloman Moser). The church is open Saturday at 3 for a guided tour (in German) for €6. English tours can be arranged in advance at €6 per person *for* groups of 10 or more. (Even with fewer people, you still must pay the price for 10.) You may walk around the church on your own for free between 4 and 5 PM on Saturday. ⊠*Baumgartner Höhe 1, 13th District/Hütteldorf* ☎*01/91060–11–204* 🎫*€6*

⊘*Sat. 3–4, 4–5* Ⓤ*U4/Unter-St.-Veit, then Bus 47A to Psychiatrisches Krankenhaus; or U2/Volkstheater, then Bus 48A.*

㊻ **Belvedere Palace.** One of the most splendid pieces of Baroque archi-
Fodor'sChoice tecture anywhere, the Belvedere Palace—actually two imposing pal-
★ aces separated by a 17th-century French-style garden parterre—is one
of the masterpieces of architect Lucas von Hildebrandt. Built outside
the city fortifications between 1714 and 1722, the complex originally
served as the summer palace of Prince Eugene of Savoy; much later it
became the home of Archduke Franz Ferdinand, whose assassination
in 1914 precipitated World War I. Though the lower palace is impressive in its own right, it is the much larger upper palace, used for state
receptions, banquets, and balls, that is acknowledged as Hildebrandt's
masterpiece. The usual tourist entrance for the Upper Belvedere is the
gate on Prinz-Eugen-Strasse (No. 27); for the Lower Belvedere, use the
Rennweg gate (No. 6a). But for the most impressive view of the upper
palace, approach it from the south garden closest to the South Rail
Station. The upper palace displays a wealth of architectural invention
in its facade, avoiding the main design problems common to palaces
because of their size: monotony on the one hand and pomposity on the
other. Hildebrandt's decorative manner here approaches the rococo,
that final style of the Baroque era when traditional classical motifs all
but disappeared in a whirlwind of seductive asymmetric fancy. The
main interiors of the palace go even further: columns are transformed
into muscle-bound giants, pilasters grow torsos, capitals sprout great
piles of symbolic imperial paraphernalia, and the ceilings are aswirl
with ornately molded stucco. The result is the finest rococo interior
in the city. On the garden level you are greeted by the **Sala Terrena**
whose massive Atlas figures shoulder the marble vaults of the ceiling and, it seems, the entire palace above. The next floor is centered
around a gigantic Marble Hall covered with trompe l'oeil frescoes,
while down in the Lower Belvedere palace, there are more 17th-century
salons, including the Grotesque Room painted by Jonas Drentwett and
another Marble Hall (which really lives up to its name).

Both the upper and lower palaces of the Belvedere are museums devoted
to Austrian painting. The Belvedere's main attraction is the collection
of 19th- and 20th-century Austrian paintings, centering on the work
of Vienna's three preeminent early-20th-century artists: Gustav Klimt,
Egon Schiele, and Oskar Kokoschka. Klimt was the oldest, and by the
time he helped found the Secession movement he had forged an idio-
syncratic painting style that combined realistic and decorative elements
in a way that was revolutionary. *The Kiss*—his greatest painting—is
here on display. Schiele and Kokoschka went even further, rejecting the
decorative appeal of Klimt's glittering abstract designs and producing
works that ignored conventional ideas of beauty. ⊠*Prinz-Eugen-Strasse
27, 3rd District/Landstrasse* ☎*01/795–57–134* ⊕*www.belvedere.
at* ☎*€12.50* ⊘*Daily 10–6; Lower Belvedere and Orangerie Wed.
10–9* Ⓤ*U1, U2, or U4 Karlsplatz, then Tram D/Belvederegasse.*

㊹ **Karlskirche.** Dominating the Karlsplatz is one of Vienna's greatest build-
★ ings, the Karlskirche, dedicated to St. Charles Borromeo. Before you

is a giant Baroque church framed by enormous freestanding columns, mates to Rome's famous Trajan's Column. These columns may be out of keeping with the building as a whole, but were conceived with at least two functions in mind: one was to portray scenes from the life of the patron saint, carved in imitation of Trajan's triumphs, and thus help to emphasize the imperial nature of the building; and the other was to symbolize the Pillars of Hercules, suggesting the right of the Habsburgs to their Spanish dominions, which the emperor had been forced to renounce. The end result is an architectural tour de force.

The Karlskirche was built in the early 18th century on what was then the bank of the River Wien and is now the southeast corner of the park complex. The church had its beginnings in a disaster. In 1713 Vienna was hit by a brutal outbreak of plague, and Emperor Charles VI made a vow: if the plague abated, he would build a church dedicated to his namesake, St. Charles Borromeo, the 16th-century Italian bishop who was famous for his ministrations to Milanese plague victims. In 1715 construction began, using an ambitious design by Johann Bernhard Fischer von Erlach that combined architectural elements from ancient Greece (the columned entrance porch), ancient Rome (the Trajanesque columns), contemporary Rome (the Baroque dome), and contemporary Vienna (the Baroque towers at either end). When it was finished, the church received decidedly mixed press. History, too, delivered a negative verdict: the Karlskirche spawned no imitations, and it went on to become one of European architecture's curiosities. Notwithstanding, seen lighted at night, the building is magical in its setting.

The main interior of the church utilizes only the area under the dome and is conventional despite the unorthodox facade. The space and architectural detailing are typical High Baroque; the fine vault frescoes, by J.M. Rottmayr, depict St. Charles Borromeo imploring the Holy Trinity to end the plague. If you are not afraid of heights take the panorama elevator up into the sphere of the dome and climb the top steps to enjoy an unrivalled view into the heart of the city. ⊠ *Karlsplatz, 4th District/Wieden* ☎ *01/504–61–87* 🖃 *€6* ⊙ *Daily 9–12:30 and 1–6* Ⓤ *U1, U2, or U4 Karlsplatz.*

⑥⑤ Karlsplatz. Like the space now occupied by the Naschmarkt, Karlsplatz was formed when the River Wien was covered over at the turn of the 20th century. At the time, Wagner expressed his frustration with the result—too large a space for a formal square and too small a space for an informal park—and the awkwardness is felt to this day. The buildings surrounding the Karlsplatz, however, are quite sure of themselves: the area is dominated by the classic **Karlskirche,** made less dramatic by the unfortunate reflecting pool with its Henry Moore sculpture, wholly out of place, in front. On the south side of the Resselpark, that part of Karlsplatz named for the inventor of the screw propeller for ships, stands the **Technical University** (1816–18). In a house that occupied the space closest to the church, Italian composer Antonio Vivaldi died in 1741; a plaque marks the spot. On the north side, across the heavily traveled roadway, are the **Künstlerhaus** (the exhibition hall in which the Secessionists refused to exhibit, built in 1881 and still in use) and the

Musikverein. The latter, finished in 1869, is now home to the Vienna Philharmonic. The downstairs lobby and the two halls upstairs have been restored and glow with fresh gilding. The main hall has what may be the world's finest acoustics.

Some of Otto Wagner's finest Secessionist work can be seen two blocks east on the northern edge of Karlsplatz. In 1893 Wagner was appointed architectural supervisor of the new Vienna City Railway, and the matched pair of small pavilions he designed, the **Otto Wagner Stadtbahn Pavilions**, at No. 1 Karlsplatz, in 1898 are among the city's most ingratiating buildings. Their structural framework is frankly exposed (in keeping with Wagner's belief in architectural honesty), but they are also lovingly decorated (in keeping with the Viennese fondness for architectural finery). The result is Jugendstil at its very best, melding plain and fancy with grace and insouciance. The pavilion to the southwest is utilized as a small, specialized museum. In the course of redesigning Karlsplatz, it was Wagner, incidentally, who proposed moving the fruit and vegetable market to what is now the Naschmarkt. ⊠ *4th District/Wieden* Ⓤ *U1, U2, or U4/Karlsplatz.*

④① Naschmarkt. The area between Linke and Rechte Wienzeile has for 80 years been home to the Naschmarkt, Vienna's main outdoor produce market, certainly one of Europe's—if not the world's—great open-air markets, where packed rows of polished and stacked fruits and vegetables compete for visual appeal with braces of fresh pheasant in season; the nostrils, meanwhile, are accosted by spice fragrances redolent of Asia or the Middle East. It's open Monday to Saturday 7 AM–6:30 PM (many stalls open an hour later and close two hours earlier in winter months). ■TIP➜ **Be sure you get the correct change and watch the scales when your goods are weighed.** ⊠ *Between Linke and Rechte Wienzeile, 4th District/Wieden* Ⓤ *U1, U2, or U4 Karlsplatz (follow signs to Secession).*

NEED A BREAK?

There are so many enticing snack stands in the Naschmarkt that it's hard to choose. A host of Turkish stands offer juicy *Döner* sandwiches—thinly sliced, pressed lamb with onions and a yogurt sauce in a freshly baked roll. A number of Asian noodle and sushi stalls offer quick meals, and many snack bars offer Viennese dishes. At the Karlsplatz end of the Naschmarkt is the "Nordsee" glass-enclosed seafood hut.

④⓪ Otto Wagner Houses. The Ringstrasse-style apartment houses that line the Wienzeile are an attractive, if generally standard, lot, but two stand out: **Linke Wienzeile 38 and 40**—the latter better known as the "Majolica House"—designed (1898–99) by the grand old man of Viennese fin-de-siècle architecture, Otto Wagner. A good example of what Wagner was rebelling against can be seen next door, at **Linke Wienzeile 42**, where decorative enthusiasm has blossomed into Baroque Revival hysteria. Wagner banished classical decoration and introduced a new architectural simplicity, with flat exterior walls and plain, regular window treatments meant to reflect the orderly layout of the apartments behind them. There the simplicity ended. For exterior decora-

Jugendstil Jewels

From 1897 to 1907, the Vienna Secession movement gave rise to one of the most spectacular manifestations of the pan-European style known as Art Nouveau. Viennese took to calling the look *Jugendstil,* or the "young style." In such dazzling edifices as Otto Wagner's Wienzeile majolica-adorned mansion, Jugendstil architects rebelled against the prevailing 19th-century historicism that had created so many imitation Renaissance town houses and faux Grecian temples. Josef Maria Olbrich, Josef Hoffman, and Otto Schönthal took William Morris's Arts and Crafts movement, added dashes of Charles Rennie Mackintosh and flat-surface Germanic geometry, and came up with a luxurious style that shocked turn-of-the-20th century Viennese traditionalists (and infuriated Emperor Franz Josef). Many artists united to form the Vienna Secession—whose most famous member was painter Gustav Klimt—and the Wiener Werkstätte, which transformed the objects of daily life with a sleek modern look. Today Jugendstil buildings are among the most fascinating structures in Vienna. The shrine of the movement is the Secession Building.

---

tion, he turned to his younger Secessionist cohorts Joseph Olbrich and Koloman Moser, who designed the ornate Jugendstil patterns of red majolica-tile roses (No. 40) and gold stucco medallions (No. 38) that gloriously brighten the facades of the adjacent houses so much so that their Baroque-period neighbor is ignored. The houses are privately owned. ⊠*4th District/Wieden* Ⓤ*U1, U2, or U4/Karlsplatz.*

66 **Schwarzenbergplatz.** The center of this square off the Ring is marked by an oversize equestrian sculpture of Prince Schwarzenberg—he was a 19th-century field marshal for the imperial forces. See if you can guess which building is the newest—it's the one on the northeast corner (No. 3) at Lothringer Strasse, an exacting reproduction of a building destroyed by war damage in 1945 and dating only from the 1980s. The military monument occupying the south end of the square behind the fountain is the **Russian War Memorial,** set up at the end of World War II by the Soviets; the Viennese, remembering the Soviet occupation, call its unknown soldier the "unknown plunderer." South of the memorial is the stately **Schwarzenberg Palace,** designed as a summer residence by Johann Lukas von Hildebrandt in 1697 and completed by Fischer von Erlach father and son. ⊠*Schwarzenbergplatz, 3rd District/ Landstrasse* Ⓤ*Tram: Schwarzenbergplatz.*

43 **Secession Building.** If the Academy of Fine Arts represents the conservative attitude toward the arts in the late 1800s, then its antithesis can be found in the building immediately behind it to the southeast: the Secession Pavilion, one of Vienna's preeminent symbols of artistic rebellion. Rather than looking to the architecture of the past, like the revivalist Ringstrasse, it looked to a new antihistoricist future. It was, in its day, a riveting trumpet-blast of a building, and is today considered by many to be Europe's first example of full-blown 20th-century architecture.

The Secession began in 1897, when 20 dissatisfied Viennese artists, headed by Gustav Klimt, "seceded" from the Künstlerhausgenossenschaft, the conservative artists' society associated with the Academy of Fine Arts. The movement promoted the radically new kind of art known as Jugendstil, which found its inspiration in both the organic, fluid designs of Art Nouveau and the related but more geometric designs of the English Arts and Crafts movement. (The Secessionists founded an Arts and Crafts workshop of their own, the Wiener Werkstätte, in an effort to embrace the applied arts.) The Secession building, designed by the architect Joseph Olbrich and completed in 1898, was the movement's exhibition hall. The lower story, crowned by the entrance motto *Der Zeit Ihre Kunst, Der Kunst Ihre Freiheit* ("To Every Age Its Art, To Art Its Freedom"), is classic Jugendstil: the restrained but assured decoration (by Koloman Moser) complements the facade's pristine flat expanses of cream-color wall. Above the entrance motto sits the building's most famous feature, the gilded openwork dome that the Viennese were quick to christen "the golden cabbage" (Olbrich wanted it to be seen as a dome of laurel, a subtle classical reference meant to celebrate the triumph of art). The plain white interior—"shining and chaste," in Olbrich's words—was also revolutionary; its most unusual feature was movable walls, allowing the galleries to be reshaped and redesigned for every show. One early show, in 1902, was a temporary exhibition devoted to art celebrating the genius of Beethoven; Klimt's *Beethoven Frieze* was painted for the occasion, and is on display in a special, temperature-controlled room. ⊠ *Friedrichstrasse 12, 4th District/Wieden* 🖀 *01/587–5307–0* ⊕ *www.secession.at* 🖃 *€4.50 exhibition, €6 exhibition with Beethoven Frieze, €1.50 guided tour* ☉ *Tues.–Sun. 10–6, Thurs. 10–8, guided tours Sat. at 3 and Sun. at 11.*

㊺ Wien Museum Karlsplatz (*Museum of Viennese History*). Housed in an incongruously modern building at the east end of the regal Karlsplatz, this museum possesses Viennese historical artifacts and treasures: everything from 16th-century armor to paintings by Schiele and Klimt and the preserved facade of Otto Wagner's *Die Zeit* offices. ⊠ *Karlsplatz, 4th District/Wieden* 🖀 *01/505–8747–0* ⊕ *www.wienmuseum.at* 🖃 *€6* ☉ *Tues.–Sun. 9–6* Ⓤ *U1, U2, or U4 Karlsplatz.*

ALSO WORTH SEEING
㊷ Akademie der bildenen Künste (*Academy of Fine Arts*). If the teachers here had admitted Adolf Hitler as an art student in 1907 and 1908 instead of rejecting him, history might have proved very different. The Academy was founded in 1692, but the present Renaissance Revival building dates from the late 19th century. The idea was conservatism and traditional values, even in the face of a growing movement that scorned formal rules. The Academy includes a museum focusing on Old Masters. The collection is mainly of interest to specialists, but Hieronymus Bosch's *Last Judgment* triptych hangs here—an imaginative, if gruesome, speculation on the hereafter. ⊠ *Schillerplatz 3, 1st District* 🖀 *01/588–16–225* ⊕ *www.akademiegalerie.at* 🖃 *€7* ☉ *Tues.– Sun. 10–6* Ⓤ *U1, U2, or U4 Karlsplatz.*

Dritte Mann Museum (*Third Man Museum*). This shrine for film aficionados is close to the Naschmarkt and offers an extensive private collection of memorabilia dedicated to the classic film directed by Carol Reed and shot entirely on location in Vienna. Authentic exhibits include cinema programs, autographed cards, movie and sound recordings, and first editions of Graham Greene's novel, which was the basis of the screenplay. Also here is the original zither used by Anton Karas to record the film's music, which started a zither boom in the '50s. Karas, born in Vienna in 1906, had his 100th birthday celebrated with commemorative performances of the music that made history: the "Harry Lime Theme." Listen to the original shellac that's played on an old music cabinet. In the reading corner, you can browse through historic newspaper articles about the film. ⊠*Pressgasse 25, 4th District* ☎*01/586–4872* ⊕*www.3mpc.net* ✉*€7.50* ⊙*Sat. 2–6* Ⓤ*U4/ Kettenbrückengasse.*

OFF THE BEATEN PATH **Zentralfriedhof.** Taking a streetcar out of Schwarzenbergplatz, you can make a pilgrimage to the **Zentralfriedhof** (Central Cemetery), which contains the graves of most of Vienna's great composers: Ludwig van Beethoven, Franz Schubert, Johannes Brahms, the Johann Strausses (father and son), and Arnold Schönberg, among others. The monument to Wolfgang Amadeus Mozart is a memorial only; the approximate location of his unmarked grave can be seen at the now deconsecrated St. Marx-Friedhof at Leberstrasse 6–8. ⊠*Simmeringer Hauptstrasse, 11th District/Simmering* Ⓤ*Tram: 71 to St. Marxer Friedhof, or on to Zentralfriedhof Haupttor/2.*

THE HABSBURGS' SCHÖNBRUNN PALACE

The glories of imperial Austria are nowhere brought together more convincingly than in the Schönbrunn Palace (Schloss Schönbrunn) complex. Imperial elegance, interrupted only by tourist traffic, flows unbroken throughout the grounds. This is Austria's primary tourist site, although few stay long enough to discover the real Schönbrunn (including the fountain with the little maiden carrying the water jar, after whom the complex is named). The outbuildings served as entertainment centers when the court moved to Schönbrunn in summer, accounting for the zoo, the priceless theater, the fake Roman ruins, the greenhouses, and the walkways. In Schönbrunn you step back 270 years into the heart of a powerful and growing empire and follow it through to defeat and demise in 1918.

A GOOD WALK

The usual start for exploring the Schönbrunn complex is the main palace. There's nothing wrong with that approach, but as a variation, consider first climbing to the **Gloriette** ❽ on the hill overlooking the site for a bird's-eye view to put the rest in perspective (take the stairs to the Gloriette roof for the ultimate experience). While at the Gloriette, take a few steps west to discover the **Tiroler House** ❽ and follow the zigzag path downhill to the palace; note the picture-book views of the main building through the woods. Try to take the full tour of **Schön-**

brunn Palace ❽❾ rather than the truncated version. Check whether the ground-floor back rooms (Berglzimmer) are open for viewing. After the palace guided tour, take your own walk around the grounds. The Schöner Brunnen, the namesake fountain, is hidden in the woods to the southeast; continue along to discover the convincing (but fake) Roman ruins. At the other side of the complex to the west are the **Tiergarten** ❽❺ (zoo), and **Palmenhaus** ❽❻ (tropical greenhouse). Closer to the main entrance, both the **Wagenburg** ❽❽ (carriage museum) and Schlosstheater (palace theater) are frequently overlooked treasures. Before heading back to the city center, visit the **Hofpavillon** ❽❼, the private subway station built for Emperor Franz Josef, to the west across Schönbrunner Schlossstrasse.

TIMING If you're pressed for time, the shorter tour will give you a fleeting impression of the palace itself, but try to allot at least half a day to take the full tour and include the extra rooms and grounds. The 20-minute hike up to the Gloriette is a bit strenuous but worthwhile, and there's a café as reward at the top. The zoo is worth as much time as you can spare, and figure on at least a half hour to an hour each for the other museums. Tour buses begin to unload for the main building by 9 AM; start early or go during the noon lull to avoid the worst crowds. The other museums and buildings in the complex are far less crowded.

WHAT TO SEE

❽❸ **Gloriette.** At the crest of the hill, topping off the Schönbrunn Schlosspark, sits a Baroque masterstroke: Johann Ferdinand von Hohenberg's Gloriette, now restored to its original splendor. Perfectly scaled, the Gloriette—a palatial pavilion that once offered royal guests a place to rest and relax on their tours of the palace grounds and that now houses a welcome café—holds the vast garden composition together and at the same time crowns the ensemble with a brilliant architectural tiara. This was a favorite spot of Maria Theresa's, though in later years she grew so obese it took six men to carry her in her palanquin to the summit. ⊠ *13th District* Ⓤ *U4/Schönbrunn.*

❽❼ **Hofpavillon.** The unusual interior of the Schönbrunn Palace complex, the restored imperial subway station known as the Hofpavillon is just outside the palace grounds (at the northwest corner, a few yards east of the Hietzing subway station). Designed by Otto Wagner in conjunction with Joseph Olbrich and Leopold Bauer, the Hofpavillon was built in 1899 for the exclusive use of Emperor Franz Josef and his entourage. Exclusive it was: the emperor used the station only once. The exterior, with its proud architectural crown, is Wagner at his best, and the lustrous interior is one of the finest examples of Jugendstil decoration in the city. ⊠ *Schönbrunner Schloss-Strasse, next to Hietzing subway station, 13th District/Hietzing* ☎ *01/877–1571* 💶 *Free* 🕙 *Sun. 10:30–12:30* Ⓤ *U4/Hietzing.*

❽❻ **Palmenhaus.** On the grounds to the west of Schönbrunn Palace is a huge greenhouse filled with exotic trees and plants. ⊠ *Nearest entrance is Hietzing, 13th District/Hietzing* ☎ *01/877–5087* 💶 *€4* 🕙 *May–Sept., daily 9:30–6; Oct.–Apr., daily 9:30–5.*

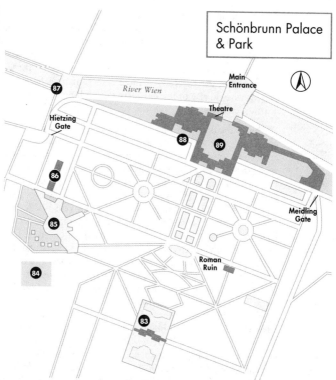

Schönbrunn Palace & Park

89 **Schönbrunn Palace.** Originally designed by Johann Bernhard Fischer von
FodorśChoice Erlach in 1696 and altered considerably for Maria Theresa 40 years
★ later, Schönbrunn Palace, the huge Habsburg summer residence, lies
within the city limits, just a few subway stops west of Karlsplatz on line
U4. The vast and elegant **gardens** are open daily from dawn until dusk,
and multilingual guided tours of the palace interior are offered daily.
A visit inside the palace is not included in most general city sightseeing
tours, which offer either a tempting drive past it, or else a short half
hour or so to explore. The four-hour commercial sightseeing-bus tours
of Schönbrunn offered by tour operators cost several times what you'd
pay if you tackled the easy excursion yourself; their advantage is that
they get you there and back with less effort. Go on your own if you
want time to wander through the grounds.

The most impressive approach to the palace and its gardens is through
the front gate, set on Schönbrunner Schloss-Strasse halfway between
the Schönbrunn and Hietzing subway stations. The vast main courtyard is ruled by a formal design of impeccable order and rigorous
symmetry: wing nods at wing, facade mirrors facade, and every part
stylistically complements every other. The courtyard, however, turns
out to be a mere appetizer; the feast lies beyond. The breathtaking view
that unfolds on the other side of the palace is one of the finest set pieces

in all Europe and one of the supreme achievements of Baroque planning. Formal *Allées* (garden promenades) shoot off diagonally, the one on the right toward the zoo, the one on the left toward a rock-mounted obelisk and a fine false Roman ruin. But these, and the woods beyond, are merely a frame for the composition in the center: the sculpted marble fountain; the carefully planted screen of trees behind; the sudden, almost vertical rise of the grass-covered hill beyond, with the **Gloriette** a fitting crown.

Within the palace, the state salons are quite up to the splendor of the gardens, but note the contrast between these chambers and the far more modest rooms in which the rulers—particularly Franz Josef—lived and spent most of their time. Of the 1,441 rooms, 40 are open to the public on the regular tour, of which two are of special note: the Hall of Mirrors, where the six-year-old Mozart performed for Empress Maria Theresa in 1762 (and where he met seven-year-old Marie Antoinette for the first time, developing a little crush on her), and the Grand Gallery, where the Congress of Vienna (1815) danced at night after carving up Napoléon's collapsed empire during the day. Ask about viewing the ground-floor living quarters (Berglzimmer), where the walls are painted with palm trees, exotic animals, and tropical views. As you go through the palace, glance occasionally out the windows; you'll be rewarded by a better impression of the formal gardens, punctuated by hedgerows and fountains. These window vistas were enjoyed by rulers from Maria Theresa and Napoléon to Franz Josef. ⊠ *Schönbrunner-Schloss-Strasse, 13th District/Hietzing* ☎ *01/81113–239* ⊕ *www.schoenbrunn. at* ✍ *Guided grand tour of palace interior (40 rooms) €14.40, self-guided tour €12.90* ☉ *Apr.–June, Sept., and Oct., daily 8:30–5; July and Aug., daily 8:30–6; Nov.–Mar., daily 8:30–4:30. Park Apr.–Oct., daily 6 AM–dusk; Nov.–Mar., daily 6:30 AM–dusk* Ⓤ*U4/Schönbrunn.*

⑧⑤ **Tiergarten.** Claimed to be the world's oldest, the Tiergarten zoo has
Ⓒ retained its original Baroque decor, but new settings have been created for both animals and public. In one case, the public looks out into a new, natural display area from one of the Baroque former animal houses. The zoo is constantly adding new attractions and undergoing renovations, so there's plenty to see. ⊠ *Schönbrunner Schloss-park, 13th District/Hietzing* ☎ *01/877–9294–0* ⊕ *www.zoovienna.at* ✍ *€12; combination ticket with Palmenhaus €16* ☉ *Nov.–Jan., daily 9–4:30; Feb., daily 9–5; Mar. and Oct., daily 9–5:30; Apr.–Sept., daily 9–6:30* Ⓤ*U4/Schönbrunn.*

⑧④ **Tiroler House.** This Tyrolean-style building to the west of the Gloriette was a favorite retreat of Empress Elisabeth; it now includes a small restaurant (open according to season and weather). ⊠ *Schönbrunner Schlosspark, 13th District/Hietzing* Ⓤ*U4/Schönbrunn.*

⑧⑧ **Wagenburg** *(Carriage Museum)*. Most of the carriages are still road-
Ⓒ worthy, and in fact Schönbrunn dusted off the gilt-and-black royal funeral carriage that you see here for the burial ceremony of Empress Zita in 1989. ⊠ *Schönbrunner Schlosspark, 13th District/Hietzing* ☎ *01/877-3244* ⊕ *www.khm.at/* ✍ *€4.50* ☉ *Apr.–Oct., daily 9–6; Nov.–Mar., daily 10–4* Ⓤ*U4/Schönbrunn.*

1

**OFF THE
BEATEN
PATH**

Technisches Museum. About a 10-minute walk from Schönbrunn Palace is the **Technical Museum,** which traces the evolution of industrial development over the past two centuries. On four floors you'll find actual locomotives from the 19th century, a Tin Lizzie, airplanes from the early days of flying, as well as examples of factory life, how electric lighting took the place of gas lamps, and how mountain highway tunnels are constructed. And, appropriate for such a music-loving city, a whole section is devoted to the work involved in creating different musical instruments. ✉*Mariahilferstrasse 212, 14th District/ Penzing* ☎*01/899–9860–00* ⊕*www.tmw.at* ✆*€8.50* ⊘*Weekdays 9–6, weekends 10–6* Ⓤ*U3 or U6/Westbahnhof, then Tram 52 or 58/ Penzingerstrasse.*

WHERE TO EAT

To appreciate how far the restaurant scene in Vienna has come in recent years, it helps to recall the way things used to be. Up until about 10 years ago, Austria was still dining in the 19th century. Most dinners were a *mittel-europäisch* sloshfest of *Schweinebraten, Knödeln,* and *Kraut* (pork, dumplings, and cabbage). No one denies that such courtly delights as *Tafelspitz*—the blush-pink boiled beef famed as Emperor Franz Josef's favorite dish—is delicious, but most traditional carb-loaded, nap-inducing meals left you stuck to your seat like a suction pad. If you consumed a plate-filling schnitzel and were able to eat anything after it, you were looked upon as a phenomenon—or an Austrian. A lighter, more nouvelle take on cuisine had difficulty making incursions because many meals were centered around *Rehrücken* (venison), served up in wine-cellar recipes of considerable—nay, medieval—antiquity.

Today, Vienna's dining scene is as lively, experimental, and as good as it is thanks in part to changing epicurean tastes and a rising generation of chefs dedicated to taking the culinary heritage of the nation to a new phase of *Neu Wiener Küche* (New Vienna Cuisine). No longer tucked away in anonymous kitchens, cooks now create signature dishes that rocket them to fame; they earn fan clubs and host television shows; there are star Austrian chefs in Vienna the way there are in New York and Hollywood, and these Viennese chefs want to delight an audience hungry for change. Schmaltzy schnitzels have been replaced by Styrian beef, while soggy *Nockerl* (small dumplings) are traded in for seasonal delights like Carinthian asparagus, Styrian wild garlic, or the common alpine-garden stinging nettle. The old goulash and bratwurst have given way to true gustatory excitement, though you can always find the time-honored standards of Wiener Küche at the *Beisln,* Vienna's answer to Paris's bistros and London's gastro-pubs.

■TIP➔ The basket of bread put on your table is not free. Most of the older-style Viennese restaurants charge €0.70–€1.70 for each roll that is eaten, but more establishments are charging a per-person cover charge (anywhere from €1.50 to €7.50), which includes all the bread you want, plus usually an herb spread and butter.

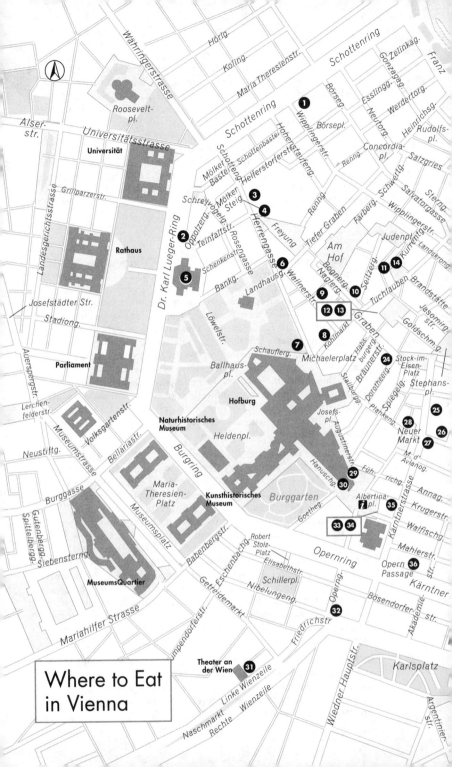

Where to Eat in Vienna

1

Oberе Donaustrasse
Danube Canal
Holländstr.
Taborstr.
osefs Kai
olsdorfg.
Salztorg.
Salztorbr.
Marc-Aurel-Str.
Morzin-
pl.
Danube
Judengasse
Praterstr.
Franz
Josefs Kai
Canal
Schweden-
pl.
Raben Steig
Fleischmarkt
Laurenzer
berg
Köllnerhof.
Postg.
Dominikanerbastei
Bäckerstr.
Sonnenfelsg.
Schön latern g.
Wollzeile
Postg.
Biberstr.
Domg.
Schulerstr.
Zedlitzg.
Blutg.
Grünangerg.
Riemerg.
Kumpfg.
Dr. Karl
Luegerpl.
Singerstr.
Stubenbastei
Liebenbg.
Franziskaner-
pl.
Ballg.
Seilerstätte
Weihburgg.
Parkring
Johannesg.
Schellingg.
Stadtpark
Fichteg.
Hegelg.
Schwarzenbergstr.
Schubertring
Johannesg.
Lothringerstr.
ring
usikverein
Konzerthaus
Schwarzenberg-
pl.
Am Heumkt.
Salesianerg.
Prinz Eugen-
Str.
Rennweg

0   1/4 mi
0   1/4 km

KEY

i *Tourist Information*

WHAT IT COSTS IN EUROS					
	¢	$	$$	$$$	$$$$
AT DINNER	under €10	€10–€16	€17–€22	€23–€28	over €28

Prices are per person for a main course at dinner.

RESTAURANTS

$$$$ ✕ **Julius Meinl am Graben.** A few doors down from the Hofburg Palace,
Fodor's Choice Meinl opened as a caterer to the Habsburgs in 1862 and has remained
★ Vienna's poshest grocery store as well as ranking among the city's best
restaurants. On the first floor up is a cozy salon, all deep-orange banquettes and dark wood. The window tables have stunning views over
the pedestrian crossroads of Graben/Kohlmarkt. The maestro here is
Joachim Gradwohl, who has several times been crowned "Cook of
the Year." Allow the excellent staff to guide you through the daily
changing menu with their expertise, serenity, and charm. ⊠ *Graben 19
(entrance after 7 PM from outdoor elevator on Naglergasse), 1st District* ☎*01/532–3334–99* ⚐*Reservations essential* ⊟*AE, DC, MC, V*
⊘*Closed Sun.* Ⓤ*U3/Herrengasse.*

$$$$ ✕ **Steirereck.** Possibly the most raved-about restaurant in Austria, Steir-
Fodor's Choice ereck is in the former Milchhauspavilion, a grand Jugendstil-vintage
★ dairy overlooking the Wienfluss promenade in the Stadtpark, the main
city park on the Ringstrasse. Winning dishes include delicate smoked
catfish, turbot in an avocado crust, or char in white garlic sauce. At
the end of the meal, an outstanding selection of more than 60 cheeses
from Steirereck's own cheese cellar await. If you don't want the gala
Steirereck experience, opt for a bite in the more casual lower-floor
"Meierei," which is still stylish with its hand-painted floor and furniture in shades of milky white. ⊠ *Im Stadtpark; Am Heumarkt 2A,
3rd District/Landstrasse* ☎*01/713–3168* ⚐*Reservations essential*
⊟*AE, DC, MC, V* Ⓤ*U4/Stadtpark.*

$$$–$$$$ ✕ **Anna Sacher.** The Sachertorte is the culmination of a family saga that
began with Franz Sacher, Prince von Metternich's pastry chef. Franz's
son and his wife Anna, Vienna's hostess with the mostest, opened the
19th-century hotel. The restaurant Anna Sacher, a showcase for *inter-
nationale und typische Wiener Küche,* seeps the monarchical magic of
former glory: wainscoted oak walls and sparkling chandeliers create
a suitably aristo ambience. Sacher offers some of the city's best Tafel-
spitz (boiled beef), garnished with creamed spinach and hash-brown
potatoes, with chive cream sauce and apple horseradish adding extra
flavor to this favorite dish of Emperor Franz Josef. ⊠*Philharmoni-
kerstrasse 4, 1st District* ☎*01/5145–6840* ⚐*Reservations essential*
⚐*Jacket and tie* ⊟*AE, DC, MC, V* ⊘*Closed Mon.* Ⓤ*U1, U2, or
U4/Karlsplatz/Opera.*

$$$–$$$$ ✕ **Zum Schwarzen Kameel.** Back when Beethoven dined at "the Black
Fodor's Choice Camel," it was already a foodie landmark. Since then, this provisioner
★ split into a *Delikatessen* and a restaurant. You can use the former if
you're in a hurry—fresh sandwiches are served at the counter. If time

is not an issue, dine in the elegant, intimate Art Nouveau dining room. Let the head waiter, the one with the Emperor Franz Josef mustache, rattle off the specials of the day in almost perfect English; the food is expertly prepared by one of Austria's best chefs, Christian Domschitz. ⊠*Bognergasse 5, 1st District* ☎*01/533–8125* ⚖*Reservations essential* ☐*AE, DC, MC, V* ⊗*Closed Sun.* Ⓤ*U3/Herrengasse.*

$$$ ✕**Bauer.** Unpretentious and hidden away in one of the quietest quarters of historic Vienna this is a temple for taste enthusiasts who look for the very best in fine creative cuisine. The quality-crazy owner, Walter Bauer, has over the years encouraged some of Austria's greatest chefs to perform their very best in his kitchen, using only the finest ingredients. Tommy Möbius began cooking here a year ago; try his roasted perch with crab and fennel or the pasta with *tafelspitz* filling. The best Austrian wines and friendly service make this a winner. ⊠*Sonnenfelsgasse 17, 1st District* ☎*01/512–98–71* ⚖*Reservations essential* ☐*AE, DC, MC, V* ⊗*No lunch Mon. Closed weekends and mid-July–mid-Aug.* Ⓤ*U1 or U3/Stephansplatz.*

$$–$$$ ✕**Cantino.** After a visit to the Haus der Musik, repair to its restaurant overlooking the towers, roofs, and steeples of the city. Chef Richard Rainer's lemon risotto is unbeatable, while his *Bonito del Norte* (white Spanish tuna) on arugula salad with lemon-olive oil dressing is a delight. The tapas lunch served on Sunday is particularly impressive. Wines are mainly homegrown Austrian, but there is also a fine array of Italian vintages. When you've tired of the view out the enormous windows, study the historic prints and photos decorating the slanting ceiling to see if you can recognize any of the celebrated conductors and composers. ⊠*Seilerstätte 30, 1st District* ☎*01/512–54–46* ☐*AE, DC, MC, V* ⊗*No lunch Sat., no dinner Sun. Closed mid-July–mid-Aug.* Ⓤ*U1 or U3/Stephansplatz.*

$$–$$$ ✕**Fabios.** The easiest way for Viennese to visit sleek, suave, power-
★ dining New York—short of paying for a round-trip plane ticket—is to book a table at this cool hot spot. If they can, that is. Wait-listed weeks in advance, this Modernist extravaganza has brought a touch of big-city glamour to Alt Wien, and foodies to fashionistas love it. Chef Christoph Brunnhuber has a sophisticated touch, as you'll see with his octopus carpaccio with paprika, crispy pork with orange pesto on fennel, or duckling breast on kumquat-cassis sauce with potato-olive puree. ⊠*Tuchlauben 6, 1st District* ☎*01/532–2222* ⚖*Reservations essential* ☐*AE, DC, MC, V* ⊗*Closed Sun.*

$$–$$$ ✕**Griechenbeisl.** Mozart, Beethoven, and Schubert all dined here—so
★ how can you resist? Neatly tucked away in a quiet and quaint area of the Old City, this ancient inn goes back half a millennium. You can hear its age in the creaking floorboards when you walk through some of the small, dark-wood panel rooms. Yes, it's touristy, yet the food, including all the classic hearty dishes like goulash soup, Wiener Schnitzel, and *Apfelstrudel,* is as good as in many other Beisln. The Mark Twain room has walls and ceiling covered with signatures of the famed who have been served here. ⊠*Fleischmarkt 11, 1st District* ☎*01/533–1941* ☐*AE, DC, MC, V* Ⓤ*U1 or U4/Schwedenplatz.*

$$-$$$ ✕**Theatercafe Wien.** Since the rococo Theater an der Wien next door reopened as a repertory opera house 2006, celebrities and divas can be seen eating here after the show, and artsy shooting star chef Herbert Malek, dubbed a "food designer," has given the dishes here a particularly artistic look. In addition to the weekday business lunch (a two-course classic Viennese meal and a drink, all for €10.90), there's a great choice of Asian, Mediterranean, and, for good measure, Viennese delights served here in the evening. Saturday brings great egg-spectations, from 10 AM on. The latest addition to the location is a stylish cigar club lounge. ⊠*Linke Wienzeile 6, 6th District/Mariahilf* 🕾*01/585-6262* ⚑*Reservations essential* 🚾*AE, DC, MC, V* ☻*No lunch Sun.* Ⓤ*U4/Karlsplatz.*

$$-$$$ ✕**Urania.** The year 1910 saw the inauguration of the Urania under the
★ auspices of Emperor Franz Josef and today this beautifully restored Jugendstil building is one of Vienna's trendiest locations. The interior design is cool, modern, and urban; its biggest boon besides the great food is the view from the terrace across the water. Chef Norbert Fiedler's creations include fillet of trout on chanterelle risotto and tender duck served with ginger ravioli, all brought to table by some of the handsomest waiters in town (rumor has it they are mostly models). Open times are an accommodating 9 AM until 2 AM, but the big event on Sunday is brunch. ⊠*Uraniastrasse 1, 1st District* 🕾*01/7133066* ⚑*Reservations essential* 🚾*AE, DC, MC, V* Ⓤ*U1 or U4/Schwedenplatz.*

$$-$$$ ✕**Vestibül.** Attached to the Burgtheater, this was once the carriage ves-
★ tibule of the emperor's court theater. Today, the Marmorsaal dining room with marble Corinthian columns, coffered arcades, and candle-light adds romance, but don't expect high drama: as an example of Ringstrasse architecture, the Burgtheater offers splendor at its most staid. In fact, you might opt instead for a lighter meal in the adjoining bar salon, with its views of the boulevard. The menu changes frequently, and may include veal goulash and Wiener Schnitzel as well as some classic *Beuschel* (a hash made of heart and lung, Viennese-style), plus a full array of nouvelle novelties. ⊠*Burgtheater/Dr.-Karl-Lueger-Ring 2, 1st District* 🕾*01/532-4999* 🚾*AE, DC, MC, V* ☻*Closed Sun. No lunch Sat.* Ⓤ*Tram: 1 or 2.*

$$ ✕**Österreicher im MAK.** Helmut Österreicher, one of the country's pre-eminent chefs, has brought the philosophy of inexpensive, moderately portioned food to this lovely setting inside the Museum of Applied Arts. The restaurant is a destination in itself, but also a great way to extend your museum visit. The contemporary Austrian culinary creations include tomato soup with cucumber and herb Gervais cheese, spinach noodles with Austrian blue cheese, and veal meat loaf. ⊠*Stubenring 5, 1st District* 🕾*01/714-0121* 🚾*AE, DC, MC, V* Ⓤ*U3/Stubentor.*

$-$$ ✕**DO & CO Albertina.** When you're ready to drop from taking in all
FodorsChoice the art treasures at the fabulous Albertina, fall into the museum eat-
★ ery's high-back, camel-color leather seating. For exotic, try the Thai wok dish with steamed rice, oysters, and sweet chili sauce that can be served with vegetables, prawns, or beef. If you fancy just a snack, sit at the bar and enjoy the Baguette Albertina, stuffed with juicy smoked salmon, cream cheese, arugula, and sun-dried tomatoes. DO & CO is

open every day, 10 AM to midnight. In warm weather you can also sit outside on the terrace overlooking the Burggarten. ⊠*Albertinaplatz 1, 1st District* ☎*01/532–9669* ⌔*Reservations essential* ⊟*V* Ⓤ*U1, U2, or U4/Karlsplatz/Opera.*

$–$$ ✕**Weibels Wirtshaus.** Down an old cobbled lane between Singerstrasse
★ and Schulerstrasse and just a stone's throw from the cathedral, is one of the coziest places to have a lazy lunch or a delightful dinner. Try to reserve a table upstairs in the Galerie: with just a couple of tables it soon feels like home. The friendly waitstaff will help you decide on dinner; the menu changes with the season but if you're there in asparagus season the ravioli is a winner, as is the rhubarb-rice pudding. ⊠*Kumpfgasse 2, 1st District* ☎*01/512–3986* ⌔*Reservations essential* ⊟*AE, MC, V* Ⓤ*U1/U3/Stephansplatz*

$–$$ ✕**Wrenkh.** Once Vienna's vegetarian pioneer extraordinaire, Christian Wrenkh now prefers a mixed cuisine (his ex-wife keeps up the vegetarian kitchen over in the 15th District). You can still get delightful dishes like wild-rice risotto with mushrooms, Greek fried rice with vegetables, or the tofu, tomato, and basil-pesto tarts and now you can also be tempted by steak, fish, and fowl. The minimalist-style café offers inexpensive lunch specials, while the more elegant dining room adjacent is perfect for a relaxed lunch or dinner. Fortunately, Christian hasn't changed the no-smoking policy in his restaurant. ⊠*Bauernmarkt 10, 1st District* ☎*01/533–1526*⊟*AE, DC, MC, V* ☉*Closed Sun.* Ⓤ*U1 or U3/Stephansplatz.*

$–$$ ✕**Zum Finsteren Stern.** This name translates as "dark star," but the lady
★ who runs the show is a well-known, shining star on the culinary horizon of the city. It takes courage in Vienna to offer a choice of only two three-course menus, but Ella de Silva's success is undeniable. If it's available, try the rabbit with sweet-and-sour lentils or the lamb steak with polenta tomato, zucchini cakes, and red-wine shallot sauce. Opening hours are 5 PM until 1 AM; when weather permits there's a lovely seating area outside underneath an old bluebell tree. ⊠*Schulhof 8 at Parisergasse, 1st District* ☎*01/535–2100* ⊟*MC, V* ☉*Closed Sun.* Ⓤ*U3/Herrengasse.*

¢–$$ ✕**Hansen.** This fashionable establishment, in the basement of the 19th-
★ century Vienna Stock Exchange, shares an enormous space with the flower shop Lederleitner and the air is mixed with the sweet perfume of tuberoses and the tantalizing whiff of truffle. While dining you can see shoppers browsing for everything from a single rose to a $2,000 lemon tree. Although this eatery is named after Theophil Hansen—the ornament-crazy architect of the Börse—the decor is sleek and modern; note the superb contemporary artwork adorning the walls. Lunch is the main event, though you can also come for breakfast or a pretheater dinner. ⊠*Wipplingerstrasse 34, 1st District* ☎*01/532–0542* ⌔*Reservations essential* ⊟*AE, DC, MC, V* ☉*Closed Sun. and after 9* PM *weekdays. No dinner Sat.* Ⓤ*U2/Schottenring.*

$ ✕**Figlmüller.** This Wiener Schnitzel institution is known for breaded
★ veal and pork cutlets so large they overflow the plate, and it's always packed. The cutlet is so large because it's been hammered (you can hear the mallets pounding from a block away). Meat winds up wafer-thin but

delicious, because the quality, as well as the size, is unrivaled (a quarter kilo of quality meat for each schnitzel). As the Viennese say, "Schnitzel should swim," so don't forget the lemon juice. If this location is full, try the one just around the corner on Bäckerstrasse 6. ⊠ *Wollzeile 5, 1st District* ☎*01/512–6177* ⊟*AE, DC, MC, V* ⊙*Closed first 2 wks Aug.* Ⓤ*U1 or U3/Stephansplatz.*

¢–$ ✗**Gasthaus Wild.** This is the best option near the Kunsthaus Wien and
★ the Hunderwasser House. Formerly a wine tavern, it's now a revitalized, great value, down-to-earth *beisl* (the equivalent to a pub, also called a *gasthaus*). The menu changes regularly but almost always features local-favorite protein-packed dishes and Schinkenfleckerl (delicious pasta squares stuffed with ham and cabbage, best served with a leafy green salad), fine wines, and a great choice of deserts. ⊠*Radetzkyplatz 1, 3rd District/Landstrasse* ☎*01/920–9477* ⊟*AE, DC, MC, V* ⊙*Closed Mon.* Ⓤ*Tram: N and O/Radetzkyplatz.*

¢–$ ✗**Gmoa Keller.** One of the friendliest places in Vienna, this wonderful
★ old cellar—just across the street from the Konzert Haus—offers some of the heartiest home cooking in town. Come here to enjoy dishes that hail from Carinthia, one of the best being the *Kas'nudeln* (potatoes and spinach pasta filled with cheese and onion), best served with green leaf salad. Another favorite is the *Tafelspitzsulz mit Kernoel und Zwiebeln* (cold cut of beef in aspic served with onions): you'll want to use the *Semmel* (white bread roll) to sop up that last drop of dark-green pumpkinseed-oil dressing. ⊠*Am Heumarkt 25, 3rd District/Landstrasse* ☎*01/712–5310* ⊟*AE, DC, MC, V* ⊙*Closed Sun.* Ⓤ*U4/Stadtpark.*

¢–$ ✗**Gösser Bierklinik.** This engaging old-world house, which dates back four centuries, is in the heart of Old Vienna. One of the top addresses for beer connoisseurs in Austria, it serves brews, both draft and bottled, *Dunkeles* (dark) and *Helles* (light), from the Gösser brewery in Styria. Of the four eating areas, many diners opt for the covered courtyard, where beer tastes better no matter the weather. Besides the obligatory (but first-class) Wiener Schnitzel, there are substantial, whole wheat sandwiches stuffed with ham, cheese, and vegetables, along with *Kas'nocken* (pasta dumplings topped with melted Tyrolean mountain cheese). ⊠*Steindlgasse 4, 1st District* ☎*01/533–7598* ⊟*DC, MC, V* ⊙*Closed Sun.* Ⓤ*U3/Herrengasse.*

¢–$ ✗**Schon Schön.** Designers and stylists abound along Lindengasse; it's rapidly becoming the trendiest part of Vienna's young scene and deserves to be seen, so come check out Schon Schön, where a chef, a clothes designer, and a hair stylist have literally cornered the market here in this corner location. You can eat, shop for the latest apparel, and have your hair styled, too. The small, sleek, and superbly decorated eatery has a large table that seats 22, where you can dine with the locals who know that the three-course lunch menu is one of the best values in town: €8.50, either meat or vegetarian. ⊠*Lindengasse 53, corner Andreasgasse, 7th District/Neubau* ☎*06991/53777* ⊟*No credit cards* Ⓤ*U3/Zieglergasse.*

MUNCH ON THE RUN

If you don't have time for a leisurely lunch, or you'd rather save your money for a splurge at dinner, here's a sampling of the best places in the city center to grab a quick, inexpensive, and tasty bite to eat.

In the lower level of the Ringstrasse Galerie shopping mall, the gourmet supermarket **Billa Corso** (✉ *Kärntner Ring 9–13, 1st District* ☎ *01/512–6625* ⊙ *Closed Sun.*) has a good salad bar, and will prepare the sandwich of your choice at the deli counter. (The Ringstrasse Galerie is in two similar buildings, so make sure you're in the one on the Kärntner Ring.)

The best pizza by the slice can be found near St. Stephen's at **Bizi Pizza** (✉ *Rotenturmstrasse 4, 1st District* ☎ *01/513–3705*).

Next to the produce section on the ground floor of Vienna's premier gourmet grocery store, **Meinl am Graben** (✉ *Graben 19, 1st District* ☎ *01/532–3334* ⊙ *Closed Sun.*) is a smart, stand-up café where you can choose from a selection of soups, sandwiches, or antipasti (don't confuse it with the full-service restaurant upstairs).

Near the Freyung, the epicurean deli **Radatz** (✉ *Schottengasse 3a, 1st District* ☎ *01/533–8163* ⊙ *Closed Sun.*) offers made-to-order sandwiches from a vast selection of mouthwatering meats and cheeses.

Around the corner from Am Hof, **Zum Schwarzen Kameel** (✉ *Bognergasse 5, 1st District* ☎ *01/533–8967* ⊙ *Closed Sun.*) serves delicious, fresh, open-faced sandwiches in its stand-up section.

A sure way to spike a lively discussion among the Viennese is to ask which *Würstelstand* serves the most delicious grilled sausages. Here are three that are generally acknowledged to be the best:

Kiosk (✉ *Schleifmühlgasse 7, 4th District*), in the trendy Freihaus quarter, serves excellent quality, scrumptious sausages from all over Europe. This is no ordinary sausage stand.

Würstelstand Albertina (✉ *Corner of Philharmonikerstrasse/Hanuschgasse, 1st District*), considered by gourmets to be the best sausage stall in the city center—behind the Opera House—entices passersby with its plump, sizzling *bratwurst*.

And then there's **Würstelstand am Hoher Markt** (✉ *Hoher Markt, corner of Marc-Aurel-Strasse, 1st District*), which, hot on the trail of that "Best Sausage" appellation, is a stall serving the best *Bürenwurst* and American-style hot dogs.

WINE TAVERNS (ALSO CALLED *HEURIGEN*)

Vienna lays claim to being the only capital city in the world to bring forth world-class wines. Four young, innovative vintners set up the group Wien Wein ("Vienna Wines") in 2006 and since then have worked together to perfect and promote the delicious wines they grow. Gone are the days when taverns were just a place to drink the "new wine"— the *heurige*, harvested every September and October in hills around the city, and drunk at suburban taverns known as *heurigen*. Tourist traps still abound in Grinzing, just outside Vienna, where for years busloads descended upon the picturesque wine village on Vienna's outskirts to drink new wine, but there are also worthy *heurigen*destinations in Stammersdorf, Sievering, Nussdorf, or Neustift (tram lines from the city center are listed in the reviews below). And these days you can usually find fine dinners to accompany the excellent wine. If you visit a *heurigen* in the fall, be sure to order a glass of *Sturm*, a cloudy drink halfway between grape juice and wine, with a delicious yeasty fizz.

Taverns or wine cellars can be found in the heart of the old city, too; hundreds of years ago Vienna's vintners started taking advantage of the cavernous spaces found below ancient monasteries and old houses by converting them into underground wine cellars. That these subterranean cellars were some of the coolest spots in summertime Vienna has always proved a big drawing card.

> ## A STRUDEL STEAL
>
> Why not take your afternoon coffee break in one of the very best restaurants in town, for less than you would pay in most Viennese cafés? At around 2 PM weekdays head to the Steiereck's "Meierei" in Stadtpark and savor the freshest *Apfelstrudel* around, when it comes out hot from the oven. It doesn't last long, though, so if you don't make it in time for this fruitiest and juiciest of Apfelstrudel, you can try for the 3 PM revelation of the creamy *Topfenstrudel*—a strudel with a creamy cheese filling, rather than apples. Either are best served warm and accompanied by a smooth, aromatic coffee.

$$–$$$ ✗**Mayer am Pfarrplatz.** Heiligenstadt is home to this *heurige*in one of
★ Beethoven's former abodes; he composed his Sixth (Pastoral) Symphony, as well as parts of his Ninth Symphony ("Ode to Joy") while staying in this town. The à la carte offerings and buffet are abundant, and the house wines are among the most excellent of all *heurigen*nectars. You'll find lots of Viennese among the tourists here. Though the Mayer family sold the property, the place fortunately remains unchanged. ⊠*Heiligenstädter Pfarrplatz 2, 19th District/Nussdorf* ☎*01/370–1287* ⊟*AE, DC, MC, V* ⊗*No lunch Mon.–Sat.* Ⓤ*Tram: D/Nussdorf from the Ring.*

$$–$$$ ✗**Weingut Reinprecht.** The grandest *heurige*in Grinzing (the town has more than 30 of them), Reinprecht is *gemütlichkeit* heaven: Tyrolean wood beams, 19th-century oil paintings, Austrian-eagle banners, portraits of army generals, globe lanterns, marble busts, trellis tables, and what is probably the greatest collection of corkscrews in Austria. The building—a former monastery—is impressive, as is the garden, which can hold up to 700 people (to give you an idea of how popular this place is). If you ignore the crowds, get a cozy corner table, and focus on the archetypal *atmosphäre*, you should have a great time. ⊠*Cobenzlgasse 20, 19th District/Grinzing* ☎*01/320–1389* ⊟*AE, DC, MC, V* ⊗*Closed Dec.–Feb.* Ⓤ*U2/Schottentor; Tram: 38/Grinzing.*

$–$$ ✗**Augustinerkeller.** Built into the old brick vaults of the 16th-century historic fortifications surrounding the old city, this is one of the last monastic wine cellars in central Vienna. The atmosphere is very *gemütlich* (cozy), with a vaulted brick ceiling, wooden "cow-stall" booths, street lanterns, Austrian bric-a-brac, and a troupe of roaming musicians in the evening. The spit-roasted chicken is excellent, as is the filling *Stelze* (roast pork knuckle). ⊠*Augustinerstrasse 1, Albertinaplatz, 1st District* ☎*01/533–1026* ⊟*DC, MC, V* Ⓤ*U3/Herrengasse.*

$-$$ ✕**Esterházykeller.** The origins here go back to 1683, when this spot opened as one of the official *Stadtheuriger* (city wine taverns). Below the Esterházy palace, the atmosphere is like that of a cozy subterranean cave, with low-hanging vaults and alpine wooden booths. The maze of rooms offers some of the best wines of any cellar in town, plus a typical Viennese menu noontime and evenings, and a hot and cold buffet. ⊠*Haarhof 1, 1st District* ☎*01/533–3482* ⊟*No credit cards* ⊘*Closed weekends in summer. No lunch weekends* Ⓤ*U1 or U4/Stephansplatz.*

$-$$ ✕**Wolff.** Located in the heart of the vine village of Neustift am Walde, the *heurige*Wolff, open since 1609, sticks to tradition and offers, besides a great meal, a great show. Daily from mid-April to mid-September singers present a selection of well-known arias from the favorite operettas. It's €45 for a three-course meal including drinks and show, starting at 8:15 PM. ⊠*Neustift am Walde 19, 19th District/Grinzing* ☎*01/524–7478* ⊟*AE, DC, MC, V* Ⓤ*U4/U6/Spittelau; Bus: 35A/ Neustift am Walde.*

¢-$ ✕**Melker Stiftskeller.** Down and down you go, into one of the friendliest cellars in town, where *Stelze* (roast pork) is a popular feature, along with outstanding wines by the glass or, rather, mug. Part of the Melkerhof complex—dating from 1438 but rebuilt in the 18th century— this was originally the storehouse for wines from the Melk Abbey in the Danube Valley. It is a complex of six cavernous rooms, and the most atmospheric has low-arched vaults right out of a castle dungeon. ⊠*Schottengasse 3, 1st District* ☎*01/533–5530* ⊟*AE, DC, MC, V* ⊘*Closed Sun. and Mon. No lunch* Ⓤ*U2/Schottentor.*

¢-$ ✕**Passauerhof.** If you want live folk music (offered nightly) to accompany your meal, this is the place, though you may have to share the experience with the tour groups that descend on Grinzing. The food from the menu, such as roast chicken and Wiener Schnitzel, is tasty, while the buffet offers a limited selection. It's a pleasant five-minute walk up the hill from the town center. ⊠*Cobenzlgasse 9, 19th District/ Grinzing* ☎*01/320–6345* ⊟*AE, DC, MC, V* ⊘*Closed Jan. and Feb. No lunch* Ⓤ*U2/Schottentor; Tram: 38/Grinzing.*

¢-$ ✕**Schreiberhaus.** In Neustift am Walde, the Schreiberhaus has one of the prettiest terraced gardens in the city, with picnic tables stretching up into the vineyards. The buffet has treats like spit-roasted chicken, salmon pasta, and a huge selection of tempting grilled vegetables and salads. The golden *traminer* wine is excellent. ⊠*Rathstrasse 54, 19th District/Neustift am Walde* ☎*01/440–3844* ⊟*AE, DC, MC, V* Ⓤ*U4, U6/Spittelau; Bus 35A/Neustift am Walde.*

¢-$ ✕**Wieninger.** The driving force behind the WienWein group, this vintner knows his business better than many. He exports his Vienna wines to the United States and elsewhere, but luckily there are some left to be savored in this pleasant, tree-shaded inner courtyard and tavern. The food is very good, too. It's across the Danube in Stammersdorf, one of Vienna's oldest *heurige*areas. ⊠*Stammersdorferstrasse 78, 21st*

CLOSE UP

Wine-Wien-Wein-Vienna

For a memorable experience, sit at the edge of a vineyard on the Kahlenberg with a tankard of young white wine and listen to the *Schrammel* quartet playing sentimental Viennese songs. The wine taverns, called *Heurigen* (the singular is *Heurige*) after the new wine that they serve, sprang up in 1784 when Joseph II decreed that owners of vineyards could establish their own private wine taverns; soon the Viennese discovered it was cheaper to go out to the wine than to bring it inside the city walls, where taxes were levied. The Heurige owner is supposed to be licensed to serve only the produce of his own vineyard, a rule more honored in the breach than the observance. These taverns

in the wine-growing districts on the outskirts of the city vary from the simple front room of a vintner's house to ornate settings. The true Heurige is open for only a few weeks a year to allow the vintner to sell a certain quantity of his production, tax-free, when consumed on his own premises. The choice is usually between a "new" and an "old" white (or red) wine, but you can also ask for a milder or sharper wine according to your taste. Most Heurigen are happy to let you sample the wines before you order. You can also order a *Gespritzter*, half wine and half soda water. The waitress brings the wine, usually in a ¼-liter mug or liter carafe, but you serve yourself from the food buffet.

District/Floridsdorf ☎01/292–4106 ▤V ⊙*Closed late Dec.–Feb. No lunch Mon.–Sat.* ⓊU2, U4/Schottenring; Tram: 31/Stammersdorf.

¢–$ ✕**Zimmermann.** East of the Grinzing village center, the Zimmermann *heurige*has excellent wines, an enchanting tree-shaded garden, and a seemingly endless series of small paneled rooms and vaulted cellars. You can order from the menu or choose from the tempting buffet. ⊠*Armbrustergasse 5/Grinzingerstrasse, 19th District/Grinzing* ☎01/370–2211 ▤AE, DC, MC, V ⊙*No lunch* ⓊU2/Schottentor; Tram: 38/Grinzing.

CAFÉS & COFFEEHOUSES

Is it the coffee they come for or the coffeehouse? This question is one of the hot topics in town, as Vienna's café scene has become overpopulated with Starbucks branches and Italian outlets. The ruckus over whether the quality of the coffee or the *atmosphäre* is more important is not new, but is becoming fiercer as competition from all sides increases. The result is that the landmark Wiener Kaffeehäuser—the cafés known for centuries as "Vienna's parlors," where everyone from Mozart and Beethoven to Lenin and Andy Warhol were likely to hang out—are smarting from the new guys on the block. On the plus side, their ageless charms remain mostly intact, including the sumptuous red-velvet padded booths; the marble-top tables; the rickety yet indestructible Thonet bentwood chairs; the waiter, dressed in a Sunday-best outfit; the pastries, cakes, strudels, and rich tortes; the newspapers, magazines, and journals; and, last but not least, a sense that here time stands still. To savor the traditional coffeehouse experience, set aside a morning or an afternoon, or at least a couple of hours, and settle down in the one you've chosen. Read a while, catch up on your letter writing, or plan tomorrow's itinerary: there's no need to worry about overstaying your welcome, even over a single small cup of coffee—though don't expect refills. (Of course, in some of the more opulent coffeehouses your one cup of coffee may cost as much as a meal somewhere else.)

In Austria coffee is never merely coffee. It comes in countless forms and under many names. Ask a waiter for *ein Kaffee* and you'll get a vacant stare. If you want a black coffee, you must ask for a *kleiner* or *grosser Schwarzer* (small or large black coffee, small being the size of a demitasse cup). If you want it strong, add the word *gekürzt* (shortened); if you want it weaker, *verlängert* (stretched). If you want your coffee with cream, ask for a *Brauner* (again *gross* or *klein*); say *Kaffee Creme* if you wish to add the cream yourself (or *Kaffee mit Milch extra, bitte* if you want to add milk, not cream). Others opt for a *Melange*, a mild roast with steamed milk (which you can even get *mit Haut,* with skin, or *Verkehrter,* with more milk than coffee). The usual after-dinner drink is espresso. Most delightful are the coffee-and-whipped-cream concoctions, universally cherished as *Kaffee mit Schlag,* a taste that is easily acquired and a menace to all but the very thin. A customer who wants more whipped cream than coffee asks for a *Doppelschlag.* Hot black coffee in a glass with one knob of whipped cream is an *Einspänner* (literally, "one-horse coach"—as coachmen needed one hand free to hold the reins). Or you can go to town on a *Mazagran,* black coffee with ice and a tot of rum, or *Eiskaffee,* cold coffee with ice cream and whipped cream. Or you can simply order *eine Portion Kaffee* and have an honest pot of coffee and jug of hot milk. Most coffeehouses offer hot food until about an hour before closing time.

¢–$ ✕**Café Central.** This is the coffeehouse *supreme.* Made famous by its illustrious guests, the Café Central is right up there with Florian's in Venice. But don't expect a cozy hole-in-the-wall Kaffeehaus: with soaring ceiling and gigantic columns giving it the look of an apse strayed from St. Stephen's cathedral, Café Central provided a rather sumptuous home-away-from-home for Leon Trotsky, who mapped out the Russian Revolution here beneath portraits of the imperial family. Piano music fills the marble pillared hall in the afternoon; it's worth putting on your must-see list. ⊠*Herrengasse 14, corner Strauchgasse, 1st District* ☎*01/5333–76424* Ⓤ*U3/Herrengasse.*

¢–$ ✕**Café Frauenhuber.** Repair here to find some peace and quiet away from the *Kärntnerstrasse's* busy shoppers. The original turn-of-the-20th-century interior with its obligatory red-velvet seating and somewhat tired upholstery (if you don't suffer from back problems you'll be fine), is a visual treat and breakfast here is legendary. You'll find fewer tourists here than in other typical Viennese cafés, and more of a local feel, which its had since it first opened its doors in 1824. ⊠*Himmelpfortgasse 6, 1st District* ☎*01/512–4323* Ⓤ*U1 or U3/Stephansplatz.*

¢–$ ✕**Café Griensteidl.** Once the site of one of Vienna's oldest coffeehouses and named after the pharmacist Heinrich Griensteidl—the original dated back to 1847 but was demolished in 1897—this café was resurrected in 1990. Karl Kraus, the sardonic critic, spent many hours here writing his feared articles, and it's also here that Hugo von Hofmannsthal took time out from writing libretti for Richard Strauss. Although this establishment is still looking for the patina needed to give it real flair, locals are pleased by the attempt to re-create the historic atmosphere. Numerous newspapers and magazines hang on the rack (many are in English). It's also entirely no-smoking. ⊠*Michaelerplatz 2, 1st District* ☎*01/533–2692* Ⓤ*U3/Herrengasse.*

¢–$ ✕**Café Hawelka.** Practically a shrine—indeed, almost a museum—the beloved Hawelka has been presided over for more than 70 years by Leopold Hawelka, in person, day in, day out. This was the hangout of most of Vienna's modern artists, and the café has acquired quite an admirable art collection over the years. As you enter the rather dark interior, wait to be seated—which is unusual in Vienna—but then you can ask to have a look at the guest book, itself a work of art, with entries including some very illustrious names (Elias Canetti, Andy Warhol, Tony Blair, et al.). Back in the 1960s, the young John Irving enjoyed the atmosphere here, too, as you can see when reading *The Hotel New Hampshire*. The Hawelka is most famous for its Buchteln, a baked bun with a sweet filling that goes down well with a melange. The café can be pretty smoky when the doors are closed, but there are some tables outside if the air gets too thick. ⊠*Dorotheergasse 6, 1st District* ☎*01/512–8230* Ⓤ*U1 or U3/Stephansplatz.*

¢–$ ✕**Café Landtmann.** A recent $500,000 government-sponsored renovation has brought new luster to the chandeliers of Landtmann, a century-old favorite of politicians, theater stars (the Burg is next door), and celeb-watchers. Sigmund Freud, Burt Lancaster, Hillary Rodham Clinton, and Sir Paul McCartney are just a few of the famous who have patronized this café, whose glass-and-brass doors have been open since 1873. If you want a great meal at almost any time of the day, there are few places that can beat this one. Since early 2008 an air-conditioned glass veranda has added contemporary flair to this venerable location. ⊠*Dr.-Karl-Lueger-Ring 4, 1st District* ☎*01/532–0621* Ⓤ*U2/ Schottenring.*

¢–$ ✕**Café Mozart.** Graham Greene, staying in the Hotel Sacher next door, ★   loved having his coffee here while working on the script for *The Third Man* (in fact, Greene had the café featured in the film, and Anton Karas, the zither player who did the Harry Lime theme, wrote a waltz for the place). The café was named after the monument to Mozart (now in the Burggarten) that once stood outside the building. Although the place is overrun with sightseers, the waiters are charming and manage to remain calm even when customers run them ragged. Crystal chandeliers, a brass-and-oak interior, comfortable seating, and delicious food—the excellent *tafelspitz* here has to be mentioned—add to its popularity. With the Opera just behind the café, this is a fine place for an after-performance snack; be on the lookout for opera divas here for the same reason. ⊠*Albertinaplatz 2, 1st District* ☎*01/2410–0210* Ⓤ*U1, U2, or U4/Karlsplatz/Opera.*

¢–$ ✕**Café Museum.** The controversial architect Adolf Loos (famed for his pronouncement "Ornament is a sin") laid the foundation stone for this puristically styled coffeehouse in 1899. Throughout the 20th century, this was a top rendezvous spot for Wien Secession artists, along with actors, students, and professors because of its proximity to the Secession Pavilion, the Academy of Fine Arts, the Theater an der Wien, and Vienna's Technical University. Gustav Klimt, Egon Schiele, and Josef Hoffmann all enjoyed sipping their *melange* here. Today, after years of intensive and painstaking restoration (following Loos's detailed documents discovered in the Albertina), it once again lives up to its former glory. The daily menu special is one of the best bargains in town. ✉ *Operngasse 7, 1st District* ☎ *01/586–5202* Ⓤ *U1, U2, or U4/Karlsplatz/Opera.*

¢–$ ✕ **Café Sacher.** This legend began life as a *Delikatessen* opened by Sacher, court confectioner to Prince von Metternich, the most powerful prime minister in early-19th-century Europe and a fervent chocoholic—it was for him that the Sachertorte was created. War-weary Metternich must have been amused to see a battle break out between Sacher and Demel—a competing confectioner—as to who served the real Sachertorte. Sacher puts its apricot jam in the cake middle, while Demel puts it just below the icing. If you're not a sweets person, try a savory alternative: Sacher Würstl: slim sausages served with fresh horseradish, mustard, and home-baked bread. Mirrors and chandeliers add glitter, and there is live piano music every day from 4:30 until 7 PM. ✉ *Philharmonikerstrasse 4, 1st District* ☎ *01/514560* Ⓤ *U1, U2, or U4/Karlsplatz/Opera.*

¢–$ ✕ **Café Schwarzenberg.** A bright-yellow facade and a large terrace welcome all to this café across from the Hotel Imperial. The location is perfect if you want a snack after a concert at the Musikverein or the Konzerthaus, both just a couple of minutes away. Wall-to-wall mirrors reflect the elegant clientele perched on dark-green leather seats. Open until midnight, it has a good choice of food and pastries, and even though the waiters can be a little condescending, the overall atmosphere is still nice enough to encourage longer stays. Piano music can be heard until late on Wednesday and Friday and from 5 until 7 PM on weekends. Sit outside when the weather allows and appreciate the new lights installation on Schwarzenbergplatz. ✉ *Kärntnerring 17, 1st District* ☎ *01/512–8998* Ⓤ *U2/Schottentor.*

¢–$ ✕ **Haas & Haas Colonial Teahouse.** If you find yourself tired of coffeehouses in Vienna (is that possible?), and are longing for a decent cuppa, head for the far end of the Ringstrassen-Galerien. Here you'll find one the coziest tea parlors in town, with a selection of more than 200 brews and an afternoon tea to die for: presented on the obligatory three-tier tea rack, the traditional finger sandwiches come with all sorts of fillings and are accompanied by scones with strawberry jam, clotted cream, and a selection of petits fours. Yum! It's open Monday through Saturday, 9:30–7. ✉ *Kärntnerring 9–13, Ringstrassen Galerien Top 65, 1st District* ☎ *01/512–6817* Ⓤ *U1, U2, or U4 Karlsplatz.*

Vienna's Sweetest Vice

Many think that the chief contribution of the people who created the Viennese waltz and the operetta comes with the dessert course in the form of rich and luscious pastries, and in the beloved and universal *Schlagobers* (whipped cream).

First stop for sweet lovers, pastry fans, and marzipan maniacs has to be **Demel** (⊠ *Kohlmarkt 14, 1st District* ☎ *01/535-1717-0*), a 200-year-old confectioner famous for its sweetmeats that make every heart beat faster (and eventually slower). The display cases are filled to the brim; all you have to do is point at what you want and then go and sit where you want. But don't forget to watch the pastry chef at work in the glassed-over, glassed-in courtyard. Beyond the shop proper are stairs that lead to dining salons where the decor is almost as sweet as the goods on sale. Chocolate lovers will want to try the Viennese Sachertorte (two layers of dense chocolate cake, with apricot jam sandwiched between, and chocolate icing on top) debate by sampling Demel's version and then comparing it with its rival at the **Café Sacher**, in the Hotel Sacher. **Gerstner** (⊠ *Kärntnerstrasse 13–15* ☎ *01/5124963*), in the heart of the bustling Kärntnerstrasse, is one of the best places for dark, moist, mouthwatering poppyseed cake (*Mohntorte*), carrot cake, and

chocolate-dipped strawberries. Rumor has it that the best strudel in town is to be had here. Its decor is modern, but the place has been here since the mid-18th century

Oberlaa (⊠ *Neuer Markt 16* ☎ *01/513-2936* ⊠ *Babenbergerstrasse 7, opposite Kunsthistoriches Museum* ☎ *01/5867-2820* ⊠ *Landstrasser Hauptstrasse 1* ☎ *01/7152-7400*) has irresistible confections such as the *Oberlaa Kurbad* cake, truffle cake, and chocolate mousse cake. Popular with the locals and great value for money, there are now six Oberlaa branches to choose from. The good lunch menu includes vegetarian dishes. **Sperl** (⊠ *Gumpendorferstrasse 11, 6th District/Mariahilf* ☎ *01/586-4158*), founded in 1880, has an Old Viennese ambience.

It doesn't really matter which of the many branches of **Aida** (⊠ *Neuer Markt 16* ☎ *01/513-2936* ⊠ *Opernring 7* ☎ *01/533-1933* ⊠ *Bognergasse 3* ☎ *01/533-9442* ⊠ *Stock-im-Eisen-Platz 2* ☎ *01/512-2977* ⊠ *Wollzeile 28* ☎ *01/512-3724* ⊠ *Praterstrasse 78* ☎ *01/216-2137* ⊠ *Rotenturmstrasse 24* ☎ *01/58-2585*) you visit—they're all quite similar. Aida is most famous for the cheapest cup of (excellent) coffee in town, but the incredibly inexpensive pastries are just fantastic.

WHERE TO STAY

If you're lucky enough to stay at one of Vienna's better hotels, chances are you'll be deposited at one of the grand Ringstrasse palaces that once housed assorted Imperial Highnesses. Their red velvet–gilt mirror–and–crystal chandelier opulence still stands supreme even in today's world of lavish hospitality, and these establishments pride themselves on staff that appear to anticipate, like fairy guardians, your every desire. For those with more modest requirements and purses, ample rooms are available in less costly but still alluring hotels. Our lower-price options offer the best in location, value, and, in many instances, a quaint echo of Alt Wien (Old Vienna) atmosphere.

If you have only a short time to spend in Vienna, you'll probably choose to stay in the inner city (the 1st District, or 1010 postal code), to be within walking distance of the most important sights, restaurants, and shops. Outside the 1st, though, there are many other delightful neighborhoods in which to rest your head. The "Biedermeier" quarter of Spittelberg, in the 7th District of Neubau, has cobblestone streets, lots of 19th-century houses, a wonderful array of art galleries and restaurants, and, increasingly, some good hotel options. Just to its east is the fabulous MuseumsQuartier, an area that has some very nice hotel finds. Schwedenplatz is the area fronted by the Danube Canal—a neighborhood that is one of the most happening in the city, although just a stroll from the centuries-old lanes around Fleischmarkt. Other sweet hotel options can be found in the 8th District of Josefstadt, an area noted for antiques shops, good local restaurants, bars, and theater.

Because of the Christmas markets, the weeks leading up to the holidays are a popular time to visit, as is the week around New Year's (*Silvester*), with its orchestral concerts. Expect to pay accordingly, and, at the very top hotels, a lot (around €300–€550 a night). Summer months are not as busy, perhaps because the opera is not in season. You'll find good bargains at this time of year, especially in August. Air-conditioning is customary in the top-category hotels only, but since Vienna has very few extremely hot days, with temperatures cooling off at night, it's usually not missed.

Assume that all guest rooms have air-conditioning, room phones, and room TVs unless noted otherwise.

WHAT IT COSTS IN EUROS					
	¢	$	$$	$$$	$$$$
FOR TWO PEOPLE	under €80	€80–€120	€121–€170	€171–€270	over €270

Prices are for two people in a standard double room. Assume that hotels operate on the European Plan (EP, with no meals provided) unless we note that they use the Breakfast Plan (BP).

$$$$ **Ambassador.** Franz Lehár, Marlene Dietrich, the Infanta Isabel of Spain, and Mick Jagger are just a few of the celebrities who have stayed at this old dowager (from 1866). The lobby is small but grand, and the high-ceiling guest rooms, differing only in size, are uniformly decorated with pale-yellow-striped wallpaper, deep-blue carpets, and faux Empire furniture. Unless you want the excitement of a direct view onto the lively pedestrian Kärntnerstrasse, ask for one of the quieter rooms on the Neuer Markt side. The Ambassador also houses the top-flight restaurant Mörwald, which has stunning views of the square. **Pros:** great location for shopaholics and casino lovers (casino just across the street). **Cons:** noisy neighborhood at times. ⊠*Kärntnerstrasse 22/Neuer Markt 5, 1st District* ☎*01/961610* ⊕*www.ambassador.at*

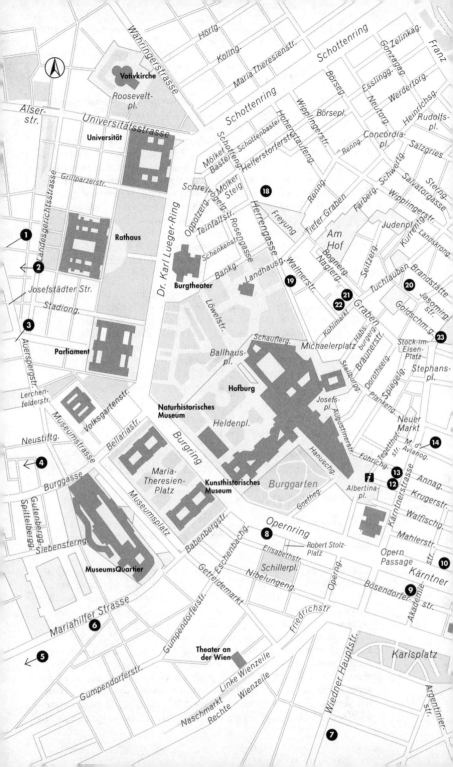

Where to Stay in Vienna

Altstadt **4**
Ambassador **14**
Am Stephansplatz **23**
Astoria **13**
Benediktushaus **18**
Das Triest **7**
Das Tyrol **6**
Grand Hotel Wien **10**
Hollmann Beletage **26**
Imperial **11**
König von Ungarn **25**
Le Méridien **8**
Levante Parliament **3**
Mailberger Hof **15**
Palais Coburg **16**
Pension Domizil **24**
Pension Nossek **21**
Pension Pertschy **22**
Pension Zipser **1**
Radisson **17**
Rathaus Wine & Design **2**
The Ring **9**
Sacher **12**
Stadthalle **5**
Style Hotel Vienna **19**
Wandl **20**

1

KEY

i *Tourist Information*

◄*86 rooms* &*In-hotel: restaurant, bar, Internet, Wi-Fi* ⊟*AE, DC, MC, V.*

$$$$
Fodor'sChoice
★
Grand Hotel Wien. With one of the great locations on the Ringstrasse, just across from the Musikverein and a minute on foot from the Opera, the Grand Hotel Wien (the first luxury hotel in Vienna) rose to new splendor in the early 1990s. The interior has a palatial feel, thanks to its exquisite fabrics and rare antiques, and the rooms are elegant, with dark-wood walls and pastel accents. Three restaurants—Le Ciel, Unkai, and the Grand Café—offer Viennese, Japanese, and European culinary delights, and an additional boon here is the adjoining Ringstrassen-Galerien shopping mall connected to the hotel by a glass bridge. **Pros:** great restaurants in-house; good shopping next door. **Cons:** desk staff can be haughty. ⊠*Kärntnerring 9, 1st District* ☎*01/515–800* ⊕*www.grandhotelwien.com* ◄*205 rooms* &*In-hotel: restaurant, bar, gym, no-smoking rooms, Wi-Fi* ⊟*AE, DC, MC, V.*

$$$$
Fodor'sChoice
★
Hotel Sacher. The legendary Sacher dates from 1876 but by adding two extra floors and a spa the hotel has augmented its historic aura with luxurious, modern-day comfort. The corridors of the hotel serve as a veritable art gallery, and guest rooms are furnished with antiques, heavy fabrics, and original artwork. The rooftop apartment has a view to die for. The location, directly behind the Opera House, could hardly be more central, and the ratio of staff to guests is more than two to one. **Pros:** intimate, cozy feel; great location. **Cons:** small, cramped elevator; booking by phone can be frustrating. ⊠*Philharmonikerstrasse 4, 1st District* ☎*01/514–56–0* ⊕*www.sacher.com* ◄*152 rooms* &*In-hotel: 2 restaurants, bar, no-smoking rooms, Wi-Fi* ⊟*AE, DC, MC, V.*

$$$$
Fodor'sChoice
★
Imperial. One of the landmarks of the Ringstrasse, this hotel has exemplified the grandeur of imperial Vienna ever since it was built. Adjacent to the Musikverein concert hall, the emphasis here is on Old Vienna elegance and privacy, which accounts for a guest book littered with names like Elizabeth Taylor, José Carreras, and Bruce Springsteen. The main lobby looks as opulent as a Hofburg ballroom and the ground-floor showpiece, the Marmorsaal, or Marble Hall, where you can dine amid Corinthian columns, is quite spectacular. Guest rooms are furnished with sparkling chandeliers, gorgeous swagged fabrics, and original 19th-century paintings. Suites come with a personal butler. **Pros:** service is top-class. **Cons:** some rooms are on the small side; bathrooms can be tiny. ⊠*Kärntnerring 16, 1st District* ☎*01/501–10–0* ⊕*www.luxurycollection.com/imperial* ◄*138 rooms* &*In-hotel: restaurant, bar, gym, no-smoking rooms, Internet, Wi-Fi* ⊟*AE, DC, MC, V.*

$$$$
★
Le Méridien. Le Méridien's supercool "art and tech" lobby in its Vienna outpost is adorned with Mies van der Rohe–style sofas and ottomans and nouvelle fluorescent-light panels. Guest rooms are white and decorated with glass headboards, contemporary vases, and other cutting-edge items. Cloudlike mattresses, flat-screen plasma TVs, and roomy "tower of power" showers with three massaging jets pour on the luxe. Outside, visual excitements continue, as the tranquil, soundproofed rooms offer views of the Hofburg, Burggarten, and Ring. Add to this a complimentary minibar and Internet service, and you have the makings of a truly pampered stay. **Pros:** next door to museums, opera,

1

and Hofburg. **Cons:** lacks "Vienna" character. ⊠*Opernring 13, 1st District* ☎*01/588–900* ⊕ *www.austria.starwoodhotels.com* ⇆*294 rooms* ⚿*In-hotel: restaurant, bar, pool, gym, no-smoking rooms, Internet, Wi-Fi* ▭*AE, DC, MC, V.*

$$$$ ⬚ **Palais Coburg.** In this 19th-century regal residence the lobby is all white stone and plate-glass Modernism, embodying the hotel's philosophy of "preserving the past—shaping the future." There are 35 deluxe modern or imperial-style suites; many of them are spectacular, two-story showpieces, the best done in gilded-yellow Biedermeier or Empire style. All have fresh flowers; fully equipped kitchenettes with a complimentary stock of champagne, wine, beer, and soft drinks; espresso makers; laptops with free Internet; and two bathrooms, some with gigantic whirlpool baths and saunas. Popular in its own right is the house restaurant, Restaurant Coburg, which is manned by one of the most famous chefs in the country, Christian Petz, and which has one of the best wine cellars in Europe. **Pros:** luxurious atmosphere; excellent on-site dining. **Cons:** room decor can feel a bit over the top; pricey. ⊠*Coburgbastei 4, 1st District* ☎*01/51818–0* ⊕*www.palaiscoburg. at* ⇆*33 suites* ⚿*In-room: kitchen, Internet. In-hotel: restaurant, bar, pool, gym, Wi-Fi* ▭*AE, DC, MC, V.*

$$$$ ⬚ **The Ring.** Following the trend toward smaller boutique properties,
★ this new luxury accommodation takes its place alongside some of the Vienna's opulent grand hotels, at a somewhat more reasonable price. The 1860 historic facade remains, as does the old-fashioned wrought-iron elevator, but otherwise the house oozes sumptuous modernity, with a soothing color scheme fitting to the city: *café au lait* with splashes of pistachio throughout. The elegant entrance is discreet but welcoming and the rooms have modern amenities like flat-screen TVs and Nespresso machines. The spa and gym area on the top floor is state of the art, with a steam bath and sauna that has views overlooking the church of St. Charles. **Pros:** has the best vodka bar in Vienna; you can often find good last-minute deals. **Cons:** trams frequently thunder around the block. ⊠*Kärntner Ring 8, 1st District* ☎*01/221–22–0* ⊕*www.theringhotel.com* ⇆*68 rooms* ⚿*In-hotel: restaurant, bar, gym, Wi-Fi*▭*AE, DC, MC, V .*

$$$–$$$$ ⬚ **Am Stephansplatz.** You can't get a better location than this, directly across from the front entrance of St. Stephen's Cathedral, and, after a recent renovation, a sleek, peaceful, and stunning hotel has emerged. Dom Café on the first floor has been transformed into a showy, ultra-chic breakfast lounge—a loss for the Viennese but a gain for hotel guests, since this is the best spot in Vienna from which to admire the "Giant's Gate" and the throngs of worshippers entering the church. Parquet flooring, light-oak furniture paired with dark-brown leather, light-color walls, and triple-glazed windows make this a hotel with flair. **Pros:** top location; great breakfast-bar views, excellent staff. **Cons:** noisy area at night. ⊠*Stephansplatz 9,1st District* ☎*01/53405–0* ⊕*www.hotelamstephansplatz.at* ⇆*56 rooms* ⚿*In-hotel: restaurant, bar, gym, Wi-Fi* ▭*AE, DC, MC, V* �a�*BP.*

$$$ ⬚ **Astoria.** Built in 1912 and still retaining the outward charm of that era, the Astoria is one of the grand old Viennese hotels and enjoys a

superb location on the Kärnterstrasse, between the Opera and St. Stephen's. The wood-paneled lobby is an essay in Wiener Werkstätte style and all four floors have a soft contemporary style with pretty fabrics in beige tones, polished dark wood, and Oriental rugs. Before deciding where to stay in Vienna, try the Astoria for packages and special rates. **Pros:** location hard to beat; some special (cheap) rates available. **Cons:** charge for Internet; no air-conditioning. ⊠ *Kärntnerstrasse 32–34, 1st District* ☎ *01/51577* ⊕ *www.austria-trend.at/asw* ⤳ *118 rooms* ⟳ *In-room: no a/c. In-hotel: bar, Internet* ⊟ *AE, DC, MC, V* ⦿ *BP.*

$$$
Fodor's Choice
★

🎬 **Das Triest.** An ultrasleek ocean-liner look is Sir Terrence Conran's nod to the past of this former postal-coach station on the route between Vienna and the port city of Trieste. The original cross vaulting remains in the lounges and some suites, but otherwise the interior and furnishings are what you'd expect from Conran. In the rooms, beige-on-beige fabrics are offset by glowing pine wall-size headboards. Blue carpeting and honey-hue woods radiate elegance and comfort, and even the doorknobs feel good to the touch. The hotel also allures with an excellent Austro-Italian restaurant, Collio. Das Triest may be a bit off the beaten track, but is still within easy walking distance of the city center. **Pros:** best barkeep in the city; quiet surroundings. **Cons:** a bit out of the hub. ⊠ *Wiedner Hauptstrasse 12, 4th District/Wieden* ☎ *01/589–180* ⊕ *www.dastriest.at* ⤳ *72 rooms* ⟳ *In-room: no a/c (some). In-hotel: restaurant, bar, gym, Internet, Wi-Fi* ⊟ *AE, DC, MC, V* ⦿ *BP.*

$$$

🎬 **König von Ungarn.** In a dormered, 16th-century house in the shadow of St. Stephen's Cathedral, this hotel began catering to court nobility in 1746. The complex is also joined to the Mozarthaus, where Mozart lived when he wrote *The Marriage of Figaro.* Wolfie would undoubtedly enjoy this hostelry, now outfitted with the Mozartstuberl restaurant that is aglow in "Maria Theresa yellow"; a courtyard atrium (so gigantic a tree sprouts in the middle of it); and guest rooms that radiate charm. Some rooms with Styrian wood–paneled walls are furnished with country antiques and have walk-in closets and double sinks in the sparkling bathrooms. The eight suites are two stories, and two have balconies with rooftop views of Old Vienna. **Pros:** staff extremely friendly; great location. **Cons:** a tad old-fashioned. ⊠ *Schulerstrasse 10, 1st District* ☎ *01/515–840* ⊕ *www.kvu.at* ⤳ *33 rooms* ⟳ *In-hotel: restaurant, bar, Internet* ⊟ *DC, MC, V* ⦿ *BP.*

$$$

🎬 **Levante Parliament.** This extravagant design hotel caters to seekers of luxury and high-tech, and it's arty indeed: top photographer Curt Themessl exhibits his wonderful black-and-white ballet pics and Romanian glass artist Ioan Nemtoi decorates the hotel spaces with fantastic glasswork. Breathing Bauhaus, the 1911 building is as polished outside as it is within. Bright natural stone, glass, chrome, and dark wood harmonize with the classical design of the house. The room furnishings emphasize rectangular formalism, but warm with splashes of orange and red. The huge courtyard garden is an oasis of peace. The Nemtoi Restaurant offers fabulous fusion cuisine, and the bar is an eye-catcher. You get five-star luxury here for the price of four. **Pros:** less touristy than many of the big Vienna hotels. **Cons:** entrance isn't very inviting; location a bit out of the way. ⊠ *Auerspergstrasse 9, 1st Dis-*

trict ☎*01/228–280* ⊕*www.thelevante.com* ↩*74 rooms* ⚘*In-hotel: bar, gym, Wi-Fi*☰*AE, DC, MC, V* ⍟*BP.*

$$$ ⌂**Mailberger Hof.** The Knights of Malta—the Hospitallers— knew something about hospitality, and their Baroque mansion, now family-run, continues to offer travelers a comforting welcome mat. An atmospheric carriage entrance and cobblestoned courtyard greet you in this tranquil location just off Kärntnerstrasse, away from the crowded shopping streets. It's a traditional sort of hotel, with attractive and airy rooms with golden and crimson bedspreads, reproduction furniture, and soft carpets. The rooms on the first floor are the most attractive; try to get one facing the pretty Baroque street. In summer the inner courtyard is set with tables for dining; at other times you can sample Vienna specialties and *Naturküche* under rather regal vaulted arches. **Pro:** top location; friendly staff. **Cons:** no Internet. ✉*Annagasse 7, 1st District* ☎*01/512–0641* ⊕*www.mailbergerhof.at* ↩*40 rooms, 5 apartments with kitchenettes (available by the month)* ⚘*In-hotel: restaurant* ☰*AE, DC, MC, V* ⍟*BP.*

$$$ ⌂**Radisson.** One of the handsomest of the Ringstrasse palace hotels, the Radisson combines the fin-de-siècle Palais Leitenberger and the Palais Henckel von Donnersmarck. The latter, built in 1872, was occupied by a patrician family, and its taste shows in the superbly designed facade, articulated with window pediments and caryatids. The location is also princely—directly across from the Stadtpark, Vienna's main city park. Inside, the rooms are done with an understated, traditional, and meticulous feel. Quiet and comfortable, some have pretty floral drapes and matching bedspreads, others have a more masculine Biedermeier look. The Le Siecle restaurant offers food as stylish as its decor. **Pros:** great breakfast buffet; excellent staff. **Cons:** slow elevators. ✉*Parkring 16, 1st District* ☎*01/515170* ⊕*www.radissonsas.com* ↩*246 rooms* ⚘*In-hotel: 2 restaurants, bar, gym, spa, Wi-Fi* ☰*AE, DC, MC, V.*

$$$

FodorsChoice

★

⌂**Style Hotel Vienna.** Within the hotel's Art Nouveau shell, London interior designer Maria Vafiadis has paid tribute to Viennese Art Deco and the result is über-stylish yet comfortable. Smack in the middle of the lobby is an eye-catching glass-enclosed vault; the property used to be a bank and the big bucks were stashed here, though today it serves as a wine cellar and you can enjoy a glass of wine in the elegant marble-and-wood wine bar, which has an enormous open fireplace. Rooms are full of streamlined, sedate furnishings. The location is unbeatable: step out of the hotel and you're in the Café Central, and just down the cobbled street is the Hofburg palace, and, if style is your thing, you'll love your stay here. **Pros:** excellent rates available online; quiet area of old city. **Cons:** small reception area; reception desks oddly too low. ✉*Herrengasse 12, 1st District* ☎*01/22–780–0* ⊕*www.stylehotel.at* ↩*78 rooms* ⚘*In-hotel: restaurant, bar, gym, Wi-Fi* ☰*AE, DC, MC, V* ⍟*BP.*

$$–$$$ ⌂**Altstadt.** In 2006, owner and arts patron, Otto E. Wiesenthal, hired Italian star architect Matteo Thun to revamp eight rooms and a suite; the results are are dark, velvety, sleek, and sensuous chambers oozing atmosphere from the Vienna era of Freud and Klimt. All the guest rooms are large, and differ in decor, but all have modern comforts, and throughout the property are displayed contemporary art that adds char-

acter and style. The cozy red lounge and bar has a fireplace and piano. **Pros:** huge rooms; staff are accommodating and pleasant; trendy area. **Cons:** dowdy entranceway; stairs to climb to reception area; outside city center. ⊠*Kirchengasse 41, 7th District/Neubau* ☎*01/526–3399–0* ⊕*www.altstadt.at* ⇄ *42 rooms* ⚐ *In-hotel: bar, Wi-Fi*☰*AE, DC, MC, V* ⏍|*BP.*

$$–$$$ ⊞ **Das Tyrol.** On a busy Mariahilferstrasse corner, this small, luxurious
★ hotel is a good choice for those who want to be close to the MuseumsQuartier and some fun shopping, too. Blending the old with the new, Austrian contemporary art work adorns the pleasing rooms, with fabrics and tony furniture from posh Viennese stores like Backhausen, Thonet, and Wittmann. There are other nice touches too, such as stylish high-backed chairs, fashionable lamps, and elegant drapes that dress the long windows. The neighborhood also has a host of good restaurants. **Pros:** great Internet rates available; great location. **Cons:** busy road. ⊠*Mariahilferstrasse 15* ☎*01/587–5415* ⊕*www.das-tyrol. at* ⇄*30 rooms* ⚐*In-hotel: bar, Wi-Fi*☰*AE, DC, MC, V* ⏍|*BP.*

$$–$$$ ⊞ **Hollmann Beletage.** If you want to remain anonymous this is your address. A new boutique hotel, neatly tucked away in the center of town just a short walk from the cathedral, was opened recently by a young actor-chef with a unique vision: a theater room has just been added to the hotel. Rooms are spacious, with a light, breezy flair and sleek natural-colored wood floors and furniture. A welcoming reception lounge with a library, music center, open fireplace, and comfy furniture gives the place a home-away-from-home feel. There are bikes to borrow, too. **Pros:** off the beaten track in a superb part of the old city; flat-screen TVs, bikes. **Cons:** location a bit hard to find. ⊠*Köllnerhofgasse 6, 1st District* ☎*01/961–1960–0* ⊕*www.hollmann-beletage.at* ⇄*25 rooms* ⚐*In-hotel: Wi-Fi* ☰*AE, DC, MC, V* ⏍|*BP.*

$$–$$$ ⊞ **Pension Domizil.** Around the corner from the house where Mozart wrote *The Marriage of Figaro,* the Domizil offers quiet, well-equipped rooms with rather bland contemporary furniture. Breakfast is a notch above average, though, with both hot and cold selections. The staff is pleasant, and you're right in the middle of a series of charming old-world cobblestone streets near St. Stephen's. **Pros:** top location; friendly staff. **Cons:** not much character. ⊠*Schulerstrasse 14, 1st District* ☎*01/513–3199–0* ⊕*www.hoteldomizil.at* ⇄*47 rooms* ⚐*In-room: no a/c, Wi-Fi*☰*AE, DC, MC, V* ⏍|*BP.*

$$–$$$ ⊞ **Pension Pertschy.** Housed in the former Palais Cavriani, just off the Graben, this pension is about as central as you can get. It's one of those typical Viennese mansion-turned-apartment houses, adorned with touches of bygone grandeur: case in point, the palatial grand staircase. Most rooms are spacious and all are comfortable. Some have bed canopies and chandeliers, others are decorated with repro–antique furniture that verges on the kitsch. The street outside gets a lot of horse-drawn carriages (and street sweepers at night), so opt for a courtyard room if you need peace and quiet. **Pros:** hard-to-beat location; family-run and friendly. **Cons:** rooms facing street are noisy. ⊠*Habsburgergasse 5, 1st District* ☎*01/534–49–0* ⊕*www.pertschy.com* ⇄*43 rooms* ⚐*In-room: no a/c* ☰*AE, DC, MC, V* ⏍|*BP.*

$$–$$$ 🏨 **Wandl.** The restored facade identifies this 300-year-old house that
★ has been in family hands as a hotel since 1854. You couldn't find a better location, tucked behind St. Peter's Church, just off the Graben. The
hallways are punctuated by bright openings the look out onto glassed-in inner court, making the whole feel quite airy. The rooms are modern,
but some are a bit plain and charmless, despite parquet flooring and
red accents. Ask for one of the rooms done in period furniture, with
decorated ceilings and gilt mirrors; they're rather palatial, with plush
Victorian chairs, carved-wood trim, and velvet throws. **Pros:** top location; quiet square; helpful staff. **Cons:** no Wi-Fi; rooms can get stuffy.
⊠ *Petersplatz 9, 1st District* ☎ *01/534–55–0* ⊕ *www.hotel-wandl.com*
⇗ *138 rooms* ♿ *In-room: no a/c. In-hotel: bar, Internet* ▤ *AE, DC,
MC, V* ⊺◎⊺ *BP.*

$$ 🏨 **Pension Nossek.** A family-run establishment on the upper floors of a
19th-century office and apartment building, the Nossek lies at the heart
of Vienna's pedestrian and shopping area. Rooms have high ceilings
and are eclectically but comfortably furnished; those on the street side
have a view of the Graben. Mozart worked on *The Abduction from the
Seraglio* while he lived here in the early 1780s. Do as the many regular
guests do: book early. **Pros:** perfect location; family oriented; friendly
staff. **Cons:** old-fashioned, a little drab in appearance. ⊠ *Graben 17,
1st District* ☎ *01/533–7041–0* ⊕ *www.pension-nossek.at* ⇗ *30 rooms*
♿ *In-room: Internet, no a/c* ▤ *No credit cards* ⊺◎⊺ *BP.*

$$ 🏨 **Rathaus Wine & Design.** The friendliest staff and what might be the
★ best breakfast buffet in town—see to it that your schedule allows you
to savor the spread—make this exclusive boutique hotel a worthwhile
choice. The property also pays homage to the top winemakers of Austria, and rooms are named after Austria's best winemakers, with a bottle
of the vintner's wine inside (sorry, not included in the room price). The
spacious, high-ceiling, ultramodern guest rooms have polished wooden
floors and accent wood walls, with warm orange, yellow, ocher, and
cream colors. **Pros:** top marks for staff; unbeatable breakfast; top-floor
penthouse suite has its own terrace—book way ahead. **Cons:** awkward
spiral stairs from street to reception area (elevator starts at reception).
⊠ *Langegasse 13* ☎ *01/400–1122* ⊕ *www.hotel-rathaus-wien.at* ⇗ *33
rooms* ♿ *In-hotel: bar, Wi-Fi* ▤ *AE, DC, MC, V* ⊺◎⊺ *BP.*

$–$$ 🏨 **Pension Zipser.** With an ornate facade and a gilt-trimmed coat of
arms, this 1904 house is one of the city's better values. It's in the picturesque Josefstadt neighborhood of small cafés, shops, bars, and good
restaurants, yet within steps of the J streetcar line to the city center.
The rooms are in browns and beiges, with modern furniture and well-equipped baths. The balconies of some of the back rooms overlook
tree-filled neighborhood courtyards. The accommodating staff will
help get theater and concert tickets. If available ask for a room with
balcony. **Pros:** friendly staff; quiet area. **Cons:** far from the city center. ⊠ *Langegasse 49, 8th District/Josefstadt* ☎ *01/404–540* ⊕ *www.
zipser.at* ⇗ *47 rooms* ♿ *In-room: no a/c. In-hotel: bar, Internet* ▤ *AE,
DC, MC, V* ⊺◎⊺ *BP.*

$ 🏨 **Benediktushaus.** You can stay in this guesthouse of a monastery,
in the heart of Vienna, without following the dictum *ora et labora*

(pray and work), though you will get to see how the monks live by the credo. This will be one of the most tranquil stays you've ever had. The rooms are simply furnished and without frills, and without TV; why not switch on the relax mode and go chant with the *fratres* in the Freyung? The picturesque square is just a minute from Café Central if you think you're missing out on some of the fun. **Pros:** superb location; good value. **Cons:** only the bare necessities. ⊠*Freyung 6a, 1st District* ☎*01/534–98–900* ⊕*www.schottenstift.at* ⇘*21 rooms* ⚲*In-room: no a/c* ⊟*AE, DC, MC, V* ⦿*BP.*

$ ⊡ **Stadthalle.** This budget hotel close to Vienna's main Westbahnhof
★   railway station was awarded the Austrian environment-friendly label from the Ministry for Economic Affairs in 2005: water is heated by solar cells, rainwater is recycled, and the flat roofs are used for gardening. A courtyard abounds with plants and flowers, and it's the lovely setting for the outdoor breakfast made up entirely of produce, which is free of genetically modified products. The homey rooms are quiet and individually styled; some of Austria's well-known artists have had a hand in embellishing the interiors. An additional 30 rooms are set to open in early 2009. **Pros:** eco-friendly; Sunday arrivals usually get a lower rate for whole stay; some cheap rates available via Internet. **Cons:** busy roads nearby. ⊠*Hackengasse 20, 15th District/Rudolfsheim–Fünfhaus* ☎*01/982–4272* ⊕*www.hotelstadthalle.at* ⇘*42 rooms* ⚲*In-room: no a/c, Wi-Fi* ⊟*MC, V* ⦿*BP.*

NIGHTLIFE & THE ARTS

Vienna's nightlife and arts scenes present visitors with many tantalizing choices, so it's probably good sense to do some planning if you want to maximize your entertainment. Do you want to time-warp back to the 18th century at Mozart concerts featuring bewigged musicians in the opulent surroundings at Schönbrunn Palace? Or perhaps you'd like to cheer the divas at the grandest of grand opera at the Staatoper, or dive into the Franz Josef splendor of an evening concert of Strauss waltzes, or enjoy a trombone troupe at a *Jazzkeller*? Maybe catch a Broadway-musical extravaganza devoted to the life of the tragic empress Elisabeth at the Raimund Theater? Or will it be a summer opera, dance, or concert performance at the Theater an der Wien (where Beethoven's *Fidelio* premiered in 1805)? The choices are seemingly endless, so here's some help.

THE ARTS

Getting tickets:With a city as music mad and opera crazy as Vienna, it's not surprising to learn that the bulk of major performances are sold out in advance, but, with thousands of seats to be filled every night, you may luck out with a bit of planning and the help of the State Theater Booking Office, or **Bundestheaterkassen** (⊠*Main box office for tickets, Operngasse 2* ☎*01/514–44–7880* ⊕*www.bundestheater.at*). It sells tickets for the Akademietheater, Schauspielhaus, Staatsoper, Volksoper, and Burgtheater. Call the (frequently busy) phone line weekdays 8–5.

The above address also operates as a central clearinghouse, open week-days 8–6, weekends from 9 AM to noon. Tickets for the Staatsoper and Volksoper go on sale one month before the date of performance; credit-card reservations are taken up to six days before the performance. You can also purchase tickets using the **Web site** ⊕*www.culturall.at.* As for other ticket agencies, the most trusted is **Liener Brünn** (✉ *Augustiner-strasse 7* ☎*01/533–0961* ⊕*www.viennafirsttickets.com*)—open week-days 9:30 to 5 PM, Saturday till noon, it charges a 25% markup for seats. Tickets to musicals and some events including the Vienna Festival are available at the **"Salettl" gazebo** kiosk alongside the Opera House on Kärntnerstrasse, open daily 10 AM to 7 PM. Tickets to that night's musicals are half-price after 2 PM.

DANCE

A small revolution has been brewing on the modern dance front, thanks to **Tanzquartier Wien** (✉*Museumsplatz 1, 7th District/Neu-bau* ☎*01/581–35–91* ⊕*www.tqw.at*). DanceQuarter Vienna is now Austria's foremost center for contemporary dance performances. The Tanzquartier season lasts from September through April. In May and June it's followed by the so-called "Factory Season," when the center concentrates solely on the projects presented in its dance studios. The **ballet evenings** (☎*01/514–44–0* ⊕*www.wiener-staatsoper.at*) on the Staatsoper and Volksoper seasonal schedule feature mostly contemporary choreography.

FILM

The film schedules in the daily newspapers *Der Standard* and *Die Presse* list foreign-language film showings; *OmU* means original language with German subtitles. Vienna has a thriving film culture, with many viewers seeking original rather than German-dubbed versions. The most popular venues are listed below. Just around the corner from Tuchlauben street, the **Artis** (✉*Corner of Shultergasse/Jordangasse, 1st District* ☎*01/535–6570*) has six screens altogether, showing the latest blockbusters three to four times a day. The **Burg Kino** (✉*Opernring 19, 1st District* ☎*01/587–8406*) features Carol Reed's Vienna-based classic *The Third Man,* with Orson Welles and Joseph Cotton, every Tuesday, Friday, and Sunday. Otherwise all new releases are usually shown in the original English version. The **Haydn** (✉*Mariahilferstrasse 57, 6th District/Mariahilf* ☎*01/587–2262*) is a multiplex theater. Set in the Albertina museum, the **Filmmuseum** (✉*Augustinerstrasse 1, 1st District* ☎*01/533–7054* ⊕*www.filmmuseum.at*) has one of the most ambitious and sophisticated schedules around, with original-version classics and a heavy focus on English-language films; it's closed July to September. The arty **Votiv-Kino** (✉*Währingerstrasse 12, 9th District/Alsergrund* ☎*01/317–3571*) usually features less mainstream, more alternative fare, with most films shown in their original version with German subtitles. In winter the Votiv-Kino offers a leisurely Sunday brunch–feature film package.

GALLERIES

With new and hip contemporary art museums springing up across Austria (notably the Kunsthaus in Graz and the Museum der Moderne Kunst in Salzburg), art in Vienna needs to remain cutting-edge, and it succeeds in notable galleries in two city quarters. The first is behind the MQ (MuseumsQuartier) complex, while the second is in the 4th District—the Freihaus-Quartier, where some of the most exciting contemporary galleries in town have set up shop, appropriately within range of the Secession Pavilion. Freihaus has become one of the hottest areas in Vienna for everything that's trendy, fashionable, and fun. The more traditional art galleries are still grouped around the now privatized Dorotheum auction house *(⇨Shopping)* in the city center.

Another of the Schleifmühlgasse galleries is **Gallery Christine Koenig** (⊠*Schleifmülgasse 1a, 4th District/Wieden* ☎*01/585–7474*). The leading address for contemporary galleries in the Freihaus-Quartier is Schleifmühlgasse. Here is where you'll find, in a former printing shop, **Gallery Georg Kargl** (⊠*Schleifmühlgasse 5, 4th District/Wieden* ☎*01/585–4199*), which shows art that sidesteps categorization and is a must for serious art collectors. **Gallery Hohenlohe** (⊠*Bäckerstrasse 3, 1st District* ☎*01/512–9720*) has exhibits that illustrate the diversity of contemporary art forms. The artists shown here tend to take a critical position toward patriarchal society and discrimination. A presence at cutting-edge art fairs around the world, **Krinzinger Gallery** (⊠*Schottenfeldgasse 45, 7th District* ☎*01/513–30 06*) has been going strong since the 1970s, when it pushed Vienna Actionism. Its Krinzinger Projects are among the most important blips on the contemporary Austrian art radar screen, and it is close to the MQ (MuseumsQuartier). While her father, Baron H. H. Thyssen-Bornemisza, amassed one of the greatest collections of Old Master paintings, Francesca von Habsburg has chosen to spearhead Austria's avant-garde scene at her **TB A-21** (⊠*Himmelpfortgasse 13, 1st District* ☎*01/513–9856*). New media installations, puppet rock operas, and exhibitions by hot new international artists keep people talking about Thyssen-Bornemisza Art Contemporary.

MUSIC

Vienna is one of the main music centers of the world. Contemporary music gets its due, but it's the hometown standards—the works of Beethoven, Brahms, Haydn, Mozart, and Schubert—that draw the Viennese public and make tickets to the Wiener Philharmoniker the hottest of commodities. A monthly printed program, the *Wien-Programm,* put out by the city tourist board and available at any travel agency or hotel, gives an overview of what's going on in the worlds of opera, concerts, jazz, theater, and galleries, and similar information is posted on billboards and fat advertising columns around the city. Vienna is home to four full symphony orchestras: the great Wiener Philharmoniker (Vienna Philharmonic), the outstanding Wiener Symphoniker (Vienna Symphony), the broadcasting service's ORF Symphony Orchestra, and the Niederösterreichische Tonkünstler. There are also hundreds of smaller groups, from world-renowned trios to chamber orchestras.

★ The most important concert halls are in the buildings of the Gesell-schaft der Musikfreunde, called the **Musikverein** (✉*Dumbastrasse 3, ticket office at Karlsplatz 6* ☎*01/505-8190* ⊕*www.musikverein. at*). There are six halls in this magnificent theater, but the one that everyone knows is the venue for the annually televised New Year's Day Concert—the Goldene Saal, the Gold Hall, officially called the Grosser Musikvereinssaal. Possibly the most beautiful in the world, this Parthenon of a music hall was designed by the Danish 19th-century architect Theophil Hansen, a passionate admirer of ancient Greece. For his 1869 design of the hall, he arrayed an army of gilded cary-atids in the main concert hall, planted Ionic columns in the 660-seat Brahmssaal, and placed the figure of Orpheus in the building pediment. But the surprise is that his smaller Brahmssal is even more sumptu-ous—a veritable Greek temple with more caryatids and lots of gild-ing and green malachite. What Hansen would have made of the four newly constructed (2004) subsidiary halls, set below the main theater, must remain a mystery, but the avant-garde Glass, Metal, Wooden, and Stone Halls (Gläserne, Hölzerne, Metallene, Steinerne Säle) make fitting showcases for contemporary music concerts. The Musikverein, in addition to being the main venue for such troupes as the Wiener Philharmoniker and the Wiener Symphoniker, also hosts many of the world's finest orchestras. A three-minute walk from the Musikverein, crossing Schwarzenbergplatz, is the **Konzerthaus** (✉*Lothringerstrasse 20, 1st District* ☎*01/242002* ⊕*www.konzerthaus.at*), home to the Grosser Konzerthaussaal, Mozartsaal, and Schubertsaal. The first is a room of magnificent size, with red-velvet and gold accents. The cal-endar of Grosser Konzerthaussaal is packed with goodies, including the fabulous early-music group Concentus Musicus Wien, headed by Nicolaus Harnoncourt, and concerts of the Wiener Philharmoniker and the Wiener Symphoniker.

If the whirling waltzes of Strauss are your thing, head to the Johann Strauss concerts at the **Wiener Kursalon** (✉*Johannesgasse 33, 1st Dis-trict* ☎*01/513-2477* ⊕*www.strauss-konzerte.at*), a majestic palace-like structure built in the Italian Renaissance Revival style in 1865 and set in Vienna's sylvan Stadtpark. Here, in gold-and-white salons, the Salonorchester Alt Wien performs concerts of the works of "Waltz King" Johann Strauss and his contemporaries, with waltzes, polkas, parade themes, operetta melodies and *Salonmusik* at the fore, replete with singers, dancers, and your own glass of champagne (no dancing by the audience allowed).

Happily, there is a plethora of small, period-era, jeweled concert salons in Vienna as well as the larger venues. One of the most opulent is the **Schlosstheater Schönbrunn** (✉*Schönbrunner Schloss-Strasse, 13th Dis-trict/Hietzing* ☎*0664-1111-600* ⊕*www.musik-theater-schoenbrunn. at*), built for Empress Maria Theresa in the palace's Valerie Wing, with glittering chandeliers and a gigantic ceiling fresco. For a grand evening of Strauss and Mozart in imperial surroundings, head to the Wiener Hofburgorchester concerts given in the Hofburg palace's Redouten-saal and mammoth 19th-century **Festsaal** (✉*Heldenplatz, 1st District*

The Sound—and Sights—of Music

What closer association to Vienna is there than music? Saturated with musical history and boasting one of the world's greatest concert venues (the Musikverein), two of the world's greatest symphony orchestras (Vienna Philharmonic and Vienna Symphony), and one of the top opera houses (the Staatsoper), it's no wonder that music and the related politics are subjects of daily conversation.

Music lovers can tread in the footprints of the mighty, seeing where masterpieces were committed to paper or standing where a long-loved work was either praised or damned at its first performance. Many former musicians' residences are open as museums. The most famous apartments are where Mozart wrote his last three symphonies (⇨ Mozarthaus in From St. Stephen's to the Opera House) and Beethoven's Pasqualatihaus (⇨ Baroque Gems & Cozy Cafés). Unlike most of Vienna's composers, Schubert was a native of Vienna and you can visit **Schubert's Birthplace** (✉ Nussdorferstrasse 54, 9th District ☎ 01/317-3601 Ⓤ U2/ Schottenring; Streetcar 37 or 38 to Canisiusgasse) as well as where he died at **Kettenbrückengasse 6** (✉ 4th

District ☎ 01/581-6730 Ⓤ U4/ Kettenbrückengasse). **Joseph Haydn's house** (✉ Haydngasse 19, 6th District ☎ 01/596-1307 Ⓤ U4/ Pilgramgasse or U3/Zieglergasse) includes a Brahms memorial room and is open Wednesday and Thursday 10–1 and 2–6, Friday–Sunday 10–1. **Beethoven's Heiligenstadt residence** (✉ Probusgasse 6, 19th District ☎ 01/370-5408 Ⓤ U4/Heiligenstadt; Bus 38A to Wählamt) is where at age 32 he wrote the "Heiligenstadt Testament," an anguished cry of pain and protest against his ever-increasing deafness. All the above houses contain commemorative museums. Admission is €2. Most are open Tuesday–Sunday 10–1 and 2–6, but note there are exceptions. The home of the most popular composer of all, waltz king Johann Strauss the Younger, can be visited at **Praterstrasse 54** (✉ 2nd District ☎ 01/214-0121 Ⓤ U4/ Nestroyplatz); he lived here when he composed "The Blue Danube Waltz" in 1867. Opening times here are Tuesday–Thursday 2–6, Friday–Sunday 10–1. On Sunday all houses but the Mozarthaus offer free admission.

☎ 01/587-2552 ⊕ www.hofburgorchester.at). The concerts are offered Thursday, and Saturday, May through October. The most enchanting place to hear Mozart in Vienna (or probably anywhere, for that matter) is the exquisite 18th-century Sala Terrena of the **Deutschordenskloster** (✉ Singerstrasse 7, 1st District ⊕ www.mozarthaus.at). Here, in a tiny room—it seats no more than 50 people—a bewigged chamber group offers Mozart concerts in a jewel box overrun with rococo frescoes in the Venetian style, from Thursday to Sunday. The concerts are scheduled by the nearby Mozarthaus. Said to be the oldest concert "hall" in Vienna, the Sala Terrena is part of the German Monastery, where, in 1781, Mozart worked for his despised employer, Archbishop Colloredo of Salzburg.

Although the well-known mid-May to mid-June Vienna Festival, the **Wiener Festwochen** (☎ 01/589-22-11 ⊕ www.festwochen.at), signals the end of the primary season, the rest of the summer music scene, from mid-July to mid-August, nowadays brims with activities, particularly in the Theater an der Wien.

The beloved Vienna Boys' Choir, the **Wiener Sängerknaben** (✉ *Hofburg, Schweizer Hof, 1st District* ☎ *01/533–9927* ⊕ *www.wsk.at*) isn't just a set of living "dolls" out of a Walt Disney film (remember the 1962 movie *Almost Angels?*). Its pedigree is royal, and its professionalism such that the Choir regularly appears with the best orchestras around the world. The troupe originated as a choir founded by Emperor Maximilian I in 1498, but with the demise of the Habsburg empire in 1918 it was on its own and became a private outfit, subsidizing itself by giving public performances starting in the 1920s. When the troupe lost its imperial patronage, it traded in court costume for the current charming costumes, then the height of fashion (a look even sported by Donald Duck, who was also born in that era).

From early September to late June, the apple-cheeked lads sing mass at 9:15 AM Sunday in the **Hofburgkapelle** (✉ *Hofmusikkapelle, Hofburg-Schweizerhof, Vienna*). Written requests for seats should be made at least eight weeks in advance. You will be sent a reservation card, which you exchange at the box office (in the Hofburg courtyard) for your tickets (cash only). Tickets are also sold at ticket agencies and at the box office (open Friday 11–1 and 3–5; any remaining seats may be available Sunday morning, 8:15 to 8:45). General seating costs €5, prime seats in the front of the church nave €29. ■ TIP→ Note that only the 10 side balcony seats allow a view of the choir; those who purchase floor seats, standing room, or center balcony will not have a view of the boys. On Sunday at 8:45 AM any unclaimed, preordered tickets are sold. You can also opt for standing room, which is free. If you miss hearing the choir at a Sunday mass, you may be able to catch them in a more popular program in the Musikverein.

OPERA & OPERETTA

★ The **Staatsoper** (*State Opera House* ✉ *Opernring 2, 1st District* ☎ *01/514–440* ⊕ *www.wiener-staatsoper.at*), one of the world's great opera houses, has been the scene of countless musical triumphs and a center of unending controversy over how it should be run and by whom. (When Lorin Maazel was unceremoniously dumped as head of the opera not so many years ago, he pointed out that the house had done the same thing to Gustav Mahler almost a century earlier.) A performance takes place virtually every night September to June, drawing on the vast repertoire of the house, with emphasis on Mozart, Verdi, and Wagner works. Guided tours of the opera house are given year-round.

★ Opera and operetta are also performed at the **Volksoper** (✉ *Währingerstrasse 78* ☎ *01/514–440* ⊕ *www.volksoper.at*), outside the city center at Währingerstrasse and Währinger Gürtel (third stop on Streetcars 41, 42, or 43, which run from Schottentor, U2, on the Ring). Prices here are significantly lower than at the Staatsoper, and performances can be every bit as rewarding. This theater has a packed calendar, with offerings ranging from the grandest opera, such as Mozart's *Don Giovanni,* to an array of Viennese operettas, such as Johann Strauss's *Wiener Blut* and *Die Fledermaus*, to modern Broadway musicals (in 2004, Rodgers and Hammerstein's *Sound of Music* finally received its first Austrian staging here). Most operas here are sung in German.

You'll also find musicals and operetta at a couple of theaters. The **Raimundtheater** (⊠ *Wallgasse 18* ☎*01/599–77–0* ⊕*www.musicalvienna. at*) does long-running musical productions and shows from local and international producers. One of the last—*Barbarella*—was an enormous flop taken off the bill soon after the start.

Ronacherer (⊠*Seilerstätte 9* ☎*01/588–85–0* ⊕*www.musicalvienna.at*), which reopened in 2008 after extensive restoration, shows the latest in musical smash hits from Broadway, including a German-language production of Mel Brooks's *The Producers*.

For decades the **Theater an der Wien** (⊠*Linke Wienszeile 6* ☎*01/588– 30–660* ⊕*www.theater-wien.at*), a beautiful rococo-style historic theater dating to 1801, was misused as a contemporary musical venue. Now this building—which is closely linked to Beethoven, who lived here, and to Schikaneder, the librettist who wrote *The Magic Flute* for Mozart—has renewed its role as an opera house, attracting an increasingly international crowd. It's open year-round with a premiere nearly every month. The selection of works performed here is tremendous, ranging from Janacek to Prokofiev, Monteverdi, and Bach. Opera and operetta are performed on an irregular schedule at the **Kammeroper** (⊠*Fleischmarkt 24* ☎*01/512–01–000* ⊕*www.wienerkammeroper. at*). In summer, light opera or operetta performances are given in the exquisite, formerly imperial, rococo **Schlosstheater** at Schönbrunn. (☎*0664–1111–600* ⊕*www.musik-theater-schoenbrunn.at*).

THEATER

Vienna's **Burgtheater** (⊠*Dr.-Karl-Lueger-Ring 2, 1st District* ☎*01/514– 444–440* ⊕*www.burgtheater.at*) is one of the leading German-language theaters of the world. The repertoire frequently mixes German classics with more modern and controversial pieces; particulary notorious are the works of Nobel prize winner Elfriede Jelinek, who won the 2004 Nobel Prize in Literature. The Burg's smaller house, the **Akademie theater** (⊠*Lisztstrasse 1* ☎*01/514–444–740* ⊕*www.bundesttheater. at*), draws on much the same group of actors for classical and modern plays but performances are in a more relaxing setting. Both are closed during July and August. The **Kammerspiele** (⊠*Rotenturm- strasse 20* ☎*01/42700–304*) does modern and comedy plays. The **The- ater in der Josefstadt** (⊠*Josefstädterstrasse 26, 8th District/Josefstadt* ☎*01/42700–306*) stages classical and modern works year-round in the house once run by the great producer and teacher Max Reinhardt. The theater had, of late, been seeming to gather layers of dust, but happily, the relatively new directorship of actor Herbert Föttinger has restored its reputation for more avant-garde and daring productions. The **Volk- stheater** (⊠*Neustiftgasse 1, 7th District/Neubau* ☎*01/523–3501–0*) presents dramas, comedies, and folk plays.

For theater in English (mainly classic comedy and standard plays), head for the cozy and charming **Vienna's English Theater** (⊠*Josefsgasse 12, 8th District/Josefstadt* ☎*01/402–1260*). Another option is the equally good **International Theater** (⊠*Porzellangasse 8, 9th District/Alsergrund* ☎*01/319–6272*).

NIGHTLIFE

BALLS

The gala Vienna evening you've always dreamed about can become a reality: among the many **balls** given during the Carnival season, several welcome the public—at a wide range of prices, from about €75 to €450 and up, per person. Dates change every year, but most balls are held in January and February. The dress code for all is "full dress," and they usually run between 8 or 9 PM and 3 or 4 AM. Food and drink is always available. Some of the more popular balls are the Hofburg Ball known as the Kaiserball (Emperor Ball), the Philharmoniker Ball (Philharmonic Ball), the Bonbon Ball (Confection Ball), the Blumen Ball (Florists' Ball), and the most famous and expensive of them all, the Opernball (Opera Ball). For more information see the event page of the Vienna Info (⊕*www.wieninfo.at* ⊕*www.kaiserball.at*).

BARS, LOUNGES & NIGHTCLUBS

Where once night owls had to head to Vienna's *Bermuda Dreieck* (Bermuda Triangle, around St. Ruprecht's church on the Ruprechtsplatz, two blocks south of the Danube Canal), today's club scene has blossomed with a profusion of delightful and sophisticated bars, clubs, and lounges. Many of the trendy people head to the clubs around the Naschmarkt area, then move on to nearby Mariahilferstrasse for dancing. The Freihaus Quarter sizzles with cafés and shops.

A sort of spaceship has landed smack between the Hofburg palace and the Kunsthistorisches Museum—just look for the glowing orange kiosk at the intersection of the Ring and Mariahilferstrasse and head downstairs to find **Babenberger Passage** (⊠*Ringstrasse at Babenbergerstrasse, 1st District* ☎*01/961–8800* Ⓤ*U2/MuseumsQuartier*), one of the hippest places in Vienna these days. State-of-the-art lighting systems, futuristic decor, and adaptable design elements come together in a blush-hued bar and a sizzling-blue dance room. A dazzling setting for a Viennese club is in a cavernous subway station, and **Café Carina** (⊠*Josefstädterstrasse 84/Stadtbahnbogen, 8th District/Josefstadt* ☎*01/406–4322* Ⓤ*U6/Josefstädterstrasse*) is in one of the best—an Otto Wagner original. Vienna's new subway-station clubs are proof positive that nightlife is no longer centered in and around the old city center. Carina is very off-beat, artistic, and action-packed—anything can happen here, from an air-guitar competition to an evening of 1980s hits. Near the Naschmarkt, **Kaleidoskop** (⊠*Schleifmühlgasse 13, 4th District/Wieden* ☎*01/920–3343* Ⓤ*U4/Kettenbrückengasse*) sits shoulder to shoulder with a number of top art galleries, attracting the hip and happening art crowd. Chic, chic, and once again chic, the designer café-bar **Shultz** (⊠*Siebensterngasse 31, 7th District/Neubau*

Stepping Out in Three-Quarter Time

Ever since the 19th-century Congress of Vienna—when pundits laughed "*Elle danse, mais elle ne marche pas*" (the city "dances, but it never gets anything done")—Viennese extravagance and gaiety have been world-famous. Fasching, the season of Carnival, was given over to court balls, opera balls, masked balls, chambermaids' and bakers' balls, and a hundred other gatherings, many held within the glittering interiors of Baroque theaters and palaces. Presiding over the dazzling evening gowns and gilt-encrusted uniforms, towering headdresses, flirtatious fans, *chambres séparées*, "Wine, Women, and Song," *Die Fledermaus*, "Blue Danube," hand kissing, and gay abandon was the baton of the waltz emperor, Johann Strauss. White-gloved women and men in white tie would glide over marble floors to his heavenly melodies. They still do. Now, as in the days of Franz Josef, Vienna's old three-quarter-time rhythm strikes up anew each year during Carnival, from New Year's Eve until Mardi Gras.

During January and February as many as 40 balls may be held in a single evening. Many events are organized by a professional group, including the Kaiserball (Imperial Ball), Philharmonikerball (Ball of the Philharmonic Orchestra), Kaffeesiederball (Coffee Brewers' Ball), the Zuckerbaeckerball (Confectioners' Ball), or the Opernball (Opera Ball). The latter is the most famous—some say too famous. This event transforms the Vienna Opera House into the world's most beautiful ballroom (and transfixes all of Austria when shown live on national television). The invitation reads "*Frack mit Dekorationen*," which means that ball gowns and tails are usually required for most events (you can always get your tux from a rental agency) and women mustn't wear white (reserved for debutantes). But there's something for everyone these days, including the "Ball of Bad Taste" or "Wallflower Ball." Other noted venues are the imperial Hofburg palace and the Musikverein concert hall. Prices usually run from about €75 to €450 and up per person. If you go, remember that you must dance the *Linkswalzer*—the counterclockwise, left-turning waltz that is the only correct way to dance in Vienna. After your gala evening, finish off the morning with a *Kater Frühstuck*—hangover breakfast—of goulash soup.

☎01/522–9120 ⓊU4/*Kettenbrückengasse*) seduces fashionable folk with its long drinks, retro cocktails, and Vienna Moderne setting. Back in 1870, Viennese used to come to the **Volksgarten** (✉*Burgring 2, 1st District* ☎01/532–0907 ⓊU2/3 *MuseumsQuartier*) to waltz, drink champagne, and enjoy the night in a candlelit garden. Today they come to the same site to *diskothek* the night away under pink strobes, enjoy some boogie-woogie or tango dancing in the Tanzcafe (Dance Café), and sip beer amid the greenery. A best bet when you don't know where else to head, this all-in-one club complex is set within a lush garden and has a pretty, vaguely Jugendstil dining salon with a vast curved wall of windows overlooking a terrace set with tables. Beyond lies the Pavilion, a 1950s jewel that looks airlifted from California, which serves brews and nibbles.

DANCE CLUBS

In the MuseumsQuartier, **Café Leopold** (⊠*Museumsplatz 1, Museums-Quartier, 1st District* ☎*01/523–6732* Ⓤ*U2 or 3/MuseumsQuartier*) is inside the large, modern, white cube that is the Leopold Museum, with tables outside in the plaza for after enough house and electro music. In the middle of the Freihaus Quarter, **Club Schikaneder** (⊠*Margaretenstrasse 22–24, 4th District/Wieden* ☎*01/585–2867* Ⓤ*U1, U2, or U4/Karlsplatz*) is a former movie theater that has become a multimedia art and dance center. It still screens three to five art films daily, has exhibitions, and first-class DJ lineups. "U" stands for underground and **Club U im Otto-Wagner-Café** (⊠*Karlsplatz/Kuenstlerhauspassage, 4th District/Wieden* ☎*01/505–9904* Ⓤ*U1, U2, or U4/Karlsplatz*) is just underneath one of the two Jugendstil pavilions that Otto Wagner built on the Karlsplatz square when designing Vienna's subway, which means this disco is easy to find. One of the best dance halls for alternative music, it's open on Sunday, has outdoor seating, live music, a great atmosphere, and excellent DJs who turn this place into a real Soul City most nights. **Flex** (⊠*Donaukanal/Augartenbrücke, 1st District* ☎*01/533–7525* Ⓤ*U1, U2, or U4/Karlsplatz*) is one of the best disco venues in Vienna, with unmatched acoustics due to the architecture of the underground-cave-style construction. The DJ lineup is considered by insiders to be the best in town (and there must be something in that, because the Flex crew just started a music label).

JAZZ CLUBS

★ The jazz scene in Vienna is one of the hottest in Europe. The stage might be small at **Birdland** (⊠*Am Stadtpark 3 [enter Landstrasser Hauptstrasse 2], 3rd District* ☎*01/2196–39315*), but the stars are major, and this club under the Hilton Hotel Stadtpark hosts some of the best in the world of jazz. Jazz legend Joe Zawinul named it after one of his most renowned compositions and New York City's legendary temple of jazz. Set in a cellar under St. Ruprecht's church and the granddaddy of Vienna's jazz clubs, **Jazzland** (⊠*Franz-Josefs-Kai 29, 1st District* ☎*01/533–2575*) opened more than 30 years ago when there was just a small, local jazz scene. But thanks to the pioneering work of the club's founder, Axel Melhardt, Austrian jazz musicians have vibed with the best American stars. The club also serves excellent and authentic Viennese cuisine. In the course of a few years, **Porgy & Bess** (⊠*Riemergasse 11, 1st District* ☎*01/512–8811*) has become a fixed point in the native and international jazz scene.

SHOPPING

SHOPPING DISTRICTS

The **Kärntnerstrasse, Graben,** and **Kohlmarkt** pedestrian areas in the 1st District, Inner City, claim to have the best shops in Vienna, and for some items, such as jewelry, they're probably the some of the best anywhere, but prices are quite steep. The side streets within this area have developed their own character, with shops selling antiques, art, clocks, jewelry, and period furniture. **Ringstrasse Galerie,** the indoor shopping

CLOSE UP

Vienna by Bike

Look for the special pathways either in red brick or marked with a stylized cyclist image in yellow; there are also special traffic signals at some intersections. You can take a bike on the subway (except during rush hours) for an additional half fare, but only in cars with a blue shield on the door, and only on stairs or elevators with the "bike" shield, not on escalators. The city tourist office has a brochure in German with useful cycling maps, plus a leaflet, "See Vienna by Bike," with tips in English. At most bookstores you can purchase a cycling map of Vienna put out by a local cycling organization known as ARGUS.

It's possible to rent bikes and rickshaws in the Prater. **Radverleih Hochschaubahn** (☎ 12/729–5888) is open mid-March to October and is in the Prater amusement park by the Hochschaubahn, slightly to the right after the Ferris wheel. **Pedal Power** (✉ Ausstellungsstrasse 3, 2nd District/ Leopoldstadt ⊕ www.pedalpower.at

☎ 01/729–7234) offers guided bike tours of Vienna and the surrounding vicinity in English from April to October, including the main sights of the city, or tours to the outlying vineyards for a glass of wine. It's also possible to rent a bike and do your own exploring (a half day, including hotel delivery and pickup, is five hours for €24; a full-day rental is €27. Rental for three hours including a guided tour is €23).

The cheapest way to discover Vienna in a saddle is with one of the handy **Citybikes**, available with a Citybike Tourist Card, Visa, or Master Card. After a short registration procedure hop in the saddle and off you go. Pick up the bike at one of the 54 Citybike stations all over the city. When you're finished, just deposit it at a vacant station anywhere you like. The first hour on your bike is free, the second costs €1, the third €2, and the fourth through 120th hours are €4.

plaza at Kärntner Ring 5–7, brings a number of shops together in a modern complex, though many of these stores have other, larger outlets elsewhere in the city. Outside the center, concentrations of stores are on **Mariahilferstrasse,** straddling the 6th and 7th districts; **Landstrasser Hauptstrasse** in the 3rd District; and, still farther out, **Favoritenstrasse** in the 10th District.

A collection of attractive small boutiques can be found in the **Palais Ferstel** passage at Freyung 2 in the 1st District. Another good shopping street is Landstrasser Hauptstrasse in the 3rd District, where there is also a small market. Gumpendorferstrasse, in the 6th District, is rapidly turning into one of the hippest shopping destinations in town, with small boutiques, trendy hairstylists, and great eateries. Then there's the 7th District Neubau, which is starting to compete for the title of hippest of all. On Neubaugasse, Kirchengasse, Lindengasse, and the quaint Mondscheingasse, fashionistas can find unique clothing, jewelry, and footwear in lovely little boutiques; a whole new group of designers has moved into the latter area. Not far away, at the **Spittelberg** market, on the Spittelberggasse between Burggasse and Siebensterngasse in the 7th District, are small galleries and handicrafts shops; this area is particu-

A DIP IN THE WATER

1

When the going gets hot and you're desperate for a cool dip, head to **Badeschiff** (bathing ship). Anchored between Urania and Schwedenplatz on the Donau Canal. This converted cargo ship, with its huge open-air pool and sundeck, is quite the hip social scene. Indeed, if you've cooled down enough to want to heat back up, try out the new disco floor set up beneath the pool. ⌨ Pool €7.50 day ticket ☉ May–mid-Sept., daily 10 AM–midnight Ⓤ U1 or U4/ Schwedenplatz.

If pools cramp your style, try the 24 km- (15 mi-) long **Neue Donau** (take the U1 from Schwedenplatz and there is a stop right above the area for bathing called Neue Donau), a channel of the larger Danube, where you can swim (as long as no red flag is posted) for free. If you forget your swim things, there's nude bathing there, too. Food stalls dot its length.

larly popular in the weeks before Christmas and Easter. Christmas is the time also for the tinselly **Christkindlmarkt** on Rathausplatz in front of City Hall; in protest over its commercialization, smaller markets specializing in handicrafts have sprung up on such traditional spots as Am Hof and the Freyung (1st District), also the venue for other seasonal markets.

Vienna's **Naschmarkt** (between Linke and Rechte Wienzeile, starting at Getreidemarkt) is one of Europe's great and most colorful food and produce markets. Stalls open at 6 AM, and the pace is lively until about 6 PM. Saturday is the big day, though, when farmers come into the city to sell at the back end of the market, but shops close around 5 PM. Also on Saturday is a huge flea market at the Kettenbrückengasse end. The Naschmakt is closed Sunday.

FLEA MARKETS
You should definitely haggle over prices at the flea markets.

Every Saturday (except holidays), rain or shine, from 6:30 AM to 6 PM, the **Flohmarkt** in back of the Naschmarkt, stretching along the Linke Wienzeile from the Kettenbrückengasse U4 subway station, offers a staggering collection of stuff ranging from serious antiques to plain junk. If the weather is bad and business is slack, stalls tend to close earlier. On Friday and Saturday from March until mid-November 10 AM to 8 PM, an outdoor combination arts-and-crafts, collectibles, and flea market takes place on **Am Hof**. From early May to late September, Saturday from 2 to 8 PM and Sunday from 10 AM to 8 PM, an outdoor **art and antiques market** springs up along the Danube Canal underneath the Salztorbrücke. The merchandise here is slightly better in quality than elsewhere. Lots of books are sold, some in English, plus generally less junk than at the Saturday flea market.

DEPARTMENT STORES

Steffl (⊠ *Kärntnerstrasse 19, 1st District*) is one of Vienna's most prominent department stores, stocking just about everything; it's moderately upscale without being overly expensive. Several of the larger department stores are concentrated in Mariahilferstrasse and, for clothes, the best of these is **Peek & Cloppenburg** (⊠ *Mariahilferstrasse 26–30, 6th District*). Farther up the street you'll find four floors with over 25 different stores, including housewares and electronic gadgets, at **Gerngross mall** (⊠ *Mariahilferstrasse 42–48, 6th District*). The top floor has six places to eat, including a great sushi restaurant with an outdoor rooftop terrace, for when you need to take a shopping break. **La Stafa** (⊠ *Mariahilferstrasse 120, 7th District*) is the department store closest to the Westbahnhof railway station; it has a huge supermarket in the basement and a fabulous coffee–breakfast bar on the first floor.

SPECIALTY STORES

ANTIQUES You'll find the best antiques shops in the 1st District, many clustered close to the Dorotheum auction house, along the Dorotheergasse, Stallburggasse, Plankengasse, and Spiegelgasse. There are also interesting shops in the Josefstadt (8th) District, where prices are considerably lower than those in the center of town. Wander up Florianigasse and back down Josefstädterstrasse, being sure not to overlook the narrow side streets.

Just around the corner from the Opera House, **Gallery Dr. Sternat** (⊠ *Lobkowitzplatz 1* ☎ *01/512–2063*) is one of the most traditional art galleries, with a focus on fine Austrian paintings, Viennese bronzes, Thonet furniture, and beautiful Biedermeier pieces. **Bel Etage** (⊠ *Mahlerstrasse 15* ☎ *01/512–2379*) has wonderful works by Josef Hoffmann, Dagobert Peche, and other Wiener Werkstätte masters, all of which entice onlookers to spend more than just time here.

D & S Antiquitäten (⊠ *Dorotheergasse 13* ☎ *01/512–5885*) has a striking entrance designed by Oskar Hoefinger; inside are rare Austrian clocks, 18th-century paintings, and beautiful 19th-century furniture.

Set in a beautiful historic palais, the **Dorotheum** (⊠ *Dorotheergasse 17* ☎ *01/515–60–0*), dating from 1707, when Emperor Josef I determined that he didn't want his people being exploited by pawnbrokers, the Dorotheum was privatized a couple of years ago. The place is intriguing, with goods ranging from furs to antique jewelry to paintings and furniture auctioned almost daily. Information on how to bid is available in English. Some items are for immediate cash sale. Also check out **Palais Kinsky** (⊠ *Freyung 4* ☎ *01/532–42009*) for paintings and antiques.

AUSTRIAN If you want to dress like Captain von Trapp and Maria, perhaps the
CLOTHING & best place for that extra-special piece of folklore wear is **Loden-Plankl**
TRACHTEN (⊠ *Michaelerplatz 6* ☎ *01/533–8032*), which stocks hand-embroidered
★ jackets and *lederhosen* for kids (known for being just about indestructible). The building, opposite the Hofburg, is a centuries-old treasure. Dirndls and *Trachten* (the typical Austrian costume with white blouse, print skirt, and apron) for toddlers to ladies, and cute hand-embroi-

1

CLOSE UP

A Glittering Trove

If you're looking for something truly special—an 18th-century oil portrait or a real fur, a rococo mirror or a fine silk fan, modern or retro jewelry, a china figurine or sterling-silver spoon, an old map of the Austrian Empire or even a stuffed parrot—the one place that may have the answer is the **Dorotheum** (⊠ *Dorotheergasse 17, 1st District* ☎ *01/515–60–0* ⊕ *www. dorotheum.at*), Vienna's fabled auction house. Have you ever wanted to see how the Austrian aristocracy once lived, how their sumptuous homes were furnished? Well, don't bother with a museum—you can inspect their antique furnishings, displayed as if in use, for free, and without the eagle eyes of sales personnel following your every move, in peace and quiet in the gilded salons here. This was the first imperial auction house (*oops*, pawnshop), established in 1707 by Emperor Joseph I. Occupying the

former site of the Dorothy Convent (hence the name), the Dorotheum has built up a grand reputation since it was privatized in the early 2000s. The neo-Baroque building was completed in 1901 and deserves a walk-through (you can enter from Spiegelgasse and exit on Dorotheergasse) just to have a look, even if you only admire the gorgeous stuccoed walls and palatial interiors, or peek into the glass-roofed patio stocked with early-20th-century glass, furniture, and art. With more than 600 auctions a year, this has become one of the busiest auction houses in Europe. There are auctions held frequently throughout the week, though not Saturday, and it's closed Sunday. And if you don't fancy bidding for something, there are large cash-sale areas on the ground and second floors where loads of stuff (that didn't sell at auction) can simply be bought off the floor.

dered cardigans for the kids, are all found at **Giesswein** (⊠ *Kärntnerstrasse 5–7* ☎ *01/512–4597*), with some of the best traditional clothing in town. **Resi Hammerer** (⊠ *Kärntnerstrasse 29–31* ☎ *01/512–6952*) was one of the pioneers of trendy *tracht* attire and today the store is filled with the finest and best-known fashion labels available. Fancy having your very own tailor-made Austrian dirndl dress? **Tostmann** (⊠ *Schottengasse 3a* ☎ *01/533–5331*) is the place to fulfill your wishes.

BOOKS   The biggest Harry Potter launch in Austria took place at the **British**
★   **Bookshop** (⊠ *Weihburggasse 24* ☎ *01/512–1945*), which is always well stocked with the latest English-language editions and best sellers. The staff encourages browsing. If you're planning a hiking holiday in Austria, stock up on the necessary maps at **Freytag & Berndt** (⊠ *Kohlmarkt 9* ☎ *01/533–8685*), the best place for maps and travel books. **Frick** (⊠ *Kärntnerstrasse 31* ☎ *01/513–7364*) does some of the best business in art history and guidebooks on Vienna and Austria. Staff is helpful and bargains can often be found in the trays at the door. A larger branch can be found at Graben 27.</ The biggest book store in Vienna, **Morawa** (⊠ *Wollzeile 11* ☎ *01/513–7513*), has titles on everything under the sun. Thankfully, help is always at hand if you can't find that specific one you're looking for. The magazine and newspaper section is vast, and don't pass over some of the printed gifts, such as a calendar made out of paper shopping bags (you can put the bags to

good use when the year has passed.) Art-book lovers will adore **Wol-frum** (✉*Augustinerstrasse 10* ☎*01/512–5398*) and if you have money to burn, you can also spring for a Schiele print or special art edition to take home.

CERAMICS,
GLASS &
PORCELAIN
★

The best porcelain in town can be found at **Augarten** (✉*Graben/Stock-im-Eisen-Platz 3* ☎*01/512–1494–0*) and the manufactory in the 2nd District in Vienna offers tours of the palais Augarten; you can study the steps involved in making these precious pieces. Is it a "Maria-There-sia," ornately cut diamanté chandelier with a 30%–34% lead content you're looking for? If it is, head and hunt here at **Lobmeyr** (✉*Kärnt-nerstrasse 26* ☎*01/512–0508–0*), one of the world's finest addresses for the best in glass and crystal. It's one of the only stores left in Vienna that retains its interior of imperial glory, yet allows the cutting edge of design to enter its realm (see the breathtakingly beautiful black rococo mirrors by young designer Florian Ladstätter). Even if you're not buy-ing, go upstairs and have a look at the glass museum on the second floor. Pottery from **Berger** (✉*Weihburggasse 17* ☎*01/512–1434*) may be just the gift you're looking for—how about a ceramic stove made to measure for your alpine chalet or a decorative wall plate blooming with a hand-painted flowering gentian? If you want to enter an old-fashioned interior that is little changed from the time when Empress Elisabeth shopped here, **Albin Denk** (✉*Graben 13* ☎*01/512–4439*) is the place. The shop entrance is lined with glass cases and filled with a wonderful if kitschy army of welcoming porcelain figurines. Gmunden ceramics—often with a typical green-and-white design and tiny painted buttercups, or with irregular bands of color—are found in nearly every Austrian country home; you can stock up at **Pawlata** (✉*Kärntner-strasse 14* ☎*01/512–1764*). Ireland has its Waterford, France its Bac-carat, and Austria has **Swarovski** (✉*Kärntnerstrasse 8* ☎*01/5129032*), purveyors of some of the finest cut crystal in the world and, thanks to the newer generation of Swarovskis, increasingly fashionable trinkets. You'll find your typical collector items and gifts here, but also high-style fashion accessories (Paris couturiers now festoon their gowns with Swarovski crystals the way they used to with ostrich feathers), crystal figurines, jewelry, and home accessories. This flagship store is a cave of coruscating crystals that gleam and glitter. Proving just how popular Swarovski is, two more branches opened up nearby, at Kärntnerstrasse 9 and Kärntnerstrasse 53.

GIFTS THAT
SAY "VIENNA"

Are you looking for an old postcard, a hand-carved walking stick, an old record, or even an old photograph of the Opera House from before the war? Head to **Alt-Österreich** (✉*Himmelpfortgasse 7* ☎*01/5121296*)—its name translates as "Old Austria," and this trea-sure trove has just about everything dealing with that time-burnished subject. Austria's one-and-only cooperative for arts and crafts, **Österre-ichische Werkstätten** (✉*Kärntnerstrasse 6* ☎*01/512–2418*), stocks Aus-trian handicrafts of the finest quality. It has home accessories, from brass or pewter candlesticks to linen tablecloths, and quality souve-nirs ranging from enamel jewelry to embroidered brooches. For that Alt Wien flourish, choose a needlepoint handbag, pill box, or brooch

1

from **Petit Point Kovalcec** (✉ *Kärntnerstrasse 16* ☎*01/512–4886*). Fancy a composers' portrait-bust collection? Schubert, Mozart, Beethoven, Haydn, and the rest of the gang can be had at **Souvenir in der Hofburg** (✉ *Hofburgpassage 1 and 7* ☎*01/533–5053*). While you're at it, you might want to go for a ceramic figure of a Lipizzaner stallion, too (it may not be an Augarten porcelain original, but it's certainly more affordable). Postcards, vintage booklets on Vienna, imperial memorabilia, small busts of former Habsburg rulers, and petite gifts for the folks back home will tempt connoisseurs at **Stransky** (✉ *Hofburgpassage 2* ☎*01/533–6098*).

CHRISTKINDL-MÄRKTE Vienna keeps the Christmas flame burning perhaps more brightly than any other metropolis in the world. Here, during the holiday season, no fewer than nine major *Christkindlmärkte* (Christmas Markets) proffer their wares, with stands selling enough wood-carved Austrian toys, crèche figures, and Tannenbaum ornaments to tickle anybody's mistletoes. Many of the markets have food vendors selling *Glühwein* (mulled wine) and *Kartoffelpuffer* (potato patties). In our opinion, the best markets include the following. The **Altwiener Christkindlmarkt** (✉ *The Freyung* ☎*01/5121296*) is held on one of Vienna's biggest squares. **Karlsplatz** (✉ *Karlsplatz*) has some of the more refined stands in town, selling homemade wares. The biggest holiday market is the one on **Rathausplatz,** in front of the Gothic fantasy that is Vienna's city hall. All the glitter and gilt of the season frames the market held at the Habsburgs' **Schönbrunn** (✉ *Schönbrunn Palace*). The cognoscenti love the arty market held in the enchanting Biedermeier quarter of **Spittelberg** (✉ *Burggasse and Siebensterngasse*).

JEWELRY The finest selection of watches in Vienna can be found at **Haban** (✉ *Kärntnerstrasse 2* ☎*01/512–6730–0* ✉*Kärntnerstrasse 17* ☎*01/512–6750*), and the gold and diamond jewelry selection is top-notch, too. In the city of Freud, father of psychoanalysis, what else can you expect but the sort of jewelry at the **Golden Genius** (✉ *Kohlmarkt 3* ☎*01/470–94–82*), where dream symbols are individually cast in different shades of gold as a surround for colorful precious stones. One of Vienna's purveyors to the imperial court, **A. E. Köchert** (✉ *Neuer Markt 15* ☎*01/512–5828–0*), has been Vienna's jeweler of choice for nearly two centuries. Almost 150 years ago Empress Elisabeth ordered some diamond-studded stars from here to adorn her legendary auburn hair (so long she could sit on it). Guess what? Those stars are more fashionable than ever since Köchert started reissuing them. And if you're ever in need of a crown, Köchert will craft your very own.

MEN'S CLOTHING **Grandits** (✉ *Rotenturmstrasse 10* ☎*01/512 63 89*) has a great selection from Armani, Boss, Joop, Ralph Lauren, Versace, and Zegna, all displayed in a stylish ambience. **Peek & Cloppenburg** (✉ *Mariahilferstrasse 26–30* ☎*01/525610*) is the right place for those who hate having to go to various shops to find what they're looking for. It's all here, with brand names, designer labels, and excellent value for money. **Collins Hüte** (✉ *Opernpassage* ☎*01/587–1305*) is one of the best sources in town for accessories such as scarves, gloves, and hats, including the stray sombrero (for that glaring summer sun on the slopes at Lech).

For the classic look, **Sir Anthony** ($\boxtimes$ *Kärntnerstrasse 21–23, 1st District* ☎ *01/512–6835*) is the place.

MUSIC   You just might bump into Placido, Jose, or even Dame Joan Suther-
★   land—and if you do, you know where to buy that picture postcard and
then run and have it autographed—at **Arcardia** ($\boxtimes$ *Staatsoper Opera House, Opernring 2* ☎ *01/513–9568–0*), which is stocked with not only a grand selection of the latest CD releases from the operatic world but quite a few classic rareties, too. Helpful sales assistants are at the ready if you're looking for any special titles at **EMI** ($\boxtimes$ *Kärntnerstrasse 30* ☎ *01/512–3675*)—one of the big mainstays for classical music (upstairs), plus the whole gamut from ethno to pop.

TOYS   Emperor Franz Josef in his horse-drawn carriage, the infantry cheering him on, and the Prussian emperor to meet him at the battlefield—
here at **Kober** ($\boxtimes$ *Graben 14–15* ☎ *01/533–6018*) you can find all the historic tin soldiers you'll ever need to relive the eventful last years of the empire. If you prefer something a little less military, go for the full Johann Strauss Orchestra. In the street where Mozart passed away is one of the better toy stores, **Spielzeugschachtel,** which means toy box; parents with a passion for educational games love this place, and there are also loads of games to choose from, many made of good old wood. ($\boxtimes$ *Rauensteingasse 5* ☎ *01/512–3994*).

WOMEN'S   **Doris Ainedter** ($\boxtimes$ *Jasomirgottstrasse 5* ☎ *01/532–0369*) is the place for
CLOTHING   business and leisure fashion for the trend-conscious woman; she's one of Vienna's most successful designers. **Wiener Blut** ($\boxtimes$ *Spiegelgasse 19* ☎ *01/5132015*) has lots of temptations, including Monika Bacher's zippy knitwear, striking pieces by Berlin designers, zany shoes from Canada, and the finest handbags from Italy. Fashionistas make a bee-line for the studio of Austrian designer **Schella Kann** ($\boxtimes$ *Singerstrasse 14/2* ☎ *01/513–2287*)—extravagant and trendy, these are clothes you never want to take off. For conservative, high-quality clothing, go to the **Geiger Boutique** ($\boxtimes$ *Kärntnerstrasse 19* ☎ *01/513–1398*) in the Steffl Department Store.

Vienna Environs

WORD OF MOUTH

"Some of my favourite Heurige are in Gumpol-dskirchen in the south of Vienna (about 30–40 minutes by car) . . . Are you thinking of renting a car? You will need one to get there from the airport. Gumpoldskirchen is amidst vineyards, and you are close to the Vienna Woods (perfect for hiking) and the small town of Baden bei Wien (very picturesque)."

—viennese

Updated by
Diane Naar-
Elphee

THE VIENNESE ARE UNDENIABLY LUCKY. Few populaces enjoy such glorious—and easily accessible—options for day-tripping. For many the first destination is the Wienerwald, the deservedly fabled Vienna Woods—a rolling range of densely wooded hills extending from Vienna's doorstep to the outposts of the Alps in the southwest (and not a natural park or forest, as you might think from listening to Strauss or the tourist blurbs). This region is crisscrossed by country roads and hiking paths, dotted with forest lodges and inns, and solidifies every now and then into quaint little villages and market towns.

In addition to such natural pleasures, the regions outside of Vienna offer satisfactions for every interest. Keen on history and mystery? Turning south to Mayerling leads you to the site where in 1889 the successor to the Austrian throne presumably took his own life after shooting his secret love—a mystery still unresolved. Music lover? Johann Strauss transformed the tales of the Vienna Woods into exhilarating music, and a glass of intoxicating Retzer Wein moved Richard Strauss to compose the "Rosenkavalier Waltz." Prefer scenic beauty? To the south, you can sip and taste your way down the Weinstrasse (Wine Road), along which vast expanses of vineyards produce excellent, mainly white, wines. Here, you'll find Gumpoldskirchen, one of Austria's many famous wine-producing villages and the source of one of Europe's most pleasing white wines. Another choice is to follow the trail of the defensive castles that protected the land from invaders arriving from the north; or you can even trace the early days of Masonic lore in Austria—both Haydn and Mozart were members of what was then a secret and forbidden brotherhood. For dramatic contrast, head to the elegant spa town of Baden, where Beethoven passed 15 summers and composed large sections of the Ninth Symphony.

ORIENTATION & PLANNING

GETTING ORIENTED

The region surrounding Vienna divides itself logically into two main areas. The Vienna Woods, that huge, unspoiled belt of forest green stretching westward south of the Danube, was celebrated by composers Beethoven, Schubert, and Strauss and remains beloved by the Viennese today. The towns to its south—Mödling, Baden, and Bad Vöslau—mark the east end of these rolling, wooded hills.

North of the Danube, and east of the Kamp River, are the undulating hills of the agricultural Weinviertel (Wine District), bordering on the Czech Republic and on Slovakia, where the March River flows into the Danube.

ON THE ROAD TO BADEN & MAYERLING

Taking a trip to the spa town of Baden means following the Vienna Woods southern trail past ancient monasteries, fertile plains, and colorful vineyards. The land and its people enjoy the advantage of the proximity of the capital and the quiet of the pleasant countryside

TOP REASONS TO GO

Baden & Gumpoldskirchen. Spend an afternoon discovering the attractive spa and casino town of Baden, then travel along the enchanting wine road to the pleasant village of Gumpoldskirchen.

Heiligenkreuz Abbey. Admire the Romanesque and Gothic architectural glory of this stunning abbey where, within the historic walls, Cistercian monks chant the hits.

Retz. Appreciate the beauty of this town's enormous main square both above and below the ground, then sample the excellent wines and scrumptious specialties that come from around the region.

THE WEINVIERTEL

North of the Vienna, the rolling hills, vineyards, and pleasant rural vistas invite visitors to experience a slow-moving, almost dreamy kind of lifestyle, different from the Austria of cliché; this is the region that was for years the least developed, least modern part of the country.

PLANNING

WHEN TO GO

Most of the regions around Vienna are best seen in the temperate months between mid-March and mid-November. The Waldviertel, however, with its vast stands of great forest, offers picture-book scenery throughout the year. The combination of oaks and evergreens offers a color spectrum ranging from intense, early-spring green, through the deep green of summer, and into traces of autumn foliage, particularly in the Kamp River valley; in winter, occasional spectacular displays of hoarfrost and snow-swept vistas turn the region into a glittering three-dimensional Christmas card.

GETTING HERE & AROUND

Driving through these regions is by far the best way to see them, since you can wander the byways and stop whenever and wherever you like. Buses are a good possibility for getting around, although if you're not driving, a combination of bus and train is probably a better plan in many cases.

BY BUS Frequent scheduled bus service runs between Vienna and Baden, departing from across from the Opera House in Vienna to the center of Baden. Connections are available to other towns in the area. Bus service runs between Vienna and Carnuntum-Petronell, and on to Hainburg. In the Weinviertel, bus service is fairly good between Vienna and Laa an der Thaya, Mistelbach, and Poysdorf.

GREAT ITINERARIES

The districts surrounding Vienna are compact, and each can be explored in a day or two.

IF YOU HAVE 1 DAY

East of Vienna: The elegant Baroque castle at Schlosshoff, near **Marchegg** is your destination. Tour the castle and its formal gardens before heading to the ancient Roman site of **Carnuntum**, where you can delve deeper into the past. Keep in mind: Schlosshof is only 15 mi from the center of Bratislava in Slovakia. It would be ideal to combine a day at Schlosshof with an overnight in Bratislava.

IF YOU HAVE 1 DAY

South of the Danube: To get a taste of the fringes of the Vienna Woods

to the capital's south and west, head for **Mödling** and **Baden**. Both are smaller communities with unspoiled 17th-century town centers on a scale easy to assimilate. The route to Baden runs through the band of rolling wooded hills that mark the eastern edge of the Vienna Woods. These hills are skirted by vineyards forming a "wine belt," which also follows the valleys south of Vienna.

OR

North of the Danube: To enjoy the rolling hills and vast expanses of vineyards (and to sample their output), seek out the Weinviertel to the north of Vienna. **Retz**, a charming town near the Czech border, is known for its reds, which you can taste in a windmill vinothek.

BY CAR   To reach Baden and the surrounding villages by car, take the A2 autobahn south in the direction of Graz, getting off in Baden and taking Route 210 west.

The Weinviertel is accessed by major highways but not by autobahns. Follow signs to Prague, taking Route E461 toward Mistelbach and Poysdorf if you want to go northeast. Or take the A22 toward Stockerau, changing to Route 303 or the E49 in the northwesterly direction of Horn and Retz.

The A4 autobahn is a quick way to reach the Carnuntum region. If you're going east to Carnuntum, follow signs to the A23 and the airport (Schwechat).

BY TRAIN   The train system is excellent, and reliable trains run frequently from Vienna's Schnellbahn stations to most of the destinations covered in this chapter. The main east–west train line cuts through the Vienna Woods; the main north–south line out of Vienna traverses the eastern edge of the Vienna Woods. Trains leave Vienna's Südbahnhof regularly for Baden, with stops in Gumpoldskirchen and in Mödling.

Train service in the Weinviertel is regular to Laa an der Thaya, Mistelbach, and Retz. You can get to the Weinviertel from Wien-Nord/Praterstern, then connect to buses running between the small villages.

The Schnellbahn No. 7 running from Wien-Mitte (Landstrasser Hauptstrasse) stops at Petronell, with service about once an hour. Carnuntum is about a 10-minute walk from the Petronell station. Trains go on to Hainburg, stopping at Bad Deutsch-Altenburg.

TOURS The Vienna Woods is one of the standard routes offered by the sight-seeing-bus tour operators in Vienna, and it usually includes a boat ride through the "underground lake" grotto near Mödling. These short tours give only a quick taste of the region; if you have more time, investigate further. For details, check with your hotel or with Cityrama Sightseeing. Another good option is Vienna Sightseeing Tours.

ESSENTIALS

For information on Lower Austria, call the Niederösterreich Tourismus in Vienna. Local tourist offices in the Vienna Woods, including those in Baden, Gumpoldskirchen, Mödling, and Perchtoldsdorf, are generally open weekdays. The Weinviertel region also has several tourist centers: Laa an der Thaya, Poysdorf, and Retz.

Contacts **Cityrama Sightseeing** (☎ *01/534–130*). **Vienna Sightseeing Tours** (☎ *01/712–4683–0*).

Train Information **ÖBB—Österreichisches Bundesbahn** (☎ *05/1717*).

Visitor Information **Niederösterreich Tourismus** (☎ *01/53610–6200*). **Wein viertel** (✉ *Kolpingstrasse 7, Poysdorf* ☎ *02552/3515* ⊕ *www.weinviertel.at*). **Wienerwald** (✉ *Hauptplatz 11, Purkersdorf* ☎ *02231/62176*).

ABOUT THE RESTAURANTS & HOTELS

With some exceptions, food in this region, while influenced by Viennese cuisine, is on the simple side. The basics are available in abundance: roast meats, customary schnitzel variations, game in season, fresh vegetables, and standard desserts such as *Palatschinken* (crepes filled with jam or nuts, topped with chocolate sauce). However, imaginative cooking is beginning to spread, and most places have fresh fish and other lighter fare. Look for at least one vegetarian course on the menu.

Dining in the countryside outside Vienna is a casual affair. Meal times are usually from noon to 2 for lunch and from 6 to 10 for dinner. It's rare to find a restaurant that serves all afternoon, so plan ahead. It's a good idea to reserve a table, especially for Sunday lunch, which is a popular time for families to get together. Tipping 5%–7% is customary.

In general accommodations in the countryside are pretty basic. Although this is a lightly traveled region, many hotels have received complete makeovers, so they are far more stylish than they were a generation ago. Most establishments are family-run, and somebody on staff usually speaks English. You'll probably have to carry your own bags, and sometimes climb stairs in older buildings. Booking ahead is a good idea, as most places have relatively few rooms, particularly rooms with private baths. The standard country pillows and bed coverings are down-filled, so if you're allergic to feathers ask for blankets.

Some hotels offer half-board, with dinner in addition to buffet breakfast. The half-board room rate is usually an extra €15–€30 per person. Occasionally, quoted room rates for hotels already include half-board accommodations, though a "discounted" rate is usually offered if you prefer not to take the evening meal. Inquire when booking. Room rates

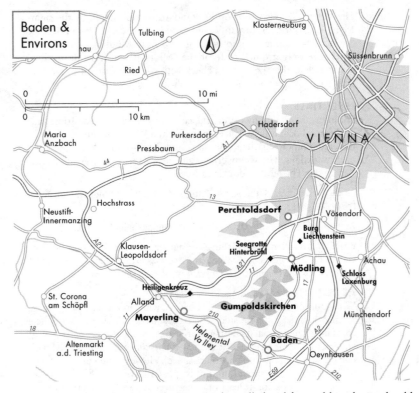

include taxes and service, and usually breakfast—although you should always ask about the latter.

WHAT IT COSTS IN EUROS				
¢	$	$$	$$$	$$$$
RESTAURANTS under €8	€8–€13	€14–€18	€19–€23	over €23
HOTELS under €70	€70–€100	€100–€135	€135–€175	over €175

Restaurant prices are per person for a main course at dinner. Hotel prices are for a standard double room in high season, including taxes and service. Assume that hotels operate on the European Plan (EP, with no meal provided) unless we note that they use the Breakfast Plan (BP), Modified American Plan (MAP, with breakfast and dinner daily, known as "halb Pension"), or Full American Plan (FAP, or "voll Pension," with three meals a day). Higher prices (inquire when booking) prevail for any meal plans.

ON THE ROAD TO BADEN & MAYERLING

This brief though history-rich tour takes you to Baden through the part of the legendary Vienna Woods that borders Vienna on the west. The hills are skirted by vineyards forming a "wine belt," which also follows the valleys south of Vienna. You can tour this area easily in a day, either by car or by public transportation, or you can spend the night in Baden, Mödling, or Alland to allow for a more leisurely exploration of Mayerling, Heiligenkreuz, and a few other sights in the area.

PERCHTOLDSDORF

12 km (7½ mi) southwest of Vienna center.

ESSENTIALS
Tourist Information Perchtoldsdorf (⊠ *Marktplatz 11* ☎ *01/86683–34*).

EXPLORING
Just over the Vienna city line to the southwest lies Perchtoldsdorf, a charming market town with many wine taverns, a 13th-century Gothic Pfarrkirche (parish church), and the overarching symbol of the town—an imposing stone tower completed in 1511, once forming a piece of the town's defense wall. Familiarly known as Pedersdorf, the town is a favorite excursion spot for the Viennese, who come mainly for the good local wines. Wander around the compact town square to admire the Renaissance houses, some with arcaded courtyards. The Pestsäule (Plague Column) in the center of the square, which gives thanks for rescue from the dread 16th-century plague, was created by the famous Baroque architect Fischer von Erlach and is similar to the Plague Column that adorns the Graben in Vienna (⇨ *Vienna's Shopwindow: From Michaelerplatz to the Graben in Chapter 1, Vienna*). Without a car, you can reach Perchtoldsdorf from Vienna by the S-Bahn, or train, from the Westbahnhof, to Liesing, and then a short cab ride to the town.

WHERE TO EAT
$$ ✗**Sonnbergwirt.** A former 19th-century carriage house, Sonnbergwirt offers country-casual dining with a friendly welcome. The restaurant serves tasty Wiener Schnitzel and other standards. Max Mitterstöger and his team serve many of the dishes in a traditional style with a number of daily specials on the menu depending on the season. The wine list is full of good Austrian labels, with a strong Styrian slant, that are very reasonably priced. Dining at a picnic table in the inviting courtyard is a delightful way to spend a summer evening. ⊠ *Sonnbergstrasse 22* ☎ *01/869–8181* ☱ *AE, DC, MC, V* ⊗ *Closed Mon. and Tues. No lunch Wed.–Sat.*

MÖDLING

20 km (12½ mi) southwest of Vienna.

Founded in the 10th century, Mödling has a delightful town center, now free of cars. Centuries-old buildings, most of them one- or two-story, give the town an intimate scale. Note the domineering Gothic **Pfarrkirche St. Othmar** on a hill overlooking the town proper, a Romanesque 12th-century charnel house (where the bones of the dead were kept), and the town hall, which has a Renaissance loggia. Later eras added Art Nouveau, which mixes happily with the several 16th-

IF YOU LIKE

BICYCLING

The Carnuntum region and the southeast corner of the Weinviertel, a region known as the Marchfeld, offer outstanding cycling, with a number of marked routes. Cycle paths follow the southern bank of the Danube past Carnuntum (Petronell) through Bad Deutsch-Altenburg to Hainburg, and other parts of the region are flat enough to offer fine cycling without over-exertion. One of the marked routes close to the March River includes the Baroque castles at Marchegg and Schlosshof.

CASTLES

Taking advantage of the natural line of defense formed by the course of the Danube, barons and bailiffs decided centuries ago to erect fortifications on the bluffs along the river. Castles were the best answer, and a wonderful string of these dot the Weinviertel, including Schloss Niederweiden and Schlosshof. A more polished estate awaits at Schloss Rohrau. The 17th- and 18th-century structures vary from turreted hilltop fortresses to more elegant moated bastions, but all were part of a chain designed to repel invaders. Several are basically intact while others have been restored, but all are impressive relics worth visiting. Castle concerts have become popular during summer months, when the buildings are open for tours as well.

HIKING & WALKING

The celebrated Vienna Woods to the west and southwest of Vienna are crisscrossed by hundreds of easy hiking paths, numbered, color-coded, and marked for destinations. Excellent hiking maps available from most bookstores will give ideas and routes. Paths will take you through woods, past meadows and vineyards, alongside streams and rivers, occasionally revealing a tavern hidden away deep in the woods where you can stop for refreshment or a cold snack. Deer, wild boar, and a host of small animals inhabit these preserves. The area is protected, and development is highly restricted, making it ideal for pleasurable hiking.

WINE

Four separate wine regions surround Vienna—the Weinviertel, or wine quarter to the north of the city; the Kamptal, which divides the Weinviertel from the Waldviertel to the west; the Carnuntum-Petronell region, just below the Danube to the southeast of Vienna; and the Thermen region, south and southwest of the capital.

The specialties are mainly white wines, with the standard types, grüner veltliner and rieslings and increasingly weissburgunder, predominating. Reds are coming more into favor, with lighter reds such as zweigelt and even rosés to be found in the northern areas. The heavier reds such as blaufränkisch and St. Laurent and the spicier gewürztraminer and Müller-Thurgau whites are found in the south. Most vintners work small holdings, so output is limited. The wine market in Poysdorf, center of one of Austria's largest wine regions, offers an opportunity to sample a wide choice of area vintages.

and 17th-century buildings. Composers Beethoven and Schubert spent time here in the early 1800s; Mödling was one of Beethoven's favored residences outside of Vienna.

ESSENTIALS

Tourist Information **Mödling** (⊠ *Elisabethstrasse 2* ☎ *02236/26727* ⊕ *www. moedling.at*).

EXPLORING

☼ A couple of miles east of Mödling is **Schloss Laxenburg,** a complex consisting of a small 14th-century Altes Schloss (Old Castle), a large Baroque Neues Schloss (New Castle), and the early-19th-century Franzensburg, a neo-Gothic castle set into the sizable lake. Of the three castles, only the **Franzensburg** (☎€6 ⊙ *Tours [in German] daily at 11, 2, and 3*) is open to the public. Weather permitting, you can also partake in the 4 PM tour of the tower and roof for an additional €5. The Altes Schloss, built in 1381 by Duke Albrecht III as his summer residence, houses the Austrian Film Archive. Several Habsburg emperors spent summers in the Neues Schloss (also called the "Blauer Hof"), which is now the International Institute of Applied Systems Analysis research institute. Opposite the Neues Schloss is the large Baroque convent of the order of the Charitable Sisters. The **Schlosspark** (☎€1.50 ⊙ *Daily*), which has been restored to its 18th- and 19th-century form, is full of birds and small game, such as roe deer and hare, and is ornamented with statues, cascades, imitation temples, and other follies. It's popular in summer for families with children because there are pony rides, a small playground, and an open-air train that runs through the park past all the sights. There are several casual restaurants and cafés with outdoor seating. ⊠ *Schlossplatz 1* ☎ *02236/712–26–0* ⊕ *www.schloss-laxenburg.at*.

☼ **Burg Liechtenstein,** an imposing medieval castle, perches formidably on a crag overlooking the Vienna Woods a couple of miles north of Mödling. The pale stone walls and turrets have withstood marauding armies and the elements for more than 800 years. It's currently not open for tours, but the exterior is well worth a look. ⊠ *Maria Enzersdorf.*

☼ West of Mödling on Route 11 is the **Seegrotte Hinterbrühl,** a fascinating but now somewhat commercialized underground lake created years ago when a mine filled up with water. You can take a 45-minute motorboat trip and look at the reflections through the arched caverns of the mine. Some of *The Three Musketeers,* starring Charlie Sheen and Chris O'Donnell, was filmed here. ⊠ *Grutschgasse 2, Hinterbrühl* ☎ *02236/26364* ☎€9 ⊙ *Apr.–Oct., daily 9–5; Nov.–Mar., weekdays 9–noon and 1–3, weekends 9–3:30.*

WHERE TO STAY

$$ 🛏 **Höldrichsmühle.** A former mill with sections dating from the 12th century, the Höldrichsmühle has been a famed country inn for more than 200 years. Legend holds that the linden tree and the well found here inspired composer Franz Schubert to compose one of his better-known pieces. The comfortable rooms are simply but adequately furnished. **Pros:** great location for hiking; popular for horseback riding. **Cons:** rooms facing the road can be noisy. ⊠ *Gaadnerstrasse 34*

☎02236/26274–0 ⊕*www.hoeldrichsmuehle.at* ⬧60 *rooms* ♿*In-room: no a/c. In-hotel: Wi-Fi* ⊟*AE, DC, MC, V* ⦿*BP.*

GUMPOLDSKIRCHEN

4 km (2½ mi) west of Mödling.

From Mödling, follow the scenic Weinstrasse (an unnumbered road to the west of the rail line) through the lush vineyard country to the famous wine-producing village of Gumpoldskirchen. This tiny village on the eastern slopes of the last Alpine rocks has lived for wine for 2,000 years, and its white wines enjoy a widespread fame. **Vintners' houses** line the main street, many of them with the typical large wooden gates that lead to vine-covered courtyards where the Heuriger (wine of the latest vintage) is served by the owner and his family at simple wooden tables with benches. Gumpoldskirchen also has an arcaded Renaissance town hall and a market fountain made from a Roman sarcophagus.

WHERE TO EAT

$ ✕**Altes Zechhaus.** Perched at the top of the Altstadt (Old Town), this centuries-old drinking tavern is still going strong. Choose from the tempting panoply of salads downstairs and then order a hearty schnitzel or spit-roasted chicken. When in season, go for the freshly picked Vienna Woods mushrooms, fried in batter or served in a creamy sauce. Try to get a table upstairs in the wood-beamed Gothic Room, where plank tables are set against ancient stone walls and mullioned windows. Check out the house wine with its bawdy label, on display in the foyer. ⊠*Kirchenplatz 1* ☎02252/62247 ⊟*V* ⊗*No lunch weekdays.*

BADEN

★ *7 km (4½ mi) south of Gumpoldskirchen, 32 km (20 mi) southwest of Vienna.*

The Weinstrasse brings you to the serenely elegant spa town of Baden. Since antiquity, Baden's sulfuric thermal baths have attracted the ailing and the fashionable from all over the world. When the Romans came across the springs, they dubbed the town Aquae; the Babenbergs revived it in the 10th century; and with the visit of the Russian czar Peter the Great in 1698, Baden's golden age began. Austria's Emperor Franz II spent 31 successive summers here. Later in the century Emperor Franz Josef was a regular visitor, his presence inspiring many of the regal trappings the city still displays. In Baden Mozart composed his "Ave Verum"; Beethoven spent 15 summers here and wrote large sections of his Ninth Symphony and *Missa Solemnis* when he lived at Frauengasse 10; Franz Grillparzer wrote his historical dramas here; and Josef Lanner, both Johann Strausses (father and son), Carl Michael Ziehrer, and Karl Millöcker composed and directed many of their waltzes, marches, and operettas here.

GETTING HERE & AROUND

A streetcar was built in the 19th century for the sole purpose of ferrying the rich Viennese from their summer houses in Baden to the Opera in Vienna—the last stop is directly in front of the opera house. The streetcar (the cars now are modern) still winds its way through Vienna's suburbs on its 50-minute journey to Baden, though things only start to get scenic about 25 minutes before Baden, as the car passes through the wine villages. A faster option is to take the train. It's about a half hour from Westbahnhof, and most of trains are double-deckers (so you can sit up top and have a great view of the countryside).

> **NOT ONLY IN VIENNA**
>
> Heurige are everywhere in this region, particularly on the main roads in and out of the villages, fronting the vineyards where the wine they serve is grown. As they usually serve only the wines they grow themselves, you will not have a huge wine selection to choose from. But the wine you get will be fresh, authentic, and delicious. The food in the heurige is almost always very simple, restricted to a small buffet with freshly made salads, cold or warm braten, and homemade pies and desserts.

ESSENTIALS

Tourist Information Baden (✉ *Brusattiplatz 3* ☎ *02252/22600–600* ⊕ *www. baden.at*).

EXPLORING

☙ For many people the primary reason for a visit to Baden is the lovely, sloping **Kurpark** in the center of town, where outdoor public concerts are held most weekend afternoons in summer. Operetta is performed under the skies in the Summer Arena (its roof closes if it rains); in winter performances are moved to the Stadttheater. People sit quietly under the old trees or walk through the upper sections of the Kurpark for a view of the town from above. The old Kurhaus now incorporates a convention hall. ■ TIP➜ **Above the park, follow the signs pointing to the Rudolfshof for lunch or a snack.** Along the 10-minute walk, children of all ages will enjoy seeing the large, fenced-in areas where goats, deer, and other animals indigenous to the region, some now endangered, are kept and cared for. When you reach the restaurant, head straight for the terrace with its spectacular view of Baden and the Wienerwald. During the Tertiary Period, the basin stretching from the Rudolfshof all the way to the Leitha Mountains in the distance was a gigantic sea, created by the flooding of the area by the waters of the Mediterranean. Baden and the surrounding countryside were deep under water. The grassy slope in front of the Rudolfshof is all that is left of the "Lido di Baden." ✉ *Kaiser Franz-Ring*.

Music lovers will want to visit the **Beethoven Haus,** just one of several addresses Beethoven called his own hereabouts—the great man was always on the run from his creditors and moved frequently. ✉ *Rathausgasse 10* ☎ *02252/86800–231* 💰 *€3* ⏱ *Tues.–Fri. 4–6, weekends 10–noon and 4–6.*

Children of all ages will enjoy the enchanting **Badener Puppen und Spielzeugmuseum** *(Doll and Toy Museum).* ⊠*Erzherzog Rainer-Ring 23* ☎*02252/41020* ⌧*€3* ⊘*Tues.–Fri. 4–6, weekends 11–noon and 4–6.*

WHERE TO STAY & EAT

$ ✕**Rudolfshof.** Enjoy a walk through the Kurpark, where you'll find this 19th-century hunting lodge. The fine restaurant serves traditional dishes from the region, with an excellent wine list highlighting local vintages, particularly St. Laurent, Zweigelt, and blaue Portugieser. Stop for lunch or just take a break with coffee and cake. When the air is clear and the weather is good, the grand vistas across the hills from the terrace mean it's hard to get a table on weekends. ⊠*Am Gamingerberg 5, Baden* ☎*02252/209–203* ⊕*www.rudolfshof.at* ⊟*DC, MC, V* ⊘*Closed Tues. May–Sept., closed Tues. and Wed. Oct.–Apr.*

$$$$ ▦**Grand Hotel Sauerhof.** Many of the rooms at this appealing country house remain in the Old Vienna style, and a few even have balconies. (Avoid those on the higher floors, as they have been rather cheaply renovated.) The hotel caters heavily to seminars and conferences, but individual guests are not ignored. Special discounted weekend packages are sometimes available. The on-site Beauty Farm is an option for pampering yourself with a full-body treatment. **Pros:** quiet location, elegant building, extensive spa. **Cons:** some rooms stuffy in summer, often feels crowded. ⊠ *Weilburgstrasse 11–13* ☎*02252/41251-0* ⊕*www.sauerhof. at* ⇌*90 rooms* ⌂*In-room: no a/c, refrigerator. In-hotel: restaurant, bar, tennis court, pool, gym, Wi-Fi* ⊟*AE, DC, MC, V* ⦿*BP.*

$$$$ ▦**Schloss Weikersdorf.** A restored Renaissance castle whose earliest
★   foundations go back to 1233, the Weikersdorf is minutes away from the center of Baden. Set on the edge of a vast public park, the hotel estate offers bonuses of a rose garden featuring 600 varieties and boating on the pristine lake. Rooms and baths are luxuriously outfitted. In fine weather tables are outside on the loggia overlooking the rose garden. The hotel sometimes offers special last-minute rates. The newly enhanced spa area of the hotel offers guests a wide variety of luxurious treatments. **Pros:** helpful staff; beautiful surroundings. **Cons:** rooms vary greatly in size; can feel crowded. ⊠*Schlossgasse 9–11* ☎*02252/48301* ⊕*www.hotelschlossweikersdorf.at* ⇌*100 rooms* ⌂*In-room: no a/c, refrigerator. In-hotel: restaurant, bar, tennis courts, pool, Wi-Fi* ⊟*AE, DC, MC, V* ⦿*BP.*

$$–$$$ ▦**Krainerhütte.** About 5 km (3 mi) from Baden, this typical Alpine
★   house (think lots of balconies and natural wood) has been given a top-to-bottom renovation. It now has an almost Scandinavian feel thanks to rooms that are sleek and modern. The site on the outskirts of town is ideal for relaxing or exploring the surrounding woods. The restaurant offers a choice of cozy dining rooms or an outdoor terrace. The menu has national and international dishes, along with fish and game from the hotel's own reserves. **Pros:** beautiful location; great for hiking. **Cons:** often gets booked up. ⊠*Helenental* ☎*02252/44511-0* ⊕*www. krainerhuette.at* ⇌*62 rooms* ⌂*In-room: no a/c, Wi-Fi. In-hotel: restaurant, tennis court, pool* ⊟*AE, MC, V* ⦿*BP.*

MAYERLING

11 km (7 mi) northwest of Baden, 29 km (18 mi) west of Vienna.

Scenic Route 210 takes you through the quiet Helenental valley west of Baden to Mayerling, scene of a tragedy that is still passionately discussed and disputed by the Austrian public, the press, and historians at the slightest provocation. On the snowy evening of January 29, 1889, the 30-year-old Habsburg heir, Crown Prince Rudolf, Emperor Franz Josef's only son, and his 17-year-old mistress, Baroness Marie Vetsera, met a violent and untimely end at the emperor's hunting lodge at Mayerling. Most historians believe it was a suicide pact between two desperate lovers (the pope had refused an annulment to Rudolf's unhappy marriage to Princess Stephanie of Belgium). There are those, however, who feel Rudolf's pro-Hungarian political leanings might be a key to the tragedy. Given information gleaned from private letters that have more recently come to light, it is also possible Rudolf was hopelessly in love with a married woman and killed himself in despair, taking Marie Vetsera with him. The bereaved emperor had the hunting lodge where the suicide took place torn down and replaced with a rather nondescript Carmelite convent. Mayerling remains remote: the village is infrequently signposted.

WHERE TO STAY

$$$$
★ **Hanner.** Many people come here just for the restaurant, because owner Heinz Hanner is one of the country's most decorated chefs. His focus is on traditional dishes updated for modern tastes, so the menu includes marinated Mediterranean scallops with truffles and duck liver with salted red beets. Breakfast (included in the room rate) includes sparkling wine, caviar, and other delicacies. The spacious rooms are filled with light, and have lots of natural wood and contemporary art. The extensive garden, pool, and spa area are the epitome of relaxation. **Pros:** unparalleled dining; beautiful rooms; and gorgeous surroundings. **Cons:** lacks traditional charm. ⊠ *Mayerling 1* ☎ *02258/2378* ⊕ *www. hanner.cc* ☞ *20 rooms* ⚏ *In-room: no a/c, Wi-Fi. In-hotel: restaurant, pool, spa* ⊟ *AE, MC, V* ⊚ *BP.*

HEILIGENKREUZ

4 km (2½ mi) west of Mayerling, 14 km (8¾ mi) west of Mödling.

Heiligenkreuz, in the heart of the southern section of the Vienna Woods, is a magnificent Cistercian abbey with a famous Romanesque and Gothic church founded in 1135 by Leopold III. Until a few years ago was a little-known place of contemplative worship and prayer. Then the monks recorded their Gregorian chants, and the resulting album topped the charts, beating out pop stars like Amy Winehouse and Madonna.

The church itself is lofty and serene, with beautifully carved choir stalls (the Cistercians are a singing order) surmounted by busts of Cistercian saints. The great treasure here is the relic of the cross that Leopold V is said to have brought back from his crusade in 1188. ⊠ *Heiligenkreuz*

1 ☎02258/8703 ⊕*www.stift-heiligenkreuz.at* ✉*Abbey free, tour €6.60. Tours in English can be arranged by calling in advance* ☉*Tours Mon.–Sat. at 10, 11, 2, 3, and 4, Sun. at 11, 2, 3, and 4.*

WHERE TO STAY

$ ⊡ **Landgasthof Zur Linde.** In the heart of the Vienna Woods, some 24 km (15 mi) northwest of Mayerling, lies the small town of Laaben bei Neulengbach—equidistant from Mayerling and Heiligenkreuz, in the shadow of the 2,900-foot Schöpfl Mountain. This family-run country inn offers an excellent base from which to explore the countryside. Rooms are modest but complete and comfortable, with rustic trimmings. The rambling restaurant, with its several wood-beam rooms, serves standard tasty Austrian fare, with seasonal specialties such as lamb, asparagus, and game. **Pros:** a hiker's paradise; friendly atmosphere. **Cons:** modest rooms; few amenities. ✉*Hauptplatz 28, Laaben bei Neulengbach* ☎*02774/8378–0* ⤡*9 rooms* ⌂*In-room: no a/c. In-hotel: restaurant* ⊟*MC, V* ☉*Hotel closed Tues. and Wed. and 1 wk in Mar.* ⧉|*BP.*

THE WEINVIERTEL

Luckily, Austria's Weinviertel (Wine District) has been largely neglected by the "experts," and its deliciously fresh wines reward those who enjoy drinking wine but dislike the all-too-frequent nonsense that goes with it. The Weinviertel is bounded by the Danube on the south, the Thaya River and the Czech border on the north, and the March River and Slovakia to the east. No well-defined line separates the Weinviertel from the Waldviertel to the west; the Kamp River valley, officially part of the Waldviertel, is an important wine region. A tour by car, just for the scenery, can be made in a day; you may want two or three days to savor the region and its wines—these are generally on the medium-dry side. Don't expect to find here the elegant facilities found elsewhere in Austria; prices are low by any standard, and village restaurants and accommodations are mainly *Gasthäuser* that meet local needs. This means that you'll be rubbing shoulders with the country folk over your glass of wine or beer.

RETZ

★ *43 km (27 mi) north of Göllersdorf, 70 km (44 mi) north of Vienna.*

ESSENTIALS

Tourist Information **Retz** (✉*Hauptplatz 30* ☎*02942/2700* ⊕ *www.retz.at*).

EXPLORING

Retz, at the northwest corner of the Weinviertel, is a charming town with an impressive rectangular central square formed by buildings dating mainly from the 15th century. Take time to explore Retz's tiny streets leading from the town square; the oldest buildings and the wall and gate-tower defenses survived destruction by Swedish armies in 1645, during the Thirty Years' War. The Dominican church (1295) at the southwest

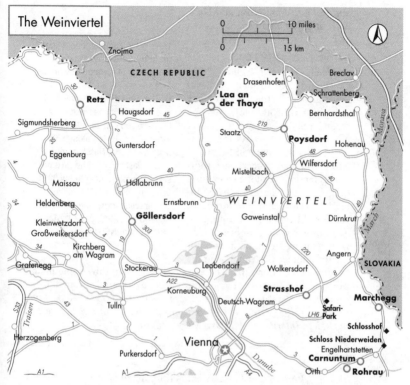

The Weinviertel

0 — 10 miles
0 — 15 km

CZECH REPUBLIC

Znojmo

Drasenhofen

Breclav

Retz

Haugsdorf 45

Laa an der Thaya

Schrattenberg

Sigmundsherberg

Staatz 219

Bernhardsthal

Guntersdorf

Poysdorf

Hohenau

Eggenburg

Mistelbach

Wilfersdorf

Maissau

Hollabrunn

W E I N V I E R T E L

Heldenberg

Ernstbrunn

Göllersdorf

Gaweinstal

Dürnkrut

Kleinwetzdorf
Großweikersdorf

Kirchberg
am Wagram

Angern

SLOVAKIA

Grafenegg

Stockerau

Leobendorf

Wolkersdorf

Tulln

Korneuburg

Strasshof

Marchegg

Deutsch-Wagram

Safari-Park

Schlosshof

Herzogenberg

Vienna

Schloss Niederweiden
Engelhartstetten

Purkersdorf

Danube

Carnuntum

Orth

Rohrau

corner of the square also survived, and it is interesting for its long, narrow design. The pastel Biedermeier facades along with the *sgraffiti* (painted facades) add appeal to the square, which is further marked by the impressive city hall with its massive Gothic tower in the center.

The landmark of the town is the pretty **Windmühle,** a 19th-century windmill set in the middle of vineyards on the edge of town, and the only remaining historic windmill in Austria that is still operable today. The windmill, with its well-preserved grinding wheel, can be visited. Follow the markers leading up to the summit, where you can sit and rest on benches offering a stunning view of the surrounding countryside. *€2.50 including tour ⊙ Tours last approx. ½ hr Apr.–Oct., weekends 10–noon and 2–5; July and Aug. also daily 11–5.*

Retz is best known for its red wines. Here you can tour the **Retzer Erlebniskeller,** Austria's (and reputedly also Europe's) largest wine cellar, tunneled 65 feet under the town, and at the same time taste wines of the area. Some of the tunnels go back to the 13th century, and at the end of the 15th century each citizen was permitted to deal in wines and was entitled to storage space in the town cellars. Entrance to the cellars is at the Rathauskeller, in the center of town. Dress warmly if you decide to go on the cellar tour, which lasts well over an hour. ⊠ *Hauptplatz* ☎ *02942/2700* 🎫 *Tour €7.50 ⊙ Tours May–Oct., daily at 10:30, 2,* and 4; Mar., Apr., Nov., and Dec., daily at 2; Jan. and Feb., weekends at 2.

WHERE TO STAY

$ 🏨**Althof.** The big, yellow "Old Courtyard"—a former medieval estate just off the town square—has a sloping terra-cotta roof, a narrow second-story loggia, and a tranquil grassy courtyard perfect for relaxing. The rooms, done in beige and white with red accents, are thoroughly modern. Although they don't quite have the charm of the building's exterior, they are spacious, comfortable, and well equipped. The house has its own health club with a sauna, steam bath, and hot tub. In summer you can dine in the beautiful cool courtyard. The excellent wines naturally come mainly from the area. **Pros:** great value; quiet grounds; centrally located. **Cons:** some rooms are dark. ⊠ *Althofgasse 14* ☎ *02942/3711–0* ⊕ *www. althof.at* 🛏 *95 rooms* 🔑 *In-room: no a/c, Wi-Fi. In-hotel: 3 restaurants, bar, Internet* 🖃 *AE, DC, MC, V* 🍽 *BP.*

> **TILTING YOUR GLASS**
>
> Wine is the common denominator in the lives of all Retzers. In the course of restoration work to Retz's windmill, the **Windmühlkeller,** an attractive vinothek, was installed in the ancient cellar. Here you can sample various wines of the region along with tasty traditional *Nussbrot* (nut bread). Tastings of either five or seven wines are offered (€4.50 or €6 per person). ⊠ *Weingut Windmühlheuriger Bergmann, Am Anger 3* ☎ *02942/2467* ⊙ *Apr.– Oct., weekends 2–6.*

LAA AN DER THAYA

39 km (24 mi) east of Retz, 65 km (41 mi) north of Vienna.

ESSENTIALS

Tourist Information Laa an der Thaya (⊠ *Stadtplatz 17/Altes Rathaus* ☎ *02522/250129*).

EXPLORING

From 1948 until about 1990, Laa an der Thaya was a town isolated by the Cold War, directly bordering what was then Czechoslovakia. Laa is considerably livelier now that the border is open. (As long as you have your passport with you, you can cross into the Czech Republic and return without complication.) A good time to visit is mid-September, during the Onion Festival, when all varieties of onions are prepared in every imaginable way in food stalls set up throughout the village. If you're traveling from Retz to Laa an der Thaya, retrace your way south on Route 30 to Route 45.

Laa is noted for its **Bier Museum,** located in the town fortress, that traces the history of beer (the nearby Hubertus Brewery has been in business since 1454) and displays an imposing collection of beer bottles. ⊠ *Burgplatz 23* ☎ *02522/85142* 🎫 *€2* ⊙ *May–Oct., weekends 2–4.*

2

WHERE TO EAT

$ ×**Gasthaus Weiler.** Chef Martin Weiler enjoys quiet fame in this out-
★ post of culinary delights. There is much experimenting going on in the
kitchen, and cooking courses are offered now and then. This restaurant is pleasantly decorated in pale woods and country accessories. In
summer meals are served in the shady garden. Try the delicate cream
of garlic soup or wild game, if it is in season. The extensive wine list
showcases many local vintages. For dessert either try the house-made
cakes, the rice with fresh apricots, or the sherry mousse. ⊠ *Staatsbahn
strasse 60* ☎ *02522/2379* ⊟ *No credit cards* ⊘ *Closed Mon., 2 wks in
Feb., and variable wks in July. No dinner Sun.*

POYSDORF

*22 km (13 mi) southeast of Laa an der Thaya, 61 km (38 mi) north
of Vienna.*

Impressively situated on a gently sloping hill crowned by an early-
Baroque church, Poysdorf is considered by many the capital of the
Weinviertel. Wine making here goes back to the 14th century. Poysdorf
vintages, especially the local grüner veltliner, rank with the best Austria
has to offer. Narrow paths known as *Kellergassen* (cellar streets) on the
northern outskirts are lined with wine cellars set into and under the
hills. A festival in early September marks the annual harvest.

ESSENTIALS

Tourist Information Poysdorf (⊠ *Weinmarktplatz 1* ☎ *02552/20371* ⊕ *www.
poysdorf.at*).

EXPLORING

In the center of town, the **Weinmarkt Vinothek** (⊠ *Reichensteinhof,
Weinmarktplatz 1*) in the center of town, you can taste as well as buy.
The 29 regional vintners offer over 250 of their best red, white, and
sparkling wines. The Wine Market is open June to October, daily 9 to
7, and November to May, daily 9 to 6.

The **Weinstadt-Museum Poysdorf** is dedicated primarily to the history of
wine and viticulture in the region, but also showcases other aspects
of the region's history, including many prehistoric finds. The €7 ticket
for families is a good deal. ⊠ *Brünnerstrasse 9* ☎ *02552/20371* 🖭 *€3*
⊘ *Easter–Oct., Wed. 1–6, weekends 9–noon and 1–6.*

The **Hermann Nitsch Museum** is dedicated to one of Austria's most controversial artists, Hermann Nitsch (best known for using cow's blood
in his art). More than 150 of his works, ranging from paintings to vid-
eos, are on display at this museum south of Laa. ⊠ *Waldstrasse 44–46,
Mistelbach* ☎ *02572/20719* 🖭 *€7* ⊘ *Tues.–Sun. 10–6.*

WHERE TO STAY & EAT

$–$$ ×**Zur Linde.** This family-run restaurant is setting high standards for
★ such traditional fare as roast pork, stuffed breast of veal, flank steak,
and wild game. Desserts are excellent; try the extraordinary *Apfelstrudel.* A major attraction here, besides the Saturday candlelight dinner,

is the remarkable parade of wines from the neighborhood, all offered at altogether reasonable prices. The Zur Linde, which also has several modern rooms for overnighters, is in Mistelbach, 16 km (10 mi) south of Poysdorf. ⊠ *Bahnhofstrasse 49, Mistelbach* ☎ *02572/2409* ▭ *AE, DC, MC, V* ⊗ *Closed Sat. in July and Aug. No dinner Sun.*

$$ ⌨ **Hotel Veltlin.** Near the Kellergasse on the edge of town, this fine hotel has lots to do with wine. (The name calls to mind grüner veltliner, one of the best local wines.) The elegant and spacious rooms are named after types of wine, and are furnished accordingly in appropriately rich shades. Bathrooms are well equipped, and have nice touches like fluffy robes. A balcony or terrace in each room allows wonderful views of the fields, orchards, or vineyards in the surrounding area. An extensive spa area includes a sauna and steam bath. Just past the doorstep is a fine 18-hole golf course. **Pros:** great breakfast buffet; fine restaurant; quiet surroundings. **Cons:** can get very busy. ⊠ *Am Golfplatz 9* ☎ *02552/20606* ⊕ *www.hotelveltlin.at* ◔ *31 rooms* ⌖ *In-room: no a/c, refrigerator, Wi-Fi. In-hotel: restaurant, spa, golf course, Internet* ▭ *AE, DC, MC, V* ⦿ *BP.*

STRASSHOF

⟳ *25 km (16 mi) northeast of Vienna.*

The **Eisenbahnmuseum Das Heizhaus,** north of Strasshof, is a fascinating private collection of dozens of steam locomotives and railroad cars stored in a vast engine house. Enthusiasts have painstakingly rebuilt and restored many of the engines; steam locomotives are up and running on the first Sunday of each month. The complex includes a transfer table, water towers, and a coaling station, and few can resist climbing around among many of the locomotives awaiting restoration. ⊠ *Sillerstrasse 123* ☎ *02287/3027–11* ▦ €*7* ⊗ *Apr.–Oct. 26, Tues.–Sun. 10–4.*

WHERE TO EAT

$-$$ ✕ **Marchfelderhof.** In nearby Deutsch Wagram, this sprawling complex, with its eclectic series of rooms bounteously decorated with everything from antiques to hunting trophies, has a reputation for excess in the food department as well. Eccentric owner Gerhard Bocek has a smile for every guest. The menu's standards—Wiener Schnitzel, roast pork, lamb—are more successful than the more expensive efforts at innovation, but in spring try one of the various dishes highlighting *spargel* (asparagus), the specialty of the region. Deutsch Wagram is 9 km (5½ mi) southwest of Strasshof, 17 km (11 mi) northeast of Vienna on Route 8. ⊠ *Bockfliesserstrasse 31, Deutsch Wagram* ☎ *02247/2243–0* ▭ *DC, MC, V* ⊗ *No lunch weekends.*

▌ OFF THE
BEATEN
PATH

Zur Alten Schule. Less than 40 minutes (by car) northeast of Vienna, this former 19th-century cheery yellow schoolhouse has had its classrooms turned into charming dining rooms. Chef and owner Manfred Buchinger went back to his Weinviertel roots to open a reasonably priced restaurant close to his heart. The menu changes seasonally, but look for veal with creamy mustard sauce and the Austrian standard, fried chicken with potato salad. Zur Alten Schule is in the tiny village of Riedenthal, five minutes from Wolkersdorf on the B7. ✉ *Wolkers-dorferstrasse 6, Riedenthal ob Wolkersdorf* ☎*02245/82500* ⊘*Closed Mon.–Wed.*

MARCHEGG

43 km (27 mi) east of Vienna.

This tiny corner of the lower Weinviertel is known as the Marchfeld, for the fields stretching east to the March River, forming the border with Slovakia. In this region—known as the granary of Austria—a pair of elegant Baroque castles are worth a visit; while totally renovated, these country estates have lost none of their gracious charm over the centuries.

Fodor'sChoice
★
☺

The castle at **Schlosshof** is a true Baroque gem, shining even more brilliantly now after the completion of extensive restorations. The product of that master designer and architect Johann Lukas von Hildebrandt, who in 1732 reconstructed the four-sided castle into an elegant U-shape building, the Schloss opens up on the eastern side to a marvelous Baroque formal garden that gives way toward the river. The famed landscape painter Bernardo Bellotto, noted for his Canaletto-like vistas of scenic landmarks, captured the view before the reconstruction (now that the gardens are being restored to their Baroque state, Bellotto's three paintings of the court are proving the most important sources for this work). The castle was once owned by Empress Maria Theresa, mother of Marie Antoinette, and you can now visit the suite the empress used during her royal visits, faithfully re-created down to the tiniest details, as well as the two-story chapel in which she prayed. For kids there's a menagerie and petting zoo featuring exotic wild animals and old breeds of gentle pets. You can walk through the garden and grounds without paying admission, but the castle itself is open for guided tours only. Tours in English are available. The castle is about 8 km (5 mi) south of Marchegg. ✉ *Schlosshof* ☎*02285/200000* ⊕*www.schlosshof.at* ✆*€9.50.*

About 4 km (2½ mi) southwest of Schlosshof and north of Engelhartstetten, **Schloss Niederweiden** was designed as a hunting lodge and built in 1694 by that other master of the Baroque, Fischer von Erlach. This jewel was subsequently owned in turn by Prince Eugene and Empress Maria Theresa, who added a second floor and the mansard roof. Occasional exhibits take place here, and in the **Schloss-Patisserie** you can sample scrumptious desserts, as well as the wines of the surrounding area. ☎*02285/20000* ⊕*www.schlosshof.at* ✆*€2 for occasional exhibits, gardens free* ⊘*March–Nov., daily 10–6; Schloss-Patisserie daily 10:30–6.*

CARNUNTUM

★ *32 km (20 mi) east of Vienna.*

The remains of the important Roman legionary fortress and civil town of Carnuntum, which once numbered 55,000 inhabitants, extend about 3 mi along the Danube from the tiny village of Petronell to the next town of Bad Deutsch-Altenburg. Though by no means as impressive as Roman ruins in Italy and Spain, Carnuntum still merits a visit, with two amphitheaters (the first one seating 8,000) and the foundations of former residences, baths, and trading centers, some with mosaic floors. The ruins are quite spread out, with the impressive remains of a Roman arch, the **Heidentor** (Pagans' Gate), a good 15-minute walk from the main excavations in Petronell.

Many of the finds from excavations at Carnuntum are housed 4 km (2½ mi) northeast of Petronell in the village of Bad Deutsch-Altenburg, in the **Museum Carnuntinum** (⊠ *Badgasse 40–46, Bad Deutsch-Altenburg* ☎ *2165/62480–13* ⊙ *Late Mar.–mid-Nov., daily 10–5*). The pride of the collection is a carving of Mithras killing a bull. In the summer of 2008, a huge building called Villa Urbana opened to the public. You can experience what life was like in the Roman era in this elegantly furnished palace. To reach Carnuntum, take the S7, a local train that departs from Wien-Mitte/Landstrasse or Wien-Nord/Praterstern. It stops at both Petronell and Bad Deutsch-Altenburg. ⊠ *Petronell* ☎ *02163/33770* ⊕ *www.carnuntum.co.at* 💶 *€8, includes admission to Carnuntium Museum and all archaeological sites* ⊙ *Late Mar.–mid-Nov., daily 9–5.*

Just 5 km (3 mi) south of Petronell, in the tiny village of **Rohrau,** is the birthplace of Joseph Haydn. The quaint, reed-thatched cottage where the composer, son of the local blacksmith, was born in 1732 is now a small museum, with a pianoforte he is supposed to have played, as well as letters and other memorabilia. After Haydn had gained worldwide renown, he is said to have returned to his native Rohrau and knelt to kiss the steps of his humble home. ⊠ *Hauptstrasse 60, Rohrau* ☎ *02164/2268* 💶 *€2* ⊙ *Tues.–Sun. 10–4.*

Also in Rohrau is the cream-and-beige palace **Schloss Rohrau,** where Haydn's mother worked as a cook for Count Harrach. The palace has one of the best private art collections in Austria, with emphasis on 17th- and 18th-century Spanish and Italian painting. ☎ *02164/225318* ⊕ *harrach.nwy.at* 💶 *€7* ⊙ *Apr.–Oct., Tues.–Sun. 10–5.*

Eastern Austria

WORD OF MOUTH

"Graz still is a hidden gem, compared with Vienna or Salzburg. They have a lovely preserved city. There you find the landscape next to the center, as Schlossberg rises there. There are outdoor markets, not the size as the famed Vienna Naschmarkt, but also nice to see. Try some Styrian roast chicken, try some Schilcher (a kind of rose wine grown in Styria). If you prefer beer, Gösser is a good one. Have a lettuce salad with Kernöl, an oil made from pumpkin seed, looking like black motor oil, but with an excellent taste ressembling to nut and excellent for your health."

—hhildebrandt

Updated by
Uli Ehrhardt

NO PART OF THE NATION offers a greater panoply of scenery than the area loosely defined as Eastern Austria. Long a favorite of the Austrians themselves, it has become increasingly popular with Hungarians and other Eastern Europeans. Most of these travelers, being cost-conscious, demand strict value for their money, which ensures that prices will remain lower here than in other parts of the country for some time.

You'll find a largely unspoiled land of lakes, farms, castles, villages, and vineyards. The area has a rich history and a distinguished musical past, as well as one genuine city, Graz, whose sophistication and beauty may surprise you. It also happens to be a sports-lover's paradise. This is an ideal destination for experienced travelers who have already explored Vienna, Salzburg, the Tirol, and other better-known parts of Austria.

ORIENTATION & PLANNING

GETTING ORIENTED

Eastern Austria, as it is defined here, consists mainly of Burgenland and most of Styria (Steiermark). The geography varies from haunting steppes and the mysterious Lake Neusiedl (Neusiedler See) in the east to the low, forested mountains of the south; the industrial valleys of the center and west; and the more rugged mountains of the north, where Austrian skiing began. Culturally, Eastern Austria is strongly influenced by neighboring Hungary and Slovenia, most especially in its earthy and flavorful cuisines. Along with hearty food, the region produces notable wines, many of which never travel beyond the borders.

Burgenland. This region is intriguing both for its many castles and for the natural preserve at Lake Neusiedl, where storks come in the thousands to feed. Music lovers will want to make the pilgrimage to Eisenstadt, where the great composer Joseph Haydn (1732–1809) was in the employ of Prince Esterházy.

Graz & Its Environs. Graz, Austria's second-largest city, headlines one of Europe's best-preserved Renaissance town centers, dating to an era when Graz, not Vienna, was the capital.

Styria. Here you have the chance to visit one of Europe's oldest and still-revered religious pilgrimage sites, at Mariazell. The dramatic onward route northward can be accomplished by rail or road; the latter climbs to above 3,000 feet.

PLANNING

WHEN TO GO

Spring, summer, and fall are the seasons for Eastern Austria, unless you're a winter-sports enthusiast, when downhill skiers head for Lower Austria and the less crowded slopes of Styria. Other than coming across festival goers and, in summer, visitors to the shores of Neusiedler Lake, you'll find relatively few tourists in this region. Christmas in Graz is a visual spectacle, with whole sections of the city turned into a Christmas market. Winter in the area is an enigma: the Semmering mountains

TOP REASONS TO GO

Mighty Castles. Explore the great defensive bastions of Burgenland, built to keep out invaders from the East. The best example is lofty Riegersburg, a massive fortress perched on top of a volcanic outcropping.

Regional Delicacies in Historic Settings. While the Styrian parliamentarians toil away, you can work on Styrian beef and regional wine in the Landhauskeller, a charming restaurant in Graz's ancient, arcaded provincial parliament.

Museum in a Palace. Actually there are four museums—plus the gor-geous Prunkräume (State Rooms) in Graz's Schloss Eggenberg, itself a museum piece that sheds light on Austria's past.

Picturesque Rust. Luck-bringing storks raise the next generation in their nests atop the houses in this lakeside village, not even bothering to look down on all the cameras pointed at them.

Leisurely Bike Rides. Pedal through the flat plains surrounding Neusiedler Lake, stopping to explore scenic tiny villages and eat fresh fish from the lake.

mark the eastern tail end of the Alps—north of the divide can be overcast and dreary while the area to the south basks in sunshine.

GETTING HERE & AROUND

To get to Eastern Austria you can fly into the airport in Vienna or Graz or take a EuroCity train to Vienna. Once here, driving is the most convenient and scenic way to explore the region, especially if you're visiting the smaller towns and villages. If you don't want to drive, opt for the train—rather than a bus—for the main routes and longer distances.

BY AIR The northern part of Eastern Austria is served by Vienna's international airport at Schwechat, 19 km (12 mi) southeast of the city center (⇨ *Vienna Essentials in Chapter 1*).

Graz has its own international airport at Thalerhof, just south of the city, with flights to and from Vienna, Innsbruck, Linz, Munich, Frankfurt, Düsseldorf, and Zürich. Austrian Airlines and its subsidiary Tyrolean Airways, as well as Lufthansa, are the major carriers.

Airport Information Graz Airport (GRZ ☎0316/2902-0).

BY BIKE Bicycling is enormously popular in the flatlands around Neusiedler Lake. There are places that rent bikes in Neusiedl am See, Podersdorf, Illmitz, Mörbisch, and Rust. ⇨*See the individual towns for information.*

BY BUS Blauguss Reisen is a major bus service that connects Vienna to towns in Eastern Austria. Buses run by the Austrian Railway system and those run by the Austrian Postal service cover the area thoroughly for small distances, although services are less frequent in the less populated areas more distant from city centers.

Bus Information Blaguss Reisen (☎01/501-80-0 ⊕ www.blaguss.at).

GREAT ITINERARIES

Travelers who tackle Eastern Austria usually design their trip around three different destinations: The hilltop castles in Burgenland (land of castles); the city of Graz, whose preserved Old City is a time-warp marvel; and Rust, a charming village on Neusiedler Lake with good food, fine local wines, and roofs adorned with nesting storks.

Riegersburg, site of one of Austria's great defensive bastions, and **Piber**, home to the Lipizzaner Stud Farm, whose world-famous stallions perform at the Spanish Riding School in Vienna.

If you need to stick closer to Vienna, stay in Eisenstadt or in one of the small towns around Neusiedler Lake.

IF YOU HAVE 3 DAYS
Base yourself in the welcoming city of ⬛ **Graz**, making day trips to

BY CAR Two main autobahns traverse this region: the A3 between Vienna and Eisenstadt and the heavily traveled A2 between Vienna to Graz and farther south. Northern Burgenland can be reached via the A4 autobahn east out of Vienna.

Route 10 from Vienna to Neusiedler Lake in Burgenland is the preferred scenic alternative to the A4 autobahn. For a more picturesque mountain route between Graz and Vienna, you can follow Route S6 over the Semmering Pass to Bruck an der Mur, then south through the Mur Valley.

BY TRAIN Vienna and Graz are the logical rail arrival or departure points for this part of Austria. The main international north–south route connecting Vienna and northeastern Italy runs through this region and is traversed by EuroCity trains from Munich and Salzburg.

Services on the main routes are fast and frequent. Trains depart from Vienna's Südbahnhof (South Station) every two hours to Graz for a 2½ hour ride. From the same station there are many departures for the one-hour ride to Neusiedl am See. Trains for Mariazell depart from Vienna's Westbahnhof (West Station), with a change at St. Pölten.

Train Information ÖBB—National Train Information (☎ 05/1717 ⊕ www. oebb.at).

TOURS Relatively few guided tours visit Eastern Austria, and those that do are conducted in German. General orientation tours depart from Vienna and last one to four days. The one-day tours are usually to Neusiedler Lake and include a boat ride, or to the Semmering mountain region with a cable-car ride.

VISITOR INFORMATION
The regional tourist information office for Burgenland province is the Landesverband Burgenland Tourismus. For Styria, the provincial tourist office is Steirische Tourismus. There are helpful local *Fremdenverkehrsämter* (tourist offices), listed in the individual towns.

Tour Information **Landesverband Burgenland Tourismus** (✉ *Schloss Esterhazy, A-7000, Eisenstadt* ☎ *02682/63384–0* ⊕ *www.burgenland.at*). **Steirische Tourismus** (✉ *St. Peter–Hauptstrasse 243, Graz* ☎ *0316/4003–0* ⊕ *www.steiermark.com*).

Each Apotheke (pharmacy) posts a sign with information about the nearest pharmacy that will be open late. Also, the daily regional newspaper *Kleine Zeitung* lists those pharmacies with late-night hours in the area.

ABOUT THE RESTAURANTS & HOTELS

When choosing a restaurant, keep in mind that each province has its own cooking style. In Burgenland the local Pannonian cooking, strongly influenced by neighboring Hungary, showcases such spicy dishes as *gulyas* (goulash) flavored with paprika. You'll also find fish from Neusiedler Lake, goose, game, and an abundance of fresh local vegetables. Styria, bordering on Slovenia (formerly northern Yugoslavia), has a hearty cuisine with Slavic overtones; a typical dish is *Steirisches Brathuhn* (roast chicken turned on a spit). The intensely nutty *Kürbiskernöl* (pumpkinseed oil) is used in many soup and pasta dishes, as well as in salad dressings. Such Balkan specialties as *cevapcici* (spicy panfried sausages) are also often found on Styrian menus. You are most likely to encounter the more urbane Viennese cooking in Lower Austria, where you can get the traditional Wiener Schnitzel nearly everywhere.

Many of the restaurants listed in the chapter are actually country inns that provide overnight accommodations as well as meals, as noted in the reviews.

Accommodations in Eastern Austria range from luxury city hotels to mountain and lakeside resorts to castles and romantic country inns, and all are substantially lower in price than those in Vienna or Salzburg. Every town and village also has the simpler *Gasthäuser*, which give good value as long as you don't expect a private bath. Accommodations in private homes are cheaper still. These bargains are usually identified by signs reading ZIMMER FREI (room available) or FRÜHSTÜCK-SPENSION (bed-and-breakfast).

Many hotels offer half-board, with dinner in addition to buffet breakfast (although most $$$$ hotels will charge extra for breakfast). On the chart below, hotel prices are listed for room rates that include a Continental breakfast "(CP, Continental Plan) or, if indicated, no meals (EP, European Plan) or BP (Breakfast Plan, with full breakfast including hot dishes). Higher prices prevail for board plans such as MAP (Modified American Plan, with breakfast and dinner; the half-board room rate is usually an extra €15–€30 per person). Occasionally, quoted room rates for hotels already include half-board accommodations, though a "discounted" rate is usually offered if you prefer not to take the evening meal. Inquire when booking. Pets are welcome unless otherwise noted.

WHAT IT COSTS IN EUROS					
	¢	$	$$	$$$	$$$$
RESTAURANTS	under €7	€7–€12	€13–€17	€18–€22	over €22
HOTELS	under €70	€70–€100	€100–€135	€135–€175	over €175

Restaurant prices are per person for a main course at dinner. Hotel prices are for a standard double room in high season, including taxes and service.

BURGENLAND

A region of castles, grain fields, and vineyards, Burgenland is a narrow, fertile belt of agricultural land stretching some 170 km (106 mi) from the Slovak border, along the Hungarian frontier, and south to Slovenia. Only 65 km (40 mi) across at its widest point, the region at its narrowest is a mere 4 km (2½ mi).

The name Burgenland, meaning "land of castles," dates only from 1921; prior to World War I this area was a part of Hungary. Throughout its long history it has been a battleground between east and west. It was part of the ancient Roman province of Pannonia, occupied by Celts, Roman settlers, Ostrogoths, and Slavs. After them came the Bavarians, Hungarians, and Austrians, followed by invading Turks. This legacy of conflict continued into the late 20th century, with the tensions of the Iron Curtain a stark fact of life until 1989. The opening of the Hungarian border has again brought change and increased Burgenland's appeal to tourists.

NEUSIEDLER LAKE

In the north part of Burgenland, and one of the region's chief attractions, Neusiedler Lake occupies a strange world. One of the largest lakes in Europe, it is the Continent's only true steppe lake—a bizarre body of warm brackish water. Underground springs feed it, but when they fail it dries up, which last happened in the 1860s. At present the water is not more than about 7 feet deep at any spot; its many shallower sections make it possible (but still hazardous) to wade across the lake. Its depth has varied dramatically, however, at times nearly engulfing the villages on its banks. Most of its 318-square-km (124-square-mi) surface area is in Austria, but the southern reaches extend into Hungary.

What really sets Neusiedler Lake apart is the thick belt of tall reeds—in some places more than a mile deep—that almost completely encircles it. This is the habitat of large and varied flocks of birds (more than 250 species) that nest near the water's edge. The lake is also a magnet for anglers, boaters, and windsurfers; other activities include swimming and, along its banks, bicycling.

NEUSIEDL AM SEE

51 km (32 mi) southeast of Vienna.

ESSENTIALS

Bike Rentals Hotel Wende (⊠ *Seestrasse 40, Neusiedl am See* ☎ *02167/8111–0*).

Tourist Information Neusiedl am See Tourismusbüro (⊠ *Hauptplatz 1,* ☎ *02167/2229* ⊕ *www.neusiedlamsee.at*).

EXPLORING

Neusiedl am See, at the north end of the lake for which it is named, is a pleasant resort town with good facilities. Direct hourly commuter trains from Vienna have made it very popular, so you won't be alone here. To reach the lake, where you can rent small boats, swim, or just laze on the beach, follow the main street for three blocks east of the Hauptplatz and turn right on Seestrasse.

In Neusiedel am See itself, visit the ruins of the 13th-century hill fortress Ruine Tabor and the 15th-century parish church near the town hall.

WHERE TO STAY & EAT

$$$–$$$$
Fodor's Choice
★

✕**Zur Blauen Gans.** The lakeside Blue Goose is manned by Alsatian dynamo Alain Weissberger, who is fast becoming one of the best-known chefs in the country. You can dine inside the charming, thatch-roof cottage or on the patio at the edge of a green park. The kitchen casts its own spell, with delights like *Zander* (pike perch) fillet with *Eierschwammerl* (chanterelle) mushrooms and baby asparagus, or the classic, tender *Tafelspitz* beef in a chive sauce. Desserts are bursting with flavor, such as the zingy lemon-thyme sorbet. The Blauen Gans is signposted on the main street in the small town of Weiden, 4 km (2½ mi) southeast of Neusiedl. ⊠*Seepark, Weiden am See* ☎*02167/7510* ⌂ *Reservations essential* ⊟*No credit cards* ⊗*Closed Tues. and Wed.; in summer closed Tues. only.*

$–$$
✕**Nyikospark.** On the main street of Neusiedl, this upscale yet casual eatery is ill-marked, but worth the trouble to search for (it's on the left side about halfway down as you're driving through town from north to south). One side of the unique, modern, glass-and-wood structure opens onto an inviting terrace, shaded by canvas stretched between chestnut trees. Begin with an *amuse guele* of refreshing cucumber soup with a dollop of spicy fried ground beef. Continue with big, tender chunks of veal goulash with homemade spinach *Nockerln* (similar to *Spätzle*), or opt for the *Perlhuhnbrust* (guinea fowl) with crispy fried polenta balls and *Eierschwammerl* (chanterelle) ragout. ⊠*Untere Hauptstrasse 59* ☎*02167/40222* ⊟ *AE, DC, MC, V* ⊗*Closed Mon. and Tues.*

$$$
🏨 **Hotel Wende.** This sprawling three-story hotel complex is close to the lake and has more than standard amenities; here you can get a massage or rent bicycles and set off on the path that begins at its doorstep. Don't expect the charm of a country inn; this is a modern resort hotel. The comfortable rooms are of adequate size, and the balconies facing the lake add to the feeling of space. With the indoor pool, a good res-

IF YOU LIKE

WINES & WEINSTRASSE

Eastern Austria vies with Lower Austria as a source of the country's best wines. In both Burgenland and Styria you can travel between villages along "wine routes," stopping to sample the local vintages. Outstanding white wines predominate, although increasingly there are excellent reds and rosés as well. Burgenland's vineyards, mostly around Neusiedler Lake, produce wines that tend to be slightly less dry, with perhaps the best examples coming from the villages of Rust and the areas around Donnerskirchen, Jois, Gols, and Deutschkreuz. Some of the sweet dessert wines (*Spätlese*, late harvest, and *Eiswein*, pressed from frozen grapes) are extraordinary, and all Burgenland wines are gaining a reputation for high quality. Many vintners happily share samples of their wares and will provide bread and cheese as accompaniment. In Styria the increasingly popular region south of Graz along the Slovenian border (known among Austrians as "South of Styria") offers award-winning wines. With its lush, softly rolling hills, the area is reminiscent of Tuscany, and the well-marked Weinstrasse will take you from winery to winery, where it is possible to do some tasting. Southern Styria is also known for the tart, pale orange Schilcher wine. The Schilcherstrasse offers an ideal route to stop and taste at small family-run wineries.

HIKING

Eastern Austria is prime hiking country, and most tourist regions have marked trails. You'll need a local hiking map (*Wanderkarte*), usually for sale at a town's tourist office—whose staff can also suggest short rambles in the vicinity. Some particularly good places for walks are around Neusiedler Lake and Güssing in Burgenland; in the Mur Valley of Styria, especially the Bärenschützklamm at Mixnitz; around Mariazell; and atop the Schneeberg, Rax, and Semmering in Lower Austria. For the truly ambitious, several long-distance trails cut through this region, among them the Nordalpen-Weitwanderweg past the Raxalpe to Rust, and the Oststeiermärkischer-Hauptwanderweg from western Austria to Riegersburg. There's no need to carry either food or a tent, because you stay overnight in staffed huts. Camping is strongly discouraged for both safety and environmental reasons.

HORSEBACK RIDING

The *puszta* (steppe) to the east of Neusiedler Lake is known as the Seewinkel, a perfect place for horseback riding; horses (*Pferde*) can be hired in several villages. Ask at the local tourist office. Weekends are particularly popular, so book your steed well in advance.

taurant, and the bar you can even survive a rainy day. **Pros:** friendly and knowledgeable staff; spacious lobby; very good location. **Cons:** little charm. ⊠*Seestrasse 40* ☎*02167/8111* ⊕*www.hotel-wende.at* ⇘*106 rooms* ⌂*In-room: no a/c. In-hotel: restaurant, pool, gym, spa, bicycles, Wi-Fi* ⊟*AE, D, MC, V* ⊙*Closed Christmas wk and 1st 2 wks of Feb.* ⦿*CP.*

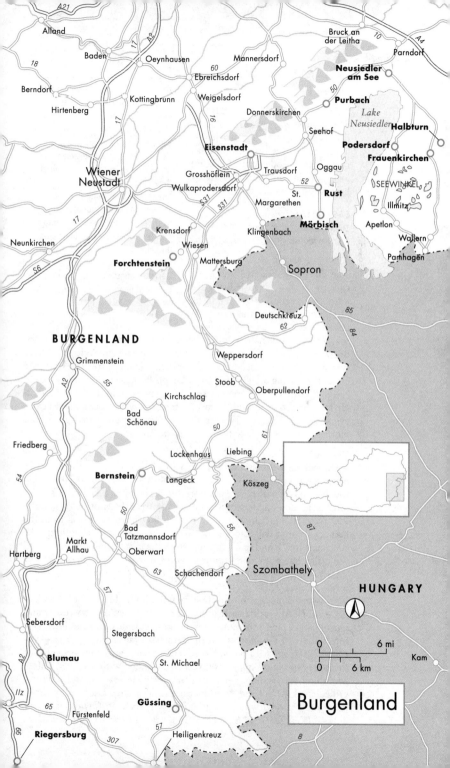

PODERSDORF

14 km (8½ mi) south of Neusiedl am See.

GETTING HERE & AROUND

The easiest way to reach Podersdorf is by car, but you can also take a train to Neusiedl Station and then take a bus to Podersdorf. In the village, walking and bicycling are the best ways to get around.

ESSENTIALS

Bike Rentals **Mike's Radverleih** (✉ *Strandgasse 9* ☎ *02177/2411*).

EXPLORING

The village of Podersdorf, on the eastern shore of Neusiedler Lake, marks the beginning of the unusual Hungarian *puszta,* the great flat steppe dotted with occasional windmills and wells with their long, characteristic wooden poles for drawing up water. Some of the picturesque houses in Podersdorf have typical thatched roofs, and in summer their chimneys are often occupied by storks nesting after wintering in Egypt. Because it's relatively free of reeds, Podersdorf is a popular spot for swimming in the lake. A circular tour of about 70 km (44 mi) by car or bicycle would cover nearly everything of interest. Twice a day, a ferry shuttles passengers—and bicycles—across the lake to the village of Rust.

> ### BICYCLING
>
> The flat plains around Neusiedler Lake, with their tiny hamlets and unspoiled scenery, are perfect for leisurely bicycling. Practically every village has a bike-rental shop (*Fahrradverleih* or *Radverleih*), but on weekends demand is so great that it's a good idea to reserve in advance. A bike route encircles the lake, passing through Hungary (you can shorten the route by taking the ferry between Illmitz beach and Mörbisch). This and many other routes are described in a German-language map-brochure called "Radeln in Burgenland," available at tourist offices.

WHERE TO STAY & EAT

$$–$$$ ✕**Gasthof zur Dankbarkeit.** The kitchen of this lovely old guesthouse offers local fare as well as creative dishes with occasional Hungarian touches, served either in a comfortable Stube or at picnic tables in an interior garden under centuries-old shady trees. Start off with some of the spicy, Hungarian-style appetizers, followed by fresh fish from the lake (the waiter will know which fish were caught that morning). The succulent steaks and goulash come from the local Apetloner cattle, and the cellar has a good selection of vintage wines. ✉ *Hauptstrasse 39* ☎ *02177/2223* ☐ *No credit cards* ☉ *Closed Wed. and Thurs.; Mon.– Thurs. from Dec. to Easter.*

$$–$$$ ✕**Presshaus.** This charming restaurant is in Illmitz, 11 km (7 mi) south of
★ Podersdorf. At first glance it seems like a traditional country restaurant, with pickled pine walls and cheerful blue curtains, but the Presshaus offers some of the most innovative Austrian cuisine in the area—seasonal *Bärlauch* (wild wood garlic) cream soup, asparagus risotto, or the house specialty, spicy ricotta strudel drizzled with browned butter. Main courses include plenty of fish choices in season, and flavorful grilled steak from local Apetloner cattle. The large selection of European and regional wines includes its own label. ✉ *Apetlonerstrasse1 3* ☎ *02175/2730* ☐ *AE, DC, MC, V* ☉ *Closed late Jan.–mid-Feb.*

and Mon. and Tues., except in July and Aug.

$$ [TV]**Seewirt and Haus Attila.** At this family-run lakefront hotel, the balconied rooms overlooking the lake are the most prized. Even the indoor pool has a lake view. Some rooms have wood floors, white walls, and simple modern furnishings, free of fuss and kitsch. Others are decorated with antique furniture. Ask for a room toward the lake, as the ones facing the square can be noisy with tourist music. At mealtime, reserve a table in the garden of the restaurant, which features local specialties, fresh fish from the lake and wine from the family winery. The family has been planting grapes for generations. **Pros:** fine food; access to water sports. **Cons:** restaurant can be noisy with day-trippers. ✉*Strandplatz 1* ☎*02177/2415* ⊕*www.seewirtkarner.at* 🛏*34 rooms* ⚒*In-room: no a/c. In-hotel: restaurant, pool, bicycles* ⊟*AE, MC, V* ⊺◎⊺*CP.*

> ### A DAY TRIP BY BIKE
>
> For an active day trip, rent a bike on Strandplatz in Podersdorf and pedal south along the lake, following cycle path No 10. It's easy going with a few small inclines. Take time to climb one of the observation towers to look west over the lake and east into the flat country. When you come to the village of Illmitz, turn left to the main road, then turn right until you reach Apetlonerstrasse 13, where you can refuel at Presshaus after your 11 km (7 mi) workout. If you still have energy, take a walk on the nature trail and visit the noted biological station in the national park in Illmitz (☎02175/3442).

FRAUENKIRCHEN

7½ km (4½ mi) east of Podersdorf, 16½ km (10¼ mi) southeast of Neusiedl am See.

Frauenkirchen is known mainly for its **pilgrimage church,** rebuilt in 1702 after its 14th-century predecessor was destroyed by invading Turks, and again restored following World War II. The Baroque interior has a much-venerated wooden statue of the Virgin from the 13th century. Note the miniature Mount Calvary depiction alongside the church.

HALBTURN

5 km (3 mi) northwest of Frauenkirchen, 14 km (8½ mi) southeast of Neusiedl am See.

★ Halbturn contains the exquisite Baroque **Schloss Halbturn,** an imperial hunting lodge built in 1710 by Lukas von Hildebrandt, the great architect of the period. This restored jewel was once used by Empress Maria Theresa as a summer residence and is noted for its ceiling frescoes. Devastated by Russian troops in the occupation following World War II, then rebuilt in the 1970s, the castle now houses special annual exhibitions. A stroll through the large, wooded surrounding park is pleasant anytime, but in late spring when the red-and-pink chestnut trees are in bloom, the spectacle easily rivals a Monet painting. In the courtyard a shop sells excellent wines from Halbturn vineyards, and a small art museum displays a copy of Gustav Klimt's impressive *Beethoven Frieze*, with the decided advantage over the Vienna original that here you can see the details up close. ⊠*Schloss Halbturn* ☎*02172/8577* ⊕*www. schlosshalbturn.at* ✑*€7* ⊙*Mid-Apr.–late Oct., Tues.–Sun. 10–6.*

PURBACH

13 km (8½ mi) southwest of Neusiedl am See.

Purbach, like the nearby wine villages of Breitenbrunn and Donnerskirchen, retains traces of its medieval fortifications. Look for the bust of a Turk atop a chimney in the town center; legend has it that when the invaders withdrew in 1532 one badly hungover, sleepy Turk missed the retreat, and fearing retribution, climbed down a chimney for safety. He was discovered, became an honored citizen, and lived in Purbach happily ever after. The wines of this area, the reds in particular, are outstanding and merit stopping for samples.

WHERE TO EAT

$$$–$$$$ ✗**Am Spitz.** This country inn at the end of an attractive row of wine cellars is known for its local Burgenland and Pannonian cooking. The restaurant is in a former cloister, and the garden is a veritable bower of flowers, looking down over the lake. The menu changes daily but always spotlights fresh fish, possibly including a spicy Hungarian fish soup, a cassoulet of lake fish in basil cream, and roast veal steak. The wines produced on the estate are available by the glass. The somewhat plain and modern associated Gasthof is pleasant but less *gemütlich* in feeling. ⊠*Waldsiedlgasse 2* ☎*02683/5519* ▤ *MC, V* ⊙*Closed Jan.– mid-Mar.; mid-Mar.–mid-Dec. Mon.–Wed.; July and Aug. Mon. and Tues.* ⏐⊙⏐*CP.*

RUST

Fodor'sChoice   *14 km (9 mi) south of Purbach, 28 km (17½ mi) southwest of Neusiedl*
★   *am See.*

ESSENTIALS

Bike Rentals **Schneeberger** (⊠*Rathausplatz 15* ☎*02685/6442*).

Tourist Information **Rust Gästeinformation** (⊠*Conradplatz 1* ☎*02685/502* ⊕*www.rust.at*).

EXPLORING

Picturesque Rust is easily the most popular village on the lake for the colorful pastel facades of its houses and for lake sports. Tourists flock here in summer to see the sight of storks nesting atop the Renaissance and Baroque houses in the well-preserved historic center. ■TIP→ **Be sure to look for** *Steckerl*, **a delicious local fish caught from Neusiedler Lake and grilled barbecue-style with spices.** It's available in most restaurants, but only in the hot months of summer. If you're heading from Purbach, leave Route 50 at Seehof and follow the local road past Oggau to arrive in Rust.

Visit the restored Gothic **Fischerkirche** (Fishermen's Church) off the west end of the Rathausplatz. Built between the 12th and 16th centuries, it is surrounded by a defensive wall and is noted for its 15th-century frescoes and an organ from 1705. ✉Conradplatz 1 ☎02685/295 or 0676/970–3316 ⚲€1, €2 with tour ⊙Apr. and Oct., Mon.–Sat. 11–noon and 2–3, Sun. 11–noon and 2–4; May–Sept., Mon.–Sat. 10–noon and 2:30–5, Sun. 11–noon and 2–5.

A causeway leads through nearly a mile of reeds to the **Seebad** beach and boat landing, where you can take a sightseeing boat either round-trip or to another point on the lake. You can also rent a boat, swim, or enjoy a waterside drink or snack at an outdoor table of the Seerestaurant Rust.

> **BOATING**
>
> You can hire boats (Bootsvermietung or Bootsverleih) around Neusiedler Lake. Expect to pay about €4 per hour for a rowboat, €7 for a pedal boat, and €10–€20 for an electric boat; sailboat prices vary widely. There are several businesses in the area, including: **Baumgartner** (✉Neusiedl am See ☎02167/2782), **Knoll** (✉Podersdorf ☎02177/2431), and **Ruster Freizeitcenter** (✉Rust ☎02685/595).

Rust is also renowned for its outstanding wines. There are wine-tasting opportunities at the **Weinakademie** (✉Hauptstrasse 31 ☎02685/6853) or at **Weingut Feiler-Artinger** (✉Hauptstrasse 3 ☎02685/237), to name just two of the many local family-run wineries.

WHERE TO STAY & EAT

$$ $$$ ✕**Rusterhof.** A lovingly renovated burgher's house—the town's oldest—at the top of the main square houses an excellent and imaginative restaurant. Light natural woods and vaulted ceilings set the tone in a series of smaller rooms; in summer there's an outside garden. The menu depends on what's fresh, and might include grilled fish or saddle of hare in *Eiswein* sauce. Finish with a rhubarb compote. The complex also includes four comfortable apartments. Under the same management is the Burgerhaus at Hauptstrasse 1, with another 10 modern, spacious apartments. ✉Rathausplatz 18 ☎02685/6162 ⊟AE, MC, V ⊙Closed Mon. ⦿CP.

$ ✕**Schandl.** The Schandl family of Rust is one of the best-known wine growers of the Neusiedl Lake area; their devotees come for wine tastings and stay for dinner. For good, simple food to go along with their excellent wine, join the locals at this popular *Buschenschank* (inn). The buffet offers a selection of sausages, salads, cheeses, and pickles, as well as a few hot dishes that change daily. You can also order entrées from the menu, such as lamb ragout with spinach noodles or goulash with sauerkraut and bread dumplings. There's a pleasant courtyard for outdoor dining in summer. ✉Hauptstrasse 20 ☎02685/265 ⊕No credit cards ⊙Closed Tues. and Nov.–Mar.

$$ ⌂**Sifkovits.** The Tomschitz family makes you feel welcome in their charming hotel, which is close to the lake and a block away from the touristy, busy center of Rust. Rooms are small but comfortable and tastefully decorated; the lounge has an open fireplace. In summer head

for the terrace to enjoy the tasty food prepared by Marcus Tomschitz. If you like fish, this is the place to come. After the meal you can relax in the large park behind the hotel. **Pros:** spacious and welcoming lobby; quiet rooms; large park behind the hotel. **Cons:** rooms facing street are sometimes noisy. ⊠ *Am Seekanal 8* ☎ *02685/360* ⊕ *www.sifkovits. at* ⬦*33 rooms* ♻ *In-room: no a/c. In-hotel: restaurant, bar, bicycles, parking (free)* ⊟ *AE, D, MC, V* ⊘ *Closed Dec.–mid-Mar.* ⦿ *CP.*

NIGHTLIFE & THE ARTS

★ Between Rust and Eisenstadt, outside the tiny village of St. Margarethen, is **Römersteinbruch** (☎ *02680/2188* ⊕ *www.roemersteinbruch. at*), a delightful rock quarry used for outdoor opera performances for six or seven weeks in July and August. It's one of the three largest outdoor opera venues in Europe, seating 7,000 nightly. Performances are a spectacular extravaganza—a run of Verdi's *Aïda* included horse-drawn chariots, a dozen galloping horses, and even two well-trained elephants. Performances also include a dazzling fireworks display. Ticket prices range from €27 to €100. It's a good idea to bring a seat cushion, if possible, because seating is on metal chairs.

MÖRBISCH

★ *5½ km (3½ mi) south of Rust.*

ESSENTIALS

Bike Rentals **Posch** (⊠ *Blumentalgasse 9* ☎ *02685/8242*).

Tourist Information **Mörbisch Tourist Info** (⊠ *Haupstrasse 23* ☎ *02685/8430* ⊕ *www.moerbischamsee.at*).

EXPLORING

Mörbisch is the last lakeside village before the Hungarian border. Considered by many to be the most attractive settlement on the lake, the town is famous for its low, whitewashed, Magyar-style houses, whose open galleries are colorfully decorated with flowers and bunches of grain. The local vineyards produce some superb white wines, especially the fresh-tasting welschriesling and the full-bodied Muscat-Ottonel. A causeway leads to a beach on the lake, where an international operetta festival is held each summer.

A leisurely activity is to tour the countryside in a typical, open **horse-drawn wagon.** Operators in several lakeside villages will arrange this, including **Johann Mad** (⊠ *Ruster Strasse 14* ☎ *02685/8250*).

Surprisingly, there is no border control here between Austria and Hungary. A small road just outside Mörbisch leads into the woods. After 50 yards or so, a sign reading "Magyarország" (Hungary) and a white marking on the road quietly announce the border crossing. You are allowed to cross on foot or on a bicycle, but not with a car. Take your passport along, in case you are stopped.

NIGHTLIFE & THE ARTS

At the **Mörbisch Lake Festival,** held on Friday, Saturday, and Sunday mid-July–August on Burgenland's Neusiedler Lake, operettas are performed outdoors on a floating stage. For information, contact the Mörbisch tourist office or the **festival office** (☎*02682/66210–0 Seefestspiele Mörbisch* ⊕*www.seefestspiele-moerbisch.at*) in Schloss Esterházy in Eisenstadt or, from June through August, in **Mörbisch** (☎*02685/8181* ☎*02685/8334*).

EISENSTADT

★ *22 km (14 mi) northwest of Mörbisch, 48 km (30 mi) south of Vienna, 26 km (16¼ mi) west of Wiener Neustadt.*

GETTING HERE & AROUND

Eisenstadt is connected to Vienna and Neusiedl am See by train and to places throughout Burgenland by bus. By car from Rust, take Route 52 west past St. Margarethen and Trausdorf to the capital.

ESSENTIALS

Eisenstadt Tourismus (⊠*Schloss Esterhazy, A-7000* ☎*02682/67390* ⊕*www. eisenstadt.at*).

EXPLORING

Burgenland's provincial capital, Eisenstadt, is a really small town. Nevertheless it has an illustrious history and enough sights to keep you busy for a half, if not quite a full, day. Although the town has existed since at least the 12th century, it only became at all significant in the 17th, when it became the seat of the Esterházys, a princely Hungarian family that traces its roots to Attila the Hun. The original Esterházy made his fortune by marrying a succession of wealthy landowning widows. Esterházy support was largely responsible for the Habsburg reign in Hungary under the Dual Monarchy. At one time the family controlled a far-flung agro-industrial empire, and it still owns vast forest resources. The composer Joseph Haydn lived in Eisenstadt for some 30 years while in the service of the Esterházys. When Burgenland was ceded to Austria after World War I, its major city, Sopron, elected to remain a part of Hungary, so in 1925 tiny Eisenstadt was made the capital of the new Austrian province.

In addition to the list below, Eisenstadt has a few other attractions that its tourist office can tell you about, including the Museum of Austrian Culture, the Diocesan Museum, the Fire Fighters Museum, Haydn's little garden house, and an assortment of churches.

Fodor'sChoice **Schloss Esterházy,** the yellow-facade former palace of the ruling princes, ★ reigns over the town. Built in the Baroque style between 1663 and 1672 on the foundations of a medieval castle and later modified, it is still owned by the Esterházy family, who lease it to the provincial government for use mostly as offices. The Esterházy family rooms are worth viewing, and the lavishly decorated **Haydn Room,** an impressive concert hall where the composer conducted his own works from 1761 until 1790, is still used for presentations of Haydn's works, with musicians often dressed in period garb. The hall can be seen on guided tours (in English on request if there is a minimum of 10 people) lasting about 30 minutes. The **park** behind the Schloss is pleasant for a stroll or a picnic. In late August the park is the site of the Burgenland wine week, during which there's a two-hour tour on wine and culture at the palace. It ends with a tasting. Inquire at the information desk. ☒ *Esterházy Platz* ☏ *02682/719–3000* ⊕ *www.schloss-esterhazy.at* ☜ *€7* ☉ *Early Apr.–mid-Nov., daily 9–5, guided tours hrly; mid-Nov.–Mar., weekdays, guided tousr at 10 and 2.*

At the crest of Esterházystrasse perches the **Bergkirche,** an ornate Baroque church that includes the strange *Kalvarienberg,* an indoor Calvary Hill representing the Way of the Cross with life-size figures placed in cavelike rooms along an elaborate path. At its highest point, the trail reaches the platform of the belfry, offering a view over the town and this section of Burgenland. The magnificent wooden figures were carved and painted by Franciscan monks more than 250 years ago. The main part of the church contains the tomb of Joseph Haydn, who died in 1809 in Vienna. ☒ *Josef Haydn Platz 1* ☏ *02682/62638* ⊕ *www.haydnkirche.at* ☜ *€2.50* ☉ *Late Mar.–Oct., daily 9–noon and 2–5; other months by appt.*

Wertheimergasse and Unterbergstrasse were boundaries of the Jewish ghetto from 1671 until 1938. During that time Eisenstadt had a considerable Jewish population; today the **Österreichisches Jüdisches Museum** *(Austrian Jewish Museum)* recalls the experience of Austrian Jews throughout history. A fascinating private synagogue in the complex survived the 1938 terror and is incorporated into the museum. ☒ *Unterbergstrasse 6* ☏ *02682/65145* ⊕ *www.ojm.at* ☜ *€3.70* ☉ *May–Oct., Tues.–Sun. 10–5; Nov.–Apr., Mon.–Thurs. 9–4, Fri. 9–1.*

The **Landesmuseum** *(Burgenland Provincial Museum)* brings the history of the region to life with displays on such diverse subjects as Roman culture and the area's wildlife. There's a memorial room to the composer Franz Liszt, along with more relics of the town's former Jewish community. ☒ *Museumgasse 1–5* ☏ *02682/6000–1234* ⊕ *www.burgenland. at* ☜ *€3* ☉ *Tues.–Sat. 9–5, Sun. 10–5.*

Joseph Haydn lived in the simple house on Joseph Haydn-Gasse from 1766 until 1778. Now the **Haydn Museum,** it contains several first editions of his music and other memorabilia. The house itself, and especially its flower-filled courtyard with the small back rooms, is quite delightful. ☒ *Joseph-Haydn-Gasse 19–21* ☏ *02682/719–3900* ⊕ *www. schloss-esterhazy.at* ☜ *€3.50* ☉ *Apr.–Oct., daily 9–5.*

WHERE TO STAY & EAT

$$$–$$$$

Fodor's Choice

★

✕ **Taubenkobel.** Consistently ranked as one of the top restaurants in Austria, the "Dovecote" is a rambling, elegantly restored 19th-century farmhouse 5 km (3 mi) from Eisenstadt in the village of Schützen. Owner–chef Walter Eselböck and his wife, Evelyne, have created a series of strikingly beautiful dining rooms. The seasonally changing menu may offer potato-and-goat-cheese soup, *Zander* from the Neusiedlersee with Rösti and fried basil, or saddle of lamb with mangold blossoms and asparagus in a saffron sauce. The former stables and outbuildings have been converted to 12 luxurious, unique bedrooms with wooden beams and cathedral ceilings. ✉*Hauptstrasse 33, Schützen am Gebirge* ☎*02684/2297* ⚓*Reservations essential* ⊘*Closed Mon. and Tues. and Jan.–Feb. 15* ➡*AE, DC, MC, V*

\$\$ 🏨**Gasthof Ohr.** This personal, family-run hotel and restaurant is an easy 10-minute walk of the town center. The immaculate rooms are comfortably attractive, done in natural woods and white with pastel accents; those in the back are quieter. The rustic wood-panel restaurant offers specialty weeks—

HAYDN FULLY AT REST

The body of composer Joseph Haydn was returned to Eisenstadt for burial at the request of Prince Esterházy in 1821. It was unaccountably headless, and although a search for the head ensued, it was not discovered until 1932. It had been under glass in the possession of the Gesellschaft der Musikfreunde, the main Viennese musical society. Finally, in 1954 Haydn's head was returned to Eisenstadt, where it was buried with his body in a crypt inside the Bergkirche.

---

goose, game, fresh asparagus—in addition to Austrian and regional standards such as schnitzel and Hungarian fish soup. A favorite is the saffron risotto with lobster and chicken. In summer the canopied outdoor dining terrace is a green oasis. Wine comes from the family vineyards. **Pros:** attractive rooms; good food. **Cons:** no real lobby; Wi-Fi very expensive. ✉*Rusterstrasse 51* ☎*02682/62460* ⊕*www.hotelohr.at* ⬅*39 rooms* ⚘*In-room: no a/c. In-hotel: restaurant, no-smoking rooms, Wi-Fi, parking (free)* ➡*MC, V* ⊘*Closed 3 wks in Feb.* ⵙ*CP.*

\$\$ 🏨**Hotel Burgenland.** This big, early-1980s hotel in the town center has everything you'd expect in a first-class establishment. The friendly staff members go out of their way to assist guests. The well-maintained, spacious rooms are classic modern, with lots of shuttered windows offering views of the town and countryside. Roomy bathrooms have a separate tub and shower. The superb restaurant showcases Austrian dishes with a Pannonian slant, thanks to the city's close proximity to Hungary. Be sure to order the special aperitif, Burgenland's own Hahnenkamp Traminer Auslese, which tastes like a fine, dry sherry. You'll need to book a year in advance for the music festivals. **Pros:** well-equipped, modern hotel. **Cons:** ambience of a business hotel. ✉*Schubertplatz 1* ☎*02682/696* ⊕*www.hotel-burgenland.at* ⬅*88 rooms* ⚘*In-room: no a/c. In-hotel: restaurant, bar, pool, Wi-Fi* ➡ *AE, DC, MC, V* ⵙ*CP.*

NIGHTLIFE & THE ARTS

Eisenstadt devotes much cultural energy to one of its favorite sons. In the first half of September it plays host to the annual **Haydn Festival** in the Esterházy Palace. Many of the concerts are by renowned performers, and admission prices vary with the event. Other concerts featuring the works of Joseph Haydn run from mid-May to early October. Contact the **Haydnfestspiele office** (☎*02682/61866–0* ⊕*www.haydnfestival. at*) in Schloss Esterházy or the local tourist office.

Eisenstadt's **Schloss Trio Eisenstadt, Haydn Quartet, and Haydn Brass,** in 18th-century costumes, play short matinee concerts of the master's works at 11 AM Wednesday, Thursday, and Friday in July and August at the **Esterházy Palace** (☎02682/719–3000 ⊕*www.schloss-esterhazy. at*). Tickets are €8.

EN ROUTE
Heading southwest from Eisenstadt brings you to the waist of Burgenland, the narrow region squeezed between Lower Austria and Hungary. The leading attraction here is Forchtenstein; take Route S31 for 20 km (12½ mi) to Mattersburg, then a local road 3 km (2 mi) west.

FORCHTENSTEIN

23 km (14½ mi) southwest of Eisenstadt.

In summer people throng to the small village of Forchtenstein for its strawberries, but its enduring dominant landmark is the medieval hilltop castle **Burg Forchtenstein.** This formidable fortress was built in the early 14th century, then enlarged by the Esterházys around 1635, and twice it successfully defended Austria against invading Turks. Captured enemy soldiers were put to work digging the castle's 466-foot-deep well, famous for its echo. As befits a military stronghold, there is a fine collection of weapons in the armory and booty taken from the Turks; there's also an exhibition of stately carriages. ⊠*Burgplatz 1* ☎*02626/63125* ⊕*www.forchtenstein.at* ☜*€8* ☉*Apr.–Oct., daily 9–6.*

WHERE TO EAT

$$–$$$ ✕**Reisner.** The delicately prepared traditional food served at this popular restaurant attracts people from all over the region. You can eat in the somewhat formal dining room or in the rustic tavern favored by the locals. Some typical dishes are grilled salmon, trout with asparagus tips, or chicken breast filled with mushroom risotto, and, for dessert, a nougat charlotte. Of course you can also get traditional dishes, such as Wiener schnitzel or steaks. ⊠*Hauptstrasse 141* ☎*02626/63139* ▤*No credit cards* ☉*Closed Mon. and Tues.*

EN ROUTE
To get to Bernstein from Forchtenstein, return to the highway from Burg Forchtenstein and take S31 and Route 50 south past Weppersdorf and Stoob, the latter famous for its pottery. The road then goes through Oberpullendorf and close to Lockenhaus, where a renowned music festival is held each summer in the 13th-century castle *(⇨ Nightlife & the Arts in Bernstein, below).*

BERNSTEIN

73 km (45 mi) south of Forchtenstein.

The small village of Bernstein is one of the very few sources of *Edelserpentin,* a dark green serpentine stone also known as Bernstein jade.

Jewelry and objets d'art made locally from the town's stone are on display in the **Felsenmuseum** *(Stone Museum),* housed partly within a former mine. ⊠*Potsch, Hauptplatz 5* ☎*03354/6620–0* ⊕*www.felsenmuseum.*

The Castle Road

If you are heading south from Vienna to Graz on the A2 autobahn, the flat plains give way suddenly to steeply wooded hills and rocky gorges, with tantalizing glimpses of proud and seemingly inaccessible castles perched atop craggy promontories. More than a dozen castles along the Schlösserstrasse (Castle Road) have withstood the invading armies of the Huns and Turks to repose today in all their splendor as museums or hotels.

Begin by dipping into the eastern edge of Styria, leaving the autobahn at the Hartberg exit to visit **Schloss Hartberg,** a castle dating from the 13th century and now a museum and the venue for occasional summer concerts.

From Hartberg take Highway 54 south to Kaibing, where there will be signs for St. Johann bei Herberstein and **Schloss Herberstein,** with its Florentine-style courtyard, animal and nature park, weaponry collection, and Baroque garden. **Schloss Stubenberg,** north along the lakeside drive Stubenbergsee, is a fortresslike structure with an impressive ceramics display and summer concerts.

The Allhau exit off the A2 autobahn a short distance north of Hartberg takes you to Highway 50 and Bernstein. This is the home of **Burg Bernstein,** now a hotel but once the castle owned by Count Almásy, the character played by Ralph Fiennes in *The English Patient.*

East of Bernstein on Highway 50 is **Lockenhaus** (☎ *02616/239480* 🖷 *02616/2766*), the castle with the most grisly history in Austria. In the 16th century Countess Elisabeth Bathory was infamous for luring peasant girls to her employ with promises of a dowry after two years' servitude;

most girls never made it out alive. Obsessed with retaining her beauty, the depraved countess tortured and killed more than 500 girls, believing that their virginal blood would keep her young. As a member of the nobility, the countess was never tried for her crimes. The castle is now a very nice hotel, with a medieval restaurant serving simple food like roast chicken and sausages.

Highway 50 south of Bernstein takes you to Stadtschlaining, home of **Burg Schlaining,** with its weaponry collection, chapel, and palatial rooms (closed Monday).

Highway 57 south of Highway 50 leads to **Burg Güssing,** not far from the Slovenian and Hungarian borders. After this the Castle Road continues on into Styria, southeast of Graz.

A drive along the Castle Road can take anywhere from four or five hours to a couple of days, depending on how many of the castles you stop to visit. If you're in a hurry, it's relatively easy to get off and on the A2 autobahn to visit a castle.

The best time to visit this area is between April and October, because most of the castles are closed during the winter months. For more information, contact the **Büro Die Schlösserstrasse** (⊠ *Schloss Stubenberg, Stubenberg am See* ☎ *03176/20050* ⊕ *www.schloesserstrasse.com*).

–Bonnie Dodson

at ⬚€5 ⊙*Mar. 2–June, Sept., and Oct., daily 9–noon and 1:30–6; Nov.–Dec. 23, daily 9–noon and 1:30–5; July and Aug., daily 9–6.*

OFF THE
BEATEN
PATH

South Burgenland Open-Air Museum. South of Bernstein in Bad Tatzmannsdorf is the Freilichtmuseum (South Burgenland Open-Air Museum), which displays wonderfully restored old barns, farmhouses, and stables from the region, giving a feeling of life as experienced a century or more ago. You can arrange in advance for a personal guided tour. ⊠*Josef-Hölzel-Allee 2* ☎*03353/7015* ⬚€1 ⊙*Apr.–Oct., daily 9–5; Nov.–Mar., daily 9–4.*

WHERE TO STAY

$$$–$$$$
★
🏨 **Burg Bernstein.** This massive medieval castle, built in the 12th century, became a hotel in 1953, with indoor plumbing being the only concession to modern life. It's owned today by a descendant of the Count Almásy family. You can still find the Count's books on the shelves in the corridors, and his room is preserved the way he left it. The large guest rooms look much as they must have in the mid-1800s; the reception salons are decorated with antique writing tables and armoires. Dinners, prepared by Countess Berger-Almásy herself, are served with regional wines in the Rittersaal, a baronial hall in the 18th-century style. **Pros:** genuine historical surroundings; no tourists; restaurant and facilities for house guests only. **Cons:** often sold out. ⊠*Schlossweg 1,* ☎*03354/6382* ⊕*www.burgbernstein.at* ⊷*10 rooms* ♿*In-room: no a/c, no phone, no TV. In-hotel: restaurant, pool* ☞*2-night minimum* ⊟*AE, DC, MC, V* ⊙*Closed mid-Oct.–Apr.* ⦿*CP.*

NIGHTLIFE & THE ARTS

The **International Chamber Music Festival** (*Kammermusikfest* ☎*02616/2225* ⊕*www.lockenhaus.at*) of Lockenhaus, 15 km (9½ mi) east of Bernstein, takes place during the first half of July in a 13th-century castle. World-famous musicians are invited to this intimate festival, and the audience may attend morning rehearsals. Call for information, reservations, and accommodations.

GÜSSING

54 km (34 mi) south of Bernstein, 13 km (8½ mi) north of Heiligenkreuz, Hungary.

Güssing is yet another of Burgenland's castle-dominated villages.

The classic 12th-century fortress **Burg Güssing,** perched high on a solitary volcanic outcrop, has wonderful views of the surrounding countryside. It also has a fine collection of Old Master paintings (including portraits by Lucas Cranach), weapons and armor, and a Gothic chapel with a rare 17th-century cabinet organ. The castle has special exhibits. ⊠ *Batthyanystrasse 10A-7540* ☎*03322/43400* ⬚€5.50 ⊙*Apr.–Oct., Tues.–Sun. 10–5.*

☺ If you stop in Güssing to explore its castle, consider also visiting the nearby game park, **Naturpark Raab-Örsg-Goricko,** where wild animals indigenous to Eastern Austria reside in more than a square mile of open space. ■TIP→ Observation posts are scattered throughout, and you should exercise patience—the animals need time to come to you. The park is in Jennersdorf, 1 km (½ mi) northeast of Güssing. ✉ *Eisenstädter-strasse 11* ☎*03329/48453* ⊕*www.naturpark-raab.at* ✎*Free* ⊘*Daily dawn–dusk.*

WHERE TO EAT

¢–$ ✕ **Gasthof Gerlinde Gibiser.** Its proximity to Hungary has inspired the creative dishes served at this classic, white, villa-style country inn. The Pannonian cuisine combines the best of Austrian and Hungarian culinary traditions to produce such specialties as cabbage soup and steak stuffed with goose liver. The wine list also indicates that you are on the border of two wine-producing countries. On a nice day, head for the terrace. For overnighters there are 12 quiet rooms, plus a few rustic thatch-roof cottages surrounded by gardens. ✉ *Heiligenkreuz Obere Hauptstr. 81* ☎*03325/4216* ▤*MC, V* ⊘*Closed Mon.*

RIEGERSBURG

57 km (35 mi) southwest of Güssing, 56 km (34¾ mi) east of Graz.

Rising some 600 feet above the valley is the mighty and well-restored **Schloss Riegersburg,** one of Austria's great defensive bastions. The massive fortress perches atop an extraordinary volcanic outcropping with breathtaking views from the top. Originally built in the 11th century on the site of Celtic and Roman strongholds, it has never been humbled in battle; the present structure dates from the 17th century. Archaeological finds have established that there were settlements here more than 6,000 years ago. The castle has weapons displays and rooms with period furnishings, as well as the Burgmuseum (castle museum) and a museum on witches and sorceresses. Until the beginning of this century, you had to climb a winding path for half an hour to get inside; now you can board a glass elevator that whisks you up slanting rails to fabulous views. ☎*03153/82131* ⊕*www.veste-riegersburg.at* ✎*€9.50, elevator €4* ⊘*Castle and elevator Apr.–Oct., daily 9–5; Nov.–Mar. daily 10–5; last admission to castle at 4; last elevator trip at 6.*

Next door to the Riegersburg Castle you can observe free-flying birds of prey at **Greifvogelwarte Riegersburg** *(Birds-of-Prey Keep).* At various hours falcons and eagles are set loose from a stand within the aviary preserve (always returning to the keepers' care—and tempting meals, of course). ☎*03153/7390* ✎*€7* ⊘*Apr.–Oct., Mon.–Sat. 11 and 3, Sun. 11, 2, and 4, weather permitting.*

NEED A BREAK?

To celebrate your climb you may want to visit the Taverne, situated just before the drawbridge of the castle gates. You can pick a snack or a hot dish from a self-service counter and head—weather permitting—for the garden to enjoy a stunning look far into Austria.

WHERE TO EAT

$-$$ ✕**Gasthof Fink Zur Riegersburg.** This venerable, family-run country inn near the foot of the castle is prettily adorned with flower boxes and shutters. Its large, paneled restaurant—complete with ceiling beams—is bright and airy, and there's also garden dining in season. The Austrian cuisine is hearty, with such dishes as bratwurst with sauerkraut and dumplings, and roast beef with fried polenta. A fine selection of Styrian wines is offered. The new guest rooms looking far into the quiet valley may entice you to stay settle in here for a few days. ⊠ *Riegersburg 29* ☎ *03153/8216* ⊟ *AE, DC, MC, V* ⊘ *Closed Thurs. and 3 wks in winter* ⊙ *CP.*

BLUMAU

60 km (37 mi) northeast of Graz.

Midway between Vienna and Graz, this tiny hamlet was known until recently as one of the poorest farming communities in the country. Then in the late 1970s an oil-exploration company drilling for gas unexpectedly found a thermal spring instead. Not realizing its value, they blocked it up, but the people in the area didn't forget about it. It wasn't until the mid-1990s that permission was granted to drill again, and when the volcanic springs were released the area became fashionable for spa treatments and cures.

WHERE TO STAY

$$$$ 🛏 **Bad Blumau.** Designed by the late visionary artist Friedensreich Hun-
★   dertwasser, this phenomenal spa-hotel complex has undulating walls covered by a brilliant checkered patchwork, with turrets, mismatched windows, sloping rooftop gardens, and multicolored ceramic pillars. Rooms have curved walls, soothing fabrics, and oddly angled bathrooms. Take an evening swim (even in winter) in the outdoor thermal pool, whose natural hot springs keep the water at a constant 34°C (92°F). Your days can be filled with spa treatments, from sound therapy to hay wraps—for an additional charge. The spa restaurants serve tasty Austrian fare, using produce and meat provided by local farmers. **Pros:** spacious lobby and guest rooms; good food; amazing architecture. **Cons:** expensive. ⊠ *A-8283, Blumau* ☎ *03383/5100–0* ⊕ *www.blumau.com* 🛏 *271 rooms, 59 suites* ⚄ *In-room: no a/c, Wi-Fi. In-hotel: 2 restaurants, bar, pool, gym, spa* ⊟ *AE, DC, MC, V* ⊙ *MAP.*

GRAZ & ITS ENVIRONS

★ *200 km (125 mi) southwest of Vienna, 285 km (178 mi) southeast of Salzburg.*

Austria's second-largest city, Graz is graceful, welcoming, and very untouristed. Instead of visitors, it's the large university population who keep the sidewalk cafés, trendy bars, and chic restaurants humming in the vibrant Altstadt. The modern art museum, the Kunsthaus, has a startling biomorphic blue shape that looms over rooftops like some alien spaceship. Along with this, the annual Styriarte summer music festival has become one of the most prestigious cultural draws in the country, and the city opera theater now attracts top companies like the Bolshoi. Graz is far from the cultural backwater it once was; in fact, it was designated the 2003 "European Capital of Culture."

With its skyline dominated by the squat 16th-century clock tower, this stylish city has a gorgeous and well-preserved medieval center whose Italian Renaissance overlay gives it, in contrast to other Austrian cities, a Mediterranean feel. The name Graz derives from the Slavic *gradec*, meaning "small castle"; there was probably a fortress atop the Schlossberg hill as early as the 9th century. By the 12th century a town had developed at the foot of the hill, which in time became an imperial city of the ruling Habsburgs. Graz's glory faded in the 17th century when the court moved to Vienna, but the city continued to prosper as the provincial capital of Styria, especially under the enlightened 19th-century rule of Archduke Johann.

In 1811, the Archduke founded the Landesmuseum Joanneum, making it the oldest public music in Austria. This museum complex, with 12 locations, has notable collections of art, archaeology and armor, as well as fossils and folk life. A €7 day ticket allows you entry to all collections and exhibitions.

GETTING HERE & AROUND

Streetcars and buses are an excellent way of traveling within the city. Single tickets (€1.70) can be bought from the driver, and one-day and multiple-ride tickets are also available. All six streetcar routes converge at Jakominiplatz near the south end of the Old City. One fare may combine streetcars and buses as long as you take a direct route to your destination. Driving in the Graz city center is not advisable, because there are many narrow, one-way, and pedestrian streets and few places to park. In Graz, taxis can be ordered by phone.

If you're pressed for time, choose which part of the Old City you'd rather see: the lower section, with its churches, historical houses, and museums, or the upper town, with its winding wooded paths, famous clock tower, and the Schlossberg, the lookout point of the city. The best time to visit is between April and October, when the weather is at its most inviting.

WALKING TOURS
Guided walking sightseeing tours of Graz in English and German are conducted Tuesday and Wednesday and Friday–Sunday at 2:30, April–October, and on Saturday at 2:30 between November and March. The meeting point for these tours is Tourist Information at Herrengasse 16. The cost is €8.50.

ESSENTIALS

Bus Information **Stadtbus Verkehr** (☎ 0316/887411). **Graz Airport** (*GRZ* ☎0316/2902–0). **Taxis** (☎0316/1718, 0316/222, or 0316/2801).

Tourist Information **Grazer Tourismus** (✉ *Herrrengasse 16* ☎0316/80750 ⊕ *www.graztourismus.at*).

EXCURSIONS

The lush, wine-terraced area 30 minutes south of Graz is home to some of the best wineries in the country. The **Graz tourist office** (☎ *0316/8075-0* ⊕ *www.graztouris-mus.at*) offers several bus excursions on Saturday to the area, as well as to the castle in Riegersburg or to Piber, home of the famous white horses of the Spanish Riding School. Ask at the office for the detailed brochure in English, "Excursions Around Graz," with suggestions as well as travel directions. Three favorite trips—to Stübing bei Graz, Piber, and Bärnbach—can each be done in a few hours. On all the bus excursions you'll be treated to the modestly named *Brettljause* (literally: a snack on a little board), which is really a wooden platter piled with an array of home-grown and -cured meats.

EXPLORING

8 **Burg.** The scanty remains of this former imperial palace now house government offices. Most of this uninspired structure is from the 19th and 20th centuries, but two noteworthy vestiges of the original 15th-century stronghold remain: the **Burgtor** (palace gate), which opens into the sprawling **Stadtpark** (municipal park), and the unusual 49-step, 26-foot carved stone double-spiral **Gothic staircase** of 1499, in the hexagonal tower at the far end of the first courtyard.

7 **Domkirche.** On the cathedral's south exterior wall is a badly damaged 15th-century fresco called the *Landplagenbild,* which graphically depicts contemporary local torments—the plague, locusts, and the Turks. Step inside to see the outstanding high altar made of colored marble, the choir stalls, Raphael Donner's 1741 tomb of Count Cobenzl, and Konrad Laib's *Crucifixion* from 1457. The 15th-century reliquaries on either side of the triumphal arch leading to the choir were originally the hope chests of Paola Gonzaga, daughter of Ludovico II of Mantua. The Baroque **Mausoleum** of Emperor Ferdinand II, who died in 1637, adjoins the cathedral. Its sumptuous interior is partly an early design by native son Fischer von Erlach, and his only work to be seen in Graz. ⊠ *Burggasse 3* ☎ *0316/821683* 🏛 *Domkirche, free; Mausoleum €4.50* ⊙ *Domkirche daily 11–dusk; mausoleum, Nov., Dec., and early Jan.–Apr., daily 10:30–noon and 1:30–4; May–Oct. daily 10–noon and 1:30–4.*

6 **Glockenspielplatz.** Every day at 11 AM and 3 and 6 PM two mullioned windows open in the mechanical clock high above the square, revealing a life-size wooden couple, the man adorned in lederhosen, a tankard of beer in his upraised fist, accompanied by a dirndl-clad Austrian maiden. An old folk tune plays and they dance on the window ledges before returning to their hidden perch. The musical box was erected in 1903 by the owner of the house. Look into the courtyard at No. 5, which has an impressive 17th-century open staircase. The house at No. 7 has an arcaded Renaissance courtyard.

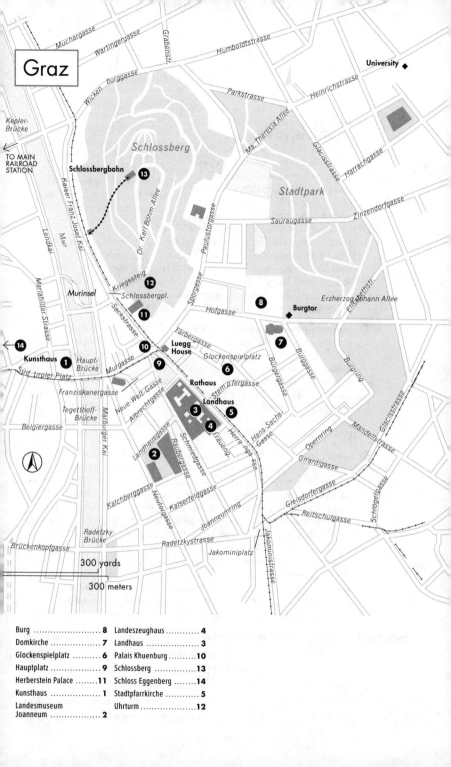

Graz

Kepler-Brücke

TO MAIN RAILROAD STATION

Muchargasse
Wartingergasse
Grabenstr.
Humboldtstrasse
Wickenburggasse
Parkstrasse
Heinrichstrasse
University
Schlossberg
Schlossbergbahn **13**
Stadtpark
Dr. Karl Böhm-Allee
Ma. Theresia Allee
Glacisstrasse
Harrachgasse
Zinzendorfgasse
Saurugasse
Erzherzog Johann Allee
Kaiser Franz Josef Kai
Mur
Lendkai
Kriegssteig
Sachstrasse
Schlossbergpl.
12
11
Murinsel
Mariahilfer-Strasse
Ellisabethstr.
Paulustorgasse
Sporgasse
Hofgasse
8
Burgtor
Burgring
Färbergasse
Luegg House
7
10
Glockenspielplatz
6
Bürgergasse
Burggasse
14
Kunsthaus **1**
Haupt-Brücke
Süd-tiroler-Platz
Murgasse
9
Rathaus
Stempfergasse
Neue-Welt-Gasse
Albrechtgasse
Landhaus
3
5
Herrengasse
Hans-Sachs-Gasse
Franziskanergasse
Tegetthoff-Brücke
Marburger Kai
Landhausgasse
2
Schmiedgasse
Raubergasse
4
Opernring
Frauengasse
Girardigasse
Belgiergasse
Glacisstrasse
Mandellstrasse
Schlögelgasse
Kalchberggasse
Neutorgasse
Kaiserfeldgasse
Gleisdorfergasse
Reitschulgasse
Radetzky-Brücke
Joanneumring
Jakoministrasse
Brückenkopfgasse
Radetzkystrasse
Jakominiplatz

300 yards
300 meters

9 Hauptplatz (*Main Square*). This triangular area was converted from a swampy pastureland to a town square by traveling merchants in 1164; it's used today as a lively open-air produce market. In its center stands the **Erzherzog Johann Brunnen** (Archduke Johann Fountain), dedicated to the popular 19th-century patron whose enlightened policies did much to develop Graz as a cultural and scientific center. The four female figures represent what were Styria's four main rivers; today only the Mur and the Enns are still within the province. The **Luegg House**, at the corner of Sporgasse, is noted for its Baroque stucco facade. On the west side of the square are Gothic and Renaissance houses. The spectacular, late-19th-century **Rathaus** (City Hall) totally dominates the south side. From the Neue-Welt-Gasse and Schmiedgasse you get a superb view of the Hauptplatz.

> ### GRAZ'S "BERMUDA TRIANGLE"
>
> Mehlplatz is lined with historic houses and has a number of bars. This is popularly known as the Bermuda Triangle, because the university students have such a good time here that they "never come out again." In summer it's perfect for sipping a beer or wine while watching the passing crowd.

11 Herberstein Palace. Another instance of old and new colliding magnificently in time-burnished Graz, this 17th-century former city residence of the ruling princes now houses the **Neue Galerie** (New Gallery), which features an array of temporary modern-art exhibitions of the newest trends in Styrian art. The permanent collection dates back to the 19th century, with works by such masters as Egon Schiele. ⊠ *Sackstrasse 16* ☎ *0316/829155* ⊕ *www.neuegalerie.at* 🎫 *€7. Ticket also valid on day of purchase for all other museums of Landesmuseum* ⊙ *Tues.–Sun. 10–6.*

1 Kunsthaus. Across the River Mur from the Altstadt is a new modern-art museum nicknamed the "Friendly Alien"—and indeed, it does look like an alien ship landed smack in the middle of the town's medieval orange-tile, gabled roofs. Designed by London-based architects Peter Cook and Colin Fournier, with an aim at forging an interaction between the traditional landmarks of Graz and the avant-garde, it resembles a gigantic blue beached whale with spiky tentacles—which light up at night. Inside, the vast exhibition rooms are linked by escalators and spiraling walkways, with an open arena at the top offering spectacular views. There is no permanent collection here, only temporary exhibits of renowned modern artists. ⊠ *Lendkai 1* ☎ *0316/8017–9200* ⊕ *www. kunsthausgraz.at* 🎫 *€7. Ticket also valid on day of purchase for all other museums of Landesmuseum* ⊙ *Tues.–Sun. 10–6.*

NEED A BREAK?

If you need a break after visiting Graz's many churches and museums, head to Murinsel island. It's actually not an island but a floating platform, designed by Modernist artist Vito Acconci in 2003 in honor of the city's designation as the European Capital of Culture. You can access it below the Kunsthaus, where a pedestrian walkway leads from the Haupt-Brucke bridge to the steel structure in the shape of a sea shell. Murinsel includes a trendy

café, amphitheater, and playground made of ropes. Mothers beware: your kids will love the ropes.

2 **Landesmuseum Joanneum.** The oldest public museum in Austria is a vast
★ complex. Its center is in Raubergasse, where its natural history collections are located. The holdings of the **Department of Geology and Paleontology** (☎ *0316/8017–9730*), which was founded in 1892, take you through 500 million years of Styrian geology. Shells and corals show that Styria was once a sea. Later fossils reveal its mammal inhabitants, now extinct. The **Mineralogy Collection** (☎ *0316/8017–9740*) contains more than 13,000 minerals collected in Styria. The **Department of Zoology** (☎ *0316/8017–9760*) includes more than 500,000 items and shows reconstructions of typical Styrian habitats with the animals that populate them. The **Botanic Collection** (☎ *0316/8017–9750*) was started by Archduke Johann. Since then, it has grown to include more than 400,000 dried specimens. The main focus of the collection is on ferns and flowering plants; there are no greenhouses or gardens. ⊠ *Raubergasse 10* ☎ *0316/8017–9660* ⊕ *www.museum-joanneum.at* ☑ *€7. Ticket also valid on day of purchase for all other museums of Landesmuseum* ☉ *Tues.–Sun. 10–6.*

4 **Landeszeughaus.** This provincial arsenal is possibly the most noted
☾ attraction in Graz. Virtually unchanged since it was built in 1643, the four-story armory still contains the 16th- and 17th-century weapons intended for use by Styrian mercenaries in fighting off the Turks. Nearly 30,000 items are on display, including more than 3,000 suits of armor (some of which are beautifully engraved), thousands of halberds, swords, firearms, cannons, and mortars. Probably the most important collection of its type in the world, the sheer quantity of displays can be daunting, so thankfully the most unusual items are highlighted, sometimes in striking displays. ⊠ *Herrengasse 16* ☎ *0316/8017–9810* ⊕ *www.zeughaus.at* ☑ *€7. Ticket is also valid on day of purchase for all other museums of Landesmuseum* ☉ *Tues.–Sun. 10–6.*

3 **Landhaus.** The Styrian provincial parliament house was built between 1557 and 1565 by Domenico dell'Allio in the Renaissance Lombard style. Its three-tier arcaded courtyard is magnificently proportioned and surrounds a 16th-century fountain that is an unusually fine example of old Styrian wrought-iron work. ⊠ *Herrengasse 16.*

10 **Palais Khuenburg.** This was the birthplace in 1863 of Archduke Franz Ferdinand, heir to the throne of the Austro-Hungarian Empire. His assassination at Sarajevo in 1914 led directly to the outbreak of World War I. The palace is now home to the **Stadtmuseum** (City Museum), whose exhibits trace the history of Graz and include an old-time pharmacy. ⊠ *Sackstrasse 18* ☎ *0316/822580* ☑ *€2* ☉ *Tues.–Sun. 10–6.*

13 **Schlossberg** (*Palace Mountain*). The view from the summit of Graz's midtown mountain takes in all of the city and much of central Styria. A zigzagging stone staircase beginning at Schlossbergplatz leads to the top, but since it's a 395-foot climb, you may prefer to use the **Schlossbergbahn** funicular railway (Kaiser-Franz-Josef-Kai 38) for €1.70, or an elevator, carved through the rock face, that leaves from Schlossbergplatz (€0.50; 8:30 AM–midnight). The defensive fortress, whose ramparts were built to prevent the invading Turks from marching up the Mur Valley toward Vienna, remained in place until 1809, when a victorious Napoléon had them dismantled after defeating the Austrians. The town paid a large ransom to preserve two of the castle's towers, but the rest was torn down and is today a well-manicured and popular park. Atop the Schlossberg and a few steps east of the funicular station is the **Glockenturm** (bell tower), an octagonal structure from 1588 containing Styria's largest bell, the famous 4-ton Liesl, in the upper belfry. It resounds three times daily (7, noon, and 7) with 101 chimes. The **Open-Air Theater,** just yards to the north, is built into the old casements of the castle and has a sliding roof in case of rain. Both opera and theater performances are presented here in summer. ☎0316/887–404 ✉€2 ⊗ Funicular May–Sept., daily 9 AM–midnight; Oct.–Apr., daily 10–10. Open-Air Theater Tues.–Sun. 10–6.

NEED A BREAK? At the top of the Schlossberg is **Aiola** (☎0316/818797), a tony café and bar serving drinks and light snacks. Relax under crisp, white, canvas umbrellas while sipping a glass of Styrian wine or coffee with all of Graz spread out below you.

⑭ **Schloss Eggenberg.** This 17th-century palace is on the very eastern edge of
Fodor'sChoice the city and is surrounded by a large deer park. Built around an arcaded
★ courtyard lined with antlers, this fine example of the high Baroque style contains the gorgeous **Prunkräume** (State Rooms) noted for their elaborate stucco decorations and frescoes. They can be visited on a guided tour only. The **Alte Galerie** (Old Gallery ☎0316/8017–9770) is a world-famous collection of art from the Middle Ages through the Baroque period. Among its treasures are works by Pieter Brueghel the Younger and both Hans and Lucas Cranach, the noted Admont Madonna wood carving from 1400, and a medieval altarpiece depicting the murder of Thomas à Becket. The **Abteilung für Vor- und Frühgeschichte** (Archaeological Museum) has a remarkable collection of Styrian archaeological finds, including the small and rather strange Strettweg Ritual Chariot dating from the 7th century BC. The **Münzensammlung** (Numismatic Museum) is tucked away in a corner on the ground floor. Styria's time as a Roman province is documented with artifacts in the **Provinzialrömische Sammlung** (Roman Provincial Collection). ■TIP→ The attractive outdoor café in the park that surrounds the castle is the perfect place to fortify yourself between museum visits. ⊠ Eggenberger Allee 90 ☎0316/583–264–9532 ✉€7. Ticket is also valid on day of purchase for all other museums of Landesmuseum. Deer park only, €1 ⊗ Tues.–Sun. 10–6. State room tours Apr.–Oct., Tues.–Sun. 10, 11, noon, 2, 3, and 4.

❺ **Stadtpfarrkirche.** The city parish church was built early in the 16th century, and later received its Baroque facade and 18th-century spire. Tintoretto's Assumption of the Virgin decorates the altar. Badly damaged in World War II, the stained-glass windows were replaced in 1953 by a Salzburg artist, Albert Birkle, who included portrayals of Hitler and Mussolini as malicious spectators at the scourging of Christ (left window behind the high altar, fourth panel from the bottom on the right). Across the street begins a narrow lane named after Johann Bernhard Fischer von Erlach, the great architect of the Austrian Baroque, who was born in one of the houses here in 1666. ⊠*Herrengasse 23* ☎*0316/829684–20* ⊙*Daily 7–7.*

⑫ **Uhrturm** *(Clock Tower).* This most famous landmark of Graz dates from the 16th century, though the clock mechanism is two centuries younger. The clock has four giant faces that might at first confuse you—until you realize that the *big* hands tell the hour and the *small* hands the minutes. At the time the clock was designed, this was thought to be easier to read at a distance. The 16th-century wooden parapet above the clock was once a post for firefighters, who kept a lookout on the city and sounded the alarm in case of fire.

WHERE TO EAT

$$$$ ✕**Grand Hotel Wiesler.** Dinner in the hotel's stylish and striking modern restaurant features one of the best and most daring menus in town—Austrian cooking with an international flair. No foodie should miss the spruce-needle melon sherbet, lamb chop on balsamic lentils, or rabbit with asparagus-orange risotto. Also noteworthy is the hearty breakfast buffet served in the elegant Grand Café, an Art Nouveau jewel; it offers salmon, ham, blackberry muffins and more for the reasonable price of €15 for nonhotel guests. The Jazz Brunch, held on Sundays from October through June, has become a real favorite, so early reservations are advised. ⊠ *Grieskai 4–8* ☎*0316/7066–0* ▭ *AE, DC, MC, V* ⊙*Closed Sun. except for Jazz Brunches.*

$$$–$$$$ ✕**Iohan.** A flickering torch marks the Renaissance portal entrance to this chic restaurant, set under a low vaulted ceiling and enhanced by dramatic lighting from wall sconces and candles. Start with a selection of fish on a skewer over a bed of mango rice and shiitake mushrooms, then go on to grilled salmon and sautéed greens, or veal with a light cheese crust and crisp shoestring potatoes. The homemade mango sherbet with coconut milk is sublime. Two or three times in summer the chef arranges a candlelight barbecue in the Renaissance courtyard. Reserve a table and you will not regret it. ⊠*Landhausgasse 1* ☎*0316/821312* ☞*Reservations essential* ▭*AE, DC, MC, V* ⊙*Closed Sun. and Mon. No lunch.*

$$–$$$ ✕**Hofkeller.** With its vaulted ceiling and dark, gleaming wainscoting, the
★ elegantly appointed Hofkeller offers the most innovative Italian cuisine in the city. The engaging waitstaff lets you linger over complimentary appetizers—Gaeta olives, cheese sticks, fresh-baked breads and a plate of Parma ham, which is thinly sliced before your eyes on a big oak table in the center of the room—before bringing the huge blackboard menu to your table. Look for the generous arugula salad with shaved Parmesan, pasta with salami and cherry tomatoes, and lightly fried John Dory atop a mound of grilled vegetables. Guests are invited to sample a wine before ordering by the glass. ⊠*Hofgasse 8* ☎*0316/832439* ▭*MC, V* ⊙*Closed Sun.*

$$–$$$ ✕**Landhauskeller.** The magnificent centuries-old Landhaus complex,
Fodor'sChoice which houses Graz's provincial parliament and its armory, also includes
★ a favorite traditional restaurant containing a labyrinth of charming

old-world dining rooms set within the ancient arcaded Landhaus itself. Weather permitting, try to get a table in the historic courtyard. Styrian beef is the main event here, but there are lots of other very tasty dishes to choose from, such as chicken breast in a sesame crust with herbed buttered noodles; *Kässpätzle,* little pasta dumplings in baked cheese with fried onions; and some very delicious fish dishes. ⊠*Schmiedgasse 9* ☎*0316/830276* ⊟*AE, DC, MC, V* ☉*Closed Sun. and late Dec.–mid-Jan.*

$$ ✕**Altsteirische Schmankerlstub'n.** Arguably the best place in the city to experience authentic Styrian cooking, this old Graz institution is reminiscent of a cozy country cottage. Salads are a must here, prepared with that Styrian specialty, *Kürbiskernöl,* pumpkinseed oil. Main courses include *Rinderschulterscherzl,* boiled beef with pumpkin puree and roasted potatoes, or chicken breast in a creamy herb sauce. A vegetarian menu, with choices like potato strudel with sour-cream dip and spaetzle sprinkled with leeks and cheese, is always offered. Often, every table in the Schmankerlstub'n is taken, so if you're alone, you may be asked if others could share your table. ⊠*Sackstrasse 10* ☎*0316/833211* ⊟*No credit cards.*

$$ ✕**Sacher.** Joining the expanding enterprise of Sacher cafés in Austria's most prominent cities, the Graz Sacher's imperious location at the junction of the Hauptplatz and Herrengasse lets you know it's *the* café in town. It's everything you would expect from a Sacher Café—lots of gilt, crimson upholstery, and sparking chandeliers, and Viennese dessert, including the rich chocolate Sachertorte. If you're hungry for a meal, there are breakfast and lunch specialties; try the Viennese plate, with several small Wiener Schnitzel made from different meats. In the adjoining Sacher Wein-Snackbar you can choose tasty snacks to blend with a full-bodied Austrian white wine or champagne. ⊠*Herrengasse 6* ☎*0316/8005–0* ⊟*AE, DC, MC, V* ☉*Closed Sun.*

¢–$ ✕**Mangolds Vollwertrestaurant.** In the block parallel to the Grand Hotel
★ Wiesler, this popular vegetarian restaurant offers tasty dishes served cafeteria-style. You can choose between at least five main courses, four salads, six desserts (including whole-grain cakes), freshly squeezed juices, two good wines, and five kinds of coffee—their *Eiskaffee mit Schlag* (iced coffee plus vanilla ice cream and whipped cream) is addictive. Very reasonable prices make this a place for the cost- and health-conscious, especially students and young families. ⊠*Griesgasse 11* ☎*0316/718002* ⊟*No credit cards* ☉*Closed Sun. No dinner Sat.*

WHERE TO STAY

$$$$ ⌖**Erzherzog Johann.** Travelers who prefer a traditionally elegant city
★ hotel will be happy with this historic establishment in a 16th-century building. It has a perfect location on the corner of the Hauptplatz in the Old City. Rooms are furnished charmingly, some in Biedermeier style, some with exotic themes and canopied beds in red or purple velvet. All rooms open onto a sunny atrium. The Wintergarden Restaurant, in the hotel's Baroque-style inner courtyard, serves lunch and dinner with an Italian accent; Café Erzherzog Johann is the perfect place for traditional Viennese pastries and coffee. **Pros:** perfect location; historical rooms; nice café; very helpful staff. **Cons:** parking in a public garage.

✉Sackstrasse 3–5 ☎0316/811616 🌐www.erzherzog-johann.com ⇒62 rooms ☝In-room: no a/c, Internet. In-hotel: 2 restaurants, bar, gym ⊙Restaurant closed 3 weeks in Aug., and Mon. and Tues. ▭AE, DC, MC, V 🍽CP.

$$$$ **Grand Hotel Wiesler.** With a supreme location just across the Mur River from the Old City, the Wiesler is the grande dame of Graz hotels. It dates from the turn of the last century, as evidenced by its high ceilings and gracious proportions, and the decoration has Secessionist echoes. The modern guest rooms are fetching with cherrywood accents, plush carpeting, and striking fabrics. Rooms facing the front have an exceptional view over the old town toward the Schlossberg. The breakfast served in the Grand Café is a real treat, and the fine-dining restaurant is not to be missed. Ask for weekend rates. **Pros:** spacious guest rooms with high ceilings; good restaurant. **Cons:** restaurant closed Sunday. *✉Grieskai 4–8 ☎0316/7066–0 🌐www.hotelwiesler.com ⇒98 rooms ☝In-hotel: 2 restaurants, bar, Wi-Fi, parking (fee), no-smoking rooms ▭AE, DC, MC, V 🍽EP.*

$$$$ ★ **Schlossberg Hotel.** This robin's-egg-blue town house tucked up against the foot of the Schlossberg was turned into a hotel in 1982. The owner's wife is an avid art collector, and the tastefully furnished rooms display provincial antiques as well as 18th-century portraits, while the corridors are filled with modern artworks and an interesting display of old Styrian lamps. The excellent breakfast in the pretty dining room will give you strength to follow the owner's suggestions for a great day of sightseeing. The outdoor pool, on a rocky terrace, offers a spectacular view of the city. **Pros:** tastefully furnished rooms; pool with a view. **Cons:** no restaurant. *✉Kaiser-Franz-Josef-Kai 30 ☎0316/8070–0 🌐www.schlossberg-hotel.at ⇒55 rooms ☝In-hotel: bar, pool, gym, Wi-Fi, parking (paid) ▭AE, DC, MC, V 🍽CP.*

$$$–$$$$ **Gollner.** A popular hotel since the mid-1800s and family-owned for four generations, the friendly Gollner is close to the Jakominiplatz and about a 10-minute walk from the Old City. Rooms are mostly contemporary in design, with soothing beige walls, soundproof windows, and plentiful space for toiletries in the bathrooms. More than half of Gollner's rooms are no-smoking, and there is no smoking allowed at breakfast. Sassy is the only word to describe the resident parrot. For families and longer stays, the Gollner offers apartments with fully equipped kitchens. Ask for weekend and special rates. **Pros:** family-owned property with personalized service. **Cons:** no restaurant; not in the center of town; some rooms need remodeling. *✉Schlögelgasse 14 ☎0316/822521–0 🌐www.hotelgollner.at ⇒50 rooms ☝In-room: no a/c, Wi-Fi. In-hotel: bar, Wi-Fi, parking (fee) ▭AE, DC, MC, V 🍽CP.*

$$$ **Augartenhotel.** A glass-and-chrome structure in the middle of a residential neighborhood, the Augarten is Graz's newest, chicest hotel. It is also a modern-art gallery (make sure to take the stairs instead of the elevator to view the art at each landing). The spacious guest rooms, all with terraces, are decorated with a cool, lean touch, yet offer the ultimate in luxury—heated wood floors, feather beds, and eye-catching, expensive fabrics. Want to go for a midnight swim in the heated indoor pool? No problem—all facilities are open 24 hours. Breakfast is

especially good, with extras like candlelight and fresh-squeezed orange juice. **Pros:** thoughtfully designed rooms; good food in adjacent restaurant. **Cons:** a bit cold feeling; not in the city center. ⊠*Schönaugasse 53* ☎*0316/20800* ⊕*www.augartenhotel.at* ⌁*56 rooms* ⌂*In-hotel: restaurant, bar, pool, gym, Internet terminal, parking (paid)* ⊟*AE, DC, MC, V* ¶○¶*CP.*

$$$ ⊞**Kirchenwirt.** An inn has stood on this lofty knoll since 1695, initially providing beds to those who made the pilgrimage to Mariatrost, the magnificent Rococo, daffodil-yellow basilica next door. Just 4 km (2.5 mi) northeast of Graz, the cheerful Kirchenwirt, now a Best Western hotel, is in the middle of the lushly rolling countryside. A charming exterior of yellow walls and green shutters gives way to modern, pleasant rooms with gorgeous vistas. The restaurant is truly outstanding; in fine weather you can enjoy a Wiener Schnitzel with beer or a fillet of perch with an Austrian wine served outdoors under huge chestnut trees. **Pros:** historic building with modern rooms. **Cons:** no elevator to lobby; no staff to carry heavy bags. ⊠*Kaiser-Franz-Josef-Kai 30* ☎*0316/391112–0* ⊕*www.kirchenwirtgraz.at* ⌁*55 rooms* ⌂*In-room: no a/c, refrigerator, Internet. In-hotel: restaurant, parking (free), no-smoking rooms* ⊟*AE, DC, MC, V* ¶○¶*CP.*

$$$ ⊞**Zum Dom.** Occupying the 18th-century Palais Inzaghi, the Dom has, hands down, the best location in Graz, smack in the center of the lively Altstadt. The high-ceiling rooms are whimsically decorated, some with eye-popping color combinations, and each door has its own delightfully grotesque figurehead. The hotel strives to indulge in the senses, and provides CD players and designer perfume to scent the room (a different fragrance in each). The rooftop suite has a Jacuzzi on a secluded terrace. **Pros:** great location; luxury in a historic building. **Cons:** baths on the small side; restaurant closed. ⊠*Bürgergasse 14* ☎*0316/824800* ⊕*www.domhotel.co.at* ⌁*28 rooms, 7 suites* ⌂*In-room: no a/c (some). In-hotel: bar, Wi-Fi, parking (fee)* ⊟*AE, DC, MC, V* ¶○¶*CP.*

$ ⊞**Mariahilf.** A comfortable hotel in the center of things, the Mariahilf is across the river from the Old City close to the Kunsthaus. Though the modern rooms are nothing fancy, the hotel is in a pedestrian zone, so the only noises you'll hear will be church bells and the sound of people hurrying to and fro. A tram stop is just steps away to take you to the city center, or you can cross one of the two nearby bridges and reach the Altstadt on foot after a short walk. **Pros:** quiet central location; modern rooms, good price. **Cons:** nondescript rooms; no restaurant. ⊠*Mariahilferstrasse 9* ☎*0316/713163* ⊕*www.hotelmariahilf. at* ⌁*44 rooms* ⌂*In-room: no a/c. In-hotel: Internet station, parking (fee)* ⊟*AE, DC, MC, V* ¶○¶*CP.*

¢ ⊞**Strasser.** This friendly budget hotel two blocks south of the main train station offers acceptable accommodations at rock-bottom prices—and your breakfast is included. The lobby is painted burnt-orange and crammed with leather chesterfields and bold paintings. The modern rooms are bright, clean and comfortable; showers are equipped with massage heads. Snacks are available round the clock from the café-bar. Credit cards are not accepted for stays of only one night. **Pros:** close to main station; good for limited budgets. **Cons:** small rooms; those facing the busy street are noisy; no restaurant. ⊠*Eggenberger Gürtel 11* ☎*0316/713977* ⊕*www.hotelstrasser.at* ⬐*40 rooms* ⬭*In-room: no a/c, no TV (some). In-hotel: parking (fee)* ⊟*AE, D, MC, V* |◎|*CP.*

NIGHTLIFE & THE ARTS

Graz is noted for its avant-garde theater and its opera, concerts, and jazz.

The **Styriarte** festival (late June to mid-July), under the direction of native son Nikolaus Harnoncourt—one of the most famous names in the early-music world—gathers outstanding musicians from around the world. Performances take place at the Helmut-List-Halle, with some at Schloss Eggenberg. Contact **Styriarte** (⊠ *Sackstrasse 17* ☎*0316/825000* ⊕*www.styriarte.com*).

A 19th-century opera house, the **Graz Opernhaus** (⊠*Kaiser-Josef-Platz 10* ☎*0316/8000* ⊕*www.buehnen-graz.com*), with its resplendent Rococo interior, is a showcase for young talent and experimental productions as well as more conventional works; it stages three to five performances a week during its late September–June season. Tickets are generally available until shortly before the performances; call for information.

Graz, a major university town, has a lively theater scene known especially for its experimental productions. Its **Schauspielhaus,** built in 1825, is the leading playhouse, and there are smaller theaters scattered around town. Contact the tourist office for current offerings.

Graz's **after-hours scene** is centered on the area around Prokopigasse, Bürgergasse, Mehlplatz, and Glockenspielplatz. Here you'll find activity until the early-morning hours.

The **Casino Graz** (⊠*Landhausgasse 10* ☎*0316/832578*), at the corner of Landhausgasse and Schmiedgasse in the Old City, is open daily from 3 PM. It offers French and American roulette, blackjack, baccarat, and punto banco. Entry is free, but you have to buy chips for €25 to get in. A passport is required, you must be at least 21, and men are expected to wear a jacket and tie, though it is not required.

SHOPPING

Graz is a smart, stylish city with great shopping. In the streets surrounding Hauptplatz and Herrengasse you'll find top designer boutiques and specialty shops. Be on the lookout for traditional skirts, trousers, jackets, and coats of gray and dark-green loden wool; dirndls; modern sportswear and ski equipment; handwoven garments; and objects of wrought iron. Take time to wander around the cobblestone streets of the Altstadt near the cathedral, where you'll come across several little specialty shops selling exotic coffees, wine, and cheese. The **Heimatwerk** shops at Paulustorgasse 4 and Herrengasse 10 are associated with the local folklore museum and stock a good variety of regional crafts and products. For a wide selection of wine and cheese, as well as hard-to-find Styrian cheese varieties, go to **Alles Käse,** at Paradeisgasse 1, near the Hauptplatz. The **English Bookshop** (⊠*Tummelplatz*

7 ☎*0316/826266*) is the only English-language bookstore in Graz, offering a great collection of current hardbacks as well as paperbacks and magazines.

STÜBING BEI GRAZ

☾ *15 km (9 mi) northwest of Graz.*

It's worth the ride to Stübing bei Graz to visit the **Austrian Open-Air Museum** *(Österreichisches Freilichtmuseum)*, which blankets some 100 acres of hilly woodland. A fascinating collection of about 80 authentic farmhouses, barns, Alpine huts, working water mills, forges, and other rural structures dating from the 16th century through the early 20th century has been moved to this site from seemingly every province of Austria. Buildings that otherwise would have been lost in the rush to "progress" have been preserved complete with their original furnishings. Most are open to visitors, and in several of them artisans can be seen at work, sometimes in period costume. There is a restaurant and outdoor café by the entrance. You can reach Stübing bei Graz by car from Graz via Route 67 to Gratkorn, by train (15 minutes) to Stübing and a 2-km (1½-mi) walk from there, or by municipal bus (40 minutes) from Lendplatz. ⊠*Stübing bei Graz* ☎*03124/53700* ⊕ *www.freilicht museum.at* ☒ *€8* ⊙*Apr.–Oct., Tues.–Sun. 9–5; last admission at 4.*

PIBER

44 km (27 mi) west of Graz.

★ The hamlet of Piber on the northeast outskirts of Köflach is devoted to
☾ raising horses. The world-famous stallions that perform at the Spanish Riding School in Vienna come from the **Lipizzaner Stud Farm.** These snow-white horses trace their lineage back to 1580, when Archduke Karl of Styria established a stud farm at Lipica, near Trieste, using stallions from Arabia and mares from Spain. After World War I, when Austria lost Lipica, the farm was transferred to the estate of Piber Castle (which can be seen when concerts are offered during the summer months). Born black, the steeds gradually turn white between the ages of two and seven. To get to Piber from Graz, follow Route 70 west or take a train to Köflach and then a railway bus to Piber. The whole trip takes about an hour. There is a fine and festive restaurant, the Spanish Caballero, on-site in the castle. ⊠*Bundesgestüt Piber* ☎*03144/3323* ⊕*www.piber.com* ☒*Tour €11* ⊙*Nov.–Mar., daily 11 and 3; Apr.– Oct., Tues.–Sun. 9–5:30; last entrance at 4.*

BÄRNBACH

33 km (21 mi) west of Graz, 3 km (2 mi) north of Voitsburg.

Bärnbach offers the amazing vision of the **Church of St. Barbara.** Completely redone in 1988 by the late Austrian painter and architect Friedensreich Hundertwasser, its exterior is a fantasy of abstract religious symbols

in brilliant colors and shapes. ✉ Kirchplatz ☎ 03142/62581 ⊕www.
kunsthauswien.com/english/st-barbara.htm 🎫Free.

At the interesting **Stölzle Glass Center** you can watch glassblowing
and purchase original glass articles. ✉Hochtregisterstrasse 1–3 ☎03142/
62950 ⊕www.stoelzle.com 🎫€5.50 ⊗May–Oct. weekdays 9–5, Sat.
9–1. Last admission 1 hr prior to closing.

STYRIA

3

The mountainous green heartland of the province of Styria (Steiermark) embraces a region where ancient Romans once worked the surrounding mines of what are accurately called the Iron Alps. Here the
atmosphere can change abruptly from industrial to tourist. The province's prime destination is Mariazell. In the past, royalty—not only
the Habsburgs but princes of foreign countries as well—traveled here
both for pleasure and for religious reasons, for Mariazell has a double
personality, as a summer and winter pleasure resort and as renowned
place of pilgrimage. The evening candlelight processions through the
village to its famed basilica are beautiful and inspiring. To tour this
region, head north from Graz, enjoying a scenic ride through the Mur
Valley to the historic crossroads of Bruck an der Mur. Here, where
several highways and rail lines converge, you can head north to Mariazell and then continue on one of the country's most scenic mountain
drives (or rail trips) back to the Danube Valley. The most direct route
from Bruck an der Mur northward to Vienna is also in some ways the
most interesting. It takes you through the cradle of Austrian skiing,
past several popular resorts, and over the scenic Semmering Pass, and
offers an opportunity to ride a 19th-century steam cogwheel train to
the top of the highest mountain in this part of the country, a peak that
often remains snowcapped into summer.

PEGGAU

20 km (12 mi) north of Graz.

Just north of the industrial town of Peggau is the famous **Lurgrotte,** the
largest cave in Austria. Guided tours lasting an hour follow a subterranean stream past illuminated sights, and there is a small restaurant
at the entrance. To get to Peggau from Graz, head north on Route 67,
driving through the heavily forested, narrow Mur Valley toward Bruck
an der Mur. (A rail line parallels the road, with trains every hour or two
making local stops near the points of interest. The rail stop for Lurgrotte is Peggau-Deutschfeistritz.) ☎03127/2580 ⊕www.lurgrotte.
com 🎫1-hr tour €5, 2-hr tour €8 ⊗Apr.–Oct., daily 9–4.

MIXNITZ

20 km (12 mi) north of Peggau.

Mixnitz is the starting point for a rugged 4½-hour hike through the wild **Bärenschützklamm**, a savage gorge that can be negotiated only on steps and ladders but is nevertheless worth visiting for its spectacular foaming waterfalls. Beyond it are peaceful mountain meadows and finally the 5,650-foot Hochlantsch mountain.

BRUCK AN DER MUR

15 km (10 mi) north of Mixnitz, 55 km (34 mi) north of Graz.

Bruck an der Mur is known primarily as Styria's major traffic junction, a point where four valleys and two rivers converge and where several highways and main rail lines come together. Although most of the busy town is devoted to industry, its compact historic center, dating partially from the 13th century, is well worth a short visit.

ESSENTIALS

Tourist Information (⊠ *Koloman-Wallisch-Platz 1* ☎ *03862/890–121* ⊕ *www.bruckmur.at/wirtschaft/u1194.htm*).

EXPLORING

The architecturally distinguished main square, **Koloman-Wallisch-Platz,** is four blocks west of the train station.

On the square's northeast corner stands the late-15th-century **Kornmesserhaus,** a magnificent example of secular architecture in the late-Gothic style, noted especially for its elaborate loggia and arcades.

The filigreed **Eiserner Brunnen** is across the square. This ornamental wrought-iron well housing dating from 1620 is considered to be the best piece of ironwork in Styria, a province noted for fine metalwork.

On the hill behind the square is the **Pfarrkirche** (*Parish Church*), built between the 13th and 15th centuries, which has an interesting late-Gothic sacristy door of wrought iron.

Overlooking the town, two blocks northeast of its center, are the remains of **Burg Landskron,** a 13th-century fortress that once defended the confluence of the Mur and Mürz rivers. Today only its clock tower remains intact, but the view is worth the short climb. The small park surrounding the Landskron ruins, on the Schlossberg hill, makes a wonderful spot for a picnic. Buy your supplies at one of the shops in the streets below.

MARIAZELL

Fodor'sChoice *50 km (29 mi) north of Bruck an der Mur.*
★
An excursion to Mariazell—famed for its pilgrimage church and gingerbread—is an adventure, thanks to the winding road that brings you to this Alpine region of northern Styria. The town has been a place

of pilgrimage since 1157, when the Benedictines established a priory here. After Louis I, king of Hungary, attributed his victory over the Turks in 1377 to the intervention of its Virgin, Mariazell's reputation for miracles began to spread. As a year-round resort, Mariazell offers a wide panoply of sports and recreation; in winter there's a good ski school for beginners and young people.

ESSENTIALS

Tourist Information **Mariazell Tourismusverband** (⊠ *Hauptplatz 13* ☎ *03882/2366* 🖷 *03882/3945*).

EXPLORING

The impressive **Mariazeller Basilica** stands resolutely over the town square. The present structure replaced the original church during the 14th century and was itself enlarged in the late 17th century by the Italian architect Domenico Sciassia. Its exterior is unusual, with the original Gothic spire and porch flanked by squat, bulbous Baroque towers. Step inside to see the elaborate plasterwork and paintings. In the **Gnadenkapelle** (Chapel of Miracles), the nave holds the main object of pilgrimage: the 12th-century statue of the Virgin of Mariazell. It stands under a silver baldachin (canopy) designed in 1727 by the younger Fischer von Erlach and behind a silver grille donated by Empress Maria Theresa, who took her first communion here. Don't miss the **Schatzkammer** (treasury) for its collection of votive offerings from medieval times to the present. 🖾 *Basilica free, Schatzkammer €3* 🕓 *Schatzkammer May–Oct., Tues.–Sat. 10–3, Sun. 11–4.*

Pay a visit to the **Heimatmuseum** (*Regional Museum of Local Life* ⊠ *Wienerstrasse 35* ☎ *03382/236*).

Bruno Habertheuer's **mechanical Nativity figurines** are at the **stations of the cross** (⊠ *Kalvarienberg 1*) on Calvary Hill. The nativity scene with its 130 moving figures took 18 years to build. Admission to the museum is €3.50.

🕄 The **Museumtramway,** the world's oldest steam tramway, dating from 1884, operates between Mariazell and the Erlaufsee, for a 20-minute ride of about 3½ km (2 mi) to a lovely lake. ■TIP➔ **For €10 extra, you can accompany the engineer in the cab.** ⊠ *Bahnhof Mariazell* ☎ *03882/3014* 🖾 *Round-trip €8* 🕓 *July–Sept., weekends 10–5.*

The famous narrow-gauge **Mariazellerbahn** rail line ambles over an 84-km (52½ mi) route between Mariazell and St. Pölten, coursing through magnificent valleys and surmounting mountain passes in the process. This remarkable engineering achievement—the line incorporates 21 tunnels and 75 bridges and viaducts—was built in 1907 and electrified in 1911. The cars are modern but the sensation is one of ages long past. About five trains a day traverse the route in each direction. In St. Pölten, the narrow-gauge line connects with the main east–west rail route. For schedules, contact the Tourist Office (☎ *03882/2366).*

WHERE TO STAY

$$ ⊡**Alpenhotel Gösing.** A breathtaking Alpine road leads to this gabled
★ early-20th-century hotel, which looks like it was the setting for Alfred
Hitchcock's *The Lady Vanishes.* There is nothing up here except the
hotel, a story-book train station, the woods with hiking trails, and gor-
geous scenery. The spacious, *gemütlich* lobby with its cozy groupings of
chintz-covered chairs and sofas is the perfect place to relax with a book
and a cup of tea. The charming rooms have cheery floral curtains and
duvets in pastel shades. Ask for one with a panoramic balcony facing
Ötscher mountain. Half-pension is optional, but the remote location
doesn't give you much choice. **Pros:** perfect for nature enthusiasts and
people who want to get away from it all. **Cons:** Remote. ⊠ *Gösing
an der Mariazellerbahn* ☎ *02728/217* ⊕ *www.goesing.at* ⇦ *74 rooms*
⚿ *In-room: no a/c. In-hotel: restaurant, bar, pool, gym, Wi-Fi* ⊟ *DC,
MC, V* ⦿ *CP.*

SPORTS

The skiing on 4,150-foot **Bürgeralpe** is quickly reached by the Bürg-
eralpebahn cable car from a lower station just two blocks north of
the basilica. Paths from the upper station fan out in several directions
for country walks in summer. ⊠ *Wienerstrasse 28* ☎ *03882/2555*
⊟ *Round-trip €13.30* ⊙ *Daily 9–5.*

SHOPPING

Parts of town are permeated by the spicy aroma of baking **gingerbread,**
for which Mariazell is famous, and you'll see the decorated cookies
everywhere.

MÜRZZUSCHLAG

*37 km (23 mi) northeast of Bruck an der Mur, 92 km (57 mi) north
of Graz.*

The resort town of Mürzzuschlag is popular with the Viennese for both
winter and summer sports. From Bruck an der Mur, head northeast on
S6, past the industrial town of Kapfenberg, and take the exit marked
for the resort. It is regarded as the birthplace of Austrian skiing and, in
a sense, of the Winter Olympics, since the first Nordic Games were held
here in 1904, but the main focus of ski activity has long since moved
west to the Tirol.

Mürzzuschlag preserves its past glories in the excellent **Winter-Sports-
Museum,** which displays equipment past and present from around the
world. Film clips will lead you across glaciers and capture an avalanche
thundering into the valley; you can be a virtual participant in an ice-
hockey match or downhill ski race. A brochure with explanations in Eng-
lish is available at the reception desk. ⊠ *Wienerstrasse 13* ☎ *03852/3504*
⊕ *www.wintersportmuseum.com* ⊠ *€5* ⊙ *Tues.–Sun. 10–5.*

The **Brahms Museum,** Austria's only museum dedicated to composer
Johannes Brahms, a German who adopted Austria as his home, is in
Mürzzuschlag, where he spent many summers. He spent two of them in
this house, which now also hosts chamber music concerts and recitals.

✉ *Wienerstrasse 4* ☎ *03852/3434* ⊕ *www.brahmsmuseum.at* 💶 *€4* ☺ *Daily 10–noon and 2–5.*

SEMMERING

★ *14 km (8½ mi) northeast of Mürzzuschlag, 90 km (56¼ mi) southwest of Vienna.*

Climbing along Route 306, high atop the Semmering Pass, at a height of 3,230 feet, lies the boundary between the provinces of Styria and Lower Austria. A bridle path has existed on this mountainous route since at least the 12th century, and the first road was built in 1728. Today's highway is an engineering wonder, particularly on the Lower Austrian side, where the road, high on concrete stilts, leaps over deep valleys; the old road snakes up in a series of switchback curves. The Styrian side is less dramatic, but offers distant Alpine vistas. Given the technologies of the era, the railway—completed in 1854—that crosses the divide is a technical marvel, with its great viaducts and tunnels, and is still the main north–south rail route. At the top is Semmering, the first town in Lower Austria, a resort on a south-facing slope overlooking the pass. Sheltered by pine forests and built on terraces reaching as high as 4,250 feet, Semmering is considered to have a healthy atmosphere and has several spa-type hotels and pensions. In the early 20th century Sigmund Freud, Oskar Kokoschka, Arthur Schnitzler, and Gustav Mahler were frequent visitors. Wealthy Viennese also came here for their *Sommerfrische* (summer vacation), and many built grand villas for the purpose, whose exteriors you can admire.

The Semmering area plus the nearby Rax and Schneeberg regions are where most Viennese first learn to ski, meaning that there are slopes ranging from gentle inclines to the more challenging, although they are no match for the rugged Alpine stretches of Tirol and Salzburg province.

OFF THE BEATEN PATH

Höllental. A delightful side trip can be made from Semmering into the Höllental (Valley of Hell), an extremely narrow and romantic gorge cut by the Schwarza stream between two high mountains, the Raxalpe and the Schneeberg. From Hirschwang, at the beginning of the valley, you can ride the **Raxbahn cable car** to a plateau on the Raxalpe at 5,075 feet. ☎ *02666/52497* 💶 *Round-trip €17* ☺ *Mid-May–Sept., weekdays 8–5; Oct.–mid-May weekdays 9–4.*

WHERE TO STAY

$$$–$$$$ 🏨 **Hotel Panhans.** Built in 1888, this classic and popular mountain-lodge
★   resort is near the center of town. The main lodge has retained its characteristic Art Nouveau ambience, while a luxurious modern annex is connected by an enclosed walkway to the main building. Rooms are quite large, some with faux French Empire furniture and others with alcove-equipped sleeping areas and a Jugendstil slant. A few rooms offer balconies, but all have spectacular views. Poached char in a crayfish-butter sauce with cilantro noodles and crispy duck breast with leek ravioli are among the entrées at the elegant Wintergarten restaurant. Wines are excellent, and the hotel's vinothek offers tastings. **Pros:** ame-

nities of modern grand hotel; huge lobby setting you back 100 years. **Cons:** faded glory of the beginning of the 20th century. ⊠*Hochstrasse 32* ☎*02664/8181–0* ⊕*www.panhans.at* ⬎*113 rooms* &*In-room: no a/c. In-hotel: 2 restaurants, bar, pool, gym, spa, Wi-Fi*⊟*AE, DC, MC, V* ⦿|*CP.*

$$$ ▦**Panoramahotel Wagner.** One of a handful of "bio" (ecologically
★ friendly) hotels in Austria, this unique family-owned establishment offers modern rooms with beech-wood floors, attractive unbleached fabrics, clean-lined furniture entirely free of nails, and balconies with panoramic views. Walls are a serene sea green or butterscotch. Baths are state-of-the-art, with temperature-controlled showers and heated towel racks. Dedicated owner Josef Wagner is also the chef, and his delicious buffet dinners are a tribute to the organic produce of the area. The hotel is no-smoking. **Pros:** wonderful views; friendly staff makes you feel at home; heaven for any "health freak." **Cons:** too far to walk to town; "modern-health-bohemian" atmosphere. ⊠*Hochstrasse 267* ☎*02664/2512–0* ⊕*www.panoramahotel-wagner.at* ⬎*24 rooms* &*In-room: no a/c, no TV. In-hotel: restaurant* ⊟*MC, V* ⊗*Closed various wks in Nov. and Apr.* ⦿|*CP.*

PUCHBERG AM SCHNEEBERG

33 km (21 mi) north of Semmering.

People flock to the quiet mountain resort of Puchberg am Schneeberg mostly to ride to the top of the Schneeberg mountain, Lower Austria's highest peak. From Vienna, the railroads have a package ticket that includes the regular rail connection, the cog railway, and a chit for lunch at one of the mountaintop restaurants. Trains also serve Puchberg from Wiener Neustadt. During a hot spell, the cooler mountain air is a relief.

EXPLORING

Ⓒ The marvelous old narrow-gauge **Puchberg cog-wheel steam train** ascends to a plateau near Schneeberg's summit on weekends in summer. Allow the better part of a day for this trip, since the ride takes nearly 90 minutes each way. ▪**TIP➡ This excursion is very popular; make reservations well in advance—particularly during holidays—at any rail station in Europe.** If you haven't already made them, be sure to make reservations at Puchberg for the return trip before you board for the trip up. Bring along a light sweater or jacket even in summer; it can be both windy and cool at the top. On weekdays the diesel train **Salamander** makes the trip (and at a faster pace).

The steam engines, dating from the 1890s, are built at a peculiar angle to the ground to keep their fireboxes level while climbing. The wooden cars they haul are of equal vintage, with hard seats. Near the upper station hut at an altitude of 5,892 feet are the small **Elizabeth Chapel** and the **Berghaus Hochschneeberg**, a simple lodge with a restaurant and overnight guest facilities. From here, you can walk to the **Kaiserstein** for a panoramic view and to the **Klosterwappen** peak, at 6,811 feet.

Allow about two to three hours total for these walks. Maps are available at the lodge. Real stick-to-your-ribs mountain food, draft beer, and plenty of gemütlichkeit are served up at the inexpensive **Damböck Haus**, a rustic hut operated by the Austrian Touring Club (ÖTK). It's only a 15-minute walk from the upper station of the Puchberg line. ⊠*Schneeberg Bahn, Bahnhof Puchberg* ☎*02636/3661–20* ⊕*www.schneebergbahn.at* ✉*Salamander diesel train, round-trip €28, cogwheel steam train surcharge €7* ☉*Cog-wheel steam train, late June–early Sept., weekends; Salamander diesel train, late Apr.–early Nov.* ☞*Call or see Web site for exact schedules.*

⟳ Don't miss a drive along the **Hohe Wand** *(High Wall)*, a scenic nature park east of Puchberg (from Puchberg, go east past Grünbach to Oberhöflein, where you turn left at the sign for Hohe Wand). The spectacular route has many twists and turns leading to the limestone plateau, and there are several simple country inns along the way that provide good bases for hiking. The 4-km (2½-mi) road ends at the top at Kleine Kanzel in the west and Herrgottschnitzerhaus in the east, so you must retrace your route down along the Panoramastrasse, unless you're mountain biking or hiking.

Also worth a visit is the **Heimatmuseum** (open mid-April to mid-September, on Saturday 3–5 and Sunday 9:30–11:30 and 3–5), with displays of local artifacts.

WHERE TO STAY

$$–$$$ 🏨**Schneeberghof.** Not far from the train station is this 100-year-old
★ chalet-hotel with a modern annex and a spacious indoor pool, all set within a small park. Rooms are large, with contemporary furnishings and pastel fabrics, and all have balconies. The restaurant serves a selection of delicious fish and meat dishes, including grilled *Welsfilet* (catfish) and pork medallions in a honey-herb sauce. In the evening you can relax with a good Austrian wine or a stronger drink at the pleasant and well-stocked bar. The year-round special weekend offers are a great value. **Pros:** pretty setting; all the amenities of a modern seminar hotel. **Cons:** the charm and clientele of a modern seminar hotel. ⊠*Wiener Neustädterstrasse 24* ☎*02636/3500* ⊕*www.schneeberghof.com* ➳*74 rooms* ♿*In-room: no a/c. In-hotel: restaurant, bar, tennis courts, pool, gym, Wi-Fi* ▤*AE, DC, MC, V* ⫴*CP.*

The Danube Valley

WORD OF MOUTH

"You may want to look into the Wachau Valley. It takes just about an hour via car to reach Melk from Linz. The Wachau Valley is gorgeous. In addition to the magnificent abbey in Melk, you could easily rent bikes and bike along the Danube. We did this a few years ago, stopping in little towns to taste wine and schnapps, and it made for a wonderful day. there is a nice, relatively flat bike path. I would skip Linz if possible. It definitely looks more industrial than touristy!"

—tcreath

Updated by
Diane Naar-
Elphee

A TRIP ALONG THE AUSTRIAN Danube unfolds like a treasured picture book. Roman ruins (some dating to Emperor Claudius), remains of medieval castles-in-air, and Baroque monasteries with "candle-snuffer" cupolas perching precariously above the river stimulate the imagination with their historic legends and myths. This is where Isa—cousin of the Lorelei—lured sailors onto the shoals; where the Nibelungs—later immortalized by Wagner—caroused operatically in battlemented forts; and where Richard the Lion-Hearted was locked in a dungeon for a spell. Today, thanks to the technology of modern dams, travelers have the luxury of tamely observing this part of Austria from the deck of a comfortable river steamer. In clement weather the nine-hour trip upriver from Vienna to Linz is highly rewarding. If your schedule allows, continuing onward to Passau may be less dramatic but gives more time to take in the picturesque vineyards and the castles perched on crags overlooking the river.

Even more of the region's attractions can be discovered if you travel by car. Climb Romanesque towers, explore plunging Gothic streets, then linger over a glass of wine in a Weinkeller. Many visitors classify this as one of Europe's great trips: you feel you can almost reach out and touch the passing towns and soak up the intimacy unique to this stretch of the valley.

ORIENTATION & PLANNING

GETTING ORIENTED

This chapter follows the course of the Danube upstream from Vienna as it winds through Lower Austria (Niederösterreich) and a bit of Upper Austria (Oberösterreich) to Linz, on the way passing monasteries and industrial towns, the riverside vineyards of the lower Weinviertel, and fragrant expanses of apricot and apple orchards.

It is, however, the Danube itself, originating in Germany's Black Forest and emptying into the Black Sea, that is this chapter's focal point. The route that brought the Romans to the area and contributed to its development remains one of Europe's most important waterways, with four national capitals on its banks—Vienna, Bratislava, Budapest, and Belgrade. The expression "Whoever controls the Danube controls all Europe" is attributed to the Romans, but the Kuenringer (robber knights who built many of the hilltop castles) followed suit, thriving by sacking the baggage caravans of the early Crusaders. With the passing of time, castles came to be financed through somewhat more commercial means—Frederick Barbarossa, leading his army downstream, had to pay a crossing toll at Mauthausen. Subsequently, settlements evolved into ports for the salt, wood, ores, and other cargo transported on the river, and today modern railroads and highways parallel most of the blue Danube's course.

The Wachau: Along the North Bank of the Danube. Dürnstein, Krems, and many other small medieval towns offer a peaceful respite to the wandering traveler. Wine taverns abound and good home cooking in quaint restaurants is a perfect way to end the day.

TOP REASONS TO GO

The Melk Abbey. Magnificent Benedictine Baroque splendor leaves you breathless. The enormous edifice, stately royal rooms, lovely library, and golden, glittering church are incomparable.

Dürnstein. Meander down medieval cobbled lanes and take a seat in a vine-adorned courtyard to admire terrific views of the Danube and hills while sipping a glass of the best wine.

Linz. As the saying goes, "It begins in Linz." Designated the Cultural Capital of Europe 2009, the capital of the province of Upper Austria has awakened to a new future, taking a leading role in contemporary art, style, and design.

Wachau Valley. Travel in tranquillity by boat or bike between the historic towns of Krems and Melk and experience the Danube Valley's most picturesque and verdant vistas.

Kreuzenstein Castle. This huge fairy-tale fortress perched on a hill, complete with ramparts, armory, torture chamber, and kitchen, takes you back in time to the Middle Ages.

Linz. The 2009 European cultural capital basks in amazing cutting-edge design. Experience exciting insights into modern day's latest technology at one of the incredible museums.

Excursions from Linz. Leave Upper Austria's busy capital to discover the quiet rural countryside, 1,000-year-old monasteries, and other hidden treasures along the way.

The Wachau: Along the South Bank of the Danube. Travel through picturesque vineyards and orchards to the mighty Melk Abbey. Pass by ruins of old castles, or stop and hike through the woods for a closer look at the remnants. The views across the Danube will reward you for your toil.

PLANNING

WHEN TO GO

This glorious landscape becomes fairy-tale-like when apricot and apple trees are in bursting blossom, late April to mid-May. One of the best ways to discover the region is to take a bike ride alongside the blossoming orchards and the bright-orange poppy fields.

Others might prefer the early- to mid-autumn days, when the vineyards on the terraced hills turn reddish-blue and a bracing chill settles over the Danube. From mid-September till the beginning of October the Bruckner Festival in Linz joins forces with Ars Electronica and Klangwolke to combine the classic with the contemporary.

Throughout the region, winter can be drab. Seasons notwithstanding, crowds jam the celebrated abbey at Melk; you're best off going first thing in the morning, before the tour buses arrive, or at midday, when the throngs have receded.

No matter when you come, be sure to try some fruits in a Linzertorte (a filling of brandy-flavored apricots, raspberries, or plums under a latticed pastry crust), a treat as rich and satisfying as the scenic wonders of the Danube Valley itself.

GETTING HERE & AROUND

The easiest way of getting around the area is by car. Train and bus travel requires more planning. Timetables change from season to season (be sure to check for the latest update), and connections are not always favorable. Local trains that stop in every station take a long time to get anywhere, but if you have a lot of time to spare, train rides can be fun.

BY AIR   The Blue Danube Airport Linz is a good alternative to Vienna's Schwechat Airport if you want to start your journey in calmer surroundings. Located just 15 minutes from the city center by car or train, the airport is serviced regularly by Lufthansa, Austrian Airlines, and several low-cost airlines.

BY BOAT   You can take a day trip by boat from Vienna or Krems and explore one of the stops, such as Dürnstein or Melk. Boats run from May to late September. There are two boat companies that ply the Danube. ⇨ *For full information on cruises offered by the Blue Danube Schifffahrt/DDSG (Vienna to Dürnstein) and Brandner Schifffahrt (Krems to Melk), see Danube River Cruises elsewhere in this chapter. Along this stretch of the river, bridges are few and far between.* Old-fashioned tow ferries, attached to cables stretched across the river, allow a speedy crossing for people, cars, and bikes for a small fee and available upon request.

BY BUS   If you link them together, bus routes will get you to the main points in this region and even to the hilltop castles and monasteries, assuming you have the time. If you coordinate your schedule to arrive at a point by train or boat, you can usually make reasonable bus connections to outlying destinations. The main bus route links Krems and Melk. You can book bus tours in Vienna or Linz by calling central bus information, listed below.

Bus Information Central bus information (☎ 01/71101).

BY CAR   Driving is certainly the most comfortable way to see this region, as it conveniently enables you to pursue the byways. The main route along the north bank of the Danube is Route 3; along the south bank, there's a choice between the autobahn Route A1 and a collection of lesser but good roads. Roads are good and well marked, and you can switch over to the A1 autobahn, which parallels the general east–west course of the Danube Valley route. Car rental is best in Vienna or Linz.

BY TRAIN   Fast services from Vienna run as far as Stockerau; beyond that, service is less frequent. Rail lines parallel the north and south banks of the Danube, and while trains reach all the larger towns and cities in the region, they miss the smaller towns of the Wachau Valley along the Danube's south bank. You can combine rail and boat transportation along this route, taking the train upstream and crisscrossing your way back on the river.

Train Information ÖBB—Österreichisches Bundesbahn (☎ 05/1717).

GREAT ITINERARIES

IF YOU HAVE 3 DAYS

Start out early from Vienna, planning for a stop to explore the medieval center and contemporary art world of **Krems** along the northern side of the Danube. You can opt to spend a night in a former cloister, now the elegant Richard Löwenherz hotel, in ⛪**Dürnstein**, probably the most famous, if not prettiest, town of the Danube Valley. Here you'll find the ruined castle where Richard the Lion-Hearted was imprisoned—an early-morning climb up to the ruin or a jog along the Danube shoreline will reward you with great views. Take time to explore enchanting Dürnstein before heading west along the Danube, crossing over to ⛪**Melk**, one of the greatest abbeys in Europe. This is High Baroque at its most glorious. Follow the river road back east to ⛪**Göttweig** and have lunch on the terrace at the abbey. The abbey's 17th-century chapel is breathtaking. Continuing eastward, follow the river as closely as possible (signs indicate Zwentendorf and Tulln) to **Klosterneuburg**, the imposing abbey that was once the seat of the powerful Babenburger rulers, and onward to Vienna.

IF YOU HAVE 5 DAYS

A more leisurely schedule would follow the same basic route but permit a visit at either the fairy-tale castle of Burg Kreuzenstein, near **Korneuburg** or the more staid and mammoth castle of **Schloss Grafenegg,** near **Haitzendorf,** before stopping in attractive **Krems** to tour its "Kunstmeile" (art mile) and then overnighting in ⛪**Dürnstein**. Spend the morning exploring Dürnstein, including the colorfully restored Baroque Stiftskirche. In the afternoon, discover the wine villages of **Weissenkirchen** and **Spitz**. Plan on two overnights in the capital city of the region, ⛪**Linz,** to tour the entire city. On Day 4 take in the spectacular abbey of **St. Florian** (where composer Anton Bruckner spent a good deal of time) and the palatial halls of the abbey at **Kremsmünster,** both southeast of Linz and south of the Danube; then proceed east to the grandest abbey of all, ⛪**Melk**. The fifth day will be full, but start with the Melk abbey, then continue east to the religious complex at **Göttweig** and move onward to the abbey at **Klosterneuburg.**

TOURS Tours out of Vienna take you to Melk and back by bus and boat. Companies include Cityrama and Vienna Sightseeing Tours. These tours usually run about eight hours, with a stop at Dürnstein. Bus tours operate year-round except as noted, but the boat runs only April–October.

Contacts Cityrama Sightseeing (✉ *Börsegasse 1* ☎ *01/534–130*). **Vienna Sightseeing Tours** (✉ *Graf Starhemberggasse 25* ☎ *01/712–4683–0* ⊕ *www.viennasightseeingtours.com*).

VISITOR INFORMATION

For general information on the area, check with the district tourist offices: Lower Austria, Upper Austria, Linz, Mühlviertel, and Wachau. In Linz you can pick up the latest *Guests Magazine* in English as well as

German. Most towns have a local *Fremdenverkehrsamt* (tourist office); these are listed below, under each town.

Tourist Information Lower Austria (⊠ *Niederösterreich Werbung GmbH, Fischhof 3/3, Vienna* ☎ *01/53610–6200*). **Upper Austria** (⊠ *Freistaedter Strasse 119, Linz* ☎ *0732/221022* ⊕ *www.oberoesterreich.at*). **Wachau** (⊠ *Schlossgasse 3, Spitz an der Donau* ☎ *02713/300–6015* ⊕ *www.wachau.at*). **Waidhofen an der Ybbs** (⊠ *Freisingerberg 2* ☎ *07442/511255* ⊕ *www.waidhofen.at*).

ABOUT THE RESTAURANTS & HOTELS

Wherever possible, restaurants make the most of the river view, and alfresco dining overlooking the Danube is one of the region's delights. Simple *Gasthäuser* are everywhere, but better dining is more often found in country inns. Restaurants, whether sophisticated and stylish or plain and homey, are often rated by their wine offerings as much as by their chefs' creations. In some of the smaller villages you can sample the vintner's successes right on the spot in his cellars.

Accommodation options range from castle-hotels, where you'll be treated like royalty, to quiet and elegant country inns (often family-managed), to standard city hotels in Linz. The region is compact, so you can easily lodge in one place and drive to a nearby locale to try a different restaurant. Rates reflect the quality of service and amenities but usually include breakfast, which may range from a fast to a feast. Some hotels offer half-board, with dinner included in addition to buffet breakfast (although most $$$$ hotels charge extra for breakfast). The half-board room rate is usually an extra €15–€30 per person. Occasionally, quoted room rates for hotels already include half-board, though a "discounted" rate may be available if you prefer not to take the evening meal. Inquire about any pension food plans when booking. Room rates include taxes and service, and usually breakfast—although, again, always ask. In summer, nights are generally cool, but days can get uncomfortably hot. Most older hotels don't have air-conditioning, and rooms can get stuffy; whenever possible, see the room first before checking in.

WHAT IT COSTS IN EUROS				
	¢	$	$$	$$$	$$$$
RESTAURANTS	under €8	€8–€13	€14–€18	€19–€24	over €25
HOTELS	under €70	€70–€100	€100–€135	€135–€175	over €175

Restaurant prices are per person for a main course at dinner. Hotel prices are for a standard double room in high season, including taxes and service. Assume that hotels operate on the European Plan (EP, with no meal provided) unless we note that they use the Breakfast Plan (BP), Modified American Plan (MAP, with breakfast and dinner daily, known as halb pension), or Full American Plan (FAP, or voll pension, with three meals a day). Higher prices (inquire when booking) prevail for any meal plans.

THE WACHAU: ALONG THE NORTH BANK OF THE DANUBE

The loveliest stretches of the Danube's Austrian course run from the outskirts of Vienna, through the narrow defiles of the Wachau to the Nibelungengau—the region where the mystical race of dwarfs, the Nibelungs, are supposed to have settled, at least for a while. If you're taking the tour by train, take Streetcar 3 to Vienna's Franz Josef Bahnhof for your departure point. If you're driving, the trickiest part may be getting out of Vienna. Follow signs to Prague to get across the Danube, but once across, avoid the right-hand exit marked Prague—which leads to the autobahn—and continue ahead, following signs for Prager Strasse and turning left at the traffic light. Prager Strasse (Route 3) heads toward Langenzersdorf and Korneuburg.

4

KORNEUBURG

18 km (11¼ mi) northwest of Vienna.

Fodor's Choice ★ Castle lovers, prepare yourself. Seemingly lifted from the pages of a Germanic fairy tale, **Burg Kreuzenstein**, bristling with storybook turrets and towers, might have made Albrecht Dürer drop his sketch pad. Sitting atop a hillside 3 km (2 mi) beyond Korneuburg along Route 3, "Castle Cross-stone," in fact, is a 19th-century architectural fantasy built to conjure up "the last of the knights"—Emperor Maximilian I himself. Occupying the site of a previously destroyed fort, the enormous structure was built by Count Nepomuk Wilczek between 1879 and 1908 to house his collection of late-Gothic art objects and armor, including the "Brixner Cabinet" dating from 15th-century Salzburg. Using old elements and Gothic and Romanesque bits and pieces, the castle was carefully laid out according to the rules of yore, complete with a towering Burgtor, "kennel" corridor (where attackers would have been cornered), Gothic arcades, and tracery parapet walls. The Burghof courtyard, with its half-timbered facade and Baltic loggia, could be a stand-in for a stage set for Wagner's *Tannhäuser*. Inside, the medieval thrills continue with rooms full of armaments, a festival and banquet hall, a library, a stained-glass chapel (available for weddings), vassal kitchens, and the Narwalzahn, a room devoted to hunting trophies (if you've ever wanted to see a "unicorn horn," here's your chance).

A group of falconers keeps peregrine falcons and other birds of prey near the castle grounds. ■TIP➔ **Eagles and falcons take flight, hunt, and return to their trainer's arm with the catch at least twice a day, taking part in a sport that goes back nearly 4,000 years.** Shows, which run from April through October, are scheduled every day except Monday at 11 AM and 3 PM and on Sunday at 11 AM and 2 and 4 PM. Tickets cost €7.50 each.

It is possible to reach Kreuzenstein from Vienna via the suburban train (S-Bahn) to Leobendorf, followed by a ¾-hour hike up to the castle. Until recently, the town of Korneuburg was the center of Austrian shipbuilding, where river passenger ships, barges, and transfer cranes were built to order for Russia, among other customers. Stop for a look at the imposing

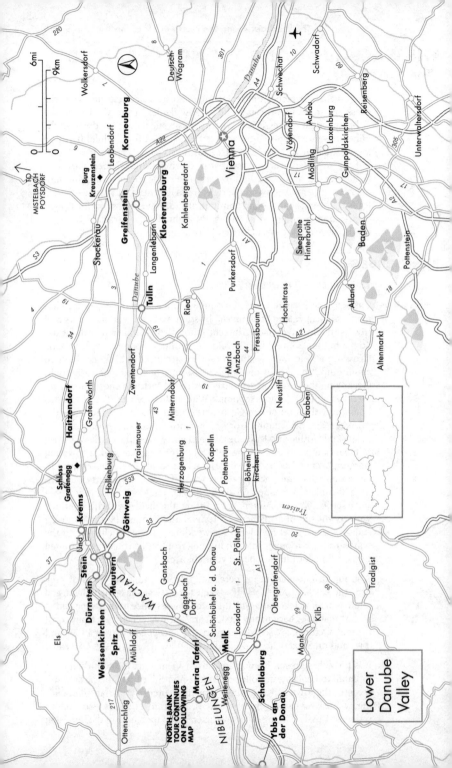

Lower Danube Valley

neo-Gothic city hall (1864), which dominates the central square and towers over the town. ✉*Leobendorf bei Korneuburg* ☎*0664–422–53–63, 01/283–0308 falconer* ⊕*www.kreuzenstein.com* 🎫*€8* ⊙*Mid-Mar.–Oct., Mon.–Sat. 10–4, Sun. 10–5; guided tour on hr.*

HAITZENDORF

51 km (38½ mi) west of Korneuburg.

The tiny farming community of Haitzendorf (to reach it from Korneuburg, take Route 3, 33 km [21 mi] past Stockerau, then turn right at Graftenwörth) is landmarked by a church dating from the 14th century. In early summer the vast strawberry fields surrounding the town yield a delicious harvest, which you can pick yourself.

★ A lush meadow and woodland area also surrounds the best-known site, **Schloss Grafenegg.** The moated Renaissance castle dating from 1533 was stormed by the Swedes in 1645 and rebuilt from 1840 to 1873 in the English Gothic Revival style, although its dominant feature is a gigantic central tower in the Bohemian style, complete with four mini-turrets like those of spooky Prague Castle. Greatly damaged during the 1945–55 occupation, the vast structure was extensively restored in the 1980s and has been owned for centuries by the Metternich-Sándor family. Inside, there's a Bibliothek (library), Rittersaal (Knights' Hall), and Wappenstube (coat of arms room). Look for such fascinating details as the gargoyle waterspouts, and don't miss the chapel. The outstanding Grafenegg Auditorium, which seats up to 1,300 people, and the extraordinary outdoor *Wolkenturm* (Cloud Tower) stage, are grand venues for the arts, particularly classical music. From late August to early September, these stages are home to an international festival of classical music, featuring performances by world-renowned musicians and the orchestra in residence, the Tonkünstler. ☎*02735/2205–17* ⊕*www.grafenegg.com* 🎫*€5* ⊙*Late Apr.–Oct., Tues.–Sun. 10–5.*

WHERE TO EAT

$$–$$$ ✕**Zur Traube.** Just past the manicured lawns of Schloss Grafenegg, this
★ elegant tavern was the beginning of the culinary empire founded by fiercely ambitious owner Toni Mörwald, and—after some near financial disasters—his sanctuary. The seasonal menu of classic Austrian dishes with a fresh slant may include Waldviertler duck with asparagus and *Schupfnudeln* (Austrian-style gnocchi), or grilled *Saiblingsfilet* (char) with tomato and zucchini risotto. Mörwald has his own winery and distillery, and a glass of his golden Gelbe Muskateller or sauvignon blanc provides the perfect accompaniment. He offers 10 different cooking-lesson programs and overnight packages in his four-star hotel-villa opposite. ✉*A-3485 Feuersbrunn* ☎*02738/2298–0* 🗋*AE, DC, MC, V.*

KREMS

★ *10 km (6 mi) west of Haitzendorf, 80 km (50 mi) northwest of Vienna.*

Krems marks the beginning (when traveling upstream) of the Wachau section of the Danube. The town is closely tied to Austrian history; here the ruling Babenbergs set up a dukedom in 1120, and the earliest Austrian coin was struck in 1130. In the Middle Ages Krems looked after the iron trade, while neighboring Stein traded in salt and wine, and over the years Krems became a center of culture and art. Today the area is the heart of a thriving wine-producing area, and Krems is most famed for the cobbled streets of its Altstadt (Old Town), which is virtually unchanged since the 18th century. The lower Old Town is an attractive pedestrian zone, while up a steep hill (a car can be handy) you'll find the upper Old Town, with its Renaissance Rathaus and a parish church that is one of the oldest in Lower Austria. Krems new Arts Mile boosts the contemporary cultural aspect of the area. It includes, besides galleries and eateries, the Karikaturmuseum; the Kunsthalle Krems; the brand new Frohner Museum, dedicated to the late Austrian graphic artist and painter; and the Lower Austria literature center.

ESSENTIALS

Tourist Information **Krems/Stein** (⊠ *Utzstrasse 1* ☎ *02732/82676* ⊕ *www. krems.at*).

EXPLORING

The **Karikaturmuseum** *(Caricature Museum)* houses more than 250 works of cartoon art from the 20th century to the present, including a large collection of English-language political satire and caricature. ⊠ *Steiner Landstrasse 3a* ☎ *02732/908020* ⊕ *www.karikaturmuseum. at* ☎ *€8* ⊙ *Daily 10–6.*

The **Kunsthalle Krems,** located in the old tobacco factory, concentrates on changing exhibits of art by known and unknown artists from the 19th to 21st centuries, for example, Joseph Beuys, and Duane Hanson. ⊠ *Franz-Zeller-Platz 3* ☎ *02732/908010* ⊕ *www.kunsthalle.at* ☎ *€9* ⊙ *Daily 10–6; Nov.–Mar. 10–5.*

A 14th-century former Dominican cloister now serves as the **Weinstadt Museum Krems,** a wine museum that holds occasional tastings. ⊠ *Körnermarkt 14* ☎ *02732/801-567* ⊕ *www.weinstadtmuseum.at* ☎ *€4* ⊙ *Mar.–Nov., Wed.–Sat. 10–6.*

WHERE TO STAY & EAT

$$–$$$ ✕ **Zum Kaiser von Österreich.** At this landmark in Krems's Old City district, you'll find excellent regional cuisine along with an outstanding wine selection (some of these vintages come from the backyard). The inside rooms are bright and pleasant, and the outside tables in summer are even more inviting. Owner-chef Haidinger, awarded a toque from Gault Millaut, learned his skills at Bacher, across the Danube in Mautern, so look for refined fish dishes along with specialties such as potato soup and roast shoulder of lamb with scalloped potatoes. He's also well known for creating mouthwatering savory and sweet

mozzarella dishes. Try the one with sour cherries. ⊠*Körnermarkt 9* ☎*02732/86001* 🖷*02732/86001–4* ♿*Reservations essential* ▭*AE, DC, V* ⊘*Closed Sun., Mon., and last 2 wks in July–1st wk in Aug.*

\$–\$\$ ✕**Jell.** In the heart of Krems's medieval Altstadt, this storybook stone cottage run by Ulli Amon-Jell (pronounced "Yell") is a cluster of cozy rooms with lace curtains, dark-wood banquettes, candlelight, and Biedermeier knickknacks on the walls. Wild-mushroom omelets with home-cured bacon or figs stuffed with Roquefort and ham are two examples of Ulli's delightful cooking. There are always fish and vegetarian dishes on the menu if you want something lighter, but the chef's motto is "None goes home hungry from my tavern." In summer book ahead for a table under the grape arbor in the small, secluded outdoor dining area. ⊠*Hoher Markt 8–9* ☎*02732/82345* ♿*Reservations essential* ▭*AE, DC, MC, V* ⊘*Closed Mon. and 1st 2 wks in July. No dinner weekends.*

\$–\$\$ ✕**M. Kunst. Genuss.** Strikingly minimalistic, cathedral-roofed and glass-
★ sided, this popular, hip museum café is located in the **Kunsthalle Krems,** which makes it ideal for a respite from sightseeing. It belongs to entrepreneur Toni Mörwald, who also owns Zur Traube in Haitzendorf; its name signifies "Mörwald, Art, and Pleasure." The international cuisine has a Mediterranean influence; look for the salad of field greens topped with a generous skirt steak, or the perfectly cooked wild salmon fillet with basmati rice and a profusion of colorful grilled vegetables. Wines from the adjacent cellars of Kloster Und are excellent. Service is without fault. ■**TIP**➔ **This is one of the few restaurants in the area open for lunch all day.** ⊠*Franz-Zeller-Platz 3* ☎*02732/908–0102–1* ▭*AE, DC, MC, V.*

\$\$\$ 🖫**Am Förthof.** Set back from the busy main road, with a large garden shaded by 200-year-old chestnut trees, this charming, romantic hotel has rooms done in tranquil, pale pastels with antique pieces. Those in front have views of the river and abbeys, whereas the back rooms overlook a swimming pool. The hotel was recently given a complete overhaul, and it now warrants its four-star ranking. Breakfast is a feast with fresh-baked *Wachauer Semmeln,* sweet strawberries, red currants, and apricots picked from the *Marillen* trees of the neighboring village of Stein. **Pros:** great location; gourmet cooking; free bikes for use. **Cons:** some rooms on the small side; rooms can get hot in summer. ⊠*Förthofer Donaulände 8* ☎*02732/83345* ⊕*www.gourmethotel-foerthof.at* 🖙*20 rooms* ♿*In-room: no a/c. In-hotel: restaurant, pool, Internet terminal, parking (free), no-smoking rooms* ▭*AE, DC, MC, V* ⊘*Closed Jan. and Feb.* ⊠❘*BP.*

¢–\$ 🖫**lte Post.** The oldest inn in Krems, for centuries the mail-route post-
★ house for the region, this hostelry is centered on an adorable Renaissance-style courtyard, which is topped with a flower-bedecked arcaded balcony and storybook mansard roof. If you're a guest here, you're allowed to drive into the pedestrian zone of the Old Town and pull up next to the Steinener Tor (Stone Gate) to find this inn. Rooms are comfortable and decor is pleasant country-style, but the real draw here is dining on regional specialties or sipping a glass of the local wine in the courtyard. The staff is friendly and cyclists are welcome. **Pros:** excellent restaurant; large portions. **Cons:** old-fashioned; some rooms have neither shower nor toilet and have to share facilities. ⊠*Obere Land-*

4

CLOSE UP

Grape Expectations

The epitome of Austrian viticulture is found in the Wachau, those few precious kilometers of terraced vineyards along the north bank of the Danube River. There are few pleasanter ways to spend an afternoon than to travel to the fabled wineries of the valley and sample the golden nectar coaxed from the vines. It's usually possible to stop in and meet the winemaker, who will be happy to pour you a taste from the latest vintage and share some of the secrets of the trade. A late-spring drive through the charming villages of Weissenkirchen and Dürnstein, when the apricots are in blossom, is an experience not easily forgotten.

Here you can discover some of the finest white wines in Europe. The elegant, long-lived rieslings are world-renowned, but the special glory of Austria is the grüner veltliner, an indigenous grape that can produce anything from simple Heurigen thirst-quenchers to wines of a nobility that rival the best of Burgundy.

The area has its own unique three-tiered classification system, ranging from the young, fresh Steinfeder and medium-bodied Federspiel to the rich, ripe smaragd. Some of the already legendary vintners include Toni Zöhrer, F.X. Pichler, Prager, Knoll, and Hirtzberger, as well as the exemplary cooperative of the Freie Weingärtner Wachau. For a fine Web site on Wachau wineries, log on to ⊕**www. vinea-wachau.at.**

Straddling both sides of the Danube is the Kremstal, centering on the medieval town of Krems, the hub of the area's wine trade. The range of grape varieties expands here to include intensely fragrant traminer, grauburgunder (more familiar as pinot gris),

and even some full-bodied reds from cabernet sauvignon and pinot noir. To sample some of these wines, you may be tempted to make an excursion to one of the nearby wineries like Nigl, Salomon, Malat, or Zöhrer. Toni Zöhrer runs vineyard rally tours—his wines have been among the most successful in recent challenges.

Venturing farther from the Danube takes you through lush, rolling hills to the Kamptal, the valley that follows the winding course of the gentle Kamp River. Here is another premium wine region, this one dominated by Langenlois, the country's largest wine-producing town. The **Loisium** (⊠*Kornplatz, Langenlois* ⊕*www. loisium.at*), a sleek, ultramodern emporium, provides a comprehensive selection of wines and other delectables from the area. It has a new wine bar and offers slow food (local, organic cuisine) and picnics in the surrounding vineyards. Top producers include Hirsch, Loimer, and Bründlmayer, who makes one of Austria's best sparkling wines as well as chardonnay and *Alte Reben* (old-vine) grüner veltliner and riesling of exceptional character.

After you've had your fill of wine tasting, you might want to relax over a good meal at one of these distinguished wineries. Several have very nice restaurants on-site, including Jamek, near Dürnstein, and Bründlmayer in Langenlois.

—Gary Dodson

strasse 32 ☎02732/82276–0 🌐www.altepost-krems.at 23 rooms, 4 with bath In-room: no a/c. In-hotel: restaurant No credit cards ⊗Closed Dec.–Mar. BP.

STEIN

5 km (3 mi) west of Krems.

A frozen-in-time hamlet that has, over the years, become virtually a suburb of the adjacent city of Krems, Stein is dotted with lovely 16th-century houses, many on the town's main street, Steinlanderstrasse. The 14th-century **Minoritenkirche,** just off the main street in the pedestrian zone, now serves as a museum with changing exhibits. A few steps beyond the Minoritenkirche, an imposing square Gothic tower identifies the 15th-century **St. Nicholas parish church,** whose altar painting and ceiling frescoes were done by Kremser Schmidt. Stein was the birthplace of Ludwig Köchel, the cataloger of Mozart's works, which are still referred to by their Köchel numbers.

DÜRNSTEIN

★ *4 km (2½ mi) west of Stein, 90 km (56 mi) northwest of Vienna, 34 km (21¼ mi) northeast of Melk.*

If a beauty contest were held among the towns along the Wachau Danube, chances are Dürnstein would be the winner—as you'll see when you arrive along with droves of tourists. The town is small; leave the car at one end and walk the narrow streets. The main street, Hauptstrasse, is lined with picturesque 16th-century residences. **■ TIP→ The trick is to overnight here—when the day-trippers depart, the storybook spell of the town returns.** The top night to be here is the summer solstice, when hundreds of boats bearing torches and candles sail down the river at twilight to honor the longest day of the year—a breathtaking sight best enjoyed from the town and hotel terraces over the Danube. In October or November the grapes from the surrounding hills are harvested by volunteers from villages throughout the valley—locals garnish their front doors with straw wreaths if they can offer tastes of the new wine, as members of the local wine cooperative, the Winzergenossenschaft Wachau.

ESSENTIALS

Tourist Information Dürnstein (*✉Rathaus ☎02711/200*).

EXPLORING

Set among terraced vineyards, the town is landmarked by its gloriously Baroque **Stiftskirche,** dating from the early 1700s, which sits on a cliff overlooking the river. This cloister church's combination of luminous blue facade and stylish Baroque tower is considered the most beautiful of its kind in Austria.

After taking in the Stiftskirche, head up the hill, climbing 500 feet above the town, to the famous **Richard the Lion-Hearted Castle** where Leopold V held Richard the Lion-Hearted of England, captured on his way back home from the Crusades. Leopold had been insulted, so the story goes, by Richard while they were in the Holy Land and when the English nobleman was shipwrecked and had to head back home through Austria, word got out—even though Richard was disguised as a peasant—and Leopold pounced. In the tower of this castle, the Lion-Hearted was imprisoned (1192–93) until he was located by Blondel, the faithful Minnesänger (troubadour). It's said that Blondel was able to locate his imprisoned king when he heard his master's voice completing the verse of a song Blondel was singing aloud—a bit recycled in Sir Walter Scott's *Ivanhoe* (and the Robert Taylor MGM film). Leopold turned his prisoner over to the emperor, Henry VI, who held him for months longer until ransom was paid by Richard's mother, Eleanor of Aquitaine.

■ **TIP** → The rather steep 30-minute climb to the ruins will earn you a breathtaking view up and down the Danube Valley and over the hills to the south.

WHERE TO STAY & EAT

$$$–$$$$ ✕ **Loibnerhof.** It's hard to imagine a more idyllic frame for a memorable
★ meal, especially if the weather is fine and tables are set out in the fragrant apple orchard. One of the oldest restaurants in the area, its kitchen offers inventive variations on regional themes: Wachau fish soup, crispy roast duck, and various grilled fish (fresh from the aquarium) or lamb specialties. The house is famous for its *Butterschnitzel*, an exquisite variation on the theme of ground meat (this one's panfried veal with a touch of pork). To reach Loibnerhof, look for the Unterloiben exit a mile east of Dürnstein. ✉ *Unterloiben 7* ☏ *02732/82890–0* ⌕ *Reservations essential* ▤ *MC, V* ⊘ *Closed Mon. and Tues. and early Jan.–mid-Feb.*

$$$$ 🏨 **Schloss Dürnstein.** Once the preserve of the princes of Starhemberg,
★ this 17th-century early-Baroque castle on a rocky terrace with exquisite views over the Danube is one of the most famous hotels in Austria. Many a regal visitor and a bevy of celebs have enjoyed its classic elegance and comfort. The best rooms face the river and all are elegantly decorated, in grand style. Biedermeier armoires and country antiques grace the public rooms. The restaurant—try pike perch from the Danube—is nestled under coved ceilings; tables on the outside terrace overlook the river. **Pros:** indoor and outdoor pools; exquisite views from the terrace. **Cons:** no air-conditioning. ✉ *3601 Dürnstein 2* ☏ *02711/212* ⊕ *www.schloss.at* ➦ *47 rooms* ⌕ *In-room: no a/c. In-hotel: restaurant, bar, pools, gym* ▤ *AE, DC, MC, V* ⊘ *Closed Nov.–Mar.* ⌑ *BP.*

$$$–$$$$ 🏨 **Richard Löwenherz.** Built up around the former church of a vast 700-year-old convent, this noted inn overlooks the Danube. The beautifully furnished interior with antiques, open fire, grandfather clock and bowls of fresh roses make this one of the most romantic of the Romantik Hotels group. Though all rooms are spacious and comfortable, the balconied guest rooms in the newer part of the house have more modern furnishings. Wander through the grounds among the roses, oleanders, and fig trees, all set against the dramatic backdrop of 600-year-old stone walls. The outstanding restaurant is known for its local wines and regional specialties. **Pros:** river view; vaulted reception rooms; spacious guest rooms. **Cons:** rooms can get hot in summer; no elevator. ✉ *Dürnstein 8* ☏ *02711/222* ⊕ *www.richardloewenherz.at* ➦ *37 rooms* ⌕ *In-room: no a/c. In-hotel: restaurant, bar, pool* ▤ *AE, DC, MC, V* ⊘ *Closed Nov.–Easter or mid–Apr.* ⌑ *BP.*

$–$$ ⚏**Sänger Blondel.** Nearly under the shadow of the Baroque spire of Dürnstein's parish church, this *Gasthof-Pension* welcomes you with a lovely, sunny-yellow, flower-bedecked facade. Owned by the same family since 1729, the inn—named after the minstrel famous for tracking Richard the Lion-Hearted—has a large garden, quite the treat in the heart of town. The simply furnished, country-style rooms are of medium size. The staff is particularly helpful and can suggest excursions in the area. The hotel's restaurant serves hearty Austrian food, and in summer, meals are served in the pretty courtyard under a huge chestnut tree. **Pros:** great value for money; beautiful garden; quiet area. **Cons:** no elevator; simple, drab styling. ✉*No. 64* ☎*02711/253–0* ⊕*www.saengerblondel.at* ⇆*16 rooms* ♿*In-room: no a/c. In-hotel: restaurant* ☰*MC, V* ⊘*Closed mid-Nov.–mid-Mar.* ❦*BP.*

WEISSENKIRCHEN

5 km (3 mi) west of Dürnstein, 22 km (14 mi) northeast of Melk.

Tucked among vineyards, just around a bend in the Danube, is Weissenkirchen, a picturesque town that was fortified against the Turks in 1531.

ESSENTIALS

Tourist Information Weissenkirchen (✉*Donaulände 262* ☎*02715/2600* ⊕*www.weissenkirchen-wachau.at*).

A fire in 1793 laid waste to much of the town, but the 15th-century parish church of **Mariä Himmelfahrt,** built on earlier foundations, largely survived. The south nave dates from 1300, the middle nave from 1439, the chapel from 1460. The Madonna on the triumphal arch goes back to the Danube school of about 1520; the Baroque touches date from 1736; and to complete the picture, the Rococo organ was installed in 1777.

On the Marktplatz, check out the 15th-century **Wachaumuseum,** which has a charming Renaissance arcaded courtyard. The building now contains many paintings by Kremser Schmidt. ✉*Marktplatz* ☎*02715/2268* ⊕*www.weissenkirchen.at/museum.php* 💶*€5* ⊘*Apr.–Oct., Tues.–Sun. 10–5.*

EN ROUTE One of the prettiest drives in the Wachau leads from Weissenkirchen to the renowned Gasthaus Erwin Schwarz in Nöhagen. From the main entrance to the town of Weissenkirchen, follow the road (Route L7094) north through the village, veering to your right and continuing upward. Soon the village gives way to a forested incline, after which you'll emerge into a verdant landscape of soft-contoured hills and vineyards and an occasional old farmhouse, passing through Weinzierl on Route L7090 on your way north to Nöhagen. From Nöhagen, take Route L7040 east toward Reichau, then to sleepy, rambling Senftenberg ("Mustard Mountain") with its romantic castle ruin perched above the town. A few kilometers east of Senftenberg, change to Route 218, going northeast to Langenlois. From here there will be signs to Vienna or back to Krems.

WHERE TO STAY & EAT

$$–$$$ ✕**Gasthaus Erwin Schwarz.** Natives will tell you this is one of the best
★   restaurants in the area, offering delicious regional cooking in a former
farmhouse and butcher shop. The village of Nöhagen, which is 7 km
(4½ mi) north of Weissenkirchen, offers little otherwise, yet people
come from miles around to dine here. The restaurant raises its own
animals, and all produce is grown on the premises. You're in luck if
the succulent crispy duck with *Rotkraut* (red cabbage) is on the menu;
the dumplings were voted the best in the region. For information on
the pleasant drive to this countryside spot, ⇨ *see the En Route below.*
⊠*Nöhagen 13* ☎*02717/8209* ⊕*www.gasthaus-schwarz.at* ⚭*Reservations essential* ▤*AE, MC, V* ⊗*Closed Mon. and Tues. Also closed
Wed. and Thurs. Nov.–Easter.*

$$–$$$ ✕**Jamek.** The Jamek family's country inn on the Danube is well known
throughout Austria for its fine cuisine. You can dine either in one of
several rooms tastefully decorated with 19th-century touches or outdoors in the shady garden. Start with the vegetable torte gratin, and
then go on to lightly fried *Zanderfilet* (pike perch) on a bed of garlicky
spinach. Don't miss the house specialty, the surprisingly light chocolate cake with whipped cream and chocolate sauce. Wines are from
the nearby family vineyards; guided tours of the vineyards take place
regularly. Jamek is just west of Weissenkirchen in Joching. ⊠*Joching
45* ☎*02715/2235* ⚭*Reservations essential* ▤*DC, MC, V* ⊗*Closed
weekends and mid-Dec.–mid-Jan.*

$$ ▥**Raffelsbergerhof.** This lovely Renaissance building (1574), once a ship-
master's house, has been tastefully converted into a hotel with every
comfort, including a new steam bath and sauna. The friendly family
management and peaceful surroundings make this a good lodging choice.
Guest rooms, with beautiful, original, wooden floors, are furnished with
charming country pieces, pretty fabrics, and fresh flowers, and most
have sitting areas. Baths are spacious, modern and well-equipped. The
buffet breakfast is excellent. There's an extra charge of €5 per person
for stays of only one night. **Pros:** helpful, friendly staff; beautiful gar-
den. **Cons:** no elevator; reservations needed well in advance. ⊠*A-3610*
☎*02715/2201* ⊕*www.raffelsbergerhof.at* ⮍*15 rooms* ♨*In-room: no
a/c, Wi-Fi*▤*DC, MC, V* ⊗*Closed Nov.–Easter* ⦿*BP.*

SPITZ

*5 km (3 mi) southwest of Weissenkirchen, 17 km (10½ mi) northeast
of Melk.*

Picturesque Spitz is off the main road and set back from the Danube,
sitting like a jewel in the surrounding vineyards and hills. One vine-
yard, "Thousand Bucket Hill," is so called for the amount of wine it is
said to produce in a good year. A number of houses in Spitz go back to
the 16th and 17th centuries.

The late-Gothic, 15th-century **parish church** contains Kremser Schmidt's
altar painting of the martyrdom of St. Mauritius. Note the carved-wood
statues of Christ and the 12 apostles, dating from 1380, on the organ loft.

Just beyond Spitz and above the road is the ruin of the **castle Hinterhaus,** to which you can climb.

WHERE TO STAY

$$–$$$ [hotel] **Burg Oberranna.** About 7 km (4½ mi) beyond the village of Mühldorf, directly west of Spitz, stands this out-of-the-way, well-preserved castle-hotel, surrounded by a double wall and dry moat. The original structure dates from the early 12th century, and the St. George chapel, with frescoes and Romanesque interior, possibly even earlier, make a point of seeing this fascinating site before you leave. Some of the charming antiques-filled suites include a kitchenette and sitting room. This is a great base for hiking and also perfect for those who just want peace and quiet. **Pros:** very helpful, friendly staff. **Cons:** creaky floors; breakfast area far from most rooms. ⊠ *Ober-Ranna 1, Mühldorf* ☎ *02713/8221* ⊕ *www.schlosshotels.co.at* ⊅ *5 rooms, 7 suites* ⚏ *In-room: no a/c, kitchen. In-hotel: restaurant* ☐ *AE, DC, MC, V* ♥ *Closed Nov.–end Apr.* ⦿ *BP.*

EN ROUTE The vistas are mainly of the other side of the Danube, looking across at Schönbühel and Melk, as you follow a back road via Jauerling and Maria Laach to Route 3 at Aggsbach. Shortly after Weitenegg the Wachau ends, and you come into the part of the Danube Valley known as the **Nibelungengau,** where the Nibelungs—who inspired the great saga *Das Nibelungenlied,* source of Wagner's *Ring*—are supposed to have settled for a spell. If you have always thought of the Nibelungs as a mythical race of dwarfs known only to old German legends and Wagner, dismiss that idea. The Nibelungs actually existed, though not as Wagner describes them, and this area was one of their stomping grounds.

MARIA TAFERL

49 km (31 mi) southwest of Spitz, 13 km (8 mi) west of Melk, 7½ km (4¾ mi) northeast of Persenbeug/Ybbs an der Donau.

Crowning a hill on the north bank is the two-towered **Maria Taferl Basilica,** a pilgrimage church with a spectacular outlook. It's a bit touristy, but the church and the view are worth the side trip.

About 5 km (3 mi) up a back road is **Schloss Artstetten,** a massive square castle crowned with no fewer than seven "candle-snuffer" turrets—a touch of *Mitteleuropa* style befitting this family seat of the Austro-Hungarian Habsburgs. This was the former country retreat of Archduke Franz Ferdinand and his wife Sophie, whose double assassination in 1914 in Sarajevo was one of the immediate causes of World War I. The castle has rooms given over to their collected memorabilia as well as their marble vaults. ⊠ *Artstetten* ☎ *07413/8006* ⊕ *www.schloss-artstetten.at* ⊠ *€7* ♥ *Apr.–Nov., daily 9–5:30.*

WHERE TO STAY

$$ [hotel] **Hotel Schachner–Krone & Kaiserhof.** The Schachner family completely overhauled and refurbished its hotels Krone and Kaiserhof in 2006, creating this complex with two separate but neighboring buildings. Whirlpools, an indoor swimming pool, and three different types of saunas are in the

BIKING ALONG THE RIVERBANK

You don't have to be Lance Armstrong to bike the Danube River trail. The stretch of relatively even terrain from Upper Austria to Vienna is an almost-effortless pleasure, even for the inexperienced cyclist. From mid-April until the end of October, from the budding apricot orchards in spring to the copper-red leaves in the vineyards in fall, the natural beauty of this river landscape, not to mention its historic sites and towns, makes this route the most popular Austrian cycle track.

From Passau, Germany or Schärding, Austria (roughly 17 km south of Passau), the circa-330-km trip (an elevation change of 150 m) can take up to a week, depending on your sightseeing urges, stamina, and curiosity. For much of the way (with the exception of the Korneuburg–Krems stretch) you can bike along either side of the river.

The best Web site for planning a trip, with information about where to start, stop, and stay, is ⊕**www. upperaustria.at**. It's the official site for the tourist office of Upper Austria, and it has comprehensive advice in English on cycling tours in Austria in general and on the Danube route in particular. Another site, ⊕**www.donauradweg.com,** covers the whole of Upper Austria and offers lots of information about bike-rental agencies and hotels. The tourist office of Lower Austria also has a Web site, ⊕**www.niederoesterreich.at,** which offers a brochure in English, the "Danube Cycle Track." Their brochure "Radfahren" is in German, but lists contact numbers for cycle rentals throughout Austria.

The Upper Austria Web site offers tailor-made packages and deals for cycle adventures in Austria, but, if you are adventurous enough, it's not difficult to tackle the bike routes alone. Paths are well signposted, and there are outfitters and repair stations along most tracks. Many hotels and B&Bs will even arrange to pick up you and your bike from the cycle path and/or from the train station. Since cycling has become so popular, bikes for rent can be found in most towns in the Danube Valley and even at train stations.

If you decide to return to your starting point by train or to take a shortcut on the rails, it's best to check in advance whether or not there is room for bikes, as space can be limited. The ÖBB call center (☎0043 (0)5-1717) will help with reservations if necessary.

BIKE RENTALS & TOURS

Donau Touristik. This operator offers easygoing seven-day Danube trips from Passau to Vienna, including B&Bs, bike rental, baggage transfer, and more at reasonable prices. Depending on the season, costs per person for double-room occupancy run €399–€507. ⊠ *Lederergasse 4–12, Linz* ☎ *0732/2080* ⊕ *www. donautouristik.com.*

Pedal Power. Based in Vienna, this venerable outfitter has a very good reputation and a great guidebook in English, "The Danube Bike Trail" for €13 (€21 if mailed to the United States). They have bikes for rent and guided bike tours of Vienna. ⊠ *Ausstellungsstrasse 3, Vienna* ☎ *01/729-7234* ⊕ *www.pedal power.at.*

Krone, while a magnificent garden with an outdoor pool adjoins the Kaiserhof. The Krone is also home to the Smaragd, an intimate restaurant with superb views of the Danube Valley. For sports lovers there's horseback riding, tennis, Nordic walking, and golf at a nearby course. Check out last-minute deals on its Web site. **Pros:** spacious, modern rooms; located on what's considered a "power place" of spiritual energy and healing. **Cons:** difficult to reach without your own transportation. ⊠*A-3672* ☏*07413/6355–0* ⊕*www.hotel-schachner.at* ⇋*84 rooms* ᴄ*In-room: no a/c. In-hotel: 3 restaurants, bar, tennis courts, pools, bicycles, Wi-Fi* ⊟*AE, DC, MC, V* ☉*Closed Nov.–Feb.* ⦿*BP.*

> ### HIKING
>
> You could hardly ask for better hiking country: from the level ground of the Danube Valley hills rise on both sides, giving great views when you reach the upper levels. There are *Wanderwege* (marked hiking paths) virtually everywhere; local tourist offices have maps and route details. You can hike in the Mühlviertel from Freistadt to Grein and even arrange to get your pack transferred from hotel to hotel. Around Linz you might retrace the route of the Linz–Budweis horse-drawn tramway, Continental Europe's first railway, or trek from one castle to another.

GREIN

32 km (20 mi) west of Maria Taferl, 20 km (12 mi) west of Persenbeug/ Ybbs an der Donau.

Set above the Danube, Grein is a picture-book town complete with castle. The river bend below, known for years as the "place where death resides," was one of the river's most hazardous stretches until the reefs were blasted away in the late 1700s.

ESSENTIALS

Tourist Information Grein (⊠*Stadtplatz 7* ☏*07268/7055*).

EXPLORING

Take time to see the intimate Rococo **Stadttheater** in the town hall, built in 1790 and still occasionally used for concerts or plays. ⊠*Rathaus* ☏*07268/7055* ⊕*www.grein.ooe.gv.at* ⛁*€3* ☉*May–Oct., Mon.–Sat. 9–10 and 1:30–5, Sun. 1:30–4.*

BAUMGARTENBERG

11 km (7 mi) west of Grein, 17½ km (11 mi) east of Mauthausen.

The small village of Baumgartenberg is worth a visit for its ornate Baroque **parish church.** Note the lavish stuccowork and exquisitely carved 17th-century pews—and the unusual pulpit supported by a tree trunk. The church is the only reminder of a once-famed Cistercian abbey, founded in 1141 by Otto von Machland, that formerly stood here.

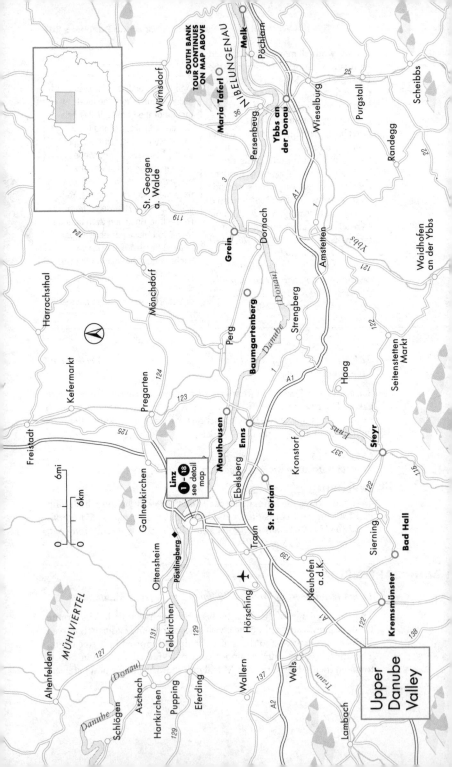

Upper Danube Valley

Outside the town is the picturesque **castle of Klam,** which used to belong to Swedish playwright August Strindberg; it now contains a small museum. 🗋€6 ⊙ *May 2–Oct. 26, daily 10 –5.*

LINZ: "RICH TOWN OF THE RIVER MARKETS"

48 km (22 mi) northwest of Baumgartenberg, 130 km (81 mi) northeast of Salzburg, 185 km (115 mi) west of Vienna.

Linz, the capital of Upper Austria—set where the Traun River flows into the Danube—has a fascinating Old City core and an active cultural life, which will be even more dynamic throughout 2009 as Linz celebrates its status as the European Capital of Culture with a yearlong calendar of special events, exhibits, and concerts. In 1832 its horsedrawn train to Czechoslovakia functioned as the first rail line on the Continent. Once known as the "Rich Town of the River Markets" because of its importance as a medieval trading post, it is today the center of Austrian steel and chemical production, both started by the Germans in 1938. Linz is also a leader in computer technology—every September the city hosts the internationally renowned Ars Electronica Festival, designed to promote artists, scientists, and the latest technical gadgets. A city where past and present collide, Linz has Austria's largest medieval square and one of the country's most modern multipurpose halls, the Brucknerhaus, which is used for concerts and conventions.

Linz can cast a spell, thanks to the beautiful old houses on the Hauptplatz; a Baroque cathedral with twin towers and a fine organ over which composer Anton Bruckner once presided; and its "city mountain," the Pöstlingberg, with a unique railway line to the top. Mozart *en famille* often stayed here as his family relentlessly traveled up and down Europe, most notably in November 1783, when he was a guest of Count Johann Thun-Hohenstein at his Thun Palace. Today extensive redevelopment, ongoing restoration, and the creation of traffic-free zones and biking paths through the city continue to transform Linz.

■ TIP→ **If you will be in Linz for a day or more, consider purchasing the Linz City Ticket available at the Tourist Office and in most hotels. It's a great bargain.** This €20 booklet of vouchers grants huge savings on most of the must-see sites, including admission to 11 of the city's museums, a ticket valid for a ride up and down on the Pöstlingberg tram, and a day ticket for public transport.

GETTING HERE & AROUND

Linz is served mainly by Austrian Airlines, Lufthansa, Swissair, and Tyrolean. Regular flights connect with Vienna, Amsterdam, Berlin, Düsseldorf, Frankfurt, Paris, Stuttgart, and Zürich.

The Linz airport is in Hörsching, about 12 km (7½ mi) southwest of the city. Buses run between the airport and the main train station according to flight schedules.

Fast trains connect German cities via Passau with Linz.

The city center is easy to manage on foot. The heart of the city—the Altstadt (Old City)—has been turned into a pedestrian zone; either leave your car at your hotel or use the huge parking garage under the main square in the center of town. Distances are not great, and you can take in the highlights in the course of a two- or three-hour walking tour.

Easy-to-use trams take visitors to sites of interest not directly in the city center. If in doubt grab a cab; there are many taxi stands in Linz.

From Linz the delightful LILO (Linzer Lokalbahn) interurban line makes the run up to Eferding. A charming narrow-gauge line meanders south to Waidhofen an der Ybbs.

ESSENTIALS

Information **Linz Blue Danube airport** (☎ 07221/600–0). **LILO** (☎ 0732/600703 or 0732/707–0145–0). **ÖBB—Österreichisches Bundesbahn** (☎ 05/1717).

Tourist Information **Linz** (✉ Hauptplatz 1, Linz ☎ 0732/707–0177–1 ⊕ www. linz.at).

A GOOD WALK

Numbers in the text correspond to numbers in the margin and on the Linz map.

The center of the Old City (Altstadt) is the Hauptplatz, with its pretty pastel town houses. Dominating the square is the **Pillar to the Holy Trinity** ⓰, erected in 1723 in gratitude for Linz's survival after threats of war, fire, and the dreaded plague. Head down Klostergasse to the magnificent **Minoritenkirche** ❻. The adjacent **Landhaus** ❺, once Linz's college and the place where famed astronomer Johannes Kepler taught, occupies a rambling Renaissance building with two inner courtyards. In the arcarded courtyard is the Fountain of the Planets, with Jupiter the crowning glory.

At No. 20 Klostergasse is the Thun Palace, now known as the **Mozart Haus** ❹, where Mozart stayed as a guest of the Count of Thun-Hohenstein and composed the Linz Symphony in his "spare time." Turn right at the corner onto Altstadtgasse. At No. 10 is the **Kremsmünsterhaus** ❸, with its turrets and onion domes, where Emperor Friedrich III supposedly died in August 1493. Turn left from Altstadtgasse onto Hofgasse (one of the prettiest corners in the city), and climb the quaint narrow street that leads up to the Rudolfstor, one of the entrances to **Schlossmuseum Linz** (Linz Castle) ❷. Since its early days as a prime fortress on the Danube, it has served as a hospital, army barracks, and even a prison, before becoming a provincial museum. The view from the castle promontory is one of the most impressive in Linz. Walk through the castle grounds to the end of the parking lot and turn left, going through the archway to the **Martinskirche**, one of the oldest churches in Austria, whose nave dates from 799.

Go back along Römerstrasse, which veers right down the hill. At the bottom it becomes the Promenade. Go straight on the Promenade, following it around to the left, then turn right onto Herrenstrasse. Where

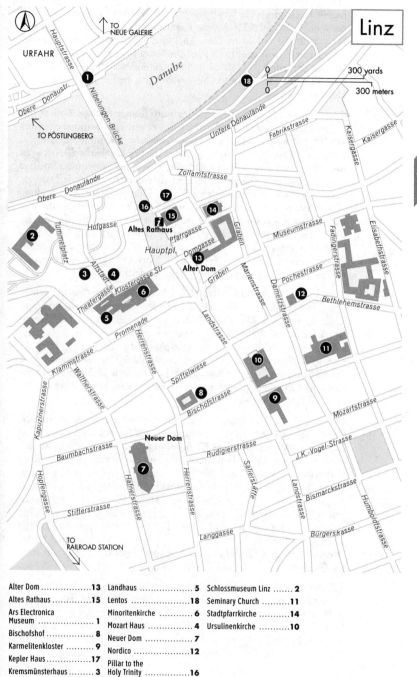

Linz

TO NEUE GALERIE

URFAHR

Danube

TO PÖSTLINGBERG

0   300 yards
0   300 meters

4

Bichofstrasse meets Herrenstrasse is the **Bischofshof** ❽, which was built between 1721 and 1726 for the Kremsmünster monastery and is still the seat of the bishop of Linz. The west end of Bishofstrasse angles onto Baumbachstrasse, the site of the **Neuer Dom** ❼, a massive 19th-century cathedral capable of holding 20,000 worshippers. Note the Linz Window, depicting the history of Linz, before heading back to Herrenstrasse.

Turn right and shortly afterward left onto Rudigierstrasse. Follow this to Landstrasse, where you'll make another left. Two Baroque churches are located here, that of the **Karmelitenkloster** ❾, modeled after St. Joseph's in Prague, and down the street the **Ursulinenkirche** ❿. Between these two churches is Harrachstrasse, which holds another Baroque gem, the **Seminary Church** ⓫, located shortly after you cross Dametz-gasse. After inspecting the high altar by Hildebrandt, backtrack along Harrachstrasse to Dametzstrasse, where you'll turn right. At the corner of Dametzstrasse and Bethlehemstrasse is the **Nordico** ⓬, the city museum, which was originally an early-17th-century town house used by the Kremsmünster monastery for nearly 200 years as a Jesuit training center for young Scandinavian men. Now it houses a collection that ranges from archaeological finds to the Biedermeier era.

Keep going along Dametzstrasse until you reach the Graben, where you turn left and walk for a short while before turning right on Dom-gasse. Here is the **Alter Dom** ⓭, the old city cathedral where Anton Bruckner played the organ for 12 years beginning in 1856. From here, follow Domgasse around to the **Stadtpfarrkirche** ⓮, near the intersection to Kollegiumgasse. This was originally a Romanesque basilica before being rebuilt in the Baroque style in the mid-17th century. In the entrance hall and approach to the tower staircase you can see Gothic cross-ribbing on the vaulted ceiling.

Go left from the church into Kollegiumgasse, then left into the Pfarrplatz. From the northwest edge of the square, head down Rathausgasse to No. 5 to view the **Kepler Haus** ⓱, home of astronomer Johannes Kepler. He lived here with his family for 10 years, beginning in 1612. More than 100 years later, Linz's first printing shop was established here. Opposite the Kepler house, head across the Rathausgasse into the neo-Renaissance courtyard of Linz's **Altes Rathaus** ⓯—a neo-Renaissance Town Hall. Back at the central Hauptplatz square, you can decide to chill out at a café or blast forward to the 21st century by heading across the Nibelungen Bridge to see two hypermodern sights, the **Ars Electronica Museum** ❶ and the dazzling contemporary art museum, **Lentos** ⓲, gleaming on the bank of the Danube.

TIMING The best time to visit Linz is between May and September, but the main tourist attractions are open year-round. Touring the Old City takes two to three hours, depending on how many of the sights you stop to visit. If you're pressed for time, head straight for Linz Castle. You'll pass through the loveliest parts of the city, and from the heights of the castle grounds you'll be able to enjoy stupendous views of the Danube.

CLOSE UP

On a Clear Day You Can Flee Forever

When you want to escape the hustle and bustle of Linz, just hop on the **Pöstlingbergbahn**, an electric railway, for a scenic ride up to the famous mountain belvedere, the **Pöstlingberg**. The narrow-gauge marvel has been making the 16-minute journey since 1898 and has recently undergone a complete overhaul. To reach the base station for the railway, take Streetcar 3 to the Bergbahnhof stop, which crosses the river to Urfahr, Linz's left bank. Note the railway's unusual switches, necessary because the car-wheel flanges ride the outside the rails rather than (the usual) inside. Europe's steepest non-cog mountain railway gains 750 feet in elevation in a journey of roughly 3 km (2 mi), with neither pulleys nor cables to prevent it from slipping, tackling a gradient of nearly 1:10. In summer the old open-bench cars are used. On a clear day the view from the top of the Postlingberg is superb, with the city and the wide sweep of the Danube filling the foreground and the snowcapped Alps on the horizon. With a glass of chilled white wine in hand, drink in the grand vista over Linz and the Danube from the terrace of the **Pöstlingberg-Schlössl** restaurant, located at the top of Linz's "city mountain." There are also cafés and beer gardens at the summit, along with the **Church of the Seven Sorrows of the Virgin** (Sieben Schmerzen Mariens), an immense and opulent twin-towered Baroque pilgrimage church (1748) visible for miles as a Linz landmark. Also on the mountain is the **Märchen-grotte (Fairy-tale Grotto) Railroad.** ☎ 0732/7801–7002 ⊕ www.linzag.at ✉ Round-trip €3.60, combined ticket with Streetcar 3 €6.20 (combination tickets only available at Tourist Information). Both sites are included in the Linz City Ticket booklet for free ⊙ Mon.–Sat. every 30 min 5 AM–8 PM; Sun. every 30 min 7 AM–8 PM.

MAIN ATTRACTIONS

1 **Ars Electronica Museum.** Just across the Nibelungen Bridge from the Hauptplatz, this futuristic museum allows visitors to try out all kinds of modern technology gadgets. In the "cave," the most popular of all the installations, experience, with the aid of 3-D glasses, the sensation of flying over Renaissance cathedrals, speeding through a labyrinth of underground tunnels, or entering a painting. Instructions for all exhibits are also in English. Allow at least a whole morning or afternoon to experience all the cybersites. When you need a break, visit the Sky Media Loft on the third floor for refreshments and a spectacular view overlooking the Danube and Lentos Museum. ⊠ Hauptstrasse 2 ☎ 0732/72720 ⊕ www.aec.at ✉ €6 ⊙ Wed.–Fri. 9–5, weekends 10–6.

18 **Lentos.** Taking its name from the ancient Celtic settlement that was the origin of the city of Linz, this contemporary art museum hugs the banks of the Danube on the Altstadt side of the river. Designed by Zürich architects Weber and Hofer, its long, low-slung "shoe-box" gray-glass structure picks up the reflection of the water and, at night, lit in shimmering blue or red, really stands out. The collection contains an impressive number of paintings by Austrian Secession artists Klimt, Schiele, and Kokoschka, along with works by other artists, including sculptures by Alfred Hrdlicka and one of those famous silkscreen portraits of Marilyn Monroe by Andy Warhol. All in all, the museum has about 1,500 artworks, more than 10,000 sketches, and nearly 1,000 photographs. The excellent restaurant has an outdoor terrace with beautiful views of the river. ⊠ *Ernst-Koref-Promenade 1* ☎ *070/7070–3600–0* ⊕ *www.lentos.at* ⊠ *€6.50* ⊙ *Daily 10–6, Thurs. until 9.*

❼ Neuer Dom (*New Cathedral*). In 1862 the bishop of Linz engaged one of the architects of Cologne cathedral to develop a design for a grand cathedral in the French neo-Gothic style to accommodate 20,000 worshippers, at that time one-third of the population of Linz. According to legend, the tower was not to be higher than that of St. Stephen's in Vienna. The result was the massive 400-foot tower, shorter than St. Stephen's by a scant 6½ feet. The cathedral contains gorgeous stained-glass windows and offers organ recitals. ⊠ *Herrenstrasse 26* ☎ *0732/771–506* ⊠ *Free* ⊙ *Mon.–Sat. 7:30–7, Sun. 8–7.*

⓰ Pillar to the Holy Trinity. One of the symbols of Linz is the 65-foot Baroque column in the center of the Hauptplatz. Made in 1723 from white Salzburg marble, the memorial offers thanks from an earthly trinity—the provincial estates, city council, and local citizenry—for deliverance from the threats of war (1704), fire (1712), and plague (1713). ■TIP→ From March through October there's a flea market here each Saturday (except holidays), from 7 AM to 2 PM.

❷ Schlossmuseum Linz (*Linz Castle*). The massive four-story building on
★ Tummelplatz was rebuilt by Friedrich III around 1477, literally on top of a castle that dated from 799. Note the **Friedrichstor** (the Frederick Gate), with the *A.E.I.O.U.* monogram (some believe it stands for the Latin sentence meaning "Austria will last until the end of the world") and two interior courtyards. This is widely known as one of the best provincial museums in the country. The interior of the castle is well worth a visit, with a 17th-century inlaid walnut portal from Schloss Hartheim, historical musical instruments (including Beethoven's Hammerklavier), re-creations of rooms from 19th-century Austrian homes, fine 19th-century portraits and landscapes by Dutch and Austrian artists, as well as weaponry, coins, and ceramics. ⊠ *Tummelplatz 10* ☎ *0732/774–419* ⊕ *www.schlossmuseum.at* ⊠ *€4.50* ⊙ *Tues.–Fri. 9–6, weekends 10–5.*

ALSO WORTH SEEING

⓭ Alter Dom (*Old Cathedral*). Hidden away off the Graben, a narrow side street off the Taubenmarkt above the Hauptplatz, is this Baroque gem (1669–78), whose striking feature is its single nave with side altars. Anton Bruckner was the organist here from 1856 to 1868. ⊙ *Daily 7–7.*

⓯ Altes Rathaus (*Old City Hall*). At the lower end of the main square, the original 1513 building was mostly destroyed by fire and replaced in 1658–59. Its octagonal corner turret and lunar clock, as well as some vaulted rooms, remain, and you can detect traces of the original Renaissance structure on the Rathausgasse facade. The present exterior dates from 1824. The approach from Rathausgasse 5, opposite the Kepler Haus, leads through a fine, arcaded courtyard. On the facade here you'll spot portraits of Emperor Friedrich III, the mayors Hoffmandl and Prunner, the astronomer Johannes Kepler, and the composer Anton Bruckner. ⊠ *Hauptplatz.*

⑧ Bischofshof (*Bishop's Residence*). At the intersection of Herrenstrasse and Bischofstrasse is this impressive mansion, which dates from 1721. The residence of Mozart's friend Count Herberstein, who was later appointed Bishop of Linz, this remains the city's most important Baroque secular building. Graced by a fine wrought-iron gateway, the building was designed by Jakob Prandtauer, the architectural genius responsible for the glorious Melk and St. Florian abbeys.

⑪ Seminary Church. Dating from 1723, this yellow-and-white Baroque treasure has an elliptical dome designed by Johann Lukas von Hildebrandt, who also designed its high altar. ⊠ *Harrachstrasse 7* ☎ *0732/771205* ⊙ *Daily 7–5.*

⑨ Karmelitenkloster. This magnificent Baroque church on Landstrasse was modeled after St. Joseph's in Prague. ⊠ *Landstrasse 33* ☎ *0732/770217* ⊙ *Daily 7–noon and 2–6:30, Sun. 6–11:30 and 3–6:30.*

⑰ Kepler Haus. The astronomer Johannes Kepler lived here from 1612 to 1622; Linz's first printing shop was established in this house in 1745. The interior is closed to the public. ⊠ *Rathausgasse 5.*

③ Kremsmünsterhaus. Emperor Friedrich III is said to have died here in 1493. The building was done over in Renaissance style in 1578–80, and a story was added in 1616, with two turrets and onion domes. There's a memorial room to the emperor here; his heart is entombed in the Linz parish church, but the rest of him is in St. Stephen's cathedral in Vienna. The traditional rooms house one of Linz's best restaurants, Herberstein. ⊠ *Altstadt 10.*

⑤ Landhaus. The early-Renaissance monastery adjoining the **Minoritenkirche** is now the Landhaus, with its distinctive tower, seat of the provincial government. Look inside to see the arcaded courtyard with the Planet Fountain (honoring Johannes Kepler, the astronomer who taught here when it was Linz's college) and the Hall of Stone on the first floor, above the barrel-vaulted hall on the ground floor. This hall, the Steinerner Saal, was probably the setting for a noted concert given by the Mozart children in October 1762 (from which Count Pálffy hurried back to Vienna to spread the word about the musical prodigies). For a more extensive look at the interior, inquire at the local tourist office about their scheduled guided tours. The beautiful Renaissance doorway (1570) is of red marble. ⊠ *Klosterstrasse 7.*

↻ Märchengrotte (Fairy-tale Grotto) Railroad. More than 100 years old, the "Dragon Express" hasn't aged one bit, and still runs through a colorful imaginary world full of dwarfs and other displays at the top of the **Pöstlingberg.** ☎ *0732/3400–7506* ⊕ *www.linzag.at* ⛁ *€4.50* ⊙ *Mar.– May and Sept.–Nov., daily 10–5; June–Aug., daily 10–6.*

⑥ Minoritenkirche. Situated at the end of Klosterstrasse, this church was
★ once part of a monastery. The present building dates from 1752 to

1758 and has a delightful Rococo interior with side-altar paintings by Kremser Schmidt and a main altar by Bartolomeo Altomonte. Mozart probably worshipped here when he stayed at the Thun Palace across the way. ⊠*Klosterstrasse 7* ☎*0732/7720–11364* ☉ *Apr.-Oct., daily 8–4; Nov.–Mar., daily 8* AM.*–11* AM.

4 **Mozart Haus.** This three-story Renaissance town house, actually the Thun Palace, has a later Baroque facade and portal. Mozart arrived here with his wife in 1783 to meet an especially impatient patron (Mozart was late by 14 days). As the composer forgot to bring any symphonies along with him, he set about writing one and completed the sublime Linz Symphony in the space of four days. The palace now houses private apartments, but the courtyard can be viewed (entering from Altstadt 17, around the corner). ⊠*Klostergasse 20.*

12 **Nordico.** At the corner of Dametzstrasse and Bethlehemstrasse you'll find the city museum, dating from 1610. Its collection follows local history from pre-Roman times to the mid-1880s. ⊠*Dametzstrasse 23* ☎*0732/7070–1912* ⊕*www.nordico.at* ☑*€4.50* ☉ *Weekdays 10–6, Thurs. till 9; weekends 1–5.*

14 **Stadtpfarrkirche.** This city parish church dates from 1286 and was rebuilt in Baroque style in 1648. The tomb in the right wall of the chancel contains Frederick III's heart and entrails (the corpse is in Vienna's St. Stephen's Cathedral). The ceiling frescoes are by Altomonte, and the figure of Johann Nepomuk (a local saint) in the chancel is by Georg Raphael Donner, with grand decoration supplied by the master designer Hildebrandt. ⊠*Pfarrplatz 4* ☎*0732/7761–200* ☉ *Weekdays 8–noon, Tues. and Thurs. 2–4:30.*

10 **Ursulinenkirche.** The towers at this Baroque church are one of the identifying symbols of Linz. Inside is a blaze of gold and crystal ornamentation. Note the Madonna figure wearing a hooded Carmelite cloak with huge pockets, used to collect alms for the poor. ⊠*Landstrasse 31* ☎*0732/7610–3151* ☉*Daily 7:30–6.*

WHERE TO EAT

$$$ ✕**Herberstein.** Tucked in the historic Kremsmünsterhaus you'll find an elegant and popular restaurant with a 1960s-retro look, defined by cozy tables, muted lighting, and attractive stonework. The cuisine is Austrian with a slice of Asia, as evidenced by the selection of wok dishes. Main courses include mouthwatering variations of fish, such as the pan-fried salmon trout with saffron rice and cardamom-orange sauce. On Saturday, a romantic "Dinner for 2," including a four-course meal, aperitif, and bottle of wine is offered for €89. If the weather is fine, you can opt to sit outside in the inviting, enclosed *Hof* (courtyard). ⊠*Altstadt 10* ☎*0732/786161* ⌔*Reservations essential* ▭*AE, DC, MC, V* ☉*No lunch Mon.–Sat.*

$–$$ ✕**Höfinger's.** Although it's on the Hauptplatz (main square) this place
★ can be overlooked, as it is tucked away at the end of a long passage through the doorway of No. 23. The columned courtyard is calm and cool and the restaurant inside is simply furnished—no frills—but pleasant. Home cooking prevails with ingredients that are guaranteed to

be fresh and of local provenance. The crispy *Zanderfilet* (pike perch) with gherkin linguini in a honey sauce is a winner. Some well-known favorites like Wiener schnitzel can be ordered as Klein (small portions). There are plenty of vegetarian dishes, too. ⊠*Hauptplatz 23* ☎*0732/770742* ⊟ *MC, V* ⊘*Closed Sun.*

$–$$ ✕**Promenadenhof.** The atmosphere is that of a spacious, contemporary *Gasthaus,* with a fabulous roofed garden filled with flowers. The cellar is open for you to pick your own wine, available by the glass from open bottles. The varied menu of regional cuisine is reasonably priced and has a touch of the Mediterranean. Plenty of vegetarian meals are available but go for the *Tafelspitz* if you like really good beef. Desserts include a yummy baked apple dumpling dish served with a sweet wine sauce. Service is excellent. The place is easy to find; just look for the theater in the heart of the Altstadt. ⊠*Promenade 39* ☎*0732/777661* ⊟*AE, DC, MC, V* ⊘*Closed Sun.*

$–$$ ✕**Verdi Einkehr.** The trendy, less-pricey bistro (Austrian-style) alterna-
★ tive to Verdi—a noted Linz dinner restaurant—Verdi Einkehr shares the same house and kitchen. The rooms are done in rustic chic, with stone fireplaces, chintz-covered chairs, and lots of polished wood. There is also a terrace for summer dining. Delights are many, ranging from guinea fowl with thyme gnocchi to a *Saiblingschnitzel* (golden-fried char) served with lime radicchio risotto. If you don't have a car, you'll need a taxi to get here. It's set in Lichtenberg, about 3 km (2 mi) north of the center, off Leonfelderstrasse. You must specify that you want to be seated in the Einkehr. ⊠*Pachmayrstrasse 137* ☎*0732/733005* ⬩*Reservations essential* ⊟*DC, MC, V* ⊘*Closed Sun. and Mon.*

¢–$ ✕**Schloss Café.** A more pleasant spot for casual dining in Linz can
★ hardly be imagined, tucked to the side of the town's landmark castle and affording lordly views of the Danube and the opposite bank. Tables are set outside under shady trees and take full advantage of the scenery, but it's alluring inside as well, thanks to the smart red-leather banquettes and modern artwork. The menu offers dishes for every taste, from the bubbling hot spinach-and-feta crepes to a big chicken salad with pumpkinseed-oil dressing. Zipfer beer is fresh on tap, and wines from the Danube Valley are featured. ⊠*Tummelplatz 10* ☎*0732/781574* ⊟*MC, V.*

¢ ✕**Traxlmayr.** Proud with the patina of age, this is one of Austria's great
★ old-tradition coffeehouses, and the only one of its kind in Upper Austria. You can linger all day over a single cup of coffee, reading the papers (*Herald Tribune* included) in their bentwood holders, and then have a light meal. In winter it's extremely smoky from European cigarettes, but in summer you can sit outside on the terrace, enjoy the cleaner air, and watch passersby. Ask for the specialty, Linzertorte (almond cake with jam), with your coffee, or try the homemade Apfelstrudel. ⊠*Promenade 16* ☎*0732/773353* ⊟*No credit cards.*

WHERE TO STAY

$$–$$$$ ⊞**Arcotel Nike.** Next door to the Brucknerhaus concert hall, the Arcotel Nike is a good 10-minute walk from the Altstadt. Rooms in this modern, relatively uninspiring high-rise on the banks of the Danube are smallish, but comfortable and well-equipped. Just recently the hotel

4

was given an overhaul and a "feel-good" oasis with steam bath, sauna, and pool was added. Executive rooms on floors 7 to 11 are equipped with Internet and flat-screen TVs. There's a generous breakfast buffet for an extra charge. Check for special low rates and packages at certain times of the year. **Pros:** modern rooms; spacious spa area. **Cons:** lacks charm. ⊠ *Untere Donaulände 9* ☎ *0732/76260* ⊕ *www.arcotel. at* ⤜ *172 rooms* ⚭ *In-hotel: 2 restaurants, bars, pool, gym, Internet terminal, parking (paid)* ⊟ *AE, DC, MC, V* ⦿ *CP.*

$$$ 🏨 **Drei Mohren.** Legend has it that three Moors were stranded here in a
★ snowstorm in 1770 and took such a liking to the place that they made Linz their home. You, too, may cotton to this inn, which faces Landhaus Park in the very heart of the city center. Occupying three 16th-century buildings (with lots of modernizations), this pretty, family-owned hotel has some guest rooms beautifully decorated in regal blue and gold with large, state-of-the art baths; others are smaller and more modestly furnished. The showpiece is the elegant drawing room, replete with card tables, wing chairs, and a fireplace. **Pros:** elegant, spacious rooms; weekend rates; good breakfast buffet. **Cons:** lots of regulars; often full. ⊠ *Promenade 17* ☎ *0732/772626–0* ⊕ *www.drei-mohren.at* ⤜ *25 rooms* ⚭ *In-room: no a/c. In-hotel: bar, parking (free)* ⊟ *AE, DC, MC, V* ⦿ *BP.*

$$–$$$ 🏨 **Landgraf.** Set in a turn-of-the-century redbrick building, this new, ultrachic hotel is next door to the Ars Electronica Museum and just a five-minute walk across the bridge from the Altstadt. Guest rooms are enormous, so big that even though they have a good-size bed, desk, bookcases, and seating arrangements, they still seem rather bare. Rolf Benz designed the striking leather furniture in the three suites and the Philippe Starck–designed bathrooms feature an open-style bath. If you don't book a suite, request a room on the rear side of the house; these are much quieter. **Pros:** spacious rooms; very trendy interior. **Cons:** busy area; can get noisy at night. ⊠ *Hauptstrasse 12* ☎ *0732/700712* ⤜ *35 rooms* ⚭ *In-room: no a/c. In-hotel: restaurant, bar, Internet terminal, parking (fee)* ⊟ *AE, DC, MC, V* ⦿ *BP.*

$$ 🏨 **Wolfinger.** A 500-year-old former nunnery, the centrally located Wolfinger has been a hostelry since the late 1700s. Some rooms have real charm, with vaulted ceilings and antique headboards; others are furnished with a mixture of kitsch and modern pieces. Those in the front on the busy square are less quiet but offer a view of city activities. The breakfast room allures with flowing curtains and Baroque-style chandeliers—a lovely way to greet the day. The tourist information office is right across the square. **Pros:** great location for museums and restaurants; charming rooms; very helpful and friendly staff. **Cons:** creaking floorboards; old fittings in some rooms. ⊠ *Hauptplatz 19* ☎ *0732/773291–0* ⊕ *www.hotelwolfinger.at* ⤜ *45 rooms, 4 without bath* ⚭ *In-room: no a/c. In-hotel: Internet terminal, parking (paid)* ⊟ *AE, DC, MC, V* ⦿ *BP.*

$–$$ 🏨 **Zum Schwarzen Bären.** The birthplace of the renowned Mozart tenor Richard Tauber (1891–1948), the "Black Bear" is a traditional house filled with memorabilia. It sits on a quiet side street in the center of the Old City, a block from the pedestrian zone. The floors and walls are of gleaming wood, sprightly curtains decorate the windows, and the low, modern beds have fluffy white comforters. Some rooms contain imaginative bathrooms with brick-and-gray-tile bathtubs set out in the open. Room differ considerably in size; ask to see your room first, if possible. The hotel also has a very good *Heurige*-style restaurant. Pros: quiet location; some rooms have waterbeds. Cons: old-fashioned interior. ⊠*Herrenstrasse 9–11* ☎*0732/772477–0* ⊕*www. linz-hotel.at* ⇆*35 rooms* ♿*In-room: no a/c. In-hotel: restaurant, bar, Internet terminal, parking (paid)* ☐*MC, V* ⫿⦿*BP.*

SWEET TOOTH?

The cuisine of the Danube Valley usually runs along traditional lines, but the desserts are often brilliant inventions. First among these is the celebrated Linzertorte, with its filling of brandy-flavored apricots, raspberries, or plums under a latticed pastry crust. Less well-known are Linzer Augen, jam-filled cookies. A specialty found only in the Wachau region of the Danube Valley is the *Wachauer Semmel,* a freshly baked roll that is crisped golden on the outside and dense and chewy inside.

NIGHTLIFE & THE ARTS

Linz is far livelier than even most Austrians realize. The local population is friendlier than that of either Vienna or Salzburg, and much less cliquish. And Linz hasn't lagged behind other Austrian cities in developing its own fashionable neighborhood, known as the Bermuda Triangle. Around the narrow streets of the Old City (Klosterstrasse, Altstadt, Hofgasse) are dozens of fascinating small bars and lounges; as you explore, you'll probably meet some Linzers who can direct you to the current "in" location.

THE ARTS The talented **Linz opera company** often mounts venturesome works and productions. Most performances are in the Landestheater, with some in the Brucknerhaus.

The tourist office's monthly booklet "Was ist los in Linz und Oberösterreich" ("What's On in Linz and Upper Austria") will give you details of theater and concerts.

Two **ticket agencies** are the **Linzer Kartenbüro** (⊠*Herrenstrasse 4* ☎*0732/778800*) and **Kartenbüro Pirngruber** (⊠*Landstrasse 34* ☎*0732/772833*).

A vast array of concerts and recitals are presented in the noted **Brucknerhaus,** the modern hall on the bank of the Danube. From early to late September it's home to the International Bruckner Festival. In mid-June the hall hosts the biggest multimedia event in the area, the Ars Electronica, a musical and laser-show spectacle. ⊠*Untere Donaulände 7* ☎*0732/775230* ⊕*www.brucknerhaus.at* ☯*Box office Sept.–June, weekdays noon–6:30, Sat. 10–1; July and Aug. Mon.–Sat. 10–1.*

NIGHTLIFE A good starting point, where both the young and the older will feel comfortable, is the below-stairs, fanciful, Moroccan-style bar in the **Landgraf Hotel** (⊠*Hauptstrasse 12*), which is just across the bridge from the Altstadt and open Tuesday–Saturday from 6 PM until the wee hours.

The Linz **casino,** with roulette, blackjack, poker, and slot machines, is in the Hotel Schillerpark; the casino complex includes a bar and the Rouge et Noir restaurant. A passport is required for admission. Parking in the garage is free. The less formal Jackpot Casino, which does not require a jacket and tie, opens at noon. ⊠ *Rainerstrasse 2–4* ☎ *0732/654487–0* 🎫 *€23, includes €25 worth of tokens* ⊙ *Daily 3* PM–*3* AM.

There are a number of good late-night locations in the city, but for lovers of good beer and whiskey the **Chelsea Pub** (⊠ *Domgasse 5* ☎ *0732/779409*) is probably the best place in Linz. Located in the heart of Linz behind the old cathedral, it's open daily from 6 PM to around midnight or later depending on the crowd, Friday and Saturday till 2 PM. **Josef Stadtbräu** (⊠ *Landstrasse 49* ☎ *0732/773165*) is another hopping establishment with its own home-brewed beer on tap, light snacks, and hearty regional dishes, open every day from 11 AM until very late.

SHOPPING

Linz is a good place to shop; prices are generally lower than those in resorts and the larger cities, and selections are varied. The major shops are found in the main square and the adjoining side streets, in the old quarter to the west of the main square, in the pedestrian zone of the Landstrasse and its side streets, and in the Hauptstrasse of Urfahr, over the Nibelungen Bridge across the Danube.

For local handmade goods and good-quality souvenirs, try **O.Ö. Heimatwerk** (⊠ *Landstrasse 31* ☎ *0732/773–3770*), where you'll find silver, pewter, ceramics, fabrics, and some clothing. Everything from clothing to china is sold at the **Flea Market,** open every Saturday from 7 to 2 on the Hauptplatz (main square). Check with the tourist office about other flea markets. At the state-run **Dorotheum auction house** (⊠ *Fabrikstrasse 26* ☎ *0732/773132–0*), auctions take place on varying days—see the auction calendar on the Dorotheum Web site. The auction house is open to the public weekdays 9–5.

For antiques, head for the Old City and these shops on the side streets around the main square. **Otto Buchinger** (⊠ *Bethlehemstrasse 5* ☎ *0732/770117*) is the place to go for modern drawings and 19th-century furniture and artworks. **Richard Kirchmayr** (⊠ *Bischofstrasse 3a* ☎ *0732/797711*) has a tempting collection of paintings and furniture. **Kunst-Haus Dr. Pastl** (⊠ *Wischerstrasse 26* ☎ *0699/117221–44*) is known throughout Linz for the great selection of sculpture and 18th-century paintings, ceramics, and porcelain. **Ferdinand Saminger** (⊠ *Waldeggstrasse 20* ☎ *0732/654081*) sells antique paintings and objets d'art.

There are two superior places in the city center to shop for elegant jewelry at reasonable prices, **Juwelier Mayrhofer** (⊠ *Hauptplatz 22* ☎ *0732/775649*) and **Atelier Almesberger** (⊠ *Hofgasse 7* ☎ *0732/790561*), where individual, handmade pieces catch the eye. For nice, less costly jewelry and souvenirs, go to **Le Clou** (⊠ *Landstrasse 17–25* ☎ *0732/782980*).

SPORTS & THE OUTDOORS

BICYCLING Cyclists appreciate the relatively level terrain around Linz, and within the city there are 89 km (55 mi) of marked cycle routes. Get the brochure "Cycling in Linz" from the tourist office. You can rent a bike through **LILO Bahnhof** (⊠*Coulinstrasse 30* ☎*0732/600703*) or **Donau Touristik** (⊠*Lederergasse 4–12* ☎*0732/2080*). The latter also runs guided cycling tours along the Danube River. If you prefer to glide and not pedal take the two- to three-hour Segway tour for €48 that leaves from the Tourist Information Office (⊠ *Hauptplatz 1* ☎*0732/7070–2009*).

EXCURSIONS FROM LINZ

4

Many travelers find Linz the most practical point of departure for visits to nearby towns, which are filled with noteworthy Gothic and Baroque sights. You'll be dazzled by two masterworks of the Austrian Baroque, the great abbeys of St. Florian and Kremsmünster, in towns of the same name. In the spa town of Bad Hall, you can "take the cure." Steyr—a gorgeous, Gothic-flavored market town once home to the great composer Anton Bruckner—merits an overnight itself.

To the west of Linz, south of the Danube, lies the Innviertel, named for the Inn River (which forms the border with Germany before it joins the Danube), a region of broad fields and meadows and enormous woodland tracts ideal for cycling, hiking, and riding. To the south, the hilly landscape introduces the foothills of the Austrian Alps.

ST. FLORIAN

13 km (8 mi) southeast of Linz.

St. Florian is best known for the great Augustinian abbey, considered among the finest Baroque buildings in Austria. Composer Anton Bruckner (1824–96) was organist here for 10 years and is buried in the abbey.

Fodor'sChoice Built to honor the spot on the river Enns where St. Florian was drowned
★ by pagans in 304 (he is still considered the protector against fire and flood by many Austrians), the **Stift St. Florian** *(St. Florian Abbey)* over the centuries came to comprise one of the most spectacular Baroque showpieces in Austria, landmarked by three gigantic "candle-snuffer" cupolas. In 1686 the Augustinian abbey was built by the Italian architect Carolo Carlone, then finished by Jakob Prandtauer. More a palace than anything else, it is centered on a mammoth **Marmorsaal** (Marble Hall)—covered with frescoes honoring Prince Eugene of Savoy's defeat of the Turks—and a sumptuous library filled with 140,000 volumes. In this setting of gilt and marble, topped with ceiling frescoes by Bartolomeo Altomonte, an entire school of Austrian historiographers was born in the 19th century. Guided tours of the abbey begin with the magnificent figural gateway, which rises up three stories and is covered with symbolic statues. The Stiegenhaus, or Grand Staircase, leads to

the upper floors, which include the **Kaiserzimmer,** a suite of 13 opulent salons (where you can see the "terrifying bed" of Prince Eugene, fantastically adorned with wood-carved figures of captives). The tour includes one of the great masterworks of the Austrian Baroque, Jakob Prandtauer's **Eagle Fountain Courtyard,** with its richly sculpted figures. In the over-the-top **abbey church,** where the ornate surroundings are somewhat in contrast to Bruckner's music, the Krismann organ (1770–74) is one of the largest and best of its period, and Bruckner used it to become a master organist and composer. Another highlight is the **Altdorfer Gallery,** which contains several masterworks by Albrecht Altdorfer, the leading master of the 16th-century Danube School and ranked with Dürer and Grunewald as one of the greatest northern painters. ⊠*Stiftstrasse 1* ☎*07224/8902–0* ⊕*www.stift-st-florian.at* ⊠*€7* ⊗*70-min tour Easter–Oct., daily at 10, 11, 2, 3, and 4.*

NIGHTLIFE & THE ARTS

Summer concerts are held weekends in June and July at the Kremsmünster and St. Florian abbeys; for tickets, contact **Oberösterreichische Stiftskonzerte** (⊠*Domgasse 12* ☎*0732/776127* ⊕*www.stiftskonzerte.at*).

A series of **concerts** (☎*0732/221022* ⊕*www.florianer.at* ⊗*May–Sept., Mon. and Wed.–Fri. 2:30* ⊠*€4*) on the Bruckner organ are given in the church of St. Florian during the summer months. Also look for the annual Christmas concert by the St. Florian choir boys (*Sängerknaben*). For details, check its Web site.

KREMSMÜNSTER

36 km (22½ mi) south of Linz.

★ The vast Benedictine **Stift Kremsmünster** was established in 777 and remains one of the most important abbeys in Austria. Inside the church is the Gothic memorial tomb of Gunther, killed by a wild boar, whose father, Tassilo, duke of Bavaria (and nemesis of Charlemagne), vowed to build the abbey on the site. Centuries later, the initial structures were replaced in the grand Baroque manner, including the extraordinary tower. Magnificent rooms include the Kaisersaal and the frescoed library with more than 100,000 volumes, many of them manuscripts. On one side of the Prälatenhof courtyard are Jakob Prandtauer's elegant fish basins, complete with sculpted saints holding squirming denizens of the deep (which can be consumed in the abbey restaurant, if desired), and opposite is the Abteitrakt, whose art collection includes the Tassilo Chalice, from about 765. The seven-story observatory (*Sternwarte*) houses an early museum of science, which includes (among lots of other treasures) the sextant used by Johannes Kepler. Most travelers arrive here by taking Route 139 (or the train) heading southwest from Linz. ☎*07583/5275–151* ⊕*www.kremsmuenster.at* ⊠*Rooms and art gallery €5, observatory and tour €6.50* ⊗*Rooms and art gallery tour (minimum 5 people) Easter–Oct., daily at 10, 11, 2, 3, and 4; Nov.–Easter, Tues.–Sun. at 11 and 2. Observatory tour (minimum 5 people) May–Oct., daily at 10 and 2.*

Schloss Kremsegg has a collection of rare musical instruments, including the personal collection of Austrian pianist Friedrich Gulda. A number of rooms are dedicated to Franz Schubert, with personal letters and an audio room for listening to his works. ✉ *Kremseggerstrasse 59* ☎ *07583/52470* ⊕ *www.schloss-kremsegg.at* 🎟 *€5* ⊙ *Apr.–Oct., Wed.–Mon. 10–5. Open in winter by arrangement.*

WHERE TO EAT

$$–$$$ ✕ **Gasthof Moser.** North of Kremsmünster on Highway 139 in the village
★ of Neuhofen, the Moser is known throughout the countryside for its good cooking. Built in 1640, it retains a time-stained ambience with its vaulted ceilings, curving, thick, white walls, and dark wood. During the week, it's a gathering spot for chess aficionados from the surrounding area. The menu ranges from old standards like turkey cordon bleu to the innovative cannelloni stuffed with *Zanderfilet* (pike perch) on a bed of roast zucchini and tomatoes. The pork roast with homemade bread dumplings, sauerkraut, and gravy is always a good choice. ✉ *Marktplatz 9, Neuhofen an der Krems* ☎ *07227/4229* ✍ *Reservations essential* 🖃 *DC, V* ⊙ *Closed Mon. and 1st 3 wks in Aug. No lunch Tues.* ⏍ *BP.*

BAD HALL

9 km (5½ mi) southeast of Kremsmünster, 36 km (22 mi) south of Linz.

Bad Hall is a relic from earlier days, when "taking the cure" was in vogue in Europe. It's still a spa, and its saline-iodine waters are prescribed for both internal and external complaints.

The town makes for an enjoyable stop, with its turn-of-the-20th-century frills and houses. ■**TIP➜** During a stroll through the center of town, take a break and enjoy a coffee accompanied by the homemade Bad Haller Torte at the best patisserie in the area, Cafe Pürstinger at Hauptplatz 11. There are music festivals in summer and numerous sports offerings during warm weather—including excellent opportunities for golf and tennis.

WHERE TO STAY & EAT

$–$$ ✕ **Gasthof Hametner-Innviertlerhof.** Right in the middle of town, very close to the huge spa, this popular restaurant is reminiscent of a large, venerable farmhouse, with lots of cozy rooms. The friendly staff, good service, and home-style cooking makes this a fine choice for lunch or dinner. Authentic regional specialties might include fillet of veal in a zucchini mousse or a hearty dish of pork fillet with potato dumpling and sauerkraut. The pride of the house, though, has to be the scrumptious calorie-charged original *Hametner Torte*. There are 11 rather plain bedrooms here, too. ✉ *Kirchenstrasse 12* ☎ *07258/2082* ⊕ *www.gasthof-hametner.at* 🖃 *MC, V* ⊙ *Closed Wed. and Thurs.*

$$$$ 🖫 **Hotel Miraverde.** This luxurious, completely revitalized and modern-
★ ized hotel located in the middle of a beautiful park is a quiet, tranquil choice. The hotel has its own spa, with indoor and outdoor thermal pools and a wealth of therapeutic and wellness treatments; guests also

have access to the huge public spa in Bad Hall. The rooms are furnished in a blend of Art Nouveau and contemporary style with warm colors and dark and light wood features and floors. Some rooms have balconies and views of the park. The bathrooms are spacious and well fitted, with bathrobes and slippers. **Pros:** excellent staff; quiet location; terrific spa amenities. **Cons:** spa can be busy at times. ⊠*Parkstrasse 4* ☎*07258/799–6600* ⊕*www.eurothermen.at* ⤻*70 rooms* ☐ *In-hotel: restaurant, pool, parking (free)* ☐*AE, DC, MC, V* |◯|*MAP.*

STEYR

★ *18 km (11 mi) east of Bad Hall, 40 km (25 mi) south of Linz. If you travel to Steyr from Kremsmünster, follow Rte. 139 until it joins Rte. 122, and take road another 17 km (10½ mi).*

Steyr is one of Austria's best-kept secrets, a stunning Gothic market town that watches over the confluence of the Steyr and Enns rivers. Today the main square is lined with Baroque facades, many with Rococo trim, all complemented by the castle that sits above. The Bummerlhaus at No. 32, in its present form dating from 1497, has a late-Gothic look. On the Enns side, steps and narrow passageways lead down to the river. Across the River Steyr, St. Michael's Church, with its Bohemian cupolas and gable fresco, presides over the postcard-perfect scene. In the center of town is the Stadtplatz, lined with arcaded houses, along with a Rococo-era town hall and a late-Gothic burgher's house.

In Steyr you are close to the heart of Bruckner country. He composed his Sixth Symphony in the parish house here, and there is a Bruckner room in the Meserhaus, where he composed his "sonorous music to confound celestial spheres." Schubert also lived here for a time. So many of the houses are worthy of attention that you'll need to take your time and explore. Excitement is guaranteed if you accompany the night watchman on his tour of the historic center (for info, contact the tourist board). Given the quaintness of the town center, you'd hardly guess that in 1894 Steyr had Europe's first electric street lighting.

ESSENTIALS
Tourist Information **Steyr** (⊠*Stadtplatz 27* ☎*07252/53229–0).*

EXPLORING
The **Steyrertalbahn** (☎*0664–5087664 or 07257/7102* ⊕*www.steyrtal bahn.at*), a narrow-gauge vintage railroad, wanders 17 km (10½ mi) from Steyr through the countryside from late May to late September. It also runs in December on weekends, on the 6th (as the St. Nikolaus train), and on the 31st.

In a Gothic building on Michaelerplatz, the **Austrian Christmas Museum** houses the world's largest private collection of antique Christmas-tree decorations. There are more than 10,000 ornaments created out of glass, porcelain, metal, and many other materials. In addition, there are more than 200 parlor dolls, doll houses, and doll tea-cozies from Biedermeier time to post–World War II. A thoroughly eccentric Viennese lady named Elfriede Kreuzberger collected this treasure and decided that Steyr was the right place to deposit her hoard. There's also a cute, tiny, single-seater train that takes you up two floors, past Nativity scenes, to the attic with its angel workshop. ⊠ *Michaelerplatz 2* ☎ *07252/80659, 07252/53229 tourist board* ⛛ *€3, combination train and museum €7* ☉ *Late Nov.–early Jan., daily 10–5. For visits outside these dates call tourist board.*

The **Museum Industrielle Arbeitswelt** *(Industrial Museum)*, set in former riverside factories, is a reminder of the era when Steyr was a major center of iron making and armaments production; hunting arms are still produced here, but the major output is powerful motors for BMW cars, including some assembled in the United States. Interactive installations and exhibitions make for a worthwhile visit. ⊠ *Wehrgrabengasse 7* ☎ *07252/77351* ⊕ *www.museum-steyr.at* ⛛ *€5* ☉ *Sept.–July, Tues.–Sun. 9–5.*

WHERE TO STAY & EAT

$$$–$$$$
★
✕ **Rahofer.** You'll have to search for this popular restaurant, which is hidden at the end of one of the passageways off the main square. Inside it's warm and cozy, with dark-wood accents and candlelight. The focus here is Italian, from the Tuscan bread and olives brought to your table on your arrival to the selection of fresh pastas and lightly prepared meat and fish dishes. Individual pizzas are baked to perfection with a thin, crispy crust and toppings ranging from arugula and shaved Parmesan to tuna and capers. The wines come mainly from vineyards in Friuli, Toscana, and Piemont. ⊠ *Stadtplatz 9* ☎ *07252/54606* ☐ *AE, DC, MC, V* ☉ *Closed Sun. and Mon.*

$$–$$$$
🏨 **Minichmayr.** From this traditional hotel the view alone—out over the confluence of the Enns and Steyr rivers, up and across to the Schloss Lamberg and the Baroque cupolas of St. Michael's Church—will make your stay memorable. Some rooms have modern-style Biedermeier furnishings, complementing the old-world charm of the building's exterior and public rooms, and others have traditional cherrywood furniture. Try to get a room on the river side—the front of the hotel overlooks a busy street. The restaurant, with a Secession-style bar, offers classic Austrian cuisine, specializing in fresh fish. **Pros:** beautiful location; charming staff; very good restaurant. **Cons:** front rooms can be noisy. ⊠ *Haratzmüllerstrasse 1–3* ☎ *07252/53410–0* ⊕ *www.hotel-minichmayr.at* 🛏 *47 rooms* ⚷ *In-room: no a/c. In-hotel: restaurant, bar, Internet terminal* ☐ *AE, DC, MC, V* ⏐⌾⏐ *BP.*

$$
🏨 **Hotel Mader.** This gabled house in the Gothic style, erected more than 500 years ago, is now a charming, family-run hotel with pleasant and well-equipped modern rooms. Although it may be noisier to have a room that faces the front, it's worth it for the view overlooking the beautiful town square. The restaurant offers solid local and traditional fare, with outdoor dining in a delightful garden area within the ancient courtyard. You can also dine by candlelight in the romantic wine cellar. **Pros:** the building oozes historic charm; very friendly staff; great location. **Cons:** some rooms on the small side; difficult to find parking in front of the hotel. ⊠ *Stadtplatz 36* ☎ *07252/53358–0* ⊕ *www.mader.*

4

at ⟨▷60 *rooms* ⚬*In-room: no a/c, Internet (some). In-hotel: restaurant* ⊟*AE, DC, MC, V* ⦿|*BP.*

Waidhofen an der Ybbs. Well worth a slight detour from the more traveled routes, this picturesque river town (30 km [18 mi] east of Steyr) developed early as an industrial center, where Styrian iron ore was turned into swords, knives, sickles, and scythes. These weapons proved successful in the defense against the invading Turks in 1532; marking the decisive moment of victory, the hands on the north side of the town tower clock remain at 12:45. In 1871 Baron Rothschild bought the collapsing castle and assigned Friedrich Schmidt, architect of Vienna's City Hall, to rebuild it in neo-Gothic style. Stroll around the two squares in the Altstadt to see the Gothic and Baroque houses and to the Graben on the edge of the Old City for the delightful Biedermeier houses and churches and chapels.

THE WACHAU: ALONG THE SOUTH BANK OF THE DANUBE

The gentle countryside south of the Danube and east of Linz is crossed by rivers that rise in the Alps and eventually feed the Danube. In this prosperous country of light industry and agriculture, there's little remaining evidence that the area was heavily fought over in the final days of World War II. From 1945 to 1955 the River Enns marked the border between the western (U.S., British, and French) and eastern (Russian) occupation zones. The great attraction here—and the adjective is entirely appropriate—is a string of Baroque-era abbeys, including the incomparable Stift Melk, set above the Danube.

ENNS

20 km (12 mi) southeast of Linz.

Enns has been continuously settled since at least AD 50; the Romans set up a major encampment shortly after that date. Contemporary Enns is dominated by the 184-foot-high city tower (1565–68) that stands in the town square. A number of Gothic buildings in the center have Renaissance or Baroque facades.

Visit the **Basilika St. Laurenz,** built on the foundations of a far earlier church, west of the town center, to view the glass-encased archaeological discoveries. And outside, look for the Baroque carved-wood Pontius Pilate disguised as a Turk, alongside a bound Christ, on the balcony of the old sanctuary.

Guided tours (☎07223/82777) of the town's highlights, starting at the tower, are available daily early May–mid-September. The cost is €23 for the 1½-hour tour. If there are more than 10 people, the price is €5 per person.

WHERE TO STAY

$ ⬚**Lauriacum.** You might overlook this plain postwar building, set as it is among Baroque gems in the center of town, but it's the best place to stay. Some of the rooms have been given a recent face-lift and have bright, colorful interiors. Most of the furnishings are plain but comfortable and the bathrooms are well equipped and clean. If there is more than one spare room, have a look at a few before checking in. The quiet garden is a welcoming spot in fine weather. **Pros:** excellent location in the heart of Enns; helpful staff; bikes available for rent. **Cons:** front of hotel can be noisy at night. ✉ *Wienerstrasse 5–7* ☎ *07223/82315* ⊕ *www.lauriacum.at* ➘*30 rooms* ⌂ *In-room: no a/c. In-hotel: restaurant, bar, Internet terminal* ▭ *AE, DC, MC, V* ⦿|*BP.*

4

MAUTHAUSEN

14 km (8½ mi) southeast of Linz, 6 km (4 mi) north of Enns.

In the midst of all the beauty of the Wachau Valley, horror. Adolf Hitler had the **Mauthausen Konzentrationslager,** the main concentration camp in Austria, built here along the bank of the Danube in the town of the same name. The pretty town of Mauthausen, with numerous 15th- and 16th-century buildings, was selected as the site for a concentration camp because of the granite quarries nearby, which would provide material needed for the grandiose buildings projected in Hitler's "Führer cities." The grim, gray fortress was opened in August 1938 for male prisoners (including boys), and the conditions under which they labored were severe even by SS standards. Beginning in the early 1940s women were also admitted as prisoners. More than 125,000 people lost their lives here before the camp was liberated by the American army in May 1945. Much of the camp is preserved exactly as it was left after the liberation, and it's possible to walk through many of the low, wooden buildings. An impressive visitor information center has semiprivate cubicles with headphones for listening to videotaped testimonies of survivors. The site also includes a small museum and memorials, as well as a bookstore. From Linz, follow signs to Enns and Perg, and then to the EHEMALIGE KZ DENKMAL, the concentration-camp memorial. ✉ *Erinnerungsstrasse 1* ☎ *07238/2269* ⊕ *www.mauthausen-memorial.at* ▦ *€2* ⊙ *Daily 9–5:30.*

YBBS AN DER DONAU

69 km (43 mi) east of Linz.

Floods and fires have left their mark on Ybbs an der Donau, but many 16th-century houses remain, their courtyards vine-covered and shaded.

The parish church of **St. Laurence** has interesting old tombstones, a gorgeous gilt organ, and a Mount of Olives scene with clay figures dating from 1450. To get to Ybbs an der Donau from Waidhofen an der Ybbs, make your way back to the Danube via routes 31 and 22 east, then take Route 25 north through the beer-brewing town of Wieselburg.

MELK

★ *22 km (13 mi) east of Ybbs an der Donau, 18 km (11 mi) west of St.*
Pölten, 33 km (21 mi) southwest of Krems.

One of the most impressive sights in all Austria, the abbey of Melk is
best approached in mid- to late afternoon, when the setting sun ignites
the abbey's ornate Baroque yellow facade. As one heads eastward par-
alleling the Danube, the abbey, shining on its promontory above the
river, comes into view. It easily overshadows the town—located along
Route 1—but remember that the riverside village of Melk itself is worth
exploring. A self-guided tour (in English, from the tourist office) will
head you toward the highlights and the best spots from which to photograph the abbey.

ESSENTIALS

Tourist Information **Melk** (⊠ *Babenbergerstrasse 1* ☎ *02752/52307–410*).

EXPLORING

Fodor'sChoice   By any standard, **Stift Melk** (*Melk Abbey*) is a Baroque-era masterpiece.
★   Part palace, part monastery, part opera set, Melk is a magnificent
vision thanks greatly to the upward-reaching twin towers capped with
Baroque helmets and cradling a 208-foot-high dome, and a roof bristling with Baroque statuary. Symmetry here beyond the towers and
dome would be misplaced, and much of the abbey's charm is due to
the way the early architects were forced to fit the building to the rocky
outcrop that forms its base. Erected on the site of an ancient Roman
fort, used by Napoléon as his Upper Austrian redoubt, exploited as the
setting for part of Umberto Eco's *Name of the Rose* and still a working
monastery, the Benedictine abbey has a history that extends back to the
11th century, as it was established in 1089. The glorious building you
see today is architect Jakob Prandtauer's reconstruction, completed in
1736, in which some earlier elements are incorporated; two years later
a great fire nearly destroyed the abbey and it had to be rebuilt. A tour of
the building includes the main public rooms: a magnificent library, with
more than 100,000 books, nearly 2,000 manuscripts, and a superb ceiling fresco by the master Paul Troger; the **Marmorsaal**, whose windows
on both sides enhance the ceiling frescoes; and the glorious **Stiftskirche**
(abbey church) of Saints Peter and Paul, an exquisite example of the
Baroque style. The **Stiftsrestaurant** (closed November–April) offers
standard fare, but the abbey's excellent wines elevate a simple meal to
a lofty experience—particularly on a sunny day on the terrace. ⊠ *Abt
Berthold Dietmayr-Strasse 1* ☎ *02752/555–232* ⊕ *www.stiftmelk.at*
🎫 *€7.50; with tour €9.30* ⊙ *End of Mar.–Apr. and Oct., daily 9–4:30,
ticket office closes at 4; May–Sept., daily 9–5:30, ticket office closes at
5. Guided tours in English May–Oct., daily 10:55 and 2:55; Apr. and
May, daily 2:55.*

WHERE TO STAY & EAT

$$–$$$ ✗**Tom's.** The Wallner family has given son Tom full creative control
★   of the kitchen in this Melk landmark, and to show its approval even
changed the name from Stadt Melk to Tom's. Nestled below the golden
abbey in the center of the village square, the elegant outpost (whose

DANUBE RIVER CRUISES

A cruise up the Danube to the Wachau Valley is a tonic in any season. A parade of storybook-worthy sights—fairy-tale castles-in-air, medieval villages, and Baroque abbeys crowned with "candle-snuffer" cupolas—unfolds before your eyes. Remember that it takes longer to travel north: the trip upstream to Krems, Dürnstein, and Melk will be longer than the return back to Vienna, which is why many travelers opt to return to the city by train, not boat. Keep your fingers crossed: rumor has it that on some summer days the river takes on an authentic shade of Johann Strauss blue.

Blue Danube Schifffahrt/DDSG. The main company offering sightseeing cruises is based in Vienna. Boats depart from the company's piers at Handelskai 265 (by the Reichsbrücke bridge) every Sunday between May 11 and September 28 at 8:35 AM, arriving in Krems at 1:55 PM and Dürnstein at 2:30 PM, and return from Dürnstein at 4:40 PM, and Krems at 5PM, getting back to Vienna by 9 PM. One way is €19.50 (round-trip €26). The ticket office is at the Vienna piers (take the U-Bahn line U1 to Vorgartenstrasse). ✉ *Friedrichstrasse 7, Vienna* ☎ *01/588–800* ⊕ *www. ddsg-blue-danube.at.*

Brandner Schifffahrt. Another way to cruise the Danube is to leapfrog ahead by train from Vienna to Krems. A short walk takes you to the Schiffstation Krems piers, where river cruises run by Brandner Schifffahrt depart (10:10 AM and 3:40 PM) for a ride to glorious Melk Abbey and Dürnstein. One-way tickets are €18, but its Web site offers an enticing array of extra goodies—oompah band concerts, wine cruises, and the like—for an extra fee. ✉ *Ufer 50, Wallsee* ☎ *07433/2590–21* ⊕ *www. brandner.at.*

guest roster includes the Duke and Duchess of Windsor) maintains its high standards. The seasonal menu may include zucchini Parmesan lasagna with truffles or fresh grilled crayfish drizzled with butter and lemon. Desserts are irresistible, such as chocolate pudding with a Grand Marnier parfait or cheese-curd soufflé with homemade pistachio ice cream. ✉ *Hauptplatz 1* ☎ *02752/52475* ▤ *AE, DC, MC, V* ⊙ *Closed some wks in winter.*

$–$$ ▥ **Hotel zur Post.** Here in the center of town you're in a typical village hotel with the traditional friendliness of family management. The spacious rooms are nicely furnished, very comfortable, and impeccably clean. Some afford views of the abbey, which can be easily reached on foot, but because of its close vicinity, the bell ringing can be a bit of a nuisance. The restaurant offers solid, standard fare. **Pros:** the location for visits to the abbey is perfect; friendly and accommodating; hearty breakfast. **Cons:** parking area behind the hotel is small. ✉ *Linzer Strasse 1* ☎ *02752/52345* ⊕ *www.post-melk.at* ⇌ *27 rooms* ⌂ *In-room: no a/c. In-hotel: restaurant, bar, room service, bicycles, Wi-Fi* ▤ *DC, MC, V* ⊙ *Closed Jan. and Feb.* ❙◎❙ *BP.*

SCHALLABURG

6 km (4 mi) south of Melk.

From Melk, take a road south marked to Mank to arrive at the restored **Schloss Schallaburg** (dating from 1573), a castle featuring an imposing two-story arcaded courtyard that is held to be the area's finest example of Renaissance architecture. Its ornate, warm-brown–terra-cotta decoration is unusual. The yard once served as a jousting court. Many centuries have left their mark on the castle: inside, the Romanesque living quarters give way to an ornate Gothic chapel. The castle now houses changing special exhibits. ⊠*Schloss Schallaburg 1 A-3382* ☎*02754/6317* ⊕*www.schallaburg.at* ☜*€8* ☾*May–early Nov., weekdays 9–5, weekends 9–6; last admission 1 hr before closing.*

EN ROUTE To return to the Wachau from Schallaburg, head back toward Melk and take Route 33 along the south bank. This route, attractive any time of year, is spectacular (and thus heavily traveled) in early spring, when apricot and apple trees burst into glorious bloom. Among the palette of photogenic pleasures is **Schönbühel an der Donau,** whose picturesque castle, perched on a cliff overlooking the river, is unfortunately not open to visitors. Past the village of Aggsbachdorf you'll spot, on a hill to your right, the romantic ruin of the 13th-century Aggstein Castle, reportedly the lair of pirates who preyed on river traffic.

MAUTERN

34 km (21 mi) northeast of Melk, 1 km (½ mi) south of Stein.

Mautern, opposite Krems, was a Roman encampment mentioned in the tales of the Nibelungs. The old houses and the castle are attractive, but contemporary Mautern is known for one of Austria's top restaurants, in an inn run by Lisl Wagner-Bacher; another culinary landmark, Schickh, near Göttweig Abbey, is also excellent and run by her brother and sister.

WHERE TO EAT

$$$$
Fodor's Choice
★

✕**Landhaus Bacher.** This is one of Austria's best restaurants, elegant but entirely lacking in pretension. Lisl Wagner-Bacher, one of the top female chefs in the country, bases the dishes served here on the seasons. In fall look for pumpkin-cream soup and pheasant breast with chestnut ravioli; in winter, scallops with sautéed chicory and pike perch with crispy cabbage lasagna; in spring, Bärlauch (wild garlic) spaghettini and tender veal fillet with prosciutto and fresh asparagus; in summer, local grilled trout or corn-fed chicken with citrus-ginger noodles. You can dine in the garden in summer. The 10-room guesthouse has exquisite bedrooms. ⊠*Südtirolerplatz 2A-3512* ☎*02732/82937* ⊕*www. landhaus-bacher.at* ☜*Reservations essential* ☰*DC, V* ☾*Closed Mon. and Tues. and Jan. 7–Feb.*

GÖTTWEIG

4 km (2½ mi) south of Mautern, 7 km (4½ mi) south of Krems.

★ You're certain to spot the "Austrian Montecassino," **Stift Göttweig** *(Göttweig Abbey)*, as you drive along the riverside road. Vast and squat like its famous Italian counterpart, this vast Benedictine abbey sits high above the Danube Valley atop a mountain gateway to the Wachau. Göttweig's exterior was redone in the mid-1700s in the classical style, which you'll note from the columns, balcony, and relatively plain side towers. The inside is a monument to Baroque art, with marvelous ornate decoration against the gold, brown, and blue. The stained-glass windows behind the high altar date from the mid-1400s. The abbey's public rooms are splendid, particularly the **Kaiserzimmer** (Emperor's Rooms), in which Napoléon stayed in 1809; these are reached via the elegant Emperor's Staircase. During the summer the abbey presents concerts. Try to arrange your visit to include lunch on the terrace of the monastery restaurant, which offers fine wines, local specialties, and beautiful vistas of the Danube Valley. There are rooms for overnight guests. To reach it, cross the river from Krems in the direction of Mautern and then follow signs to Stift Göttweig. ✉*Furth bei Göttweig* ☎*02732/85581* ⊕*www.stiftgoettweig.or.at* ✉*€7, €9 with guided tour* ☉*Mid-Mar.–mid-Nov., daily 10–6, last admittance at 5; guided tours weekdays at 11 and 3, weekends at 11, noon, 1, 2, 3 and 4. Mid.-Nov.–mid-Mar. by appt.*

WHERE TO EAT

$$–$$$ ✕**Schickh.** This rambling yellow restaurant, tucked away next to a brook
★ and among lovely old trees below the north side of Göttweig Abbey, is worth looking for. Chef Christian Schickh creates new versions of traditional Austrian dishes while his sister Eva makes sure everything runs smoothly. One of the tastiest dishes is the organic Waldviertler duck and homemade dumplings. Be sure to save room for the house dessert, *Cremeschnitte*, a light cream pastry. To reach Schickh, cross the river from Krems in the direction of Mautern and Furth bei Göttweig, continuing on a couple of kilometers to the tiny village of Klein Wien. ✉*Klein-Wien 2, Furth bei Göttweig* ☎*02736/7218–0* ⊕*www.schickh.at* ⌕*Reservations essential* ▭*MC, V* ☉*Closed Wed. and Thurs. and mid-Jan.–Mar.*

TULLN

42 km (26 mi) west of Vienna.

ESSENTIALS

Tourist Information Tulln (✉*Minoritenplatz 2* ☎*02272/6900* ⊕*www.tulln.at*).

EXPLORING

At Tulln you'll spot a number of charming Baroque touches in the attractive main square.

The **Egon Schiele Museum** honors the great modern artist (1890–1918) who was born here; the museum, which shows a selection of his works,

CLOSE UP

The Danube Waltzes On

The whole world sighs when it hears the opening strains of Johann Strauss II's "The Blue Danube" waltz. When Strauss composed this piece he was living on Vienna's Praterstrasse, a river's-breath away from the Danube Canal, and enamored of a poem by Karl Beck, whose refrain "By the Danube, beautiful blue Danube" he couldn't get out of his mind. It may come as a surprise to learn that the Waltz King was a terrible dancer and never took to the floor. But if you listen to the first motif of "An der schonen blauen Donau" (Strauss's title)—developing from the D major triad (D–F#–A)—it seems the composer must have been a wonderful swimmer. The melody suggests flowing waters—to be exact, the interplay of main current and subsidiary little

whirlpools you often find on the Danube as you cruise its banks. Strauss composed "On the Beautiful Blue Danube" for a war memorial concert given by the Men's Choral Association at Vienna's Imperial Winter Riding School in 1867, where it was politely applauded, then forgotten the next week. Austria had been trounced by Prussia the year before and was licking its wounds, so hopes were high for the premiere, when the piece was accompanied by a chorus singing lyrics by poet Josef Weyl—"Vienna, be gay!"—but once the chorus was banished (the words fight the waltz rhythm), and once it was taken up at the World Exposition held that year in Paris, "The Blue Danube" exploded around the world.

is in the one-time district prison, with a reconstruction of the cell in which Schiele—accused of producing "pornography"—was locked up in 1912. ⊠ *Donaulände 28* ☎ *02272/64570* ⊠ *€5, more for special exhibits* ⊙ *Apr.–Nov., Tues.–Sun. 10–noon and 1–5.*

A former **Minorite cloister** houses the interesting **Römermuseum** (Roman Museum), which recalls the early Roman settlements in the area. Also look inside the well-preserved, late-Baroque (1750) Minorite church next door. ⊠ *Marc-Aurel-Park 1b* ☎ *02272/65922* ⊠ *€3* ⊙ *Mar.– Nov., Tues.–Sun. 10–noon and 1–5.*

WHERE TO STAY & EAT

$$$–$$$$ ✕**Zur Sonne.** This popular gourmet Gasthaus, owned by the Sodoma family, is elegant yet unpretentious. Zur Sonne has high ceilings, large windows, and fresh flowers. The seasonally changing menu may include *Saibling* (char) lasagna with garden vegetables, organic pork in a creamy mushroom-cabbage sauce with *Erdäpfelpuffer* (hash browns), or saltimbocca of chicken breast with herb risotto. Austrian wines by the glass are very reasonable. End your meal with the homemade apple strudel, which comes warm out of the oven. It's a 20-minute train ride from the Heiligenstadt or Franz Josef stations in Vienna, and a five-minute walk from the Tulln train station. ⊠ *Bahnhofstrasse 48* ☎ *02272/64616* ⚐ *Reservations essential* ▭ *No credit cards* ⊙ *Closed Sun. and Mon.*

$$–$$$ ✕**Floh.** Charmingly homey and cozy, this corner Gasthaus is on the
★ main street of tiny Langenlebarn, close to Tulln. Josef Floh, the young and creative chef, trained at top restaurants in the Salzkammergut and

Tirol before setting up his own establishment. You're in luck if you're here in spring, when you can enjoy Tullnerfeld asparagus dressed with local organic melted butter and Parmesan. For a heartier dish, try the perfectly grilled beef with light, creamy, semolina dumplings. Round off the meal with homemade sorbets, pancake delights, or cheese from Vorarlberg, together with light Austrian wines from the area. ⊠ *Tullner Strasse 1* ☎ *02272/62809* ⚴ *Reservations essential* ⊟ *AE, DC, MC, V* ☉ *Closed Tues. and Wed.*

$ ▦ **Nibelungenhof.** Located almost directly on the banks of the Danube with a shady terrace and garden, this small, charming hotel was recently reopened after a renovation. The 18 spacious and inviting rooms in the two-story building have been updated with elegant touches and painted in deep, warm shades of red or green. Wooden floors are accented with silk carpets. There is no need for air-conditioning in this location as the cool air from the river does the job in summer. **Pros:** cozy, pleasant atmosphere; cool in summer. **Cons:** mosquitoes can be a problem if summers are wet. ⊠ *Donaulände 34* ☎ *02272/62658* ⊕ *www.nibel ungenhof.at* ⇌ *18 rooms* ⚴ *In-room: no a/c. In-hotel: restaurant, bar* ⊟ *MC, V* ⑩ *BP.*

GREIFENSTEIN

10 km (6½ mi) northeast of Tulln.

Greifenstein is east of Tulln along Route 14; turn left at St. Andrä-Wördern and stay on the bank of the Danube.

Atop the hill at Greifenstein, yet another **castle** with spectacular views looks up the Danube and across to Stockerau. Its earliest parts date from 1135, but most of it stems from a thorough but romantic renovation in 1818. The view is worth the climb, even when the castle and inexpensive restaurant are closed. Due to a recent huge fire there are no visits allowed at the present time. ⊠ *Kostersitzgasse 5.*

KLOSTERNEUBURG

13 km (8 mi) northwest of Vienna.

ESSENTIALS

Tourist Information Klosterneuburg (⊠ *Rathausplatz1* ☎ *02243/34396* ⊕ *www. klosterneuburg.net/tourismus*).

EXPLORING

★ The great Augustinian abbey **Stift Klosterneuburg** dominates the town. The structure has undergone many changes since the abbey was established in 1114, most recently in 1892, when Friedrich Schmidt, architect of Vienna's City Hall, added neo-Gothic embellishments to its two identifying towers. Klosterneuburg was unusual in that until 1568 it housed both men's and women's religious orders. In the abbey church look for the carved-wood choir loft and oratory and the large 17th-century organ. Among Klosterneuburg's treasures are the beautifully enameled 1181 Verdun Altar in the Leopold Chapel, stained-glass windows from the 14th and 15th centuries, Romanesque candelabra from the 12th century, and gorgeous ceiling frescoes in the great marble hall. In an adjacent outbuilding there's a huge wine cask over which people slide; the exercise, called *Fasslrutsch'n,* is indulged in during the Leopoldiweinkost, the wine tasting around St. Leopold's Day, November 15. The **Stiftskeller,** with its atmospheric underground rooms, serves standard Austrian fare and wine bearing the Klosterneuberg label. ⊠*Stiftsplatz 1* ☎*02243/411–0* ⊕*www.stift-klosterneuburg.at* ☎*€8* ⊙*May–Nov., daily 9–6; tours in English weekends at 2.*

The **Sammlung Essl** contemporary art museum, somewhat alarmingly resembling a sports center from the outside, was designed by Heinz Tesar to showcase art created after 1945. The permanent collection includes works by such regional artists as Maria Lassnig, Hermann Nitsch, and Arnulf Rainer, and changing exhibitions focus on contemporary artists, including the recently deceased Nam June Paik. The emphasis here is on "new," including special evening concerts that highlight the works of modern composers. To get to the Sammlung Essl museum take the free pink-and-blue shuttle bus from Albertinaplatz 2 (outside Café Mozart) at 10, noon, 2, or 4 (return at 11, 1, 3, or 6). The bus is free only if you purchase a ticket to the museum on board. Every Wednesday evening the public is offered free entrance to the museum from 6 to 9 PM. ⊠*An der Donau–Au 1* ☎*02243/370–5015–0* ⊕*www.sammlung-essl.at* ☎*€7* ⊙*Tues.–Sun. 10–6, Wed. 10–9.*

OFF THE BEATEN PATH

Kahlenbergerdorf. Near Klosterneuburg and just off the road tucked under the Leopoldsberg promontory is the charming small vintners' village of Kahlenbergerdorf, an excellent spot to stop and sample the local wines. You're just outside the Vienna city limits here, which accounts for the crowds (of Viennese, not international tourists) on weekends.

Salzburg

WORD OF MOUTH

"Salzburg is thoroughly Baroque in its appearance (well, except for the Fortress above everything, which is definitely medieval), although many of the Baroque facades cover much older buildings. Also, some of the old buildings were demolished to make some of the squares during Baroque remodeling. Both times I've visited have been in winter and the snow on the city looked absolutely charming. I've heard it said that everyone who visits Salzburg thinks he(she) sees it at the prettiest time. The river running through the city adds to the visual charm."

—noe847

Updated by
Horst Erwin
Reischenböck

"ALL SALZBURG IS A STAGE," Count Ferdinand Czernin once wrote. "Its beauty, its tradition, its history enshrined in the grey stone of which its buildings are made, its round of music, its crowd of fancy-dressed people, all combine to lift you out of everyday life, to make you forget that somewhere far off, life hides another, drearier, harder, and more unpleasant reality." Shortly after the count's book, *This Salzburg,* was published in 1937, the unpleasant reality arrived; but having survived the Nazis, Salzburg once again became one of Austria's top drawing cards. Art lovers call it the Golden City of High Baroque; historians refer to it as the Florence of the North or the German Rome; and, of course, music lovers know it as the birthplace of one of the world's most beloved composers, Wolfgang Amadeus Mozart (1756–91). If the young Mozart was the boy wonder of 18th-century Europe and Salzburg did him no particular honor in his lifetime, it is making up for it now. Since 1920 the world-famous Salzburger Festspiele (Salzburg Festival), the third-oldest on the continent, have honored "Wolferl" with performances of his works by the world's greatest musicians.

Ironically, many who come to this golden city of High Baroque may first hear the instantly recognizable strains of music from the film that made Salzburg a household name: from the Mönchsberg to Nonnberg Convent, it's hard to go exploring without hearing someone humming "How Do You Solve a Problem Like Maria?" A popular tourist exercise is to make the town's acquaintance by visiting all the sights featured in that beloved Hollywood extravaganza *The Sound of Music,* filmed here in 1964. Just like Mozart, the Trapp family—who escaped the Third Reich by fleeing their beloved country—were little appreciated at home; Austria was the only place on the planet where the film failed, closing after a single week's showing in Vienna and Salzburg. It is said that the Austrian populace at large didn't cotton to a prominent family up and running in the face of the Nazis.

ORIENTATION & PLANNING

GETTING ORIENTED

Salzburg lies on both banks of the Salzach River, at the point where it is pinched between two mountains, the Kapuzinerberg on one side, the Mönchsberg on the other. In broader view are many beautiful Alpine peaks.

Salzburg's rulers pursued construction on a grand scale ever since Wolf-Dietrich von Raitenau began his regime in the latter part of the 16th century. At the age of only 28, Wolf-Dietrich envisioned "his" Salzburg to be the Rome of the Alps, with a town cathedral grander than St. Peter's, a Residenz as splendid as a Roman palace, and his private Mirabell Gardens flaunting the most fashionable styles of Italianate horticulture. After he was deposed by the rulers of Bavaria, other cultured prince-archbishops took over. Johann Ernst von Thun and Franz Anton von Harrach commanded the masters of Viennese Baroque, Fischer von Erlach and Lukas von Hildebrandt, to complete Wolf-Dietrich's vision. The result is that Salzburg's many fine buildings blend into a harmonious whole. Perhaps nowhere else in the world is there so cohesive a flowering of Baroque architecture.

But times change and the Salzburgians with them. It is not surprising to learn that Salzburg is now home to one of the most striking museums: the Museum der Moderne. The avant-garde showcase stands on the very spot where Julie Andrews "do-re-mi"-d with the von Trapp brood; where once the fusty Café Winkler stood atop the Mönchsberg mount, a modern, cubical museum of cutting-edge art now commands one of the grandest views of the city.

The Altstadt: In Mozart's Footsteps. Salzburg is the only city in the world with 1,300 years of continuous music history, which you can experience in concert halls, churches, restaurants and bars, and even outdoors in city squares.

Across the River Salzach: From the Fortress to the New Town. Here you can simultaneously enjoy outstanding old and new architecture and beautiful nature, from gardens to the hills.

PLANNING

GETTING HERE & AROUND

BY AIR Salzburg Airport, 4 km (2½ mi) west of the city center, is Austria's second-largest international airport. There are direct flights from London and other European cities to Salzburg, but not from the United States. From the United States you can fly to Munich and take the 90-minute train ride to Salzburg, or you can take a bus run by Salzburger Mietwagenservice. Taxis are the easiest way to get downtown from the Salzburg airport; the ride costs around €13–€14 and takes about 20 minutes. City Bus No. 2, which makes a stop by the airport every 15 minutes, runs down to Salzburg's train station (about 20 minutes), where you can change to Bus No. 3 or 5 for the city center.

BY BOAT For a magically different vantage point, take a round-trip boat ride along the relentlessly scenic Salzach River, departing at the Markartsteg in the Altstadt from April until October. The boat journeys as far south as Hellbrunn Palace (depending on the water level). In June, July, and August you can also take the cruise as you enjoy a candlelight dinner—the real dessert is a floodlit view of Salzburg.

BY BUS A tourist map (available from tourist offices in Mozartplatz and the train station) shows all bus routes and stops; there's also a color-coded map of the public transport network, so you should have no problem getting around. Virtually all buses and trolleybuses (O-Bus) run via Mirabellplatz and/or Hanuschplatz. Single bus tickets bought from the driver cost €1.80. Special multiple-use tickets, available at tobacconists (*Tabak-Trafik*), ticket offices, and tourist offices, are much cheaper. You can buy five single tickets for €1.60 each (not available at tourist offices), a single 24-hour ticket for €3.40.

BY CAR If driving, the fastest routes into Salzburg are the autobahns. From Vienna (320 km [198 mi]), take A1; from Munich (150 km [93 mi]),

A8 (in Germany it's also E11); from Italy, A10. The only advantage to having a car in Salzburg itself is that you can get out of the city for short excursions. The Old City on both sides of the river is a pedestrian zone, and the rest of the city, with its narrow, one-way streets, is a driver's nightmare.

BY TRAIN   Yours truly, can get to Salzburg by rail from most European cities. Salzburg Hauptbahnhof is a 20-minute walk from the center of town in the direction of Mirabellplatz. The bus station and the suburban railroad station are at the square in front. A taxi to the center of town should take about 10 minutes and cost €9.

TOURS   The Old City, composed of several interconnecting squares and narrow streets, is best seen on foot. Salzburg's official licensed guides offer a one-hour walking tour through the Old City every day at 12:15, which starts in front of the Information Mozartplatz (€9—owners of the Salzburg Card get a reduced fee).

Several local companies conduct 1½- to 2-hour city tours. The tour will be in a minibus, since large buses can't enter the Old City. Tours briefly cover the major sights in Salzburg, including Mozart's Birthplace, the festival halls, the major squares, the churches, and the palaces at Hellbrunn and Leopoldskron. Bob's Special Tours is well known to American visitors—the company offers a 10% discount to Fodor's readers who book directly with them without help from their hotel. Salzburg Panorama Tours and Salzburg Sightseeing Tours offer similar tours.

VISITOR INFORMATION
All the major highways into town have their own well-marked information centers. The Salzburg-Mitte center is open April–October, daily 9–7, and November–March, Monday–Saturday 11–5; the Salzburg-Süd, April–October, daily 9–7; and the Salzburg-Nord Kasern service facility is open June–mid-September, daily 9–7.

ESSENTIALS
Airport Contacts Flughafen München (MUC) (☎08997500 ⊕ www.munich-airport. de). **Salzburg Airport (SZG)** (✉ Innsbrucker Bundesstrasse 96 ☎0662/8580 ⊕ www. salzburg-airport.com). **Salzburger Mietwagenservice** (✉ Ignaz-Harrer-Strasse 79a ☎0622/8161–0).

Boat Contacts Salzburger Festungskonzerte GmbH (✉ Anton-Adlgasser-Wegasse 22 ☎0662/825769–12 ⊕ www.salzburgschifffahrt.at).

Bus Contacts Salzburger Verkehrsverbund (Main ticket office) (✉ Schrannengasse 4 ☎0662/44801500).

Medical Assistance St. Johannsspital-Landeskrankenanstalten (✉ Müllner Hauptstrasse 48 ☎0662/44820).

Taxis Radio Cab (☎0662/8111). **Salzburg Panorama Tours** (☎0662/883211–0 ⊕ www.panoramatours.com).

Train Information ÖBB (⊕ www.oebb.at). **Salzburg Hauptbahnhof** (✉ Südtirolerplatz ☎05/1717).

Tour Info Bob's Special Tours (✉ Rudolfskai 38, Salzburg ☎0662/849511 ⊕ www.

GREAT ITINERARIES

IF YOU HAVE 1 DAY

Start at the **Mozartplatz ❶**, not just to make a pit stop at the tourist information office, but to sweeten your tour with a few Mozartkugeln from the nearby chocolate manufacturers Fürst. Flower-bedecked cafés beckon, as does the palatial **Residenz ❹**, home to the great prince-archbishops and the center of Baroque Salzburg. Nearby is the **Dom ❺**, Salzburg's grand 17th-century cathedral. Across the Domplatz is the Franciscan church, **Franziskanerkirche ❽**. A bit to the south is the Romanesque-turned-Rococo **Stiftkirche St. Peter ❼**, where, under the cliffs, you'll find the famous **Petersfriedhof ❻**—St. Peter's Cemetery, whose wrought-iron grills and Baroque vaults shelter the final resting place of Mozart's sister and much of Old Salzburg. Take the Festungsbahn cable car (it's just behind the cathedral) up to the **Fortress Hohensalzburg ❿**—the majestic castle atop the Mönchsberg peak that overlooks the city. Enjoy a rest at the Stadt Alm restaurant or picnic in a quiet corner. Descend back to the city via the Mönchsberg express elevators. Head over to the **Pferdeschwemme ⓭**—the Baroque horse trough that is a somewhat bewildering tribute to the equine race—then over to the **Getreidegasse**. In this venerable merchant's quarter, posh shops set in pastel-covered town houses announce their wares through the overhanging wrought-iron scroll signs, and some of the houses have hidden courtyards set with timber-lined balconies. Next up is the most famous address in town: No. 9 Getreidegasse—**Mozarts Geburtshaus ⓱**, the birthplace of Mozart. After paying your respects, head over to the **Alter Markt ⓲** to welcome twilight with a *Kaffee mit Schlag* (coffee with whipped cream) at Café Tomaselli.

IF YOU HAVE 3 DAYS

With three days, you can explore the **Altstadt**—the Old City—and the **New Town** as described in the two walking tours below. Try to catch an evening concert—perhaps of Mozart's music. For your third day, try one of four options: book a *Sound of Music tour*, then, in the afternoon, take a ride up the **Untersberg**; or opt for a boat trip along the Salzach river south to the 17th-century Hellbrunn Palace with its mischievous water fountains; or take an excursion to the picture-book towns of the **Salzkammergut**. A fourth idea is to walk for about two hours over the Mönchsberg, starting in the south at the **Nonnberg Convent ⓴** and continuing on to the **Richterhöhe** to enjoy the southwestern area of the city. Above the Siegmundstor, the tunnel through the mountain, there is a nice belvedere to take in a city view. But the most fascinating view is from the terrace in front of the new **Museum der Moderne ⓰**, which you reach after passing the old fortifications from the 15th century. Continue on to the Augustinerbräu, the large beer cellar at the northern end of the hill for some of the best brews and conviviality in town.

5

bobstours.com). **Salzburg Panorama Tours** (⊠ *Schrannengasse 2/2, Salzburg* 🕾 *0662/883211-0* ⊕ *www.panoramatours.com*). **Salzburg Sightseeing Tours** (⊠ *Am Mirabellplatz 2, Salzburg* 🕾 *0662/881616* ⊕ *www.welcome-salzburg.at*).

Visitor Info **Railway Station Information** (⊠ *Platform 2A* 🕾 *0662/88987-330*). **Salzburg City Tourist Office** (⊠ *Auerspergstrasse 6* 🕾 *0662/88987-0* ⊕ *www.salzburginfo.at*). **Salzburg-Süd Information** (⊠ *Park & Ride-Parkplatz, Alpensiedlung-Süd, Alpenstrasse 67* 🕾 *0662/88987-360*).

EXPLORING SALZBURG

Getting to know Salzburg is not too difficult, for most of its sights are within a comparatively small area. The Altstadt (Old City) is a compact area between the jutting outcrop of the Mönchsberg and the Salzach River. The cathedral and interconnecting squares surrounding it form what used to be the religious center, around which the major churches and the old archbishops' residence are arranged (note that entrance into all Salzburg churches is free). The Mönchsberg cliffs emerge unexpectedly behind the Old City, crowned to the east by the Hohensalzburg Fortress. Across the river, in the small area between the cliffs of the Kapuzinerberg and the riverbank, is Steingasse, a narrow medieval street where working people lived. Northwest of the Kapuzinerberg lie Mirabell Palace and its gardens.

It's best to begin by exploring the architectural and cultural riches of the Old City, then go on to the fortress and after that cross the river to inspect the other bank. Ideally, you need two days to do it all. An alternative, if you enjoy exploring churches and castles, is to go directly up to the fortress, either on foot or by returning through the cemetery to the funicular railway.

■ TIP→ **If you are doing this spectacular city in just one day, consider taking a walking tour run by city guides; one sets out every day at 12:15 PM, from the tourist information office, Information Mozartplatz, at Mozart Square (closed on some Sundays during off-season).** There are also escorted bus tours through the city but because much of Salzburg's historic city center is for pedestrians only, the bus doesn't get you close to some of the best sights.

THE ALTSTADT: IN MOZART'S FOOTSTEPS

Intent on becoming a patron of the arts, the prince-archbishop Wolf-Dietrich lavished much of his wealth on rebuilding Salzburg into a beautiful and Baroque city in the late 16th and early 17th centuries. In turn, his grand townscape came to inspire the young Joannes Chrysostomus Wolfgangus Amadeus (Theophilus) Mozart. In fact, by growing up in the center of the city and composing already at five years of age, Mozart set lovely Salzburg itself to music. He was perhaps the most purely Austrian of all composers, a singer of the smiling Salzburgian countryside, of the city's gay Baroque architecture. So even if you are

TOP REASONS TO GO

The view from Fortress Hohensalzburg. Go up to the fortress on the peak and see what romantic visitors in the 19th century enjoyed so much—the soul-stirring combination of gorgeous architecture in a stunning natural location.

A pilgrimage to the Rome of the North. See the magnificent Baroque churches built not only to honor God but also to document of the importance of the ruling prince-archbishops during the 17th century.

Concerts, operas, and more. Feel the spirit of 1,300 years of musical history as you listen to the music of Wolfgang Amadeus Mozart, the greatest composer who ever lived, in the Marble Hall of Mirabell Palace.

Or perhaps you would prefer an opera performed by marionettes or a mass sung in the cathedral. You'll run out of time, not options, in Salzburg.

Medieval city. After exploring the Altstadt's grand churches and squares, cross the river Salzach to take in the completely different atmosphere of the narrow, 16th-century Steingasse, where working people once lived and shops, galleries, and clubs now beckon.

Rulers' delights. Drive, bike, walk, or take the boat out to Schloss Hellbrunn, a Renaissance-inspired pleasure palace with trick fountains and the gazebo that witnessed so much wooing in *The Sound of Music.*

not lucky enough to snag a ticket to a performance of *The Marriage of Figaro* or *Don Giovanni* in the Grosses Festspielhaus, you can still enjoy his melodies just by strolling through his streets.

Ever since the 1984 Best Film Oscar-winner *Amadeus* (remember Tom Hulse as "Wolfie"?), the composer has been the 18th-century equivalent of a rock star. Born in Salzburg on January 27, 1756, he crammed a prodigious number of compositions into the 35 short years of his life, many of which he spent in Salzburg (he moved to Vienna in 1781). Indeed, the Altstadt (or Old Town) revels in a bevy of important sights, ranging from his birthplace on the Getreidegasse to the abbey of St. Peter's, where the composer's "Great Mass in C Minor" was first performed. Beyond the Altstadt—the heart of the Baroque Salzburg familiar to the young prodigy—other Mozart-related sights are included in our second Salzburg tour. As you tour the composer's former haunts, why not listen to Papageno woo Papagena on your iPod?

A GOOD WALK

For this city there is no more appropriate center-of-it-all than **Mozartplatz ❶**, the square named to honor Salzburg's native genius. Get in the mood by noticing, near the statue of Mozart, the strolling street violinists, who usually play a Mozart sonata or two. Walk into the next square, the Residenzplatz, centered by the 40-foot-high fountain, which is often illuminated at night. Take in the famous **Glockenspiel ❷** (chances are the tunes it plays will be by you-know-who), set atop the Neubau Palace, now the city's **Salzburg Museum ❸**. Then cross the plaza to enter the **Residenz ❹**, the opulent Baroque palace of Salzburg's prince-archbishops and Mozart's patrons. From the Residenzplatz,

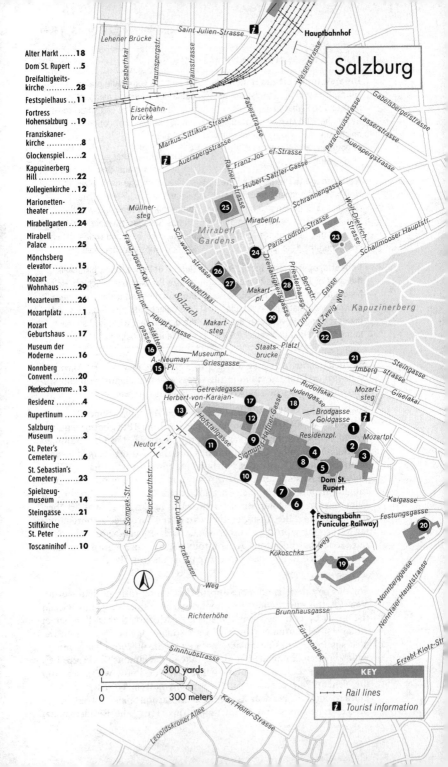

Salzburg

Hauptbahnhof

KEY

⊢—⊢ Rail lines

🛈 Tourist information

walk through the arches into Domplatz, the city's majestic Cathedral Square—in August, set out with seats for the annual presentation of Hofmannsthal's play *Jedermann*. The **Dom** ❺ (Salzburg Cathedral) is among the finest Italian-style Baroque structures in Austria. Walk into the Kapitelplatz through the arches across the square and go through two wrought-iron gateways into **St. Peter's Cemetery** ❻—one of the most historic and beautiful places in Salzburg. Enter the church of **Stiftkirche St. Peter** ❼.

As you leave St. Peter's, look up to the right to see the thin Gothic spire of the **Franziskanerkirche** ❽. Leave the courtyard in this direction, cross the road, and enter around the corner by the main entrance (the side entrance is closed). It will bring you into the Gothic apse crowned by the ornate red-marble altar designed by Fischer von Erlach. Return back up the Romanesque aisle and exit on Sigmund-Haffner-Gasse. Opposite is the rear entrance to one of Salzburg's galleries of contemporary art, the **Rupertinum** ❾. Turn left around the corner into **Toscaninihof** ❿, the square cut into the dramatic Mönchsberg cliff. The wall bearing the harp-shape organ pipes is part of the Haus für Mozart, one of three theaters that constitute the **Festspielhaus** ⓫. The carved steps going up the Mönchsberg are named for Clemens Holzmeister, architect of the new festival hall. If you climb them, you get an intimate view of the Salzburg churches at the level of their spires, and if you climb a little farther to the right, you can look down into the open-air festival hall, the Felsenreitschule, cut into the cliffs. From Hofstallgasse—the main promenade (sometimes floodlighted and adorned with flags during the festival) connecting the main festival theaters—you can either walk directly up to Herbert-von-Karajan-Platz or, preferably, walk around by Universitätsplatz to take a look at one of Johann Bernhard Fischer von Erlach's Baroque masterpieces, the **Kollegienkirche** ⓬, or Collegiate Church. In Herbert-von-Karajan-Platz is another point at which building and cliff meet: the **Pferdeschwemme** ⓭, a horse trough decorated with splendid Baroque-era paintings. To the left is the Siegmundstor, the impressive road tunnel blasted through the Mönchsberg in 1764. The arcaded Renaissance court on your left houses the **Spielzeugmuseum** ⓮ (Toy Museum), and a fine collection of ancient musical instruments.

Pass by the tiny church of St. Blasius, built in 1350, and follow the road on through the Gstättentor to the **Mönchsberg elevator** ⓯ for a trip up the hill to Salzburg's most famous outlook, now the site of a large "white marble brick" (as critics carp), the **Museum der Moderne** ⓰, or Museum of Modern Art. After descending from the heights, turn left into the short street leading to Museumsplatz, where you could explore the Haus der Natur, one of Europe's finest museums of natural history. Walk back toward the Blasius church, which stands at the beginning of the Old City's major shopping street, **Getreidegasse**, hung with numerous signs depicting little wrought-iron cobblers and bakers (few people could read centuries ago). Amid the boutiques and Salzburg's own McDonald's (featuring its own elegant sign) is **Mozarts Geburtshaus** ⓱, the composer's birthplace. Continue down the street past the Rathaus

(Town Hall), and enter the **Alter Markt** ⑱, the old marketplace, adorned with historic buildings.

TIMING   The Old City—the left bank of the Salzach River—contains many of the city's top attractions. Most of your exploring will be done on foot, since this historic section of town bans cars. The center city is compact and cozy, so you can easily cover it in one day. Note that many churches close at 6 PM, so be sure to visit during the daylight hours.

MAIN ATTRACTIONS

⑱ **Alter Markt** (*Old Market*). Right in the heart of the Old City is the Alter Markt, the old marketplace and center of secular life in past centuries. The square is lined with 17th-century middle-class houses, colorfully hued in shades of pink, pale blue, and yellow ocher. Look in at the old royal pharmacy, the **Hofapotheke,** whose ornate black-and-gold Rococo interior was built in 1760. Inside, you'll sense a curious apothecarial smell, traced to the shelves lined with old pots and jars (labeled in Latin). These are not just for show: this pharmacy is still operating today. You can even have your blood pressure taken—but preferably not after drinking a *Doppelter Einspänner* (black coffee with whipped cream, served in a glass) in the famous Café Tomaselli just opposite. In warm weather the café's terrace provides a wonderful spot for watching the world go by as you sip a *Mélange* (another coffee specialty, served with frothy milk), or, during the summer months, rest your feet under the shade of the chestnut trees in the Tomaselli garden at the top end of the square. Next to the coffeehouse you'll find the **smallest house in Salzburg;** note the slanting roof decorated with a dragon gargoyle. In the center of the square, surrounded by flower stalls, is the marble **St. Florian's Fountain,** dedicated in 1734 to the patron saint of firefighters.

⑤ **Dom** (*Cathedral*). When you walk through the arches leading from Resi-
★ denzplatz into **Domplatz,** it's easy to see why Max Reinhardt chose it in August of 1920 as the setting for what has become the annual summer production of Hugo von Hofmannsthal's *Jedermann* (*Everyman*). The plaza is one of Salzburg's most beautiful urban set pieces. In the center rises the Virgin's Column, and at one side is the cathedral, considered to be the first early Italian Baroque building north of the Alps. Its facade is of marble, its towers reach 250 feet into the air, and it holds 10,000 people. There has been a cathedral on this spot since the 8th century, but the present structure dates from the 17th century. The cathedral honors the patron saint of Salzburg, St. Rupert, who founded Nonnberg Abbey around 700, and also the Irish St. Virgil, the founder of the first cathedral consecrated in 774, whose relics lie buried beneath the altar. Archbishop Wolf-Dietrich took advantage of the old Romanesque-Gothic cathedral's destruction by fire in 1598 to demolish the remains and make plans for a huge new structure facing onto the Residenzplatz to reaffirm Salzburg's commitment to the Catholic cause. His successor, Markus Sittikus, and the new court architect, Santino Solari, started the present cathedral in 1614; it was consecrated with great ceremony in 1628 during the Thirty Years' War. The church's simple sepia-and-white interior, a peaceful counterpoint to the usual

Baroque splendor, dates from a later renovation. To see remains of the old cathedral, go down the steps from the left-side aisle into the crypt where the archbishops from 1600 on are buried. Mozart's parents, Leopold and Anna-Maria, were married here in 1747. Mozart was christened, the day after he was born, at the 14th-century font here, and he later served as organist from 1779 to 1781. Some of his compositions, such as the *Coronation Mass,* were written for the cathedral. ■TIP➔ **On Sunday and all Catholic holidays, mass is sung at 10 AM—the most glorious time to experience the cathedral's full splendor.** This is the only house of worship in the world with five independent fixed organs, which are sometimes played together during special church-music concerts. Many of the church's treasures are in a special museum on the premises. ✉*Domplatz* ☎*0662/844189* ⊕*www.kirchen.net/dommuseum* ✉*Museum €5* ⊙*Early May–late Oct., Mon.–Sat. 10–5, Sun. and holidays 11–6.*

★ **Getreidegasse.** For centuries, this has been the main shopping street in the Old City center. According to historians, the name means "trade street"—not "grain street," as many believe. Today you'll find elegant fashion houses, international shoe chains, and a McDonald's (note its wrought-iron sign—one of many on the street—with classy bronze lettering: like all the other shops, it has conformed with Salzburg's strict Old City conservation laws). Besides coming to shop, crowds flock to this street because at No. 9 is Mozart's birthplace, the **Mozarts Geburtshaus.** In summer the street is densely packed with people. You can always escape for a while through one of the many arcades—mostly flower-bedecked and opening into delightful little courtyards—that link the Getreidegasse to the river and the Universitätsplatz. At No. 37 you'll find one of the most glamorous hotels in the world, the Goldener Hirsch—just look for its filigree-iron sign showing a leaping stag with gilded antlers. ■TIP➔ **The Goldener Hirsch's interiors are marvels of Salzburgian gemütlichkeit, so, if you're appropriately attired, you may wish to view the lobby and enjoy an aperitif in its gorgeous bar, *the* watering hole of chic Salzburg.** The southern end of Getreidegasse becomes Judengasse, part of the former Jewish ghetto area, which is also festooned with more of Salzburg's famous wrought-iron signs.

❷ **Glockenspiel.** The famous carillon tower is perched on top of the **Neue Residenz** (New Residence), Prince-Archbishop Wolf-Dietrich's government palace. The carillon is a later addition, brought from today's Belgium in 1695 and finally put in working order in 1704. The 35 bells play classical tunes (usually by Mozart or Haydn) at 7 AM, 11 AM, and 6 PM—with charm and ingenuity often making up for the occasional musical inaccuracy. From Easter to October, the bells are immediately followed by a resounding retort from perhaps the oldest mechanical musical instrument in the world, the 200-pipe "Bull" organ housed in the Hohensalzburg Fortress across town. Details about the music selections are listed on a notice board across the square on the corner of the Residenz building. ✉*Mozartplatz 1.*

❶ **Mönchsberg Elevator.** Just around the corner from the Pferdeschwemme horse-fountain, at Neumayr Platz, you'll find the Mönchsberg elevator, which carries you up through solid rock not only to the new **Museum der Moderne** but also to wooded paths that are great for walking and gasping—there are spectacular vistas of Salzburg. In summer this can be a marvelous—and quick—way to escape the tiny crowded streets of the Old City. ⊠ *Gstättengasse 13* ⊠ *Round-trip €2.90, one-way €1.80* ⊙ *Oct.–May, daily 9–9; June–Sept., daily 9 AM–11 PM.*

🔟 **Museum der Moderne.** Enjoying one of Salzburg's most famous scenic spots, the dramatic museum of modern and contemporary art reposes atop the sheer cliff face of the Mönchsberg. The setting was immortalized in *The Sound of Music*—this is where Julie and the kids start warbling "Doe, a deer, a female deer . . ." Clad in minimalist white marble, the museum (2004) was designed by Friedrich Hoff Zwink of Munich. It has three exhibition levels, which bracket a restaurant with a large terrace—now, as always, the place to enjoy the most spectacular view over the city while sipping a coffee. ■TIP➔ **Visit in the evening to see the city illuminated.** ⊠ *Mönchsberg 32* ☎ *0662/842220* ⊕ *www.museumdermoderne.at* ⊠ *€8* ⊙ *Tues. and Thurs.–Sun. 10–6, Wed. 10–9.*

❹ **Residenz.** At the very heart of Baroque Salzburg, the Residenz over-
★ looks the spacious Residenzplatz and its famous fountain. The palace in its present form was built between 1600 and 1619 as the home of Wolf-Dietrich, the most powerful of Salzburg's prince-archbishops. The Kaisersaal (Imperial Hall) and the Rittersaal (Knight's Hall), one of the city's most regal concert halls, can be seen along with the rest of the magnificent **State Rooms** on a self-guided tour. Of particular note are the frescoes by Johann Michael Rottmayr and Martino Alto-monte depicting the history of Alexander the Great. Upstairs on the third floor is the **Residenzgalerie,** a princely art collection specializing in 17th-century Dutch and Flemish art and 19th-century paintings of Salzburg. On the state-room floor, Mozart's opera *La Finta Semplice* premiered in 1769 in the Guard Room. Mozart often did duty here, as, at age 14, he became the first violinist of the court orchestra (in those days, the leader, as there was no conductor). Today the reception rooms of the Residenz are often used for official functions, banquets, and concerts, and might not always be open for visitors. The palace courtyard has been the lovely setting for Salzburg Festival opera pro-ductions since 1956—mostly the lesser-known treasures of Mozart. ⊠ *Residenzplatz 1* ☎ *0662/8042–2690, 0662/840451 art collection* ⊕ *www.residenzgalerie.at* ⊠ *€8.20 for both museums; art collection only, €6* ⊙ *Mar.–Jan., daily 10–5.*

❸ **Salzburg Museum** (*Neugebäude*). The biggest "gift" to Mozart was the
Fodor's Choice opening, one day shy of his 250th birthday, when, on January 26,
★ 2006, Salzburg's mammoth 17th-century **Neue Residenz** (New Resi-dence) welcomed visitors to an exhibition entitled "Viva! Mozart." The setting is splendid, as this building was Prince-Archbishop Wolf-Dietrich's "overflow" palace (he couldn't fit his entire archiepiscopal court into the main Residenz across the plaza). As such, it features 10 state reception rooms that were among the first attempts at a *stil Renaissance* in the North. Highlights of the archaeological collection include Hallstatt Age relics, remains of the town's ancient Roman

ruins, and the famous Celtic bronze flagon found earlier this century on the Dürrnberg near Hallein (15 km [10 mi] south of Salzburg). Pride of place is given to the spectacular **Sattler Panorama,** one of the few remaining 360-degree paintings in the world, which shows the city of Salzburg in the early 19th century. Also here is the original composition of "Silent Night," composed by Franz Gruber in nearby Oberndorf in 1818. ✉ *Mozartplatz 1* ☎ *0662/620808–700* ⊕ *www.salzburg museum.at* ✉ *€7* ⊗ *Tues., Wed., and Fri.–Sun. 9–5, Thurs. 9–8.*

> **GET CARDED**
>
> Consider purchasing the Salzburg Card. SalzburgKarten are good for 24, 48, or 72 hours for €24–€37, and allow no-charge entry to most museums and sights, use of public transportion, and special discount offers. Children under 15 pay half.

❼ ★ Stiftkirche St. Peter (*Collegiate Church of St. Peter*). The most sumptuous church in Salzburg, St. Peter's is where Mozart's famed *Great Mass in C Minor* premiered in 1783, with his wife, Constanze, singing the lead soprano role. Wolfgang directed the orchestra and choir and also played the organ. During every season of the city's summer music festival in August, the work is performed here during a special church-music concert. The porch has beautiful Romanesque vaulted arches from the original structure built in the 12th century; the interior was decorated in the voluptuous late-Baroque style when additions were made in the 1770s. Note the side chapel by the entrance, with the unusual crèche portraying the Flight into Egypt and the Massacre of the Innocents. Behind the Rupert Altar is the "Felsengrab," a rock-face tomb where—according to a legend—St. Rupert himself was originally buried. To go from the sacred to the profane, head for the abbey's legendary Weinkeller restaurant, adjacent to the church. ✉ *St. Peter Bezirk* ☎ *0662/844578–0* ✉ *Free* ⊗ *Apr.–Sept., daily 6:30 AM–7 PM; Oct.–Mar., daily 6:30–6.*

ALSO WORTH SEEING

⓫ Festspielhaus (*Festival Hall Complex*). With the world-famous Salzburg Festival as their objective, music lovers head for the Hofstallgasse, the street where the three festival theaters are located. Arrow-straight and framing a grand view of the Fortress Hohensalzburg, the street takes its name from the court stables once located here. Now, in place of the prancing horses, festival goers promenade along Hofstallgasse during the intervals of summer performances, showing off their suntans and elegant attire. ■TIP→ **If you want to see the inside of the halls, it's best to go to a performance, but guided tours are given and group tours can be booked on request.** The festival complex consists of three theaters. The first is the **Haus für Mozart** (House for Mozart), formerly the Kleines Festspielhaus, or Small Festival Hall. It seats about 1,600 and is used for productions of Mozart's operas. The center ring is occupied by the famous **Grosses Festspielhaus** (Great Festival Hall), leaning against the solid rock of the Mönchsberg. Opened in 1960, it seats more than 2,150. In recent times the Grosses Festspielhaus, nicknamed the Wagner Stage because of headline-making productions of the *Ring of the*

Nibelungs, has been the venue for spectacular operas and concerts by the world's top symphony orchestras. Stage directors are faced with the greatest challenge in the third theater, the **Felsenreitschule** (the Rocky Riding School), the former Summer Riding School, which—hewn out of the rock of the Mönchsberg during the 17th century by architect Fischer von Erlach—offers a setting that is itself more dramatic than anything presented on stage. Max Reinhardt made the first attempt at using the Summer Riding School as a stage in 1926. With its retractable roof it gives the impression of an open-air theater; the three tiers of arcades cut into the rock of the Mönchsberg linger in the mind of fans of *The Sound of Music* film, for the von Trapps were portrayed singing "Edelweiss" here in their last Austrian concert (according to Hollywood—in fact, the 1950 Festival farewell by the Trapp Family Singers, conducted by Franz Wasner, was given in the Mozarteum and at the cathedral square). The theaters are linked by tunnels (partially in marble and with carpeted floors) to a spacious underground garage in the Mönchsberg. ⊠*Hofstallgasse 1* ☎*0662/849097* ⊕*www.salzburg festival.at* ⬚*Guided tours €5* ⊘*Group tour Jan.–May and Oct.–Dec. 20, daily at 2; June and Sept., daily at 2 and 3:30; July and Aug., daily at 9:30, 2, and 3:30.*

8 **Franziskanerkirche** (*Franciscan Church*). The graceful, tall spire of the Franciscan Church stands out from all other towers in Salzburg; the church itself encompasses the greatest diversity of architectural styles. There was a church on this spot as early as the 8th century, but it was destroyed by fire. The Romanesque nave of its replacement is still visible, as are other Romanesque features, such as a stone lion set into the steps leading to the pulpit. In the 15th century the choir was built in Gothic style, then crowned in the 18th century by an ornate red-marble and gilt altar designed by Austria's most famous Baroque architect, Johann Bernhard Fischer von Erlach. Mass—frequently featuring one of Mozart's compositions—is celebrated here on Sunday at 9 AM. ⊠*Franziskanergasse 5* ☎*0662/843629–0* ⬚*Free* ⊘*Daily 6:30 AM–7 PM.*

12 **Kollegienkirche** (*Collegiate Church*). Completed by Fischer von Erlach in 1707, this church, sometimes called the Universitätskirche, is one of the purest examples of Baroque architecture in Austria. Unencumbered by Rococo decorations, the modified Greek cross plan has a majestic dignity worthy of Palladio. At this writing, the church was undergoing renovations. ⊠*Universitätsplatz* ☎*0662/841–327–72* ⊘*Mon.–Sat. 9–7, Sun. 10–7 (winter closing hrs approximately 3 hrs earlier).*

1 **Mozartplatz** (*Mozart Square*). In the center of the square stands the statue of Wolfgang Amadeus Mozart, a work by sculptor Ludwig Schwanthaler unveiled in 1842 in the presence of the composer's two surviving sons. It was the first sign of public recognition the great composer had received from his hometown since his death in Vienna in 1791. The statue, the first for a non-noble person in old Austria, shows a 19th-century stylized view of Mozart, draped in a mantle, holding a page of music and a copybook. A more appropriate bust of the composer, modeled by Viennese sculptor Edmund Heller, is found on the Kapuzinerberg.

⓱ Mozarts Geburtshaus (*Mozart's Birthplace*). As an adult, the great composer preferred Vienna to Salzburg, complaining that audiences in his native city were no more responsive than tables and chairs. Still, home is home, and this was Mozart's—when not on one of his frequent trips abroad—until the age of 17. Mozart was born on the third (in American parlance, the fourth) floor of this tall house on January 27, 1756, and his family lived on this floor, when they were not on tour, from 1747 to 1773.

As the child prodigy composed many of his first compositions in these rooms, it is fitting and touching to find Mozart's tiny first violin and his viola on display. The second-floor displays focus on the day-to-day living and traveling circumstances of his day, while the third floor has an exhibition called "Mozart on Stage." American artist Robert Wilson redesigned the whole fourth floor, and his sometimes surprising installation uses architecture, light, sound, and design objects with the intention of transforming the museum-like character of the apartment. Most of the rooms here are fitted out with modern museum vitrines and there is not much from Mozart's time. ⊠ *Getreidegasse 9* ☎ *0662/844313* ⊕ *www.mozarteum.at* ☜ *€6.50; combined ticket for Mozart residence and birthplace €10* ☾ *Sept.–June, daily 9–5:30; July and Aug., daily 9–8.*

⓭ Pferdeschwemme (*Horse Pond*). If Rome had fountains, so, too, would Wolf-Dietrich's Salzburg. The city is studded with them, and none is so odd as this monument to the equine race. You'll find it if you head to the western end of the Hofstallgasse to find Herbert-von-Karajan-Platz (named after Salzburg's second-greatest musical son, maestro Herbert von Karajan, the legendary conductor and music director of the Salzburg Festival for many decades. On the Mönchsberg side of the square is the Pferdeschwemme—a royal trough where prize horses used to be cleaned and watered, constructed in 1695; as they underwent this ordeal they could delight in the frescoes of their pin-up fillies on the rear wall. The Baroque monument in the middle represents the antique legend of the taming of a horse, Bellerophon and his mount, Pegasus. ⊠ *Herbert-von-Karajan-Platz.*

Rathaus (*Town Hall*). Where Sigmund-Haffner-Gasse meets the Getreidegasse you will find the Rathaus, an insignificant building in the Salzburg skyline—no doubt reflecting the historical weakness of the burghers vis-à-vis the Church, whose opulent monuments are evident throughout the city. On the other hand, this structure is a prime example of the Italian influence in Salzburg's architecture. Originally this was a family tower (and the only one still remaining here), but it was sold to the city in 1407. ⊠ *Getreidegasse and Sigmund-Haffner-Gasse.*

⓽ Rupertinum. If you are interested in 20th-century art, don't miss the chance to see changing exhibitions of graphic art on display in this gallery, now part of Salzburg's **Museum der Moderne** (which you can spot, shining in white marble atop the Mönchsberg hill, from the Rupertinum's main entrance). ⊠ *Wiener-Philharmoniker-Gasse 9* ☎ *0662/842220–451* ⊕ *www.museumdermoderne.at* ☜ *€6* ☾ *Tues. and Thurs.–Sun. 10–6, Wed. 10–9.*

CLOSE UP

Mozart: Marvel & Mystery

"Mozart is sunshine." So proclaimed Antonin Dvorak—and how better to sum up the prodigious genius of Wolfgang Amadeus Mozart (January 27, 1756–December 5, 1791)? Listening to his Rococo orchestrations, his rose-strewn melodies, and his insouciant harmonies, many listeners seem to experience the same giddiness as happiness. Scientists have found Mozart's music can cause the heart to pound, bring color to the cheeks, and provide the expansive feeling of being thrillingly alive. Yet, Mozart must have sensed how hard it is to recognize happiness, which is often something vaguely desired and not detected until gone. It is this melancholy undertow that makes Mozart modern—so modern that he is now the most popular classical composer, having banished Beethoven to second place. Shortly after *Amadeus* won the 1984 Oscar for best film—with its portrayal of Mozart as a giggling, foulmouthed genius—*Don Giovanni* began to rack up more performances than *La Bohème*. The bewigged face graces countless "Mozartkugeln" chocolates, and Mostly Mozart festivals pay him homage. But a look behind the glare of the spotlights reveals that this blond, slightly built tuning-fork of a fellow was a quicksilver enigma.

Already a skilled pianist at age three, the musical prodigy was dragged across Europe by his father Leopold to perform for empresses and kings. In a life that lasted a mere 35 years, he spent 10 on the road—a burden that contributed to making him the first truly *European* composer. Growing up in Salzburg, the *Wunderkind* became less of a *Wunder* as time went by. Prince-Archbishop Hieronymus von Colloredo enjoyed dissing his resident composer by commanding him to produce "table music" with the same disdainful tone he commanded his chef's dinner orders. Being literally forced to sit with those cooks, Mozart finally rebelled. In March 1781 he married Constanze Weber and set out to conquer Vienna.

Hated by Mozart's father, Constanze is adored today, since we now know she was Mozart's greatest ally. Highly repressed by stuffy Salzburg, Mozart came to like his humor glandular (he titled one cantata "Kiss My XXX") and his women globular, a bill Constanze adequately filled. She no doubt heartily enjoyed the fruits of his first operatic triumph, the naughty *Abduction from the Seraglio* (1782). His next opera, *The Marriage of Figaro* (1786), to no one's surprise, bombed. Always eager to thumb his nose at authority, Mozart had adapted a Beaumarchais play so inflammatory in its depiction of aristos as pawns of their own servants, it soon helped ignite the French Revolution. In revenge, wealthy Viennese gave a cold shoulder to his magisterial *Don Giovanni* (1787). Mozart was relegated to composing, for a lowly vaudeville house, the now immortal *Magic Flute* (1790), and to ghosting a *Requiem* for a wealthy count. Sadly, his star only began to soar after a tragic, early death. But in company with fellow starblazers Vincent van Gogh and Marilyn Monroe, we assume he must be enjoying the last laugh.

–Robert I. C. Fisher

6 **St. Peter's Cemetery.** The eerie but intimate Petersfriedhof, or St. Peter's Cemetery, is the oldest Christian graveyard in Austria, in the present condition dating back to 1627. Enclosed on three sides by elegant wrought-iron grilles, Baroque arcades contain chapels belonging to Salzburg's old patrician families. The graveyard is far from mournful: the individual graves are tended with loving care, decorated with candles, fir branches, and flowers—especially pansies (because the name means "thoughts"). In Crypt XXXI is the grave of Santino Solari, architect of the cathedral; in XXXIX that of Sigmund Haffner, a patron for whom Mozart composed a symphony and named a serenade. The final communal crypt LIV (by the so-called "catacombs") contains the body of Mozart's sister Nannerl and the torso of Joseph Haydn's younger brother Michael (his head is in St. Peter's church). The cemetery is in the shadow of the Monchsberg mount; note the early Christian tombs carved in the rock face. ⊠ *St. Peter Bezirk* ☎ *0662/844578-0* ⊙ *Daily dawn–dusk.*

14 **Spielzeugmuseum** (*Toy Museum*). On a rainy day this is a delightful diversion for both young and old, with a collection of dolls, teddy bears, model trains, and wooden sailing ships. At 3 on Tuesday, Wednesday, and the first Friday of the month, special Punch and Judy–style puppet shows are presented. Performance days change in the summer, so call ahead. The museum also has a collection of ancient instruments, including Michael Haydn's own fortepiano. ⊠ *Bürgerspitalplatz 2* ☎ *0662/620808-300* ⊕ *www.salzburgmuseum.at* 🎫 *€3* ⊙ *Daily 9–5.*

10 **Toscaninihof** (*Arturo Toscanini Courtyard*). The famous Italian maestro Arturo Toscanini conducted some of the Salzburg Festival's most legendary performances during the 1930s. Throughout the summer months the courtyard of his former festival residence is a hive of activity, with sets for the stage of the "House for Mozart" being brought in through the massive iron folding gates.

Wiener Philharmoniker-Gasse. Leading into Max-Reinhardt-Platz at the head of the grand Hofstallgasse, this street was named after the world-famous Vienna Philharmonic Orchestra in recognition of the unique contribution it has made annually to the Salzburg Festival, playing for most opera productions and for the majority of orchestral concerts. ■ TIP→ **The street blooms with an open-air food market every Saturday morning; note that there is a fruit-and-vegetable market on Universitätsplatz every day except Sunday and holidays.**

ACROSS THE RIVER SALZACH: FROM THE FORTRESS TO THE NEW TOWN

According to a popular saying in Salzburg, "If you can see the fortress, it's just about to rain; if you can't see it, it's already raining." Fortunately there are plenty of days when spectacular views can be had of Salzburg and the surrounding countryside from the top of this castle. Looking across the River Salzach to the Neustadt (New Town) area of historic Salzburg, you can pick out the Mirabell Palace and Gardens, the Landestheater, the Mozart Residence and the Mozarteum, the

Church of the Holy Trinity, and the Kapuzinerkloster perched atop the Kapuzinerberg. Ranging from the "acropolis" of the city—the medieval Fortress Hohensalzburg—to the celebrated Salzburg Marionette Theater, this part of Salzburg encapsulates the city's charm. If you want to see the most delightful Mozart landmark in this section of town, the Zauberflötenhäuschen—the mouthful used to describe the little summerhouse where he finished composing *The Magic Flute*—it can be viewed when concerts are scheduled in the adjacent Mozarteum.

A GOOD WALK

Start with Salzburg's number one sight—especially at night, when it is spectacularly spotlighted—the famed **Fortress Hohensalzburg** ⑲, the 11th-century castle that dominates the town. Take the Mönchsberg elevator or the Festungsbahn cable car on Festungsgasse, located behind the cathedral near St. Peter's Cemetery. If it's not running, you can walk up the zigzag path that begins a little farther up Festungsgasse; it's steep in parts but gives a better impression of the fortress's majestic nature. Once you've explored it, head back to the footpath, but instead of taking the steps back into town, turn right toward the **Nonnberg Convent** ⑳. Explore the church—the real Maria von Trapp almost found her calling here—then return along the path to the first set of steps, take them down into Kaigasse, and continue on to Mozartplatz. From here you can cross the Salzach River over the oldest extant footbridge in the city, Mozartsteg. Cross the road and walk west a minute or two along Imbergstrasse until you see a bookstore on the corner. Here a little street runs into **Steingasse** ㉑—a picturesque medieval street, and the old Roman street coming into town from the south. After exploring this "time machine," walk through the Steintor gate, past the chapel of St. Johann am Imberg to the Hettwer Bastion on the **Kapuzinerberg Hill** ㉒ for another great vista of the city.

Continue up the path to the Kapuziner-Kloster. From here, follow the winding road down past the stations of the cross. Turn right at the bottom of the road into Linzergasse, the New Town's answer to the Getreidegasse. Continue up this street to St. Sebastian's Church on the left. An archway will lead you into the tranquil **St. Sebastian's Cemetery** ㉓— if it looks somewhat familiar, that's because it inspired the scene at the end of *The Sound of Music*, where the von Trapps are nearly captured. When you leave the cemetery, walk north through a passageway until you reach Paris-Lodron-Strasse. To the left as you walk west down this street is the Loreto Church. At Mirabellplatz, cross the road to the **Mirabell Gardens** ㉔—the Pegasus Fountain (remember "Do-Re-Mi"?) and the Dwarfs' Garden are highlights here.

Take in Prince-Archbishop Wolf-Dietrich's private Xanadu, the adjacent **Mirabell Palace** ㉕ and its noted 18th-century Angel Staircase. Turn left out of the garden park onto busy Schwarzstrasse. Along this road you will find the famous center of Mozart studies, the **Mozarteum** ㉖, whose Great Hall is often the setting for concerts (during which you can view the "Magic Flute" House in the nearby Bastionsgarten). Next door is the **Marionettentheater** ㉗—home to those marionettes known around the world. Turn left at the corner, around the Landestheater, and continue onto Makartplatz, dominated at the far end by Fischer von Erlach's **Dreifaltigkeitskirche** ㉘. Across from the Hotel Bristol is the second-most-famous Mozart residence in the city, the **Mozart Wohnhaus** ㉙, where you can complete your homage to the city's hometown deity. Just to its right is the house where another famous Salzburger, the physicist Christian Doppler (remember the Doppler effect?), was born in 1803.

TIMING Allow half a day for the fortress, to explore it inside and out. Call the Mozarteum to see if there will be evening recitals in its two concert halls; hearing the *Haffner* or another of Mozart's symphonies could be a wonderful conclusion to your day.

MAIN ATTRACTIONS

⑲ **Fortress Hohensalzburg.** Founded in 1077, the Hohensalzburg is Salzburg's acropolis and the largest preserved medieval fortress in Central Europe. Brooding over the city from atop the Festungsberg, it was originally founded by Salzburg's Archbishop Gebhard, who had supported the pope in the investiture controversy against the Holy Roman Emperor. Over the centuries the archbishops gradually enlarged the castle, using it originally only sometimes as a residence, then as a siege-proof haven against invaders and their own rebellious subjects. The exterior may look grim, but inside there are lavish state rooms, such as the glittering **Golden Room,** the **Burgmuseum**—a collection of medieval art—and the **Rainer's Museum,** with its brutish arms and armor. Politics and Church are in full force here: there's a torture chamber not far from the exquisite late-Gothic **St. George's Chapel** (although the implements on view came from another castle and were not used here). The 200-pipe organ from the beginning of the 16th century, played during the warmer months daily after the carillon in the Neugebäude, is best heard from a respectful distance, as it is not called "the Bull" without reason. ■TIP→ Climb up the 100 tiny steps to the Recturm, a grand lookout post with a sweeping view of Salzburg and the mountains. Children will love coming here, especially as some rooms of the castle are now given over to a special exhibition, the **Welt der Marionetten,** which offers a fascinating view into the world of marionettes—a great preview of the treats in store at the nearby Marionettentheater.

To reach the fortress, walk up the zigzag path that begins just beyond the Stieglkeller on Festungsgasse. Note that you don't need a ticket to walk the footpath. The more-than-110-year-old **Festungsbahn** (*funicular railway* ✉*Festungsgasse 4* ☎*0662/4480–9750* ⊕*www.festungsbahn.at* ◔*Every 10 min Oct.–Apr., daily 9–5; May–Aug., daily 9–10; Sept., daily 9–9*) is the easy way up (advisable with young children). It's behind St. Peter's Cemetery. A round-trip pass including the entrance fee to all the museums in the fortress is €10, and a one-way ticket down is €2.10. Visitor lines to the fortress can be long, so try to come early. ⊠*Fortress Hohensalzburg, Mönchsberg 34* ☎*0662/620808–400* ⊕*www.salzburgmuseum.at* 🎫€7 ⊗*Jan.–Apr. and Oct.–Dec., daily 9:30–5; May–Sept., daily 9–7.*

㉒ Kapuzinerberg Hill. Directly opposite the Mönchsberg on the other side of the river, Kapuzinerberg Hill is crowned by several interesting sights. By ascending a stone staircase near Steingasse 9 you can start your climb up the peak. At the top of the first flight of steps is a tiny chapel, **St. Johann am Imberg,** built in 1681. Farther on are a signpost and gate to the **Hettwer Bastion,** part of the old city walls. ■TIP➔ **Hettwer Bastion is one of the most spectacular viewpoints in Salzburg.** At the summit is the gold-beige **Kapuzinerkloster** (Capuchin Monastery), originally a fortification built to protect the one bridge crossing the river. It is still an active monastery and thus cannot be visited, except for the church. The road downward—note the Stations of the Cross along the path— is called Stefan Zweig Weg, after the great Austrian writer who rented the **Paschingerschlössl** house (on the Kapuzinerberg to the left of the monastery) until 1934, when he left Austria after the Nazis had murdered chancellor Dollfuss. As he was one of Austria's leading critics and esthetes, his residence became one of the cultural centers of Europe.

㉗ Marionettentheater (*Marionette Theater*). The Salzburger Marionetten-
★ theater is both the world's greatest marionette theater and—surprise!—
☾ a sublime theatrical experience. Many critics have noted that viewers quickly forget the strings controlling the puppets, which assume life-like dimensions and provide a very real dramatic experience. The Marionettentheater is identified above all with Mozart's operas, which seem particularly suited to the skilled puppetry; a delightful production of *Così fan tutte* captures the humor of the work better than most stage versions. The theater itself is a Rococo concoction. The company is famous for its world tours, but is usually in Salzburg around Christmas, during the late-January Mozart Week, at Easter, and from May to September (schedule subject to change). ⊠*Schwarzstrasse 24* ☎*0662/872406–0* ⊕*www.marionetten.at* 🎫€18–€35 ⊗*Box office Mon.–Sat. 9–1 and 2 hrs before performance; Salzburg season May–Sept., Christmas, Mozart Week (Jan.), Easter.*

㉔ Mirabellgarten (*Mirabell Gardens*). While there are at least four entrances
Fodor'sChoice to the Mirabell Gardens—from the Makartplatz (framed by the statues
★ of Roman gods), the Schwarzstrasse, and Mirabell Square—you'll want
☾ to enter from the Rainerstrasse and head for the Rosenhügel (Rosebush Hill): you'll arrive at the top of the steps where Julie Andrews and her seven charges showed off their singing ability in *The Sound of Music.* This is also an ideal vantage point from which to admire the formal gardens and one of the best views of Salzburg, as it shows how harmoniously architects of the Baroque period laid out the city. The center of the gardens—one of Europe's most beautiful parks, partly designed by Fischer von Erlach as the grand frame for the Mirabell Palace—is dominated by four large groups of statues representing the elements water,

fire, air, and earth, and designed by Ottavio Mosto, who came to live in Salzburg from Padua. A bronze version of the horse Pegasus stands in front of the south façade of the palace in the center of a circular water basin. The most famous part of the Mirabell Gardens is the **Zwerglgarten** (Dwarfs' Garden), which can be found opposite the Pegasus fountain. Here you'll find 12 statues of "Danubian" dwarves sculpted in marble—the real-life models for which were presented to the bishop by the landgrave of Göttweig. Prince-Archbishop Franz Anton von Harrach had the figures made for a kind of stone theater below. The **Heckentheater** (Hedge Theater) is an enchanting natural stage setting that dates from 1700. The Mirabell Gardens are open daily 7 AM–8 PM. Art lovers will make a beeline for the **Barockmuseum** (✉ *Orangeriegarten* ☎ *0662/877432*), beside the Orangery of the Mirabell Gardens. It houses a collection of late-17th- and 18th-century paintings, sketches, and models illustrating the extravagant vision of life of the Baroque era—the signature style of Salzburg. Works by Giordano, Bernini, and Rottmayr are the collection's highlights. The museum is open Tuesday to Sunday 10 to 5. Admission is €4.50.

㉕ Mirabell Palace. The "Taj Mahal of Salzburg," Schloss Mirabell was built in 1606 by the immensely wealthy and powerful Prince-Archbishop Wolf-Dietrich for his mistress, Salomé Alt, and their 15 children. It was originally called Altenau in her honor. Such was the palace's beauty that it was taken over by succeeding prince-archbishops, including Markus Sittikus (who renamed the estate), Paris Lodron, and finally, Franz Anton von Harrach, who brought in Lukas von Hildebrandt to give the place a Baroque facelift in 1727. A disastrous fire hit in 1818, but happily, three of the most spectacular set-pieces of the palace—the Chapel, the Marble Hall, and the Angel Staircase—survived. The Marble Hall is now used for civil wedding ceremonies, and is regarded as the most beautiful registry office in the world. Its marble floor in strongly contrasting colors and its walls of stucco and marble ornamented with elegant gilt scrollwork are splendid. The young Mozart and his sister gave concerts here, and he also composed *Tafelmusik* (Table Music) to accompany the prince's meals. ■TIP➔ **Candlelight chamber music concerts in the Marble Hall provide an ideal combination of performance and atmosphere.** The magnificent marble Angel Staircase was laid out by von Hildebrandt and has sculptures by Georg Rafael Donner. The staircase is romantically draped with white marble putti, whose faces and gestures reflect a multitude of emotions, from questioning innocence to jeering mockery. The very first putto genuflects in an old Turkish greeting (a reminder of the Siege of Vienna in 1683). Outdoor concerts are held at the palace and gardens May though August, Sunday mornings at 10:30 and Wednesday evenings at 8:30. ✉ *Off Makartplatz* ☎ *0662/889-87-330* 💲 *Free* 🕙 *Weekdays 8–6.*

㉙ Mozart Wohnhaus (*Mozart Residence*). The Mozart family moved from ★ its cramped quarters in Getreidegasse to this house on the Hannibal ☾ Platz, as it was then known, in 1773. Wolfgang Amadeus Mozart lived here until 1780, his sister Nannerl stayed here until she married in 1784, and their father Leopold lived here until his death in 1787. The house is accordingly referred to as the Mozart Residence, signifying that it was not only Wolfgang who lived here. During the first Allied bomb attack on Salzburg in October 1944, the house was partially destroyed, but was reconstructed in 1996. Mozart composed the "Salzburg Symphonies" here, as well as all five violin concertos, church music and some sonatas, and parts of his early operatic masterpieces, including *Idomeneo*. Besides an interesting collection of musical instruments (for example, his own pianoforte), among the exhibits on display are books from Leopold Mozart's library. Autograph manuscripts and letters can be viewed, by prior arrangement only, in the cellar vaults. One room offers a multimedia show and wall-size map with more personal details about Mozart, like his numerous travels across Europe. Another salon has been decorated in the domestic decor of Mozart's day. ⊠ *Makartplatz 8* ☎ *0662/874227* ⊕ *www.mozarteum.at* 🖃 *Mozart residence €6.50, combined ticket for Mozart residence and birthplace €10* ⊘ *Sept.–June, daily 9–5:30; July and Aug., daily 9–8.*

⑳ Nonnberg Convent. Just below the south side of the Fortress Hohensalzburg—and best visited in tandem with it—the Stift Nonnberg was founded right after 700 by St. Rupert, and his niece St. Erentrudis was the first abbess (in the archway a late-Gothic statue of Erentrudis welcomes the visitor). ■ TIP→ **Spend the extra €1 to illuminate the frescoes just below the steeple. They are some of the oldest in Austria, painted in the Byzantine style during the 10th century.** The church is more famous these days as "Maria's convent"—both the one in *The Sound of Music* and that of the real Maria. She returned to marry her Captain von Trapp here in the Gothic church (as it turns out, no filming was done here—"Nonnberg" was re-created in the film studios of Salzburg-Parsch). Each evening in May at 7 the nuns sing a 15-minute service called Maiandacht in the old Gregorian chant. Their beautiful voices can be heard also at the 11 PM mass on December 24. Parts of the private quarters for the nuns, which include some lovely, intricate woodcarving, can be seen by prior arrangement. ⊠ *Nonnberggasse 2* ☎ *0662/841607–0* ⊘ *Fall–spring, daily 7–5; summer, daily 7–7.*

㉓ St. Sebastian's Cemetery. Memorably re-created for the escape scene in
★ *The Sound of Music* on a Hollywood soundstage, final resting place for many members of the Mozart family, and situated in the shadows of St. Sebastian's Church, the Friedhof St. Sebastian is one of the most peaceful spots in Salzburg. Prince-Archbishop Wolf-Dietrich commissioned the cemetery in 1600 to replace the old cathedral graveyard, which he planned to demolish. It was built in the style of an Italian *campo santo,* (sacred field) with arcades on four sides, and in the center of the square he had the Gabriel Chapel, an unusual, brightly tiled Mannerist mausoleum, built for himself, in which he was interred in 1617 (now closed to visitors). Several famous people are buried in this cemetery, including the medical doctor and philosopher Theophrastus Paracelsus, who settled in Salzburg in the early 16th century (his grave is by the church door). Around the chapel is the grave of Mozart's widow, Constanze, her second husband, Georg Nikolaus Nissen, and probably also the one of Genoveva Weber, the aunt of Constanze and the mother of

Carl Maria von Weber (by the central path leading to the mausoleum). According to the latest research, Mozart's father Leopold came to rest in the unmarked community grave here, too. If the gate is closed, enter through the back entrance around the corner in the courtyard. ⊠ *Linzergasse* ⊙ *Daily 9–6.*

㉑ Steingasse. This narrow medieval street, walled in on one side by the bare cliffs of the Kapuzinerberg, was originally the ancient Roman entrance into the city from the south. The houses stood along the riverfront before the Salzach was regulated. Nowadays it's a fascinating mixture of shops and nightclubs, but with its tall houses the street still manages to convey an idea of how life used to be in the Middle Ages. The **Steintor** marks the entrance to the oldest section of the street; here on summer afternoons the light can be particularly striking. House No. 23 on the right still has deep, slanted peep-windows for guarding the gate. House No. 31 is the birthplace of Josef Mohr, the poet of "Silent Night, Holy Night" fame (not No. 9, as is incorrectly noted on the wall).

ALSO WORTH SEEING

㉘ Dreifaltigkeitskirche (*Church of the Holy Trinity*). The Makartplatz—named after Hans Makart, the most famous Austrian painter of the mid-19th-century—is dominated at the top (east) end by Fischer von Erlach's first architectural work in Salzburg, built 1694–1702. It was modeled on a church by Borromini in Rome and prefigures von Erlach's Karlskirche in Vienna. Dominated by a lofty, oval-shape dome—which showcases a painting by Michael Rottmayr—this church was the result of the archbishop's concern that Salzburg's new town was developing in an overly haphazard manner. The church interior is small but perfectly proportioned, surmounted by its dome, whose trompe-l'oeil fresco seems to open up the church to the sky above. ⊠ *Dreifaltigkeitsgasse 14* ☎ *0662/877495* ⊙ *Mon.–Sat. 6:30–6:30, Sun. 8–6:30.*

Mozart Audio and Video Museum. In the same building as the Mozart Wohnhaus (Residence) is the Mozart Audio and Video Museum, an archive of thousands of Mozart recordings as well as films and video productions, all of which can be listened to or viewed on request. ⊠ *Makartplatz 8* ☎ *0662/883454* ⊕ *www.mozarteum.at* ⎙ *Free* ⊙ *Mon., Tues., and Fri. 9–1, Wed. and Thurs. 1–5.*

㉖ Mozarteum. Two institutions share the address in this building finished just before World War I—the International Foundation Mozarteum, set up in 1870, and the University of Music and Performing Arts, founded in 1880. Scholars come here to research in the **Bibliotheca Mozartiana,** the world's largest Mozart library (for research only and therefore not open to public). The Mozarteum also organizes the annual Mozart Week festival in January. Many important concerts are offered from October to June in its two recital halls, the Grosser Saal (Great Hall) and the Wiener Saal (Vienna Hall).

Behind the Mozarteum, sheltered by the trees of the Bastiongarten, is the famous **Zauberflötenhäuschen**—the little summerhouse where Mozart composed parts of *The Magic Flute*, with the encouragement

"Oh, the Hills Are Alive . . ."

Few Salzburgers would publicly admit it, but *The Sound of Music,* Hollywood's interpretation of the trials and joys of the local Trapp family, has become their city's most eminent emissary when it comes to international promotion. The year after the movie's release, international tourism to Salzburg jumped 20%, and soon *The Sound of Music* was a Salzburg attraction.

Perhaps the most important *Sound* spin-offs are the tours offered by several companies, including **Salzburg Panorama Tours** (✉ *Schrannengasse 2/2, Salzburg* ☎ *0662/883211–0* ⊕ *www.panoramatours.com*) and **Salzburg Sightseeing Tours** (✉ *Am Mirabellplatz 2, Salzburg* ☎ *0662/881616* ⊕ *www.welcome-salzburg.at*). Besides showing you some of the film's locations (usually very briefly), these four-hour rides have the advantage of giving a very concise tour of the city. The buses generally leave from Mirabellplatz; lumber by the "Do-Re-Mi" staircase at the edge of the beautifully manicured Mirabell Gardens; pass by the hardly visible Aigen train station, where in reality the Trapps caught the escape train; and then head south to Schloss Anif. This 16th-century water castle, which had a cameo appearance in the opening scenes of the film, is now in private hands and not open to the public.

First official stop for a leg-stretcher is at the gazebo in the manicured park of Schloss Hellbrunn at the southern end of the city. Originally built in the gardens of Leopoldskron Palace, it was brought out here to give the chance for taking pictures. This is where Liesl von Trapp sings "I Am Sixteen Going on Seventeen" and where

Maria and the Baron woo and coo "Something Good." The simple little structure is the most coveted prize of photographers. The bus then drives by other private palaces with limited visiting rights, Schloss Frohnburg and Schloss Leopoldskron, with its magical water-gate terrace, adorned with rearing horse sculptures and site of so many memorable scenes in the movie. The bus continues on to Nonnberg Convent at the foot of the daunting Hohensalzburg fortress, then leaves the city limits for the luscious landscape of the Salzkammergut. You get a chance for a meditative walk along the shore of the Wolfgangsee in St. Gilgen before the bus heads for the pretty town of Mondsee, where, in the movie, Maria and Georg von Trapp were married at the twin-turreted Michaelerkirche.

Tour guides are well trained and often have a sense of humor, with which they gently debunk myths about the movie. Did you know, for example, that Switzerland was "moved" 160 km (100 mi) eastward so the family could hike over the mountains to freedom (while singing "Climb Every Mountain")? It all goes to show that in Hollywood, as in Salzburg and its magical environs, almost anything is possible.

For something different, try the **Sternbräu Dinner Theater** (✉ *Griesgasse 23* ☎ *0662/826617*). Its dinner show features those unforgettable songs from the movie, as well as traditional folksongs from Salzburg and a medley of Austrian operettas. The cost of the dinner show is €43; without dinner it's €31.

of his frantic librettist, Emanuel Schikaneder, who finally wound up locking the composer inside to force him to complete his work. The house was donated to the Mozarteum by Prince Starhemberg. It is much restored: back in the 19th century, the faithful used to visit it and snatch shingles off its roof. The house can generally be viewed only when concerts are offered in the adjacent Grosser Saal. ⊠ *Schwarzstrasse 26* ☎ *0662/88940–21* ⊕ *www.mozarteum.at* ☉ *Summerhouse: only during Grosser Saal concerts.*

SHORT SIDE TRIPS FROM SALZBURG

Gaisberg and Untersberg. Salzburg's "house mountains" are so called because of their proximity to the city settlements. You can take the bus to the summit of the Gaisberg, where you'll be rewarded with a spectacular panoramic view of the Alps and the Alpine foreland. In summer Dr. Richard/Albus bus (☎ *0662/424–000–0*) leaves from Mirabellplatz at 10, noon, 2, and 5:15, and the journey takes about a half hour. The Untersberg is the mountain Captain von Trapp and Maria climbed as they escaped the Nazis in *The Sound of Music.* In the film they were supposedly fleeing to Switzerland; in reality, the climb up the Untersberg would have brought them almost to the doorstep of Hitler's retreat at the Eagle's Nest above Berchtesgaden. A cable car from St. Leonhard (about 13 km [8 mi] south of Salzburg) takes you up 6,020 feet right to the top of the Untersberg, giving you a breathtaking view. In winter you can ski down (you arrive in the village of Fürstenbrunn and taxis or buses take you back to St. Leonhard); in summer there are a number of hiking routes from the summit. ⊠ *Untersbergbahn* ☎ *06246/72477–0* ⊕ *www.untersberg.net* ⊠ *Round-trip €19* ☉ *Mid-Dec.–Feb., daily 9–4; Mar.–June and Oct., daily 8:30–5; July–Sept., daily 8:30–5:30.*

Hallein. The second-largest town of the region, 15 km (10 mi) south of Salzburg, Hallein was once famed for its caves of "white gold"—salt. "Hall" is the old Celtic word for salt, and this treasure was mined in the neighboring Dürrnberg mountain. To learn all about Hallein, head to the **Keltenmuseum** (*Museum of the Celts* ⊠ *Pflegerplatz 5* ☎ *06245/80783* ⊠ *€6*), where more than 30 rooms explore the history of the region's Celtic settlements (before the birth of Christ). In the three state rooms more than 70 oil paintings show the working conditions of the salt mines and the salina. You can get to Hallein by regular bus system, by car along the B159 Salzachtal-Bundesstrasse, or by bicycle along the River Salzach. Once in Hallein, you can pay your respects to Franz Gruber, the composer of "Silent Night," who lies in the only grave still extant next to the town's parish church.

Oberndorf. This little village 21 km (13 mi) north of Salzburg has just one claim to fame: it was here on Christmas Eve, 1818, that the world-famous Christmas carol "Silent Night," composed by the organist and schoolteacher Franz Gruber to a lyric by the local priest, Josef Mohr, was sung for the first time. The church was demolished and replaced in 1937 by a tiny commemorative chapel containing a copy of the original composition (the original is in the Museum Salzburg), stained-glass windows depicting Gruber and Mohr, and a Nativity scene. ■TIP➔ **Every December 24 at 5 PM, a traditional performance of the carol—two male voices plus guitar and choir—in front of the chapel is the introduction to Christmas.** About a 10-minute walk from the village center along the riverbank, the local **Heimatmuseum** (✉ *Stille-Nacht-Platz* 7 ☎ *06272/4422–0*), opposite the chapel, documents the history of the carol. The museum is open daily 9–noon and 1–5; admission is €2.50. You can get to Oberndorf by the local train (opposite the main train station), by car along the B156 Lamprechtshausener Bundesstrasse, or by bicycle along the River Salzach.

Fodor'sChoice **Schloss Hellbrunn** (*Hellbrunn Palace*). Just 6½ km (4 mi) south of Salz-
★ burg, the Lustschloss Hellbrunn was the prince-archbishops' pleasure
☉ palace. It was built early in the 17th century by Santino Solari for Markus Sittikus, after the latter had imprisoned his uncle, Wolf-Dietrich, in the fortress. The castle has some fascinating rooms, including an octagonal music room and a banquet hall with a trompe-l'oeil ceiling. Hellbrunn Park became famous far and wide because of its **Wasserspiele,** or trick fountains: in the formal gardens, a beautiful example of the Mannerist style including a later-added outstanding mechanical theater, some of the exotic and humorous fountains spurt water from strange places at unexpected times—you will probably get doused (bring a raincoat). A visit to the gardens is highly recommended: nowhere else can you experience so completely the realm of fantasy that the grand Salzburg archbishops indulged in. The **Monatsschlösschen,** the old hunting lodge (built in one month), contains an excellent folklore museum. Following the path over the hill you find the **Steintheater** (Stone Theater), an old quarry made into the earliest open-air opera stage north of the Alps. The former palace deer park has become a **zoo** featuring free-flying vultures and Alpine animals that largely roam unhindered. You can get to Hellbrunn by Bus 25, by car on Route 159, or by bike or on foot along the beautiful Hellbrunner Allee past several 17th-century mansions. On the estate grounds is the little gazebo filmed in *The Sound of Music* ("I am 16, going on 17")—the doors are now locked because a person once tried to repeat the movie's dance steps, leaping from bench to bench, and managed to fall and break a hip. ✉ *Fürstenweg 37, Hellbrunn* ☎ *0662/820372* ⊕ *www.hellbrunn.at* 🎫 *Tour of palace and water gardens €8.50* ☉ *Apr. and Oct., daily 9–4:30; May–Sept., daily 9–5:30; evening tours July and Aug., daily on the hr 6–10.*

WHERE TO EAT

Salzburg has some of the best—and most expensive—restaurants in Austria, so if you happen to walk into one of the Altstadt posheries without a reservation, you may get a sneer worthy of Captain von Trapp. Happily, the city is plentifully supplied with pleasant eateries, offering not only good, solid Austrian food (not for anyone on a diet), but also exceptional Italian dishes and newer-than-now *neue Küche* (nouvelle cuisine) delights. There are certain dining experiences that are quintessentially Salzburgian, including restaurants perched on the town's peaks that offer "food with a view"—in some cases, it's too bad the food isn't up to the view—or rustic inns that offer "Alpine evenings" with entertainment. Some of the most distinctive places in town are the fabled hotel restaurants, such as those of the Goldener Hirsch or the "Ratsherrenkeller" of the Hotel Elefant.

For fast food, Salzburgers love their broiled-sausages street stands. Some say the most delicious are to be found at the Balkan Grill at Getreidegasse 33 (its recipe for spicy Bosna sausage has always been a secret). ■TIP➔ **For a quick lunch on weekdays, visit the market in front of the Kollegienkirche—a lot of stands offer a large variety of boiled sausages for any taste, ranging from mild to spiced.**

> ## BICYCLING
>
> As most Salzburgers know, one of the best and most pleasurable ways of getting around the city and the surrounding countryside is by bicycle. Bikes can be rented, and local bookstores have maps of the extensive network of cycle paths. The most delightful ride in Salzburg? The **Hellbrunner Allee** from Freisaal to Hellbrunn Palace is a pleasurable run, taking you past Frohnburg Palace and a number of elegant mansions on either side of the tree-lined avenue. The more adventurous can go farther afield, taking the **Salzach cycle path** north to the village of Oberndorf, or south to Golling and Hallein.

In the more expensive restaurants the set menus give you an opportunity to sample the chef's best; in less expensive ones they help keep costs down. Note, however, that some restaurants limit the hours during which the set menu is available. Many restaurants are open all day; otherwise, lunch is served from approximately 11 to 2 and dinner from 6 to 10. In more expensive restaurants it's always best to make a reservation. At festival time most restaurants are open seven days a week, and have generally more flexible late dining hours.

WHAT IT COSTS IN EUROS					
	¢	$	$$	$$$	$$$$
AT DINNER	Under €7	€7–€12	€13–€17	€18–€22	over €22

Prices are per person for a main course at dinner.

$$$$ ✕**Gasthof Hohlwegwirt.** It's worth a detour on the way to Hallein along
★   the B159 Salzachtal-Bundesstrasse about 10 km (6 mi) south of Salzburg to dine at this inviting inn, run by the same family for more than 130 years. Enjoy the cooking, the wine cellar filled with more than 100 different vintages, and the unmistakable atmosphere of this *stile Salzburg* house with its nicely decorated salons. Chef Ernst Kronreif uses his mother's recipes for the delicious *Butternockerlsuppe* (soup broth with buttered dumplings), the *Kalbsbries* (calf's sweetbreads), or the *Salzburger Bierfleisch* (beef boiled in beer)—all Salzburgian classics and yet always so up-to-date. ⊠*Salzachtal-Bundesstrasse Nord 62, Hallein-Taxach* ☎*06245/82415–0* ⌖*Reservations essential* ⊘*Closed Mon., except during summer festival* ▤*MC, V.*

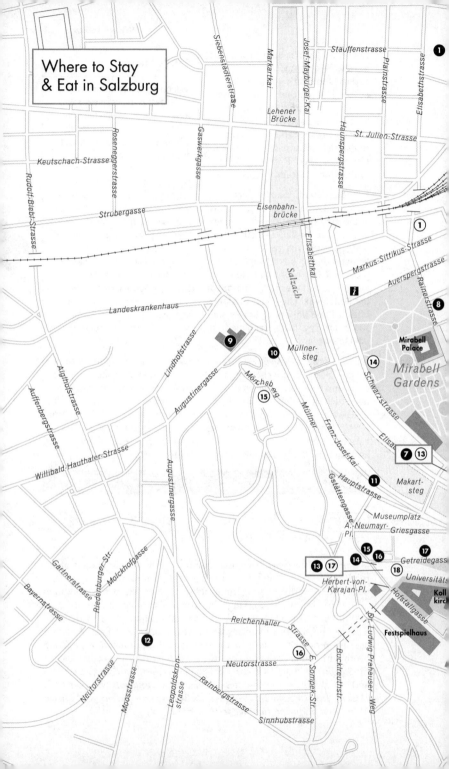

Where to Stay & Eat in Salzburg

Stauffenstrasse
Plainstrasse
Elisabethstrasse
Josef-Mayburger-Kai
Markatkai
Siebenstädterstrasse
Haunspergstrasse
St. Julien-Strasse
Lehener Brücke
Keutschach-Strasse
Roseneggerstrasse
Gaswerkgasse
Rudolf-Biebl-Strasse
Strubergasse
Eisenbahn-brücke
Elisabethkai
Salzach
Markus-Sittikus-Strasse
Auerspergstrasse
Rainerstrasse

1

1

i

8

Mirabell Palace

Mirabell Gardens

14

Landeskrankenhaus
Lindhofstrasse
Aiglhofstrasse
Auffenbergstrasse
Willibald-Hauthaler-Strasse
Augustinergasse
Mönchsberg
Müllner-steg
Müllner-
Schwarzstrasse
Elisa

9

10

15

7 **13**

Franz-Josef-Kai
Hauptstrasse
Gstättengasse
A.-Neumayr-Pl.
Museumplatz
Griesgasse
Getreidegass
Universitäts
Koll kirch
Herbert-von-Karajan-Pl.
Hofstallgasse
Festspielhaus

Makart-steg

11

15 **16**

17

13 **17**

14

18

Gartnerstrasse
Riedenburger Str.
Molckhofgasse
Bayernstrasse
Neutorstrasse
Moosstrasse
Leopoldskron-strasse
Reichenhaller Strasse
Neutorstrasse
Rainbergstrasse
Dr.-Ludwig-Prahauser-Weg
Sinnhubstrasse
Bucklreuthstr.
F.-Sompek-Str.

12

16

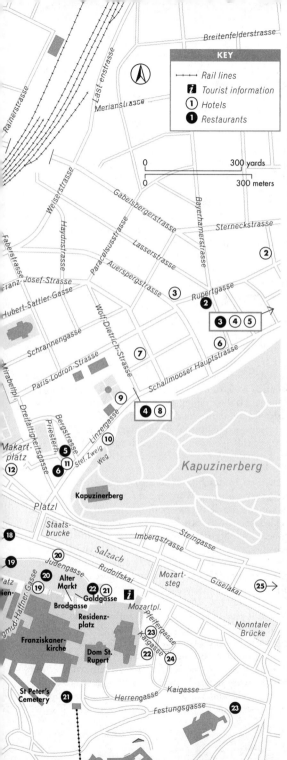

KEY

┝━━┥ Rail lines

ℹ Tourist information

① Hotels

❶ Restaurants

0   300 yards

0   300 meters

5

\$\$\$\$ ✕**Pfefferschiff.** The "Pepper Ship" is one of the most acclaimed res-
★ taurants in Salzburg—though it's 3 km (2 mi) northeast of the center.
It's in a pretty, renovated rectory, dated 1640, adjacent to a pink-and-
cream chapel. Klaus Fleishhaker, an award-winning chef, makes you
feel pampered in the country-chic atmosphere, adorned with polished
wooden floors, antique hutches, and tabletops laden with fine bone
china and Paloma Picasso silverware. The menu changes seasonally. A
taxi is the least stressful way of getting here, but if you have your own
car, drive along the north edge of the Kapuzinerberg toward Hallwang
and then Söllheim. ⊠*Söllheim 3, Hallwang* ☎*0662/661242* ⚒*Reservations essential* ▤*AE.*

\$\$\$–\$\$\$\$ ✕**Pan e Vin.** This tiny trattoria is easy to find, as it stands next to one of
the few remaining city gates. It has only a handful of tables, and they're
hard to obtain, since the Italian specialties on tap are top-flight. Feel
the spirit of the city called the "Rome of the North" here: burnt-sienna
walls are lined with wine bottles, colorful ceramic plates, and Italian
dry stuffs, and the chef cooks in full view. The upstairs restaurant of
the same name has a more extensive menu, but it's also much more
expensive. ⊠*Gstättengasse 1* ☎*0662/844666* ⚒*Reservations essential* ▤*AE, DC, MC, V* ☉*Closed Sun. and Mon.*

\$\$–\$\$\$\$ ✕**Stiftskeller St. Peter.** Legends swirl about the famous St. Peter's Beer
Fodor'sChoice Cellar. Locals claim that Mephistopheles met Faust here, others say
★ Charlemagne dined here, and some believe Columbus enjoyed a glass
of its famous Salzburg Stiegl beer just before he set sail for America in
1492. But there is no debating the fact that this place—first mentioned
in a document dating back to 803—is Austria's oldest restaurant. It is
also one of the most dazzling dining experiences in Salzburg. Choose
between the fairly elegant, dark-wood-panel Prälatenzimmer (Prelates'
Room) or one of several less-formal banqueting rooms. Along with
other Austrian standards, you can dine on fish caught in local rivers
and lakes. ⊠*St. Peter Bezirk 4* ☎*0662/841268–0* ⊕*www.haslauer.at*
▤*AE, DC, MC, V.*

\$–\$\$\$\$ ✕**Carpe Diem.** Dietrich Mateschitz (who also invented the Red Bull
★ energy drink) together with Jörg Wörther did, and they came up with
something truly unique: small dishes—both savory and sweet—served
in "cones." Pickled perch with artichokes and asparagus tips arrives
in a polenta cone, while a potato cone bursts with prime beef with
creamed spinach and horseradish. Mix and match to create a delicious
meal. For dessert, try the cold-warm dark chocolate with refried apricot. You can either sit inside in the barlike atmosphere or, in summer,
on the open terrace. ⊠*Getreidegasse 50* ☎*0662/848800* ⚒*Reservations essential* ▤*AE, DC, MC, V.*

\$\$–\$\$\$ ✕**Blaue Gans.** In a 500-year-old building with vaulted ceilings and win-
★ dows looking out onto the bustling Getreidegasse, the old-fashioned
menu at this restaurant in the Blaue Gans Hotel has been revamped
to showcase a more innovative style of Austrian cooking. The fresh
flavors are evident in dishes like the *Wolfsbarsch* (perch), which comes
with a cilantro-chili cream sauce. There are always vegetarian choices.
The service is top-notch, and you can peer through a glass floor to
study an old cellar—the site of the oldest inn in Salzburg. It's men-

tioned in documents from the 15th century. ⊠ *Getreidegasse 41–43* ☎ *0662/842491–0* ⊟ *AE, DC, MC, V* ⊘ *Closed Tues.*

$$-$$$ ✕ **Mundenhamer.** Chef Ernst Breitschopf knows the repertoire of good old Upper Austrian dishes inside and out: an *Innviertler* (raw ham with horseradish, dark bread, and butter); a garlic soup with bread croutons; a roast pork chop served in a pan with bread dumplings and warm bacon-cabbage salad; homemade spaetzle with braised white cabbage and bacon; a Salzburger Schnitzel (scallop of veal filled with minced mushrooms and ham) with buttered finger dumplings. Dessert? Nobody can resist the Mohr im Hemd (Moor-in-a-shirt), the warm chocolate cake garnished with fruits, chocolate sauce, vanilla ice cream, and whipped cream. ⊠ *Rainerstrasse 2* ☎ *0662/875693* ⊟ *AE, DC, MC, V* ⊘ *Closed Sun.*

$$-$$$ ✕ **Zum Eulenspiegel.** What has Till Eulenspiegel, a 14th-century jester,
★ to do with Salzburg? Not much, but when Hans Grassl opened this restaurant in 1950, he decided to go for it. Spiffily restored, the restaurant allures with rustic wooden furniture, old folio volumes, antique weapons, and open fireplaces. Tables gleaming with white linen are set in wonderful nooks and crannies reached by odd staircases and charming salons, like the tiny "women's apartment." The unique setting is matched by the delicious food. Try the potato goulash with chunks of sausage and beef in a creamy paprika sauce, or the house specialty, fish stew Provençal. ⊠ *Hagenauerplatz 2* ☎ *0662/843180–0* ⚫ *Reservations essential* ⊟ *AE, DC, MC, V* ⊘ *Closed Sun. except during festival, and Jan.–mid-Mar.*

$-$$$ ✕ **Café Sacher.** Red-velvet banquettes, sparkling chandeliers, and lots of gilt mark this famous gathering place, a favorite of well-heeled Salzburgers and an outpost of the celebrated Vienna landmark. It's a perfect choice for a leisurely afternoon pastry. The most popular choice is the famous house-made chocolate Sachertorte, but there is also a large variety of cakes. Don't pass up the coffee, which is second to none. Full meals are also served, and the restaurant offers a no-smoking room. ⊠ *Schwarzstrasse 5–7* ☎ *0662/889770* ⊟ *AE, DC, MC, V.*

$$ ✕ **Die Weisse.** This *Weissbierbrauerei* occupies one of Salzburg's most
★ historic breweries, and many locals consider it to be the ultimate private retreat (so much so that from Wednesday through Saturday it's best to make a reservation). The beer garden really hits the spot on a hot summer day, but all year long you can delight in traditional Bavarian goodies (veal sausages with sweet mustard) as well as the usual array of tempting Salzburg delights. ⊠ *Rupertgasse 10* ☎ *0662/8722460* ⊟ *MC, V* ⊘ *Closed Sun.*

$$ ✕ **Kuglhof.** In Maxglan, a famous Austrian "farmer's village," now part
★ of the city tucked behind the Mönchsberg and next to the Stiegl Brewery (best, therefore, reached by taxi), Alexander Hawranek perfects Old Austrian specialties by giving them a nouvelle touch. The setting is your archetypal black-shuttered, yellow-hue, begonia-bedecked Salzburgian farmhouse, oh-so-cozily set with a tile oven, mounted antlers, embroidered curtains, and tons of gemütlichkeit. The menu is seasonal, so you might not be able to enjoy the signature *Beuschl* (calf's lights) with dumplings. Best bet for dessert is the *Apfelschmarrn,* sliced pan-

5

cake with apples. In summer opt for a table out in the shady garden. ⊠ *Kuglhofstrasse 13* ☎*0662/832626* ⊕*www.kuglhof.at* ▤*AE, DC, MC, V* ⊘*Closed Mon. and Tues.*

$–$$ ✕**Ährlich.** Just because this restaurant is all-organic doesn't mean it isn't fun. The dining room has a country casual ambience with cozy booths. It's a good historic-district choice for vegetarians. ⊠ *Wolf-Dietrich-Strasse 7* ☎*0662/871275* ▤*AE, DC, MC, V* ⊘*Closed Sun. and Mon. No lunch.*

$–$$ ✕**Café Tomaselli.** This inn opened its doors in 1705 as an example of that
Fodor'sChoice   new-fangled thing, a "Wiener Kaffeehaus" (Vienna coffeehouse). It was
★   an immediate hit. Enjoying its 11 types of coffee was none other than Mozart's beloved, Constanze, who often dropped in, as her house was just next door. The Tomasellis set up shop here in 1850, becoming noted "chocolatmachers." Feast on the famous "Tomaselliums Café" (mocha, Mozart liqueur, and whipped cream) and the large selection of excellent homemade cakes, tarts, and strudels. Inside, the decor is marble, wood, and walls of 18th-century portraits. In summer the best seats are on the terrace and at the pretty "Tomaselli-Kiosk" on the square. ⊠*Alter Markt 9* ☎*0662/844488–0* ⊕*www.tomaselli.at* ▤*No credit cards.*

$–$$ ✕**Coco Lezzone.** You'll always find a lively crowd at this popular spot on the quay on the Altstadt side of the river. Spacious with a contemporary, informal dining room, it can be a bit noisy at night. The menu changes with the seasons. ⊠*Franz-Josef-Kai 7* ☎*0662/846735* ▤*AE, MC, V* ⊘*Closed Sun. No lunch Sat.*

$–$$ ✕**Daxlueg.** If you really want to enjoy food with a view, drive 3 km (2
★   mi) north along the B1 Linzer Bundesstrasse to Mayrwies and turn right up through the woods. Here you can take in a view of Salzburg from the mountainside perch of this former Rupertialm (St. Rupert's Pasture), a famous scenic lookout even in Mozart's time. Owned by St. Peter's Monastery and now nicely renovated, this restaurant allures with the romantic charm of an Alpine chalet. Seasonal specialties of the region top the bill: not only venison and fried trout but heavenly garnishes—cress, elder blossoms, herbs from the meadows, raspberries, blueberries, *Schwammerl* (mushrooms) fresh out of the forest, cheese from goat and sheep. ⊠*Daxluegstrasse 5, Hallwang* ☎*0662/665800* ▤*MC, V.*

$–$$ ✕**Gablerbräu.** Many like to stop here for a fast bite, but you should ponder the historic vibes, too. In this old inn Richard Mayr—a star of Vienna's State Opera House—was born. He later became one of the organizers of the music festival. After studying the parlor of Mayr's parents—a dark, wood-carved, neo-Gothic interior from the end of the 19th century—head for a table and settle down to hot breads and cold beer: a selection of beers from different provinces along with a large variety of sandwiches for any taste. Other treats on the menu are northern Italian (in former days, of course, Austrian), including the polenta croquets with ratatouille and Gorgonzola cream sauce or the homemade linguine with courgettes in tomato sauce—best paired with a glass of white or red wine from Guttmann's cellars. ⊠*Linzergasse 9* ☎*0662/88965* ▤*AE, DC, MC, V.*

$–$$ ✕**K&K am Waagplatz.** This old house was once the domicile of the Freysauff family, who counted among their close friends Leopold Mozart, the composer's father. Its cellar, the downstairs section of the restaurant, is still called the Freysauff (but don't be misled—this translates into "free drinks"). The restaurant is particularly pleasant, with white-linen tablecloths, candles, and flowers, and windows opening onto the street. Menu selections consist of locally caught fish, delicious chicken-breast medallions, lentil salad with strips of goose breast, and traditional Austrian dishes and game in season. Service is friendly. ⊠ *Waagplatz 2* ☎ *0662/842156* ⊟ *AE, DC, MC, V.*

$–$$ ✕ **Fabrizi Espresso.** Named after the former Italian owner of this historic house (note the beautiful small archway passage), this is a top spot for tasting Marzemino, the red wine Don Giovanni drinks in Mozart's opera. But there are plenty of other goodies here: some of the best Italian coffees in the city; outstanding Austrian *Apfel-oder Topfenstrudel* (apple or cheese pie—worth any money, but not expensive) and the best Salzburger *Nockerl*; excellent prosecco (Italian sparkling wine); various salads; and a fine Wiener schnitzel. ⊠ *Getreidegasse 21* ☎ *0662/845914* ⊟ *No credit cards.*

$ ✕ **Krimpelstätter.** About a 15-minute walk downriver from the Altstadt
★ in the Müllner neighborhood, this is one of the top spots where the artists of the summer festival like to celebrate after their premieres. Everyone enjoys the traditional Salzburg cooking: seasonal and delicious *Bärlauch* (wild wood garlic) soup, or the potato goulash with chunks of country ham, or the homemade pork sausage with dumplings, or the *Zanderfilet* (pike perch). Happily, all this is served up in a delicious, centuries-old building with fetching accents provided by vaulted ceilings, leaded-glass windows, and homespun tablecloths. There's a big shady garden for dining in summer. ⊠ *Müllner Hauptstrasse 31* ☎ *0662/432274* ⩘ *Reservations essential* ⊟ *No credit cards* ⊙ *Closed Sun. and Mon. Sept.–Apr.*

$ ✕ **Wilder Mann.** "After a certain time all men become wild." So goes a famous Salzburg saying, perhaps coined after someone drank too much of the local "liquid bread"—Stiegl beer from the oldest private brewery in Austria. In fact, when this inn opened its doors in 1884 it became one of the most important burgher houses in the Altstadt. Today it offers a true time-stained ambience of an old Salzburg *Gasthaus,* right down to the wooden chairs next to a huge ceramic stove that generations of locals have sat on and the enormous plates of *Bauernschmaus* (farmer's dish) overflowing with veal, pork, sausage, sour cabbage, and dumplings. ⊠ *Getreidegasse 20* ☎ *0662/841787* ⊟ *No credit cards* ⊙ *Closed Sun.*

$ ✕ **Zum Fidelen Affen.** The name means "At the Faithful Ape," which
★ explains the monkey motifs in this popular Gasthaus dominated by a round copper-plated bar and stone pillars under a vaulted ceiling. Besides the beer on tap, the kitchen offers tasty Austrian dishes, such as *Schlutzkrapfen,* cheese ravioli with a light topping of chopped fresh tomatoes, or a big salad with strips of fried chicken. It's always crowded, so be sure to arrive early or book ahead. ⊠ *Priesterhausgasse 8* ☎ *0662/877361* ⩘ *Reservations essential* ⊟ *DC, MC, V* ⊙ *Closed Sun. No lunch.*

¢–$ ✕**Augustinerbräu.** One of the larg-
★ est beer cellars in Europe, the celebrated Augustinerbräu is at the
north end of the Mönchsberg. You
can even bring your own food—a
relic of the old tradition that for-
bade breweries from serving meals
in order to protect the status of
restaurants. Pick up a stone jug of
strong, frothy beer and sit in the gardens or at a dark-wood table in one
of the large refectory halls. Shops
in the huge monastery complex sell
a vast array of salads, breads, and
pastries, as well as sausage and spit-
roasted chicken. If you don't feel
up to cold beer, there's an old copper beer warmer in the main hall.
During Advent and Lent a special
beer is offered, with the blessing of past popes, one of whom com-
mented, "drinking does not interrupt fasting." ✉ *Augustinergasse 4*
☎ *0662/431246* ⊟ *No credit cards* ⊘ *No lunch.*

¢–$ ✕**Ristorante Pizzeria al Sole.** Next to the Mönchsberg elevator you sit
in this Italian restaurant upstairs in a pretty room lined with Venetian
prints or in the more casual downstairs area. Choose from an impressive menu of scrumptious thin-crust pizzas. Pasta dishes are numerous
and delicious, and may include tagliatelle with grilled shrimp or penne
with tuna and capers. ✉ *Gstättengasse 15* ☎ *0662/843284* ⊟ *AE, DC,*
MC, V ⊘ *Closed Tues. in spring and fall.*

> ## ON THE MENU
>
> Many restaurants favor the *neue Küche*—a lighter version of the somewhat heavier traditional specialties of Austrian cooking, but with more substance than nouvelle cuisine. Salzburgers also have a wonderful way with fish—often a fresh catch from the nearby lakes of the Salzkammergut. Favorite fish dishes are usually *gebraten* (fried). The only truly indigenous Salzburg dish is *Salzburger Nockerln*, a snowy meringue of sweetened whisked egg whites with a little bit of flour and sugar.

WHERE TO STAY

It's difficult for a Salzburg hotel not to have a good location—you can
find a room with a stunning view over the Kapuzinerberg or Gaisberg
or one that simply overlooks a lovely Old City street—but it's possible.
Salzburg is not a tiny town, and location is important. It's best to be
near the historic city center; it's about a mile from the railway station to
historic Zentrum (center), right around the main bridge of the Staats-
brücke. The Old City has a wide assortment of hotels and pensions, but
there are few bargains. Also note that many hotels in this area have to
be accessed on foot, as cars are not permitted on many streets. If you
have a car, you may opt for a hotel or converted castle on the outskirts
of the city. Many hostelries are charmingly decorated in *Bauernstil*—
the rustic look of Old Austria; the ultimate in peasant-luxe is found at
the world-famous Hotel Goldener Hirsch.

If you're looking for something really cheap (less than €50 for a double), clean, and comfortable, stay in a private home, though the good
ones are all a little way from downtown. The tourist information offices

don't list private rooms; try calling Eveline Truhlar of **Bob's Special Tours** (☎0662/849511–0), who runs a private-accommodations service.

If you're planning to come at festival time (July and August), you must book as early as possible; try to reserve at least two months in advance. Prices soar over the already high levels—so much so that during the high season a hotel may edge into the next-higher price category.

Room rates include taxes and service charges. Many hotels include a breakfast in the room rate—check when booking—but the more expensive hostelries often do not. A property that provides breakfast and dinner daily is known as *halb pension,* and one that serves three meals a day is *voll pension.* If you don't have a reservation, go to one of the tourist information offices or the accommodations service (*Zimmernachweis*) on the main platform of the railway station.

WHAT IT COSTS IN EUROS					
	¢	$	$$	$$$	$$$$
FOR TWO PEOPLE	Under €80	€80–€120	€120–€170	€170–€270	over €270

Prices are for a standard double room in high season, including taxes and service.

$$$$ ★ **Altstadt Radisson SAS.** "Venerable" describes this 1372 building, one of the city's oldest inns. The exterior is a charmer, done up in buff pink, white trim, sash windows, and iron lanterns. The interior has been renovated to within an inch of its life, but stone arches, beamed ceilings, and tasteful antiques abound. On one side, rooms overlook the river and the picturesque hilltop cloister; on the other, those on upper floors sneak a peek at the fortress. Rooms are spacious and light filled, and most are furnished with reproduction antiques and traditional accents. The Symphonie Restaurant is elegance personified, with royal-blue and gold hues ashimmer under Rococo chandeliers. Added bonuses are the central yet quiet location and generous buffet breakfast. **Pros:** central location; quiet street; generous buffet. **Cons:** inconvenient location if you have a car; chain-hotel feel. ⊠*Judengasse 15/Rudolfskai 28* ☎*0662/848571–0* ⊕*www.austria-trend.at/ass* ⇆*42 rooms, 20 suites* △*In-hotel: restaurant, bar* ⊟*AE, DC, MC, V* ⍝*BP.*

$$$$ Fodor'sChoice ★ **Goldener Hirsch.** Celebrities from Picasso to Pavarotti have favored the "Golden Stag" for its legendary Gemütlichkeit, patrician pampering, and adorable decor. It's near the most popular sites, but double-paned windows ensure you won't hear a thing once you enter this special, private world. Inside it's delightfully rustic, with hand-carved wood, peasant-luxe furniture, and some of the lowest ceilings in town; the stag motif is even on lamp shades, which were hand-painted by an Austrian countess. As it's a historic treasure, expect some rooms to have snug, yet cozy, dimensions (some readers have written in alarm about some far-flung rooms tucked under the eave). There are two restaurants: the regal dining room and a smaller bistro. The latter is set on the pretty Sigmundsplatz, and locals love its cozy, timbered look and the house specialty, *Nürnberger Bratwürstl* (half a dozen little roasted Nürnberg sausages served with sauerkraut and served on pewter heart-shaped plates). **Pros:** unbeatable location; top-notch dining; charm to spare. **Cons:** noisy neighborhood; now part of a chain. ⊠ *Getreidegasse 37* ☎*0662/8084–0* ⊕*www.goldenerhirsch.com* ⚟*64 rooms, 5 suites* ⚐ *In-room: refrigerator. In-hotel: 2 restaurants, bar, parking (paid), Internet terminal* ▤*AE, DC, MC, V.*

$$$$ ⊡ **Sacher Salzburg.** On the Salzach River, this mammoth hotel has
★   attracted guests from the Beatles and the Rolling Stones to Hillary and Chelsea Clinton. It's owned by the Gürtler family, who make sure that even if you don't have a Vuitton steamer trunk you'll feel welcome. The main atrium is a symphony in marble, while the grand staircase still looks like the Empress Sisi could make a dazzling entrance amidst its ferns. Upstairs, guest rooms are so lovely there is a danger you won't want to leave (especially if you get one with picture-perfect views of the Old City). Each is different, but all are exquisitely decorated. In nice weather tables are set outside on the terrace, where you can enjoy a salad or hamburger (called a "Salzburger") for lunch while gazing across at the fortress. Restaurants include haute, tavern, and the Salzburg outpost of Vienna's fabled Café Sacher—enjoy your slice of Sachertorte at the latter. **Pros:** some great views; delicious buffet breakfast; plenty of dining options. **Cons:** gets overcrowded during festival. ⊠ *Schwarzstrasse 5–7* ☎*0662/88977* ⊕*www.sacher.com* ⚟*118 rooms* ⚐ *In-room: refrigerator, Internet. In-hotel: 5 restaurants, bar, gym, parking (paid), no-smoking rooms, Wi-Fi* ▤*AE, DC, MC, V* ⎮◉⎮*BP.*

$$$$ ⊡ **Schloss Mönchstein.** With gorgeous gardens and hiking trails, it's little
★   wonder the 19th-century naturalist Alexander von Humboldt called this retreat outside the city a "small piece of paradise." Catherine of Russia and the Duchess of Liechtenstein are just two of the notables who have stayed in the gable-roofed, tower-studded mansion. Inside, a series of lovely rooms are hung with tapestries and adorned with painted chests and Old Master daubs. The wedding chapel is particularly popular with American and Japanese couples. Getting to town means a taxi, unless you are willing to negotiate steps or take the nearby Mönchsberg elevator, which is about an eight-minute walk away. **Pros:** luxurious rooms; lovely views; feels far from the city. **Cons:** outside the city center; need a car to get around. ⊠ *Mönchsberg 26* ☎*0662/848555–0* ⊕*www. monchstein.com* ⚟*23 rooms* ⚐ *In-room: refrigerator. In-hotel: bar, tennis court, parking (free)* ▤*AE, DC, MC, V.*

$$$$ ⊡ **Sheraton Salzburg.** With the lovely Mirabell park and gardens virtually at its back door, this modern hotel tastefully blends in with the Belle Époque buildings that surround it. Rooms are soothing in tone with contemporary furniture, and contain all the little extras and then some. Try to get a room facing the gardens. The buffet breakfast is outstanding—enough to keep you going all day. The house café, with attractive garden seating, bakes all its tempting pastries and strudels on the premises. It's about a 10-minute walk from the Altstadt across the river. **Pros:** spacious rooms; outstanding breakfast. **Cons:** often filled with conferences; chain-hotel feel. ⊠ *Auerspergstrasse 4* ☎*0662/889990* ⊕*www.sheraton.at* ⚟*163 rooms* ⚐ *In-room: refrigerator. In-hotel: 2 restaurants, bar, gym, parking (paid), no-smoking rooms, Internet terminal* ▤*AE, DC, MC, V* ⎮◉⎮*BP.*

$$$–$$$$ 🏨**Blaue Gans.** "The Blue Goose" has always been a popular option—its location on the main shopping drag of Getriedegasse is tops. It has a 400-year-old pedigree and still retains its ancient wood beams, winding corridors, and low archways. Works by avant-garde artists such as Erich Shobesberger, Christian Ecker, and Waldemar Kufner adorn the walls. Upstairs, the guest rooms have whitewashed walls with cheeky framed posters and cheerful curtains; a few have skylights. The popular restaurant has lively contemporary art on the walls and nouvelle Austrian delights on the dishes. Now that Salzburg's profile in the modern-art world has expanded considerably with its new Museum der Moderne, artists and curators are touching down here, so be sure to make reservations well in advance. **Pros:** spacious rooms; near the sights; close to shopping. **Cons:** on a noisy street. ✉ *Getreidegasse 43* ☎ *0662/842491–0* ⊕ *www.blauegans.at* 📞 *40 rooms* ♿ *In-room: no a/c (some), refrigerator, Wi-Fi. In-hotel: restaurant, bar, parking (paid), Internet terminal* ⊟ *AE, DC, MC, V* ⦿ *BP.*

$$$–$$$$
★   🏨**Bristol.** Just across the river from the Altstadt, this pale-yellow palace has hosted Emperor Franz Josef I, Sigmund Freud, and the cast of *The Sound of Music*. The sunny lobby showcases a huge ancient tapestry along one wall and works by the Salzburg-born painter Hans Makart, and the piano bar contains framed black-and-white photos of prominent guests (including Max, the Captain, and Liesl from the film cast). No two rooms are alike, but all have impressive fabrics, chandeliers, and marble baths (some have inner doors with their original etched glass). A few rooms are done in a whimsical Napoleonic style with tented ceilings. The classy rooftop suite, known simply as "The View," has arguably the most stupendous views in the entire city. **Pros:** unbeatable views; charming accommodations. **Cons:** not in the old city; some rooms are better than others. ✉ *Makartplatz 4* ☎ *0662/873557* ⊕ *www.bristol-salzburg.at* 📞 *60 rooms* ♿ *In-room: refrigerator, Wi-Fi. In-hotel: restaurant, bar, parking (paid)* ⊟ *AE, DC, MC, V* ⦿ *Closed Feb. and Mar.* ⦿ *BP.*

$$$ 🏨**Neutor.** A two-minute walk from the Old City and next to the historic tunnel that plows through the Mönchsberg, this modern but classy option, run by the Schwärzler hotel group, is divided between two buildings on opposite sides of the street. The decor is bright and shiny—a real blessing on a gray, rainy day—and all rooms are equipped with modern technology. Children ages six and under are free. There are a few parking spaces behind the hotel, but if they're occupied you'll have to pay to park either along the street or in a garage. **Pros:** excellent location; cheerful rooms. **Cons:** on a busy street; not enough parking. ✉ *Neutorstrasse 8* ☎ *0662/844154–0* ⊕ *www.schwaerzler-hotels. com* 📞 *89 rooms* ♿ *In-room: no a/c. In-hotel: restaurant, bar, parking* ⊟ *AE, DC, MC, V* ⦿ *BP.*

$$$ 🏨**Stieglbräu/Imlauer.** Named after a noted Salzburg brewery, this hotel has some leafy gardens and serves up the old-fashioned treats the beer coachmen of yore liked, such as *Liptauer* (hot spiced cheese served with radish, bacon, cold pork, sausages, butter, and bread, along with a mug of the fresh beer on tap). Stieglbräu/Imlauer has comfortably equipped rooms with soundproof windows. The hotel is midway

5

between the train station and the Mirabell Gardens; the No. 1 bus takes you to the city center. **Pros:** nice gardens; tasty food. **Cons:** faces a busy street. ⊠*Rainerstrasse 12–14* 🕿*0662/88992* ⊕*www.imlauer. com* 🗪*99 rooms* ⚹*In-hotel: restaurant, parking (free)* ⊟*AE, DC, MC, V* ⎜⊙⎜*BP.*

$$–$$$ 🏨 **Auersperg.** Would you like to start your mornings with a stroll by a pool flowered with water lilies? You'll find this green oasis between the two buildings that comprise the Auersperg—the hotel, built in 1892 by the noted Italian architect Ceconi, and its neighboring "villa." The lobby welcomes you with Biedermeier antiques, while upstairs, the rooms contain mostly modern pieces accented with classic ornaments. A rich breakfast buffet and a rooftop sauna and steam bath are included. You're five minutes from the historic section. A big plus: just around the corner is that Salzburg treasure of a restaurant–beer garden, Die Weisse. **Pros:** historic hotel; great breakfast. **Cons:** on a busy intersection. ⊠*Auerspergstrasse 61* 🕿*0662/88944* ⊕*www.auersperg.at* 🗪*51 rooms* ⚹*In-room: no a/c, Wi-Fi. In-hotel: parking (free), Internet terminal* ⊟*AE, DC, MC, V* ⎜⊙⎜*BP.*

$$–$$$ 🏨 **Elefant.** An old-time favorite, this hotel was once graced by the real Maria von Trapp (her personal check, written when she stayed here in 1981, is set under glass on the second floor). But we mean really old: this 700-year-old house began life as an inn run by Salzburg citizen Hans Goldeisen, host to the likes of Maximilian II, who on his way from Spain via Italy to Vienna was accompanied by his new pet, an Indian elephant named Soliman. That's also the reason why guests are welcomed by the sight of an elephant sculpture in the lobby. Some rooms are alluring, with pale-yellow striped wallpaper and blue accents, but others are much more generic. For real history, repair to the hotel's "Ratsherrenkeller," one of Salzburg's most famous wine cellars in the 17th century. Today it's the restaurant Bruno, and serves alluring candlelight dinners. **Pros:** lots of history; some rooms have antique-style furniture. **Cons:** chain-hotel feel. ⊠*Sigmund-Haffner-Gasse 4* 🕿*0662/843397* ⊕*www.elefant.at* 🗪*31 rooms* ⚹*In-room: refrigerator. In-hotel: restaurant, parking (paid), Internet terminal* ⊟*AE, DC, MC, V* ⎜⊙⎜*BP.*

$$–$$$ 🏨 **Rosenvilla.** A haven of peace and tranquillity, this upscale bed-and-breakfast is across the Salzach River from the Altstadt. You enter the pretty suburban villa through an arbored garden gate. Guest rooms, all designed with taste, are a seductive mixture of contemporary, French Empire, and Biedermeier accents, with pretty fabrics and lots of light. Some have balconies overlooking the soothing garden with its expanse of velvet green lawn, tiled pathways, and a little pond with ducks. A special three-day offer includes dinner at the owners' top-ranked restaurant, Pfefferschiff. The Rosenvilla is a 20-minute walk from the center. **Pros:** quiet location; tasteful rooms. **Cons:** long walk away from downtown. ⊠*Höfelgasse 4* 🕿*0662/621765* ⊕*www.rosenvilla.sbg.at* 🗪*14 rooms* ⚹*In-room: no a/c. In-hotel: parking (free)* ⊟*AE, DC, MC, V* ⎜⊙⎜*BP.*

$$ 🏨 **Amadeus.** There isn't much here to clue you into why the hotel has adopted Mozart's second name, but dig a bit. You'll learn that this 500-year-old, rather ramshackle yet charming house is not far from the

St. Sebastian church and cemetery where many members of his family are booked for an eternal stay. The hotel site was once home to one of Salzburg's communal baths. Back in Wolfgang's time there was no running water in houses, so travelers—especially those arriving through the nearby Linz Gate—would immediately repair to this official bath after their long trip along dusty roads. Today travelers still make a beeline here. The guest rooms are each decorated differently, with several featuring charming wood armoires and beds, others in a calm and modern fashion. Downstairs, greet the day in one of the cutest breakfast nooks in Salzburg, festively done up in red, white, and green. But if you have a problem with Salzburg's incessantly ringing church bells, beware—there is a church next door and its bell goes off every quarter hour. It stops at 11 PM but will prove a rather loud alarm clock at 5 AM. **Pros:** huge breakfast; historic house. **Cons:** church bells are a noisy alarm clock. ⊠ *Linzergasse 43–45* ☎ *0662/871401* ⊕ *www.hotelamadeus.at* ⟵ *23 rooms* ⚬ *In-room: no a/c* ⊟ *AE, DC, MC, V* †◎│ *BP.*

$$ ⊞ **Gersberg Alm.** A picture-perfect Alpine chalet on the lofty perch of
★ the Gersberg high above Salzburg, this hotel is less than 15 minutes by car from the center of the city. Inside, it has all the warmth and rustic coziness you would expect in a country house; indeed, it was originally a 19th-century farmhouse. Guest rooms have contemporary furniture and have wooden balconies overlooking the mountain scenery. The house restaurant is excellent—top choices include ravioli stuffed with spinach in a tomato-butter sauce, or lightly fried pike perch in a tomato-olive crust with pesto spaghetti. Be sure to try the warm apricot fritters for dessert. The wine list has an outstanding selection of Austrian wines. **Pros:** beautiful location; pleasant rooms. **Cons:** outside the city. ⊠ *Gersberg 37* ☎ *0662/641257* ⊕ *www.gersbergalm.at* ⟵ *43 rooms* ⚬ *In-room: no a/c, refrigerator. In-hotel: restaurant, pool, parking (free)* ⊟ *AE, DC, MC, V* †◎│ *BP.*

$$ ⊞ **NH Salzburg.** Run by a Spanish hotel chain, this pretty building has Art Nouveau awnings, Secession-style sash windows, and white stone trim. Inside all is sleek and comfy. The location is nice—you're around the corner from Linzergasse, the shopping street leading to the Salzach river or five minutes away from the beautiful Mirabell Gardens. There is a rich buffet-style breakfast and the restaurant has a garden terrace. **Pros:** situated in historic setting; tasty breakfast. **Cons:** noisy common areas. ⊠ *Franz-Josef-Strasse 26* ☎ *0662/8820410* ⊕ *www.nh-hotels. com* ⟵ *140 rooms* ⚬ *In-room: no a/c, Wi-Fi. In-hotel: restaurant, bar, parking (paid)* ⊟ *AE, DC, MC, V* †◎│ *BP.*

$$ ⊞ **Pension Wolf.** The embodiment of Austrian Gemütlichkeit, just off Mozartplatz, the small, family-owned, in-the-center-of-everything Wolf offers spotlessly clean and cozy rooms in a rustic 1429 building. Rooms are idiosyncratically arranged on several upper floors, connected by narrow, winding stairs, and are decorated with a pleasing Salzburg mix of rag rugs and rural furniture. This is popular, so be sure to book far in advance. **Pros:** plenty of atmosphere; in a historic house. **Cons:** parking is a problem. ⊠ *Kaigasse 7* ☎ *0662/843453–0* ⊕ *www.hotelwolf. com* ⟵ *12 rooms* ⚬ *In-room: no a/c. In-hotel: parking (paid)* ⊟ *AE* ⊗ *Closed early Feb.–early Mar.* †◎│ *BP.*

$$ 🏨**Stadtkrug.** Snuggled under the monument-studded Kapuzinerberg and a two-minute walk from the bridge leading to the center of the Altstadt, the Stadtkrug (dated 1353) hits an idyllic, romantic, and quiet vibe, thanks to its mountainside setting. A traditional wrought-iron sign greets you, the lobby tinkles with chandeliers, and the main-floor restaurant is your archetypal, white, classic, vaulted Salzburg sanctorum. Upstairs you find a charming atmosphere and rustic rooms. Head up to the roof to enjoy a restaurant that is terraced into the mountainside and set with statues, potted begonias, echoes of Italy, and lovely views. **Pros:** good location; lots of charm. **Cons:** on a busy street. ⊠ *Linzergasse 20* ☎*0662/873545–0* ⊕*www.stadtkrug.at* ⇆*34 rooms* ⚐*In-room: no a/c. In-hotel: 2 restaurants* ☰*AE, DC, MC, V* ⏃*BP.*

$$ 🏨**Weisse Taube.** In the heart of the pedestrian area of the Altstadt, the centuries-old "White Dove" is around the corner from Mozartplatz, the Salzburg Museum, and the Residenz. Comfortably renovated into a hotel—now family-run for four generations—this 14th-century burgher's house has been traditionally restored, but some time-burnished touches remain: uneven floors, ancient stone archways, and wood-beam ceilings. Guest rooms are simply furnished, with dark-wood accents. Several no-smoking rooms are available, and the main section of the breakfast room is also no-smoking. **Pros:** excellent location for walkers; friendly staff. **Cons:** noisy area at night. ⊠ *Kaigasse 9* ☎*0662/842404* ⊕*www.weissetaube.at* ⇆*33 rooms* ⚐*In-room: no a/c. In-hotel: bar, parking (paid), no-smoking rooms, Internet terminal* ☰*AE, DC, MC, V* ⊘*Closed 2 wks in Jan.* ⏃*BP.*

$$ 🏨**Wolf-Dietrich.** Two houses sit opposite each other: the Altstadt and
★ the Residenz. Some of the guest rooms in this small, family-owned hotel across the river from the Altstadt are decorated with Laura Ashley fabrics—two "romantic" apartments are designed like stage settings for Mozart's *The Magic Flute*—and have extra amenities, such as attractive sitting areas. Those in the back look out over the looming Gaisberg and the cemetery of St. Sebastian. The staff is warm and helpful. **Pros:** elegantly decorated rooms; nice views. **Cons:** church bells ring constantly. ⊠ *Wolf-Dietrich-Strasse 7* ☎*0662/871275* ⊕*www.salzburg-hotel.at* ⇆*32 rooms* ⚐*In-room: no a/c, Internet. In-hotel: restaurant, pool, parking (paid), no-smoking rooms* ☰*AE, DC, MC, V* ⏃*BP.*

$ 🏨**Am Dom.** Tucked away on a tiny street near Residenzplatz, this small pension in a 14th-century building offers simply furnished rooms, some with oak-beam ceilings. Note the beautiful hand-carved Renaissance reception desk. The selling point here is the great location in the heart of the Altstadt. **Pros:** rustic atmosphere; well-kept rooms. **Cons:** few amenities. ⊠ *Goldgasse 17* ☎*0662/842765* ⊕*www.amdom.at* ⇆*15 rooms* ⚐*In-room: no a/c, no TV* ☰*AE, DC, MC, V* ⊘*Closed 2 wks in Feb.* ⏃*BP.*

$ 🏨**Bergland.** A 10-minute walk from the train station, this cheerful, pleasant, family-owned pension offers modern, comfortable rooms with breakfast included in the price. The sitting room includes an English library. **Pros:** quiet location; very good value. **Cons:** long walk to the center; basic accommodations. ⊠ *Rupertgasse 15* ☎*0662/872318* ⊕*www.berglandhotel.at* ⇆*17 rooms* ⚐*In-room: no a/c. In-hotel:*

parking (free), no-smoking rooms ⊟*AE, DC, MC, V* ⊗*Closed Nov.– Christmas* ⑂|*BP.*

$ ⊡**Cordial Theaterhotel.** Music lovers will enjoy studying the myriad pro-
duction posters and photographs of famous artists that festoon the
lobby here. Part of a classy chain, this is a modern option with comfy
guest rooms. The location is about a 10-minute walk from the city
center, as are the auditoriums on both sides of the Salzach River. **Pros:**
pleasant rooms; close to performance spaces. **Cons:** on a noisy street.
⊠*Schallmooser Hauptstrasse 13* ☎*0662/881681–0* ⊕*www.cordial.at*
⤶*58 rooms, 10 apartments* ⚭*In-room: no a/c. In-hotel: restaurant,
bar* ⊟*AE, DC, MC, V* ⑂|*BP.*

$ ⊡**Turnerwirt.** In the former farmer's village of Gnigl, part of Salzburg's
outskirts, this is a quaint complex of buildings. The most charming is the
small "Villa," an adorable mansion fitted out with begonia-hung windows, red storybook roof, and fairy-tale turret. Out front is the massive
Gasthaus—an Alpine roof and its name picked out in Gothic lettering
on the front makes the building look on sabbatical from an Albrecht
Dürer engraving. Rooms are decorated in a traditional and pleasing style.
The largest suites have three and four bedrooms. By car, the Turnerwirt
can be reached from Salzburg by taking the motorway and exiting after
2 mi (1 km) at Salzburg Nord or Wallersee. **Pros:** family-run friendli-
ness; lots of charm. **Cons:** outside city center. ⊠*Linzer Bundesstrasse 54*
☎*0662/640630* ⊕*www.turnerwirt.at* ⤶*62 rooms* ⚭*In-room: no a/c,
Wi-Fi. In-hotel: parking (free)* ⊟*AE, DC, MC, V* ⑂|*BP.*

¢ ⊡**Schwarzes Rössl.** Once a favorite with Salzburg regulars, this traditional Gasthof now serves as student quarters for most of the year, but is
well worth booking when available. Rooms are fresh and immaculate,
if not charming, and the location is excellent—close to the nighttime
action. **Pros:** near city center. **Cons:** few amenities. ⊠*Priesterhausgasse
6* ☎*0662/874426* ⊟*01/401–76–20* ⤶*51 rooms, 4 with bath* ⚭*In-
room: no a/c* ⊟*AE, DC, MC, V* ⊗*Closed Oct.–June* ⑂|*BP.*

NIGHTLIFE & THE ARTS

THE ARTS

Before you arrive in Salzburg, do some advance research to determine
the city's music schedule for the time you will be there, and book reservations; if you'll be attending the summer Salzburg Festival, this is
a must. After you arrive in the city, any office of the Salzburg Tourist
Office and most hotel concierge desks can provide you with schedules
for all the arts performances held year-round in Salzburg, and you can
find listings in the daily newspaper, *Salzburger Nachrichten.*

THE SALZBURG MUSIC FESTIVAL

The biggest event on the calendar—as it has been since it was first
organized by composer Richard Strauss, producer Max Reinhardt, and
playwright Hugo von Hofmannsthal in 1920—is the world-famous
Salzburger Festspiele (⊠*Hofstallgasse 1, Salzburg* ☎*0662/8045–
500 for summer festival, 0662/8045–361 for Easter festival* ⊕*www.*

salzburgfestival.at). The main summer festival is usually scheduled for the last week of July through the end of August. In addition, the festival presents two other major annual events: the Easter Festival (early April), and the Pentecost Baroque Festival (late May).

The most star-studded events—featuring the top opera stars and conductors such as Riccardo Muti and Nikolaus Harnoncourt—have tickets ranging from €22 to €340; for these glamorous events, first-nighters still pull out all the stops—summer furs, Dior dresses, and white ties stud the more expensive sections of the theaters. Other performances can run from €8 to €190, with still lesser prices for events outside the main festival halls, the **Grosses Festspielhaus** (Great Festival Hall) and the **Haus für Mozart**

A LOT OF NIGHT MUSIC

Salzburg is most renowned for the Salzburger Festspiele. But much of Salzburg's special charm can be best discovered and enjoyed off-season. Music lovers face loads of riches, including chamber concerts held in Mirabell Palace, the Fortress, or at St. Blasius. Salzburg concerts by the Mozarteum Orchestra and the Camerata are now just as popular as the Vienna Philharmonic's program in the Musikverein in Vienna. The Landestheater season runs from September to June. And no one should miss the chance to be enchanted and amazed by the skill and artistry of the Salzburg Marionette Theater.

(House for Mozart), located shoulder to shoulder on the grand promenade of Hofstallgasse. This street, one of the most festive settings for a music festival, is especially dazzling at night, thanks to the floodlighted Fortress Hohensalzburg, which hovers on its hilltop above the theater promenade. Behind the court stables first constructed by Wolf-Dietrich in 1607, the Festspielhäser (festival halls) are modern constructions—the Grosses Haus was built in 1960 with 2,200 seats—but are actually "prehistoric," being dug out of the bedrock of the Mönchsberg mountain. There are glittering concerts and operas performed at many other theaters in the city. You can catch Mozart concertos in the 18th-century splendor of two magnificent state rooms the composer himself once conducted in: the Rittersaal of the Residenz and the Marble Hall of the Mirabell Palace. Delightful Mozart productions are offered by the Salzburger Marionetten Theater. In addition, many important concerts are offered in the two auditoriums of the Mozarteum.

■TIP→ Since you *must* order your tickets as early as possible, make your decisions as soon as the program comes out (usually in the middle of November). Many major performances are sold out two or three months in advance, as hordes descend on the city to enjoy staged opera spectacles, symphony concerts by the Vienna Philharmonic and other great orchestras, recitals, church oratorios, and special evenings at the Mozarteum year after year. Tickets can be purchased directly at the box office, at your hotel, or, most conveniently, at the festival Web site listed above. Next to the main tourist office is a box office where you can get tickets for Great Festival Hall concerts Monday through Friday, 8 to 6: **Salzburger Kulturvereinigung** (⊠ *Waagplatz 1A* ☎*0662/845346*). The following agencies also sell tickets: **American Express** (⊠*Mozartplatz 5* ☎*0662/8080–0* ☎*0662/8080–9*). **Polzer** (⊠*Residenzplatz 3,* ☎*0662/846500*). **Salzburg Ticket Service** (⊠*Mozartplatz 5,* ☎*0662/840310*).

MUSIC

There is no shortage of concerts in this most musical of cities. Customarily, the Salzburg Festival hosts the Vienna Philharmonic, but other orchestras can be expected to take leading roles as well. Year-round there are also the Palace-Residenz Concerts and the Fortress Concerts, while in the summer there are Mozart Serenades in the Gothic Room at St. Blase's Church. In addition, there are the Easter Festival, the Pentecost Baroque Festival, Mozart Week (late January), and the Salzburg Cultural Days (October). Mozart Week is always special; in recent seasons Nikolaus Harnoncourt, Zubin Mehta, and Sir Charles Mackerras have conducted the Vienna Philharmonic, while Sir Neville Marriner, Daniel Harding, and Sir Roger Norrington were in charge with other orchestras.

Fodor'sChoice The **Salzburger Schlosskonzerte** (⊠*Theatergasse 2* ☎*0662/848586* ⊕*www.*
★ *salzburger.schlosskonzerte.at* ☜*€29–€35*) presents concerts in the legendary Marmorsaal (Marble Hall) at **Mirabell Palace,** where Mozart performed.

The **Salzburger Festungskonzerte** (⊠*Fortress Hohensalzburg* ☎*0662/ 825858* ⊕*www.mozartfestival.at* ☜*€31–€38*) are presented in the grand Prince's Chamber at Festung Hohensalzburg. Concerts often include works by Mozart. A special candlelight dinner and concert-ticket combo is often offered.

Organizer of the important Mozart Week held every January, the **Mozarteum** (⊠*Schwarzstrasse 26* ☎*0662/88940–21* ⊕*www.mozarteum.at*) center is open to scholars only. However, thousands flock here for its packed calendar of important concerts. The two main concert rooms are in the main facility on Schwarzstrasse.

OPERA

The great opera event of the year is the **Salzburger Festspiele,** which mount a full calendar of operas every year. These performances are held in the Grosses Festspielhaus (Great Festival Hall), the Haus für Mozart (House for Mozart), the Landestheater, the Felsenreitschule, the Mozarteum, and numerous other smaller venues, where lieder recitals and chamber works predominate. Prices range from €5 to €600.

Fodor'sChoice The delightful, acclaimed **Salzburger Marionettentheater** (⊠*Schwarz-*
★ *strasse 24* ☎*0662/872406–0* ⊕*www.marionetten.at*) is also devoted
♨ to opera, with a particularly renowned production of *Così fan tutte* to its credit. The Marionettentheater not only performs operas by Mozart, but also goodies by Rossini, the younger Strauss, Offenbach, Humperdinck, and Mendelssohn (who wrote the music for the troupe's delightful show devoted to William Shakespeare's *A Midsummer Night's Dream*). Performances are staged during the first week of January, during Mozart Week (late January), from May through September, and December 25 through January 7. Tickets usually range

from €18 to €35. The box office is open Monday through Saturday 9–1 and two hours before the performance.

THEATER

The morality play *Jedermann* (*Everyman*), by Hugo von Hofmannsthal, is famously performed annually (in German) in the forecourt of the **Cathedral** (✉ *Salzburger Festspiele Postfach 140*, ☎ *0662/8045–500* ⊕ *www.salzburgfestival.at*). This is a spine-tingling presentation, and few of the thousands packing the plaza are unmoved when at the height of the banquet the voice of Death is heard calling "Jedermann—Jedermann—Jed-er-*mann*" from the Franziskanerkirche tower, and is then followed with echoes of voices from other steeples and from atop the Fortress Hohensalzburg. As the sun sets, the doors of the great cathedral hover open and the sounds of its organ announce the salvation of Everyman's soul.

NIGHTLIFE

Music in Salzburg is not just *Eine Kleine Nachtmusik*. The city's nightlife is livelier than it is reputed to be. The "in" areas include the "Bermuda Triangle" (Steingasse, Imbergstrasse, and Rudolfskai) and Kaigasse; young people tend to populate the bars and discos around Gstättengasse.

Salzburg loves beer, and has some of the most picturesque Bierkeller in Austria. The Augustinerbräu is a legendary Munich-style beer hall. A top beer paradise is the **Stieglkeller** (✉ *Festungsgasse 10* ☎ *0662/842681* ⏱ *May–Sept.*), by the funicular station of the Hohensalzburg tram. The noted local architect Ceconi devised this sprawling place around 1901. The Keller is partly inside the Mönchsberg hill, so its cellars guarantee the quality and right temperature of the drinks. The gardens here have chestnut trees and offer a marvelous view above the roofs of the Old City—a lovely place to enjoy your Bauernschmaus (farmer's dish). The **Sternbräu** (✉ *Griesegasse 23* ☎ *0662/842140*) is a mammoth Bierkeller with eight rambling halls festooned with tile stoves, paintings, and wood beams. The chestnut-tree beer garden or the courtyard are divine on hot summer nights. Many travelers head here for the **Sound of Salzburg Dinner Show**, presented May through October, daily 7:30 to 10 PM, which includes some Mozart in addition to the best of *The Sound of Music*. A three-course meal and show costs €40, or you can arrive at 8:15 PM to see the show and just have Apfelstrudel and coffee for €25.

SHOPPING

For a small city, Salzburg has a wide spectrum of stores. The specialties are traditional clothing, like lederhosen and loden coats, jewelry, glassware, handicrafts, confectionary, dolls in native costume, Christmas decorations, sports equipment, and silk flowers. A *Gewürzsträussl* is a bundle of whole spices bunched and arranged to look like a bouquet of flowers (try the markets on Universitätsplatz). This old tradition goes back to the time when only a few rooms could be heated, and people and their farm animals would often cohabitate on the coldest days. You can imagine how lovely the aromas must have been—so this spicy room-freshener was invented.

At Christmas there is a special **Advent market** on the Domplatz, offering regional decorations, from the week before the first Advent Sunday until December 24, daily from 9 AM to 8 PM. Stores are generally open weekdays 10–6, and many on Saturday 10–5. Some supermarkets stay open until 7:30 on Thursday or Friday. Only shops in the railway station, the airport, and near the general hospital are open on Sunday.

SHOPPING STREETS

The most fashionable specialty stores and gift shops are found along Getreidegasse and Judengasse and around Residenzplatz. Linzergasse, across the river, is less crowded and good for more practical items. There are also interesting antiques shops in the medieval buildings along Steingasse and on Goldgasse.

SPECIALTY STORES

ANTIQUES
Internationale Messe für Kunst und Antiquitäten (⊠ *Residenzplatz 1* ☎ *0662/8042–2690*) is the annual antiques fair that takes place from Palm Sunday to Easter Monday in the state rooms of Salzburg's Residenz.

Ilse Guggenberger (⊠ *Brodgasse 11* ☎ *0662/843184*) is the place to browse for original Austrian country antiques. **Marianne Reuter** (⊠ *Gstättengasse 9* ☎ *0662/842136*) offers a fine selection of porcelain and 18th-century furniture. **Schöppl** (⊠ *Gstättengasse 5* ☎ *0662/842154*) has old desks, hutches, and some jewelry. For an amazing assortment of secondhand curiosities, try **Trödlerstube** (⊠ *Linzergasse 50* ☎ *0662/871453*).

CONFECTIONARY
If you're looking for the kind of *Mozartkugeln* (chocolate marzipan confections) you can't buy at home, try the store that claims to have invented them in 1890: **Konditorei Fürst** (⊠ *Brodgasse 13* ☎ *0662/843759–0*). It still produces the candy by hand according to the original recipe that the family never gave away. Stock up at one of its four locations while you're in town—Konditoriei Fürst does not offer overseas shipping. **Konditorei Schatz** (⊠ *Getreidegasse 3, Schatz passageway* ☎ *0662/842792*) makes its own version of Mozartkugeln and other delectable goodies.

CRAFTS
Christmas in Salzburg (⊠ *Judengasse 10* ☎ *0662/846784*) has rooms of gorgeous Christmas-tree decorations, some hand-painted and hand carved. **Fritz Kreis** (⊠ *Sigmund-Haffner-Gasse 14* ☎ *0662/841768*) sells ceramics, wood carvings, handmade glass objects, and so on. **Gehmacher** (⊠ *Alter Markt 2* ☎ *0662/845506–0*) offers whimsi-

cal home decorations. **Salzburger Heimatwerk** (⊠ *Residenzplatz 9* ☎*0662/844110–0*) has clothing, fabrics, ceramics, and local handicrafts at good prices.

TRADITIONAL CLOTHING

Dschulnigg (⊠ *Griesgasse 8, corner of Münzgasse* ☎*0662/842376–0*) is a favorite among Salzburgers for lederhosen, dirndls, and *Trachten,* the typical Austrian costume with white blouse, print skirt, and apron. For a wide selection of leather goods, some made to order, try **Jahn-Markl** (⊠ *Residenzplatz 3* ☎*0662/842610*). **Lanz** (⊠ *Schwarzstrasse 4* ☎*0662/874272*) sells a good selection of long dirndls, silk costumes, and loden coats. **Madl am Grünmarkt** (⊠ *Universitätsplatz 12* ☎*0662/845457*) has more flair and elegance in its traditional designs.

SOUVENIR SWEETS

Mozartkugeln, candy balls of pistachio-flavored marzipan rolled in nougat cream and dipped in dark chocolate, which bear a miniportrait of Mozart on the wrapper, are omnipresent in Salzburg. Taste-test and compare to find the best. Those handmade by Konditorei Fürst cost more but can be purchased individually. In hot summer months, ask for a thermos bag to prevent melting. Industrial products like those from Mirabell—500,000 pieces every day—or from the German competitor Reber you get almost everywhere. Special cheap offers are easy to find in supermarkets or in duty-free shops at the airport.

Salzkammergut

WORD OF MOUTH

"By the time we entered St. Gilgen (about 30 km from Salzburg) it was raining lightly, but even the inclement weather could not detract form the breathtaking beauty of the area. We all immediately fell in love with the place—the mountains, the lakes, the villages . . . Just all of it! I personally think this must be one of the most beautiful places I have ever visited and I loved every single day of our stay, even though the weather was not very kind to us."

—PRLCH

Updated by
Horst Erwin
Reischenböck

REMEMBER THE EXQUISITE OPENING SCENES of *The Sound of Music*? Castles reflected in water, mountains veiled by a scattering of downy clouds, flower-strewn valleys dotted with cool blue lakes: a view of Austria as dreamed up by a team of Hollywood's special-effects geniuses—so many thought. But, no, except for the bicycle ride along the Mondsee, those scenes were filmed right here, in Austria's fabled Salzkammergut region. The Lake District of Upper Austria, centered on the region called the Salzkammergut (literally, "salt estates"), presents the traveler with stunning sights: soaring mountains and needlelike peaks; a glittering necklace of turquoise lakes; forested valleys populated by the *Rehe* (roe deer) immortalized by Felix Salten in *Bambi*— this is Austria at its most lush and verdant. Some of these lakes, like the Hallstätter See, remain quite unspoiled, partly because the mountains act as a buffer from busier, more accessible sections of the country. Another—historic—reason relates to the presence of the salt mines, which date back to the Celtic era; with salt so common and cheap nowadays, many forget it was once a luxury item mined under strict government monopoly, and he Salzkammergut was closed to the casually curious for centuries, opening up only after Emperor Franz Josef made Bad Ischl—one of the area's leading spa towns (even then, studded with *salt*water swimming pools)—his official summer residence in 1854.

ORIENTATION & PLANNING

GETTING ORIENTED

To the west of Bad Ischl are the best known of all the Salzkammergut's 76 lakes—the Wolfgangsee, the Mondsee, and the Attersee (*See* is German for "lake"). Not far beyond these lakes lies one of Austria's loveliest spots, Gosau am Dachstein. Here the Gosau lakes are backdropped by a spectacular sight that acts as a landmark for many leagues: the Dachstein peak. Another scenic wonder is the storybook village of Hallstatt, huddled between mountain and lake.

Whether you start out from Salzburg or set up a base in Bad Ischl—the heart of the Lake District—it's best to take in the beauties of the Salzkammergut in perhaps two separate courses: first around the Mondsee, the Wolfgangsee, and Bad Ischl; then southwest to Gosau am Dachstein, back to the Hallstätter See, and east to Bad Aussee and the Altausseer See, returning via the Pötschen mountain pass.

On the Road to St. Wolfgang & Bad Ischl. Between its romantic lakes surrounded by alpine peaks, this region is perfect for both water sports in summer and skiing in winter. The charming Bad Ischl's old-fashioned buildings document the town's importance in days of the Habsburgs.

Gosau, Hallstatt & Bad Aussee. The sight of the high Dachstein mountain range gives the impression of being on top of the world. The picturesque towns in this region are full of Austrian folklore and tradition, and have inspired many composers, painters, and poets.

GREAT ITINERARIES

IF YOU HAVE 4 DAYS

Setting out early from Salzburg or Vienna, head to the core of the Lake District, 🖼 **Bad Ischl**. Check out Franz Josef's summer residence and stop in at Zauner in the center of the town for some of the best pastry in Europe. Delicious, but beware: *two* to a person will be plenty. Spend the night here at this history-rich spa—today it is one of the best equipped in Austria—and the next morning head south on Route 145 toward Hallstatt. After Bad Goisern bear right past Au, then turn right over the bridge to cross the River Traun into Steeg (don't worry about the factory smokestack—it's an isolated affair in these parts). Twenty-nine kilometers (18 mi) from Bad Ischl you'll come to a junction with Route 166. Here you should turn right into the ravine of the Gosaubach river. After heading through very scenic territory framed by steep wooded slopes for some 32 km (20 mi), you'll reach 🖼 **Gosau am Dachstein**, which spreads out over a comfortable north–south valley, at the end of which lie the famous Gosau lakes. You have now reached one of Austria's most beautiful spots. There are three lakes here, several miles apart from each other and all framed by the craggy heights of the Dachstein range. After taking in the views, spend the night in the village and awaken to a dazzling dawn glistening over the snow-swept Bischofsmütze peak.

On your third morning, head back to Route 145 and south to 🖼 **Hallstatt**, called the "world's prettiest lakeside village." After spending quality time with your Nikon (do your photography in the morning when the village is nicely lit), check out two natural wonders: the salt mines above Hallstatt and, continuing around the southern end of the lake for 5 km (3 mi), the **Dachstein Ice Caves** at Obertraun. On your fourth morning, leave Upper Austria and head for 🖼 **Bad Aussee** along the romantic old road that follows the Traun River. It is still in part covered with hand-hewn paving stones and has at one point an impressive gradient of 23% (sometimes closed in winter). After exploring the town's picturesque 15th- and 16th-century architecture, you should still have time for a stroll around neighboring **Altaussee**, whose romantic landscape has inspired many artists and poets. Return to Bad Aussee, then catch Route 145 north across the Pötschen pass to Bad Ischl, enjoying spectacular vistas along the way back.

6

PLANNING

WHEN TO GO

Year-round, vacationers flock to the Lake District; however, late fall is not the best time to visit the region, for it could be rainy and cold, and many sights are closed or operate on a restricted schedule. By far the best months are July and September. August sees the countryside overrun with families on school holidays and music lovers from the nearby Salzburg Music Festival (even so, who can resist a visit on to Bad Ischl on August 18, when Emperor Franz Josef's birthday is still celebrated). Another seasonal highlight is the annual Narcissus Festival held in May or June at Bad Aussee (the town is blanketed with flowers). Bad Aussee also has a special Carnival celebration (in February, with varying dates year to year), with men dressed as women and banging drums (the so-called *Trommelweiber*) on one day, then the *Flinserln* parading in costumes bedecked with silvery paillettes on the next day. Others like to visit Hallstatt for its annual procession across the lake, held on Corpus Christi day (weather permitting, around the last weekend in May, or the Sunday after)—a Catholic, and therefore, state holiday all over Austria. December finds several small picturesque markets in the villages around the Wolfgangsee.

GETTING HERE & AROUND

BY AIR   By air, the Lake District is closer to Salzburg than to Linz. The Salzburg airport is about 53 km (33 mi) from Bad Ischl, heart of the Salzkammergut; the Linz airport (Hörsching) is about 75 km (47 mi).

BY CAR   Driving is by far the easiest and most convenient way to reach the Lake District; traffic is excessive only on weekends (although it can be slow on some narrow lakeside stretches). From Salzburg you can take Route 158 east to Fuschl, St. Gilgen, and Bad Ischl or the A1 autobahn to Mondsee. Coming from Vienna or Linz, the A1 passes through the northern part of the Salzkammergut; get off at the Steyrermühl exit or the Regau exit and head south on Route 144/145 to Gmunden, Bad Ischl, Bad Goisern, and Bad Aussee. From the Seewalchen exit, take Route 152 down the east side of the Attersee, instead of the far less scenic Route 151 down the west side. Remember: gasoline is expensive in Austria.

BY TRAIN   The geography of the area means that rail lines run mainly north–south. Where the trains don't go, buses do, so if you allow enough time you can cover virtually all the area by public transportation. The main bus routes through the region are: Bad Aussee to Grundlsee; Bad Ischl to Gosau, Hallstatt, Salzburg, and St. Wolfgang; Mondsee to St. Gilgen and Salzburg; St. Gilgen to Mondsee; Salzburg to Bad Ischl, Mondsee, St. Gilgen, and Strobl.

TOURS   Daylong tours of the Salzkammergut, offered by Dr. Richard/Albus/Salzburg Sightseeing Tours and Salzburg Panorama Tours, whisk you all too quickly from Salzburg to St. Gilgen, St. Wolfgang, and Mondsee.

VISITOR INFORMATION

Most towns in the Salzkammergut have their own *Fremdenverkehrsamt* (tourist office), which are listed below, in the specific towns. The main tourist offices for the provinces and regions covered in this chapter are Salzkammergut/Salzburger Land, Styria, Tourismusverband Ausseerland, and Upper Austria. Styria, Upper Austria, and Salzburg Province all comprise the backbone of the Dachstein range.

ESSENTIALS

Bus Contacts **Zentrale Busauskunft** (☎ *05/1717-4* ⊕ *www.oebb.at*).

Medical Assistance **St. Johannsspital-Landeskrankenanstalten** (✉ *Müllner Hauptstrasse 48, Salzburg* ☎ *0662/44820*).

TOP REASONS TO GO

Fairy-tale landscape. The lakes and mountains resemble the pictures in a children's book, especially in the Styrian region.

Bad Iscl. This town, where the rich and famous have long come for the healing waters, was Emperor Franz Josef's summer retreat in the 19th century.

The Attersee. The region's largest lake has long attracted artists, including the great Gustav Klimt, who have come to sketch its magical shores

Cradle of culture. Vienna and Salzburg may get all the credit, but the composers who made these cities cultural capitals came to this part of Austria to hear the music in the air.

Sports abound. Everyone knows about the region's great ski resorts, but there is an endless array of summer sports as well.

6

Tour Information Dr. Richard/Albus/Salzburg Sightseeing Tours (⊠ *Mirabellplatz 2, Salzburg* ☎*0662/881616* 🖷*0662/878776*). **Salzburg Panorama Tours** (⊠ *Schrannengasse 2/2, Salzburg* ☎*0662/883211* 🖷*0662/871628*).

Train Information ÖBB—Österreichisches Bundesbahn (☎*05/1717–2* ⊕*www. oebb.at*).

Visitor Info Salzkammergut/Salzburger Land (⊠ *Wirerstrasse 10, Bad Ischl* ☎*06132/26909–0* ⊕*www.salzkammergut.at*). **Tourismusverband Ausseerland** (⊠ *Chlumeckyplatz 44, Bad Aussee* ☎*03622/54040–0* ⊕*www.ausseerland.at*). **Upper Austria** (⊠ *Schillerstrasse 50, Linz* ☎*0732/6002–219* ⊕*www.oberoes terreich.at*).

ABOUT THE RESTAURANTS & HOTELS

Culinary shrines are to be found around Mondsee. However, in many of the towns of the Salzkammergut you'll find country inns with dining rooms but few independent restaurants, other than the occasional, simple *Gasthäuser.*

In the grand old days, the aristocratic families of the region would welcome paying guests at their charming castles. Today most of those castles have been, if you will, degentrified: they are now schools or very fine hotels. But you needn't stay in a castle to enjoy the Salzkammergut—there are also luxurious lakeside resorts, small country inns, even guesthouses without private baths; in some places the *Herr Wirt,* his smiling wife, and his grown-up children will do everything to make you feel comfortable. Although this chapter's hotel reviews cover the best in every category, note that nearly every village, however small, also has a Gasthaus or village inn. Many hotels offer half-board, with dinner in addition to buffet breakfast (although most $$$$ hotels will often charge extra for breakfast). The half-board room rate is usually an extra €15–€30 per person. Occasionally quoted room rates for hotels already include half-board accommodations, though a "discounted" rate is usually offered if you prefer not to take the evening meal. Inquire when booking. Happily, these hotels do not put their breathtakingly beautiful natural surroundings on the bill.

WHAT IT COSTS IN EUROS					
	¢	$	$$	$$$	$$$$
RESTAURANTS	under €7	€7–€12	€13–€17	€18–€22	over €22
HOTELS	under €70	€70–€100	€100–€135	€135–€175	over €175

Restaurant prices are per person for a main course at dinner. Hotel prices are for a standard double room in high season, including taxes and service. Assume that hotels operate on the European Plan (EP, with no meal provided) unless we note that they use the Breakfast Plan (BP), Modified American Plan (MAP, with breakfast and dinner daily, known as halb pension), or Full American Plan (FAP, or voll pension, with three meals a day). Higher prices (inquire when booking) prevail for any meal plans.

ON THE ROAD TO ST. WOLFGANG & BAD ISCHL

The mountains forming Austria's backbone may be less majestic than other Alps at this point, but they are also considerably less stern; glittering blue lakes and villages nestle safely in valleys without being constantly under the threatening eye of an avalanche from the huge peaks. Here you'll find what travelers come to the Lake District for: elegant restaurants, Baroque churches, meadows with getaway space and privacy, lakeside cabanas, and forests that could tell a tale or two.

MONDSEE

35½ km (22 mi) east of Salzburg, 100 km (62 mi) southwest of Linz.

Mondsee is the gateway to the Salzkammergut for many tourists and Salzburgers alike. *Mondsee* means "Moon Lake," a name whose origins are the subject of some debate. Some say this body of water (11 km [7 mi] long and 2 km [1 mi] wide), which vaguely resembles a crescent moon, was named after a prehistoric lunar deity, although the Mondsee Monastery had its own story about a Bavarian duke being saved from falling into the lake water by a full moon that showed him a safe passage, after which he vowed to found a monastery. The water is warmer than that of any of the other high-altitude lakes, which makes it a good place for swimming, sailing, and windsurfing (head to the tourist office at Dr-Franz-Müller-Strasse 3, near the town bus stop, for all the info). In addition, Mondsee has some of the best dining the Salzkammergut has to offer.

ESSENTIALS
Tourist Information Mondsee (⊠*Dr-Franz-Müller-Strasse 3,* ☎*06232/2270* ⊕*www. mondsee.org).*

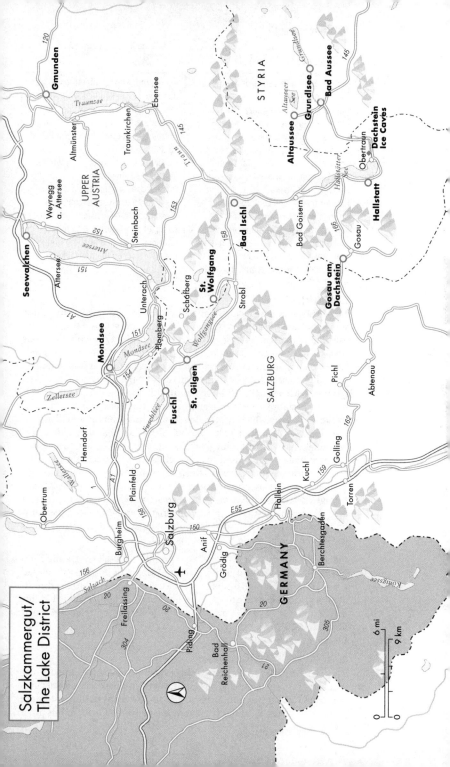

Salzkammergut/The Lake District

Gmunden
120
Traunsee
Altmünster
Traunkirchen
Ebensee
145
Traun

STYRIA
Grundlsee
Grundlsee
Bad Aussee
145
Altaussee
Altaussee
Obertraun
Dachstein Ice Caves

UPPER AUSTRIA
Weyregg a. Attersee
Steinbach
152
Attersee
153
Bad Ischl
Hallstätter See
Bad Goisern
Gosau
166
Hallstatt

Seewalchen
Attersee
151
A1
Unterach
Schafberg
Plomberg
St. Wolfgang
158
Strobl
Wolfgangsee
Gosau am Dachstein

Mondsee
151
Mondsee
154
Zellersee
Irrsee
St. Gilgen
Pichl
Abtenau

Fuschl
Fuschlsee
SALZBURG
162

Hennдorf
Wallersee
Golling
159
Kuchl

Obertrum
1
AT
Plainfeld
Torren

Burgheim
158
Salzburg
E55
Hallein
150
Anif
Grödig
Pichl
Berchtesgaden

156
Salzach
20
Freilassing
304
Piding
20
GERMANY
305
Königssee

Bad Reichenhall
21

6 mi
9 km

ON THE MENU

Fresh, local lake fish is on nearly every menu in the area, so take advantage of the bounty. The lakes and streams are home to several types of fish, notably trout, carp, and perch. They are prepared in numerous ways, from plain breaded (*gebacken*), to smoked and served with *Kren* (horseradish), to fried in butter (*gebraten*). Look for *Reinanke*, a mild whitefish straight from the Hallstättersee. Sometimes at country fairs you will find someone charcoaling fresh trout wrapped in aluminum foil with herbs and butter: it's worth every euro. *Knödel*—bread or potato dumplings usually filled with either meat or jam—are a tasty specialty. Desserts are doughy as well, though *Salzburger Nockerl*, a sabayon-based soufflé worthy of the gods, consist mainly of sugar, beaten egg whites, and air. And finally, keep an eye out for seasonal specialties: in summer restaurants often serve chanterelle mushrooms (*Eierschwammerl*) with pasta, and in October it's time for delicious venison and game during the *Wildwochen* (game weeks).

EXPLORING

Most travelers first head for the town square, adorned with pretty, somewhat gaudily colored houses, to visit the marvelous Baroque twin-towered **Michaelerkirche** *(St. Michael's)*, built in 1470, with a famous twin-towered facade dating from the 18th century. This is the second-largest church in Upper Austria, thanks to the fact that it was originally part of a powerful Benedictine monastery—the *monasterium altissimum* (the Most High)—founded in the 8th century, closed in 1791. It holds a special place in the hearts of many travelers who remember it as the church in which Maria finally wed her Captain von Trapp in *The Sound of Music.* Don't overlook the gilded Baroque side altars decorated by Meinrad Guggenbichler (1649–1723), a famed Swiss sculptor, said to have used his own children as models for the little angels festooning the Corpus Christi Altar (halfway down the nave on the left side). Today, the monastery building is the site of the Mondseetage (⊕ *www.mondseetage.com*), an annual chamber music festival held during the first week in September. The monastery complex also houses a small museum, with sculptures ranging from prehistoric finds to Guggenbichler models.

On a hillock behind St. Michael's is a primitive **Rauchhaus.** Dating from 1420, this farmhouse is a rare extant example of a medieval smoke-house, in which smoke from the fireplace was directed up to the threshing floor above in order to dry corn and meats. A family resided in this dwelling as late as 1950, and it remains a fascinating relic of peasant life. ⊠€2.20 ⊙*May–Aug., Tues.–Sun. 10–6; Sept., Tues.–Sun. 10–5; Oct., weekends 10–5.*

WHERE TO STAY

$$$–$$$$
★
⌖**Schloss Mondsee.** Adjacent to the golden-hued church, this former monastery is now a hotel. The centuries-old complex has a lovely garden courtyard; the accent notes of the sleekly renovated interiors are plate-glass windows and scrubbed monastic stone. Guest rooms are a

bit spartan, although most are duplexes, complete with living room, bedroom, and kitchenette. Chances are you won't be using the latter too often, as the hotel has two excellent restaurants, the casual Gewölbe and the intimate, but ambitious Monchsküche. Menu delights may include beef carpaccio with shaved Parmesan and pesto, pork medallions with zucchini spaghetti, or grilled *Saiblingsfilet* (char) on a bed of sautéed spinach. In summer, tables are set outside in the pretty Blumenhof courtyard. **Pros:** large rooms; great dining options. **Cons:** many tour groups; basic decor. ⊠*A-5310Mondsee* ☎*06232/5001* ⊕*www.schlossmondsee.at* ⊅*67 rooms* ⌂*In-room: no a/c, kitchen. In-hotel: 2 restaurants, bar, pool, gym, parking (free), Internet terminal* ▤*AE, DC, MC, V* ❘❍❘*BP, MAP.*

$$ **Seegasthof-Hotel Lackner.** A 10-minute walk west from the center of Mondsee village, this flower-bedecked modern inn glows in ochre-hue stone, putting you in mind of a Tuscan villa. Inside, faux-Romanesque columns, terra-cotta walls, and enchanting lake views also allure. The range of rooms is wide here, but whether you go for simple and standard or a larger suite, always opt for a room with a balcony overlooking the lake. After enjoying the natural beach, head back to enjoy the critically praised cuisine cooked up by owner, Martin Lackner. His signature tomato soup, spaghetti with rabbit ragout, or dessert of cheese dumplings with plums can all be enjoyed with a noted selection of Austrian wines. **Pros:** beautiful natural beach; near the center. **Cons:** on a busy road. ⊠*Mondseestrasse 1, Mondsee* ☎*06232/2359–0* ⊕*www. seehotel-lackner.at* ⊅*16 rooms* ⌂*In-room: no a/c. In-hotel: restaurant, parking (free)* ▤*AE, DC, MC, V* ❘❍❘*MAP.*

$ **Gasthof Drachenwand.** "Preserve the old, discover the new" is the
★ motto of the Eder family, and that is certainly followed at this lovely, off-the-beaten-track inn—a traditional *Gasthof* chalet, complete with Tyrolean hipped roof and a facade dotted with hunter-green shutters. Next to a small Baroque church and a former stop of the old *Salzkammergutlokalbahn* local railway, the inn enjoys a scenic backdrop: the Dragon Wall, a soaring limestone rock cliff west of the lake. Inside, the inn's rooms have been sleekly renovated. A five-minute walk from the hotel's shady garden will get you to the lakeside beach. The restaurant is supplied by local farmers and the menu is reasonably priced. **Pros:** rooms have rustic local furniture; lots of atmosphere. **Cons:** restaurant doesn't take credit cards. ⊠*St. Lorenz 32, St. Lorenz/Mondsee* ☎*06232/3356* ⊕*www.drachenwand.at* ⊅*7 rooms* ⌂*In-room: no a/c. In-hotel: restaurant* ☉*Restaurant closed Mon. and Tues. during Oct.–Apr. and Mon. during May–Sept.* ▤*AE, DC, MC, V* ❘❍❘*MAP.*

FUSCHL

20 km (12 mi) south of Mondsee, 30½ km (19 mi) east of Salzburg.

Fuschl is so close to Salzburg that many attendees of the Salzburger Festspiele choose to stay in a hotel here, enjoying urban comforts while getting to savor rural pleasures at the same time. On Route 158, the town is on the Fuschlsee—a gem of a clear, small, deep lake whose bluishgreen water is ideal for swimming and windsurfing—surrounded by a nature preserve once the hunting domain of Emperor Franz Josef himself. There's not much to do in Fuschl, the beaches being very limited in number, though those willing to hike can reach an extremely narrow strip on the northern shore that is especially popular with nudists. The town is noted for its many good places to eat and spend the night, including Schloss Fuschl, one of the finest establishments in the Salzkammergut.

WHERE TO STAY & EAT

$$–$$$ ✕**Brunnwirt.** You'll have to knock to be admitted, but once inside you'll find elegantly set tables in this atmospheric 15th-century house. It's not only worth seeing, but also worth the trip so you can enjoy real local meals. Frau Brandstätter presides over a kitchen that turns out good-size portions of excellent Austrian and regional dishes. You might be offered game (in season) or roast lamb, always prepared with a light touch. Fish fresh from the lake is a regular specialty. During the winter seafood is another possibility. ⊠*Brunn 8* ☎*06226/8236* ═*AE, DC, MC, V* ☾*Closed Mon. and Tues. No lunch except during Salzburg Festival.*

$$$–$$$$ ▥**Schloss Fuschl.** This dramatic 15th-century castle enjoys a spectacu-
FodorśChoice   lar perch atop a promontory over the Fuschlsee. About 16 km (10 mi)
★   from Salzburg, this former hunting lodge has been warmed up with quaint red-and-white shutters. Inside, finely frescoed ceilings, intriguing passageways lined with antique furniture, and a sumptuously outfitted restaurant make an haute Alpine splash. The suites and superior rooms are regally splendid, and though the standard rooms are more modern, some are surprisingly small. In fine weather dining is outdoors on the magically beautiful stone terrace. Opt for the trout caught in the lake (which is unpolluted by motorboats) and then delicately smoked in the smokehouse on the premises. The hotel presides over an 85-acre estate, replete with 9-hole golf course, sailing, and a gorgeous private beach and pier. **Pros:** splendid suites; spectacular views of the lake. **Cons:** need a car to get around. ⊠*Hof bei Salzburg* ☎*06229/2253–0* ⊕*www.Schlossfuschl.at* ⇗*110 rooms* ⌂*In-room: no a/c, refrigerator, Wi-Fi. In-hotel: restaurant, pool* ═*AE, DC, MC, V* ⧉*MAP.*

ST. GILGEN

10 km (6 mi) south of Fuschl, 34 km (21 mi) east of Salzburg.

Though its modest charms tend to be overshadowed by neighboring St. Wolfgang, St. Gilgen has a pretty main square and a nice beach (the northernmost strand on the Wolfgangsee). ◾**TIP➔ A combination ticket sold in the village pairs a boat ride with a trip up the cable car for fantastic views. You can see just about every lake in the entire region as well as the pilgrimage church below.**

ESSENTIALS

Tourist Information St. Gilgen (⊠*Mozartplatz 1* ☎*06227/2348* ⊕*www.wolf gangsee.at*).

EXPLORING

A fountain of Mozart in the town square commemorates the fact that his mother, Anna Pertl, was born here on December 25, 1720. Later his sister Nannerl resided in the same house when she married a town magistrate, Baron Baptist von Berchtold zu Sonnenberg. Their house, the **Mozart-Haus St. Gilgen**, stands near the dock and is devoted to the town's Mozart legacy. After exploring the small town—more than Mozart himself ever did, since he never came here—you can see its small Baroque parish church (where Mozart's grandparents and sister married and his mother was baptized), then take the Zwölferhornbahn cable car (next to the bus station) up to the summit of the majestic Zwölferhorn peak. ⊠ *Mozarthaus: Ischler Strasse 15* ☎ *06227/2642* ✆ *€3.50* ⊙ *June–Sept., Tues.–Sun. 10–noon and 2–6.*

WHERE TO EAT

$$$–$$$$ ✕ **Timbale.** Cozy (with only five tables) and cheerful, Timbale is one of
★   the premier restaurants in the Salzkammergut, known far and wide for regional specialties done just so. The taste treats start with the corn, whole wheat, and French breads baked on the premises, and dazzle on to the *Stubenküken* (chicken breast) stuffed with a cheese soufflé and wild mushrooms, or the *Kalbsrücken* (veal) with risotto and grilled shallots. Your eyes, as well as your stomach, will be happy—the crocheted red flower petals on periwinkle-blue tablecloths make everyone smile. ⊠ *Salzburgerstrasse 2* ☎ *06227/7587* ≛ *Reservations essential* ▭ *No credit cards* ⊙ *Closed Thurs. No lunch Fri. Sept.–July.*

WHERE TO STAY

$$$–$$$$ ⛻ **Parkhotel Billroth.** Theodor Billroth was a member of the famous Viennese medical school, a surgeon who specialized in stomach ailments. Like many doctors, he was musically talented, playing violin and viola and becoming president of the Gesellschaft der Musikfreunde (Society of Friends of Music) in Vienna: its chorus master Johannes Brahms often came to see his friend at this summer residence. After Billroth's death his house was replaced by this villa, set in a huge park close to the lake. The house is pleasantly worn at the edges yet spaciously arranged and luxuriously appointed, with a fine dining room. Sun terraces are particularly inviting. **Pros:** 19th-century style; quiet location. **Cons:** long walk to the village. ⊠ *Billrothstrasse 2* ☎ *06227/2217* ⊕ *www.billroth.at* ◁ *44 rooms* ⚿ *In-room: no a/c. In-hotel: restaurant, bar, tennis court, beachfront* ▭ *MC, V* ⊙ *Closed mid-Dec.–mid-Jan.* ⊖ *MAP.*

$$–$$$ ⛻ **Fürberg.** If you drive down from Winkl to the northeastern corner of
★   the Wolfgangsee (not far from a famous pilgrimage route used to get to St. Wolfgang), you'll leave the crowds of St. Wolfgang far behind and immerse yourself in the peace and scenic splendors of the mountains. To savor it all, this old inn in the typical Salzkammergut style offers a perfect perch. Flower-decorated balconies and bathing jetties, an excellent breakfast buffet, and the elegant Stüberl restaurant (with a finely carved wooded ceiling) are some of the allures here. Fishing is possible, the use of rowboats free, and the kitchen may even do the honors in cooking up your afternoon haul. **Pros:** comfortable guest rooms; peaceful set-

ting. **Cons:** many day-trippers stop here. ⊠*A-5340* ☎*06227/2385–0* ⊕*www.fuerberg.at* ⟲*25 rooms* ⌂*In-room: no a/c. In-hotel: bicycles, no-smoking rooms* ⊟*AE, DC, MC, V* ⦿*FAP, MAP.*

$$–$$$ 🏨**Hotel Gasthof zur Post.** An inn since 1415, the family-owned Post is one of the most attractive houses in town, a former domicile of Mozart's grandfather. A beautiful old sprucewood staircase leads to rooms with stunning views of the village and the Wolfgangsee (most rooms have balconies). Owner Norbert Leitner is also a top chef—his seasonal menus might include a salad of wild greens with duck breast, spinach and garlic soup with slivers of smoked freshwater salmon, and *Tafelspitz* (boiled beef). On Friday evenings from September to mid-November the restaurant offers live folk music. Be sure to have a glass of wine in the Vinothek, with its original 12th-century entrance. And get to know the secret behind the old hunting-scene fresco in the main parlor (with hidden motifs symbolizing "hunted" Lutherans). **Pros:** spacious rooms; contemporary furnishings. **Cons:** some rooms face noisy main square. ⊠*Mozartplatz 8* ☎*06227/2157* ⊕*www.gasthofzurpost. at* ⟲*18 rooms* ⌂*In-room: no a/c. In-hotel: restaurant* ⊟*AE, DC, MC, V* ⊙*Closed 1 month (variable) in winter. Restaurant closed Wed. and Thurs., Nov.–Apr.* ⦿*MAP.*

SPORTS & THE OUTDOORS

SKIING **Zwölferhorn** (⊠*St. Gilgen* ☎*06227/2348* 🖷*06227/72679* 🚠*Cable car* €*19 round-trip,* €*14 one-way* ⊙ *Sept.–June, daily 9–5; July and Aug., daily 9–6),* reached via cable car, has two runs totaling 10 km (6 mi) for expert ski, and offers a ski school.

ST. WOLFGANG

Fodor's Choice *19 km (12 mi) east of St. Gilgen, 50 km (31 mi) east of Salzburg.*
★

GETTING HERE & AROUND

A delightful way to enter the picture-book town of St. Wolfgang is to leave your car at Strobl, at the southern end of the Wolfgangsee, and take one of the steamers that ply the waters of the lake. Strobl itself is a delightful village but not as fashionable as St. Wolfgang; if you prefer a quiet vacation base, this may be its attraction for you. Between St. Wolfgang and Strobl the Wolfgangsee retains its old name of "Abersee." One of the earliest paddleboats on the lake is still in service, a genuine 1873 steamer called the *Kaiser Franz Josef.* Service is regular from May to mid-October. The view of the town against the dramatic mountain backdrop is one you'll see again and again on posters and postcards. If you decide to drive all the way to town, be prepared for a crowd. Unless your hotel offers parking, you'll have to park on the fringes of town and walk a short distance, as the center is a pedestrian-only zone.

ESSENTIALS

Tourist Information **St. Wolfgang** (✉ *Au 140* ☎ *06138/800381* ⊕ *www.wolf gangsee.at*).

EXPLORING

The town has everything: swimming and hiking in summer, cross-country skiing in winter, and natural feasts for the eye at every turn. Here you will find yourself in the Austria of operetta. Indeed, St. Wolfgang became known around the world thanks to the inn called the **Weisses Rössl,** which was built right next to the landing stage in 1878. It featured prominently in a late-19th-century play that achieved fame as an operetta by Ralph Benatzky in 1930. Ironically, the two original playwrights, Gustav Kadelburg and Oskar Blumenthal, had another, now destroyed, Weisses Rössl (along the road from Bad Ischl to Hallstatt) in mind. In the years following World War II the composers Samuel Barber and Gian Carlo Menotti spent summer vacations here, too.

You shouldn't miss seeing Michael Pacher's great altarpiece in the 15th-century **Wallfahrtskirche** *(pilgrimage church)*, one of the finest examples of late-Gothic wood carving to be found anywhere. This 36-foot masterpiece took 10 years (1471–81) to complete. As a winged altar, its paintings and carvings were used as an *Armenbibel* (a Bible for the poor)—illustrations for those who couldn't read or write. You're in luck if you're at the church on a sunny day, when sunlight off the nearby lake dances on the ceiling in brilliant reflections through the stained-glass windows. ⊙ *May–Sept., daily 9–5; Oct.–Apr., daily 10–4; altar closed to view during Lent.*

OFF THE BEATEN PATH

Schafberg. From May to mid-October the rack railway trip from St. Wolfgang to the 5,800-foot peak of the Schafberg offers a great chance to survey the surrounding countryside from what is acclaimed as the "belvedere of the Salzkammergut lakes." On a clear day you can almost see forever—at least as far as the Lattengebirge mountain range west of Salzburg. Figure on crowds, so reserve in advance or start out early. The **train** (☎ *06138/2232–0* 🖶 *06138/2232–12*) itself is a curiosity dating from 1893, and does not run in bad weather. It departs daily from May to October every hour from 8:25 AM to 7:55 PM. Allow at least a good half day for the outing, which costs €27.

WHERE TO EAT

$$–$$$ ★ ✕**Hupfmühle.** A hot tip for fish lovers: this romantic old mill is simply a must for either fresh trout or *Reinanke,* the mild, local fish, right out of the Hutterer family's own pond nearby. And the warm *Apfel-* or *Topfenstrudel* is the ideal dessert afterward. Hupfmühle is a short distance along the rather steep road parallel to the Schafbergbahn. Then take a few steps down to the restaurant, by the murmuring water of the Dittelbach. It's well worth the walk. ✉ *Au 1,* ☎ *06138/2579* 🍴 *Reservations essential* 🚫 *No credit cards* ⊙ *Closed Tues. Sept.–June.*

WHERE TO STAY

$$$$ 🏨 **Landhaus zu Appesbach.** Secluded and quiet and offering excellent service, this old ivy-covered manor hotel is away from the hubbub of the village. Public salons are charmingly furnished with Biedermeier

pieces, while guest rooms are a mixture of country antiques and modern pieces, with grand overtones. Some have large balconies overlooking the lake. The Duke of Windsor and writer Thomas Mann once enjoyed respites here. The hotel has its own restaurant for guests. The menu is seasonal, but a staple is the fantastic antipasti buffet. Half-pension is included in the room price, or you can opt for a reduction without. **Pros:** peaceful atmosphere; quiet location. **Cons:** need a car to get around. ⊠ *St. Wolfgang am See* ☎*06138/2209* ⊕*www.appesbach. com* ⇌*26 rooms* ⌂*In-room: no a/c, refrigerator. In-hotel: restaurant, tennis court, beachfront* ⊟*AE, DC, MC, V* ⊗*Closed varying wks in Nov. and last 3 wks of Jan.* ⫿◎⫿*MAP.*

$$$–$$$$ 🔲 **Weisses Rössl.** The "White Horse" has been family-owned since the
★ 1800s. Guest rooms are full of country charm, with pretty chintz fabrics and quaint furniture. Many have a balcony with a lake view. Baths are luxurious, complete with controls to set the exact water temperature you desire. An added attraction is the outdoor pool, situated directly on the lake and heated to a constant 86°F year-round. The dining terraces, built to float over the water, are enchanting, and there you can enjoy the noted leek cream soup with scampi, *Forelle Müllerin* ("Miller's Daughter," a trout fried in butter), or corn-fed chicken in a rosemary gravy. The hotel is world-famous, so book well in advance, especially for the summer. **Pros:** cozy rooms; outstanding breakfast. **Cons:** very touristy; noisy location in the center. ⊠ *Markt 74* ☎*06138/2306–0* ⊕*www.weissesroessl.at* ⇌*72 rooms* ⌂*In-room: no a/c, refrigerator. In-hotel: 2 restaurants, bar, tennis court, pools, water sports* ⊟*AE, DC, MC, V* ⊗*Closed Nov.–mid-Dec.* ⫿◎⫿*MAP.*

$$$ 🔲**Cortisen am See.** A large chalet-style structure with a glowing yellow
★ facade, "At the Court" has become one of St. Wolfgang's most stylish and comfortable hotels. It has a lakeside perch with its own beach, rowboats, terrace dining, and plenty of mountain bikes. Inside, all is Gemütlichkeit nouvelle—chintz fabrics, tin lanterns, Swedish woods, and sash windows. The restaurant sparkles with a mix of 19th-century fabrics and gleaming white trim. The menu is mighty spiffy, and owner Roland Ballner is proud to offer not only the largest wine selection in the area but also its most exotic cigar collection. **Pros:** in the center of the village; a quiet place to relax. **Cons:** no children under 12. ⊠ *Markt 15* ☎*06138/2376–0* ⊕*www.cortisen.at* ⇌*36 rooms* ⌂*In-room: no a/c. In-hotel: restaurant, bar, gym, no children under 12* ⊟*AE, DC, MC, V* ⫿◎⫿*MAP.*

$–$$ 🔲**Gasthof Zimmerbräu.** This pretty, pleasant, budget Gasthof is four centuries old and was once a brewery, though for the last hundred years it has been an inn run by the Scharf family. Centrally located, the Zimmerbräu is not near the lake but does maintain its own bathing cabana by the water. The decor is appealingly rustic in some rooms, contemporary in others, but all rooms have balconies, and there is a lovely sitting room with Biedermeier furnishings on the first floor. Half-pension is offered in the summer season only. **Pros:** reasonable rates; pretty views. **Cons:** Not on the lake; noisy during the day. ⊠ *Im Stöck 85* ☎*06138/2204* ⊕*www.zimmerbraeu.com* ⇌*25 rooms* ⌂*In-room: no a/c. In-hotel: restaurant, bar* ⊟*MC, V* ⊗*Closed Nov.–Dec. 26* ⫿◎⫿*MAP.*

NIGHTLIFE & THE ARTS

Free brass-band concerts are held on the Marktplatz in St. Wolfgang every Saturday evening at 8:30 in May, and on both Wednesday and Saturday at 8:30 PM from June to September. Folk events are usually well publicized with posters (if you're lucky, Benatzky's operetta *Im Weissen Rössl* might be on schedule). Not far from St. Wolfgang, the town of Strobl holds a Day of Popular Music and Tradition in early July— "popular" meaning brass band, and "tradition" being local costume. Check with the regional tourist office for details.

BAD ISCHL

56 km (35 mi) east of Salzburg, 16 km (10 mi) southeast of St. Wolfgang.

Many travelers used to think of Bad Ischl primarily as the town where Zauner's pastry shop is located, to which connoisseurs drove miles for the sake of a cup of coffee and a slice of *Guglhupf,* a lemon sponge cake studded with raisins and nuts. Pastry continues to be the best-known drawing card of a community that symbolizes, more than any other place except Vienna itself, the Old Austria of resplendent uniforms and balls and waltzes and operettas.

Although the center is built up, the town is charmingly laid out on a peninsula between the Rivers Traun and Ischl. Bad Ischl was the place where Emperor Franz Josef chose to establish his summer court, and it was here that he met and fell in love with his future empress, the troubled Sisi, though his mother had intended him for Sisi's elder sister. Today you can enjoy the same sort of pastries *mit Schlag* (whipped cream) that the emperor loved. Afterward, you can hasten off to the town's modern spa, one of the best-known in Austria.

GETTING HERE & AROUND

Bad Ischl is accessed easily via various routes. From St. Wolfgang, backtrack south to Strobl and head eastward on Route 158. To get to the town directly from Salzburg, take the A1 to Mondsee, then routes 151 and 158 along the Wolfgangsee and the Mondsee. There are many buses that depart hourly from Salzburg's main railway station; you can also travel by train via the junction of Attnang-Puchheim or Stainach-Irdning (several transfers are required)—a longer journey than the bus ride, which is usually 90 minutes. There are also many regular bus and train connections between Gmunden and Bad Ischl.

ESSENTIALS

Tourist Information Bad Ischl (✉ *Bahnhofstrasse 6* ☎ *06132/277570* ⊕ *www. badischl.at*).

EXPLORING

You'll want to stroll along the shaded **Esplanade,** where the pampered and privileged of the 19th century loved to take their constitutionals, usually after a quick stop at the **Trinkhalle,** a spa pavilion in high 19th-century Austrian style, still in the middle of town on Ferdinand-Auböck-Platz.

★ In Bad Ischl the quickest way to travel back in time to the gilded 1880s is to head for the mammoth **Kaiservilla**, the imperial-yellow (signifying wealth and power) residence, which looks rather like a miniature Schönbrunn: its ground plan forms an "E" to honor the empress Elisabeth. Archduke Markus Salvator von Habsburg-Lothringen, great-grandson of Franz Josef, still lives here, but you can tour parts of the building to see the ornate reception rooms and the surprisingly modest residential quarters (through which sometimes even the archduke guides guests with what can only be described as a very courtly kind of humor). It was at this villa that the emperor signed the declaration of war against Serbia, which officially marked the start of World War I. The villa is filled with Habsburg and family mementos, none more moving than the cushion on which the head of Empress Elisabeth rested after she was stabbed by an Italian assassin in 1898, which is on view in the villa's chapel. ⊠*Kaiserpark* ☏*06132/23241* ⊕*www.kaiservilla.at* 🎫*Grounds €4; combined ticket, including tour of villa, €10* ☉*Easter, Apr. weekends, and May–mid-Oct., daily 9:30–4:45.*

Don't overlook the small but elegant "marble palace" built near the Kaiservilla for Empress Elisabeth, who used it as a teahouse; this now houses a **photography museum.** The marriage between Franz Josef and Elisabeth was not an especially happy one; a number of houses bearing women's names in Bad Ischl are said to have been quietly given by the emperor to his various lady friends (such as Villa Schratt, given to Katharina Schratt, the emperor's nearly official mistress). You'll first need to purchase a ticket to the museum to enter the park grounds. ⊠*Kaiserpark* ☏*06132/24422* 🎫*€2* ☉*Apr.–Oct., daily 9:30–5.*

Fascinating is the only word to describe the **Museum der Stadt Ischl,** which occupies the circa 1880 Hotel Austria—the favored summer address for Archduke Franz Karl and his wife Sophie (from 1834 on). More momentously, the young Franz Josef got engaged to his beloved Elisabeth here in 1853. After taking in the gardens (with their Brahms monument), explore the various exhibits, which deal with the region's salt, royal, and folk histories. Note the display of national folk costumes, which the emperor wore while hunting. From December until the beginning of February, the museum shows off its famous *Kalss Krippe,* an enormous mechanical Christmas crèche. Dating from 1838, it has about 300 figures. The townsfolk of Ischl, in fact, are famous for their Christmas "cribs," and you can see many of them in tours of private houses opened for visits after Christmas until January 6. ⊠*Esplanade 10* ☏*06132/30114* ⊕*www.stadtmuseum.at* 🎫*€4.70* ☉*Jan.–Mar., Fri.–Sun. noon–5; Apr.–Oct. and Dec., Sun.–Tues. and Thurs.–Sat. 10–5, Wed. 2–7.*

In the center of town, **St. Nikolaus** parish church graces Ferdinand-Auböck-Platz. It dates back to the Middle Ages, but was enlarged to its present size during Maria Theresa's time in the 1750s. The decoration inside is in the typically gloomy style of Franz Josef's days (note the emperor's family portrayed to the left above the high altar). Anton Bruckner used to play on the old church organ.

A steady stream of composers followed the aristocracy and the court to Bad Ischl. Anton Bruckner, Johannes Brahms (who composed his famous *Lullaby* here as well as many of his late works), Johann Strauss the Younger, Carl Michael Ziehrer, Oscar Straus, and Anton Webern all spent summers here, but it was the Hungarian born Franz Lehár, composer of *The Merry Widow,* who left the most lasting musical impression—today, Bad Ischl's summer operetta festival always includes one Lehár work. With the royalties he received from his operettas, he was able to settle into the sumptuous **Villa Lehár,** in which he lived from 1912 to his death in 1948. Now a museum, it contains a number of the composer's fin-de-siècle period salons, which can be viewed on guided tours. ⊠ *Lehárkai 8* ☎ *06132/26992* ⊡ *€5* ☼ *May–Sept., daily 9–noon and 2–5.*

WHERE TO EAT

$$$–$$$$
Fodor's Choice
★

✕ **Villa Schratt.** About a mile outside of Bad Ischl on the road to Salzburg is this enchanting villa, fabled retreat of the actress Katharina Schratt. "Kati"—star of Vienna's Hofburgtheater (Imperial and Royal Court Theater)—was Emperor Franz Josef's mistress in his later years, and almost every summer morning the emperor would stroll over here for his breakfast. Over the course of their time together, most of Europe's royalty dropped in for a visit. Nowadays the Villa Schratt is one of the best places to dine in the area. Choose between two dining rooms— one with a Jugendstil slant, the other country style with chintz curtains, a ceramic stove, and a hutch displaying homemade jams. Try the *Zanderfilet* (pike perch) on a bed of delicate beets soaked in port wine, or beef tenderloin strips with oyster mushrooms in a cream sauce. For dessert, order the traditional Guglhupf, Franz Josef's favorite—it even comes warm out of the oven. Upstairs are four lovely, antiques-filled bedrooms for overnighters. ⊠ *Steinbruch 43* ☎ *06132/27647* ⊕ *www.villaschratt.at* ✍ *Reservations essential* ⊟ *AE, MC* ☼ *Closed Wed.*

$–$$
✕ **Rettenbachmühle.** A shady walk of about 20 minutes east from Bad Ischl's town center follows a brook and deposits you at this former farmhouse, once thought to be the supplier of eggs and milk for the imperial breakfast table (a nice story, though probably not true). The Vierthaler family, the present owners, swear, however, that this was the very locale where the *Kaiserschmarrn* was born. The name literally translates to "emperor's nonsense," but many consider it to be the most delicious dessert in Austria—a raisin-studded pancake covered with powdered sugar. It makes for a lovely time to stop here to enjoy this treat along with an afternoon coffee. ⊠ *Hinterstein 6* ☎ *06132/23586* ⊟ *AE, MC* ☼ *Closed Mon. and Tues.*

$–$$
★

✕ **Weinhaus Attwenger.** Once the summer residence of composer Anton Bruckner (who journeyed here to be the emperor's organist in the town parish church), this turn-of-the-19th-century gingerbread villa is in a shady garden overlooking a river, with the Villa Lehár perched next door. The tranquil garden is ideal for summer dining, and inside the house the cozy, wood-panel rooms are decorated with antique country

Landscape as Muse

For nearly two centuries the Salzkammergut Lake District has been a wellspring of inspiration to great artists and composers. Richard Strauss, Gustav Klimt, and Franz Léhar are just a few of the great names who ventured here to holiday and, as souvenirs of their trips, left behind immortal symphonies and paintings.

It was in the 19th century that the region was discovered. French philosopher Jean Jacques Rousseau's "back to nature" theories and the Romantic movement of the 19th century made tourism fashionable. And the Salzkammergut was opened for the first time to visitors (previously, the "saltmine" region was a private preserve of the Habsburgs).

Following the example of Emperor Franz Josef and other royals, painters and poets soon began flocking to this region to enjoy the "simple life." The region's spas also attracted aristos by the boatload. Archduke Rudolf—brother of the emperor and pupil of Beethoven (for whom the composer

wrote his *Missa solemnis*)—was the first Habsburg to enjoy the cure in Bad Ischl. The sensitive souls of the composers of the Romantic era were highly attracted by the beauty of the landscape. Little wonder that listeners can hear its reflection in the music written here: drive along the Attersee and listen to the Scherzo movement of Gustav Mahler's Third Symphony and you'll know where its cuckoo-theme and wistful post horn come from. Then when the Salzburg Music Festival hit its stride in the 1930s, many of the great artists involved—Hugo von Hofmannsthal and Richard Strauss among them—liked to escape to summer houses in the hills after performing in town. Just as Johannes Brahms used to walk over a meadow on a sunny day or through a silent forest, or climb a mountain to renew mind and spirit, they followed his example and footsteps. So should you. The "Via Artis" route in Bad Aussee links locales that inspired many different artists.

---

knickknacks. Order the crispy duck in a honey-ginger sauce or the basket of country-fried chicken, or ask for seasonal recommendations; the fish and game dishes are particularly good. ⊠ *Lehárkai 12* ☎ *06132/23327* ⊟ *No credit cards* ⊗ *Closed Wed., Thurs., and 2 wks in Mar.*

¢-$ ✕ **Café Zauner.** If you haven't been to Zauner, you've missed a true high-
★ light of Bad Ischl. There are two locations, one on the Esplanade overlooking the River Traun (open only in summer) and the other a few blocks away on Pfarrgasse. ■ TIP→ **The desserts—particularly the house creation, *Zaunerstollen*, a chocolate-covered confection of sugar, hazelnuts, and nougat—have made this one of Austria's best-known pastry shops.** Emperor Franz Josef used to visit every day for a Guglhupf, a lemon sponge cake. ⊠ *Pfarrgasse 7* ☎ *06132/23522* ⊟ *MC* ⊗ *Closed Tues.*

WHERE TO STAY

$-$$ 🏨 **Goldener Ochs.** The "Golden Ox" is in a superb location in the town center, with the sparkling River Traun a few steps away. Rooms are modern with blond-wood furniture; some have balconies, and there are a few large rooms designed for families. The kitchen prides itself on its health-oriented cooking. **Pros:** close to the sites; modern rooms. **Cons:**

traffic noise. ⊠*Grazerstrasse 4* ☎*06132/235290* ⊕*www.tiscover. com/goldener-ochs* ↩*48 rooms* ♿*In-room: no a/c. In-hotel: restaurant, gym, Internet terminal* ⊟*AE, DC, MC, V* ⦿*FAP, MAP.*

NIGHTLIFE & THE ARTS

The main musical events of the year in the Salzkammergut are the July and August operetta festivals held in Bad Ischl.

In addition, performances of at least two operettas (*The Merry Widow* is a favorite standard) take place every season in the **Kongress- und Theaterhaus** (☎*06132/23420*), where tickets are sold. For early booking, contact the **Operettengemeinde** (⊠*Kurhausstrasse 8, Bad Ischl* ☎*06132/23839*).

GMUNDEN

76 km (47 mi) northeast of Salzburg, 40 km (25 mi) southwest of Linz, 32 km (20 mi) northeast of Bad Ischl.

Gmunden, at the top of the Traunsee, is an attractive town to stroll about in. The tree-lined promenade along the lake is reminiscent of past days of the idle aristocracy and artistic greats—the composers Franz Schubert, Johannes Brahms, Béla Bartók, Arnold Schoenberg, and Erich Wolfgang Korngold and the Duke of Württemberg were just some who strolled under the chestnut trees.

ESSENTIALS

Tourist Information **Gmunden** (⊠*Am Graben 2* ☎*07612/64305* ⊕*www. oberoesterreich.at/gmunden*).

EXPLORING

The gloriously ornate, arcaded yellow-and-white **town hall,** its corner towers topped by onion domes, can't be overlooked; it houses a famous carillon, with bells fashioned not from the local clay but from fabled Meissen porcelain (which gives a better sound) decorated in the Gmunden style.

You can easily walk to the **Strandbad,** the swimming area, from the center of town. The beaches are good, and you can sail, water-ski, or windsurf.

Be sure to head out to the town's historic castles: the "lake" castle, **Schloss Orth,** on a peninsula known as Toskana, was originally built in the 15th century. It was once owned by Archduke Johann, who gave up his title after marrying an actress and thereafter called himself Orth. He disappeared with the casket supposedly holding the secret of the Mayerling tragedy after the death of Emperor Franz Josef's son Rudolf.

Music lovers will enjoy the Brahms memorial collection—the world's largest—on display in the **Stadtmuseum** *(City Museum)* at the town Kammerhof. Other exhibitions are devoted to the town's history and the region's salt and mineral resources. ⊠*Kammerhofgasse 8* ☎*07612/794420* ☞*€6* ⊙*May–Oct., Dec., and Jan., Mon.–Sat. 10– noon and 2–5, Sun. 10–noon.*

★ From Gmunden, take a lake trip on the *Gisela,* built in 1872, the oldest coal-fired steam side-wheeler running anywhere. It carried Emperor Franz Josef in the last century and is now restored. For departure times, check with **Traunseeschiffahrt Eder** (☎07612/66700 ⊕*www.traunsee schifffahrt.at*). The boat route crisscrosses the whole 12-km (7-mi) length of the lake.

From beyond the railroad station, a 12-minute cable-car ride brings you to the top of the **Grünberg**. From here you will have a superb view over the Traunsee, with the Dachstein glacier forming the backdrop in the south. In winter there are good ski runs here. ⊠*Freygasse 4* ☎07612/64977–0 ⊠*Round-trip €11.80, one-way €8.20* ⊗*Apr.–June and Sept., daily 9–5; July and Aug., daily 9–6; Oct., daily 9–4:30.*

To get to Bad Ischl from Gmunden, take Route 145 along the western shore of the Traunsee—note the Traunstein, Hochkogel, and Erlakogel peaks on the eastern side, the latter nicknamed "Die schlafende Griechen" ("The Slumbering Greek Girl")—and then along the Traun River. At **Ebensee** is the chance to enjoy the overwhelming karst scenery of the limestone Alps from above by using the **cable car** (⊠*Rudolf-Ipplisch-Platz 4* ☎06133/52190 ⊠*€17* ⊗*May 15–Oct. 10, hrs vary*) up the Feuerkogel mountain. You can also take a train to Gmunden via Attnang-Puchheim from Salzburg, or from the main station in Linz.

OFF THE BEATEN PATH

Traunkirchen. About 4½ km (3 mi) north of Ebensee on Route 145 you'll come to Traunkirchen, a little village where Arnold Schoenberg invented his 12-tone method of composition; stop for a look at the famous "fishermen's pulpit" in the parish church next to a convent founded by the nuns from Nonnberg in Salzburg. This 17th-century Baroque marvel, carved from wood and burnished with silver and gold, portrays the astonished fishermen of the Sea of Galilee pulling in their suddenly full nets at Jesus' direction.

WHERE TO STAY

$$$ 🏨 **Schloss Freisitz Hotel Roith.** Crowning the eastern shores of the Traunsee, this landmark draws all eyes, thanks to the flapping flag atop its white turret, its *Mitteleuropisch* Baroque pediments, and expansive "hunting lodge" facade. Gracing a castle site from 1550, it was renovated in 1887 by Gustav Faber. In 1964 the mansion became a hotel, and now anyone can experience the 19th-century luxe that Faber, the famous German pencil maker, once enjoyed—Oriental carpets and Art Nouveau furniture. The breakfast buffet is almost as beautiful. **Pros:** breathtaking vistas of the lake; lots of atmosphere. **Cons:** need a car to get around. ⊠*Traunsteinstrasse 87* ☎07612/64905 ⊕*www.freisitzroith.at* ⇆*14 rooms* ♿*In-hotel: restaurant, gym*⊟*AE, DC, MC, V* .

$$ 🏨 **Grünberg am See.** This sprawling, multilevel chalet hotel makes a pretty picture along the lakeshore opposite Gmunden's city center. Rooms are spacious with contemporary blond-wood furniture, and many have balconies with stunning views. The popular restaurant serves good local cuisine, emphasizing fish fresh from the lake. The hotel offers superb sports opportunities, from hiking to cycling to swimming. Half-pension plans are offered for a stay of three days or more. **Pros:** stun-

ning views; restful location. **Cons:** A little far from the city. ⊠ *Traunsteinstrasse 109* ☎*07612/777–00* ⊕*www.gruenberg.at* ⃕*30 rooms* ⌂*In-room: no a/c. In-hotel: restaurant, bar, beachfront, bicycles* ▤*AE, DC, MC, V* ⊗*Closed 2 wks in Feb.* ⦿*MAP.*

$$ ⊞**Hois'n Wirt.** This large, modern-chalet complex enjoys a swooningly idyllic Traunsee setting. Now run by the fourth generation of the Schallmeiner family, it's geared to please. The restaurant has a glittering glass window wall overlooking the lake, the kitchen uses the lake as its larder, cooking up some of the best trout and Reinanke around, and guest rooms are pretty, light-filled, and casual-modern, with balconies overlooking the lakeside beach. Many guests check in and then immediately dive in. In a house not far away from the hotel, Arnold Schoenberg composed his first official string quartet and started painting. **Pros:** eye-popping views; quiet spot. **Cons:** far from the city. ⊠*Traunsteinstrasse 277* ☎*07612/77333* ⊕*www.hoisnwirt.at* ⃕*16 rooms* ⌂*In-room: no a/c. In-hotel: beachfront* ▤*AE, DC, MC, V* ⦿*FAP, MAP.*

> ## GMUNDEN CRAFTS
>
> Among the many souvenirs and handicrafts you'll find in Salzkammergut shops, the most famous are the handcrafted ceramics of Gmunden. The green-trimmed, white, country ceramics are decorated with blue, yellow, green, and white patterns, including the celebrated 16th-century *Grüngeflammte* design, solid horizontal green stripes on a white background. You'll find them at **Gmundner Keramik** (⊠*Keramikstrasse 24* ☎*07612/786–0*).

SEEWALCHEN

19 km (12 mi) west of Gmunden, 57 km (35 mi) northeast of Salzburg.

Heading northwest from Gmunden it's easy to reach the Attersee, whose length of 21 km (13 mi) makes it the largest lake in the Salzkammergut and the second largest in Austria. Here in Seewalchen and other Attersee lake towns you can attend the Attersee Klassik, a music festival held mainly in village churches, from the end of July until end of August. Along the Attersee, between Seewalchen and Steinbach, there are 19 locations that inspired the great Secessionist painter Gustav Klimt. From 1900 until two years before his death in 1918 he often vacationed in this area, and used its landscape motifs in more than 50 of his paintings. From May to September special guided tours (via foot, bus, or ferry) are given by the regional tourist office to show the areas he immortalized along a route running some 45 km (28 mi). Don't fail to stop in at the village's noted Konditorei Rohringer, an excellent pastry shop famous for its cookies.

ESSENTIALS

Tourist Information **Tourismusverband Attersee** (⊠*Hauptstrasse 1, Schörfling* ☎*07662/2578* ⊕*www.attersee.at*).

EXPLORING

From Seewalchen, head south along the road lining the eastern shore of the Attersee and go to **Steinbach**, another refuge for an Austrian cultural giant, in this case, Gustav Mahler, who wrote some of his *Des Knaben Wunderhorn* songs here, the second to sixth movements of his Second Symphony, and his entire Third Symphony during four holidays beginning in 1893. Music lovers make a beeline for the composer's *Komponierhäuschen*, the little wooden hut he had built so that he could work undisturbed in total isolation next to the lake (it figures prominently in Ken Russell's film about the composer). Head for the **Gasthof Föttinger** (☎07663/8100) to get the key for the hut (don't forget to lock the door afterward and bring the key back). Mahler's pupil, the great conductor Bruno Walter, visited him here and was overwhelmed with the beauty of the landscape. Mahler only grumbled, "You don't have to pay attention to it—I composed it already!"

WHERE TO STAY

$$$-$$$$ ⊞**Residenz Häupl.** On the prettiest side of the Attersee, this inn has roots going back to 1831 (the seventh generation of the same family is running it). They have kept it up to date with a spiffy renovation. This is a sports Valhalla, with its own golf course, boating on a 400-horsepower boat, tennis, mountain biking, beach facility, rafting on the Traun river, and Nordic walking. Inside, guest rooms are charming, most of them with balconies and lush views. Best of all, the restaurant is so good it's a member of the celebrated culinary society the Châine des Rotisseurs. **Pros:** elegant rooms; plenty of activities. **Cons:** a bit pricey. ⊠*Hauptstrasse 20* ☎*07662/6363* ⊕*www.residenz-haeupl.at* ↩*33 rooms* ⌂*In-room: no a/c. In-hotel: restaurant, golf course, tennis court, bicycles* ⊟*AE, DC, MC, V* ⏃*FAP, MAP.*

GOSAU, HALLSTATT & BAD AUSSEE

It's hard to imagine anything prettier than this region of the Salzkammergut, which takes you into the very heart of the Lake District. The great highlight is Gosau am Dachstein—a beauty spot that even the least impressionable find hard to forget. But there are other notable sights, including Hallstatt, the Dachstein Ice Caves, and the spa of Altaussee. Lording over the region is the Dachstein Range itself—the backbone of Upper Austria, Styria, Land Salzburg, and a true monarch of all it surveys.

GOSAU AM DACHSTEIN

Fodor'sChoice   *10 km (6 mi) west of the Hallstättersee.*
    ★

GETTING HERE & AROUND

Lovers of scenic beauty should not leave the Hallstatt region without taking in Gosau am Dachstein, considered the most beautiful spot in Austria by 19th-century travelers but unaccountably often overlooked today. This lovely spot is 10 km (6 mi) west of the Hallstätter See, just before the Geschütt Pass: you travel either by bus (eight daily from Bad

Ischl to Gosau) or car. The village makes a good lunch stop, and, with its many *Gasthöfe* and pensions, could be a base for your excursions.

ESSENTIALS

Tourist Information **Gosau am Dachstein** (✉ *Tourismusverband Gosau* ☎ *06136/8295* ⊕ *www.gosau.at*).

EXPLORING

Instead of driving around the area, it's worthwhile to take a serious walk (about 2½ hours, depending on your speed), departing from the tourist information office not far from the crossroads known as the Gosaumühle. Passing by churches, the road follows the valley over the meadows. From Gosauschmied Café on, it's a romantic way through the forest to the first Gosau lake, the Vorderer Gosausee (Front Gosau Lake), which is the crown jewel, some 8 km (5 mi) to the south of the village itself. Beyond a sparkling, almost fjordlike basin of water rises the amazing Dachstein massif, majestically reflected in the lake's mirrorlike surface. Aside from a restaurant and a gamekeeper's hut, the lake is undefiled by man-made structures. At the right hour—well before 2:30 PM, when due to the steepness of the mountain slopes the sun is already withdrawing—the view is superb. Then you may choose to endure the stiff walk to the other two lakes set behind the first and not as spectacularly located (in fact, the third is used by an electric power station and therefore not always full of water, yet it remains the closest place from which to view the glittering Dachstein glacier). Hiking to the latter two lakes will take about two hours. You can also take a cable car up to the Gablonzer Hütte on the Zwieselalm (you might consider skiing on the Gosau glacier); or tackle the three-hour hike up to the summit of the Grosser Donnerkogel.

At day's end, head back for Gosau village, settle in at one of the many Gasthöfe (reserve ahead) overhung with wild gooseberry and rose-bushes (or stay at one of Gosau's charming *Privatzimmer* accommodations). Cap the day off with a dinner of fried *Schwarzrenterl,* a delicious regional lake fish. To get to Gosau, travel north or south on Route 145, turning off at the junction with Route 166, and travel 36 km (20 mi) east through the ravine of the Gosaubach river.

WHERE TO STAY & EAT

$$-$$$ ✕**Kirchenwirt.** Adjacent to Gosau's pretty parish church, this inn is evidence of the venerable tradition of locating town restaurants next to houses of worship (on Sunday all the farmers would attend the service and afterward head for the nearest table and discuss what happened during the past week). Mentioned in town records as early as 1596, the inn here has now been much restored and built up in typical modern Alpine decor—woodwork, mounted antlers, hunter greens, bright reds. The current hosts, the Peham family, are proud of their restaurant and its rich breakfast buffet. Best bets for other meals include broth with strudel of minced meat, or the homemade noodles with cheese and white cabbage salad, or the plums with vanilla ice cream and whipped cream. In August the inn hosts some festive concerts with a traditional Trachtenmusikkapelle, a brass band dressed in folkloric costume. ⊠*Gosau 2* ☎*06136/8196* ▤*MC.*

$$$$ 🏨**Hotel Koller.** One of the most charming hotels in Gosau, the Koller
★   was originally the home of famed industrialist Moriz Faber. With peaked gables and weather vanes, the Koller has a fairy-tale aura when seen from its pretty park. Inside are an open fireplace and warm woodwork. Many of the guest rooms have breathtaking views. Try to get a room in the main house. Special highlights are the tavern's gala dinners, featuring regional barbecued specialties and health foods supplied fresh by the farmers of Gosau. **Pros:** cheerful decor; pretty views. **Cons:** half-board is required. ⊠*A-4824, Gosau am Dachstein* ☎*06136/8841* ⊕*www.hotel-koller.com* 🛏*17 rooms* ♿*In-room: no a/c. In-hotel: 2 restaurants, bar, pool* ▤*V* ⊘*Closed Nov. and 1 month around Easter (dates vary)* ⦿*MAP.*

$$$ 🏨**Sommerhof.** In the center of the extended village of Gosau, this modern resort is surrounded by blooming Alpine meadows in summer, and in winter it makes a great perch for skiers heading to Dachstein West, the largest ski region in the province of Salzburg. The yellow-and-green chalet is studded with "Rapunzel" balconies, the guest rooms are traditional in decor and very comfy, and the grounds are filled with facilities for children, including a Mini Club playground and a *Kaiserbad* (emperor's bath) with heated water. Hikers, skiers, and families will love this hotel. At night the Vinothek and the café-bar come into their own. **Pros:** cheerful decor; family-friendly vibe. **Cons:** ski lifts are noisy. ⊠*Gosau 25* ☎*06136/8258* ⊕*www.sommerhof.at* 🛏*48 rooms* ♿*In-room: no a/c. In-hotel: restaurant* ▤*No credit cards* ⦿*FAP, MAP.*

HALLSTATT

Fodor'sChoice   *89 km (55 mi) southeast of Salzburg, 19 km (12 mi) south of Bad Ischl.*
★

As if rising from Swan Lake itself, the town of Hallstatt is the subject of thousands of travel posters. "The world's prettiest lakeside village" perches precariously on what seems the smallest of toeholds, one that nevertheless prevents it from tumbling into the dark waters of the Hallstättersee. Down from the steep mountainside above it crashes the Mühlbach waterfall, a sight that can keep you riveted for hours. Today, as back when—Emperor Franz Josef and his Elisabeth took an excursion here on the day of their engagement—the town is a magnet for tourists, and accordingly a bit too modernized, especially considering that Hallstatt is believed to be the oldest community in Austria. More than 1,000 graves of prehistoric men have been found here, and it has been such an important source of relics of the Celtic period that this age is known as the Hallstatt epoch.

GETTING HERE & AROUND

Arriving in Hallstatt is a scenic spectacle if you come by train. The Hallstatt station is on the opposite side of the lake. After you leave the train, a boat, the *Hemetsberger* (⊠*Hallstättersee-Schiffahrt* ☎*06134/8228* ⊕*www.hallstatt.net/schiffahrt*), takes you across the Hallstättersee to the town, leaving every hour. ■TIP➔ **This is widely celebrated as the most beautiful way to arrive, because it's the only chance to see the entire village arrayed across the lakefront.** If you miss out on arriving by ferry, you can also opt for a boat tour around the lake via Obertraun, available May–September daily at 1, 2, and 3; July and August also at 11 and 4:15. There are also boat tours around the lake via Steeg July and August daily at 10:30, 1:30, and 3:30. Embark via train for Hallstatt from Bad Ischl or via the Stainach-Irdning junction. From Bad Ischl you can also take a half-hour bus ride to Hallstatt. To get to Hallstatt from Bad Ischl via car, head south on Route 145 to Bad Goisern (which also has curative mineral springs but never achieved the cachet of Bad Ischl). Just south of town, watch for signs for the turnoff to the Hallstätter-see. Since the lake is squeezed in between two sharply rising mountain ranges, the road parallels the shore, with spectacular views.

ESSENTIALS

Tourist Information Hallstatt (⊠ *Seestrasse 169* ☎ *06134/8208* ⊕ *www. oberoesterreich.at/hallstatt*).

EXPLORING

★ The Hallstatt market square, now a pedestrian area, is bordered by colorful 16th-century houses. Be sure to visit the **Michaelerkirche** (*St. Michael's*), which is picturesquely sited near the lake. Within the 16th-century Gothic church you'll find a beautiful winged altar, which opens to reveal nine 15th-century paintings. The charnel house beside the church is a rather morbid but regularly visited spot. Because there was little space to bury the dead over the centuries in Hallstatt, the custom developed of digging up the bodies after 12 or 15 years, piling the bones in the sun, and painting the skulls. Ivy and oak-leaf wreaths were used for the men, Alpine flowers for the women, plus names, dates, and often the cause of death. The myriad bones and skulls are now on view in the *Karner* (charnel house) in the back of the cemetery, which has a stunning setting overlooking the lake. Each year at the end of May the summer season kicks off with the Fronleichnahm (Corpus Christi) procession, which concludes with hundreds of boats out on the lake.

Most of the early relics of the Hallstatt era are in Vienna (including the greatest Iron Age totem of them all, the Venus of Willendorf, now a treasure of Vienna's Naturhistorisches Museum), but some are here in the **World Heritage Museum,** the former Prähistorisches Museum. ⊠*Seestrasse 56* ☎*06134/828015* ⊕*www.museum-hallstatt.at* ☎€7.50 ☽Nov.–Mar., Tues.–Sun. 11–3; Apr. and Oct., daily 10–4; May–Sept., daily 9–6.

Salt has been mined in this area for at least 4,500 years, and the Hallstatt mines of the Salzberg (not "burg") mountain are the oldest in the world. These "show mines" are known as the **Schaubergwerk,** and are set in the Salzbergtal valley, accessed either by paths from the village cemetery or, much more conveniently, via a funicular railway that leaves from the southern end of the village. From the railway a 10-minute walk takes you to a small-scale miner's train (tall people, beware), which heads deep into the mountain. Inside, you can famously slide down the wooden chutes once used by the miners (watch out, or you'll get a bad case of "hot pants") all the way down to an artificial subterranean lake, once used to dissolve the rock salt. At the entrance to the mines you'll find an Iron Age cemetery and a restaurant. ⊠ *Salzberg* ☎ *06132/200–2490* ⊕ *www.salzwelten.at* 🚠 *Funicular railway round-trip €10, one-way €6, mine and tour €16, combination cable car and salt mines €22* ☉ *Late Apr.–late Sept., daily 9–4:30; late Sept.–Oct. 27, daily 9:30–3.*

WHERE TO STAY

$$–$$$ 🏨 **Grüner Baum.** Glowing with a daffodil-yellow facade, sitting directly on the shore of the lake, and at the foot of a picture-perfect square, this traditional inn is one of Hallstatt's most memorable accommodations. Dating from 1760, it was the house of the most important salt trader in town. Today its renovated interiors are friendly and homey; family pets sit near the reception desk on 19th-century armchairs, offering a special welcome. Rooms are simply furnished; try to get one with a balcony facing the lake. **Pros:** on the lake; pretty views. **Cons:** old-fashioned rooms. ⊠ *Marktplatz 104* ☎ *06134/8263* ⊕ *www.gruenerbaum. cc* 🛏 *20 rooms* ⚒ *In-room: no a/c, no phone, no TV (some), refrigerator. In-hotel: restaurant, bar, Internet terminal* ☐ *AE, DC, MC, V* ☉ *Closed late Oct.–Apr.* ⦾ *MAP.*

$ 🏨 **Bräugasthof.** With an idyllic lakeside perch, this former 16th-century brewery, or Bräugasthof, offers distinctive charm. Outside is a pretty terrace set with trees and umbrella tables. Beyond the beer-hall restaurant (open May to October), you'll find Hallstatt gemütlichkeit in excess—cozy-nooked rooms, leaded-glass windows, Tyrolean armoires, tapestried chairs, coved hallways, antique chandeliers. Upstairs, the guest rooms are fetching in their simplicity, and give a taste of the "pension"-style rooms so prevalent in Hallstatt (the tourist office can often place visitors for overnights in actual homes in the village); most have wooden balconies. The Lobisser family are your hosts and can tell you all about the brewery's connection to Emperor Maximilian I. **Pros:** cozy rooms; lakefront setting. **Cons:** noisy during the day. ⊠ *Seestrasse 120* ☎ *06134/8221* ⊕ *www.brauhaus-lobisser.com* 🛏 *8 rooms* ⚒ *In-room: no a/c. In-hotel: restaurant* ☐ *MC, V* ☉ *Restaurant closed mid-Oct.–Easter* ⦾ *BP.*

SPORTS & THE OUTDOORS

BOATING   The lakes of the Salzkammergut are excellent for **canoeing** because most prohibit or limit powerboats. Try canoeing on the Hallstätter See. For information, contact **Alois Zopf** (⊠ *Hauptstrasse 237, Bad Goisern* ☎ *06135/8254* ⊕ *www.bogensport-zopf.at*). For white-water **kayaking** on the Traun River, call **Fritz Schiefermeyer** (☎ *06134/8338*).

HIKING   There are many great hiking paths around Hallstatt; contact the local tourist office for information about the path along the Echerntal to Waldbachstrub past pleasant waterfalls, or the climb to the Tiergartenhütte, continuing on to the Wiesberghaus and, two hours beyond, the Simony-Hütte, spectacularly poised at the foot of the Dachstein glacier. From here, mountain climbers begin the ascent of the Hoher Dachstein, the tallest peak of the Dachstein massif.

DACHSTEIN ICE CAVES

5 km (3 mi) east of Hallstatt.

★ Many travelers to Hallstatt make an excursion to one of the most impressive sights of the eastern Alps, the **Dachstein Ice Caves**. From Hallstatt, take the scenic road around the bottom of the lake to Obertraun; then follow the signs to the cable car, the *Dachsteinseilbahn*, which will ferry you up the mountain (you can hike all the way up to the caves if you prefer). From the cable-car landing, a 15-minute hike up takes you to the entrance (follow signs to DACHSTEINEISHÖHLE) of the vast ice caverns, many of which are hundreds of years old and aglitter with ice stalactites and stalagmites, illuminated by an eerie light. The most famous sights are the **Rieseneishöhle** (Giant Ice Cave) and the **Mammuthöhle** (Mammoth Cave), but there are other caves and assorted frozen waterfalls. The cave entrance is at about 6,500 feet, still well below the 9,750-foot Dachstein peak farther south. ■TIP→ **Be sure to wear warm, weatherproof clothing and good shoes; inside the caves it is very cold, and outside the slopes can be swept by chilling winds.** ☎06134/8208 ⊕*www. dachsteinwelterbe.at* ✉*Cable car round-trip €14.40. Giant Ice Cave €9.80, Mammoth Cave €9.80, combined ticket for both caves €14.90. Cable car including both caves €29.30* ⊙*Mammoth Cave: late May–late Oct., daily 9:30–3; Giant Ice Cave: May–Oct. 15, daily 9:30–4.*

BAD AUSSEE

81 km (50 mi) southeast of Salzburg, 24 km (15 mi) west of Hallstatt.

ESSENTIALS

Tourist Information **Bad Aussee** (✉*Bahnhofstrasse 138, entrance on Pratergasse* ☎*03622/52323* ⊕*www.badaussee.at).*

EXPLORING

Following the bumpy old road westward (often closed in winter) from Hallstatt, you'll find yourself in company with the railroad and the Traun River (watch out for the precipitous 23% gradient at one point) and entering a region dotted with small lakes. The heart of this region is Bad Aussee, a great lure in the summertime, for the town's towering mountains and glacier-fed lake keep the area cool. In the town, several miles from the lake, salt and mineral springs have been developed into a modern spa complex, yet the town retains much of its 15th- and 16th-century character in the narrow streets and older buildings, particularly in the upper reaches. To see its quaintest corners, head for Chumeckyplatz, lined with centuries-old houses. Here you will also find the town **Heimatmuseum,** set in a Gothic Kammerhof, renovated in early 2005; inside are exhibits on regional costume and the 18th-century landscape frescoes of the Kaiserssal room. ✉*Hauptstrasse 48.*

The 1827 marriage of Archduke Johann (notoriously nicknamed the "father of Styria"—at last count, he had 1,200 descendants) to Anna Plochl, the daughter of the local postmaster, brought attention and a burst of new construction, including some lovely 19th-century villas. Of special note is the little late-Gothic hospital church, with its 16th-century frescoes. In the mid-19th century musicians flocked here to relax and compose. Nikolaus Lenau worked on his version of *Faust* here, Mahler began his Fourth Symphony in 1899, and right after the turn of the century Hugo von Hofmannsthal wrote his famous *Jedermann* play as well as the beloved libretti for Richard Strauss's operas *Der Rosenkavalier* and *Ariadne auf Naxos*. You can walk along a marked "Via Artis" here and in Altaussee to see all the different locales that gave inspiration to such famed creative souls. Aussee is a good base for hiking in the surrounding countryside in

---

FISHING

The Salzkammergut is superb fishing country, whether casting or trolling—the main season runs June–September—but you will need a license. Many townships have their own licensing offices. A number of hotels in the Altaussee–Bad Aussee area have packages that combine a week's stay with the fishing license.

Steirischer Tourismus (⊠ *St. Peter-Hauptstrasse 243, Graz* ☎ *0316/4003-0* 🖷 *0316/4003–1*) provides information about and bookings for fishing trips.

---

summer and for excellent skiing in winter. Many travelers come to Bad Aussee via the train from Salzburg, making a connection southward at the Attnang–Puchheim junction.

WHERE TO STAY & EAT

¢   ✕ **Lewandofsky.** This popular café in the center of town is *the* place to meet, especially in summer, when tables are spread under the chestnut trees overlooking the main square. Choose from tempting pastries (marzipan-topped gingerbread!) to go along with the excellent coffee. ⊠ *Kurhausplatz 144* ☎ *03622/53205* ▭ *No credit cards.*

$$$–$$$$ 🏨 **Erzherzog Johann.** A golden-yellow facade identifies this traditional house, which, although in the center of town, is remarkably quiet. A direct passageway connects the hotel to a spa next door, with a heated Olympic-size swimming pool and cure facilities. The rooms are spacious and have balconies. Extras include complimentary coffee and cake in the afternoon and a van that fetches guests at the train station free of charge. The elegant restaurant serves the best creative cooking in the area; look for poached salmon and wild rice or baby lamb with potato strudel. **Pros:** contemporary-style rooms; good location. **Cons:** limited parking. ⊠ *Kurhausplatz 62* ☎ *03622/52507* ⊕ *www.erzher zogjohann.at* ➮ *62 rooms* ⚙ *In-room: no a/c, refrigerator. In-hotel: restaurant, bar, pool, gym, spa, Internet terminal* ▭ *AE, DC, MC, V* ⊗ *Closed late Nov.–mid-Dec.* ⦿ *FAP, MAP.*

$ 🏨 **Villa Kristina.** In a lovely wooded park, this adorably charming 19th-century hotel comes replete with Tyrolean wood balconies, regional antiques, antlers, and trophies; its guest rooms are appropriately outfitted with older furniture. **Pros:** traditional atmosphere. **Cons:** long walk to town center. ⊠ *Altausseer Strasse 54* ☎ *03622/52017* ⊕ *www. villakristina.at* ➮ *12 rooms* ⚙ *In-room: no a/c. In-hotel: restaurant* ▭ *AE, DC, MC, V* ⊗ *Closed Nov. and Apr.* ⦿ *MAP.*

GRUNDLSEE

8 km (5 mi) west of Bad Aussee.

From Bad Aussee, journey into deepest, darkest Salzkammergut with a trip to the Styrian end of the region. Head to the Grundlsee, a small, scenic lake, and take, from its eastern end, a walk of 15 minutes to arrive at nearly hidden, even smaller Toplitzsee. Legend has it that the Nazis loaded it up with their golden plunder. Diver teams of the Allied forces, however, came up empty.

WHERE TO STAY

¢ ★ ⛆ **Gasthof Ladner.** Located 3 km (2 mi) east of Grundlsee village, this is one of the oldest family-owned inns and cafés in Austria: Empress Maria Theresa herself ordained its opening back in 1745, and other Austrian royals later made merry here. The great composer Richard Strauss often came for a visit and ultimately immortalized this inn in the "Ball at Ladner" scene in his opera *Intermezzo*. For all its pedigree, the inn itself is unpretentious and rather modest. Enjoy the rustically furnished rooms with the view of the lake from the balconies. When dining (local *Saibling* char or trout with parsley potatoes), be sure to sit in the old dark and wooden Erzherzog Johann Stube. **Pros:** historic house; laid-back vibe. **Cons:** need a car to get around. ⊠ *Gössl 1, Grundlsee* ☎ *03622/8211* ⊕ *http://members.eunet.at/ladner/* ⇆ *10 rooms* ♨ *In-room: no a/c. In-hotel: restaurant* ⊟ *AE, MC, V* ❍ *MAP.*

6

ALTAUSSEE

4 km (2½ mi) north of Bad Aussee.

Taking a fairly steep road from Bad Aussee, you'll find Altaussee tucked away at the end of a lake cradled by gentle mountains. This is one of the most magical spots of the Salzkammergut. As Austrian poet Friedrich Torberg put it: "Whoever comes to Altaussee does not want to go anywhere else, and if he would, he couldn't. Altaussee is a crowning conclusion. The mountains not only lie around the lake, they surround and protect it. Like a fortress, they make you feel cozy and secure."

During the war, Nazi leaders were ordered to store stolen art in underground caverns near Altaussee. In their hurry to get the job done, they skipped a few details; one story has it that a famous painting from Vienna, possibly a Rubens or a Rembrandt, was overlooked and spent the remaining war years on the porch of a house near the entrance to the mines.

ESSENTIALS

Tourist Information Altaussee (⊠ *Fischerndorf 44* ☎ *03622/71643* ⊕ *www. ausseerland.at*).

EXPLORING

The town is completely unspoiled, perfect for those who simply want an Alpine idyll: to do nothing, hike in the meadows, climb the slopes, or row on the lake. The end of May to the beginning of June is perhaps the best time to visit; the field flowers have burst forth and Bad Aussee holds its famous Narcissus Festival, which includes a procession to Altaussee.

☾ Salt is still dug in the nearby Sandling Mountain, and the **mines** are open to visitors. Check with the tourist office or phone for details of guided tours. ☎*06132/200–2551* ✉*€15.50* ☾*Late Apr.–late Sept., daily 10–4; late Sept.–late Oct., daily 10–2.*

If time allows and you feel fit enough, do the approximately 2½-hour walk up the **Loser Mountain** that begins at the end of Altaussee (follow the colored marks and occasional signs), where at the top of the Panorama Strasse you can rest and refuel at your choice of two restaurants: the cafeteria-style Loser-Berg (at the very top of the mountain) or the Loserhütte. Richard Strauss also walked up the Loser, which is said to have inspired his great *Alpensinfonie* (*Alpine Symphony*). A much easier way to reach the top of the Panorama Strasse is to drive, but you pay for the privilege—€15 for your car.

WHERE TO EAT

¢ ✕**Loserhütte.** A short walk down a well-marked path just before the crest of Loser Mountain leads to this chalet restaurant with a wrap-around terrace affording panoramic views of the surrounding mountains and the sparkling lake below. Dishes are local and hearty, such as the *Pfandl*, a mixture of home-fried potatoes, pork, and cheese served in a blackened skillet. Don't confuse this restaurant with the Loser-Berg cafeteria, which is a little bit farther up the mountain. The Loserhütte also has seven simply furnished bedrooms for overnighters on the floor above. ✉*Fischerndorf 80* ☎*03622/71202* ▤*No credit cards* ☾*Closed Nov.–mid-Dec. and late Apr.–mid-May.*

▐ **EN ROUTE**

To get back to Bad Ischl, your best bet is to return to Bad Aussee and then take Route 145 north. It's only 28 km (18 mi), but a great deal of this consists of precipitous ups and downs, the highest point being at 3,200 feet before you head down through the Pötschen Pass. The views are spectacular; don't miss the lookout point at a hairpin turn at Unter, far above the Hallstätter See.

Carinthia

WORD OF MOUTH

"Klagenfurt is a great little city (visit the Lindwurm). We always got a kick out of Minimundus, miniatures of world landmarks in a open-air park. Burg Hochosterwitz is my favorite castle/fortress ever."
—elberko

Updated by
Karin Hanta

WHEN MANY PEOPLE THINK OF Austria, they imagine the superb, mountainous terrain of Tirol with its snowy peaks and powdery slopes perfect for skiing and dotted with storybook Alpine chalets clustered around a village church. The cities of Salzburg and Vienna also come to mind. But there is another, less-well-known part of Austria that beckons with its own set of spectacular mountain ranges, abundant forests, and some of the most gorgeous, glass-clear resort lakes in all Europe. This is the southern province of Carinthia—Kärnten to the Austrians—located directly above Italy and Slovenia.

Art lovers gravitate to such architectural landmarks as the Romanesque Gurk Cathedral, a host of Baroque town halls, and the medieval fantasy of the 9th-century castle Hochosterwitz. Most delightfully, there is also the gaiety bubbling up in such waterside resorts as Velden and Pörtschach, set within the spectacular pleasure-land that is the "Austrian Riviera." The province's summer season is custom-tailored for bicycling, fishing, hiking, and water sports.

ORIENTATION & PLANNING

GETTING ORIENTED

Carinthia is protected in the northwest by the vast Hohe Tauern range and the impossibly high and mighty Grossglockner. Along its northern borders are the bulky Nockberge and the massive crests of the Noric mountain range, and to the east are the grassy meadows on the slopes of the Saualpe and Koralpe. Completing the circle in the south and bordering Slovenia and Italy, are the steep, craggy Karawanken mountains and Carnic Alps. Lying serenely in the valleys between these rocky mountains are the long, meandering Drau and Gail rivers and more than 100 lakes, including the best-known and largest, the Wörther See, as well as the Ossiacher See and Faaker See.

Klagenfurt & the Southern Lakes. On the eastern end of Wörther See, the region's biggest lake, the Carinthian capital Klagenfurt prides itself on its charming city center and mellow lifestyle. Villach, Carinthia's second biggest city, is situated in close proximity to the lakes and serves as springboard to the spas of Warmbad Villach and Bleiberg and the mountains of Gerlitze and Nassfeld.

The Gurktal Region. Located a bit off the beaten track, the unspoiled Gurktal region attracts both hikers and art lovers. Blessed with a verdant forests and Romanesque architecture, the northeastern corner of Carinthia enchants visitors with its pristine landscape.

PLANNING

WHEN TO GO

Because of the bulwark of mountains that protect it from the cold winds of the north, the Carinthian climate is milder than that of the rest of Austria, and it also boasts more sunshine. Consequently, the lakes maintain an average summer temperature of between 75°F and 82°F.

TOP REASONS TO GO

The Wörther See. In the summer, this area turns into Austria's version of the Hamptons. Pleasure-seekers check into mansions-turned-hotels, boat on the crystalline lake, and party until the wee hours.

The other Carinthian lakes. Faaker See, Ossiachersee, Millstätter See, Weissensee, and Pressegger See give Salzburg's lake region a run for its money. The area is dotted with little towns that host arts events all summer.

Bad Bleiberg. For true pampering head to this area of thermal pools west of Villach. Another set of natu-ral hot tubs can be found at Warm-bad Villach.

Burg Hochosterwitz. Walt Disney drew the inspiration for Snow White from this magnificent castle on top of a mountain. Not even the Turks were able to pass through its 14 gates.

Gurk Cathedral. Supported by 100 marble pillars, the most splendid of all the region's Romanesque churches features the original chair of St. Hemma. When women sit in it, they supposedly have a nice surprise nine months later.

To see the province in its best festive dress of blue and emerald lakes framed by wooded hills and rocky peaks, and also do some swimming, come between mid-May and early October. Early spring, when the colors are purest and the crowds not yet in evidence, and fall, are perhaps the best times for quiet sightseeing.

FESTIVALS

Lovers of classical music will enjoy Carinthischer Sommer, a festival in July and August with a heavy emphasis on sacred and chamber music. In July, the Musikforum Viktring near Klagenfurt brings together world-renowned classical, electronic, and jazz artists. Through the summer and early fall, villages big and small celebrate their patron saints. These festivals are called Kirtag and feature music, dance, horseback-riding competitions, and lots of wine and beer. This is also the only time that villagers will wear their century-old costumes.

GETTING HERE & AROUND

BY AIR Klagenfurt–Wörther See airport, just northeast of Klagenfurt, is served by Austrian, Lufthansa, and German low-cost carrier TUIfly airlines. Several flights daily connect the provincial capital with Vienna and Frankfurt, Germany. In summer, charter flights will take you from here to several popular Mediterranean tourist destinations.

BY CAR If you are driving, the most direct route from Vienna is via the Semmering mountain pass through Styria, entering Carinthia on Route 83 just above Friesach and going on to Klagenfurt. From Salzburg, the A10 autobahn tunnels beneath the Tauern range and the Katschberghöhe to make a dramatic entry into Carinthia, although the parallel Route 99, which runs "over the top," is the more scenic route. A pretty alternative here that leads you straight into the Nock Mountains or Gurk Valley is to leave the A10 at St. Michael after the Tauern Tunnel, head toward

GREAT ITINERARIES

IF YOU HAVE 3 DAYS

Base yourself in the Austrian Riviera, the perfect balm for travelers who wish simply to sun and soak. Start off with a visit to the provincial capital **Klagenfurt** before heading out to the most popular lake, the Wörther See. You can make stops along the way at resorts such as **Pörtschach**, before spending the night and next day in chic ⚁**Velden**. For the next night, head to chic ⚁**Maria Wörth**, with its postcard-perfect spired chapel overlooking the lake. On your final day, take in the idyllic town of Maria Gail and **Egg am Faaker See**.

IF YOU HAVE 7 DAYS

If you plan on a week's worth of wonders, on your third day continue west into ⚁**Villach**—one of Carinthia's most historic cities—for your next overnight. Start your visit in this town nestled on the banks of the Drau River by wandering through the meandering lanes of the Altstadt (Old Town). Spend the night in the city or head for the nearby spa of **Warmbad Villach**, where you can

relax with a massage or soak in the soothing hot-spring water, and then check out the imposing ruins of Landskron Castle. Spend your fourth day enjoying the resort town of ⚁**Ossiach** and its 11th-century monastery, where the sounds of music waft softly through summer nights during the annual music festival. After your overnight, your fifth day is packed, so get an early start on the day's full schedule of sightseeing attractions, including the medieval city of **Feldkirchen**; the massive Romanesque cathedral at **Gurk**; and a stop in **Strassburg**, formerly the seat of the bishopric. On your fifth night pull into ⚁**Friesach**, where it's easy to imagine lords and ladies descended from the Middle Ages living in this village. On the sixth day discover **St. Veit an der Glan**, Carinthia's capital until the 16th century; then move on to the amazing castle-fortress of **Hochosterwitz**. For your last evening and day, return to ⚁**Klagenfurt**.

Tamsweg, and then take Route 97 through the Mur Valley; at Predlitz the pass road begins its climb over the steep Turracherhöhe into the Nock Mountains. The fork to Flattnitz, the most scenic way into the Gurk Valley, is at Stadl. Several mountain roads cross over from Italy, but the most traveled is Route 83 from Tarvisio.

BY TRAIN As in all of Austria, post-office or railway (*Bundesbahn*) buses go virtually everywhere, but you'll have to allow plenty of time and coordinate schedules carefully so as not to get stranded in some remote location.

The main rail line south from Vienna parallels Route 83, entering Carinthia north of Friesach and continuing on to Klagenfurt and Villach. From Salzburg, a line runs south, tunneling under the Tauern mountains and then tracing the Möll and Drau river valleys to Villach.

TOURS The official tourist office for the province is Kärnten Werbung in Velden. The Kärnten Card costs €35, lasts for any two consecutive weeks between April and October, and allows you free access to more than 100 museums, attractions, lifts, and other sites of interest in the

IF YOU LIKE

LAKESIDE ELEGANCE

Set just miles away from Italy, studded with picture-book lakes, and adorned with some of Austria's most elegant and enchanting resort hotels, the southern lake region of Carinthia easily gives the famous Salzkammergut lake district a run for its money. One of the peaks of Austrian *dolce far niente* is reclining on your chaise longue on a flower-bedecked bathing pier at one of the soigné castle-hotels of Pörtschach, Velden, or Maria Wörth. For comfort and smartness, these hotels lack for nothing and make the most alluring retreats—even on a wet day.

HIKING

The hills and mountains scattered across Carinthia have a wealth of hiking opportunities (bookstores in your resort will have hiking maps). There is a network of footpaths comprising more than 625 mi and ranging from gentle to strenuous. Most tourist regions have marked trails and local hiking maps, called *Wanderkarte*, including treks to the many castle ruins that dot the landscape, and more leisurely strolls on well-marked lakeside paths. If you are planning high-altitude hiking, remember that cable cars tend to be closed for repairs out of season. Always take protection against the rain, an extra layer of clothing, and tell your hotel desk where you are going. A nice surprise: rain in the valleys may give way to sunshine above 3,000 feet.

WATER SPORTS

The Austrian Riviera resorts are a paradise for water sports—from windsurfing to sailing—with lakes that have public beaches and water pure enough to drink. Swimmers delight in the late-summer water temperatures, which can reach 25°C (75°F) due to the presence of subterranean thermal springs. Most beaches also have wading or supervised areas for small children. To avoid the crowds, book at a hotel that has its own private beach—most do.

7

province. Many hotels offer the card to their guests for free for the duration of their stay.

ESSENTIALS

Visitor Information **Kärnten Werbung** (✉ *Velden* ☎ *04274/521000* ⊕ *www. kaernten.at*).

ABOUT THE HOTELS & RESTAURANTS

Through much of Carinthia you'll discover that, other than simple Gasthäuser, most dining spots are not independent establishments but belong to country inns. Carinthia's peasant tradition is reflected in its culinary specialties, such as *Kärntner Käsnudeln* (giant ravioli stuffed with a ricottalike local cheese and a whisper of mint), *Sterz* (polenta served either sweet or salty), and *Hauswürste* (smoked or air-cured hams and sausages, available at butcher shops).

Accommodations range from luxurious lakeside resorts to small inns, and even include guesthouses without private baths. Summers are never too hot, and it cools off delightfully at night, which means that most hotels are not equipped with air-conditioning. Some hotels offer half-board, which includes dinner in addition to buffet breakfast (although most $$$$ hotels will charge extra for breakfast). The half-board room rate is usually an extra €15–€30 per person. Occasionally quoted room rates for hotels already include half-board accommodations, though a "discounted" rate is usually available if you prefer not to take the evening meal. Inquire when booking.

WHAT IT COSTS IN EUROS					
	¢	$	$$	$$$	$$$$
RESTAURANTS	under €7	€7–€12	€13–€17	€18–€22	over €22
HOTELS	under €70	€70–€100	€100–€135	€135–€175	over €175

Restaurant prices are per person for a main course at dinner. Hotel prices are for a standard double room in high season, including taxes and service. Assume that hotels operate on the European Plan (EP, with no meal provided) unless we note that they use the Breakfast Plan (BP), Modified American Plan (MAP, with breakfast and dinner daily, known as halb pension), or Full American Plan (FAP, or voll pension, with three meals a day). Higher prices (inquire when booking) prevail for any meal plans.

KLAGENFURT & THE SOUTHERN LAKES

Because of the resorts, the elegant people, the cultural events, and the emphasis on dawn-to-dawn indulgences, the region surrounding Carinthia's pleasure lakes vies with the Salzkammergut for the nickname "Austria's Riviera." They have become tourist draws for one reason: they are flat-out beautiful. The most popular of the Fünf Schwesterseen (Five Sister Lakes) is certainly the central lake, the Wörther See, sprinkled with such resorts as Velden, Pörtschach, Krumpendorf, and Maria Wörth. The Wörther See is 17-km (10½-mi) long and the warmest of Carinthia's large lakes; people swim here as early as May. ■TIP→ A great way to see the lake is from one of the boats that cruise from end to end, making frequent stops along the way. Try to book passage on the S.S. *Thalia*, built in 1908 and now beautifully restored. You can follow the north shore to Velden by way of Pörtschach, or swing south and take the less-traveled scenic route; in any case, you should visit picturesque Maria Wörth on the south shore.

KLAGENFURT

★ *329 km (192 mi) southwest of Vienna, 209 km (130 mi) southeast of Salzburg.*

Klagenfurt became the provincial capital in 1518, so most of the delightful sights you can see date from the 16th century or later. However, a group of attention-getting Carinthian architects have also breathed new life into old buildings. The town is also an excellent base for excursions to the rest of Carinthia. In the city center you can hardly overlook the *Lindwurm*, Klagenfurt's emblematic dragon with a curled tail beside a

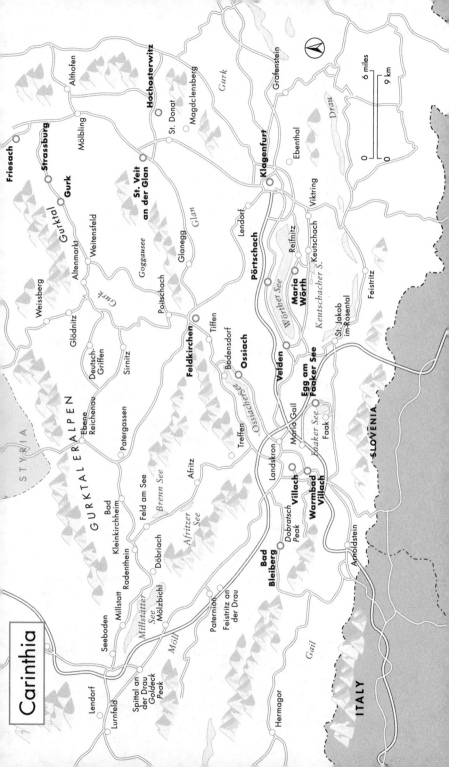

Carinthia

STYRIA

ITALY

SLOVENIA

Friesach
Strassburg
Gurk
Althofen
Hochosterwitz
Mölbling
Mölbling
St. Donat
Magdclensberg
Gurk
Gräfenstein
Drau
Klagenfurt
St. Veit an der Glan
Weitensfeld
Altenmarkt
Weissberg
Glödnitz
Gurk
Deutsch-Griffen
Sirnitz
Ebene Reichenau
Patergassen
GURKTALER ALPEN
Goggausee
Glanegg
Poilschach
Glan
Lendorf
Pörtschach
Reifnitz
Maria Wörth
Wörther See
Keutschach
Keutschacher S.
Viktring
Ebenthal
Feistritz
St. Jakob im Rosental
Velden
Ossiach
Bodensdorf
Tiffen
Feldkirchen
Ossiacher See
Treffen
Afritz
Brenn See
Feld am See
Bad Kleinkirchheim
Afritzer See
Radenthein
Millstatt
Döbriach
Millstätter See
Mölzbichl
Seeboden
Spittal an der Drau
Goldeck Peak
Lendorf
Lurnfeld
Hermagor
Möll
Paternion
Feistritz an der Drau
Bad Bleiberg
Dobratsch Peak
Villach
Warmbad Villach
Landskron
Maria Gail
Faak
Faaker See
Egg am Faaker See
Arnoldstein
Gail

6 miles
9 km
0
0

tower, which adorns the fountain on Neuer Platz (New Square). Legend has it that the town was founded on the spot where the beast was destroyed by resident peasants back in days of yore (but the notion of Klagenfurt's dragon became more intriguing when the fossilized cranium of a prehistoric rhinoceros was found nearby).

ESSENTIALS

Bike Rentals **Impulse Radverleih Klagenfurt** (⊠ *Pischeldorferstrasse 20* ☎ *0463/516310* ⊕ *www.impulse.co.at*).

Tourist Information **Klagenfurt** (⊠ Neuer Platz 1 ☎ *0463/537–2223* ⊕ *www. klagenfurt-tourismus.at*).

EXPLORING

Through the Kramergasse you reach the **Alter Platz,** the city's oldest square and the center of a pleasant pedestrian area with tiny streets and alleys.

South of Neuer Platz (take Karfreitstrasse and turn left on Lidmansky-Gasse) is the **Domkirche** *(cathedral)*, completed as a Protestant church in 1591, given over to the Jesuits and reconsecrated in 1604, and finally declared a cathedral in 1787. The 18th-century side-altar painting of St. Ignatius by Paul Troger, the great Viennese Rococo painter and teacher, is a fine example of the qualities of transparency and light he introduced to painting.

North of Neuer Platz (go along Kramergasse for two blocks, then angle left to the Pfarrplatz), is the parish church of **St. Egyd,** with its eye-catching totem-pole bronze carving by Austrian avant-garde artist Ernst Fuchs in the second chapel on the right. In the next chapel is the crypt of Julian Green (1900–98), the noted French-born American novelist whose works include *The Closed Garden* and *The Other One.* On a visit to Klagenfurt several years before his death for the production of one of his plays, he perceived the city as a sanctuary of peace in the world and decided he wanted to be buried here.

One of the most notable sights of the city is the **Landhaus** *(district government headquarters)*, with its towers and court with arcaded stairways. It was completed in 1591, and at the time formed a corner of the city wall. The only interior on view is the dramatic **Grosser Wappensaal** (Great Hall of Heraldry), which contains 665 coats of arms of Carinthia's landed gentry and a stirring rendition of the Fürstenstein investiture ceremony portrayed by Fromiller, the most important Carinthian painter of the Baroque period. **The Gasthaus im Landhaushof, on the ground floor, is well worth a stop for lunch.** ⊠ *Alter Platz* ☎ *0463/57757* ⊕ *www.landesmuseum-ktn.at* 🖾 *€4* 🕙 *Apr.–Oct., daily 9–5.*

Museum Moderner Kunst Kärnten displays works by modern and contemporary artists. It pays special attention to avant-garde artists with roots in Carinthia. Maria Lassnig, Arnulf Rainer, and Bruno Gironcoli, some of the heavyweights of post–World War II art, hail from the region. The museum also fosters the young art scene by showing works by emerging artists such as Hans Schabus and Heimo Zobernig. ⊠ *Burggasse 8* ☎ *050/53630–542* ⊕ *www.mmkk.at* 🖾 *€8* 🕙 *Tues.–Fri. 10–6.*

From Klagenfurt, bypass the autobahn and instead take Villacher Strasse (Route 83) to the Wörther See, Austria's great summer resort area. You'll pass by the entrancing **Minimundus**, literally "miniature world," with more than 175 1:25 scale models of such structures as the White House, Independence Hall, the Eiffel Tower, and the Gur-Emir Mausoleum from Uzbekistan. ⊠ *Villacher Strasse 241* ☎ *0463/21194* ⊕ *www.minimundus.at* ☜ *€12* ☉ *Apr. and Oct., daily 9–6; May, June, and Sept., daily 9–7; July and Aug., Thurs.–Tues. 9–8, Wed. 9 AM–10 PM.*

Adjacent to Minimundus is the **Reptilien Zoo**, featuring crocodiles, cobras, rattlesnakes, and several kinds of hairy spiders, as well as colorful fish from the nearby Wörther See. ⊠ *Villacher Strasse 237* ☎ *0463/23425* ⊕ *www.reptilienzoo.at* ☜ *€9.50* ☉ *May–Oct., daily 8–6; Dec.–Apr., daily 9–5.*

OFF THE BEATEN PATH

Pyramidenkogel. On the shore of the Keutschacher See, about 8 km (5 mi) west of Klagenfurt, lies the town of Keutschach, with the Romanesque church of St. George, a Baroque castle, and an 800-year-old linden tree. A winding 5-km (3-mi) road ascends to the 2,790-foot observation tower, the Pyramidenkogel; take its elevator up to its three platforms and you can see out over half of Carinthia. ⊕ *www.pyramidenkogel. info* ☜ *€6* ☉ *Apr. and Oct., daily 10–6; May and Sept., daily 9–7; June, daily 9–8; July and Aug., daily 9–9.*

Klopeinersee. With water temperatures averaging 28°C (82°F) from spring to fall, this lake is a popular spot for sunbathing. Surrounded by gentle mountains, it is 1½-mi long and ½-mi wide, and motorboats are not allowed. To reach the Klopeinersee, take the west Völkermarkt/Tainach exit from the A2 autobahn and follow signs to the lake. It's about a 30-minute drive east of Klagenfurt. For information on lakeside hotels and pensions, contact **Klopeinersee Tourismus** (⊕ *www. klopeinersee.com*).

WHERE TO EAT

$$$ ✕**Bistro 151.** A haunted-house chandelier on the front porch of this
★ sprawling establishment leads the way to 1930s-style salons with crimson accent walls, sofas, gilt sconces, naughty modern art, petite low-light table lamps, and a fireplace (with a video monitor of a fire playing). The restaurant is a haven for trendsetters, so you may want to don your best duds. Best bets include the seasonal cream of asparagus soup with a generous amount of crayfish, the butter-knife-tender filet mignon, and the delicate duck ravioli. The bistro is five minutes by car outside of town along the way to the Wörther See. ⊠ *Höhenweg 151* ☎ *0463/281653* ♨ *Reservations essential* ▭ *AE, DC, MC, V* ☉ *Closed Sun. Sept.–June.*

$$$ ✕**Dolce Vita.** Small and exclusive, this tucked-away establishment in the city center offers cutting-edge Austrian cuisine with an Italian slant. Though the tiny peach-color interior is appealing, the secluded garden is the real draw. Your meal begins with a colorful sampling of soups arranged like an artist's palette: saffron potato, white asparagus, and gazpacho. Frequent offerings include the Venetian *sarde in saor* (sardines in a sweet-and-sour sauce) or the silky tagliatelle with prosciutto

and asparagus. The restaurant uses organic products and locally caught fish in dishes like turbot fillet with foie gras and artichokes. Be sure to save room for homemade ice cream. ⊠ *Heuplatz 2* ☎ *0463/55499* ⚑ *Reservations essential* ▤ *AE, DC, MC, V* ☉ *Closed weekends.*

$$ ✕**Maria Loretto.** Gorgeous is the word to describe this spot's perch,
★ which offers a view over the Wörther See and makes a fitting backdrop for some of the area's best seafood. This former villa offers several romantic dining rooms in champagne and red tones, or you can sit outdoors on the wraparound terrace overlooking the glistening water. Don't miss the appetizer of delicate trout caviar and smoked salmon on crispy toast points, then try the grilled calamari or *Seeteufel* medallions (monkfish drizzled with garlic butter). For dessert, try the sinfully good Grand Marnier parfait. You'll need a taxi to get here. ⊠ *Lorettoweg 54* ☎ *0463/24465* ⚑ *Reservations essential* ▤ *MC, V* ☉ *Closed Jan. and Feb. Closed Tues. Mar.–Apr. and mid-Sept.–Nov.*

$$ ✕**Oscar.** This bustling, modern restaurant with floor-to-ceiling windows, crimson glass chandeliers, and close-set tables has a revolving menu of innovative Italian dishes and seafood, and portions are large. Start with spinach crepes in a light cheese sauce or mushroom risotto with chicory, then move on to pork medallions stuffed with local cheese in a sage sauce with vegetables. Pizza is also tempting. In the summer months, the chef prepares dishes using fresh chanterelle and cèpe mushrooms gathered from the local forests. If you're game for venison, come in the autumn. ⊠ *St. Veiter Ring 43* ☎ *0463/5001–77* ▤ *AE, DC, MC, V* ☉ *Closed Sun.*

$ ✕**Hamat'le.** Like a little farmhouse in the center of the city, this homey establishment just off the Villacher Ring is the place to go for Kärntner Käsnudeln, a Carinthian specialty resembling large, round ravioli. They're light as a feather and delicately stuffed with your choice of spinach, cheese, or minced beef. Schnitzels and other Austrian specialties are also featured. On Saturday, the restaurant serves its signature Schweinsbraten, pork roast with slow-cooked sauerkraut. The sommelier knows everything about Austrian wines. ⊠ *Linsengasse 1* ☎ *0463/555700* ▤ *AE, DC, MC, V* ☉ *Closed Mon.*

WHERE TO STAY

$$$$ 🏨**Das Salzamt Palais Hotel Landhaus.** Dating from the Renaissance, this
FodorśChoice majestic palace in the city center was known as the Salzamt—the town
★ salt tax office—from the late-18th century until 1935. It is now a very trendy hotel in the pedestrian quarter. Its guest rooms are lushly decorated with deep, comfortable chairs and sofas, red- or blue-and-cream bed skirts, fluffy duvets, stuffed headboards that invite you to sit up in bed and read, and floral window shades flanked by long, elegantly striped curtains. Some rooms are whimsically regal, with fun red and gilt over-the-top furniture decorated with portraits and leopard-skin hearts. The house restaurant is in the massive, light-filled atrium and features Continental cuisine. **Pros:** historic flair; presidential suite features medieval frescoes. **Cons:** lobby very hot in the summer months. ⊠ *Landhaushof 3* ☎ *0463/590959* ⊕ *www.landhaushof.at* ⇲ *27 rooms* ♻ *In-room: no a/c, refrigerator, Internet. In-hotel: restaurant, bar* ▤ *AE, DC, MC, V* ⦿| *BP.*

$$$ 🏨**Moser-Verdino.** With a facade of dusky rose and wrought-iron balconies, this central hotel has been around for more than a century. In 2008, the new owners renovated their property from top to bottom. While retaining the building's Art Nouveau facade and staircases, they redecorated the public areas and rooms in a sultry red-and-black scheme. Guest rooms feature high-tech touches like flat-screen TVs and DVD/CD players. Mixologist to the stars Rainer Husar is now in charge of the hotel restaurant. **Pros:** state-of-the-art amenities; comfortable mattresses. **Cons:** those who knew the old decor will miss it; not enough parking. ⊠ *Domgasse 2* ☎ *0463/57878* ⊕ *www.arcotel. cc* ⇙ *71 rooms* ♿ *In-room: no a/c. In-hotel: restaurant, parking (free).* ▤ *AE, DC, MC, V* ৩ৎ *BP.*

$$$ 🏨**Sandwirth.** A thriving hotel for more than a century, the Sandwirth
★ was *the* watering hole of Klagenfurt society until it fell on hard times by the last decade. Enter an ambitious private buyer, a Carinthian architect, and local artisans who together came to revamp the interior while retaining the 19th-century yellow facade. Its newest wing features streamlined furniture and innovative works of art that recast vintage landscape photographs in a new light. Guest rooms are subtly elegant and modern, with beige-and-cream accents, while the baths have unique beveled tiles. Be sure to have the house's signature hazelnut pudding in the café's "library," now once again the most popular rendezvous in town. **Pros:** ideal for large conference groups; extremely friendly staff. **Cons:** old wing less attractive than new wing; no a/c in some rooms. ⊠ *Pernhartgasse 9* ☎ *0463/56209* ⊕ *www.sandwirth.at* ⇙ *98 rooms* ♿ *In-room: no a/c (some), refrigerator, Internet. In-hotel: restaurant* ▤ *AE, DC, MC, V* ৩ৎ *BP.*

$ 🏨**Schlosshotel Wörthersee.** At the end of the lake and on its own beach, this gorgeous pale-yellow mansion with soaring red mansard roof, flower-bedecked balconies, storybook woodwork, and Rapunzel towers immediately conjures up "holiday." Despite an exterior redolent of the era of grand hotels, the guest rooms are plainly furnished in traditional style, but you can't really expect more at these extremely reasonable room rates; preferred rooms overlook the lake. The hotel is open year-round and offers a dazzling parade of sports facilities, both summer and winter. **Pros:** right on the lake; fairy-tale exterior. **Cons:** rooms have seen better days; beach gets crowded. ⊠ *Villacher Strasse 338* ☎ *0463/21158–0* ⊕ *www.schloss-hotel.at* ⇙ *35 rooms* ♿ *In-room: no a/c. In-hotel: restaurant, bar, beachfront, bicycles, Internet terminal* ▤ *MC, V* ৩ৎ *BP, MAP.*

NIGHTLIFE & THE ARTS

Operas and operettas are performed year-round at the Stadttheater in Klagenfurt, an inviting Art Nouveau building designed by the famous theater architects Helmer and Fellner of Vienna and completed in 1910. Many are performed in the **Stadttheater Klagenfurt** (⊠ *Theaterplatz 4* ☎ *0463/54064* ⊕ *www.stadttheater-klagenfurt.at*). The box office is open Monday–Saturday 9–1 and 2–6. If musicals like *Evita* are your thing, don't miss the summer entertainment at the **Wörtherseebühne** (⊠ *Lake Wörth Stage, Metnitzstrand* ☎ *0463/220300* ⊕ *www.*

woertherseefestspiele.com), which is built right on the lake. Seats cost €15–€145.

For a true after-hours scene in Klagenfurt, head for the Pfarrplatz-Herrengasse area, where you'll find a number of intimate bars and cafés. In the Old City the young crowd gathers at the **Augustiner Bierhaus** (⊠ *Pfarrhofgasse 2* ☎ *0463/ 513992*). It's closed Sunday. For some of the best-mixed drinks in town, visit the discreetly marked **Palais Egger Helldorff** (⊠ *Herrengasse 12*), once the palace where Napoléon camped out during the French occupation in 1797. Within its courtyard are two hip bars and a trendy Mexican restaurant.

> ### FRESH CATCHES
>
> Carinthia is full of lakes and rivers that abound with carp, pike, perch, eel, bream, crawfish (in a rather short season), and, best of all, a large variety of trout. The most popular way of serving Austrian brook trout and rainbow trout is *blau* (blue), the whole fish simmered in a court bouillon and served with drawn butter. Or try it *Müllerin*—sautéed in butter until a crisp brown. In summer, try *kalte Räucherforelle* (cold smoked trout) with lemon or horseradish as a delicate hors d'oeuvre.

PÖRTSCHACH

★ *16 km (10 mi) west of Klagenfurt.*

Midway along the idyllic Wörther See is Pörtschach, known as the Hamptons of Austria because of its posh, relaxed elegance. You'll find dozens of places to stay and even more things to do under the stars. In the summer, the nightlife here is as varied as the daytime activities. Elegant villas and lakeside promenades line the peninsula, which is abloom with flowers and verdant foliage during the summer months.

ESSENTIALS
Tourist Information **Pörtschach Tourist Office** (⊠ *Hauptstrasse 153* ☎ *04272/2354* ⊕ *www.poertschach.at*).

WHERE TO EAT

$$ ✕ **Anna W.** The best place in town to see and be seen, Anna W. has a tropical theme. The bar servesBrazilian caipirinhas and Cuban mojitos and reserves a corner for cigar aficionados. Menu items are on the light side: gazpacho with artichokes is a great starter, especially when followed by fillet of trout with leaf spinach and saffron foam. No store-bought noodles find their way into the pot: all pasta dishes are made from scratch. ⊠ *Hauptstrasse 218* ☎ *04272/4060* ▭ *DC, MC, V.*

¢ ✕ **Wienerroither.** The Wienerroither is proof that not all great coffeehouses are in Vienna. This cheery Konditorei and bakery fronts the main street and offers a dazzling menu of coffees, teas, mouthwatering desserts (such as the marzipan-and-pistachio-laced Mozarttorte), breads, and cakes. Breakfast is also popular, due to the sumptuous choice of fresh fruits and cheeses. Light lunches such as ciabatta breads and freshly made salads can be enjoyed on the terrace. The Wienerroither family also has several bakeries in Klagenfurt, including one in the center at Wienergasse 7. ✉ *Hauptstrasse 145* ☎ *04272/2261* 🍴 *DC, MC, V.*

WHERE TO STAY

$$$$ 🏰 **Schloss Leonstain.** The great composer Johannes Brahms raved about
Fodor's Choice   his stay at this magisterially charming retreat. Set in a 500-year-old
★   manor house replete with Bohemian cupola, Tyrolean red-and-white
doors, and one of the most enchanting half-timber Renaissance court-
yards in all Austria, this hotel also enjoys seclusion despite its address
along the main street. The restaurant is among the best in the region
and is well worth a visit on its own; the hotel offers a wide array of
pension plans. In summer, dine on the courtyard terrace underneath
ancient linden trees. Guest rooms can be super-pretty—adorned with
Tyrolean painted beds, for instance—or plain but sweetly gemütlich.
No one will want to miss the lakeside pier—pure Alpine bliss. It's not
surprising to learn that Brahms was inspired to write his Second Sym-
phony here. **Pros:** medieval charm; some of the best food in the region.
Cons: no a/c in rooms; private beach is across a street. ✉ *Leonstain-
erstrasse 1* ☎ *04272/2816–0* ⊕ *www.leonstain.at* 🛏 *33 rooms* 🔒 *In-
room: no a/c, Internet. In-hotel: restaurant, tennis court* 🍴 *DC, MC,
V* ⊙ *Closed early Oct.–early May* ᵀᴼᴵ *BP, MAP.*

$$$$ 🏰 **Schloss Seefels.** On a gorgeous spot along the shore of the Wörther
★   See, this grand resort welcomes you with a porte-cochere in Austrian
Baroque style. But the formality stops as soon as you walk around to
the back of the hotel to find a rambling lakeside manor with green
shutters, wrought-iron balconies, elegant sash windows, lots of stone
balconies, terraces, and jetties, all shadowed by a pretty pepper-pot
tower, part of the original estate. The best rooms are the junior suites,
which, though not large, have wraparound terraces, cozy sitting rooms,
and snug, odd-angled bedrooms. The grounds are full of little private
nooks with heated whirlpools looking out over the lake, and comfort-
able lounge chairs. The outdoor pool on the lake is heated year-round,
and the hotel will ferry you by motorboat to the golf course. **Pros:** spec-
tacular views; old-world charm. **Cons:** nearby condos ruin the intimate
feel. ✉ *Töschling 1* ☎ *04272/2377* ⊕ *www.seefels.com* 🛏 *71 rooms*
🔒 *In-room: Internet. In-hotel: 4 restaurants, bar, tennis courts, pool,
gym* 🍴 *AE, DC, MC, V* ⊙ *Closed Nov.* ᵀᴼᴵ *BP, MAP.*

SPORTS & THE OUTDOORS

Strandbad Pörtschach (*Pörtschach Beach* ☎ *04272/281013* ⊙ *May–
Sept., daily 9–8*) is one of the nicest public beaches on the lake. Located
in town, the area has its own island, two cafés, a dock, diving boards,
and a waterslide. Waterskiing and wakeboard services are also avail-
able. ■ TIP➔ **If the nearby parking lots are full, try the parking lot at the
train station.** Pörtschach is a center of activity for windsurfing, paras-
ailing, and sailing. Check **Herbert Schweiger** (✉ *10-Oktober-Strasse 33*
☎ *04272/2655*) for rentals. Several hotels on the Wörther See offer
sailing and water-sports packages.

7

VELDEN

12 km (8 mi) from Pörtschach.

ESSENTIALS

Tourist Information Velden (✉ *Villacherstrasse 19* ☎ *04274/2103–0* ⊕ *www. velden.at*).

EXPLORING

Velden, the largest resort on the lake, is at the western end of the Wörther See. The atmosphere here strives to retain its international chic. The fact that a casino has settled here says a lot about Velden, which otherwise has very little in the way of sights. The town's most famous beauty spot is the lakeside promenade, accented by turn-of-the-century lamps and mansions. However, if you're looking for a tranquil holiday, Velden may be too exuberant. The town gets pricey in the July and August main season.

Casino Velden, in the center of town, is a focal point of the evening. Along with the gambling tables and slot machines, the complex includes a disco, bars, and a restaurant, whose terrace overlooks the lake. You'll need your passport to enter. ✉ *Am Corso 17* ☎ *04274/2064* ⊙ *Daily noon–3 or 4* AM. ▭ *DC, MC, V.*

WHERE TO EAT

$$$$ ✕**Schlossstern.** Considered one of the best restaurants in Carinthia,
Fodor'sChoice this place is a favorite with foodies. Chef Silvio Nickol creates culinary
★   delights with impossibly long names, but amazing flavor combinations. At tables on the balcony of Schloss Hotel Velden and inside classically styled dining rooms, you'll savor such dishes as scallops and crawfish with coriander risotto or Canadian lobster. There's an à la carte menu, but seriously consider the five- or seven-course prix-fixe lunch or dinner options. The cart with handmade chocolate truffles adds the last touch of perfection. ✉ *Schlosspark 1* ☎ *04274/520000* ▭ *AE, DC, MC, V.*

$$$ ✕**Goritschnigg's.** Local butcher Goritschnigg has enriched the restaurant world with this exciting concept: during the day, his Wurstsalon serves up delicious brats and Leberkäse (ground corned beef, bacon, and onions baked in a loaf pan). The self-serve restaurant also prepares daily specials running the gamut of Austrian cuisine, from crispy Wiener Schnitzel stuffed with ham and cheese to Tyrolean roasted potatoes with bacon and onions. At night, the modern eatery turns into a steak house where locals and tourists mix and mingle. The butchers know how to make desserts, too. The chocolate mousse is rich and creamy. ✉ *Seecorso 6* ☎ *04274/2475* ▭ *DC, MC, V* ⊙ *No dinner Jan.–Mar.*

$$ ✕**Sweetlife.** If you're looking for dining room with a view, this place in the Casino Velden offers a wondrous vista over the lake. The menu includes many regional specialties, as well as international favorites. Some dishes are only available seasonally, so keep an eye out for chanterelle mushrooms in summer and venison around the end of September. The casino complex is limited to those 18 and over, and you'll need to show your passport. ✉ *Am Corso 17* ☎ *04274/20–64–500* ▭ *AE, DC, MC, V.*

WHERE TO STAY

$$$$ **Casino Velden Hotel.** Gambling aficionados need not stray far from the action. The ultrahip Casino Hotel Velden is located right across the street from the gaming tables. In 2006, architects Walter Höscl and Ernst Mayer designed 41 rooms inspired by different games of chance. Roulette fans will appreciate the "Rouge et Noir" room, featuring the game's trademark red and black. The sleek "Queen of Hearts" room has all-white environment. Every room features a clever piece of furniture that serves both as a comfortable armchair and as a suitcase rack. The hotel's first floor is reserved for smokers, the second floor for nonsmokers. **Pros:** stylish surroundings; good dining options. **Cons:** not on the lake; no breakfast options. ✉ *Am Corso 10* ☎ *04274/51–233* 🌐 *www.casino-hotel-velden.at* *41 rooms* *In-room: refrigerator, Internet. In-hotel: restaurant, bar* 💳 *AE, DC, MC, V.*

$$$$ ★ **Hubertushof.** Comprised of two houses, the Lake Villa and Garden Villa, the Hubertushof offers plenty of privacy. The vaguely Secession-style Lake Villa has a superb location with a lawn sloping down to the water and a front entrance next to the casino. The owner scours estate sales and travels frequently to London and Italy to get furniture pieces and fabrics for the pleasingly decorated, sunny rooms. Color schemes range from earth tones to tropical shades of hot pink and mint green. Rooms either have a garden or lake view and most have balconies. Breakfast is served on the garden patio. **Pros:** family atmosphere; nice breakfast buffet. **Cons:** patio may get crowded in the summer. ✉ *Europaplatz 1* ☎ *04274/2676–0* 🌐 *www.hubertus-hof.info* *45 rooms* *In-room: no a/c, refrigerator. In-hotel: 2 restaurants, pool, gym* 💳 *AE, DC, MC, V* ⏲ *Closed mid-Oct.–mid-Apr.* 🍽 *BP, MAP.*

7

$$$$ Fodor's Choice ★ **Schloss Velden.** After a major renovation, the region's brightest star has started to shine again. The neo-Renaissance castle on the main promenade features lavishly appointed rooms in the historic building and more minimalist digs in the new wing. They leave nothing to be desired: regal beds, flat-screen TVs, splendid views of the rose garden and the lake, and the obligatory house-made praline candies before bedtime. With its private cabanas and comfortable lounge chairs, the hotel's private beach is a dream come true. Equally impressive is the Auriga Spa, where nimble fingers perform different types of massages based on the lunar cycles. **Pros:** modern-design fans adore new wing; gorgeous pool area. **Cons:** steep rates; pets are allowed to roam the beach. ✉ *Schlosspark 1* ☎ *04274/520–000* 🌐 *www.schlossveldencapella.com* *105 rooms* *In-room: refrigerator, Wi-Fi. In-hotel: 2 restaurants, pool, gym, spa, beachfront* 💳 *AE, DC, MC, V.*

$$$$ **Seeschlössl Velden.** In a wooded area near a secluded shore of the lake, this glowingly yellow fin-de-siècle villa sits on the outskirts of town but is within walking distance of all the action. Resembling a luxurious vacation home from a bygone age, its public rooms are furnished with polished Biedermeier antiques and Oriental carpets. The only sound you'll hear is the gentle lapping of water and the ticking of the grandfather clock. Rooms, some of which have a loft for sleeping, are contemporary in style, with gleaming wooden floors and cool white sofas and chairs. A few have terraces overlooking the lake, but all have gorgeous

views. **Pros:** tranquil settings; soothing decor. **Cons:** several minutes to the center of town. ⊠ *Klagenfurterstrasse 34*, ☎ *04274/2824* ⊕ *www. seeschloessl.at* ⇨ *14 rooms* ⚘ *In-room: no phone* ☐ *AE, DC, MC, V* ⊙ *Closed Nov.–mid-Mar.* ⦿ *BP*.

SPORTS & THE OUTDOORS
Velden is another good location for windsurfing, parasurfing, and sailing. Rentals are available at **Sportschule Wörther See** (⊠ *Seecorso 40/ Saag 15* ☎ *0664/420–2118*).

OFF THE BEATEN PATH

Maria Gail. The Romanesque parish church here has an unusually fine 14th-century Gothic winged triptych altarpiece. To get to Maria Gail, 15 km (9 mi) west of Velden, take Villacher Strasse, Route 83, out of Velden. If you're heading on to Faaker See, you'll pass, several miles beyond Maria Gail, one of the most famous roadside shrines in Austria: framed by lake and mountain, it's a great photo op.

MARIA WÖRTH

★ *10 km (6 mi) west of Klagenfurt.*

ESSENTIALS
Tourist Information **Maria Wörth/Reifnitz** (⊠ *Seepromenade 5* ☎ *04273/ 2240–0*).

EXPLORING
The spire of Maria Wörth's parish church reflected in the waters of the Wörther See is one of Austria's most photographed sights. This unpretentious little town is on a wooded peninsula jutting out toward the center of the lake, and is almost entirely surrounded by water. It actually has two notable churches, both dating from the 12th century.

The smaller **Rosenkranzkirche** *(Rosary church)* in the town itself is basically Romanesque with later Gothic additions. The interior has a Romanesque choir with fragments of 12th-century frescoes of the apostles, a stained-glass Madonna window from 1420, and Gothic carved-wood figures.

The larger **Pfarrkirche** *(parish church)*, despite its Romanesque portal, is mainly Gothic, with a Baroque interior, revealing all the "wrinkles" acquired since the days of its appearance in the 9th century. Skulls and bones can still be seen in the round Romanesque charnel house in the cemetery.

Using one of the ferries that ply the Wöther See, you can head across the waters from Pörtschach to the village of Maria Wörth (note that these ferries operate only from May through September, and cars are not allowed on them; as the lake is 1½-km [1-mi] wide and 17-km [10½-mi] long, it's not far to drive around).

WHERE TO STAY
$$$$ ★ ▦ **Aenea.** This concrete-and-glass pavilion is quite a change from the usual "rustic" resort look. The place prides itself on having no "preordained hotel rhythm"—everything is designed to soothe and pamper its

guests, down to the placement of two four-poster beds in the outdoor "loungerie." Setting the style are the lobby and bar, adorned with black leather chairs, gleaming red walls, and plate-glass windows with great views of the south side of the Wörther See. The suites are decorated in cool white with bold accents. The bathrooms by Philippe Starck are fabulous. Each suite has a nice-size terrace with great lake views. **Pros:** an oasis of absolute tranquility; sublime design; excellent wellness facilities. **Cons:** need a car to get around; very pricey. ⊠ *Süduferstrasse 86, Reifnitz* ☎ *04273/26220* ⊕ *www.aenea.at* ↗ *15 suites* ♿ *In-room: no a/c (some), Internet. In-hotel: restaurant, bars, tennis court, pool* ▭ *AE, DC, MC, V* ⊙ *Closed Oct.May* ◯ *BP.*

EGG AM FAAKER SEE

4 km (2½ mi) east of Maria Gail.

With turquoise-green waters that seem almost Mediterranean, the Faaker See presents an idyllic setting for swimming and boating. Boating aficionados take to the lake in droves, with a rainbow of sails skimming across the horizon (motorboats are not allowed); even so, the round lake—with its tiny island in the middle—remains less crowded than other resort areas here. Watching over all is the mighty pyramid of the Mittagskogel of the Karawanken range.

ESSENTIALS

Bike Rentals **Faak am See Bike Center** (⊠ *Egg am See 80* ☎ *04254/4224*).

WHERE TO STAY & EAT

$ ✕**Tschebull.** This popular spot near the Faaker See has a lot of fans, including chef Wolfgang Puck whenever he's in the area. You won't find a lake view here—people venture here for the food, served in a large sunny hall looking out over the rolling hills or in an intimate room with mullioned windows and stag antlers on the walls. The crispy duck comes with homemade dumplings, baked apple, and steamed vegetables, and the juicy pork from the owner's farm is served with a mound of buttery green beans and golden fried Rösti. ⊠ *Egger Seeuferstrasse 26* ☎ *04254/2191* ▭ *MC, V.*

$$$$ ⚏**Karnerhof.** Blessed with one of the region's most spectacular lake
★ views, this huge chalet has the Karawanken mountains serving as a scenic backdrop. Overnighters will enjoy the rustic rooms. An exotic vibe permeates the wellness area, where the masseurs perform techniques ranging from Ayurveda to Massai African. The wonderful Götzelstube restaurant serves such regional specialties as chanterelle-mushroom ravioli with crayfish and grilled local fish. The hotel's sauna is directly on the lake, so you can jump into the water right after sweating it all out. **Pros:** great views; excellent restaurant. **Cons:** decor is a little tacky; sometimes closes in winter. ⊠ *Karnerhofweg 10* ☎ *04254/2188* ⊕ *www.karnerhof.com* ↗ *98 rooms* ♿ *In-room: no a/c. In-hotel: restaurant, tennis court, pool, spa* ▭ *AE, DC, MC, V* ⊙ *Closed Nov.* ◯ *BP, MAP.*

7

OSSIACH

★ *19 km (12 mi) northeast of Warmbad Villach via Rte. 83.*

ESSENTIALS

Tourist Information **Ossiach Lake area** (✉ *Ossiach 8* ☎ *04243/497* ⊕ *www.ossiach.at*).

EXPLORING

Home of the Carinthian Summer Festival, Ossiach is overflowing

with tourists during the high season. Ossiach has other attractions, including the 11th-century **Stift Ossiach,** a typical monastery with a chapel at the side. The chapel, despite its stern, conservative exterior, is wonderfully Baroque. Legend has it that in the 11th century the Polish king Boleslaw II lived incognito in the monastery for eight years, pretending to be mute, in penance for murdering the bishop of Kraków. A tombstone and a fresco on the church wall facing the cemetery commemorate the tale.

WHERE TO EAT

$$ ✕**Stiftsschmiede.** Near the Stift Ossiach, this pretty chalet serves some of the freshest fish you're likely to find in Austria. Caught in the restaurant's own pond, the rainbow trout and char are grilled or breaded and fried, making a memorable meal, especially if the weather is fine and you're sitting on the terrace overlooking the lake. Even though the selection of meat entrées is limited, the sirloin steaks and pork medallions are top quality and should be washed down with a pint of Villacher beer. To satisfy your sweet tooth, try Topfencreme (Austrian-style ricotta cream) with fresh berries. ✉ *Stift Ossiach* ☎ *04243/45554* ▭ *No credit cards* ☉ *May–Sept., closed Sun. Oct.–Apr., closed Sun.–Tues. No lunch.*

NIGHTLIFE & THE ARTS

Fodor'sChoice   Even though Ossiach is a very small town, it hosts an internation-
★ ally renowned music event, the **Carinthischer Sommer** (✉ *Stift Ossiach, Ossiach* ☎ *04243/2510* ⊕ *www.carinthischersommer.at*). Held in July and August, the *Carinthian Summer Festival* emphasizes 20th-century compositions. However, along with Benjamin Britten's opera *The Prodigal Son* you might also hear some Mozart and Vivaldi, plus a little jazz and even some klezmer. Chamber concerts are all the more attractive for being presented in the chapel or the monastery.

THE OUTDOORS

BICYCLING   The area around the Ossiacher See is excellent for cycling, and many of the main roads have parallel cycling paths. Rental bicycles are in great demand throughout this area, so reserve in advance. **Feriendorf Ossiach** (✉ *Alt-Ossiach 37* ☎ *04243/2202*) is a popular place to rent bikes.

FELDKIRCHEN

6 km (4 mi) northeast of Ossiach.

Feldkirchen is one of Carinthia's oldest communities, having been mentioned in documents dating from 888. Though small, Feldkirchen is an important crossroads: one road (Route 93) goes to Gurk, another (Route 94) heads to St. Veit an der Glan, and yet another (Route 95) traverses the remote Nock Mountains up to the Turracher Höhe, a high pass between Carinthia and Styria with a dangerous 23% gradient, a mountain summer resort, and a fine skiing center on a pretty lake.

EN ROUTE Heading north along Route 93 out of Feldkirchen are myriad small roads leading to colorful villages.

Goggau has a small but charming lake.

Sirnitz has an interesting little castle called Schloss Albeck that has a fine restaurant.

At **Deutsch-Griffen,** with a picturesque fortified church accessed by a long covered staircase, an easy hike up the Meisenberg takes you through Carinthia's first bird sanctuary, an initiative by Gottfried Topf, a retired German businessman who moved to the village permanently in 1990.

In **Glödnitz** a road leads up to Flattnitz, a solitary but very beautiful spot with a little skiing and a few isolated houses.

VILLACH

50 km (30 mi) west of Klagenfurt.

Carinthia's "other" capital (Klagenfurt is the official one) sits astride the Drau River. The Romans may have been the first to bridge the river here to establish the settlement of Bilachium, from which the present name Villach is derived. The city is compact, with narrow, twisting lanes (restricted to pedestrians) winding through the Old City south of the river. Small, attractive shops are tucked into arcaded buildings, and each corner turned brings a fresh and surprising perspective.

ESSENTIALS

Tourist Information Villach (✉ *Bahnhofstrasse 3* ☎ *04242/205–2900* ⊕ *www. villach.at*).

EXPLORING

The late-Gothic 14th-century **St. Jacob** *(St. James's)* was Protestant during the mid-1500s, making it Austria's first Protestant church. Its marble pulpit dates from 1555; the ornate Baroque high altar contrasts grandly with the Gothic crucifix. If the stair entry is open and you don't mind the rather steep climb, the view from the 310-foot tower is marvelous.

Near the river, at the intersection of Ossiacher Zeile and Peraustrasse, the pinkish **Heiligenkreuz** *(Holy Cross Church)*, with two towers and a cupola, is a splendid example of fully integrated Baroque.

In summer a particularly lovely way to explore the Drau River from Villach is to take a cruise on the *Landskron* (⊠ *Wirthstrasse 21b* ☎ *04242/219577* ⊕ *www.schifffahrt.at/drau*). Watching the sun set over the mountains while you dine on board makes for a memorable evening.

OFF THE BEATEN PATH **Landskron.** This ruined castle, which has spectacular views over Villach, the Ossiacher See, and the Karawanken mountain range to the south, makes for an interesting stopping point. The original castle here dated from 1351 and was destroyed by fire in 1861; since then, sections have been rebuilt. It is also a keep for birds of prey, which are trained for shows. To get here, take Route 83 about 4 km (2½ mi) northeast of Villach. There is a small fee, about €2, to drive your car up the road. From September to June you can drive up without paying the fee if you leave before 10 AM or after 4:30 PM.

WHERE TO EAT

$$$ ✕**Romantik Stadtrestaurant zur Post.** Housed in the Hotel Post, the Stadtrestaurant is known among locals as the best restaurant in town (in fact, this is where culinary giant Wolfgang Puck got his start— he worked here briefly as an apprentice chef before heading to Los Angeles to open his famed restaurant Spago). Dine in country-casual comfort on wild duck carpaccio followed by Kärtner Käsnudeln, that favorite Carinthian specialty of large, round ravioli stuffed with cheese. Vegetables and herbs are straight from the bountiful hotel garden. In summer tables are set outdoors in the Orangerie, where wild roses and ivy climb the courtyard walls. ⊠ *Hauptplatz 26* ☎*04242/26101–0* ⌂ *Reservations essential* ⊟ *AE, DC, MC, V.*

$ ✕**Hofwirt.** This country-style restaurant just off the main square serves fresh, traditional Carinthian specialties like *Käsnudel Suppe* (cheese noodle soup) without all the fuss. The kitchen also prepares a killer beef goulash and pork roast. When the weather's fitting, sit outside on the shady terrace and savor a local beer or linger over coffee with apple strudel or Palatschinken (Austrian-style pancakes with apricot jam or chocolate). ⊠ *Hauptplatz 10* ☎ *04242/24994* ⊟ *MC, V.*

WHERE TO STAY

$$$ ⚏ **Feuerberg Mountain Resort.** Those who want to savor the mountain views on Gerlitzen Alpe for more than a few hours should check in at the Feuerberg Mountain Resort. Third-generation owner Erwin Berger has turned the hotel into a Zen wellness oasis. Throughout the building, works of art and poems remind guests of what's really important in life. Every year, the owner invites artists to create sculptures. Guests are also welcome to help redesign the garden. The new sauna and pool have a magnificent view of the surrounding mountains. Rooms are simple, but will be renovated in the next two years. **Pros:** mountain views; excellent wellness center. **Cons:** rooms need renovation. ⊠ *Bergalm 1* ☎ *04248/2880* ⊕*www.hotel-feuerberg.at* ⇥ *60 rooms, 60 apartments* ⌂ *In-room: no a/c. In-hotel: restaurant, bar, pools, gym, Internet terminal* ⊟ *AE, MC.*

$$$ ⚏ **Hotel Post.** This beautifully adapted Renaissance palace, dating from
★   1500, sits in the heart of the Old City. Over the centuries the house has

played host to royalty, including Empress Maria Theresa way back in the 1700s. Architects have cleverly created an elegant, stylish hotel while preserving the building's arcaded inner court. Rooms are attractively furnished with polished mahogany and lovely floral fabrics, some in tones of pale apricot and mauve; a few have balconies overlooking the pretty courtyard. **Pros:** nicely appointed rooms; some great views. **Cons:** creaky wooden floors; small rooms on third floor.

> **FEAST DAY**
>
> A good time to visit Villach is around August 1, when the townspeople and people from surrounding villages don traditional clothes and celebrate *Kirtag*—the traditional feast day of each town's patron saint—with music, folk dancing, and general merrymaking. See ⊕ *www.villacherkirchtag.at* for details.

✉ *Hauptplatz 26* ☎ *04242/26101–0* ⊕ *www.romantik-hotel.com* ⇆ *69 rooms* ⚬ *In-room: no a/c, refrigerator, Wi-Fi. In-hotel: restaurant, bar, parking (free)* ▤ *AE, DC, MC, V* ◑ *BP, MAP.*

THE OUTDOORS

HIKING Southwest of Villach, the extremely scenic 16-km (10-mi) Villach Alpine highway climbs the mountain ridge to about 5,000 feet. From there, a lift gets you up to Hohenrain; then you can hike the marked trail—or take the train—up to the peak of the **Dobratsch,** towering 7,040 feet into the clouds and providing a spectacular view. Close to Parking Lot 6, at 4,875 feet, is an Alpine botanical garden, which is open mid-June–August, daily 9–6. The cost is €3.50 per person. The 11 parking and outlook points along the highway offer great panoramas.

When Villachers want to go on a quick hike, they head to **Gerlitzen Alpe,** a popular mountain resort. From May to October, you can take the long and winding Gerlitzen Gipfelstrasse almost to the summit. From there you will find easy hiking trails all the way to the cross on the summit.

WARMBAD VILLACH

3 km (2 mi) southwest of Villach.

On the southern outskirts of Villach lies Warmbad Villach, its name reflecting the hot mineral springs, believed to combat aging as well as a wide range of ailments. This remains one of the classic spa resorts of Carinthia—one discovered by the Romans—and people come to enjoy its thermal springs and swimming pools for various rheumatic conditions. Even if you're not staying in one of the spa hotels, you can enjoy the thermal springs for a day.

Many hotels have been built around the **Kurpark,** the wooded grounds of the spa. There are a variety of spa treatments available. ☒ *€9.50.*

WHERE TO STAY

$$$$ 🏨 **Warmbaderhof.** With a tranquil park and a comfortable, meandering
★ house seducing you into relaxation, the cure's the thing here. Rooms are elegantly appointed, with subtle tones, soft carpets, contemporary fur-

nishings, and state-of-the-art baths. Most have nice-size terraces. Ask for one overlooking "Napoléon's Meadow," where the general's troops once encamped. The very fine Bürgerstube restaurant offers regional and national specialties, and the twice-weekly buffets are extravagant. Half-pension, with dinner in the Bürgerstube, is included in the room price. Das Kleine Restaurant, with windows looking out over the woods, changes its offerings with the seasons—in warm weather, sit on the terrace. **Pros:** beautiful grounds; delicious food; lovely rooms. **Cons:** small spa; expensive rates. ⊠ *Kadischenallee 22–24* ☎ *04242/3001–0* ⊕ *www.warmbad.at* ↩ *114 rooms* ⚇ *In-hotel: 2 restaurants, bar, pool, gym, Internet terminal* ▤ *AE, DC, MC, V* ⧮ *BP, MAP.*

BAD BLEIBERG

25 km (17 mi) west of Villach.

Carinthia's other major spa area (and many believe its best) is Bad Bleiberg. From here you have a splendid view of the imposing Dobratsch Mountain, which has supplied the region not only with thermal springs, but also with lead mines.

When the lead mines were exhausted in the 1980s, entrepreneurs came up with the clever idea for **Terra Mystica**. In Terra Mystica and its sister attraction, Terra Montana, you can experience what it was like to work the mines. A sophisticated sound-and-light show highlights the mysteries of the underground world. ⊠ *9531 Bleiberg-Nötsch 91* ☎ *04244/2255* ⊕ *www.terra-mystica.at* ⧉ *€15. May, June, Sept., and Oct., Terra Mystica tours daily 11 and 3, Terra Montana tours at 3. July and Aug., Terra Mystica tours daily at 9:30 and 3, Terra Montana tours daily at 4. Nov.–Apr., Sat. at 3.*

WHERE TO STAY

$$$

Fodor'sChoice

★

Falkensteiner Hotel & Spa Bleiberger Hof. One of Carinthia's finest wellness hotels is hidden in an inconspicuous building dating from the 1970s. The staff here makes every effort to keep the guests happy. The outdoor wellness area is comprised of a natural thermal pond and swimming pool. Inside, guests unwind in the steam room and the saunas. The wellness team only uses plants from the surrounding mountains to create massage oils and creams. The specious guest rooms are newly renovated well equipped. Room price includes half board in an excellent restaurant. Guests savor dishes such as carrot puree with rosemary foam. **Pros:** mountain setting; nice rooms. **Cons:** charmless façade; no whirlpool in spa. ⊠ *Drei Lärchen 150* ☎ *04244/2205* ↩ *106 rooms* ⚇ *In-room: Wi-Fi. In-hotel: restaurant, spa* ▤ *AE, DC, MC, V.*

THE GURKTAL REGION

Storybook names such as Snow White, Tannhäuser, and the Holy Hemma are encountered throughout the Gurktal region of Carinthia. The region is populated with medieval strongholds, idyllic lakes, and towns brimming with charm down to the last cobblestone.

GURK

34 km (21 mi) northeast of Feldkirchen.

Gurk's claim to fame is its massive Romanesque **Dom** *(cathedral)* topped by two onion cupolas and considered the most famous religious landmark in Carinthia. It was founded in the 11th century by Hemma, Countess of Zeltschach, who after losing her two sons and husband decided to turn to religious works. She had two oxen tied before a cart and let them walk until they stopped on their own. At that spot she founded a cloister and gave all her belongings to the church for building a cathedral. Construction on the cathedral itself began in 1040 and ended in 1200.

Hemma wasn't canonized until 1938. Her tomb is in the crypt, whose ceiling, and hence the cathedral itself, is supported by 100 marble pillars. The Hemma-Stein, a small green-slate chair from which she personally supervised construction, is also there and alleged to bring fertility to barren women. In the church itself, the high altar is one of the most important examples of early Baroque in Austria. Note the *Pietà* by George Rafael Donner, who is sometimes called the Austrian Michelangelo. The 900-square-foot Lenten altar cloth of 1458 shows 99 scenes from the Old and New Testaments—a beautiful example of a *Biblia Pauperum*, a "poor man's Bible," meant to teach the Scriptures to those who could not read. It is displayed from Ash Wednesday to Good Friday. Make sure to visit the bishop's chapel, which features rare late-Romanesque and Gothic frescoes, among the oldest in Europe and in perfect condition (the guidebook in English is helpful).

At the end of August and in early September a concert series is held in the cathedral. Tours are restricted by church services, but in summer 90-minute tours are usually scheduled for 10:30, 1:30, and 3 (though tours can be arranged just about any time), and include the bishop's chapel. ☎ 04266/8236–0 ✉ *Short tour including crypt €4.60; long tour €7.50* ☉ *Daily 9–5.*

🔆 The **Zwergenpark** is a vast natural preserve filled with amusing garden statuary, consisting largely of typically Austrian-German garden gnomes; children can traverse the park via a miniature railway. ☎ 04266/8077 ⊕ *www.zwergenpark.com* ✉ *€4.80* ☉ *May–late June, daily 10–4; late June–late Aug., daily 10–6; late Aug–mid-Sept., daily 11–4.*

STRASSBURG

3 km (2 mi) northeast of Gurk.

The seat of the Gurk bishopric until 1787, Strassburg is dominated by the episcopal palace, which houses small museums covering the history of the valley and of the diocese. The Gothic parish church, one of the most beautiful in Carinthia, has stained-glass windows dating from 1340. Also of note is the Heilig-Geist-Spital Church, constructed in the 13th century.

Across the highway from the Schloss Pöckstein is the northern terminus of a small narrow-gauge railway, the **Gurkthaler Museumbahn.** Under steam power, the train meanders for 30 minutes down to Treibach on weekends and holidays from late June to mid-September. For an additional contribution you can ride in the locomotive alongside the engineer. ☎ *0664/1707136* ⊕ *www.gurkthalbahn.at* ✉ *Round-trip €5* ⊗ *Hrs vary.*

EN ROUTE At Zwischenwässern and Hirt, Route 93 joins Route 83 coming from Klagenfurt. Heading north (toward Friesach), you'll come to **Brauerei Hirt** (☎ *04268–2050–45* ⊕ *www.hirterbier.at*), a brewery since 1270. Sip a draft under the huge tree in the garden, in the shade of a Renaissance arcade, or in one of the paneled rooms. The food is good, standard Austrian fare, and inexpensive. Brewery tours may be arranged by calling ahead.

FRIESACH

★ *16 km (9 mi) northeast of Strassburg via Rte. 83/E7.*

ESSENTIALS
Tourist Information Friesach (✉ *Hauptplatz 1* ☎ *04268/4300* ⊕ *www.friesach.at*).

EXPLORING
The oldest settlement in Carinthia, romantic Friesach is great for wandering. You'll immediately find the **Hauptplatz** (main square), with its old town hall and gleaming, multicolor pastel facades, and as you stroll you'll discover aspects of the medieval-era town: beautiful stone houses, the double wall and the towers, gates, and water-filled moat. Among the medieval tournaments of gallantry that took place here, 600 knights participated in a famous one of May 1224; the Styrian minnesinger Ulrich von Liechtenstein, who appeared dressed and equipped all in green, alone broke 53 of his adversaries' lances.

The 12th-century Romanesque **Stadtpfarrkirche** (parish church) on Wiener Strasse has some excellent stained glass in the choir. The 13th-century church in the **Dominican monastery** north of the moat was the first of its order in Austria. If you believe that Tannhäuser was a creation of Wagner's imagination, you will be surprised to learn that descendants of his family were Salzburg administrators in Friesach; a **Tannhäuser Chapel** was erected in 1509 in this church, with a red-marble tomb of Deputy Dean Balthasar Tannhäuser added after his death in 1516.

From a footpath at the upper end of the main square, take a steep 20-minute climb up to the impressive remains of **Schloss Petersberg** to see 12th- and 13th-century frescoes and a museum housed on several floors of the tower, with examples of late-Gothic metalworking and hunting rifles. There is also a well-preserved Kammerklavier. Friesach has many more medieval marvels: be sure to stop in at the tourist office for information on all of them.

WHERE TO STAY

$ **Metnitztalerhof.** This delightful hotel has overlooked the medieval town square for more than 400 years. Rooms are furnished with country charm, from the rich, dark-wood pieces to the floral fabrics covering chairs, curtains, and beds. The best rooms have balconies and overlook the spectacular castle ruins. Other rooms face the town square and are not worth the price. The hotel also hosts gatherings, from wine tastings in its 12th-century wine cellar to medieval-style feasts on the weekend. **Pros:** historic charm; in the center of town. **Cons:** some rooms have so-so views. ⊠ *Hauptplatz 11* ☎ *04268/25100* ⊕ *www.metnitztalerhof.at* ⤳ *27 rooms* ♿ *In-room: no a/c, Internet (some). In-hotel: restaurant* ▭ *AE, DC, MC, V* ⊗ *Closed 2 wks in Nov.* ⊖ *BP, MAP.*

¢ **Friesacherhof.** Incorporated into a centuries-old building on the main square, this comfortable hotel has rather plain but well-kept rooms; those in front look out over the square and the Renaissance fountain and can be somewhat noisy. A gelateria is on the premises and meal plans are available for stays of three days. **Pros:** bargain rates; newly renovated rooms. **Cons:** front rooms can be noisy. ⊠ *Hauptplatz 4* ☎ *04268/2123–0* ⊕ *www.friesacherhof.at* ⤳ *16 rooms* ♿ *In-room: no a/c, Wi-Fi. In-hotel: restaurant* ▭ *AE, DC, MC, V* ⊗ *Closed Jan. 7–31* ⊖ *BP.*

HOCHOSTERWITZ

31 km (19 mi) south of Friesach.

Fodor'sChoice The dramatic 13th-century castle of **Hochosterwitz** crowns the top of a
★ steep, isolated outcropping, looking as if it has just emerged from the
♿ pages of a fairy tale. You can hardly ignore the Disneyland effect, and in fact, this was the inspiration for Walt Disney's *Snow White* castle. Disney and his staff stayed here for many weeks studying it, and you will find Walt's fantasy to be nearly fact. The castle was first mentioned in 860, and, after a tumultuous few centuries, ended up in the possession of the counts of Khevenhüller (1571), where it has remained ever since. It was in this castle that the besieged "Pocket-Mouthed Meg"—Margarethe Maultasch, the original of Feuchtwanger's *Ugly Duchess*—slaughtered the last ox of the starving garrison and dropped it onto the heads of the attacking Tyrolese. The stratagem succeeded, and, dispirited by such apparent proof of abundant supplies, the Tyrolese abandoned the siege. The most recent fortifications were added in the late 1500s against invading Turks; each of the 14 towered gates is a small fortress unto itself. Inside, there's an impressive collection of armor and weaponry plus a café-restaurant in the inner courtyard.

There's a glass elevator (accommodating wheelchairs) from a point near the parking-lot ticket office. The hike up the rather steep path to Hochosterwitz adds to the drama. Your reward at the summit is spectacular vistas from every vantage point. Get to the castle on the back road from Treibach or via Route 83/E7. ⊠ *Laundsdorf-Hochosterwitz* ☎ *04213/2010 or 04213/2020* ⊕ *www.burg-hochosterwitz.or.at* ⊠ *€7.50 without elevator, €11.50 with elevator* ⊙ *Apr. and Oct., daily 9–5; May–Sept., daily 8–6.*

ST. VEIT AN DER GLAN

10 km (6 mi) west of Hochosterwitz via Rte. 82.

The capital of Carinthia until 1518, this old ducal city remains largely unchanged, with the town hall's Baroque facade and ancient patrician houses forming the main square. Be sure to walk into the arcaded Renaissance courtyard of the **Rathaus** (Town Hall), overflowing with flowers in summer; the main state rooms can be seen on guided tours. The 12th-century Romanesque **Pfarrkirche** (parish church) was later given Gothic overtones; note the attractive entry. The ducal palace, **Schloss St. Veit**, at the north end of town, now houses a small medieval collection; the building itself has a marvelous arcaded stairway in the courtyard.

WHERE TO STAY

$$$ 🏨 **Ernst Fuchs Palast.** The 12 signs of the zodiac are the theme of this sure-fire conversation piece designed by Austrian avant-garde artist Ernst Fuchs. The exterior brings to mind a huge, psychedelic candy cane, but rooms are much less startling and are decorated with subdued, pastel fabrics and faux-Jugendstil furniture. Each room features an original print by the master. If you tell the hotel your birth date, you'll be given a room that is most compatible with your zodiac sign. The hotel also includes a wellness area. **Pros:** one-of-a-kind architecture; unique rooms. **Cons:** over-the-top design not for everyone. ⊠ *Prof.-Ernst-Fuchs-Platz 1* ☎ *04212/4660–0* ⊕ *www.hotel-fuchspalast.com* ⤴ *60 rooms* ♿ *In-room: no a/c, refrigerator, Wi-Fi. In-hotel: restaurant, bar* ▭ *AE, DC, MC, V* ⊠ *BP, MAP.*

Eastern Alps

WORD OF MOUTH

"The highlight of our trip was the day we drove the Grossglocknerstrasse. It took us all day, we started from Zell am See, drove towards Bruck and bought picnic lunch supplies at the Merkur supermarket, which had a good selection, then drove on to the toll booth. The hefty fee of €28 per car was worth it to us. There were lots of (very fit) cyclists and loads of groups of motor cyclists too. All along the road are places to stop, cafés, toilets, picnic tables, viewing areas etc. The views of the mountains were really awesome."

—KayF

Updated by
Diane
Naar-Elphee

THE WHOLE EASTERN ALPS REGION is dramatic countryside, with breathtaking scenery and great winter sports equal to those in Switzerland. Here majestic peaks, many well over 9,750 feet, soar above slow-moving glaciers that give way to sweeping Alpine meadows ablaze with wildflowers in spring and summer. Long, broad valleys (many names have the suffix *-au,* meaning "water-meadow") are basins of rivers that cross the region between mountain ranges, sometimes meandering, sometimes plunging. The land is full of ice caves and salt mines, deep gorges, and hot springs. Today most tourism is concentrated in relatively few towns, such as Heiligenblut, but wherever you go, you'll find good lodging, solid local food, and friendly folk; it is countryside to drive and hike and ski through, where people live simply, close to the land.

Western Carinthia and East Tirol are dotted with quaint villages that have charming churches, lovely mountain scenery, and access to plenty of outdoor action—from hiking and fishing in summer to skiing in winter. Across the southern tier, a series of scenic routes passes from Carinthia to that political anomaly Osttirol (East Tirol). In 1918, after World War I, South Tirol was ceded to Italy, completely cutting East Tirol off from the rest of Tirol and the administrative capital in Innsbruck. The mountains along the Italian border and those of the Hohe Tauern, to the north, also isolate East Tirol, which has consequently been neglected by tourists.

ORIENTATION & PLANNING

GETTING ORIENTED

Austria's Eastern Alps straddle four different provinces: Carinthia, East Tirol, Salzburg, and Styria. Imposing mountain ranges ripple through the region, isolating Alpine villages whose picture-postcard perfection has remained unspoiled through the centuries. The mountainous terrain makes some backtracking necessary if you're interested in visiting the entire area, but driving through the spectacular scenery is part of the appeal of touring the region.

To Lienz, up the Defereggental & Back. An area far from the madding crowd, this region of sleepy village and ancient farmhouses maintains cultural traditions and offers spectacular untouched nature.

Across the Grossglockner Pass. There is a thrill every hundred yards along this scenic route, but your first will be sighting Heiligenblut, one of Austria's prettiest towns, at the foot of the Grossglockner.

Mountain Spas & Alpine Rambles. Mountain magic and healing waters abound in this traditional and historic area.

GREAT ITINERARIES

It's easy to feel on top of the world, which you almost literally are, if you take the Grossglockner High Alpine Highway—the most thrilling pass over the Alps. Nestled in a nearby valley is Heiligenblut, a town commemorated in a thousand picture postcards. Everywhere, breathtaking Alpine vistas and centuries-old castles dot the landscape. For many travelers the Eastern Alps, concentrated around the Grossglockner peak, represent not only the most fascinating part of Austria's mountainous landscape, but its most unspoiled region as well.

Numbers in the text correspond to numbers in the margin and on the Eastern Alps map.

IF YOU HAVE 3 DAYS

Start in the charming villages of **Hermagor** and **Kötschach-Mauthen**, stopping at the Geo-Trail, which traces 50 million years of geological history. Then spend the afternoon exploring the East Tirolean capital of ☷ **Lienz**. Castle ruins, churches, and more spectacular landscapes are in store on your second day as you visit **St. Jakob in Defereggen** and **Matrei in Ost-**tirol before returning to Lienz. On your final day, crown your trip with a visit to that Alpine jewel **Heiligenblut**, making stops at **Döllach-Grosskirchheim** and elsewhere along the imposing **Grossglockner Highway**.

IF YOU HAVE 5 DAYS

Begin your trip in East Tirol's capital, **Lienz**, before heading to picture-perfect ☷ **Heiligenblut**. As long as it's not wintertime, your second day can be spent taking the scenic **Grossglockner Highway** through the Hohe Tauern National Park to the lake resort of ☷ **Zell am See**. In winter you'll have to use the Felbertauern tunnel route, which runs between Mittersill and Matrei in East Tirol. On Day 3, make a day trip to the mountain resorts of **Saalbach-Hinterglemm** and **Saalfelden**, and descend into the depths with a tour of the **Lamprechtshöhle** (cave). On your fourth day, travel to ☷ **Bad Gastein** and "take the cure." Then use your last day to visit the Domkirche (cathedral) in **St. Johann im Pongau** and the **Liechtensteinklamm**, the deepest, most dramatic gorge in the Eastern Alps.

8

PLANNING

WHEN TO GO

Snowy conditions can make driving a white-knuckle experience, but winter also brings extensive, superb skiing throughout the region—often at a fraction of the cost of the more famous resorts in Tirol. In summer the craggy mountain peaks and lush meadows provide challenge and joy to hikers, while spelunkers head into the bowels of the behemoths. Placid lakes and meandering mountain streams attract anglers for some of the best fishing to be found in the country.

GETTING HERE & AROUND

Driving is by far the preferred means of seeing this area; the roads are good, and you can stop to picnic or just to marvel at the scenery. There is a cost to driving these roads, though, as tunnels, passes, and

TOP REASONS TO GO

Drive the Grossglockner Highway. As long as weather conditions permit this crossing, this panoramic road is Austria's most famous mountain pass and an absolute must.

Take pictures at Heiligenblut. Of all the picture book images in the country, this jewel of a photo-op town has to be the winner, with its slender church steeple and gorgeous mountain backdrop.

Visit Lienz. Besides castles and churches, Lienz is one of the best

places to stay for truely stunning views of the dolomites.

Explore the Dachstein Region. The wonderful world of the Dachstein massif, stretching for miles, is one of the best regions for hiking, caving, and climbing.

"Take the cure" at Bad Gastein. Perhaps the most famous of all alpine mountain spas.

panoramic roads often have tolls. Bus travel is also an option, and not as difficult as it may seem.

BY AIR   The busiest airport in the Eastern Alps region is in Carinthia at Klagenfurt, 50 km (31 mi) east of Villach. The Salzburg airport is larger and has even more connections. Both have frequent connections to other Austrian cities and points in Europe, but neither has scheduled overseas direct flights.

BY BUS   As is typical throughout Austria, where trains don't go, the buses do, though some side routes are less frequently covered. Coordinating your schedule with that of the buses is not as difficult as it sounds. Austrian travel offices are helpful in this regard, or bus information is available in Villach and in Salzburg. You can take a post bus from the Zell am See rail station up and over the mountains to the glacier at Kaiser-Franz-Josefs-Höhe, a 2½-hour trip, or from the Lienz rail station via Heiligenblut to the glacier, about two hours on this route. Buses run from early June to mid-October.

BY CAR   If you're coming from northern Italy, you can get to Villach on the E55/A13 in Italy, which becomes the A2 and then the A10; from Klagenfurt, farther east in Carinthia, taking the A2 autobahn is quickest. The fastest route from Salzburg is the A10 autobahn, but you will have to take two tunnels into account at a total cost of €10.20 (Tauern- and Katschbergtunnel). In summer on certain weekends (especially during Germany's official holidays), the A10 southbound can become one very long parking lot, with hour-long waits before the tunnels. Taking the normal road over the passes, although long, is a very attractive option, but you will not be the only person who thought of it. If coming from abroad, don't forget to buy the autobahn *vignette* (sticker) for Austria (⇨ *Driving in Travel Smart Austria*).

ROAD CONDITIONS

Be aware that the Grossglockner High Alpine Highway is closed from the first heavy snow (mid-November or possibly earlier) to mid-May or early June. Though many of the other high mountain roads are kept open in winter, driving them is nevertheless tricky, and you may even need chains.

BY TRAIN Villach and Salzburg are both served by frequent rail service from Vienna. Villach is also connected to Italy and Salzburg, which in turn is well connected to Germany. You can reach most of the towns in the Eastern Alps by train, but the Grossglockner and Dachstein mountains are reachable in a practical sense only by road. If you do travel by rail, you can go from Villach to Hermagor, to Lienz, and northward (north of Spittal an der Drau) via Mallnitz and Bad Gastein to the main line at Schwarzach. There you can cut back westward to Zell am See or continue onward to Bischofshofen, connecting there via Radstadt to Schladming, or staying on the main line north to Salzburg.

VISITOR INFORMATION

For information about Carinthia, contact Kärntner Tourismus. The central tourist board for East Tirol is Osttirol Information. For information about Salzburg Province, contact Salzburger Land Tourismus. The main tourist bureau for Styria is Steiermark Information.

Many individual towns have their own *Fremdenverkehrsamt* (tourist office); they are listed under the specific towns.

ESSENTIALS

Bus Information **Post Bus** (☎ *01/711–01* ⊕ *www.postbus.at*).

Train Information **Österreichisches Bundesbahn** (☎ *05/1717* ⊕ *www.oebb.at*).

Tourist Information **Kärntner Tourismus** (☎ *0463/3000* ⊕ *www.kaernten. at*). **Osttirol Information** (✉ *Wilhelm-Greil-Strasse 17, Innsbruck* ☎ *0512/7272* ⊕ *www.tirol.at*). **Salzburger Land Tourismus** (✉ *Wiener Bundesstrasse 23, Post-fach 1, Hallwang bei Salzburg* ☎ *0662/6688–0* ⊕ *www.salzburgerland.com/eng*). **Steiermark Information** (✉ *St. Peter-Hauptstrasse 243, Graz* ☎ *0316/400–30* ⊕ *www.steiermark.com*).

ABOUT THE RESTAURANTS & HOTELS

While this region contains fine restaurants—in fact, two of the country's top dozen dining establishments are here—most of the dining in the small towns of the Eastern Alps will take place in *Gasthöfe* or *Gasthäuser* (country hotels or inns)—chalet-style inns with flower-decked balconies and overhanging eaves. The dining rooms are not necessarily separate restaurants frequented by nonguests. Note that in many cases such inns are closed in the off-season, particularly November and possibly April or May.

This part of Austria is relatively inexpensive, except for the top resort towns of Saalbach–Hinterglemm, Bad Gastein, and Zell am See. Even there, however, cheaper accommodations are available outside the center of town or in pensions. Note that room rates include taxes and service and almost always breakfast, except in the most expensive hotels, and one other meal, which is usually dinner. *Halb pension* (half-board), as this plan is called, is de rigueur in most lodgings. However, most will offer a breakfast-buffet-only rate if requested. Most hotels offer in-room phones and TVs. A few of the smaller hotels still take no credit cards, or if they do they will add a surcharge of between 3% and 5%. In the prominent resorts summer prices are often as much as 50% lower than during ski season.

WHAT IT COSTS IN EUROS					
	¢	$	$$	$$$	$$$$
RESTAURANTS	under €7	€7–€12	€13–€17	€18–€22	over €22
HOTELS	under €70	€70–€100	€100–€135	€135–€175	over €175

Restaurant prices are per person for a main course at dinner. Hotel prices are for a standard double room in high season, including taxes and service. Assume that hotels operate on the European Plan (EP, with no meal provided) unless we note that they use the Breakfast Plan (BP), Modified American Plan (MAP, with breakfast and dinner daily, known as halb pension), or Full American Plan (FAP, or voll pension, with three meals a day). Higher prices (inquire when booking) prevail for any meal plans.

TO LIENZ, UP THE DEFEREGGENTAL & BACK

Take Route 86 south out of Villach, through Warmbad Villach, and then Route 83 to Arnoldstein, about 10 km (6 mi) away. You're in the Gail River valley here, with the magnificent Julische Alpen rising in Slovenia on your left. Just beyond Arnoldstein, turn right onto Route 111, marked for Hermagor. On the way up, the views will now be on the right, the dramatic Gailtal Alps in the background as you head west.

HERMAGOR

46 km (29 mi) west of Villach.

ESSENTIALS
Tourist Information Hermagor (✉ *Gösseringlände 7* ☎ *04282/2043-0* ⊕ *www.hermagor.at*).

EXPLORING
The swift Gail flows along the southwest edge of Carinthia through small scattered villages with ancient churches and aged, often wooden, farmhouses. The narrow valley is peacefully soft, with many old linden trees, but its fir-treed slopes rise steeply, particularly on the south side, and craggy peaks peer from behind them. The main town in the Gail valley is Hermagor, situated approximately in its center. Hermagor is best known as a summer resort, offering hiking, climbing, and swimming in the nearby Pressegger See, but it also has skiing in winter.

During the Middle Ages villagers believed that the decorated keystones in Hermagor's late-Gothic **Pfarrkirche** *(parish church)* symbolized Jesus Christ's efforts to hold the framework of the church together. Dating from 1484, the church is also notable for its intricately carved and painted winged altar in the south Wolkenstein Chapel, which dates back to 1510.

Gartnerkogel mountain, south of Hermagor off Route 90, fascinates geologists. Discover why by following the **Geo-Trail,** along which you can gather fossils and trace 50 million years of geological history. Maps are available from the local tourist office. Botanists are equally intrigued by the blue Wulfenia, which blankets the Nassfeld mountain area farther along Route 90 on the Italian border each June. The flower, which is protected under Austrian law, can be found only here and in the Himalayas.

EN ROUTE

★ From Hermagor, both Route 87, running northwest to Greifenburg, and Route 111 up to the adjoining villages of Kötschach and Mauthen offer gorgeous views, and the distances to Lienz on both are about 55 km (35 mi). If you choose Route 87, you can turn right shortly before Greifenburg for a detour to the blue-green **Weissensee,** a relatively undeveloped narrow lake 11 km (7 mi) long, tucked in between high mountain ridges, where the fishing and boating are excellent and, in winter, ice-skating and cross-country skiing are as well. At Greifenburg turn west onto Route 100 up the Drau River valley toward Lienz. Or, from Kötschach, drive north on Route 110 to reach Oberdrauburg, then west onto Route 100.

WHERE TO STAY

$$ ⛴ **Seehotel Enzian.** This oasis of wellness and relaxation overlooks the pristine Weissensee. The hotel was built in 1926, and has been run by the same family for four generations. With its own sandy beach, sunny terrace, and boathouse, it's great for those who love the outdoors. There's a spa that looks out directly on the water and a sprawling breakfast buffet featuring locally produced foods. The rooms are elegantly furnished in warm shades of red, and most have balconies overlooking the shimmering lake. **Pros:** peaceful location; elegant interior. **Cons:** some rooms are noisy. ⊠*Neusach 32, Kärnten* ☏*04713/2221–0* ⊕*www.cieslar.at* ⌨*20 rooms* ⌕*In-room: no a/c. In-hotel: restaurant, spa, beachfront* ▤*AE, DC, MC, V.*

KÖTSCHACH-MAUTHEN

25 km (16 mi) west of Hermagor.

ESSENTIALS

Tourist Information **Kötschach-Mauthen** (⊠ *Kötschach-Mauthen 390,* ☏*04715/8516* ⊕ *www.koemau.at*).

EXPLORING

Most sightseers travel to Kötschach and Mauthen, its twin across Route 111, to enjoy the natural beauty the area has to offer and to pay a call on Kellerwand, one of Austria's top restaurants. The year-round resort is a good base for excursions via the Plöcken Pass over the border into Italy or up the Lesach Valley through the Austrian Dolomites.

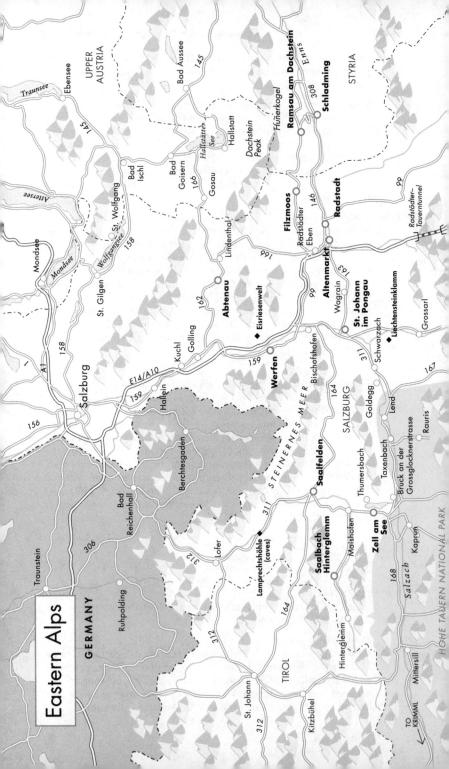

Eastern Alps

GERMANY

UPPER AUSTRIA

STYRIA

SALZBURG

TIROL

HOHE TAUERN NATIONAL PARK

Traunsee

Ebensee

Bad Aussee

145

Ramsau am Dachstein

Schladming

308

Hünerkogel

Dachstein Peak

Mondsee

Attersee

Mondsee

Wolfgangsee

St. Wolfgang

158

Bad Ischl

Bad Goisern

166

Gosau

Hallstätter See

Hallstatt

Radstädter

Filzmoos

Eben

146

Radstadt

99

Radstädter-Tauerntunnel

St. Gilgen

158

Lindenthal

991

166

Abtenau

162

Altenmarkt

99

Wagrain

163

St. Johann im Pongau

Liechtensteinklamm

Grossarl

Eisriesenwelt

Kuchl

Golling

159

Werfen

Bischofshofen

311

Schwarzach

167

Salzburg

E14/A10

159

Hallein

STEINERNES MEER

164

Goldegg

Lend

156

Berchtesgaden

Saalfelden

SALZBURG

Thumersbach

Taxenbach

Bruck an der Grossglocknerstrasse

Rauris

Bad Reichenhall

311

Maishofen

Zell am See

Kaprun

Traunstein

306

Lofer

Lamprechtshöhle (caves)

Saalbach Hinterglemm

Salzach

168

312

Ruhpolding

164

Hinterglemm

AT

St. Johann

312

Kitzbühel

TO KRIMML

Mittersill

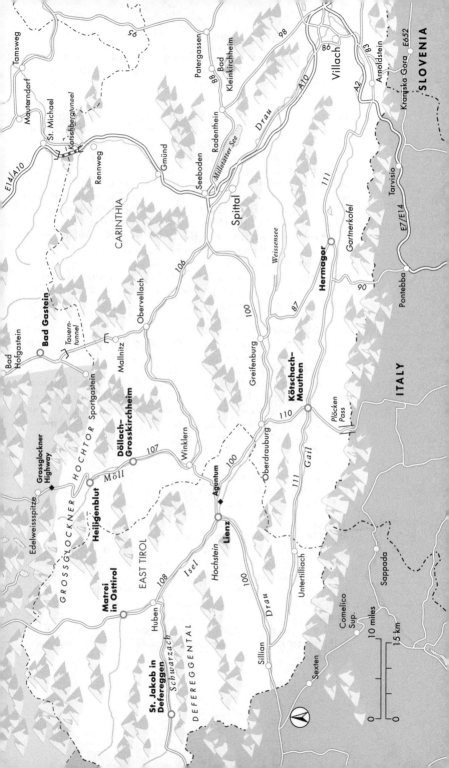

The early frescoes and unusual decorated vaulted ceiling that adorn Kötschach-Mauthen's **Pfarrkirche** *(parish church)*, which dates from 1527, make it worth a stop, too.

WHERE TO STAY & EAT

$$–$$$ ✕**Kellerwand.** Elegant tables, beamed ceilings, and a relaxed atmo-
★ sphere highlight the superb food by Frau Sonnleitner, one of the most celebrated chefs in Austria. Her kitchen is known for regional dishes served in inventive ways. If you fall in love with the place, there are a handful of rooms and a couple of suites attractively decorated in a peaceful blue-and-white country style. As can be imagined with having such a great chef at the helm, the breakfast buffet is one of the best available. ✉*Mauthen 24, Mauthen* ☎*04715/269–0* ⊕*www.sissy-sonn leitner.at* ⊟*AE, DC, MC, V* ⊗*Closed Mon. and Tues.*

$$$ 🏨**Schlank-Schlemmer Hotel Kürschner.** You'll want for nothing at this
☮ lovely lodging, as the owners have your comfort in mind. All the rooms are well equipped and furnished with natural wood. There is an extensive offering of spa treatments including hay baths for all kinds of ailments. Creative and tasty cuisine is available in all variations, and this hotel is particularly well known for its weight-reduction regimen. **Pros:** great last-minute deals; wide range of spa treatments. **Cons:** extra charge short stays. ✉*Schlanke Gasse 74* ☎*04715/259* ⊕*www.hotel-kuerschner.at* ⮑*32 rooms* ⌂*In-room: no a/c, refrigerator, Wi-Fi. In-hotel: restaurant, gym, spa, children's programs (ages 1–9)* ⊟*AE, DC, MC, V* ⊗*Closed mid-Nov.–early Dec.* ⦿*BP, MAP.*

$$–$$$ 🏨**Naturabenteuer Hotel Post.** This eccentric house, with odd balconies and a triangular garden, sits in the center of town. Rooms are attractively decorated, and some have balconies. Summer climbing and rafting excursions are offered. The main reason people stay here, however, is its fly-fishing trips. The hotel closes in late October and reopens in April. **Pros:** the place for anglers; lovely old building. **Cons:** you've got to love fishing. ✉*Hauptplatz 66, Kötschach–Mauthen* ☎*04715/221–0* ⊕*www.flyfish-hotelpost.com* ⮑*24 rooms* ⌂*In-room: no a/c, safe (some). In-hotel: restaurant, bar, pool, gym, Internet terminal* ⊟*MC, V* ⊗*Closed late Oct.–mid-Apr.* ⦿*BP, MAP.*

▌EN
ROUTE The scenic Route 110 north over the Gailberg will bring you, after about 14 km (9 mi) and some dramatic twists and turns, to Route 100 at Oberdrauburg. From here to Lienz (20 km [12 mi]), the highway follows the Drau River valley, with splendid views up into the Kreuzeck mountain range on your right. The Romans recognized the strategic importance of the region and in about AD 50 established **Aguntum** here to protect the important trade route against possible attack by native tribes. About 4 km (2½ mi) before you reach Lienz, you'll come to the excavations to the right of the road. You can explore the site, where archaeologists have been unearthing remains of this ancient settlement, quite freely.

LIENZ

34 km (21 mi) northwest of Kötschach-Mauthen.

ESSENTIALS

Tourist Information **Lienz** (✉ *Europaplatz 1* ☎ *04852/65265* ⊕ *www.lienz-tour ismus.at*).

EXPLORING

Tucked in at the confluence of the Drau and Isel rivers, the resort town of Lienz is the capital of the region. The awe-inspiring peaks rising around the town might make your first impression one of human insignificance in the face of overwhelming power and glory. Such feelings of reverence may account for the number of notable churches in Lienz.

The **St. Andrä Pfarrkirche** *(Parish Church)* on Patriadorferstrasse, can be reached by walking up Muchar Gasse and Schweizergasse or by following the Rechter Iselweg along the river. A Romanesque lion crowns the doorway, attesting to the church's early roots. The present-day Gothic edifice was completed in 1457, while the interior is Baroque, from the winged high altar to the vividly colored ceiling fresco (1761). Note the ornate marble tombstones of the noble Görz family.

Three blocks from St. Andrä—cross the Pfarrbrücke into Beda Weber-Gasse and turn left into Patriadorferstrasse—you'll find the **War Memorial Chapel,** designed in 1926 by Clemens Holzmeister, the architect responsible for Salzburg's Festspielhaus and Felsenreitschule (the two festival theaters). The wall paintings are by Albin Egger-Lienz (1868–1926), who is renowned for his ability to portray human strength and weakness and who is also buried here.

Close to the center of town, the **Franciscan Church** on Muchargasse was originally part of a Carmelite cloister, founded in 1349 by the Countess Euphemia of Görz. The church was taken over by the Franciscans in 1785 and restored in 1947–48. A Gothic pietà from about 1400 adorns the left side altar at the back; the wall frescoes are from the 15th century.

The restored 16th-century **Lieburg Palace** on the Hauptplatz, with two towers, houses provincial government offices.

A massive tower looms over **Schloss Bruck,** a battlemented residential castle that dates from 1280 and now serves as the city museum. The remarkably well-preserved castle also has a Romanesque chapel with a late 15th-century ceiling and wall frescoes. Works by Egger-Lienz and Franz Defregger (1835–1921), another Tirolean painter, are displayed here, along with Celtic and Roman relics from nearby excavations. ✉ *Iseltaler Strasse* ☎ *04852/62580–83* 🎫 *€2.50* ⊙ *Mid-May–Nov., daily 10–6.*

WHERE TO STAY

$$$–$$$$ 🏨 **Traube.** The name means "Grape," which is your first hint that this
★ hotel is a must for wine lovers. The owners are also vintners, running one of the oldest wine trades in Austria. That means there's a shop on the premises, and the restaurant serves some of the best vintages.

Centrally located, this residence has been frequented in the past by famous names, including royalty. A mix of older furniture and antiques adds elegance to the spacious, comfortable rooms. There's an enclosed rooftop pool and sauna with spectacular views of the surrounding mountains. **Pros:** great for wine enthusiasts; free parking. **Cons:** rooms on the square can be noisy. ⊠*Hauptplatz 14* ☎*04852/64444* ⊕*www.hoteltraube.at* ⇔*51 rooms* ⚿*In-room: no a/c. In-hotel: restaurant, bar, pool, Internet terminal* ⊟*AE, DC, MC, V* ⦿|*BP, MAP.*

> ### SLOW GOING
>
> Traffic into and out of Lienz can be frustrating and slow going. The B100, connecting the A10 autobahn in Carinthia with Lienz, is a winding, narrow, two-lane highway frequently overloaded with slow-moving trucks, RVs, tourists, and even cyclists. Especially if traveling this route into Lienz from the east, you may find it a challenge to keep your nerves in check. Plan on extra time for the drive here.

$-$$$ ★ **Parkhotel Tristachersee.** A little more than 4 km (2½ mi) southeast of Lienz is a small lake hidden on a hill. It's a magical setting for this grand country hotel that seems to be floating on the water. An open-air spa lets you be pampered as you enjoy great views out onto the lake. A waterfront terrace has an excellent restaurant serving regional cuisine, including fresh fish from the hotel's own ponds. Try the grilled pike-perch with homemade noodles and braised tomatoes. To get here, take the road via Amlach marked to Tristachersee. **Pros:** superb hiking; peaceful surroundings. **Cons:** charge for Internet. ⊠*Tristachersee 1* ☎*04852/67666* ⊕*www.parkhotel-tristachersee.at* ⇔*53 rooms, 4 suites* ⚿*In-room: no a/c. In-hotel: restaurant, bar, pool, spa* ⊟*DC, MC, V* ⊗*Closed Apr. and Nov.–mid-Dec.* ⦿|*BP, MAP.*

¢ **Gasthof Goldener Stern.** If you would like to stay in historic surroundings, then this budget-friendly lodging may be for you. The Golden Star was built around 1400, so it has plenty of period charm. For those looking for peace and quiet, the location is perfect. The interiors are done in simple peasant style—nothing fancy, but everything cozy. Some rooms in the newer annex have balconies overlooking the garden. There's no restaurant, but coffee and homemade cake are served in the afternoon. **Pros:** a good value; friendly staff. **Cons:** no Internet; a bit old-fashioned. ⊠*Schweizergasse 40* ☎*04852/62192* ⇔*20 rooms* ⚿*In-room: no room phones* ⊟*No credit cards* ⦿|*BP.*

SPORTS & THE OUTDOORS

HIKING   Lienz and its surrounding area have miles of marked trails, and detailed maps (available from the tourist office) show mountain lodges where you can spend the night and other facilities. Trails in Tirol are designated as easy, moderate, or difficult. Just before Schloss Bruck there is a chairlift that rises nearly to the crest of the 6,685-foot **Hochstein** mountain, from which you get a splendid panoramic view over Lienz and to the east. You'll have to hike the last kilometer (½ mi) to reach the very top.

If you want to learn to climb, contact Leo Baumgartner at the **Alpin-schule Lienz** (✉ *Gaimberg* ☎04852/68770).

WHITE-WATER RAFTING — Stretches of the **Isel River** from Matrei down to Lienz are raftable from May to mid-October. The Drau, which always has enough water, is great for beginners. Hard-core rafters will enjoy the Schwarzach in the Defereggental. For outfitters, contact the **Osttiroler Kajak Club** (☎04852/61199) in Lienz. Several companies offer rafting tours at prices beginning around €25 per person and with a minimum of five people. White-water outfitters include Dieter Messner at **Kids and Family Rafting** (✉ *Ainet 41, Ainet* ☎04853/5231). **Osttirol Adventures** (✉ *Ainet 108b, Ainet* ☎04853/200–30 ⊕*www.osttirol-adventures.at*) can help you with canyoning and paragliding.

ST. JAKOB IN DEFEREGGEN

43 km (27 mi) northwest of Lienz.

ESSENTIALS

Tourist Information **St. Jakob in Defereggen** (✉*Unterrotte 75A* ☎04873/63600 ⊕ *www.tiscover.at/defereggental*).

EXPLORING

Few American tourists venture into the Defereggen mountain range, although its craggy slopes are sprinkled with unspoiled villages. The small resort of St. Jakob in Defereggen is one of the most charming in East Tirol. Sports enthusiasts flock to the area for hiking, climbing, rafting, and fishing in summer and skiing in winter. There are also sulfur baths at nearby St. Leonhard and a waterfall at Mariahilf. To reach St. Jakob from Lienz, head northwest on Route 108, following the Isel Valley, and turn left at the village of Huben, about 19 km (12 mi) out of Lienz, onto a scenic side roadway that takes you up the valley, the Defereggental. St. Jakob is 21 km (14 mi) from Huben.

WHERE TO STAY

$$–$$$

Alpenhof. A large chalet set against a velvety green hillside is an ideal starting point for summer hiking. It's also perfect for winter skiing, particularly because it's located close to the cable car and the cross-country ski tracks. From the outside the hotel is completely out of place with the modest houses of the Defereggental, but inside the rooms are spacious and comfortable and have flower-covered balconies. The hotel pays particular attention to families with children, and has a program to take care of youngsters during the day. The restaurant showcases regional dishes. **Pros:** family-friendly vibe; peaceful surroundings. **Cons:** not for those who don't love kids. ✉*Innerrotte 35* ☎04873/5351–0 ⊕*www.alpenhof-defereggental.at* ⤶*85 rooms* ⚲*In-room: no a/c, safe, refrigerator. In-hotel: restaurant, bar, pool, children's programs (ages 3–7), Internet terminal* ⊟ *DC, MC, V* ☉*Closed May and mid-Oct.–mid-Dec.* ⏏*BP, MAP.*

MATREI IN OSTTIROL

31 km (19 mi) northeast of St. Jakob in Defereggen.

ESSENTIALS
Tourist Information **Matrei in Osttirol** (⊠ *Rauterplatz 1* ☎ *04875/6527*).

EXPLORING
Because of its strategic location on one of the easier north–south routes over the Alps, Matrei in Osttirol has a long history to look back on, including Celtic and then Roman periods.

The **Church of St. Alban** in town is definitely worth entering for its rich interior.

The real treasure, however, is the Romanesque **Church of St. Nicholas,** which is on the other side of the Isel at the beginning of the Virgen Valley. It contains some simple carvings, such as the 15th-century statue of St. Nicholas, and its late-13th-century frescoes of biblical scenes elevate it to a high work of art. Remarkably well-preserved 14th-century frescoes decorate the outside walls. Every year on the eve of St. Nicholas's Day (December 6), fantastically dressed characters with furs and bells storm through town in an old tradition called *Klaubaufgehen,* a way to frighten off bad spirits. If you find the church closed enquire for the key at the nearby farmhouse.

> ### FARMHOUSES
>
> If you fall in love with the Hohe Tauern mountains (which happens instantly for the most part) and decide you may want to stay for a while, consider booking rooms at a farmhouse. It's a wonderful way to get close to the land itself. Prices range from about €20 to €25 per person per day, and some even offer meals. The little brochure "Urlaub am Bergbauernhof" will whet your appetite, and you may consider moving to Osttirol for good. For more information, contact **Osttirol Werbung** (⊠ *Albin-Egger Strasse 17, Lienz* ☎ *04852/65333* ⊕ *www.osttirol.com*).

WHERE TO STAY

$$–$$$ ★ 🏨 **Rauter.** With an ultramodern facade, geometric lines, and slick surfaces, this fashionable hotel stands in stark contrast to the usual rustic Alpine style. Here, too, are many diversions and the best restaurant in East Tirol. The fish comes from the hotel's own waters, the lamb from the nearby mountains, and the house bakery fills the shelves at the café. A bus brings you to hiking areas in summer and ski slopes in winter. Fishing is available for those staying three days or longer, and there is horseback riding nearby. **Pros:** interesting architecture; friendly staff; lots of activities. **Cons:** expensive Internet. ⊠ *Rauterplatz 3* ☎ *04875/6611* ⊕ *www.hotel-rauter.at* 🛏 *50 rooms* ⌂ *In-room: no a/c. In-hotel: restaurant, bar, pools, gym, Internet terminal* ⊟ *DC, MC, V* ⊗ *Closed Nov.–mid-Dec.* ⧖ *BP, MAP.*

¢ ★ 🏨 **Alpengasthof Tauernhaus.** There's plenty of peace and quiet at this rustic Gasthof about 14 km (9 mi) up the Tauern Valley. The hotel began as a rest house, founded in 1207 by the archbishops of Salzburg. Frequently visited by tour groups, it can be a bit loud, but it's a good starting point for hiking and skiing. The food served in the restaurant is home cooking at its best, especially the fresh trout. **Pros:** inexpensive rates; great deal for groups. **Cons:** some rooms have partial

bathrooms. ✉A-9971 ☎04875/8811 ⊕www.matreier-tauernhaus.at
⬐41 rooms ⟁In-room: no a/c. In-hotel: restaurant ▤MC, V
⊘Closed Nov. ❙❀❙BP.

ACROSS THE GROSSGLOCKNER PASS

This is the excursion over the longest and most spectacular highway
through the Alps, the Grossglockner High Alpine Highway, an engineering achievement of the first magnitude. To explore this region, winter travelers have no choice but to drive north out of Lienz on Route
108, arriving in Mittersill in Salzburg Province via the 5-km (3-mi)
Felbertauern toll tunnel (€10 one-way, €15 day pass) under the Tauern
mountains, and taking Route 168 east to Zell am See. But if the road
is open, go north over the Grossglockner Highway. (The trip can be
done by car or bus.) Leave Lienz via Route 107, but stop on the way
up the hill outside Iselsberg-Stronach for a great panoramic view over
the city. As you go over the ridge, you'll be entering Carinthia again.
At Winklern the road follows the Möll River valley, and after about 11
km (7 mi) you'll come to Döllach-Grosskirchheim.

DÖLLACH-GROSSKIRCHHEIM

28 km (17 mi) northeast of Lienz.

ESSENTIALS

Tourist Information Döllach-Grosskirchheim (✉Döllach 47 ☎04825/521–21
⊕ www.tiscover.at/grosskirchheim).

EXPLORING

The **Gartl Waterfall** is a short stroll from the center of town—in summer,
you can safely walk through the spray to feel the water's power and
refresh yourself on a warm day.

WHERE TO STAY

$$–$$$ 🖫 **Schlosswirt.** Rooms range from somewhat spartan to elegant in
this appealing chalet hotel on the fringe of the Grossglockner. You
can climb, hike, ski, and ride horses in the gorgeous "hidden valley"
of the Graden brook. The price for the room includes half-board.
Pros: close to town; quiet location. **Cons:** mediocre meals. ✉A-9843
☎04825/211–0 or 04825/411–0 ⬐25 rooms ⟁In-room: no a/c. In-
hotel: restaurant, tennis court, Internet terminal ▤AE, DC, MC, V
⊘Closed Nov. and 3 wks in Apr. ❙❀❙BP, MAP.

HEILIGENBLUT

Fodor's Choice ★ *10 km (6 mi) north of Döllach-Grosskirchheim.*

GETTING HERE & AROUND

You can get to Heiligenblut by bus from Lienz or Zell am See (note
that some buses stop in the tiny hamlet of Winklern, directly below the
town). In winter, buses run from Heiligenblut to nearby ski runs.

ESSENTIALS

Tourist Information Heiligenblut (✉ *Hof 4* ☎ *04824/2001–21* ⊕ *www.heiligen blut.at*).

EXPLORING

One of the most photographed places in the country, Heiligenblut remains Austria's most picturesque Alpine village. With the majestic Grossglockner—Austria's highest mountain—for a backdrop, the town cradles the pilgrimage church of St. Vincent. Nowhere else does a steeple seem to find such affirmation amid soaring peaks. Some say the best time to experience this little slice of Alpine nirvana is after a leisurely dinner at one of the many Gasthöfe, gazing out at the starry firmament over the Hohe Tauern range. Others relish standing around an early morning thaw-out fire used by hikers setting out to conquer the mighty foothills of the Grossglockner peaks. It's the famed mountain-climbing school and climbing and skiing possibilities (there are 40 peaks over 10,000 feet here) that draw flocks of all-out active types.

According to local legend, St. Briccius, after obtaining a vial of the blood of Jesus, was buried by an avalanche, but when his body was recovered the tiny vial was miraculously found hidden within one of the saint's open wounds. The town gets its name, Heiligenblut (Holy Blood), from this miraculous event. Today the relic is housed in the Sakramenthäuschen, the chapel of the small but beautiful Gothic **Church of St. Vincent.** Completed in 1490 after more than a century of construction under the toughest conditions, the church is marked by its soaring belfry tower. Sublimely, the sharply pointed spire finds an impressive echo in the conical peak of the Grossglockner. St. Vincent's contains a beautifully carved late-Gothic double altar nearly 36 feet high, and the Coronation of Mary is depicted in the altar wings, richly carved by Wolfgang Hasslinger in 1520. The region's most important altarpiece, it imparts a feeling of quiet power in this spare, high church. The church also has a noble crypt and graveyard, the latter sheltering graves of those lost in climbing the surrounding mountains.

OFF THE BEATEN PATH

Alter Pocher. This 16th-century-style Goldgräberdorf (gold-mining town) was built upon historic gold mines in the Fleiss valley. The Hohe Tauern was considered one of the most important gold-mining regions of its day, and gold was mined near Heiligenblut from the 14th century until the turn of the 20th century. Many caves were created through grueling labor by thousands of miners over this period, under the most arduous conditions (of course, the owners of the mines themselves lived comfortable and rich lives). Alter Pocher, 10 minutes from Heiligenblut and over 5,906 feet above sea level, showcases the lives of the miners who dug for gold here for so many centuries; the Freilichtmuseum (open-air museum) gives an insight into their living conditions. If you get struck by gold fever, you can try panning for gold in the Fleiss stream. From mid-June through September, you can buy a ticket for an excursion in the town at the **Tourist Office** (☎ *04824/2001–21*). The price (€9) includes a visit to the museum, a guided tour and the necessary equipment and a permit to take home your finds.

WHERE TO STAY

$$$–$$$$ ⊡**Glocknerhof.** This wooden chalet in the center of the village offers old-fashioned charm and modern amenities. The elegantly furnished rooms have nice touches like flat-screen TVs. Close to climbing in summer and skiing in winter, the hotel also has its own fishing streams. Tour groups stop here on the way over the Grossglockner Highway because the restaurant is quite good. It serves its own trout and other mountain-stream fish; ask if there is *Gams* (local chamois) on the menu. **Pros:** pleasant atmosphere; friendly staff. **Cons:** some rooms on the small side. ⊠ *Hof 6-7* ☏ *04824/2244* ⊕ *www.glocknerhof.info* ⇖ *52 rooms* ⚘ *In-room: no a/c, safe, refrigerator (some). In-hotel: restaurant, bar, pool, children's programs (ages 3–7), Internet terminal* ⊟ *MC, V* ⊘ *Closed May–mid-June, Oct., and Nov.* |◯| *BP, MAP.*

$$–$$$ ⊡**Hotel Lärchenhof.** This charming hotel is a true *Panoramagasthof*—a
★   guesthouse with spectacular views. The balconies festooned with flowers overlook the eye-popping Alpine scenery. The chalet-style building is perched on a mountain slope and surrounded by lush forest, so it's easy to feel you've left civilization behind. If you need a bit of help relaxing, there's a lovely spa. Rooms are comfortably appointed with pastel fabrics and sturdy wood furniture. **Pros:** good spa; gourmet meals; quiet location. **Cons:** some double rooms on the small side. ⊠ *Hof 70* ☏ *04824/2262* ⊕ *www.ski-heiligenblut.at* ⇖ *23 rooms* ⚘ *In-room: no a/c, safe. In-hotel: restaurant, bar, spa* ⊟ *AE, DC, MC, V* |◯| *BP, MAP.*

$$ ⊡**Heiligenblut.** This family-friendly hotel sits a short distance from the
☾ town center. On weekdays the hotel runs its own kindergarten where you can leave the kids while you hit the slopes. There's even a children's disco and a kid's karaoke station. The facility is split between two buildings: an older one with apartments and a newer one with hotel rooms and a restaurant. All quarters have balconies, and you may request either a view of the mountains or of the Old Town. Meals are served buffet style, which is practical for families. **Pros:** perfect for families; lots of activities. **Cons:** not a place for peace and quiet. ⊠ *Winkl 46* ☏ *04824/4111* ⇖ *125 rooms* ⚘ *In-room: no a/c, safe. In-hotel: restaurant, bar, tennis courts, pool, gym, children's programs (ages 1–3), Internet terminal* ⊟ *AE, DC, MC, V* ⊘ *Closed Easter–May and Oct.–Dec.* |◯| *BP, MAP.*

$$ ⊡**Senger.** A peaceful location, great views, and almost always guaranteed sunshine makes this farmhouse chalet a great choice. Cleverly enlarged while keeping its original rustic appeal, its imposing wood facade has beautiful balconies covered with colorful blossoms. The white ceramic stoves in the common areas are typical of the region. The rooms and apartments, with lots of pillows and country fabrics, are well equipped. There's also a compact spa area. **Pros:** romantic feel; great place for honeymooners. **Cons:** a long way from town. ⊠ *Heiligenblut 23* ☏ *04824/2215* ⇖ *14 rooms, 8 apartments* ⚘ *In-room: no a/c. In-hotel: restaurant, bar, gym* ⊟ *MC, V* ⊘ *Closed 1 wk after Easter–June and mid-Oct.–mid-Dec.* |◯| *BP, MAP.*

8

SPORTS & THE OUTDOORS

HIKING & MOUNTAIN CLIMBING This is a hiker's El Dorado, with (in summer) more than 240 km (150 mi) of marked pathways and trails in all directions. There are relatively easy hikes to the Naturlehrweg Gössnitzfall-Kachlmoor (1½ hours), Wirtsbauer-Alm (2 hours), and the Jungfernsprung (1 hour), which arrives atop a 500-foot stone cliff above the Mölltal. Enjoyable group or private **guided tours** are available. They cost anywhere from €6 to join a short group tour to €130 per person per day for a private tour lasting from one to three days. The **National Park Programs Office** (☎04825/616114 or 04824/2700) has all the information.

GROSSGLOCKNER HIGHWAY

Grossglockner Highway is 46 km (29 mi) long.

Fodor'sChoice ★ **ESSENTIALS**

Tourist Information Grossglockner Hochalpenstrasse (✉ *Rainerstrasse 2, Salzburg* ☎ *0662/873673-0* ⊕ *www.grossglockner.at*).

EXPLORING

This is the excursion over the longest and most spectacular highway through the Alps, officially named the **Grossglockner High Alpine Highway**—the Grossglocknerstrasse. The road was completed in 1935, after five years of labor by 3,200 workers. From Heiligenblut the climb begins up the Carinthian side of the Grossglockner Mountain. The peak itself—at 12,470 feet the highest point in Austria—is to the west. The Grossglocknerstrasse twists and turns as it struggles to the 8,370-foot Hochtor, the highest point on the through road and the border between Carinthia and Salzburg Province.

A side trip on the Edelweiss-Strasse leads to the scenic vantage point at the **Edelweissspitze**. It's an unbelievable view out over East Tirol, Carinthia, and Salzburg, including 19 glaciers and 37 peaks over the 9,600-foot mark. The rare white edelweiss—the Trapps sang its praises in *The Sound of Music*—grows here. Though the species is protected, don't worry about the plants you get as souvenirs; they are cultivated for this purpose. ■TIP→ **However, it is strictly forbidden to pick a wild edelweiss (and several other plant species), should you happen to come across one.**

You can get somewhat closer to Grossglockner peak than the main road takes you by following the highly scenic but steep Gletscherstrasse westward up to the Gletscherbahn on the Franz-Josef-Plateau, where you'll be rewarded with absolutely breathtaking views of the Grossglockner peak and surrounding Alps, of the vast glacier in the valley below, and, on a clear day, even into Italy. ✉ *Grossglockner High Alpine Hwy.* ☎ *0662/873673 road information* ⊕ *www.grossglockner. at* ☎ *€28 per vehicle for a one-day pass, €35 per vehicle for 15-day pass* ☉ *Early May–late Oct., 6 AM–7:30 PM.*

Hohe Tauern National Park is one of the most varied and unspoiled landscapes on the globe—high Alpine meadows, deep evergreen woods, endless spiraling rock cliffs, and glacial ice fields—and at 1,786 square km

(690 square mi) the largest national park of central Europe. It touches on three states (Salzburg, Carinthia, and Tirol) and includes the Grossglockner group. The Grossglockner Hochalpenstrasse passes through the park. The hardier traveler may want to spend a few days hiking and lodging at any one of several refuges, where one is sometimes treated to very rustic, homemade victuals (cheeses and hams). The closest national park office is in nearby Matrei. ✉*Nationalparkverwaltung Tirol, Rauterplatz 1, Matrei in Osttirol* ☎*04875/5161–0* ⊕*www.hohetauern.at.*

HERCULES WAS HERE

Before the Grossglocknerstrasse was built, there had been no passage anywhere between the Brenner Pass and the Radstädter Tauern Pass (more than 160 km [100 mi] apart) leading over these mountains, nor was it on record that there had ever before been a regularly used route across the barrier at this point. Yet when the engineers who built the High Alpine Highway were blasting for the Hochtor tunnel they found, deep in the bowels of a mountain, a Roman statuette of, appropriately, Hercules.

ZELL AM SEE

★ *8 km (5 mi) northwest of the Grossglockner.*

GETTING HERE & AROUND

After the toll station on the north side of the Grossglockner peak, the highway finally exhausts its hairpin turns (more than 30) and continues to Bruck an der Grossglocknerstrasse. From here it's only about 8 km (5 mi) west on Route S11 and then north on Route 311 to Zell am See.

ESSENTIALS

Tourist Information Zell am See (✉*Brucker Bundesstrasse 1A* ☎*06542/770–0* ⊕*www.europasportregion.info*).

EXPLORING

This lovely lakeside town got its name from the monks' cells of a monastery founded here in about AD 790.

In the town center, visit the 17th-century Renaissance **Schloss Rosenberg,** now the town hall.

The **Kastnerturm,** built around 1300, was originally a fortified tower for an abbey and then a granary. It now houses the city museum, with an eclectic collection of old furnishings and handicrafts, open May–October, weekdays 1:30–5:30.

Unusually fine statues of St. George and St. Florian can be found on the west wall of the splendid Romanesque **St. Hippolyte Pfarrkirche** *(parish church)*, built in 1217. The tower came about two centuries later, and the church itself was beautifully renovated in 1975.

Several locations offer up stunning vistas of the town and its environs. On ground level, take a boat ride to the village of **Thumersbach,** on the opposite shore, for a wonderful reflected view of Zell am See.

For a bird's-eye view, a cable car leads virtually from the center of Zell am See up to the **Schmittenhöhe** for a 180-degree panorama that takes in the peaks of the Glockner and Tauern granite ranges to the south and west and the very different limestone ranges to the north. This sweep will impress upon you the geology of Austria as no written description ever could. In addition, there are four other cable-car trips up this mountain, offering some of the most spectacular vistas of the Kitzbühel Alps.

Ⓒ The romantic narrow-gauge **Pinzgauer Railroad** winds its way under steam power on a two-hour trip through the Pinzgau, following the Salzach River valley westward 54 km (34 mi) to Krimml. Nearby are the famous Krimmler waterfalls, with a 1,300-foot drop, which you can see from an observation platform or explore close at hand if you can manage a hike of about 3½ to 4 hours. Be sure to take a raincoat and sneakers. ☎06542/17000 ☜*Round-trip €16* ☉*Trains depart June–late Sept., Thurs. at 9:59* AM.

WHERE TO STAY

$$$$ 🍴**Salzburgerhof.** Sophisticated travelers often describe this impressive
★ chalet not far from the lake and the ski lift as the town's best hotel. It's true that at this family-managed lodging, comfort and personal service rule. Each of the attractive rooms and suites has a flower-bedecked balcony with a lovely view. The restaurant is truly excellent; try the *Tafelspitz* (boiled beef) or rack of lamb in an herb pastry crust. The pleasant garden is used for barbecues and evenings of folkloric entertainment. Golfers get a discount at the local club. **Pros:** the region's best place to stay; top-notch staff. **Cons:** rooms at rear of building are near railroad tracks; pricey Internet. ⊠*Auerspergstrasse 11* ☎06542/765–0 ⊕*www.salzburgerhof.at* ➾*36 rooms, 24 suites* 🛎*In-room: no a/c, safe, refrigerator. In-hotel: restaurant, bar, pool, gym, spa* ▤*AE, DC, MC, V* ☉*Closed Nov.* �*BP, MAP.*

$$$$ 🍴**Schloss Prielau.** With its turreted towers and striped shutters, this cas-
★ tle looks as if it belongs in a fairy tale. The elegantly furnished rooms, decked out with traditional carved-wood furniture, are a bit dim because of the narrow windows. But the service will make you feel as if you are the newest member of royalty to take up residence here. The restaurant serves classic Austrian dishes like schnitzel but with a lighter, more refined touch than you find in most other establishments. **Pros:** royal welcome; eye-popping architecture. **Cons:** outside town; need a car to get around. ⊠*Hofmannsthalstrasse* ☎06542/72911–0 ⊕*www. schloss-prielau.at* ➾*11 rooms* 🛎*In-room: no a/c, refrigerator. In-hotel: restaurant, bar* ▤*AE, DC, MC, V* ☉*Closed May* �*BP, MAP.*

$$$–$$$$ 🍴**Grand Hotel Zell am See.** In the style of the great turn-of-the-century resort hotels, this palatial lake house is the grandest place to stay in Zell. It stands on its own peninsula, is decorated with mansard roofs and whipped-cream stuccowork, and serves up some fine dining. Most of the accommodations are small apartments, some with fireplaces; the best are those farthest out in the lake. The Grand Spa, opened in 2008, lets you be pampered as you enjoy spectacular views of the water. **Pros:** a feel of luxury; great location. **Cons:** maid service can be slow. ✉ *Esplanade 4-6* ☎ *06542/788* ⊕ *www.grandhotel-zellamsee. at* ⌁ *115 rooms* ⌂ *In-room: no a/c, safe, kitchen. In-hotel: 2 restaurants, bar, pool, children's programs (ages 3–12)* ☰ *AE, DC, MC, V* ⦿ *BP, MAP.*

$-$$ ⚏ **St. Hubertushof.** On the opposite side of the lake, this sprawling resort hotel offers unbeatable views. Wood paneling and antlers over the fireplace in the lounge add to its rural feel. The hotel could do with a total renovation, and some rooms could use new furnishings. Golfers get a discount at the local course. The restaurant offers both international and local dishes, and the dance bar draws a regular crowd. **Pros:** tasty food; good service. **Cons:** rooms on lower floor can be noisy. ✉ *Seeuferstrasse 7, Thumersbach* ☎ *06542/767* ⊕ *www.zellamsee.or.at/hubertushof* ⌁ *112 rooms* ⌂ *In-room: no a/c. In-hotel: restaurant, bar* ☰ *AE, DC, MC, V* ⊙ *Closed Nov.* ⦿ *BP, MAP.*

NIGHTLIFE & THE ARTS

The emphasis in Zell is more on drinking than on dancing, but the scene does change periodically. One of the "in" places is **B17** (☎ *06542/ 47424*), a cocktail bar near the lake. Also popular is the **Crazy Daisy** (☎ *06542/72526*), a dance pub in the center of town.

SPORTS & THE OUTDOORS

BICYCLING The area around Zell am See is ideal for bicycling. If you left your wheels at home, you can rent some at **Sport Achleitner** (☎ *06542/73581*) for €10 per day for a city bike or €18 for a mountain bike. Renting by the week is cheaper. From April to October, bike tours run from south of Zell am See up to St. Johann and Salzburg via the Tauern cycle route. Mountain-bike tours are available at **Adventure Service** (✉ *Steinergasse 9, Zell am See* ☎ *06542/735251*).

FISHING The lake's tranquil waters offer fine fishing, and many hotels in the area have packages for avid anglers. Boats are for hire at the **Strandbad** (☎ *0664/2068506*) and other lakeside locations.

SKIING Nearby Kaprun and Zell am See together form **Europa-Sportregion,** offering good skiing for beginners to experts, along with a wide spectrum of terrain. Towering over Zell am See, the Schmittenhöhe has tree-lined runs that will feel familiar to Colorado and New England skiers. Kitzsteinhorn mountain, 10,499 feet above Kaprun, famous throughout Austria, offers year-round glacier skiing and was the first glacier ski area in Austria. Together these mountains offer 57 lifts, with 130 km (80 mi) of prepared slopes. In addition, there are more than 200 km (124 mi) of cross-country trails and eight ski schools. ✉ *Brucker Bundesstrasse 1A, Zell am See* ☎ *06542/770–0* ⊕ *www. europasportregion.info.*

WATER SPORTS Boating—from paddleboating to sailing—and swimming are excellent on the uncrowded Zeller See. Since powerboats are restricted on many Austrian lakes, you won't find much waterskiing, but there is a waterskiing school, **Wasserskischule Thumersbach** (✉ *Strandbad, Thumersbach* ☎ *0664/2068506*), on the lake.

SAALBACH HINTERGLEMM

17 km (9 mi) northwest of Zell am See.

ESSENTIALS

Tourist Information **Saalbach Hinterglemm** (⊠ *Saalbach Hinterglemm 550* ☎ *06541/680068* ⊕ *www.saalbach.com*).

EXPLORING

Noted skiing headliners Saalbach and its neighbor Hinterglemm are part of an area comprising also Kaprun and Zell am See, that becomes a ski circus in winter. A clever layout of lifts and trails enables you to ski slopes without duplication and still get back to your starting point. When the snow melts, the region offers sensational hiking; both towns offer a full range of sports. Take the **Kohlmais cable car** north out of Saalbach to the top of the ridge for a superb 360-degree view of the surrounding mountain ranges.

To get to Saalbach Hinterglemm from Zell am See, continue north on Route 311 to Maishofen, where the Glemm Valley opens to the west; then continue westward for about 9 km (5½ mi). For those traveling by train or bus, head first to Zell am See for transfers up the valley. Saalbach and Hinterglemm have both banned cars from their village centers. ■ TIP➔ **You can drive to your hotel to unload baggage; watch carefully for signs or ask for specific directions—the routes are convoluted and confusing.**

WHERE TO STAY & EAT

¢–$ ✕ **Iglsbergerhof.** This utterly unpretentious family-run inn serves up
★   some of the town's best and most authentic regional specialties. Start with beef bouillon with *Pinzgauer Käspressknödel* (cheese dumplings), then have *Speckknödel* (bread dumpling with bacon chunks) with sauerkraut. You'll want to finish with a delicious *Pinzgauer Bauernkrapfen* (filled doughnut). ⊠ *Vorderglemm 340, Saalbach* ☎ *06541/6491* ▤ *MC, V* ⊘ *Closed Apr. and Nov. No lunch Wed.*

$$$$ 🏨 **Saalbach Hof.** You can't miss this family-run chalet in the center of town. Just look for the rustic bell tower and overflowing pots of red geraniums against beautifully weathered wood. Warm paneling and a large fireplace welcome you as soon as you enter. The rooms are spacious and comfortable and pleasantly furnished with light wood and soft fabrics. Golfers get a discount on greens fees at Zell am See courses, and every guest gets free use of the hotel's tennis court. Half board is included in the room price. **Pros:** good deals in summer; pretty facade. **Cons:** fee for bathrobe rental. ⊠ *Dorfplatz 27* ☎ *06541/7111–0* ⊕ *www.saalbacherhof.at* ⇆ *88 rooms* ⌂ *In-hotel: 3 restaurants, bar, tennis court, pool* ▤ *MC, V* ⊘ *Closed mid-Apr.–May and mid-Oct.– early Dec.* ❑ *BP, MAP.*

$$$–$$$$ 🏨 **Glemmtalerhof.** This massive chalet is surprisingly intimate inside.
☼   Most of the pleasant paneled rooms have balconies. It's mainly a winter resort, but there's plenty to do in summer, including hiking and fishing. Prices are significantly lower in summer and last-minute online offers can be a great bargain. Golfers get a discount on greens fees at Zell am See courses. **Pros:** lots of activities; great for families. **Cons:** charge

for parking. ⊠*Dorfstrasse 150 Hinterglemm* ☎*06541/7135* ⊕*www. glemmtalerhof.at* ⇆*62 rooms, 20 apartments* ⚄*In-room: no a/c. In-hotel: 2 restaurants, bars, pool, gym, children's programs (ages 3–7), parking (paid)* ⊟*AE, DC, MC, V* ⊗*Closed Apr.–mid-May and Nov.* ⦿*BP, MAP.*

SPORTS & THE OUTDOORS

SKIING In addition to offering tobogganing, sleigh riding, and curling, Saalbach Hinterglemm has some of the finest skiing in the province of Salzburg and possibly the finest interconnected lift system in Austria. There are 55 lifts, numerous cross-country ski trails, and races and competitions are often run on the Saalbach Hinterglemm Slalom. The most popular expert run is on the Zwölferkogel mountain (a cable car takes you there from the center of Saalbach Hinterglemm), where, on high, a restaurant offers fine dining. This is an intermediate-skier's paradise, especially the north side of the mountain. Numerous ski schools provide the area with more than 200 instructors.

NIGHTLIFE

BARS Saalbach–Hinterglemm has a number of places that crowd up quickly as the slopes are vacated. For après ski, try the **Hinterhagalm** (⊠*Hinter-hagweg 43* ☎*06541/7212*). Local bands regale patrons of the **Neuhaus Taverne** (⊠*Oberdorf 38* ☎*06541/7151*). The scene is pretty and cool at the **Spitzbub** (⊠*Skiliftstrasse 302* ☎*06541/6279*).

SAALFELDEN

25 km (15 mi) northeast of Saalbach Hinterglemm.

ESSENTIALS

Tourist Information **Saalfelden** (⊠*Bahnhofstrasse 10* ☎*06582/72513* ⊕*www. alpinworld.at*).

EXPLORING

Saalfelden nestles at the foot of the **Steinernes Meer** (Sea of Stone), the formidable ridge that divides Austria from Germany. The town, farther up Route 311 from Saalbach Hinterglemm, is a climber's dream, but only for those who are experienced and who can tackle such challenges as the 9,649-feet Hochkönig. At the edge of the Steinernes Meer, signs lead you to a late-Gothic **cave chapel,** containing a winged altarpiece near a stone pulpit and hermit's cell. Saalfelden is a main stop on the Innsbruck–Salzburg train route.

Sights in town include a 19th-century Romanesque church with a late-Gothic winged altar (1539); the nearby 14th-century Farmach Castle, which is now a retirement home; and the 13th-century Lichtenberg Castle, which is now privately owned.

For many, the most interesting attraction is the museum at **Ritzen Castle**, where the Christmas manger collection of artisan Xandl Schläffer as well as exhibits on minerals, native handicrafts, and local history are on view. ⊠€3.50 ⊗*Mid-June–mid-Sept., daily 10–noon and 2–5; mid-Sept.–mid-June, Wed. and weekends 2–4.*

8

**OFF THE
BEATEN
PATH**

Lamprechtshöhle. About 14 km (8 mi) northwest of Saalfelden on Route 311 heading toward Lofer, you come to Weissbach, whose claim to fame is a system of caves totaling about 35 km (19 mi). An old legend has it that a treasure is buried here, but no one has ever found it, though not for lack of trying. ☎*06582/8343* ☜*€3.50* ☉*May–mid-Oct., daily 8–6; mid-Oct.–Dec., daily 10–5.*

WHERE TO EAT

$–$$
★

✕**Schatzbichl.** The reputation of this simple Gasthaus just east of Saalfelden draws guests from near and far. The pine-paneled interior is bright and cheerful, as is the usually overworked staff. Regional dishes are simply prepared and presented; try the garlic soup, lamb chops, or any of the local fish offered. ⊠*Ramseiden 82* ☎*06582/73281* ⚑*Reservations essential* ▤*AE, MC, V* ☉*Closed Wed. and Apr. and Nov.*

WHERE TO STAY

$$$–$$$$

⌂**Gasthof Hindenburg.** This 500-year-old inn in the center of town retains historic touches while providing modern comfort. Rooms are warm and inviting, with wood floors and a combination of antique and modern furnishings. On the top floor, above the roofs of Saalfelden, a spa area offers relaxation. There's also a rooftop terrace with awesome views. In summer the garden restaurant is particularly inviting. **Pros:** very helpful staff; discounts available in summer; free Internet. **Cons:** can get busy during conferences. ⊠*Bahnhofstrasse 6* ☎*06582/793–0* ⊕*www.hindenburg.at* ⟿*70 rooms, 6 apartments* ⌂*In-room: no a/c, safe. In-hotel: 4 restaurants, bar, spa, Internet terminal* ▤*AE, DC, MC, V* ⎇*BP, MAP.*

$$$–$$$$

⌂**Hotel Gut Brandlhof.** This sprawling ranch, about 5 km (3 mi) outside town, is perfect for an active vacation. The vast complex provides all sorts of sports facilities, including the wonderful spa and the 18-hole Saalfelden golf course. Most of the comfortable rooms are done up with traditional Alpine charm, while about a quarter are furnished in a sleek, modern style. In the wood-paneled restaurant a *Kachelofen* (ceramic tile stove) radiates warmth; the freshly cooked Austrian cuisine is first-class, with an eye to healthy meals. **Pros:** great spa; spacious rooms. **Cons:** fee for parking. ⊠*Hohlwegen 4* ☎*06582/7800–0* ⊕*www.brandlhof.com* ⟿*136 rooms, 49 suites* ⌂*In-room: no a/c, safe, refrigerator. In-hotel: restaurant, bars, golf course, tennis court, pools, gym, children's programs (ages 3–7), parking (paid)* ▤*AE, DC* ⎇*BP, MAP.*

¢

⌂**Pension Klinglerhof.** This is one of several modest bed-and-breakfasts in Saalfelden. It's simple, comfortable, and inexpensive, and the service is all by owners (the Hölzls in this case). Breakfast is a typical Austrian affair, bread rolls, cold cuts, jam, and butter. The Klinglerhof is quiet, right near the golf course, the cross-country ski trails, and the lifts. **Pros:** bargain rates; good breakfasts. **Cons:** cash only ⊠*Schinking 1* ☎*06584/7713* ▤*No credit cards* ⎇*BP.*

SPORTS & THE OUTDOORS

BICYCLING

The valley leading to Saalfelden is a great place for seeing sights on two wheels. **Bike Park Leogang** (⊠*Glemmerstrasse 21* ☎*6542/80480–25* ⊕*www.bikepark.at*) includes special downhill courses, guided tours, a rental and service center, and, most interestingly, a ticket allowing you to take your bike on the area's massive ski-lift system (in summer, of course).

MOUNTAIN SPAS & ALPINE RAMBLES

Glacier-covered Alps, hot springs, luxurious hotels, and tranquil lakes are the enticing combinations this Austrian region serves up superlatively. Gold and silver mined from the mountains were the source of many local fortunes; today glittering gold jewelry finds many buyers in the shops of Bad Gastein's Kaiser Wilhelm Promenade. To set off on this trip, head south from Salzburg on the A10 and take the Bischofshofen exit toward St. Johann im Pongau, which gets you to Route 311 and, 17 km (11 mi) later, the Route 167 junction. From Zell am See, head east on Route 311 to pass Bruck again, continue through Taxenbach to Lend, and turn south at the intersection of Route 167.

BAD GASTEIN

54 km (34 mi) southeast of Zell am See.

GETTING HERE & AROUND
Bad Gastein is serviced by many rail lines, with many expresses running from Salzberg and Klagenfurt. You can also reach the town by bus from Salzburg.

ESSENTIALS
Tourist Information **Bad Gastein, Kur & Touristikbüro** (⊠ *Kaiser-Franz-Josef-Strasse 27* ☎ *06434/2531–0* ⊕ *www.badgastein.at*).

EXPLORING
Though it traces its roots all the way back to the 15th century, this resort, one of Europe's leading spas, gained renown only in the 19th century, when VIPs from emperors on down to impecunious philosophers flocked to the area to "take the cure." Today Bad Gastein retains much of its time-burnished allure. The stunning setting—a mountain torrent, the Gasteiner Ache, rushes through the town—adds to the attraction. Most attempts at rejuvenating this turn-of-the-last-century jewel have met with failure, and everyone can be thankful for it. The old buildings still dominate the townscape, giving it a wonderful feeling of solidity and charm. The baths themselves, however, are state-of-the-art, as evidenced by the massive **Felsentherme Gastein** and the nearby **Thermalkurhaus**.

A special tradition in Bad Gastein is the old pagan *Perchtenlaufen* processions in January of every fourth year (the next is scheduled for 2010): people wearing big masks and making lots of noise chase the winter away, bringing good blessings for the new year.

8

WHERE TO STAY

$$$$ ⊡**Grüner Baum.** You're out of the center of town here, in a relaxing,
⟳   friendly village set amid meadows and woodlands. The guest list at this
incredibly charming lodge has included Austria's Empress Elisabeth and
Saudi King Saud. The wood-paneled rooms have plenty of personality.
Children are well looked after with a range of programs. The elegant
restaurant has an excellent reputation both for its Austrian fare and its
varied wine list. **Pros:** great deals in summer; lovely building. **Cons:** gets
busy during holiday season. ⊠ *Kötschachtal* ☎ *06434/2516–0* ⊕ *www.
hoteldorf.com* ⟿ *80 rooms* ⌂ *In-room: no a/c, safe, refrigerator. In-
hotel: restaurant, bar, tennis court, pools, gym, children's programs
(ages 3–7)* ⊟ *AE, DC, MC, V* ⊘ *Closed Nov.* ⧚ *BP, MAP.*

$$$$ ⊡**Hotel Weismayr.** This grand old hotel a 77-room palace with a reputa-
★   tion for luxury and service going all the way back to 1832—is without a
doubt the top address in Bad Gastein. The imposing facade may remind
you of New York City's Plaza Hotel. Everything is done to ensure your
stay will be pleasant, and even healthy: there's a spa with treatments
that pamper the body and relax the mind. The expansive dining rooms
in Biedermeier style are the setting for luxurious meals, including many
seasonal dishes. The menu also reflects the fact that you're at a spa,
so there are fresh salads and vegetarian dishes. **Pros:** luxurious rooms;
lovely spa area. **Cons:** service is a little slow. ⊠ *Kaiser-Franz-Josef-
Strasse 6* ☎ *06434/2594–0* ⊕ *www.weismayr.com* ⟿ *77 rooms* ⌂ *In-
room: no a/c, safe. In-hotel: restaurant, bar, gym, spa, Internet terminal*
⊟ *AE, DC, MC, V* ⧚ *BP, MAP.*

$$$–$$$$ ⊡**Elisabethpark.** The dining rooms and parlors go on and on in this ele-
gant hotel, which manages to marry old-school charm with modern con-
veniences. The stateliness is underscored by Oriental rugs, marble floors,
and crystal chandeliers. Rooms, with period furnishings, are particularly
comfortable. Rooms facing the park have balconies, while those over-
looking the valley have panorama windows. The majestic waterfall—
symbol of Bad Gastein—is adjacent to the hotel. The large spa area is free
of charge to guests. **Pros:** free transportation to hotel; can accommodate
special dietary needs. **Cons:** some staff members unfriendly. ⊠ *A-5640*
☎ *06434/2551–0* ⊕ *www.elisabethpark.at* ⟿ *119 rooms* ⌂ *In-room:
refrigerator. In-hotel: restaurant, bar, pool, gym, spa, children's programs
(ages 2–12), Internet terminal* ⊟ *AE, DC, MC, V* ⊘ *Closed mid-Apr.–
mid-June and Sept.–mid-Dec.* ⧚ *BP, MAP.*

$$ ⊡**Alpenblick.** Perched high above the town, this old-fashioned chalet
has a sweeping view of the valley. It's an ideal base for skiers, hikers, and
anyone who just wants a quiet stay in the most pleasant countryside. A
lovely garden has a heated outdoor pool and breathtaking views. The
rooms are furnished in the typical rustic style. There is certainly nothing particularly modern here, but everything is well maintained and the
service is congenial. **Pros:** free transportation to hotel; laid-back vibe.
Cons: 15-minute walk to town. ⊠ *A-5640* ☎ *06434/2062–0* ⊕ *www.
alpenblick-gastein.at* ⟿ *40 rooms* ⌂ *In-room: no a/c. In-hotel: restaurant, bar, pool, Internet terminal* ⊟ *AE, DC, MC, V* ⊘ *Closed Nov.–
mid-Dec.* ⧚ *BP, MAP.*

NIGHTLIFE & THE ARTS

The **Grand Hotel de l'Europe casino** (⊠ *Kaiser-Franz-Josef-Strasse 14* ☎ *06434/2465*) has baccarat, blackjack, roulette, and slot machines. A passport is required. The casino is open mid-July–September and December 25–March, daily 7 PM–3 AM. Keep an eye out also for concerts, especially at the **Kongresshaus** in the middle of town (New Year's concerts are held here, for example).

SPORTS & THE OUTDOORS

As a good spa town, Bad Gastein will keep guests entertained with all sorts of events from snowboarding competitions to llama trekking (popular with families). You will not be bored.

Although not as well known to outsiders as other resorts, **Gasteiner Tal** (Gastein Valley) is popular with Austrians. The slopes of the four areas—Dorfgastein, Bad Hofgastein, Bad Gastein, and Sportgastein— are not well connected, so you'll often have to use the free shuttle bus and do some hoofing in your ski boots. Runs are mostly intermediate, with limited advanced and beginner slopes. The other ski run near Bad Gastein is the Graukogel peak, which also offers a restaurant and great Alpine hikes.

ST. JOHANN IM PONGAU

★ *43 km (27 mi) north of Bad Gastein.*

ESSENTIALS

Tourist Information **St. Johann im Pongau** (⊠ *Ing. Ludwig Pech Strasse 1* ☎ *06412/6036* ⊕ *www.sanktjohann.com*).

EXPLORING

St. Johann has developed into a full-fledged year-round resort. The area is favored by cross-country and intermediate downhill skiers, as the gentle slopes provide an almost endless variety of runs.

The huge, twin-spired Pfarrkirche (parish church), built in 1861 in neo-Gothic style, is known locally as the **Pongau Domkirche** *(cathedral)*—a mammoth structure that rises quite majestically out of the townscape.

Every four years during the first week of January, the people of St. Johann, like the Bad Gasteiners, celebrate Perchtenlauf, which can be poetically translated to mean "away with winter's ghost." Taking to the streets, they ring huge cowbells and wear weird masks and costumes to drive away evil spirits. The next celebration will be in 2009; check with the tourist office for the exact date. St. Johann is on the rail lines connecting Munich, Klagenfurt, and Salzburg.

★ Traveling from Bad Gastein along Route 311, turn east toward Schwarzach in Pongau, where the road heads north, to find, between Schwarzach and St. Johann, the **Liechtensteinklamm,** the deepest (1,000 feet), narrowest (12½ feet), and most spectacular gorge in the Eastern Alps. At its far end is a 200-foot waterfall. A tour on a wooden walkway crisscrossing the gorge takes about one hour. ☎ *06412/8572* ⊠ *€3.50* ⊙ *Early May–late Sept., daily 8–8; Oct., daily 9–4.*

8

WHERE TO STAY

$$ **Sporthotel Alpenland.** This centrally located hotel lacks the personal service you'll find at the family-run chalets. It's one of the larger lodgings in the area, and therefore tends to attract groups and can often be noisy. But you will get an attractive room, an efficient staff, and plenty of amenities. Three restaurants offer Austrian, Italian, and international cuisine. **Pros:** good food; plenty for the kids to do. **Cons:** expensive Internet; noise from kids. *Hans-Kappacher-Strasse 7 06412/7021–0 www.alpenland.at 137 rooms In-room: no a/c. In-hotel: 3 restaurants, bars, tennis court, pool, gym, Internet terminal AE, DC, MC, V BP, MAP.*

SPORTS & THE OUTDOORS

SKIING   Linked by buses and 80 km (50 mi) of ski runs with other towns in the Pongau Valley, St. Johann remains the ski capital of the region called **Salzburger Sportwelt,** which showcases 100 lifts and more than 350 km (217 mi) of well-groomed slopes. St. Johann alone has 14 ski lifts plus several cable-car ascents. Along with other Pongau valley runs, the town offers a Drei-Täler-Skischaukel (three-valley) pass. Contact **Tourismusverband St. Johann** (*Alpendorf, St. Johann 06412/6036 www.sanktjohann.com*).

ALTENMARKT

22 km (14 mi) east of St. Johann im Pongau.

ESSENTIALS

Tourist Information **Altenmarkt-Zauchensee** (*Sportplatzstrasse 486 06452/5511 www.altenmarkt-zauchensee.at*).

EXPLORING

You cross over to Altenmarkt by leaving St. Johann im Pongau on Route 163 heading east across Wagrain and Reitdorf. Altenmarkt is small, but the **Church of St. Mary** contains the Schöne Madonna, an outstanding statue of the Virgin Mary that dates from before 1384.

Nearby streams make the town a prime fishing site in summer, and skiing takes the spotlight during the winter months. The ski mountain here is part of the extensive **Salzburger Sportwelt** ski region, so a lift ticket gives you access to 350 km (217 mi) of mostly interconnected runs.

WHERE TO STAY

$$–$$$ **Lebzelter.** Luxury permeates this small and elegant hotel in the center of the Altenmarkt. Individually furnished rooms offer a quiet, peaceful, and pleasant stay. An expansive health spa including a Finnish sauna, Roman steam bath, whirlpool, and a fitness center is open for guests every day of the week. The sun-filled country restaurant has an excellent reputation for traditional fare. The kitchen serves everything from steaks to fish to vegetarian meals. **Pros:** doting owners; friendly staff; good food. **Cons:** extra charge for short stays. *Marktplatz 79 06452/6911 www.lebzelter.com 29 rooms In-room: no a/c, refrigerator. In-hotel: restaurant, bar, gym, spa AE, DC, MC, V Closed Oct. BP, MAP.*

$$–$$$ ⌂ **Schartner.** Although it's close to the center of the Altenmarkt, this hotel has the feel of a country inn, thanks to its large garden and the adjacent meadow. Three buildings are for the accommodations, while the fourth houses the spa. The rooms differ quite a bit, but all are comfortable and spacious, and most have balconies. Summer visitors will enjoy taking their leisurely breakfast or evening meal in the outdoor *Gastgarten*. There is a wall for those who wish to practice mountain climbing. **Pros:** ideal location; excellent staff. **Cons:** cash only. ✉ *Hauptstrasse 35* ☎ *06452/5469* ⊕ *www.hotel-schartner.at* ⇥ *16 rooms, 14 suites* ⌂ *In-room: no a/c. In-hotel: restaurant, bar* ⊟ *No credit cards* ⓞ *BP, MAP.*

$$ ⌂ **Markterwirt.** This traditional house in the center of town dates back at least 900 years. The personal style of the family that runs it is reflected in the charming country decor of the comfortable rooms. A "hunting lodge" directly on the lake, with several cozy apartments, makes for a romantic getaway. The main dining room and the informal *Stube* serve delicious fare, and the bar offers the tastiest pizza in town. The recently adapted wine cellar was opened to guests and friends of the owners for wine tastings of some of the best vintages. **Pros:** great location; friendly staff; intimate feel. **Cons:** old-fashioned feel. ✉ *Marktplatz 4* ☎ *06452/5420* ⊕ *www.markterwirt.at* ⇥ *29 rooms* ⌂ *In-room: no a/c. In-hotel: restaurant* ⊟ *MC, V* ⊙ *Closed Nov.* ⓞ *BP, MAP.*

RADSTADT

4 km (2½ mi) east of Altenmarkt.

GETTING HERE & AROUND

To get to Radstadt, motorists usually take the A10 from Salzburg, about a one-hour drive. Trains and buses, too, connect Salzburg with Radstadt (occasionally with a transfer at Bischofshofen).

ESSENTIALS

Tourist Information **Radstadt** (✉ *Stadtplatz 17* ☎ *06452/7472* ⊕ *www.radstadt. com*).

EXPLORING

Despite wars and fires, the walled town of Radstadt still retains its 12th-century character. Standing guard over a key north–south route, Radstadt was once granted the right to warehouse goods and to trade in iron, wine, and salt, but the town's present prosperity is due to tourism: the area is growing in popularity as a skiing destination and has long been a lure for hikers in summer. Radstadt's north and west walls, dating from 1534, are well preserved, as are three of the towers that mark the corners of the Old Town. Most of the buildings around the square are also from the 16th century. The late-Romanesque **Pfarrkirche** (parish church), north of the square, dominates the town, but reconstructions over the ages have erased much of its original character. The interior contains several Baroque altars.

8

WHERE TO STAY

$$$–$$$$ 🏨 **Gründler's Wellness & Sporthotel.** This rambling, chalet-style resort sits on a sunny meadow right out of *The Sound of Music.* It's a great base for outdoor activities whatever the season. In summer the emphasis is on water, and the sport is fishing; the hotel gives you access to 16 km (10 mi) of the Enns River. Huge outdoor pools and a waterslide offer great fun for children. Don't stay away in winter, either: the ski slopes are nearby, and the spa is one of the nicest in town. The restaurant (for guests only) specializes in trout and other local favorites. **Pros:** pleasant house; plenty of activities. **Cons:** can get noisy. ⊠*Schlossstrasse 45* ☎*06452/5590–0* ⊕*www.gruendlers.at* 🛏*10 rooms, 18 apartments* ⚒*In-room: no a/c, safe, refrigerator (some). In-hotel: restaurant, pools* ⊟*MC, V* ⊗*Closed mid-Apr.–May and mid-Oct.–mid-Dec.* �101*BP, MAP.*

SPORTS & THE OUTDOORS

SKIING   The ski mountain here is part of the extensive **Salzburger Sportwelt** ski region, so a lift ticket gives you access to more than 350 km (217 mi) of mostly interconnected runs.

Langlaufen, or cross-country skiing, is wildly popular with many Europeans, and some resort areas such as Radstadt cater to this specialty. Sure, it takes a great deal of energy when the going is not all downhill, but gliding along through silent, snow-covered pine forests on "skinny" skis offers natural beauty and tranquility. Besides maintaining a 180-km (112-mi) groomed-trail system, Radstadt hosts annually the Internationale Tauernlauf, a cross-country ski race that attracts more than 1,000 participants each year.

SCHLADMING

20 km (13 mi) east of Radstadt.

ESSENTIALS

Tourist Information Schladming-Rohrmoos (⊠ *Rohrmoosstraße 234* ☎*03687/22268* ⊕*www.schladming-rohrmoos.com*).

EXPLORING

In the 14th and 15th centuries Schladming was a thriving silver-mining town, then in 1525 the town was burned in an uprising by miners and farmers. Most of what you see today dates from 1526, when reconstruction began, but traces of the earlier town wall and the old miners' houses stand as testament to the town's imposing earlier wealth. Dominating the skyline is the Romanesque tower of the **St. Achaz Pfarrkirche,** or parish church.

This is an area where winter sports are taken seriously; not only does it attract the world's best skiers, but it also gives beginners ample scope. In summer the area becomes a mountain-biker mecca and hosts an annual world cup downhill race. In happy contrast to fashionable resorts in Tirol and Vorarlberg, Schladming and its surrounding areas (Radstadt, Ramsau am Dachstein, and Filzmoos) are reasonably priced. To get to Schladming from Radstadt, take scenic Route 320 east along the Enns River valley for about 20 km (13 mi) over the provincial border into

Styria at Mandling, or if time is of the essence, take the A10 autobahn to the Altenmark exit and follow the signs. The town is also accessible by rail via the Salzburg–Graz line.

WHERE TO STAY

$$–$$$ ⊡**Posthotel Schladming.** This traditional lodging in the center of town
★ dates from 1618, and is notable for its rooms with vaulted ceilings. Guest rooms are cozy and comfortable. The restaurants offer good regional cuisine in an appropriately rustic atmosphere. It's the place to sit outside in summer, watch people go by, and enjoy solid Austrian cooking, cholesterol and all. Golf arrangements can be made for the nearby Dachstein-Tauern club. **Pros:** spacious rooms; lots of charm. **Cons:** front rooms can get noisy at night. ⊠*Hauptplatz 10* ☎*03687/22571* ⊕*www.posthotel-schladming.at* ⮞*40 rooms* ☝*Inroom: no a/c, refrigerator. In-hotel: 2 restaurants, bar, tennis court, spa* ⊟*AE, DC, MC, V* ⊙*BP, MAP.*

SPORTS & THE OUTDOORS

FISHING From May to mid-September you can cast a fly for trout in the nearby rivers and lakes. Contact **Gasthof Tetter** (⊠*Untertal* ☎*03687/61130*).

GOLF Schladming-Haus (Haus is a little village incorporated into Schladming) has an Alpine setting that's reason enough to play the 18-hole, par-71 course at the **Golf & Country Club Dachstein-Tauern** (⊠*6 km [4 mi] from Schladming* ☎*03686/2630–0*).

SKIING Although not well known to North Americans, Schladming is part of the **Dachstein-Tauren Region.** one of Austria's most popular downhill and cross-country ski destinations. Free ski buses connect the more remote mountains in the region, but you'll have plenty of skiing without having to leave the slopes. Schladming's so-called "Four Mountain Ski Link" connects the four largest Styrian skiing mountains allowing you to ski nonstop from Hauser-Kaibling via Planai and Hochwurzen to Reiteralm. Another lure is the bustling après-ski scene. For details, contact the **Regionalverband Dachstein-Tauern office** (⊠*Ramsauerstrasse 756 Schladming* ☎*03687/2331–0* ⊕*www.dachstein-tauern.at*).

RAMSAU AM DACHSTEIN

6 km (4 mi) north of Schladming.

GETTING HERE & AROUND

Heading north out of Schladming, you take a narrow, winding road that offers increasingly spectacular views of the Enns Valley and ends in a broad, sun-bathed valley at the foot of the mighty Dachstein range. About 4½ km (3 mi) west of Ramsau, a small toll road (€7 per car) forks to the north onto the Dachstein itself, a majestic craggy outcrop of almost 9,100 feet. To get to Ramsau without a car, take a bus from Schladming.

ESSENTIALS

Tourist Information **Ramsau am Dachstein** (⊠*Kulm 40* ☎*03687/81833* ⊕*www.ramsau.com*).

EXPLORING

Take the impressive **Dachstein cable-car ride** to the top of the Alps. A fully suspended steel cable carries up to 70 persons a distance of more than 6,600 feet in about 10 minutes to the top of the Dachstein glacier, 8,900 feet high. This glacier cable car, completed in 1969, is a remarkable engineering achievement. When you reach the top, step out onto the **Dachstein Skywalk.** This glass-floored walkway juts out into the open, 820 feet above a vertical cliff face and has breathtaking views of stupendous peaks within arm's reach, almost. To the north lie the lakes of the Salzkammergut; to the west, the Tennen mountain range. South and east lie the lower Tauern mountains. You can hike over to the Dachstein peak if you're wearing proper hiking boots. In summer the south cliff at Hunerkogel is a favorite "jumping-off spot" for paragliders.

WHERE TO STAY

$$–$$$ ⬚ **Pehab-Kirchenwirt.** *Kirchenwirt* means "inn next to the church," and that's exactly where you'll find this rustic lodging. It's been family-run for the past 200 years. Nearly all the rooms have been lovingly renovated and have cozy balconies; those in the back have the best mountain views. The interiors are inviting and warm, with wooden paneling and carpeted floors. You're close to hiking trails in summer and the hotel-operated ski lift and ski runs in winter. Hotel guests have use of the nearby indoor pool, which has a sauna and solarium. The restaurant serves good Styrian specialties. **Pros:** central location; charming rooms. **Cons:** spa area can get crowded. ⬚*A-8972* ☎*03687/81732* ⊕*www.pehab.at* ⬚*40 rooms, 5 apartments* ⬚*In-room: no a/c, Wi-Fi. In-hotel: restaurant, pool* ⊟*AE, MC* ⊘*Closed Nov. and 1 month after Easter* ⦿*BP, MAP.*

$ ⬚ **Peter Rosegger.** This rustic chalet at the forest's edge is decorated with
★ homey mementos—framed letters and embroidered mottoes—of the Styrian novelist after whom it is named. This is the place to stay when you've come for scale the heights, as Fritz Walcher heads the climbing school. Rooms are country comfortable, and the restaurant (hotel guests only) is one of the best in the area, with such local specialties as house-smoked trout, Styrian corned pork, and stuffed breast of veal. **Pros:** central location; great for outdoorsy types. **Cons:** often booked up in advance. ⬚*A-8972* ☎*03687/81223–0* ⬚*12 rooms* ⬚*In-room: no a/c. In-hotel: restaurant, gym* ⊟*MC, V* ⊘*Closed mid-Apr.–May and Nov.–mid-Dec.* ⦿*BP, MAP.*

SPORTS & THE OUTDOORS

MOUNTAIN If you're interested in learning to climb in the difficult Dachstein area,
CLIMBING contact **Alpinschule Dachstein** (⬚*Ramsau am Dachstein 233* ☎*03687/ 81223–0*). The **Bergführer Büro Ramsau am Dachstein** (☎*3687/81287* ⊕*www.bergsteigerschule.net*) is a long-established resource for mountain climbers.

SKIING The famous **Dachstein Glacier** can be skied year-round, although summer snow conditions require considerable expertise. The altitude, however, guarantees good snow conditions late into the winter season. Dachstein Glacier is part of the Dachstein-Tauern ski region; for details on skiing facilities, contact the **Tourismusverband** (✉*A-8972 Ramsau am Dachstein* ☎*03687/818–33* ⊕*www.ramsau.com*).

SHOPPING

In the nearby village of Rössing, Richard Steiner's **Lodenwalker** (☎*03687 /81930*) has been turning out that highly practical feltlike fabric made from loden since 1434. Here you can find various colors and textures at reasonable prices. It's open weekdays.

FILZMOOS

★ *14 km (9 mi) west of Ramsau am Dachstein.*

ESSENTIALS

Tourist Information Filzmoos (✉*Filzmoos 50* ☎*06453/8235* ⊕*www.filz moos.at*).

EXPLORING

Filzmoos, one of the most romantic villages in Austria, is still a well-kept secret. Though skiing in the nearby Dachstein mountains is excellent, the inexpensive winter resort (which is part of the Salzburger Sportwelt ski area) has yet to be discovered by foreign tourists. During the summer months meandering mountain streams and myriad lakes attract anglers eager for trout, while hikers come to challenge the craggy peaks.

Filzmoos calls itself a "balloon village," not only for the International Hot Air Balloon Week every January, but because it relies heavily on hot-air balloons to show its guests the region.

8

WHERE TO STAY & EAT

$$$–$$$$ ✕**Hubertus.** Every last detail from romantic furnishings to the doting ser-
Fodor'sChoice vice is done to perfection at this restaurant. It's the best in the area, if not
★ all of Alpine Austria: chef Johanna Maier's way with trout is exquisite, but don't overlook the game, roast poultry, or veal sweetbreads. Finish with *Topfenknödel* (cream cheese dumpling), a house specialty. Frau Maier offers cooking courses several times each month—call for dates. ✉*Am Dorfplatz 1* ☎*06453/8204* ⊟*AE, MC* ⊙*Closed mid-Apr.– mid-May and mid-Oct.–mid-Dec.*

$ ⌂**Alpenkrone.** From the balconies of this chalet above the town center you'll have a great view of the surrounding mountains. Rooms are done up in a simple but colorful style. The British owner provides friendly management and four-star comfort at three-star prices. This house sees many of its guests returning year after year. **Pros:** great value; friendly staff; wonderful location. **Cons:** steep climb from town. ✉*Filzmoos 133* ☎*06453/8280–0* ⊕*www.alpenkrone.com* ⇆*58 rooms* ⌂*In-room: no a/c. In-hotel: restaurant, bar, pool, gym* ⊟*MC, V* ⊙*Closed Easter–mid-May and mid-Oct.–mid-Dec.* ⊙*BP, MAP.*

EN ROUTE From Filzmoos, rejoin Route 99/E14 again at Eben im Pongau. Here you can take the A10 autobahn north to Salzburg if you're in a hurry. But if you have time for more majestic scenery and an interesting detour, continue about 4 km (2½ mi) on Route 99/E14, and turn north on Route

166, the **Salzburger Dolomitenstrasse** *(Salzburg Dolomites Highway)*, for a 43-km (27-mi) swing around the Tennen mountains. ■TIP→ Be careful, though, to catch the left turn onto Route 162 at Lindenthal; it will be marked to Golling. Head for Abtenau.

ABTENAU

44 km (28 mi) northwest of Filzmoos.

ESSENTIALS

Tourist Information Infobüro Abtenau (⊠ *Markt 34* ☎ *06243/4040–0* ⊕ *www. lammertal.info).*

EXPLORING

Abtenau is a charming little town with a pretty old village square flanked by colorful burghers' houses and the 14th-century **St. Blasius Church,** which has late-Gothic frescoes and a Baroque high altar.

A **museum** of local history, which documents primarily the life of local farmers, has been set up south of town in the Arlerhof, an ancient house built in 1325. It's open June–mid-September, Tuesday, Thursday, and Sunday 2–5.

Nearby, nature has arranged its own museum, the Trickl and Dachser **waterfalls,** with the nearby cave known as the "cold cellar" (der Kalte Keller), where beer used to be stored.

WHERE TO STAY

$$$–$$$$ ⚏**Moisl.** This cluster of typical chalet-style houses in the center of town is recognizable by the flower-laden balconies and overhanging eaves. The lodging dates back to 1764, but the services and facilities are very modern. Nearly all the rooms are furnished in a romantic country style with lots of honey-hued wood. Fresh flowers everywhere add a special touch. Candlelight dinner are common in the evenings. The spa area is extensive and there is a wonderful salon where all kinds of treatments are available. **Pros:** friendly staff; beautiful garden. **Cons:** kids' area can get noisy in summer. ⊠ *Markt 26* ☎ *06243/22320* ⊕ *www.hotelmoisl. at* ☞ *75 rooms* ♨ *In-room: no a/c, safe. In-hotel: restaurant, bar, tennis court, pool, Wi-Fi* ⊟ *MC, V* ☉ *Closed Apr. and mid-Oct.–mid-Dec.* ⊺⊙�O⊺*BP, MAP.*

$$ ⚏**Post.** This centrally located hotel may be decorated in rustic style, but has completely up-to-date facilities. Many of the nicely decorated rooms have balconies. Transportation is available right at the door: the Windhofer family also runs the town's taxi and excursion service. The restaurant is well worth a try; don't miss the rump steak or any of the other beef dishes. **Pros:** good value; friendly staff. **Cons:** too quiet for some. ⊠ *Markt 39* ☎ *06243/2209–0* ⊕ *www.hotel-post-abtenau.at* ☞ *56 rooms* ♨ *In-room: no a/c. In-hotel: restaurant, pool* ⊟ *No credit cards* ☉ *Closed Apr. and Nov.–mid-Dec.* ⊺⊙O⊺*BP, MAP.*

SPORTS & THE OUTDOORS

WHITE-WATER
RAFTING

From May to the middle of October you can raft the Salzach and Lammer rivers. The Lammer, with its "Hell's Run," is particularly wild. Runs begin at about €19 per person. For details call **Alpin Sports** (☎06243/3088 ⊕*www.alpinsports.at*). **David Zwilling Resort** (☎06243/ 3069–0 ⊕*www.zwilling-resort.at*), a standout among Abtenau's several active clubs, can also help you to experience paragliding, mountaineering, and many other adventure sports.

WERFEN

Fodor'sChoice
★

41 km (26 mi) from Abtenau.

ESSENTIALS

Tourist Information **Werfen** (✉ *Markt 24, A-5450* ☎*06468/5388* ⊕*www. werfen.at*).

EXPLORING

The small size of Werfen, adorned with 16th-century buildings and a lovely Baroque church, belies its importance, for it actually is the base for exploring three extraordinary attractions: the largest and most fabulous ice caverns in the world; one of Austria's most spectacular castles; and a four-star culinary delight, Obauer. The riches of Werfen, in other words, place it on a par with many larger, more highly touted Austrian cities.

★ From miles away you can see **Burg Hohenwerfen,** one of the most formidable fortresses of Europe (it was never taken in battle), which dates from 1077. Though fires, reconstructions, and renovations have altered the appearance of the imposing fortress, it still maintains its medieval grandeur. Hewn out of the rock on which it stands, the castle was called by Maximilian I a "plume of heraldry radiant against the sky." Inside, it has black-timber beamed state rooms and an enormous frescoed Knights' Hall. It even has a torture chamber. Eagles, falcons, and other birds of prey swoop dramatically above the castle grounds, adding considerably to the medieval feel. The castle harbors Austria's first museum of falconry, and the birds of prey are rigorously trained. Special shows with music, falconry, and performers in period costume are held at least twice a month; call ahead for dates and times. ☎06468/7603 ⊕*www.salzburg-burgen.at* ✒*€10, including tour and birds-of-prey performance; €3 for lift* ☉ *Apr., Tues.–Sun. 9:30–4; May, June, and Sept., daily 9–5; July and Aug., daily 9–6; Oct. and Nov., daily 9:30–4; Birds-of-prey performance daily at 11 and 3.*

8

OFF THE
BEATEN
PATH

Eisriesenwelt. The "World of the Ice Giants," just southwest of Abtenau, houses the largest known complex of ice caves, domes, galleries, and halls in Europe. It extends for some 42 km (26 mi) and contains a fantastic collection of frozen waterfalls and natural formations. Drive to the rest house, about halfway up the hill, and be prepared for some seriously scenic vistas. Then walk 15 minutes to the cable car, which takes you to a point about 15 minutes on foot from the cave, where you can take a 1¼-hour guided tour. You can also take a bus to the cable car from the Werfen **railroad station** (☎*06468/5293* ⊠*€5.90*), but be sure to leave at least an hour before the start of the next scheduled cave trip. The entire adventure takes about half a day. And remember, no matter how warm it is outside, it's below freezing inside, so bundle up, and wear appropriate shoes. You must be in good shape, as there are 700 steps. ☎*06468/5291 or 06468/5248* ⊠*€19, including cable car* ⊙ *Tours May–June and Sept.–Oct., daily 9:30–3:30; July and Aug., daily 9:30–4:30.*

WHERE TO STAY & EAT

$$$$

Fodor's Choice

★

✕**Obauer.** Among Austria's top dining spots, Obauer is presided over by the brothers Karl and Rudolf, who share chef-de-cuisine responsibilities. Thanks to their flair, this has become a culinary shrine, especially for Salzburgers. Trout strudel, sole with peaches and nutmeg, or stuffed duck (anyone for a garnish of mugwort?)—any of these specialties might top the nightly bill of fare. Regional delights, such as Pongau lamb, are deftly mixed with newer-than-now nouvelle garnishes, many inspired by the brothers' far-flung travels. Obauer also has a dozen sweetly traditional guest rooms. ⊠*Markt 46* ☎*06468/5212–0* ⚐*Reservations essential* ⊟*AE.*

$

⊞**Hotel-Garni Erzherzog Eugen.** You can't miss this hot-pink hotel with window boxes trailing garlands of geraniums, as it's smack in the middle of town. Though the decor is basic and a bit bland—traditional white-lace curtains and nondescript furniture—the staff extends a warm and hospitable welcome. The lodging is under the same management as the nearby Obauer. **Pros:** budget rates; friendly staff. **Cons:** often booked up in advance. ⊠*Markt 38* ☎*06468/5210–0* ⇆*12 rooms* ⚐*In-room: no a/c, safe, refrigerator. In-hotel: bar* ⊟*MC, V* ⊗*BP, MAP.*

Innsbruck & Tirol

WORD OF MOUTH

"[From Innsbruck] take the Stubaitalbahn (a narrow-gauge train) from downtown by the Bahnhof up to the end of the line at Fulpmes, a trip lasting about an hour and taking you through some great scenery. Spend a little time strolling around Fulpmes or perhaps take a cable car up the mountain for higher level hiking. Then return by the same train. The train ride alone is a delight."

—geebee14

Updated
by Daniela
Lettner and
Giambattista
Pace

THE PROVINCE TIROL IS SO different from the rest of Austria that you might think you've crossed a border, and in a way you have. The frontier between Salzburg and Tirol is defined by mountains; four passes routed over them are what make traffic possible. The faster trains cut across Germany rather than agonizing through the Austrian Alps. To the west, Tirol is separated from neighboring Vorarlberg by the Arlberg Range.

In winter you'll find masses of deep, sparkling powder snow; unrivaled skiing and tobogganing, and bizarre winter carnivals with grotesquely masked mummers. Come summer, you can enjoy breathtaking picture-postcard Alpine scenery, cool mountain lakes, and rambles through forests. Throughout the year there are yodeling and zither music, villagers in lederhosen and broad-brim feathered hats, and, of course, the sounds of those distinctive cowbells.

And what about the Tyroleans themselves? Like most other mountain peoples, the Tyroleans are proud and independent—so much so that for many centuries the natives of one narrow valley fastness had little communication with their "foreign" neighbors in the next valley. (It's still possible to find short, dark, and slender residents in one valley and blond, blue-eyed, strapping giants in the next.) But Tirol can also be very cosmopolitan, as any visitor to Innsbruck will attest. The city is Tirol's treasure house—historically, culturally, and commercially. It's also sited smack dab in the center of the Tyrolean region and makes a convenient base from which to explore. Even if you are staying at an area resort, spend a day or two in Innsbruck first: it will give you a clearer perspective on the rest of the region.

ORIENTATION & PLANNING

GETTING ORIENTED

Innsbruck makes a good starting point for exploring Tirol, but Tirol's gorgeous geography precludes the convenient loop tour from the capital city. You must go into the valleys to discover the charming villages and hotels, and a certain amount of backtracking is necessary. We've outlined four tours over familiar routes, touching on the best of the towns and suggesting side trips and some pleasures that are off the beaten track. Whether you mix or match these tours or do them all, they'll allow you to discover a cross section of Tirol's highlights: the old and the new, glossy resorts, medieval castles, and, always, that extraordinary scenery.

Innsbruck. A city that preserves the charm of ancient times, Innsbruck has everything to offer: interesting culture, stellar restaurants, and trendy nightclubs. It's the ideal starting point for visiting Tirol.

The Lower Inn Valley. Northeast of Innsbruck, this area is famous for the romantic old towns of Hall and Schwaz. It's adored by families and outdoors enthusiasts, and is one of Austria's most famous folk music regions.

TOP REASONS TO GO

The Ötz Valley. Outdoors enthusiasts love hiking through this region because of rich green pastures in summer and glittering expanses of white in winter.

Spas everywhere. Almost every hotel in Tirol has spa facilities, large sauna areas, and swimming pools, which makes this a very relaxing stay.

Fancy skiing areas. Known around the world for its posh resorts, Tirol is where high-society types gathers to experience the good life.

Tyrolean Stuben. These warm and cozy wooden parlors, often found today in hotels and restaurants, are traditionally part of old farmhouses in Tirol.

Outdoor sports. From skiing to mountain biking, Tirol is a paradise for adventurous types.

The Road to Kitzbühel. Richly decorated farmhouses line the roads here. The sunny valley has plenty of snow in winter and golf in summer. Posh resorts and a renowned ski area make Kitzbühel the region's number one holiday destination.

West from Innsbruck. Located in the very heart of Tirol, the villages of Telfs and Imst are known for tradition and culture. The Ötz valley, with its long trekking routes and outdoor facilities, is one of Tirol's most beautiful valleys.

Landeck, Upper Inn Valley & St. Anton. The western part of Tirol is a winter heaven. Steep and challenging slopes, along with well-trained instructors, made St. Anton famous. High in the mountains are the towns of Ischgl and Galtür.

9

PLANNING

WHEN TO GO

The physical geography of the Tirol makes it an ideal place in which to enjoy the outdoor life year-round. Ski-crazy travelers descend on the resorts during the winter months; in summer, when the mountains are awash with wildflowers, camping tents spring up like mushrooms in the valleys as hikers, spelunkers, mountain bikers, and climbers take advantage of the palatial peaks. High season for summer activities is from July to August, while the skiing season begins late December and ends late March or early April.

FESTIVALS

The annual Tyrolean calendar is packed with special events: the famous Schemenlaufen, a procession of carved wooden masks, held in February in Imst; the Fasching balls, which reach their peak at the end of February; the Hahnenkamm ski race and curling competition held in winter in Kitzbühel; the world-famous Gauder Fest at Zell am Ziller during the first weekend in May; the castle concerts and music

GREAT ITINERARIES

IF YOU HAVE 3 DAYS

Head straight to the heart of Tirol to the provincial capital of ⊞ **Innsbruck**. The city is conveniently situated for access to Tirol, for it lies almost exactly in the center of the province on the Inn River. Check out the beautiful buildings built by the Emperor Maximilian I—from the **Goldenes Dachl** to the **Hofburg**—and by Austria's Empress Maria Theresa, who gave her name to the principal street of the town, the Maria-Theresien-Strasse; any sightseeing in Innsbruck begins on this street, which runs through the heart of the city from north to south and is the main shopping center. Far from being exhausting to explore, Innsbruck is only a half-hour walk from one end of the Old Town to the other. The next day, let the funicular whisk you up the **Hungerburg** for the breathtaking views of Innsbruck below. You can take a leisurely hike along the mountain trail and see the flora and fauna at the Alpine zoo. Alternatively, take the **Sightseer** bus to the observation deck and restaurant atop the **Bergisel** ski jump, which has a superb view of Innsbruck and the Nordkette mountains to the north. After returning to lower ground, set out on your final day to visit **Schloss Ambras**, with its impressive collections of medieval curiosities—pack a picnic and stay for a concert if you're traveling during the summer season. More ambitious travelers should consider a quick day trip to the seriously scenic **Stubaital Valley**, one of the showpieces of the Tirol—via the narrow-gauge electric Stubaitalbahn.

IF YOU HAVE 5 DAYS

Begin your Tyrolean sojourn with two days in attraction-studded ⊞ **Innsbruck**—but don't forget to experience your first taste of the region's grand Alpine landscape by fitting in some quick excursions to the outlying **Hungerburg** peak, **Schloss Ambras**, or the **Swarovski Crystal World** in nearby Wattens. On Day 3, start off with a train ride from Innsbruck's main station to **Seefeld**, a charming Alpine resort. Wind your way up—and, at times, through—the mountain on your way to the Seefeld plateau. Splurge on a horse-drawn carriage ride around the lake, go for a round of golf, or in winter work out on the world-class cross-country ski trails. On the fourth day, spend time exploring castle ruins, Baroque churches, and yet more spectacular scenery in **Imst** and **Landeck**. For the peak experience of your trip—literally—head to the slopes on your final day at **St. Anton am Arlberg**. Keep in mind that modern highways can get you to your destination quickly, but often the most beautiful scenic views lie on off-the-beaten-track roads. If you prefer staying closer to Innsbruck on your last day, ride the old-fashioned trolley (Tram 6 departs hourly from the main train station or the Bergisel tram station) to **Igls**, on a sunny plateau south of Innsbruck overlooking the valley.

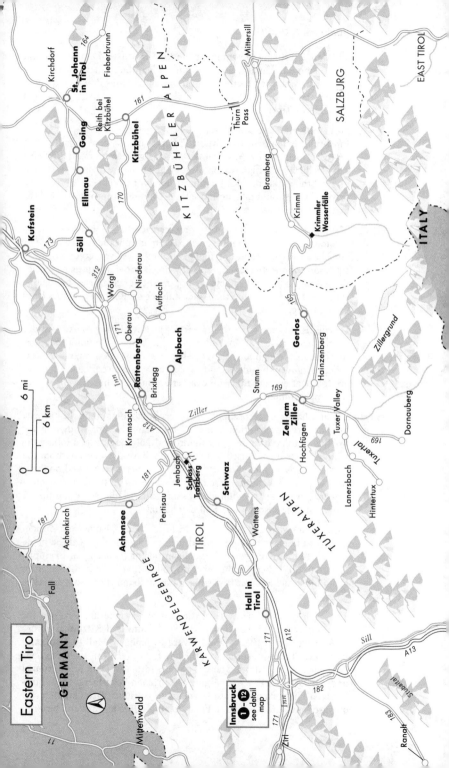

Eastern Tirol

GERMANY

EAST TIROL

ITALY

TIROL

Innsbruck ❶–⓬
see detail map

Mittenwald

Fall

Achenkirch

Pertisau

Achensee

KARWENDELGEBIRGE

Kufstein

Söll

Ellmau

Going

St. Johann in Tirol

Kirchdorf

Fieberbrunn

Reith bei Kitzbühel

Kitzbühel

ALPEN

KITZBÜHELER

Wörgl

Niederau

Oberau

Auffach

Rattenberg

Brixlegg

Kramsach

Alpbach

Ziller

Jenbach

Schloss Tratzberg

Schwaz

Wattens

Hall in Tirol

Stumm

Zell am Ziller

Hochfügen

TUXERALPEN

Tuxer Valley

Hainzenberg

Gerlos

Zillergrund

Dornauberg

Tuxertal

Lanersbach

Hintertux

Krimml

◆ **Krimmler Wasserfälle**

Bramberg

Mittersill

Thurn Pass

SALZB JRG

Sill

A12

A13

Stubaital

Ranalt

Zirl

Inn

6 mi

6 km

and dance festivals in summer, primarily in Kufstein and Innsbruck; the ceremonial Almabtrieb in autumn, when the farmers bring down their richly adorned cattle from mountain pastures down to the valley for the winter; and the many village harvest festivals in the fall throughout Tirol.

GETTING HERE & AROUND

Innsbruck Flughafen, the airport 3 km (2 mi) west of Innsbruck, is served principally by Austrian Airlines, as well as by many low-cost carriers during the high season. Buses (Line F) to the main train station in Innsbruck take about 20 minutes. Get your ticket (€1.70) from the driver. Taxis should take no more than 10 minutes into town, and the fare is about €10–€12.

BY BUS The bus is the most convenient way to reach the six major ski areas outside the city. A Club Innsbruck pass (free from the tourist office or your hotel if you spend one night or more) gives you complimentary transportation to the ski areas; many hotels provide shuttle service to the special ski bus stop. These are not the regular city buses, but deluxe ski buses that leave from the Landestheater on Rennweg, across from the Hofburg.

Driving is the best way to see Tirol, since it allows you to wander off the main routes at your pleasure or to stop and admire the view. In Tirol, as throughout Austria, where the train doesn't go, the post-office or railway bus does, and except in the most remote areas buses are frequent enough that you can get around, but bus travel requires time and planning.

BY CAR The autobahns are fastest, but for scenery you're best off on the byways. One important exception is the 1¾-km (1-mi) Europa Bridge on the Brenner autobahn running south into Italy, although if you follow the parallel route from Patsch to Pfons, you'll have the views without the traffic. Roads with particularly attractive scenery are marked on highway maps with a parallel green line. To drive on Austria's autobahn, a *vignette*, or sticker, is required, for sale at almost all service stations. A 10-day sticker costs €7.70, a 60-day €22.20.

BY TRAIN Direct trains serve Innsbruck from Munich, Vienna, Rome, and Zürich. Some of the most fascinating and memorable side trips can be made by rail: two narrow-gauge lines steam out of Jenbach, for example, one up to the Achensee, the other down to Mayrhofen in the Zillertal. From Innsbruck, the narrow-gauge Stubaitalbahn runs south to Telfes and Fulpmes.

The main railway line of Tirol runs east–west, entering Tirol via the Griessen Pass, then heading on to St. Johann and Kitzbühel before wandering over to Wörgl and onward to Jenbach, Hall in Tirol, and Innsbruck. From Innsbruck on, the line follows the Inn Valley to Landeck, then to St. Anton, where it plunges into an 11-km (7-mi) tunnel under the Arlberg range, emerging at Langen in Vorarlberg. From Innsbruck, a line runs north into Germany to Garmish-Partenkirchen and onward back into Austria, to Ehrwald and Reutte in Tirol and beyond, into Germany again. A line from Innsbruck to the south goes over the dramatic Brenner Pass (4,465 feet) into Italy.

ESSENTIALS

Airport Information **Innsbruck Flughafen Airport** (*INN* ☎ *0512/22525 flight information* ⊕ *www.innsbruck-airport.com*).

Bus Information **Postbus AG** (☎ *0512/390390 or 0810/222333* ⊕ *www. postbus.at*).

Train Information **Österreichisches Bundesbahn** (☎ *05–1717 information and reservations* ⊕ *www.oebb.at*).

Visitor Information **Austrian National Tourist Board** (⊕ *www.tirol.at*).

ABOUT THE RESTAURANTS & HOTELS

Tyrolean restaurants range from grand-hotel dining salons to little Tyrolean *Wirtshäuser,* rustic restaurants where you can enjoy hearty local specialties like *Tiroler Gröstl* (a skillet dish made of beef, potatoes, and onions), *Knödel* (dumpling) soup, or *Schweinsbraten* (roast pork with sauerkraut), while sitting on highly polished wooden seats (rather hard ones!). Don't forget to enjoy some of the fine Innsbruck coffeehouses, famous for their scrumptious cakes and cappuccino.

For one reason or another, travelers do not stay long in Innsbruck itself. Innsbruck hotels report the average stay is usually two to three days in summer and one week in winter, so there is a fast turnover and, almost always, a room to be had. Even so, if you travel during the high season (July and August) or in the winter, it's best to book in advance. If you're driving, ask in advance about parking, since some hotels have free on-site spots, while others offer parking a short distance away. Hotel rates vary widely by season, the off-peak periods being March–May and September–November. Some travelers opt to set up their base not in Innsbruck but *overlooking* it, on the Hungerburg Plateau to the north, or in one of the nearby villages perched on the slopes to the south. In any case, the official **Innsbruck Reservation Center,** online at ⊕*www. innsbruck.info* or ⊕*www.ski-innsbruck.at*, offers a one-stop booking source for Innsbruck and the surrounding villages, as well as a trove of Visitor Information.

Room rates include taxes and service and, except in the most expensive hotels, almost always breakfast and one other meal. *Halb pension* (half-board), as this plan is called, is usually the best deal. However, most will offer a breakfast buffet–only rate if requested. Most hotels now take credit cards. If you're out for savings, it's a good idea to find lodgings in small towns nearby rather than in the resorts themselves; local tourist offices may be able to help you get situated, possibly even with accommodations in pensions (simple hotels) or *Bauernhöfe* (farmhouses). Note that the most expensive hotels in the posh resort towns of Kitzbühel, St. Anton, and Seefeld have room rates higher than our price-category norm; their rooms can occasionally reach as high as €400.

⚠Keep in mind that in hotel saunas and steam baths, nude people of both genders should be expected. Children under certain ages are usually not admitted.

WHAT IT COSTS IN EUROS					
	¢	$	$$	$$$	$$$$
RESTAURANTS	under €7	€7–€12	€13–€17	€18–€22	over €22
HOTELS	under €70	€70–€100	€100–€135	€135–€175	over €175

Restaurant prices are per person for a main course at dinner. Hotel prices are for a standard double room in high season, including taxes and service. Assume that hotels operate on the European Plan (EP, with no meal provided) unless we note that they use the Breakfast Plan (BP), Modified American Plan (MAP, with breakfast and dinner daily, known as halb pension), or Full American Plan (FAP, or voll pension, with three meals a day). Higher prices (inquire when booking) prevail for any meal plans.

INNSBRUCK

★ *190 km (118 mi) southwest of Salzburg, 471 km (304 mi) southwest of Vienna, 146 km (91 mi) south of Munich.*

The capital of Tirol is one of the most beautiful towns of its size anywhere in the world, owing much of its charm and fame to its unique location. To the north, the steep, sheer sides of the Alps rise, literally from the edge of the city, like a shimmering blue-and-white wall—an impressive backdrop for the mellowed green domes and red roofs of the Baroque town tucked below. To the south, the peaks of the Tuxer and Stubai ranges undulate in the hazy purple distance.

Squeezed by the mountains and sharing the valley with the Inn River (Innsbruck means "bridge over the Inn"), the city is compact and very easy to explore on foot. Reminders of three historic figures abound: the local hero Andreas Hofer, whose band of patriots challenged Napoléon in 1809; Emperor Maximilian I (1459–1519); and Empress Maria Theresa (1717–80), the last two responsible for much of the city's architecture. Maximilian ruled the Holy Roman Empire from Innsbruck, and Maria Theresa, who was particularly fond of the city, spent a substantial amount of time here.

GETTING HERE & AROUND

Innsbruck is connected by bus to other parts of Tirol, and the Innsbruck bus terminal is beside the train station. Direct trains serve Innsbruck from Munich, Vienna, Rome, and Zürich, and all arrive at the railroad station *Innsbruck Hauptbahnhof* at Südtiroler Platz. The station is outfitted with restaurants, cafés, a supermarket, and even a post office.

In Innsbruck, most bus and streetcar routes begin or end at Maria-Theresien-Strasse, nearby Bozner Platz, or the main train station (Hauptbahnhof). You can get single tickets costing €1.70 on the bus or streetcar. You can transfer to another line with the same ticket as long as you continue in more or less the same direction in a single journey.

If you're driving, remember that the Altstadt (Old City) is a pedestrian zone. Private cars are not allowed on many streets, and parking requires vouchers that you buy from blue coin-operated dispensers found around parking areas. Each half hour normally costs €0.50–€1.

In Innsbruck taxis are not much faster than walking, particularly along the one-way streets and in the Old City. Basic fare is €5.20 for the first 1½ km (1 mi). Funktaxi is a good option if you want to call a cab.

Horse-drawn cabs, still a feature of Innsbruck life, can be hired at the stand in front of the Landestheater. Set the price before you head off; a half-hour ride will cost around €25.

The red **Sightseer** bus, a service of the Innsbruck Tourist Office, is the best way to see the sights of Innsbruck without walking. It features a recorded commentary in several languages, including English. There are two routes, both beginning from Maria-Theresien-Strasse in the Old City, but you can catch the bus from any of the nine marked stops, and jump off and on the bus whenever you like. The ride is free with your Innsbruck Card, or buy your ticket from the driver or at the tourist office.

Guided walking tours of the Old City daily at 11 and 2 highlight historic personalities and some offbeat features associated with Innsbruck.

Innsbruck's main tourist office is open daily 9–6. Tirol's provincial tourist bureau, the Tirol Werbung, is also in Innsbruck. The Österreichischer Alpenverein is the place to go for information on Alpine huts and mountaineering advice. It's open weekdays 8:30–6, Saturday 9–noon.

ESSENTIALS
Bus Information **Postbus AG** (☎ *0512/390390 or 0810/222333* ⊕ *www. postbus.at*).

Taxi Information **Funktaxi** (☎ *0512/5311*).

Train Information **Innsbruck Hauptbahnhof** (✉ *Südtiroler Platz* ☎ *0512/93000–0*). **Österreichisches Bundesbahn** (☎ *05–1717 information and reservations* ⊕ *www. oebb.at*).

Visitor Information **Innsbruck Tourist Office** (✉ *Burggraben 3A-6021* ☎ *0512/59850* ⊕ *www.innsbruck.info*). **Österreichischer Alpenverein** (✉ *Wilhelm-Greil-Strasse 15* ☎ *0512/59547*). **Tirol Werbung** (✉ *Maria-Theresien-Strasse 55,* ☎ *0512/7272* ⊕ *www.tirol.at*).

EXPLORING INNSBRUCK

MAIN ATTRACTIONS
❹ The main attraction of the Baroque **Domkirche zu St. Jakob** is the high-altar painting of the Madonna by Lucas Cranach the Elder, dating from about 1530. The cathedral was built in 1722. In the ornate Baroque interior, look in the north aisle for a 1620 monument honoring Archduke Maximilian III. ✉ *Domplatz 6* ☎ *0512/5839–02* ☜ *Free* ☻ *Nov.–Apr., Mon.–Sat. 7:30–6:30; May–Oct., daily 7:30–7:30 except during worship.*

CLUB INNSBRUCK CARD

Pick up a free Club Innsbruck card at your hotel for no-charge use of ski buses and reduced-charge ski-lift passes. For big savings, buy the **all-inclusive Innsbruck Card,** which gives you free admission to all museums, mountain cable cars, the Alpenzoo, and Schloss Ambras, plus free bus and tram transportation, including bus service to nearby **Hall in Tirol.** The card includes unlimited ride-hopping onboard the big red **Sightseer** bus, which whisks you in air-conditioned comfort to all of the major sights, and even provides recorded commentary in English and five other languages. Cards are good for 24, 48, and 72 hours at €25, €30, and €35, respectively, and are available at the tourist office, on cable cars, and in larger museums.

8 The **Ferdinandeum** (*Tyrolean State Museum Ferdinandeum*) houses Austria's largest collection of Gothic art, 19th- and 20th-century paintings, and medieval arms, along with special exhibitions. Here you'll find the original coats of arms from the Goldenes Dachl balcony. Chamber music concerts are offered throughout the year. ⊠ *Museumstrasse 5* ☎ *0512/59489–9* ⊕ *www.tiroler-landesmuseen.at* ⊠ *€8 combined ticket with Zeughaus and Hofkirche* ⊗ *Tues.–Sun. 9–6.*

NEED A BREAK? Within the Ferdinandeum, Kunstpause (⊠ *Museumstrasse 15* ☎ *512/ 572020*), the "Art pause," offers breakfast, light meals, and a wine bar in elegant but relaxed surroundings.

1 Any walking tour of Innsbruck should start at the **Goldenes Dachl**
Fodor'sChoice (*Golden Roof*), which made famous the late-Gothic mansion whose
★ balcony it covers. In fact, the roof is capped with 2,600 gilded copper tiles, and its refurbishment is said to have taken nearly 31 pounds of gold. Legend has it that the house was built in the 1400s for Duke Friedrich (otherwise known as Friedl the Penniless), and that the indignant duke had the original roof covered with gold to counter the rumor that he was poor. In truth, the 15th-century house was owned by Maximilian I, who added a balcony in 1501 as a sort of "royal box" for watching street performances in the square below. The structure was altered and expanded at the beginning of the 18th century, and now only the loggia and the alcove are identifiable as original. Maximilian is pictured in the two central sculpted panels on the balcony. In the one on the left, he is with his first and second wives, Maria of Burgundy and Bianca Maria Sforza of Milan; on the right, he is pictured with an adviser and a court jester. The magnificent coats of arms representing Austria, Hungary, Burgundy, Milan, the Holy Roman Empire, Styria, Tirol, and royal Germany are copies. You can see the originals (and up close, too) in the Ferdinandeum. The Golden Roof building houses the **Maximilianeum,** a small museum that headlines memorabilia and paintings from the life of Emperor Maximilian I. The short video presenta-

tion about Maximilian is worth a look. ⊠*Herzog-Friedrich-Strasse 15* ☎*0512/5811–11* ⊡*€4* ⊘*Oct.–Apr., Tues.–Sun. 10–5; May–Sept., daily 10–5.*

NEED A BREAK?

The small bakery and café called **Kröll** (⊠*Hofgasse 6* ☎*0512/574347*), a few steps from the Goldenes Dachl, offers homemade Strudel (sweet or savory fillings wrapped in a fine pastry) and Italian coffee specialties.

⑤ ★ One of Innsbruck's most historic attractions is the **Hofburg,** or Imperial Palace, which Maximilian I commissioned in the 15th century. Center stage is the **Giant's Hall**—designated a marvel of the 18th century as soon as it was topped off with its magnificent trompe-l'oeil ceiling painted by Franz Anton Maulpertsch in 1775. The Rococo decoration and the portraits of Habsburg ancestors in the ornate white-and-gold great reception hall were added in the 18th century by Maria Theresa; look for the portrait of "Primal" (primrose)—to use the childhood nickname of the empress's daughter, Marie-Antoinette. The booklet in English available at the ticket office will tell you more interesting tidbits about the palace than the tour guide. ⊠*Rennweg 1* ☎*0512/587186* ⊡*€5.50* ⊘ *Tours daily at 11 and 2.*

② Down the street from the Goldenes Dachl is the **Stadtturm,** a 15th-century city tower, with a steep climb of 148 steps to the top. ⊠*Herzog-Friedrich-Strasse 21* ☎*0512/5615–00* ⊡*€3* ⊘*Oct.–May, daily 10–5; June–Sept., daily 10–8.*

ALSO WORTH SEEING

⑨ The **Annasäule,** or St. Anne's Column, erected in 1706, commemorates the withdrawal of Bavarian forces in the war of the Spanish Succession on St. Anne's Day (July 26) in 1703. From here is a classic view of Innsbruck's Altstadt (Old City), with the glorious Nordkette mountain range in the background. ⊠*Maria-Theresien-Strasse.*

⑫ The ski-jumping stadium **Bergisel** now towers over Innsbruck as never before with a gloriously modern, concrete-and-glass observation deck and restaurant designed by world-celebrated architect Zaha Hadid. It's easy to reach using the **Sightseer** bus from Innsbruck. Parking a car will cost you €3.40 for 90 minutes. ⊠*Bergiselweg 3* ☎*0512/589259* ⊕*www.bergisel.info* ⊡*€8.30; free with Innsbruck Card* ⊘*Nov.–May daily 10–5; June–Oct. daily 9–6; restaurant daily 9–5.*

⑪ A visit to the 400-year-old **Grassmayr Bell Foundry** contains a fascinating little museum, and will give you an idea of how bells are cast and tuned. Guided tours in English can be arranged. Take Bus J, K, or S south to Grassmayrstrasse. ⊠*Leopoldstrasse 53* ☎*0512/59416–37* *www.grassmayr.at* ⊡*€5* ⊘*Oct.–Apr., weekdays 9–5; May–Sept., weekdays 9–5, Sat. 9–5*

③ Facing the Stadtturm is the dramatic blue-and-white **Helbling House,** originally a Gothic building (1560) to which the obvious, ornate Rococo decoration was added in 1730. ⊠*Herzog-Friedrich-Strasse 10.*

⑥ Close by the Hofburg is the **Hofkirche** (*Court Church*), built as a mausoleum for Maximilian I (although he is actually buried in Wiener

9

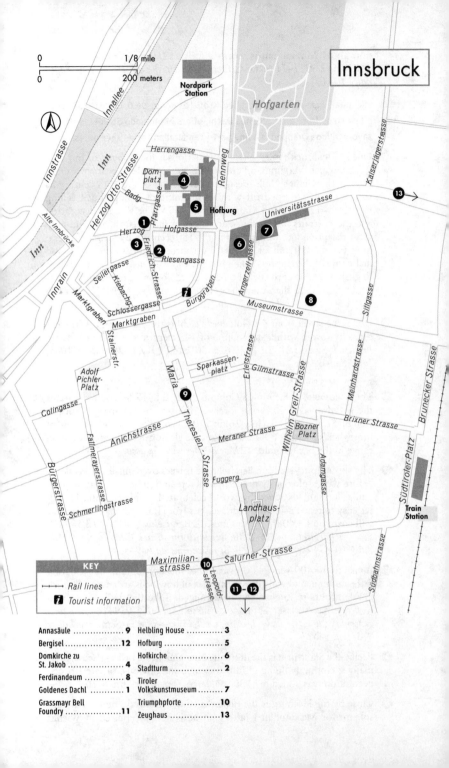

Innsbruck

0 ——— 1/8 mile
0 ——— 200 meters

Nordpark Station

Hofgarten

Innstrasse

Innallee

Inn

Herzog Otto-Strasse

Alte Innbrücke

Inn

Innrain

Herrengasse

Dom-platz

4

5 **Hofburg**

Renweg

Kaiserjägerstrasse

Universitätsstrasse

13

Badg.

Pfarrgasse

1

Herzog

Hofgasse

3

2

Riesengasse

Friedrich-Strasse

Seilergasse

Kiebachg.

Schlossergasse

Marktgraben

Stainerstr.

Marktgraben

6

7

Angerzellgasse

Burggraben

i

Museumstrasse

8

Sillgasse

Adolf Pichler-Platz

Maria

Sparkassen-platz

Gilmstrasse

Erlerstrasse

Wilhelm Greil-Strasse

Meinhardstrasse

Brunecker Strasse

Colingasse

Anichstrasse

Theresien - Strasse

Meraner Strasse

Bozner Platz

Brixner Strasse

Südtiroler-Platz

Falmerayerstrasse

Burgerstrasse

Schmerlingstrasse

9

Fuggerg.

Landhaus-platz

Adamgasse

Train Station

Maximilian-strasse

10

Salurner-Strasse

Leopold-strasse

Südbahnstrasse

11 – 12

KEY

↔ *Rail lines*

i *Tourist information*

Neustadt, south of Vienna). The emperor's ornate black-marble tomb is surrounded by 24 marble reliefs depicting his accomplishments, as well as 28 larger-than-life-size statues of his ancestors, including the legendary King Arthur of England. Andreas Hofer is also buried here. Don't miss the 16th-century **Silver Chapel,** up the stairs opposite the entrance, with its elaborate altar and silver Madonna. The chapel was built in 1578 to be the tomb of Archduke Ferdinand II and his wife, Philippine Welser, the daughter of a rich and powerful merchant family. ■TIP→ Visit the chapel for picture-taking in the morning; the blinding afternoon sun comes in directly behind the altar. ⊠ *Universitätsstrasse 2* ☎ *0512/59489–511* ⊕ *www.hofkirche.at* ⊠ *€4, €8 combined ticket with Zeughaus and Ferdinandeum* ⊘ *Mon.–Sat. 9–5, Sun. 12:30–5.*

⑦ The **Tiroler Volkskunstmuseum** (*Tyrolean Folk Art Museum*), in the same complex as the Hofkirche, exhibits Christmas crèches, costumes, rustic furniture, and entire rooms from old farmhouses and inns, decorated in styles ranging from Gothic to Rococo. Displays are somewhat static, and the information cards are in German. The small Christmas Manger Museum, on the other hand, is fascinating. At this writing it was under renovation until early 2009. ⊠ *Universitätsstrasse 2* ☎ *0512/59489–511* ⊕ *www.tiroler-volkskunstmuseum.at* ⊠ *€5* ⊘ *Mon.–Sat. 9–5, Sun. and holidays 10–5.*

⑩ The **Triumphpforte,** or Triumphal Arch, was built in 1765 to commemorate both the marriage of emperor-to-be Leopold II (then Duke of Tuscany) and the death of Emperor Franz I, husband of Empress Maria Theresa. One side clearly represents celebration, and the other, tragedy. ⊠ *Salurner-Strasse.*

⑬ The museum in the **Zeughaus** (the former weapon depot of Maximilian I) displays aspects of Tirol's culture and regional history in chronological order. ⊠ *Zeughausgasse* ☎ *0512/59489–11* ⊕ *www.tiroler-landes museen.at* ⊠ *€8 combined ticket with Ferdinandeum and Hofkirche* ⊘ *Tues.–Sun. 9–6.*

THREE EXCURSIONS FROM INNSBRUCK

NORDPARK

☾ The **Nordpark Funicular** brings you from the city center to the Hungerburg Plateau, then up the Nordkettenbahn Cableway to the top of the mountain for a commanding view of Innsbruck. The round-trip to Hungerburg costs €5.60; the round-trip to Hafelekar is €24.50, or is free with the all-inclusive Innsbruck Card. The futuristic base station can be reached in five minutes by foot from the Goldenes Dachl. The Sightseer bus also takes you to the base station. ⊠ *Rennweg* ☎ *0512/292323* ⊕ *www.nordpark.com.*

☾ The **Alpenzoo** has an unusual collection of Alpine birds and animals, including endangered species. The zoo alone is worth the trip up the Hungerburg. A ticket that includes round-trip transportation is €9. From the Markthalle bus terminal, buses marked "W" run every 30 minutes to the Alpenzoo between 7 AM and 10 PM. ⊠ *Weiherburggasse*

9

37A ☎*0512/292323* ⊕*www.alpenzoo.at* ✉*€7, children €3.50; free with Innsbruck Card* ⊙*Apr.–Oct., daily 9–6; Nov.–Mar., daily 9–5.*

SCHLOSS AMBRAS

When Archduke Ferdinand II wanted to marry a commoner for love, the court grudgingly allowed it, but the couple was forced to live outside the city limits. Ferdinand revamped a 10th-century castle for the bride, Philippine Welser, which was completed in 1556 and was every bit as luxe as what he had been accustomed to in town. Amid acres of gardens and woodland, it is an inviting castle with cheery red-and-white shutters on its many windows, and is, curiously, home to an oddball collection of armaments. The upper castle now houses rooms of noble portraits and the lower section has the collection of weaponry and armor. Be sure to inspect Philippine's sunken bath, a luxury for its time. Look around the grounds as well to see the fencing field and a small cemetery containing samples of earth from 18 battlefields around the world. The castle is 3 km (2 mi) southeast of the city. To reach it without a car, take Tram 3 or 6 to Ambras (a short walk from the castle) or Route 1 on the **Sightseer** from Maria-Theresien-Strasse. ✉*Schloss Strasse 20* ☎*0152/524745* ⊕*www.khm.at/ambras* ✉*Prices vary, check Web site* ⊙*Sept., Oct., and Dec.–July, daily 10–5; Aug., daily 10–7*

THE STUBAITAL VALLEY

The delightful little Stubai Valley, less than 40-km (25-mi) long, is one of the showpieces of the Tirol, with no fewer than 80 glistening glaciers and more than 40 towering peaks. If you just want to look, you can see the whole Stubaital in a full day's excursion from Innsbruck. The narrow-gauge electric **Stubaitalbahn** (departure from the center of Innsbruck on Maria-Theresien-Strasse and in front of the main rail station, as well as from the station just below the Bergisel ski jump) goes as far as Fulpmes, partway up the valley. You can take the bus as far as Ranalt and back to Fulpmes, to see more of the valley, then return on the quaint rail line.

Buses leave from Gate 1 of the **Autobusbahnhof** (✉*Stubaitalbahn* ☎*0512/5307–102*), just behind the rail station at Südtiroler Platz, about every hour.

WHERE TO EAT

$$$$ ✗**Lichtblick.** This little restaurant's location atop the seventh floor of the chic **Rathausgalerie might be lofty, but so is its reputation.** The all-around glass of Lichtblick (which means "bright spot") provides you with sensational views of the Old City. The kitchen, overseen by Andreas Zeindlinger, offers wonderfully creative, always captivating dishes made from the freshest local ingredients. The menu changes often and the desserts are especially good. ■**TIP→ If you're not lucky enough to get dinner reservations, score a table at the adjacent Cafe Bar Lounge 360.** ✉*Rathaus Gallery, Maria-Theresienstrasse 18* ☎*0512/566550* ⚲*Reservations essential* ▤*AE, DC, MC, V* ⊙*Closed Sun.*

$$$$ ✕**Pavillon.** In stark contrast to the surrounding stately buildings, this two-story gleaming glass box houses a café on the ground floor during the day and an au courant dining experience upstairs in the evening. Iranian-born chef Mansur Memarian keeps up a creative international menu, with a dedication to local and seasonal ingredients. Only a few fish and meat creations are listed in the menu, and these tend to change often. The Tahiti sorbet in Catalan cream foam served with seasonal fruit is a year-round favorite. Low armchairs create a fashionable and comfortable atmosphere for this hip Innsbruck landmark. ⊠ *Rennweg 4* ☎ *0512/25700–0* ⊟ *AE, DC, MC, V* ✆ *Closed Sun. and Mon. No lunch.*

$$$–$$$$ ✕**Schwarzer Adler.** This intimate, romantic restaurant on the ground floor of the Schwarzer Adler Hotel has leaded-glass windows and rustic embellishments—and in summer, dining on the rooftop terrace—offering the perfect backdrop for a memorable meal. The innovative cooks present a new menu every couple of months based on regional seasonal specialties. The year-round classics, such as the garlic soup with croutons, or three kinds of local dumplings served with sauerkraut, are delicious. ⊠ *Kaiserjägerstrasse 2* ☎ *0512/587109* ⊟ *AE, DC, MC, V.*

$$$ ✕**Europastüberl.** Cuisine that is creative, yet draws on traditional recipes, is what you'll find at this elegant and comfortable dining room of the Grand Hotel Europa. Carved wood alcoves, the typical Tirolean Stüberl, harbor intimate tables dressed with white linens and flickering candles. For the last 20 years the signature dish has been Dover sole sautéed in butter—served by the same waiter for the entire time. Seasonal regional specialties, like local game or house-made pastas, are recommended. The four- to seven-course prix-fixe menus are good choices for those who just cannot decide. ⊠ *Brixner Strasse 6* ☎ *0512/5931* ⊟ *AE, DC, MC, V.*

$$$ ✕**Pfefferkorn.** An enormous and colorful crystal chandelier makes a meal at this two-level restaurant an unforgettable experience. The modern decor–dim lighting, dark wood, and the most comfortable armchairs you're likely to find, make the time pass quickly. The cuisine is remarkable as well, including a variety of seasonal dishes culled from the specialties of the region, such as pepper steak. ⊠ *Seilergasse 8* ☎ *0512/565–444* ⊟ *AE, DC, MC, V* ✆ *Closed Mon.*

$$–$$$ ✕**Goldener Adler.** This restaurant is as popular with locals as it is with travelers. The traditional dining rooms on the arcaded ground floor and the summer-only terrace are popular places to sit. (We prefer the former, as they are more romantic and private.) Start with a glass of *Sekt* (a local sparkling wine) flavored with a dash of blackberry liqueur as you peruse the menu. The kitchen takes a modern approached to traditional dishes, so the pork medallions are topped with ham and Gorgonzola, and the veal steaks are ladled with a creamy herb sauce. ⊠ *Herzog-Friedrich-Strasse 6* ☎ *0512/5711* ⊟ *AE, DC, MC, V.*

$$ ✕**Ottoburg.** This family-run restaurant offers excellent food and an extraordinary location. This ancient landmark, built in 1180 as city watchtower, conveys an abundance of historical charm. It's fun just to explore the rabbit warren of paneled rustic rooms named after emperors. Several of the bay-window alcoves in the shuttered house

9

have great views of the main square, while others overlook the river. Try the Tafelspitz, a typical Viennese specialty of boiled beef served with vegetables and horseradish, or the Pfandl, a fillet of pork and a steak served in an old-fashioned pan. ⊠ *Herzog-Friedrich-Strasse 1* ☎ *0512/584338* ⊟ *AE, DC, MC, V* ⊘ *Closed Mon.*

$$ ✕**Seegrube.** If your plans include a Friday night stay in Innsbruck and the weather is clear, try to book a table at this restaurant in the Seegrube cableway station. The four-course dinner includes mostly Tyrolean specialties. The view of the city lights twinkling below makes a good background for a romantic dinner. During the week the self-service buffet feeds hungry hikers. ⊠ *Höhenstrasse 145* ☎ *0512/303065* ⚞ *Reservations essential* ⊟ *MC, V* ⊘ *Closed weekends.*

$$ ✕**Weisses Rössl.** In the authentically rustic dining rooms, an array of antlers adds to the charm. This is the right place for solid local standards, like *Tiroler Gröstl*, a tasty hash, and Wiener Schnitzel (veal cutlet), both of which taste even better on the outside terrace in summer. Ask about the specials that don't appear on the menu, such as wild game or freshly picked mushrooms. Because the place hosts regular local gatherings it can get quite lively here, but all you have to do is request a table in one of the smaller parlors. ⊠ *Kiebachgasse 8* ☎ *0512/583057* ⊟ *AE, MC, V* ⊘ *Closed Sun., early Nov., and mid-Apr.*

$–$$ ✕**Solo Pasta/Solo Vino.** Because "you can't invent the sun," the proud owner says, this restaurant sticks to the tried-and-true. It offers only genuine Italian products hand-chosen by the staff. That means the menu is full of top-quality Tuscan meats and cheeses, fish fresh from the Mediterranean, and freshly made pastas. The Italian wine list is outstanding. Although all the food comes from the same kitchen, the Solo Pasta section of the restaurant is more informal, while Solo Vino has a more exclusive feel. ⊠ *Universitätsstrasse 15b* ☎ *0512/587206* ⊟ *AE, DC, MC, V* ⊘ *Closed Sun. and Mon.*

$ ✕**Cammerlander.** At a given point you might want to escape from the meat-based local meals and head to the city's only real vegetarian choice. Enjoy the breezy spot along the Inn River at a table on the open terrace during the summer or in the glass-enclosed courtyard in the cooler months. Japanese-style noodle soups and pizzas are some of the offerings. Across the corridor you can let yourself be absorbed by the Latin rhythms of the adjacent Tapa Bar. ⊠ *Innrain 2* ☎ *0512/586398* ⊟ *AE, DC, MC, V.*

$ ✕**Central.** Dark wooden paneling, crystal chandeliers, and the smell of coffee make this Viennese-style café a meeting point for intellectuals, artists, and students. International newspapers and magazines are available, as is a variety of cakes and pastries. You can have breakfast any time of day, or choose a light meal from the daily menu. A typical small dish to sample is Kasnocken (cheese dumplings with brown butter). Enjoy your cappuccino with live piano accompaniment every Sunday from October to April. ⊠ *Gilmstrasse 5, in Central Hotel* ☎ *0512/5920–0* ⊟ *AE, DC, MC, V.*

$ ✕**Hofgarten.** This is *the* summer gathering place in Innsbruck, perhaps because it is so pleasant to eat and drink outdoors amid the beauty of the city's ancient and splendid park. Whether enjoying a beer and light meal on a sunny afternoon, or celebrating with friends after a show at the nearby Landestheater, this is a fine place for having fun. The place is popular with students, but on Tuesday they pack the place. ⊠ *Rennweg 6a* ☎ *0512/588871* ⊟ *AE, DC, MC, V.*

$ ✗**Thai-Li.** This Thai kitchen has quietly fashioned a reputation as one of the finest, yet most affordable, dining spots in the Old Town. Thai-Li is short on elbow room, but long on excellent food presented with elegance and efficiency. Come for lunch, when you can sit outside on the small terrace. In the evening start with skewers of grilled chicken and pork, fried prawns, and vegetables with a range of dipping sauces. For a main course try one of the curry dishes, such as duck simmered in green curry. ⊠ *Marktgraben 3* ☎ *0512/562813* ⊟ *AE, DC, MC, V* ⊘ *Closed Mon.*

$ ✗**Markthalle.** This uncommonly tidy indoor market offers plenty of farm-fresh produce, including piquant goat cheese, just-picked berries, and a wide variety of mushrooms. You'll also find pastas and other homemade delicacies. The central location makes this an ideal stop for an inexpensive lunch. Go to the bakery for your choice of breads, then browse around the stalls to find your ideal fillings. If you'd rather have someone else do the shopping, grab a seat at one of the restaurants. One favorite is Marktschiff, which serves fish selected from a nearby stall. ⊠ *Herzog-Siegmund-Ufer 1-3, Marktplatz* ☎ *0512/572562* ⊟ *No credit cards* ⊘ *Closed Sun.*

WHERE TO STAY

If you arrive in Innsbruck without a hotel room, check with the **Innsbruck Reservations Office** (⊠ *Burggraben 3* ☎ *0512/562000–0* ⊕ *www. innsbruck.info*). The downtown office, in the main tourist office in the Old City, is open weekdays 10–7 and Saturday 8–noon. The main train station branch is open daily 9–6.

9

$$$$ 🏨 **Grand Hotel Europa.** Adjacent to the train station, this elegant hotel has provided lodging to the celebrated and wealthy since it opened in 1869. It has lost none of its warmth and charm in the ensuing years. Bavarian King Ludwig II is reported to have called it "the most desirable place in Innsbruck to celebrate a festival." Inside, modern Italian interior design meets traditional Tyrolian style. Rooms are richly appointed and extremely comfortable, and the staff provides personal, attentive service. Ask for a tour of the splendid Barocksaal, a meeting room built in 1883 by Ludwig II's own architect and, thankfully, untouched by the extensive bombing the hotel sustained during World War II. **Pros:** spacious rooms; modern lobby; nice bar. **Cons:** few nice views. ⊠ *Südtirolerplatz 2* ☎ *0512/5931* ⊕ *www.grandhoteleuropa. com* ➪ *120 rooms, 10 suites* ⌂ *In-room: safe, Wi-Fi. In-hotel: restaurant, room service, bar, gym, laundry service, parking (paid), no-smoking rooms* ⊟ *AE, DC, MC, V* ⊙*BP, MAP.*

$$$$ 🏨 **The Penz.** Innsbruck's newest luxury hotel sits within the Old City. Because of this, its ultramodern steel-and-glass architecture, designed by the renowned French architect Dominique Perrault, comes as a pleasant surprise. The guest rooms are small but elegant, although

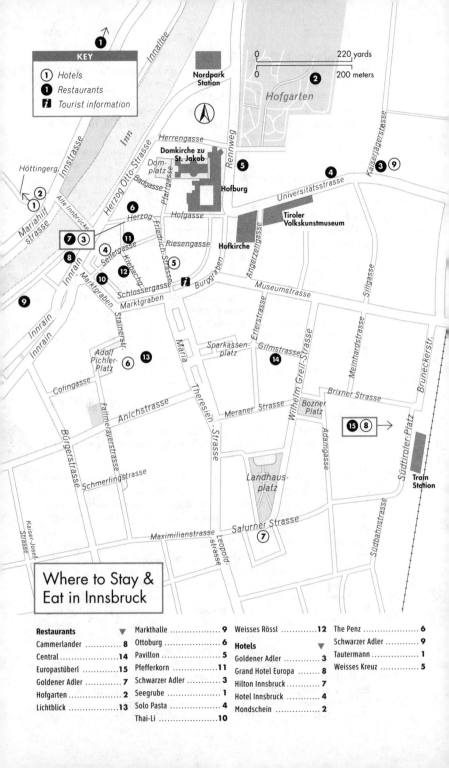

Where to Stay & Eat in Innsbruck

some find the decor a bit sterile. The rooftop American Bar makes a fine gathering spot, complete with panoramic views of the Alps. This is a business hotel, and traveling executives will feel right at home. Vacationing families might feel a bit out of place. **Pros:** sleek design; great breakfast; popular rooftop bar. **Cons:** small rooms; no spa or sauna. ⊠*Adolf-Pichler-Platz 3* ☎*0512/575657–0* ⊕*www.thepenz. com* ⌨*94 rooms* ⌂*In-room: safe, refrigerator, DVD (some), Internet, Wi-Fi. In-hotel: room service, bar, laundry service, parking (paid), no-smoking rooms* ▤*MC, V* ⏀*BP.*

$$$$ ⊞**Schwarzer Adler.** The 500-year-old building now occupied by the Black Eagle was once home of Emperor Maximilian's stables. Today it attracts those in search of a romantic experience. Most of the guest rooms are decorated with taste and creativity. For a taste of the good life, request the Swarovski Dream, a suite with a crystal bathroom. The open-air rooftop terrace offers an eye-popping view of the city and the mountains, making it the ideal place to enjoy an aperitif served by the well-trained staff. If the weather is cooperating, head to the small spa, one of the most intimate in Innsbruck. **Pros:** lovely spa; efficient staff; unique rooms. **Cons:** only one elevator; some rooms face busy street. ⊠ *Kaiserjägerstrasse 2* ☎*0512/587109* ⊕*www.deradler.com* ⌨*20 rooms, 7 suites* ⌂*In-room: Internet. In-hotel: restaurant, bar, spa, no-smoking rooms* ▤ *AE, DC, MC, V.*

$$$–$$$$ ⊞**Hilton Innsbruck.** This 14-story hotel looks a bit out of place in this historic city. Within walking distance of the train station, it's the place to go if you are looking for classic comforts, wonderful views, and a sumptuous breakfast buffet (be sure it's included in your rate or you'll have to cough up €22 for the privilege). All the guest rooms are spacious, but the contemporary interiors are slightly outdated. There's nothing particularly charming here, but it's suitable for business and leisure travelers who are not looking for surprises and like to gamble at the in-house casino. **Pros:** great views; predictably comfortable; huge breakfast buffet. **Cons:** little personality; chain-hotel feel; expensive Internet. ⊠*Salurner Strasse 15* ☎*0512/5935–0* ⊕*www.hilton.com* ⌨*176 rooms* ⌂*In-room: safe, refrigerator, Internet, Wi-Fi. In-hotel: restaurant, room service, bar, gym, spa, laundry service, parking (paid), no-smoking rooms* ▤*AE, DC, MC, V* ⏀*BP, MAP.*

$$$ ⊞**Goldener Adler.** Since 1390, this hotel has welcomed nearly every king, emperor, duke, or poet who passed through Innsbruck. Emperor Joseph II, King Ludwig II of Bavaria, Goethe, Paganini, and even the young Mozart stayed here, as the marble plate on the facade attests. In the very heart of the Old Innsbruck pedestrian area, the hotel is across the street from the Goldenes Dachl. Some of the rooms, in modern style with some Tyrolean accents, are right on the street. These can be noisy, so if you're a light sleeper ask for one of the quieter rooms upstairs. **Pros:** perfect location; free Internet; friendly and helpful staff. **Cons:** elevator can be tricky to use; some rooms can be noisy. ⊠*Herzog-Friedrich-Strasse 6* ☎*0512/571111* ⊕*www.goldeneradler.com* ⌨*33 rooms* ⌂*In-room: no a/c (some), safe, refrigerator, Internet. In-hotel: restaurant, room service, bar, laundry service, Wi-Fi, no-smoking rooms* ▤*AE, DC, MC, V* ⏀*BP, MAP.*

9

$$$ 🏨**Hotel Innsbruck.** Modern is the mood here, from the tastefully under-stated lobby to the efficient and functional guest rooms. From some rooms you have gorgeous views of the Old City, while those on the river side look out on the mountains. The indoor swimming pool in the top-floor spa area is a pleasant surprise for a city hotel. Due to its popularity with tour groups, it can get busy at times. **Pros:** lovely sauna area; heated indoor pool; great location. **Cons:** pricey parking; noisy location. ⊠*Innrain 3* ☎*0512/59868–0* ⊕*www.hotelinnsbruck. com* ⏎*110 rooms* ♿*In-room: no a/c (some), safe, refrigerator, DVD (some), Internet. In-hotel: restaurant, room service, bar, pool, gym, spa, laundry service, Wi-Fi, parking (paid), no-smoking rooms* ⊟*AE, DC, MC, V* ⦿|*BP, MAP.*

$$–$$$ 🏨**Mondschein.** Among the city's oldest houses stands the pink Moon-light Hotel, a warm and welcoming family-run establishment. Richly furnished rooms facing the Inn River offer excellent views of the Old City. There are only four standard rooms on the river side, and these are worth requesting in advance; the others face the less-appealing courtyard but cost the same. Bathrooms are big and elegant compared to the room size. **Pros:** very friendly staff; free parking; riverfront loca-tion. **Cons:** some rooms can be noisy; courtyard rooms are dark; small parking lot. ⊠*Mariahilfstrasse 6* ☎*0512/22784* ⊕*www.mondschein. at* ⏎*34 rooms* ♿*In-room: safe (some), Wi-Fi. In-hotel: room service, bar, Internet terminal, parking (free), no-smoking rooms* ⊟*AE, DC, MC, V* ⦿|*BP.*

$ 🏨**Tautermann.** This red-shuttered house within walking distance of the city center has been turned into a friendly, family-run hotel. Spacious rooms gleam with natural woods and old-fashioned style. Some upper rooms on the west side have bay windows with gorgeous views of the mountains. From the main station, Bus A to Höttinger Kirchenplatz gets you close to the door. This hotel is a good value if you're on a budget. **Pros:** very quiet location; inexpensive rates; free parking. **Cons:** basic breakfast; dated furniture. ⊠*Stamserfeld 5* ☎*0512/281572* ⊕*www.hotel-tautermann.at* ⏎*32 rooms* ♿*In-room: no a/c, refrig-erator (some). In-hotel: laundry facilities, Internet, parking (free), no-smoking rooms* ⊟*AE, DC, MC, V* ⦿|*BP.*

$ 🏨**Weisses Kreuz.** At first sight you may fall in love with this hotel, set over stone arcades in the heart of the Old City. It has quite a long his-tory, as the first guesthouse stood on this site in 1465. Guest rooms are simple but comfortable, with rustic furnishings and lots of pale wood. The service is friendly and accommodating, even though sometimes you might have to wait for a staffer to arrive. The breakfast is served in one of the building's original parlors. **Pros:** good value; family-friendly vibe; charming building. **Cons:** parking is a short walk from the hotel; noisy neighborhood. ⊠*Herzog-Friedrich-Strasse 31* ☎*0512/59479* ⊕*www.weisseskreuz.at* ⏎*40 rooms, 9 rooms without bath* ♿*In-room: no a/c. In-hotel: Internet, Wi-Fi, parking (paid), no-smoking rooms* ⊟*AE, MC, V* ⦿|*BP.*

NIGHTLIFE & THE ARTS

THE ARTS

The **Festwochen der Alten Musik** (*Festival of Early Music* ✉*Burggra-ben 3* ☎*0512/5710–32* ⊕*www.altemusik.at*) is a good reason to visit Innsbruck between mid-July and late August, as the annual festival highlights music from the 14th to 18th centuries, performed by many of Europe's finest musicians in such dramatic settings as Innsbruck's beautiful Schloss Ambras and the Hofkirche. In summer there are frequent brass-band (*Musikkapelle*) concerts in the Old Town. **Internation-aler Tanzsommer Innsbruck** (✉*Burggraben 3* ☎*0512/561–561* ⊕*www.tanzsommer.at*) brings the world's premiere dance companies to Innsbruck between mid-June and mid-July. Maracana, Brazil's Grupo Corpo, and Sankai Juku are some of the groups that have recently performed. Tickets are available online or through the tourist office, or contact the festival.

It's said that Tirol has more bandleaders than mayors. Folklore shows at the **Messehalle** and other spots around the city showcase authentic Tyrolean folk dancing, yodeling, and zither music. The tourist office and hotels have details. Concerts take place in the modern Saal Tirol of the **Kongresshaus** (✉*Rennweg 3* ☎*0512/5936–0*). Innsbruck's principal theater is the **Tiroler Landestheater** (✉*Rennweg 2* ☎*0512/52074–4* ⊕*www.landestheater.at*). Both operas and operettas are presented in the main hall, usually starting at 7:30; plays in the Kammerspiele start at 8. Obtain tickets at the box office or at the main tourist office.

NIGHTLIFE

The jazzy **casino** adjacent to the Hilton Innsbruck offers blackjack, baccarat, roulette, poker, and plenty of slot machines, as well as a bar. You must present your passport to enter the casino. ✉*Salurner Strasse 15* ☎*0512/587040–0* ⌨*€22, exchangeable for €25 worth of chips; admission free for those not playing* ⊙*Daily 3* PM–3 AM.

A popular spot among students is **Krahvogel** (✉*Anichstrasse 12* ☎*0512/580149*), a trendy beer pub on one of Innsbruck's busiest shopping streets. The beautiful people gather at **Das Stadtcafé** (✉*Universitäts Strasse 1* ☎*0512/90880*). When the weather is fine, the rooftop **Segafredo Sky Bar** (✉*Universitätsstrasse 15* ☎*0512/574910*) is the place to be. The tiny **Piano Bar** (✉*Herzog-Friedrich-Strasse 5* ☎*0512/571010*) exudes old-world charm and has occasional live music.

For dancing, the basement **Blue Chip** (✉*Wilhelm-Greil-Strasse 17* ☎*0512/565050*) is the leading hot spot on Wednesday and weekends. The upstairs **Jimmy's bar** (✉*Wilhelm-Greil-Strasse 17* ☎*0512/570473*) is wildly popular. For Latin rhythms, **Tapabar** (✉*Marktplatz, Innrain 2* ☎*0512/586398–43*) is the right place. Wednesday flamenco lessons and occasional live performances are a good warm-up for long nights of dancing.

SPORTS & THE OUTDOORS

GOLF

Golf Course Innsbruck-Igls (☎ 05223/78734 www.golfclub-innsbruck-igls. at) in Lans, about 9 km (5½ mi) outside the city, is a 9-hole, par-66 course. It's open April–November. **Golfplatz Rinn** (☎ 05223/78177) in Rinn, about 12 km (7½ mi) away, has 18 holes, with a par 71, and offers a sweeping panorama of the Inn Valley. The course is open April–October. Both courses charge greens fees of about €40 on weekdays, €45 on weekends, and discounts are offered at Rinn with the Club Innsbruck card. Several hotels—Grand Hotel Europa in Innsbruck, Sporthotel Igls, Gesundheitszentrum Lanserhof at Lans, and the Geisler at Rinn—have special golfing arrangements.

HIKING

Both easy paths and extreme slopes await hikers and climbers. From June to October holders of the Club Innsbruck card can take free, daily, guided mountain hikes. The tourist office has a special hiking brochure. If you want to learn to climb, look to the **Alpine School Innsbruck** (⊠ Natters, In der Stille 1 ☎ 0512/546000-0 ⊕ www.asi.at). If you're already an experienced *Kletterer* (rock climber), check in with the **Österreichischer Alpenverein** (⊠ Wilhelm-Greil-Strasse 15 ☎ 0512/59547-0).

HORSEBACK RIDING

Horseback riding can be arranged through **Reitclub Innsbruck** (⊠ Langer Weg 43a ☎ 0512/347174).

SKIING

Around Innsbruck you'll find everything from the beginner slopes of the Glungezer to the good intermediate skiing of the Axamer Lizum and Patscherkofel to the steep runs and off-piste skiing of Seegrube. Your Club Innsbruck membership card (free with an overnight stay in any Innsbruck hotel) will get you free transportation to the areas and reduced prices on a number of ski lifts. A Super Ski Pass covers all the ski areas of Innsbruck, the Stubai Glacier, Kitzbühel, and St. Anton, with 520 km (290 mi) of runs, 210 lifts, and all transfers. The Gletscher Ski Pass includes Innsbruck and the Stubai Glacier. If you're a summer skier (and can handle the altitude), there's year-round skiing on the Stubai Glacier, about 40 km (25 mi) from Innsbruck via the free ski shuttle bus (ask at your hotel).

You can book all your skiing needs, including lift tickets, equipment rentals, and ski lessons, with the **Ski & Snowboardschule Innsbruck** (☎ 0512/581742-17) or through the tourist office. Hotels have details on winter ski kindergartens. A good bet for ski or snowboard rentals is **Snowboard Börse** (⊠ Leopoldstrasse 4 ☎ 0512/581742-0), tucked into an alley just south of the Triumphpforte.

SWIMMING

Around Innsbruck there are plenty of lakes, but in town you have little choice other than pools, indoors and out. To swim under the sun with a panoramic view of the mountains, try the **Freischwimmbad Tivoli** (⊠ Purtschellerstrasse 1 ☎ 0512/502-7081). If the weather goes south, try the turn-of-the-20th-century indoor **Hallenbad Amraser Strasse** (✉*Amraser Strasse 3* ☎*0512/502–7051*). **Hallenbad Höttinger Au** (✉*Fürstenweg 12* ☎*0512/502–7071*) is a popular indoor facility.

SHOPPING

The best shops are along the arcaded Herzog-Friedrich-Strasse in the heart of the Altstadt, or Old City, and along its extension, Maria-Theresien-Strasse; and the adjoining streets Meraner Strasse and Anichstrasse. Innsbruck is the place to buy native Tyrolean clothing, particularly lederhosen (traditional brushed leather shorts and knickers) and loden (sturdy combed-wool jackets and vests). Look also for cut crystal and wood carvings; locally handmade, delicate silver-filigree pins make fine gifts.

> ### INNSBRUCK'S SMALLEST SHOP
>
> Definitely worth a visit is **S'Speckladele** (✉*Stiftgasse 4* ☎*0512/588816*), the smallest shop in Innsbruck. With room for only two clients at a time, it sells delicious Speck (bacon) and other smoked meats produced by local organic farms. Enjoy a sandwich and you will not be able to resist bringing something home.

For sheer holiday delight, nothing tops the traditional **Christmas Market**, open from November 23 to December 28 and featuring numerous dealers selling wooden and glass handicrafts, Christmas-tree decorations, candles, and Tyrolean toys and loden costumes. The market stalls are set up around the giant, illuminated Christmas tree just next to the Goldenes Dachl museum at Herzog-Friedrich-Strasse 15, in the heart of the Altstadt.

Rathausgalerie (✉*Maria-Theresien-Strasse, Anichstrasse, or Adolf-Pichler-Platz*) is Innsbruck's swish, centrally located, glass-roofed indoor mall, home to luxury boutiques and famous names known worldwide, where you can not only shop, but also eat and drink, in style.

Galerie Thomas Flora (✉*Herzog-Friedrich-Strasse 5* ☎*0512/577402*) sells graphics by the droll Tyrolean artist Paul Flora; there's much to smile at here, and maybe even to take home. **Hubertus Loden Steinbock** (✉*Sparkassenplatz 3* ☎*0512/585092*) is an outstanding source of dirndls, those attractive country costumes for women, with white blouse, dark skirt, and colorful apron. It also has children's clothing. **Rudolf Boschi** (✉*Kiebachgasse 8* ☎*0512/589224*) turns out reproductions of old pewterware, using the original molds when possible. Among other wares, he has locally produced, hand-decorated beer mugs with pewter lids.

S'Culinarium (✉*Pfarrgasse 1* ☎*0512/574903*) is the shop to buy Austrian wine and liquor, such as the famous Rochelt. Here you can try everything before buying and the talkative and friendly owner will be more than happy to advise you. The dazzling **Swarovski Crystal Gallery** (✉*Herzog-Friedrich-Strasse 39* ☎*0512/573100*) features almost everything from the world-renowned crystal maker, whose headquarters is in nearby Wattens, east of Innsbruck. **Tiroler Heimatwerk** (⊠ *Mer-aner Strasse 2–4* ☎*0512/582320*) is the first place to look for local mementos and souvenirs of good quality. The extremely attractive shop carries textiles and finished clothing, ceramics, carved wooden chests, and some furniture, but don't expect to bargain shop here. You can also have clothing made to order.

IGLS

5 km (3 mi) south of Innsbruck.

GETTING HERE & AROUND

Trams and buses run hourly between Innsbruck and Igls; take Tram 6, which arrives in Igls via Lans and Schloss Ambras, from either the main train station or the **Bergisel** tram station. Bus J leaves from Innsbruck Marktplatz or Landesmuseum and arrives in the center of the village in front of the Sporthotel Igls within 20 minutes.

EXPLORING

Perched on a sunny plateau ascending to the famed Brenner Pass to the south of Innsbruck, Igls (pronounced like "eagles") is one of the several lovely holiday villages minutes away from Innsbruck's city center. Here you'll find the charm and quiet of a small Austrian village with easy access to Innsbruck and its attractions. Igls is close to **Schloss Ambras** and is the best starting point for hiking or skiing the Patcherkofel mountain, whose conical shape towers volcanolike over the village.

WHERE TO STAY & EAT

$$$ ✕**Batzenhäusl.** You wouldn't expect such an elegant restaurant behind the walls of this wooden chalet. Warm tones welcome you in the contemporary ground-floor restaurant; on the upper floor you will find some very fine parlors with a more traditional feel. The two chefs conjure some very fine creations based on Austrian specialties, such as wild boar with figs or lamb with ratatouille. Menus change seasonally, and a full range of vegetarian options is always available. ⊠*Lanser Strasse 12* ☎*0512/386180* ⊟*AE, DC, MC, V* ⊗*Closed Mon.*

$$$$ 🛏 **Sporthotel Igls.** With its crackling fireplaces, elegant parlors, and winter garden, this hotel will make you feel right at home. The rooms and the lobby are spacious, warm, and inviting. The wellness area is perfect for relaxing after a day on the slopes, which are within easy reach. Complimentary tea and fresh fruit are nice treats as you wait for spa treatments. **Pros:** lovely spa and wellness area; close to Innsbruck; many activities. **Cons:** labyrinthine building; on a busy road; crowded elevator. ⊠ *Hilberstrasse 17* ☎*0512/377241* ⊕*www.sporthotel-igls.com* ⇱*74 rooms* ⚒ *In-room: no a/c, safe, refrigerator, DVD (some), Wi-Fi. In-hotel: 2 restaurant, room service, bar, pool, gym, spa, bicycles, laundry service, parking (paid), no-smoking rooms* ⊟*AE, MC, V* ⦿*BP, MAP.*

AROUND THE LOWER INN VALLEY

Northeast of Innsbruck the Inn River valley broadens out and courses right through Tirol toward Kufstein and the German border. Route 171 along the valley is a much more pleasant route than the parallel autobahn. Often overlooked by travelers zipping between Innsbruck and Salzburg on the autobahn, this region is nonetheless worth a visit for the well-preserved old towns of Hall and Schwaz and for a trip into the beautiful Zillertal (Ziller Valley), dotted with ski areas and popular as a year-round resort area.

TALER FOR DOLLAR

The famed Münze Hall (mint tower), symbol of Hall in Tirol, was moved here from Meran, and the first coins were struck here in 1477. Legend has it that Duke Sigmund the Wealthy, son of Friedl the Penniless, got his nickname by tossing handfuls of Hall-minted coins to the populace wherever he went. The Inntal (Inn Valley) gave its name to the coin, known as the *Taler,* from which came the word "dollar."

■ TIP→ **Many of the Tirol's finest folk musicians come from this valley, so if you go, ask about live music programs.**

HALL IN TIROL

9 km (5½ mi) east of Innsbruck.

GETTING HERE & AROUND

Regional trains leave every hour from Innsbruck, bringing you to Hall in Tirol in around 10 minutes. An alternative is Bus No. 4, also from the main train station, which runs more frequently but takes approximately 20 minutes.

ESSENTIALS

Visitor Information **Hall in Tirol** (✉ *Wallpachgasse 5* ☎ *05223/45544–0*).

EXPLORING

Hall in Tirol is an old city founded by salt miners. Narrow lanes running east–west, interrupted by a few short cross alleys, make up the old part of the town. Stop and look around; from the main road you cannot get a proper perspective of the fine old buildings. Every Wednesday is market day in the town.

The **Rathaus,** built in the mid-15th century, has ornately carved councillors' rooms and beautifully worked craftsmanship.

The 17th-century **monastery church** is the oldest Renaissance ecclesiastical building in Tirol.

WHERE TO STAY

$$ 🖼 **Hotel Heiligkreuz.** Ever fall asleep while watching the stars? This lodging, whose owner is passionate about astronomy, brings the night sky right into your room. Most of the rooms of this family-run hotel have glow-in-the-dark stars painted across the ceilings. Ask for a private tour of the small observatory, where you can peek at the heavens. In

9

summer you can relax in the private garden or enjoy the nearby swimming pool and tennis courts. **Pros:** breakfast with a lot of fresh fruit; free Internet. **Cons:** long walk from the center. ⊠ *Reimmichlstrasse 18* ☎ *05223/57114* ⊕ *www.holycross.at* ⇆ *34 rooms* ⌂ *In-room: no a/c (some), safe, Internet, Wi-Fi. In-hotel: restaurant, room service, bar, spa, bicycles, Internet terminal, parking (free), no-smoking rooms* ▭ *AE, DC, MC, V* ⊩ *BP, MAP.*

SHOPPING

Traveling east between Hall in Tirol and Schwaz, you'll pass the home of the Swarovski cut-crystal empire in Wattens. Stop at the **Swarovski Crystal World Shop** to browse and perhaps buy some of the famous— and now some of the chicest—crystal and glassware, or if you have more time, explore **Crystal World**, an eclectic but fascinating multimedia gallery that has become one of Tirol's most popular attractions, featuring the works of 15 or more artists including Salvador Dalí, Brian Eno, André Heller, and Andy Warhol. ⊠ *Kristallweltenstrasse 1* ☎ *05224/51080–0* ▱ *€9.50* ⊙ *Daily 9–6:30.*

SCHWAZ

16 km (10 mi) northeast of Hall in Tirol.

GETTING HERE & AROUND

To get here, take Route 171, from Hall in Tirol or Innsbruck. A quicker, but less scenic alternative is Highway A12.

ESSENTIALS

Visitor Information Schwaz (⊠ *Franz-Josef-Strasse 2* ☎ *05242/63240*).

EXPLORING

The Habsburg emperors in the 15th and 16th centuries owed much of their wealth to the silver and copper extracted from the mines here by the Fugger family, bankers and traders who emigrated from Augsburg. First mentioned in the 10th century and incorporated as a town in the 12th century, Schwaz, on the south bank of the Inn, evolved into a rich and important mining center.

The mines of the **Silberbergwerk Schwaz**—dug deep under the towering Tuxer Alps—may have provided the impetus behind the establishment of the mint in nearby Hall. ⊠ *Alte Landstrasse 3a* ☎ *05242/72372–0* ⊕ *www.silberbergwerk.at* ▱ *€15* ⊙ *May–Oct., daily 9–5; Nov.–Apr., daily 10–4.*

The 15th- and 16th-century houses built during those prosperous times still stand, and the marketplace has kept its atmosphere. Look at the vast **parish church,** the largest Gothic hall-church in Tirol. The church was expanded in 1490 and divided into two parts (once they were separated by a wooden wall): the southern chancel for the miners and the northern, or "Prince's Chancel," for the upper classes.

Another outstanding monument from the 15th and 16th centuries in Schwaz is the treasure-filled **Franciscan Church** *(Franziskanerkirche),* founded in the early 16th century by Emperor Maximilian I. This may well be the mendicant order's most beautiful church in the Alpine region.

A fascinating addition to Schwaz is the **Haus der Völker**, a museum dedicated to ethnography. Displays include ancient Asian sculptures as well as African art. ⊠ *St. Martin 16* ☎*05242/66090* ⊕*www.hausder voelker.com* ▣*€6* ⊙*Daily 10–6.*

EN ROUTE

Jenbach, 8 km (5 mi) north of Schwaz, across the river, is notable mainly as a rail and highway junction; from here Route 169 follows the Ziller Valley (Zillertal) south, past the Gerlos Valley (Route 165) and the Tuxer mountain range to Mayrhofen. The Achensee lies on the plateau to the north, fed by the Achen River rising high in the mountains beyond, on the German border. Both regions have become immensely popular with tourists.

☼ Built around 1500, **Schloss Tratzberg** is a romantic late-Gothic jewel sitting atop a vertical rock face, commanding a sweeping view of the Inn Valley. The castle, which has been a family residence for some 300 years, is accessible on foot (a 20-minute hike) or by hopping on the little trolley (€2 round-trip) from the parking area. The one-hour "walkman" tour of the castle is accompanied by guides who are happy to answer further questions. Children are offered their own, rather playful audiovisual tour, offered in a fairy-tale fashion. ⊠*Jenbach* ☎*05242/63566–20* ⊕*www.schloss-tratzberg.at* ▣*€9* ⊙*Apr.–June and Sept.–Oct., daily 10–4; June–Aug. last tour at 5.*

ACHENSEE

25 km (17 mi) north of Schwaz, 17 km (12 mi) from Jenbach.

GETTING HERE & AROUND

From Jenbach, take Route 181 to reach Achensee. The initial stretch involves challenging hairpin turns and a steep climb, but the views over the Inn Valley are exquisite.

ESSENTIALS

Tourist Information Achensee (⊠ *Rathaus 387* ☎*05246/5300* ⊕ *www. achensee.info*).

EXPLORING

The Achen Valley has fine skiing in winter, but the Achensee in summer, with water sports and excellent fishing, is the main attraction. The great mountains of the Karwendel and Rofan ranges rise from its blue-green waters, and, at 10 km (6 mi) in length, the lake is Tirol's largest and most beautiful. The lake steamer connects the villages strung along its length.

The most adventuresome and romantic way to reach the Achensee is on the steam-powered train, the **Achenseebahn** (☎*05244/62243* ⊕*www. achenseebahn.at*), built in 1889 as Tirol's first mountain cog railway. The line does its 1,300-foot climb in a nearly straight line more than 7 km (4½ mi) to the lower end of the Achensee (Seespitz).

Once at the lower end of the Achensee you can get a lake steamer operated by **Achensee Schiffahrt** (☎*05243/5253* ⊕*www.tirol-schiffahrt.at*) on to Maurach/Buchau and, at the north end of the lake, Achenkirch. From Jenbach, a round-trip train/steamer excursion takes about 4½ hours. Trains and ships run on a regular schedule between June and September.

WHERE TO STAY

$$$$ 🏨 **Posthotel Achenkirch Resort & Spa.** This comfortable chalet is also a wellness retreat, providing every convenience for taking care of relaxation, exercise, and weight loss. Horseback riders will find mounts ranging from Lipizzaners (the largest private herd in Europe) to Shetland ponies. Rooms are done up in country style and in warm, welcoming colors. Even if it is a bit out of town, you won't find yourself getting bored. **Pros:** plenty of activities; lovely spa area. **Cons:** no intimate feel; on a busy street. ⊠*Achenkirch* ☎*05246/6522–0* ⊕*www.posthotel.at* ☞*150 rooms, 54 suites* ♿*In-room: no a/c, safe, refrigerator, Internet. In-hotel: 8 restaurants, room service, bar, golf course, tennis court, pools, gym, spa, children's programs (ages 3–14), laundry service, Wi-Fi, parking (free), no-smoking rooms* ▤*AE, MC, V* ⍟|*BP, MAP.*

ZELL AM ZILLER

25 km (16 mi) southeast of Jenbach.

GETTING HERE & AROUND

From Innsbruck, take Highway A12 or Route 171. The B169 will lead you to the Ziller Valley.

ESSENTIALS

Visitor Information Zell im Zillertal (⊠*Dorfplatz 3a* ☎*05282/2281* ⊕*www.gauderfest.at*).

EXPLORING

Fodor'sChoice   The main town of the Zillertal—the biggest and most famous of the
★   many beautiful Alpine valleys of the Tirol—is noted for its traditional 500-year-old **Gauder Fest**, held on the first weekend in May, when thousands of tourists from far and wide pack the little market town for the colorful skits, music, and singing—and great quantities of *Gauderbier*, a strong brew created for the occasion. You can hear some of the country's best singing by the valley residents and listen to expert harp and zither playing, for which the valley is famous. Tradition runs strong here: witness the Perchtenlaufen, processions of colorfully masked well-wishers going the neighborhood rounds on January 5, or the annual Almabtrieb during the last September and first October days, when the cows are decorated with wreaths and bells, and, amid celebrations, herded back from the high Alpine pastures into the lower fields and barns. This is a typical Tyrolean country town, with Alpine lodges and a round-dome pink village church (note the Baroque painting of the Holy Trinity); in winter it's a center for skiing and sports.

WHERE TO EAT

$$ ✕ **Bräu.** The core of this frescoed building in the town center dates from the 16th century; subsequent renovations have brought the five-story structure up to date. The three-room restaurant serves fine fare, with emphasis on fish and game. Many products come directly from the owner's own farm and fish ponds. Make sure to taste the house beer; the on-site brewery is also the source of the *Gauderbier.* ⊠ *Dorfplatz 1* ☎ *05282/2313* ▭ *No credit cards* ⊘ *Closed Apr. and mid-Oct.–mid-Dec.*

MAYRHOFEN

10 km (6 mi) south of Zell am Ziller.

ESSENTIALS

Visitor Information Mayrhofen (⊠ *Dursterstrassse 225* ☎ *05285/6760 www. mayerhofen.at*).

EXPLORING

Mayrhofen is the end of the line for the narrow-gauge railway. This is the valley's main tourist base and a favorite summer resort for British and Dutch visitors. Mayrhofen is the starting point for summer hiking into the highly scenic valleys that branch off to the southeast, south, and southwest and for excursions into the Ziller glacier areas, at heights of 9,750 feet and more.

At Mayrhofen the valley splits into three *Täler* (valleys): the Zillergrund, Stilluptal, and Zemmgrund—prime examples of picture-postcard Alpine areas, swept at the top with glittering, pale-blue glaciers.

WHERE TO STAY & EAT

$–$$ ✕ **Wirtshaus zum Griena.** Tucked into a 400-year-old farmhouse, this restaurant is about a 10-minute drive north of Mayrhofen. It's difficult to find, but everybody knows Griena's—ask at your hotel for directions. Once you get there, you'll find yourself in rustic surroundings glowing in natural-wood paneling. Such local favorites as beer soup, potato-cheese dumplings, and schnitzel are tempting. Some recipes come have a long tradition in the Ziller Valley and are made with locally produced butter, buttermilk, cheese, and, of course, meat. The Zillertaler beer goes great with every dish. ⊠ *Dorfhaus 768* ☎ *05285/62778* ▭ *MC, V* ⊘ *Closed June–early July and Nov.–early Dec.*

$$$$ ⊞ **Elisabeth.** This modern house built in the traditional Tyrolean style radiates elegance without feeling too stuffy. The same is true of the luxurious bedrooms, some with ceramic stoves and beautiful carved walls and ceilings. Each has a balcony overlooking the mountains, and a few have fireplaces, canopy beds, and hot tubs set in windowed alcoves offering stunning views. Every Saturday evening there is a huge buffet dinner and live music. The hotel has a loyal following, so book ahead. **Pros:** wonderful spa; southern rooms have great views; friendly service. **Cons:** some traffic noise; east and west rooms face parking lot. ⊠ *Einfahrt Mitte 432* ☎ *05285/6767* ⊕ *www.elisabethhotel.com* ⇖ *32 rooms* ⌂ *In-room: no a/c, safe, Wi-Fi. In-hotel: 2 restaurants,*

9

room service, bar, pool, gym, spa, laundry service, parking (free), some pets allowed ⊟*MC, V* ⊘*Closed May and Nov.* |⊙|*BP, MAP.*

$$$–$$$$ ⊞**Kramerwirt.** In Mayrhofen, this hotel is where the crowds gather. The welcoming warmth of natural wood in the lobby and in the dining room is accented by well-chosen Tyrolean antiques. Still family-run, this hostelry has been around for centuries. The comfortable rooms, all nicely furnished, will make you feel at home. The apartments, a five-minute walk from the hotel, are a great choice for families and groups up friends traveling together. **Pros:** friendly and helpful staff; ski bus stops outside. **Cons:** spa is not free for guests. ⊠*Am Marienbrunnen 346* ☎*05285/6700* ⊕*www.kramerwirt.at* ⊃*78 rooms, 10 apartments* ⌂*In-room: no a/c, safe, kitchen (some), refrigerator (some), Wi-Fi. In-hotel: restaurant, room service, bar, laundry facilities, parking (free), some pets allowed* ⊟*MC, V* ⊘*Closed Nov.* |⊙|*BP, MAP.*

SPORTS & THE OUTDOORS

CLIMBING   For the adventuresome, Peter Habeler at the **Alpinschule u. Schischule Mount Everest** (⊠*Hauptstrasse 458* ☎*05285/62829* ⊕*www.habeler. com*) gives instruction in ice climbing. Herr Habeler, along with his climbing partner Reinhold Messner, were the first to ascend Mt. Everest without oxygen.

Action Club Zillertal (☎*05285/62977*) is the contact for adventure sports like canyoning, rafting, and mountain biking.

GERLOS

18 km (10 mi) east of Zell am Ziller.

ESSENTIALS

Visitor Information **Gerlos** (⊠*A-6281* ☎*05284/5244–0*).

EXPLORING

The sensationally scenic Route 165 climbs east out of Zell am Ziller up to Gerlos, a less glitzy but still splendid choice for a summer or winter holiday, with the 8,300-foot Kreuzjoch mountain looming in the background. Scheduled buses make the run up from Zell am Ziller. The Gerlos ski slopes are varied, and in summer the same slopes offer excellent hiking.

WHERE TO STAY

$$$$ ⊞**Almhof.** Built in typical Tyrolean style, this Alpine-style inn sits about 2 km (1 mi) out of the center. While the children are entertained with a range of activities, parents can relax in the expansive spa and sauna area. There are programs for all ages, from ski courses to hiking programs. The hotel has a small animal farm, several playrooms, and a restaurant that offers a special healthy kids' menu. Full board is required. **Pros:** family-friendly hotel; perfect for outdoors enthusiasts. **Cons:** a bit pricey; not for those without kids in tow. ⊠*Gerlos–Gmünd* ☎*05284/5323–0* ⊕*www.familyresort.at* ⊃*60 rooms* ⌂*In-room: no a/c, safe, refrigerator, Internet. In-hotel: restaurant, bar, tennis court, pool, gym, spa, children's programs (ages 6 mos–16 yrs), Wi-Fi, park-*

ing (free), no-smoking rooms ⊟*MC, V* ⊘*Closed mid-Apr.–early May and Nov.–early Dec.* ⵙ*FAP.*

$$$–$$$$ ⬚**Gaspingerhof.** Three Alpine chalets make up this family-run hotel. In the center of town, they are connected by underground passages. Rooms are done in bright colors, with plenty of natural woods. Take advantage of the summer packages, which focus on a range of outdoor activities. In winter it's a great base for skiing trips. Your children will have fun in the hotel-run programs while you indulge in the après-ski pampering. **Pros:** family-friendly environment; plenty to do no matter the season. **Cons:** like a labyrinth; too big for some. ⊠*Gerlos 153* ☎*05284/5216* ⊕*www.gaspingerhof.at* ⭋*74 rooms* ⚷*In-room: no a/c, safe. In-hotel: restaurant, bar, pools, gym, spa, children's programs (ages 2–14), Internet, no-smoking rooms* ⊟*MC, V* ⊘*Closed mid-Apr.–mid-May and mid-Oct.–early Dec.* ⵙ*BP, MAP.*

EN ROUTE Beyond Gerlos the highway climbs the 5,300-foot Gerlos Pass and plunges into the province of Salzburg in a series of double-back hairpins close to the dramatic 1,300-foot **Krimmler Wasserfälle** *(waterfalls)*. You can complete the circuit back into Tirol by continuing east to Mittersill and cutting north to Kitzbühel via the Thurn Pass.

ON THE ROAD TO KITZBÜHEL

The area between Jenbach and Kitzbühel, north of the Kitzbüheler Alps and south of the German border, is a distillation of all things Tyrolean: perfectly maintained ancient farmhouses with balconies overflowing with flowers; people who still wear the traditional lederhosen and dirndls as their everyday attire; Alpine villages and medieval castles; and wonderfully kitschy winter resorts like Kitzbühel and St. Johann. Other delightful destinations here include Kufstein, with its brooding fortress Festung Kufstein, a bevy of warm-water lakes, and Rattenberg, with its glass workshops founded by Sudeten German refugees from the Czech Republic. Everywhere the people are welcoming and the scenery is beautiful.

9

ALPBACH

24 km (15 mi) east of Jenbach.

Alpbach takes the international spotlight once a year in August, when world leaders of government and industry gather to discuss global issues at the European Forum.

GETTING HERE & AROUND

From Highway 171 at the town of Brixlegg, a small side road runs up a valley to the unspoiled picture-book village of Alpbach.

WHERE TO STAY

$$$$ ⬚**Alpbacher Hof.** A massive fireplace sets the tone at this typical chalet hotel, and the welcoming feeling carries over to the bedrooms. Yellow hues dominate the bedrooms, where comfortable armchairs help you relax after a long skiing day. The encompassing view of the valley is yours to enjoy from the large central terrace. **Pros:** best hot chocolate in town; southern rooms have nice views. **Cons:** dated decor. ✉A-6236 ☎05336/5237 ⊕www.alpbacherhof.at ➫56 rooms ⚙In-room: no a/c, refrigerator (some). In-hotel: restaurant, bar, pool, parking (paid) ➯V ⊗Closed mid-Apr.–mid-May and late Oct.–mid-Dec. ⍥MAP.

$$$ 🏠**Böglerhof.** Much of this 14th-century double chalet with heavily beamed ceilings and old stonework has been beautifully restored. A spacious lobby with inviting armchairs and a fireplace is the ideal place for reading a book or enjoying afternoon tea. The rooms are attractively decorated in Tyrolean style. The excellent restaurant, with its small *Stuben* (side rooms), is known for such Austrian specialties as cabbage soup and fillet points in light garlic sauce. **Pros:** family-friendly inn; mountain views from all sides; good breakfast buffet. **Cons:** not a party place; loud church bells. ✉A-6236 ☎05336/52270 ⊕www.boeglerhof.com ➫50 rooms ⚙In-room: no a/c, safe, kitchen (some). In-hotel: restaurant, bar, tennis court, pools, gym, spa, children's programs (ages 3–13), parking (free) ➯MC, V ⊗Closed mid-Apr.–May and late Oct.–mid-Dec. ⍥BP, MAP.

SPORTS & THE OUTDOORS

Sport Ossi (✉*Wittberg 105, Kramsach* ☎05337/63300 ⊕www.sport-ossi.at) is the area's best contact for rafting, kayaking, rock climbing, and mountain biking.

RATTENBERG

14 km (9 mi) northeast of Jenbach.

ESSENTIALS

Visitor Information Rattenberg (✉*Klostergasse 94,* ☎05337/63321).

EXPLORING

This medieval town, perhaps the smallest in Austria, was once famous for its silver mines. When the mines were exhausted, Rattenberg lapsed into a deep sleep lasting for centuries. You might think you're back in the Middle Ages as you ramble the narrow old streets full of relics of its past; the town has remained remarkably unchanged. Today Rattenburg is known for its glass and crystal artists, whose shops are mostly along Südtirolerstrasse. Local legend has it that the ruins of Emperor Maximilian's massive castle, which looms above the town, are haunted by ghosts.

WHERE TO EAT

$ ✕**Hacker.** People come from miles around to sample the scrumptious pastries and excellent coffee in this traditional café, which has been in business since 1774. You can also choose from a variety of ice-cream sundaes and other confections. The service is friendly, but can be a bit slow on busy days. In summer, tables are set outside so you can watch people passing by in the pedestrian area. ✉*Südtirolerstrasse 46* ☎05337/62322 ➯AE, MC, V ⊗Closed Nov.

SHOPPING

If you're looking for something special and different, go to **Kisslinger Kristall-Glas** (✉A-6240 ☎05337/64142) for beautiful hand-blown glass of all descriptions. You can study the artisans at work, and ogle the magnificent crystal creations on display in the multilevel showroom.

Across the river from Rattenberg lies Kramsach, a glass-production center since the 17th century. At the **Glassworks School** (☎05337/62623) you can watch craftsmen etching, engraving, and painting. Call ahead to arrange a visit.

For handcrafted ceramics, head to **Rattenberger Töpferladen** (✉*Klostergasse 66* ☎05337/67027), where two artists make and sell creative pieces.

EN ROUTE From Kramsach, follow the road on past Breitenbach toward the **Reintaler Seen** (Rein valley lakes) to the **Museum Tyrolean Bauernhöfe,** where more than a dozen complete Tyrolean farmhouses and barns, most dating back to at least the 18th century, have been brought, and restored and displayed in an idyllic setting. The museum and nearby lakes, some of the most beautiful (and warmest) in Tirol, are perfectly suited for exploring on a summer afternoon. ☎05337/62636 ⊕*www.museum-tb. at* ☑€5.50 ⊙*Apr.–Oct., daily 9–6.*

KUFSTEIN

26 km (16 mi) from Rattenberg.

ESSENTIALS

Visitor Information Kufstein (✉*Unterer Stadtplatz 8,* ☎*05372/62207*).

EXPLORING

Kufstein marks the border with Germany. The town was captured from Bavaria in 1504 by Emperor Maximilian I, who added it to the Habsburg domains.

★ Kufstein is dominated by a magnificent fortress right out of a Dürer etching, **Festung Kufstein,** originally built as a "castle for contemplation" in 1200. But Maximilian decided it was better suited for merrymaking and expanded and strengthened it in 1504, rechristening it *Lustschloss,* or "pleasure palace." The considerably renovated fortress contains a small **museum,** a panoramic windowed funicular, and an organ concert daily at noon, showcasing the famed "Heroes' Organ" (said to burst into sound when a national hero dies). With sumptuous rooms and terraced gardens, Festung Kufstein ranks among the finest of the 1,001 Tyrolean castles. ☎05372/602350 ⊕*www.festung.kufstein.at* ☑€8.90, guided tours by appt. ⊙*Nov.–mid-Mar., daily 10–4; mid-Mar.–Oct., daily 9–5.*

The center of town has some beautiful medieval-period streets, and harbors a remarkable concentration of Art Nouveau buildings, both public and private. The **Burgher's Tower** houses the Heldenorgel, the world's largest outdoor organ, with 26 registers and 1,800 pipes. The instrument is played year-round daily at noon and in summer at noon and 6 PM.

WHERE TO STAY

$$ Best Western Alpenrose. On the edge of town in green surroundings, this rustic house welcomes you immediately with its friendly lobby, which seems to continue the outdoors. The feeling of relaxed comfort carries over into the attractive bedrooms as well. The elegant restaurant is the best in the area and offers local gourmet specialties. Pros: good value; late check-out time; good for people with mobility problems. Cons: standard rooms seem small. ⊠ *Weissach Strasse 47* ☎*05372/62122* ⊕*www.bestwestern.com* ↪*19 rooms* ♿*In-room: no a/c, safe. In-hotel: restaurant, room service, bar, gym, spa, laundry service, parking (free), some pets allowed,, no-smoking rooms* ⊟ *AE, DC, MC, V* ⊙*Closed wk before and wk after Easter* ⦿*BP, MAP.*

SHOPPING

Kufstein is home to the world-famous **Riedel Glass Works** (☎*05372/ 64896–0*); a visit to the factory may be possible. Otherwise you can buy pieces at the **Riedel Factory Outlet** (⊠ *Weissachstrasse 28–34* ☎*05372/64896–0*), which is open weekdays 9–5:30, Saturday 9–1.

EN ROUTE At Wörgl most travelers begin to head east toward the great resorts of St. Johann and Kitzbühel. Route 312 takes you to St. Johann, the noted vacation center, about 30 km (19 mi) away. You can do the circuit of St. Johann and its more famous neighbor, Kitzbühel, by taking Route 161 for 12 km (7 mi) between the two resorts and returning to Wörgl via Route 170.

GOING, ELLMAU & SÖLL

10 km (6 mi) to 20 km (13 mi) south of Kufstein.

ESSENTIALS

Visitor Information **Going** (☎ *050509–510 www.wilderkaiser.info*).

EXPLORING

The villages of Going, Ellmau, and Söll have developed into attractive small winter and summer resorts. Their altitudes (and their snow) are about the same as those in Kitzbühel and St. Johann, but prices are lower, although rising as their popularity grows. Some of the region's finest restaurants and hotels are found around these villages.

The **Goinger Handwerks-Kunstmarkt,** an arts-and-crafts fair, is held one Friday each month from June through September. You can sample local specialties such as *Kässpätzle* (a noodle skillet dish with cheese and onions) and *Prügeltorte* (chocolate layer cake), along with locally distilled schnapps. Farmers and their families demonstrate crafts and skills handed down through the centuries, and if you're there at 8 PM you can hear the Going Musikkapelle (brass band) perform.

WHERE TO EAT

$$$–$$$$ ✕ **Schindlhaus.** "Four hands, two minds, one kitchen" is the motto of the two young brothers who run this acclaimed kitchen. Original variations on traditional Austrian dishes are served up in a modern setting by the Winklers. Try the lightly braised fillet of venison with red cabbage, ox served with local vegetables, or one of the fish specialties for which they are justifiably famous. The *gemütliche* atmosphere and friendly staff provide the perfect finishing touches. ⊠ *Dorf 134, Söll* ☎ *05333/516136* ▭ *DC, MC, V* ⊘ *Closed Mon., Tues. in summer.*

$$ ✕ **Restaurant Lanzenhof.** A sophisticated but festive atmosphere dominates this restaurant in a traditional Tyrolean inn. The kitchen serves impeccable traditional Tyrolean food like *Schlutzkrapfeln* (ravioli stuffed with cheese, potatoes, and spinach). The lamb chops and roast pork are particular favorites for many diners, and are always available on weekends. Produce arrives directly from local farmers. ⊠ *Dorf 23, Going* ☎ *05358/3534* ▭ *V* ⊘ *Closed Sun. and Apr. and Nov.*

WHERE TO STAY

$$$$ ▦ **Bio-Hotel Stanglwirt.** A 300-year-old coaching inn includes an expansive health-and-fitness complex. Guests can ride, swim, ski, or play tennis and squash. The tennis school is one of the best in Austria. It's also a popular mealtime stop for tour buses, so it can get crowded. Rooms in the newer section are spacious; some are studios with old-fashioned ceramic stoves, in keeping with the Tyrolean decor. Everything, from tapestry to linens and mattresses are in natural organic fibers. (There are even wood shavings in some of the pillows and duvets.) Children will enjoy the kids' farm. **Pros:** it's a "green" option; plenty of activities. **Cons:** not as charming as it once was; very expensive Internet. ⊠ *Kaiserweg 1 Going* ☎ *05358/2000* ⊕ *www.stanglwirt.com* ⤶ *62 rooms, 6 apartments* ⚷ *In-room: no a/c, safe, refrigerator, Wi-Fi. In-hotel: 2 restaurants, tennis courts, pools, gym, spa, laundry service, parking (free), some pets allowed, no-smoking rooms* ▭ *AE, DC, MC, V* ⏍ *BP, MAP.*

$$$$ ▦ **Der Bär.** Within walking distance of the center of Ellmau, "The Bear" is known throughout Austria as one of the best country inns. An elegant but relaxed vibe pervades permeates every part of the place, including the attractive Tyrolean-style guest rooms. Many outdoor activities throughout the year make this place popular with outdoorsy types. In winter you can relax in the wellness area after a morning spent skiing, while in summer you can grab your clubs and head out to the links. The kitchen does best with local dishes, such as roast lamb or wild game. **Pros:** outstanding food; something for everyone. **Cons:** outside the town center. ⊠ *Kirchbichl 9, Ellmau* ☎ *05358/2395* ⊕ *www.hotel baer.com* ⤶ *45 rooms* ⚷ *In-room: no a/c, safe, kitchen (some), refrigerator. In-hotel: restaurant, room service, bar, golf course, pools, gym, spa, children's programs (ages 3–10), laundry service, Wi-Fi, parking (free), no-smoking rooms* ▭ *AE, MC, V* ⊘ *Closed mid-Mar.–May and early Nov.–mid-Dec.* ⏍ *BP, MAP*

9

ST. JOHANN IN TIROL

32 km (24 mi) southeast of Kufstein, 12 km (7 mi) northeast of Kitzbühel.

ESSENTIALS

Visitor Information **St. Johann in Tirol** (✉ *Poststrasse 2,* ☎ *05352/63335–0*).

EXPLORING

For years St. Johann lived in the shadow of Kitzbühel, but today the town, with its colorfully painted houses, has developed a personality of its own, and for better or worse is equally mobbed winter and summer. The facilities are similar, but prices are still lower, although climbing. (The dark horses here could be Kirchdorf, 4 km [2½ mi] north of St. Johann, where costs appear to be holding, or Fieberbrunn, 12 km [7 mi] east on Route 164.)

While in St. Johann, don't miss the magnificently decorated Baroque **parish church** or the Gothic **Spitalskirche,** with its fine late-medieval stained glass, just west of town in Weitau.

WHERE TO STAY & EAT

$$$ ✗**Das Bräu.** A great place to stop between Salzburg and Innsbruck is Das Bräu, about 25 km (15 mi) northeast of St. Johann in Tirol. There are two restaurants, one for casual dining and the other for a more elegant meal. In the "rural" restaurant—with red-gingham tablecloths and cowbells, harnesses, and stirrups hanging from the wooden beams—dishes include locally caught fish, fried chicken, and grilled lamb. If you are going upscale, you'll be offered delights such as Fogosh fillet in pepper sauce with potato straws cream-cheese parfait with strawberry pulp. The desserts are scrumptious beyond belief. If you don't feel like driving on, you can stay overnight in one of the pleasant bedrooms upstairs. ✉ *Hauptstrasse 28 Lofer* ☎ *06588/82070* ⊟ *AE, DC, MC, V.*

$$ ▦**Alpenappartement Europa.** This apartment-hotel adjacent to a recreation center (where guests can pay extra for swimming, sauna, and tennis facilities) is attractively furnished with Baroque reproductions. The apartments are ample and clean and have fully equipped kitchens. Exhausted skiers can delight in knowing that breakfast (not included in the daily rate) is served until 11 AM. **Pros:** a room of one's own; feeling of independence. **Cons:** too many hidden costs. ✉ *Achen Allee 18* ☎ *05352/62285* ⊕ *www.alpenappartement-europa.at* ⟢ *15 apartments* ⚲ *In-room: no a/c, kitchen. In-hotel: parking (free), some pets allowed* ⊟ *No credit cards* ⏺|*BP.*

$–$$ ▦**Post.** The painted stucco facade identifies this traditional hotel in the center of town. Natural woods and reds carry over from the public spaces and restaurant into the guest rooms. The decor not the most modern, but the rooms are quite cozy and spacious. As the inn doesn't have any sauna or wellness area, it offers free admission to the local public swimming pool. For those who don't need too much luxury and appreciate the charm of a family-run hotel, this is the best place in St. Johann. **Pros:** centrally located; friendly staff. **Cons:** noise from the street; dated décor; smoky bar. ✉ *Speckbacherstrasse 1* ☎ *05352/62230*

⊕*www.hotel-post.tv* ➟*34 rooms* ♿*In-room: no a/c. In-hotel: restaurant, bar, bicycles, Internet, parking (paid), no-smoking rooms* ▭*AE, DC, MC, V* ☾*Closed Apr. and Nov.* ��*BP, MAP, FAP.*

KITZBÜHEL

12 km (7 mi) south of St. Johann, 71 km (44 mi) northeast of Gerlos.

ESSENTIALS
Visitor Information Kitzbühel (✉*Hinterstadt 18* ☎*05356/777*).

EXPLORING
Kitzbühel is indisputably one of Austria's most fashionable winter resorts, although the town is nowstaking a claim on its summer season as well. "Kitz" offers warm-season visitors a hefty program of hiking, cycling, and golf, along with outdoor concerts and plays, and a professional tennis tournament in July. What originally put this ski town on the map is the famous Ski Safari—a carefully planned, clever combination of lifts, cable railways, and runs that lets you ski for more than 145 km (91 mi) without having to climb a single foot. Kitzbühel is in perpetual motion, and is always packed December through February, notably at the end of January for the famed **Hahnenkamm** downhill ski race. At any time during the season there's plenty to do, from sleigh rides to fancy-dress balls.

Built in the 16th century with proceeds from copper and silver mining, Kitzbühel itself is scenic enough. Among its pleasures are its churches, such as **St. Andrew's parish church** (1435–1506), which has a lavishly Rococo chapel, the Rosakapelle, and the marvelously ornate tomb (1520) of the Kupferschmid family.

The **Church of St. Catherine,** built about 1350, houses a Gothic winged altar dating from 1515.

In summer you'll be offered a free guest card for substantial reductions on various activities (some of which are then free, like the hiking program), such as tennis, riding, and golf. The best swimming is in the nearby Schwarzsee. To see Alpine flowers in their native habitat, take the cable car up the Kitzbüheler Horn to the **Alpine Flower Garden Kitzbühel** at 6,500 feet; cars leave continuously.

WHERE TO EAT
$$$$ ✕**Tennerhof.** Thomas Dreher, Austria's youngest top-rated chef, found at Tennerehof a kitchen to give his skills full scope. Freshly picked herbs from the garden accompany almost every dish from soup to sorbet. Dishes couldn't be more creative; for example, the roasted goose liver is served with mango ravioli and a reduction of cacao. Local game is the chef's passion, so don't miss one of his seasonal creations. Food and wine are presented by the well-trained staff with white gloves in one of the four cozy parlors. Elegant dress and quiet conversations are the rule in this high-class restaurant. ✉*Griesenauweg 26* ☎*05356/63181* ⌂*Reservations essential* ▭*AE, DC, MC, V* ☾*Closed Apr.–mid-May and mid-Oct.–mid-Dec.*

$$ ✕**Hallerwirt.** In a small village about 5 km (3 mi) south of Kitzbühel,
Fodor'sChoice Hallerwirt is known for its great Austrian cuisine and charm. Old
★ wooden floors and a ceramic stove in the parlor lend a period flair to
this 400-year-old farmhouse. A colorful mix of people gathers here,
and young and old enjoy the easygoing vibe. The congenial host takes
time to give everyone some good wine suggestions. The friendly staff
serves specialties like Jerusalem artichoke soup and fillet of lamb.
⊠ *Oberaurach 4 Aurach bei Kitzbühel* ☎*05356/63181* ⌕*Reservations essential* ⊟ *MC, V.*

$–$$ ✕**Gallo.** Finding an inexpensive place in Kitzbühel is difficult, so this
modern Italian restaurant is quite a find. Located in the pedestrian area,
it's a good choice for a light meal or an afternoon cup of coffee. Sit on
the sunny terrace and enjoy a pizza from the wood-burning oven while
watching high society go by. Want something a little more substantial?
There are great Italian dishes such as risotto with arugula. ⊠ *Vorderstadt 12* ☎*05356/65862* ⊟*AE, DC, MC, V.*

$ ✕**Praxmair.** Après-ski can't begin early enough for the casually chic
crowds that pile into this famous pastry shop for its *Krapfen* (something like jelly doughnuts and available throughout Austria in January
and February). For locals the Praxmair is a meeting point for regular
get-togethers, cabaret performances, and small events. The wood decor
and a tiled stove give the special flair to this café. ⊠ *Vorderstadt 17*
☎*05356/62646* ⊟*AE, DC, MC, V* ⊗*Closed Apr. and Nov.*

WHERE TO STAY

$$$$ ▦**Golf-Hotel Rasmushof.** For year-round proximity to outdoor activities,
it's difficult to find a better address. Located on a 9-hole golf course,
it has a view of the famous Streif downhill ski run and is only steps
from the lift. All rooms have balconies and are drenched in Tyrolean
antiques and plush furnishings. The facilities are completely up-to-date,
including a large indoor swimming pool and a vast sauna. **Pros:** you
can ski right into the hotel; luxe bed linens; breathtaking views. **Cons:**
little free parking; small bathrooms on first floor. ⊠ *Hermann Reisch
Weg 15* ☎*05356/65252* ⊕*www.rasmushof.at* ⇗*49 rooms, 11 suites*
⌂ *In-room: no a/c, safe, refrigerator (some), Internet, Wi-Fi (some).
In-hotel: restaurant, room service, bar, golf course, pool, gym, spa,
laundry service, parking (paid), no-smoking rooms* ⊟*AE, DC, MC,
V* ❍*BP, MAP.*

$$$$ ▦**Romantik Hotel Tennerhof.** Adored by everyone from the Duke of
Fodor'sChoice Windsor to Kirk Douglas, this Alpine Shangri-la is set in a huge garden.
★ Inside the hilltop mountain inn you'll find a space that is at once rustic
and glamorous, with gold chandeliers hung over country cupboards
and silk-covered sofas next to shuttered windows. The guest rooms
are all different, some with ceramic stoves or even open fireplaces. The
house itself is a 400-year-old farmhouse, so don't be surprised if you
sleep in the hand-painted bed of the original owner. The public rooms
are cozy and inviting. Breakfast is served either on the terrace or in
the atmospheric parlors. **Pros:** aristocratic flair; great breakfast; nice
garden. **Cons:** some find it too formal; some standard rooms face parking lots. ⊠ *Griesenauweg 26* ☎*05356/63181* ⊕*www.tennerhof.com*
⇗*40 rooms* ⌂ *In-room: no a/c, safe, refrigerator. In-hotel: restaurant,*

room service, bar, pools, spa, laundry service, Internet, parking (free), no-smoking rooms ⊟*AE, DC, MC, V* ☉*Closed Apr.–mid-May and mid-Oct.–mid-Dec.* ⍾⃝*BP, MAP.*

$$$ $$$$ ⊞**Hotel Villa Licht.** Licht means "light" in German, and this luxurious B&B is certainly a luminous discovery. You enter through a small porch, an ideal setting for summer breakfasts, into a small reception area scented with fresh flowers. The warmly decorated rooms, some with the original wood floors, all have balconies and terra-cotta bathrooms. After enjoying the sauna in the tiny Tyrolean hut, you can jump right into the snow. Remarkable hospitality and attention to every detail are the standard here. But beware, small precious jewels come at a price; book well in advance in high season. **Pros:** a few steps from the city center; very quiet location. **Cons:** expensive rates; no restaurant. ⊠*Franz Reisch Strasse 8* ☏*05356/62293* ⊕*www.villa-licht.at* ⮐ *14 rooms, 3 suites, 3 apartments* ⚴*In-room: no a/c, safe. In-hotel: room service, bar, pool, laundry service, Wi-Fi, parking (free), no-smoking rooms* ⊟*AE, DC, MC, V* ⍾⃝*BP.*

NIGHTLIFE

Much activity centers on the **Kitzbühel Casino** in the center of the pedestrian area, which offers baccarat, blackjack, roulette, and one-armed bandits. There are a restaurant and a bar, and no set closing time. A valid passport or driver's license is needed to enter the casino. ⊠*Hinterstadt 24* ☏*05356/62300* ⮐*Free* ☉*Daily from 3* PM.

A top nightspot is **Ecco** (⊠*Hinterstadt 22* ☏*05356/71300–20*), which serves light food in an upscale setting. **Fünferl** (⊠*Franz-Reisch-Strasse 1* ☏*05356/71300–5*) in the Kitzbüheler Hof has many dedicated fans. A favorite modern bar for many is **Jimmy's** (⊠*Vorderstadt 31* ☏*05356/644–09*), which occasionally has a DJ.

The **Londoner** (⊠*Franz-Reisch-Strasse 4* ☏*05356/71428*) is a popular watering hole among young people. Established favorites include **Stamperl** (⊠*Franz-Reisch-Strasse 7* ☏*05356/62555*). The dance-club crowd moves from place to place, but check out **Take Five** (⊠*Hinterstadt 22* ☏*05356/71300–30*), the town's hot spot.

SPORTS & THE OUTDOORS

GOLF With 19 courses within an hour's drive, Kitzbühel may properly lay claim to being the "golf center of the Alps." The Golf Alpin Pass offers special deals on greens fees; it's available at some hotels and golf clubs, or from the tourist office.

Golf Eichenheim (☏*05356/66615*), an 18-hole, PGA-rated fairway, offers impressive views of the grand Kitzbühel Alps. **Golfclub Kitzbühel** (☏*05356/63007*), 9 holes, par-36, is open May–October. **Golf-Club Kitzbühel-Schwarzsee** (☏*05356/77770*), 18 holes, par-72, is open May–October. **Rasmushof Golf Club** (☏*05356/65252*) is in the finish area of the legendary "Streif" downhill run, and is the closest course to the town center.

MOUNTAIN SPORTS

HIKING & CLIMBING

Tirol has a good share of the more than 50,000 km (35,000 mi) of well-maintained mountain paths that thread the country. Hiking is one of the best ways to experience the truly awesome Alpine scenery, whether you just want to take a leisurely stroll around one of the crystalline lakes mirroring the towering mountains or trek your way to the top of one of the mighty peaks. Mountain climbing is a highly organized sport in Tirol, a province that contains some of the greatest challenges to lovers of the sport. The instructors at the Alpine School Innsbruck are the best people to contact if you want to make arrangements for a mountain-climbing holiday or if you wish to attend a mountain-climbing school.

SKIING

Downhill was practically invented in Tirol. Legendary skiing master Hannes Schneider took the Norwegian art of cross-country skiing and adapted it to downhill running. No matter where your trip takes you, world-class—and often gut-scrambling—skiing is available, from the glamour of Kitzbühel in the east to the imposing peaks of St. Anton am Arlberg in the west.

Close to the Arlberg Pass is St. Anton, which, at 4,300 feet, proudly claims one of the finest ski schools in the world. The specialty at St. Anton is piste skiing—enormously long runs studded with moguls (and few trees), some so steep and challenging that the sport is almost the equal of mountain climbing. In fact, this is the only place in Austria where you can heli-ski. It was here in the 1920s that Hannes Schneider started the school that was to become the model for all others. A short bus ride to the top of the pass brings you to St. Christoph, at 5,800 feet. Many excellent tours, served by the Galzip cable railway, start here, but the *Skihaserl,* or ski bunny, would do well to stay down at St. Anton where there are gentler—and kinder—nursery-level slopes. If you care to mingle with royalty on the lifts, then the close-by, posh winter-only villages of Zürs and Lech, on the Vorarlberg side of the Pass, are for you.

Farther along the Inn is the Ötz Valley. From the Ötztal station you can go by bus to Sölden, a resort at 4,500 feet that has become as well known for its party scene as for its superb skiing. The up-and-comer of Austrian ski resorts is Ischgl, in the Paznaun Valley bordering Switzerland, where good snow is assured by more than 120 mi of runs above 2,000 feet, and where young snowboarders are as numerous as skiers. Long, wide runs resembling those in Colorado go as far as the Swiss border. Not far from Innsbruck is Seefeld, at 3,870 feet, long popular with cross-country skiers for its miles of meticulously groomed tracks. At the farther end of Tirol lies Kitzbühel, chic and *charmant,* perhaps most famous for its "Ski Safari," a system of ski lifts and trails, some floodlighted at night, that allows skiers to ski for weeks without retracing their steps. The best time for skiing around Innsbruck is January to April.

WEST FROM INNSBRUCK

The upper Inn Valley, from Innsbruck stretching down to the Swiss border, is beautiful countryside, particularly the narrow valleys that branch off to the south. Most visitors take Route 171 west from Innsbruck along the banks of the Inn, rather than the autobahn, which hugs the cliffs along the way. This is a region of family-run farms perched on mountainsides and steep granite peaks flanking narrow valleys leading to some of Austria's finest ski areas.

TELFS

32 km (20 mi) southeast of Reutte.

EXPLORING

Mythical masked figures invade the streets of Telfs every five years just before Lent, when the town hosts its traditional Carnival celebration of **Schleicherlaufen.** This well-attended event dates back to the 16th century. Some of the grotesque masks can be seen in the local museum. The next Schleicherlaufen festival is in 2010.

WHERE TO STAY

$$$$ ☒ **Interalpen Tyrol.** Though built in Alpine style, this resort is undeniably imposing. Leave your worries–and your luggage–behind at the drive-in reception and make your way through the huge lobby crowned with two monumental chandeliers. The rooms range from Tyrolean to modern decor, and the service is excellent. Avail yourself of the massive wellness area, including a Tyrolean sauna, two pools, and a restaurant. **Pros:** great views of the Alps; huge rooms; very quiet. **Cons:** feels very isolated. *⊠ Dr.-Hans-Liebherr-Alpenstraße 1 ☎ 050809-30 ⊕ www.interalpen.com ⬅ 286 rooms ⬧ In-room: no a/c, safe, refrigerator, Internet. In-hotel: 2 restaurants, room service, bar, tennis courts, pool, gym, spa, bicycles, children's programs (ages 3–10), laundry service, Internet, public Wi-Fi, parking (free), no-smoking rooms ⊟ AE, DC, MC, V ⊗ Closed Apr.–early May and Nov.–early Dec.* ⍟ BP, MAP.

$ ☒ **Tirolerhof.** You're within a couple of blocks of the center of town in this family-run hotel, convenient also to nearby swimming pools and tennis and squash courts. Rooms are simple, done up in pale wood and colorful artwork. The hotel's main garden is a great place to relax, and some rooms have their own small gardens instead of balconies. Have a drink in the popular bar and get to know locals, or enjoy a meal in the restaurant serving regional fare with some hints of the Mediterranean. **Pros:** family-run friendliness; great restaurant; free Internet. **Cons:** small rooms; small common areas. *⊠ Bahnhofstrasse 28 ☎ 05262/62237 ⊕ www.der-tirolerhof.at ⬅ 36 rooms ⬧ In-room: no a/c, Wi-Fi. In-hotel: restaurant, room service, bar, laundry service, Internet, no-smoking rooms ⊟ DC, MC, V ⊗ Closed 2 wks around Easter and 1 wk in Oct.* ⍟ BP, MAP.

EN ROUTE   Driving west from Innsbruck or north up the mountain from Telfs you arrive at **Seefeld,** perched on a sunny plateau at 3,937 feet, only a few kilometers from the German border. As you travel, the views looking

9

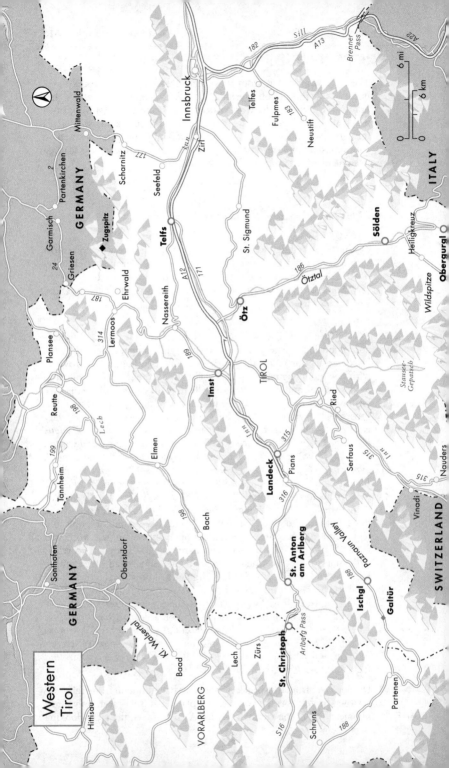

back into the Inn Valley are spectacular, and the mountains surrounding the vacation village are grand. In summer Seefeld does service as a base for climbers and hikers in the pristine Karwendel mountain preserve, and in winter attracts hordes of cross-country ski fans and downhill skiers.

IMST

35 km (22 mi) west of Telfs.

ESSENTIALS
Visitor Information Imst (✉ *Johannesplatz 4* ☎ *05412/6910–0*).

EXPLORING
Imst, a popular summer resort lying a half mile or so back from the Inn River and the railway line, makes an excellent base from which to explore the Paznaun Valley and the upper Inn Valley, leading into Switzerland and Italy.

The **Schemenlaufen,** (also called *Fastnacht*), a masked procession depicting the struggle between good and evil, usually takes place in February. Many of the magnificently carved masks worn by the mummers—especially those of the fearsome witches—are very old and qualify as works of art. The tradition is ancient, and as in Telfs you can see many of the 100-year-old carved masks in the local **museum** (✉ *Strelenegasse 6*); check with the tourist office for opening times. A great feature of these rustic carnivals is the ringing of cowbells of all shapes, sizes, and tones, and the resulting noise is quite deafening when the procession hits its stride.

Don't overlook the 15th-century frescoed **parish church** in the upper part of Imst.

WHERE TO STAY

$$ 🏨 **Best Western Hotel Stern.** This traditional Tyrolean house sits in the ☺ heart of Imst. Guest rooms are well equipped and very large; suites with balconies and mountain views are also available. The mostly regional cuisine is well-prepared and generously served. Skiers with hearty appetites will relish the evening buffet, perhaps followed by a visit to the panoramic sauna. It's a pet-friendly place, and the joke is that the "real boss" is the family dog, Waldi. **Pros:** great sauna; family-run vibe. **Cons:** guests must be dog lovers. ✉ *Pfarrgasse 42* ☎ *05412/63342* ⊕ *www.sternhotel.com* ➪ *11 rooms, 22 suites* ⚴ *In-room: no a/c, refrigerator, Internet. In-hotel: restaurant, bar, gym, parking (free), some pets allowed* 🖃 *AE, DC, MC, V* ⊙ *Closed mid-Oct.–mid-Nov.* ⦿*BP.*

$–$$ 🏨 **Schlosshotel Post.** Next to a large park, this 16th-century castle is topped with romantic onion-dome towers. The warm interior is furnished with antiques, and the modern bedrooms are cheerful. Some rooms are even located in the towers, giving them a little extra atmosphere. Even if it's not a luxury hotel, this place has its charms. The restaurant is recommended, particularly for its wild game. **Pros:** historic building; tasty restaurant. **Cons:** noisy location; a bit dated. ✉ *E. Wallnöfer-Platz 3* ☎ *05412/66555* ⊕ *www.romantikhotel-post.com* ➪ *26*

9

rooms ⚒ *In-room: no a/c, Internet (some). In-hotel: restaurant, pool, parking (paid), no-smoking rooms* ▭*DC, MC, V* ⊘ *Closed Nov.–mid-Dec.* ⊙*BP, MAP.*

$–$$ 🏨**Zum Hirschen.** This comfortable *hotel in* the center of town is a
☾   good choice for those on a budget. Rooms are equipped with only the basics, but they are spacious and cozy. The new wellness area is included in the room rate. Apartments have kitchens, although you can still arrange for breakfast or half-board. **Pros:** bargain rates; family-friendly vibe. **Cons:** lacks an intimate feel; a little spare. ⊠ *Th.-Walsch-Strasse 3* ☎*05412/6901–0* ⤶*106 rooms, 6 apartments* ⚒*In-room: no a/c, kitchen (some), refrigerator (some). In-hotel: restaurant, bar, pool, spa, Internet, Wi-Fi, parking (free), no-smoking rooms* ▭*DC, V* ⊙*BP, MAP.*

▌EN
ROUTE   The Ötz Valley climbs in a series of six great natural steps for nearly 42 km (26 mi) from the Inn River to the glaciers around Obergurgl, 6,200 feet above sea level. The entire span offers stunning scenery, the most dramatic part beginning around Sölden, where the final rise begins to the 8,100-foot pass over the Timmel Alps and across the Italian border into South Tirol. It was in this area that Ötzi, the Iceman mummy, was discovered in 1992. The body, which is more than 5,000 years old, was found by Austrians who were unaware they had crossed the Italian border. Ötzi is now in the possession of Italy, which at first wanted nothing to do with him, thinking he was a 20th-century murder victim. To reach the valley, turn south off Route 171 onto Route 186.

ÖTZ

21 km (12 mi) southeast of Imst, 23 km (14 mi) southwest of Telfs.

GETTING HERE & AROUND
The Ötz Valley is very well connected to the Innsbruck Airport by bus, and a regular shuttle connects the villages with Innsbruck.

ESSENTIALS
Visitor Information **Ötz Valley** (⊠ *Hauptstraße 66* ☎*057200/500*).

EXPLORING
Gothic houses with colorful frescoes grace this typically Tyrolean mountain village.

The parish church of **St. George and St. Nicholas,** whose tower was once a charnel house, sits on a rock promontory above the village. The small St. Michael's Chapel also has a splendid altar dating from 1683.

About 3 km (2 mi) southwest of the town lies the deep-green lake of **Piburg,** the warmest lake in Tirol. It's a nice place for swimming and hiking.

WHERE TO STAY
$ 🏨**Drei Mohren.** This century-old building at the entrance of the village will catch your attention with its wonderful collection of odd towers and onion domes. Many things have changed during the years, but fortunately a lot has been preserved, like the scent of the aged wood in

the spectacular hand-carved parlors where dinner or drinks are served, or the elegantly paneled rooms with antique furnishings. Most have balconies with views of the mountains. **Pros:** very informal; friendly staff; many activities. **Cons:** on a busy street; a bit old-fashioned. ⊠*Hauptstrasse 54* ☎*05252/6301* ⊕*www.hotel3mohren.at* ⇄*25 rooms* ⚬*In-room: no a/c, safe (some). In-hotel: restaurant, room service, tennis courts, bicycles, laundry service, Internet, parking (free), no-smoking rooms* ⊟*AE, DC, MC, V* ☾*Closed mid.-Apr.–mid.-May and Nov.–mid-Dec.* ⎆*BP, MAP.*

ÖTZTAL CARD

If you're planning to visit the Ötz Valley for a few days in summer, consider buying an Ötztal Card. The cards are good for three, seven, and 10 days for €35, €56, and €74, respectively, and are available at tourist offices in the valley or hotels. This card gives free admission to all the forms of transportation, museums, and bathing areas. Free bike rentals are also included.

SÖLDEN

28 km (18 mi) south of Ötz.

ESSENTIALS

Visitor Information **Sölden/Ötztal** (⊠*Rettenbach 466, Sölden* ☎*05254/510–0*). For information on Sölden's skiing facilities, contact the **Tourismusverband Sölden** (⊠ *Gemeindestrasse 4,* ☎*057200/200* ⊕ *www.soelden.com*).

EXPLORING

Sölden's newest addition to its already massive lift network is the "Black Blade," which carries eight at a time more than 9,800 feet to the Rettenbach glacier, completing the only lift system in Austria to boast skiing on three mountains more than 9,800 feet high. The view from any of the three peaks provides a panoramic 360-degree view of the mountains. Sölden's reputation as a wild, après-ski party town is well deserved, meaning that if you are searching for a tranquil, romantic ski holiday, or have small children, you may want to try the village of **Hochsölden**—on the slopes above town, where things are quieter—or search elsewhere.

WHERE TO STAY

$$$$ **Aqua Dome Hotel and Spa.** This monument to luxury lies 10 km (6 mi) north of Sölden in the village of Längenfeld. In addition to the spa's much-heralded thermal waters, you can avail yourself of saunas, steam rooms, and a plethora of beauty, health, and fitness treatments. Here you'll find what is reputed to be the finest hotel and spa facility in Tirol. The guest rooms, furnished under the guidance of a feng-shui expert, are soothing and elegant, with generous use of natural wood and stone. Every room is equipped with a balcony, so you can gaze out on the surrounding mountains. **Pros:** spa is open late; lovely rooms. **Cons:** spa busy on weekends; too sprawling for some. ⊠*Oberlängenfeld 140, Längenfeld* ☎*05253/6400* ⊕*www.aqua-dome.at* ⇄*141 rooms* ⚬*In-room: safe, refrigerator, Wi-Fi. In-hotel: restaurant, room service, bar,*

pool, gym, spa, children's programs (ages 3–14), laundry service, Internet, no-smoking rooms ⊟AE, DC, MC, V ⍾⃝MAP.

$$$$ ⚏**Central.** Huge arches and heavy timber beams set the mood at this massive riverside hotel. The guest rooms are spacious and luxuriously furnished, but some are slightly outdated. A five-course dinner is included in the half-board rate, but the kitchen also serves à la carte meals. The kitschy Venice-style wellness area, including a reproduction of St. Mark's Square, seems out of place but is quite relaxing. **Pros:** great service; shuttle to the slopes; nice suites. **Cons:** slopes are not within walking distance. ✉*Auweg 3* ☎*05254/2260–0* ⊕*www.central-soelden.at* ⤴*120 rooms* ⚬*In-room: no a/c, safe. In-hotel: 2 restaurants, room service, bar, pool, gym, spa, children's programs (ages 3–14), laundry service, parking (free), no-smoking rooms ⊟DC, MC, V* ⊗*Closed May–mid-July* ⍾⃝*BP, MAP.*

$$$–$$$$ ⚏**Liebe Sonne.** Ski enthusiasts will be right next to the chairlift to Hochsölden at this sprawling complex. A modern lobby and a friendly staff welcome you in this centrally located lodging. The paneled guest rooms are cozy, and all have balconies with views of the slopes. In winter, the party never stops at the nearby bars and clubs. In summer the all-inclusive plan is required, while in winter half-board is a must. **Pros:** spacious rooms; very friendly staff; nice outdoor whirlpool. **Cons:** on a noisy street. ✉*Dorfstraße 58* ☎*05254/2203–0* ⊕*www.sonnenhotels.at* ⤴*59 rooms* ⚬*In-room: no a/c, safe, refrigerator, Internet. In-hotel: restaurant, room service, bar, pools, gym, spa, children's programs (ages 3–14), laundry service, Internet terminal, parking (free), some pets allowed ⊟MC, V* ⊗*Closed May and June* ⍾⃝*MAP, FAP.*

NIGHTLIFE

The nightlife here varies from nonexistent to wild, depending on the season. In winter the more than 85 bars, discos, pubs, and eateries are packed, and many nightspots have live bands, but expect cover charges of around €5.

The most popular music bar is **Bierhimml Partyhaus** (☎*05254/50112*), with a never-ending selection of beers and decent food. Don't pass up the whimsical **Bla-Bla** (☎*05254/2646*) après-ski bar, the town's most renowned see-and-be-seen watering hole. **Fire & Ice** (☎*05254/2203*) keeps the dance floor pumped until 2 in the morning.

SPORTS & THE OUTDOORS

CLIMBING The nearby Ventertal valley burrows still farther into the Ötztal Alps, ending in the tiny village of Vent, a popular resort center. In summer the village is transformed into a base for serious mountain climbers experienced in ice and rock climbing, who want to attempt the formidable **Wildspitze** (12,450 feet) or other, even more difficult neighboring peaks. Hiring a professional local guide is strongly advised. To reach Vent from Sölden, turn off at the road marked to Heiligenkreuz.

RAFTING **Vacancia Outdoor Tirol** (✉*Hauptstrasse 438* ☎*05254/3100* ⊕*www.vacancia.at*) can provide you with what you need to enjoy the area's wild water, including guided rafting trips, and offers special outdoor adventures for kids. In winter you can secure skiing gear, lessons, and, again, children's programs.

OBERGURGL

11 km (7 mi) south of Sölden.

ESSENTIALS

Visitor Information Tourismusverband Obergurgl/Hochgurgl (✉A-6456, Ötztal ☎05256/6466 ⊕www.obergurgl.com).

EXPLORING

Austria's highest village, tiny Obergurgl gained its reputation not only for superb winter sports but also as the place where the Swiss physicist Auguste Piccard landed his famous stratospheric balloon in 1931. In winter a vast expanse of snow and ice shimmers all around you, and the great peaks and glaciers of the Ötztal Alps appear deceptively close all year.

A high Alpine road takes you from Obergurgl to the hotel settlement at **Hochgurgl,** another excellent skiing spot, and farther up to the Timmelsjoch Pass (closed in winter) through magnificent mountain scenery. Since 1988 Hochgurgl has also been accessible by cable car, bridging the two ski areas. From Hochgurgl a three-stage chairlift brings you into an area of year-round skiing.

WHERE TO STAY

$$$$ 🏨**Edelweiss und Gurgl.** This ski-in ski-out hotel is right at the base of the lifts, so you can be at the slopes in minutes. Even if it has expanded a lot—maybe too much—since it opened in 1889, the hotel still offers a nice and relaxed atmosphere. Complimentary robes and slippers await you in every room for use in the large spa area with its outdoor pool and hot tub overlooking the mountains. All rooms have natural-wood touches, but standard rooms can seem small. In winter, the outdoor Umbrella Bar serves tea and warm wine for après-ski. All the milk and butter served in the hotel comes from the adjacent farm. **Pros:** plenty of activities; close to lifts; relaxed vibe. **Cons:** rooms facing north have less impressive views; long walk to elevators. ✉ *Ramolweg 5* ☎*05256/6223* ⊕*www.edelweiss-gurgl.com* 🛏*100 rooms* ♨*In-room: no a/c, safe. In-hotel: 2 restaurants, room service, bar, pools, gym, spa, bicycles, children's programs (ages 3–10), laundry service, Internet, Wi-Fi, parking (free), no-smoking rooms* ▭*AE, DC, MC, V* ⊙*Closed May–mid-June and Oct.–Nov.* ⊙*BP, MAP.*

9

LANDECK, UPPER INN VALLEY & ST. ANTON

LANDECK

24 km (15 mi) southwest of Imst.

ESSENTIALS

Visitor Information Landeck (⊠*Malserstrasse 10* ☎*05442/65600*).

EXPLORING

On Route 171 west, Landeck is a popular place in summer and a good base from which to explore the Paznaun Valley and the upper Inn Valley, leading into Switzerland and Italy. Landeck also serves well in winter as a less-expensive base for skiing the nearby world-class slopes at St. Anton or Ischgl.

Landeck is known for an ancient and awe-inspiring rite that takes place on **"Cheese Sunday,"** the Sunday following Ash Wednesday. At dawn the young men set out to climb to the top of the great rocky crags that overshadow and hem in the Altstadt (Old City) on three sides. As dusk falls, they light huge bonfires that can be seen for miles around and then set fire to great disks of pinewood dipped in tar, which they roll ablaze down to the valley below. The sight of scores of these fiery wheels bounding down the steep slopes toward town is a fearsome spectacle worthy of Ezekiel.

The 13th-century **Burg Landeck** dominates from its position above the town. Climb up and catch the superb views from this vantage point. ⊠*Schlossweg 2* ⊕*www.schlosslandeck.at* ⊗*Apr.–Oct., Tues.–Sun. 2–6.*

Also note the 16th-century winged altar in the 15th-century Gothic **Church of the Assumption.**

WHERE TO STAY

$ ☷**Pension Haueis.** Austrian *gemütlichkeit* abounds in this family-run inn in the village of Zams. It's not fancy, but the comfortable rooms and delicious meals prepared by owner–chef Sepp Haueis have charmed many a guest. An open fireplace in the entrance hall and a nice summer terrace make the place warm and inviting throughout the year. Many signs throughout the building indicate that this is one of the oldest farms in Tirol. **Pros:** intimate feel; bargain rates. **Cons:** not luxurious; no wellness area. ⊠*Hauptplatz 1, Zams* ☎*05442/63001* ⊕*www.postgasthof-gemse.at* ⊅*15 rooms* ⅏*In-room: no a/c. In-hotel: restaurant, bar, laundry facilities, parking (free), some pets allowed* ▤*No credit cards* ⊗*Closed Easter–May and Nov.–mid.-Dec.* ⅋*BP, MAP.*

SPORTS & THE OUTDOORS

HIKING   Would-be climbers can take lessons by contacting Hugo Walter at the **Bergsteigerschule Piz Buin-Silvretta** (⊠*A-6563, Galtür* ☎*05443/8565*).

The **Zammer Lochputz** (☎*05442–65600* ⊕*www.zammer-lochputz.at*), a deep, rocky gorge across the Inn River from Zams, has been made accessible by a series of tunnels, steep metal stairways, and bridges.

Open only between May and September, the gorge provides a refreshing half-hour hike, particularly on a hot summer day.

ST. ANTON AM ARLBERG

★ *22 km (15 mi) west of Landeck.*

ESSENTIALS

Visitor Information **St. Anton am Arlberg** (✉ *Dorfstrasse 8* ☎ *05446/ 2269–0*).

EXPLORING

Tucked between the entrance to the Arlberg Tunnel and the railway, St. Anton swarms with visitors at the height of the season. The wealthy, the prominent, including, occasionally, the royal, appear regularly—some even to enjoy the winter sports. Their presence boosts prices into the very-expensive-to-outrageous category, but if you shop around you can find accommodations outside the center of the action at a bearable price. St. Anton is a particularly lovely town in summer—which has also become a fashionable season.

Thanks to an amazing system of cable cars, double chairlift, and interconnected T-bars, St. Anton can access skiers to the Arlberg's region's enormous 300-odd km (200-odd mi) of marked runs. If you decide to take to the slopes, remember that skiing remains serious business in St. Anton: many slopes are so steep you'll be sharing them with mountain climbers.

WHERE TO STAY

$$$$ ⓣ**Anton.** If you've had enough of quaint Tyrolean hotels, this wood-and-glass house is for you. The concept is modern and casual, and it's almost Zenlike in its simplicity. Many rooms can be connected, allowing the hotel to provide accommodations for almost any size group. In the evening, the live DJ turns the café into an après-ski hangout light years away from the usual beer-and-wurst scene. Book in advance, as the hotel has a loyal following. **Pros:** great architecture; funky vibe. **Cons:** party crowd can get loud. ✉ *Kandaharweg 4* ☎ *05446/2408* ⊕ *www.anton-aparthotel.com* 🛏 *14 rooms, 3 apartments* ⚒ *In-room: no a/c, safe, kitchen (some), refrigerator (some), Internet. In-hotel: restaurant, bar, spa, laundry facilities, parking (free)* ▤ *AE, DC, MC, V* ⍭ *BP.*

$$$$ ⓣ**Hotel St. Antonerhof.** The Raffl family has created a distinctive and memorable hotel filled with antiques and art of all kinds. No two rooms are alike, as each has been given its own distinctive style.

9

THE ORIGINAL SKI INSTRUCTOR

Modern ski techniques were first developed in the Vorarlberg by local Hannes Schneider (1890–1955), who as a young man was supposed to follow in his father's footsteps as a cheese maker. Instead, he founded the first ski school in St. Anton in 1921. This "Arlberg School" method, developed by Schneider in the '20s and '30s, laid down the basic principles since followed by skiing courses the world over.

The restaurant Raffl-Stubn is truly first-class, serving creative cuisine that is a delight to the last detail. The wine list is extensive, and the desserts, such as chocolate mousse on fried baby pineapple, are luscious. The hotel also rents a house with five apartments on a sunny slope with a gorgeous view of St. Anton. **Pros:** great location for skiers; well-trained staff. **Cons:** closed in summer; very expensive for what you get. ⊠*Arlbergstrasse 69* ☎*05446/2910* ⊕*www.st.antonerhof.at* ⇖*36 rooms* ⌂*In-room: no a/c, safe, refrigerator, DVD, Wi-Fi. In-hotel: restaurant, room service, bar, pool, spa, laundry service* ▤*AE, DC, MC, V* ⊘*Closed mid-Apr.– Nov.* ⦿*MAP.*

$$$$ ⊡ **Schwarzer Adler.** The beautifully frescoed facade of this 430-year-old inn in the center of town hints at what you'll find inside: open fireplaces, Tyrolean antiques, and colorful Oriental carpets. Alpine-style rooms are tastefully furnished, spacious, and full of modern conveniences. An annex across the street has somewhat less elegant, but cheaper, rooms. **Pros:** very helpful and friendly staff; best bar in St. Anton; lovely building. **Cons:** can be loud on weekends. ⊠ *Dorfstrasse 35* ☎*05446/2244–0* ⊕*www.schwarzeradler.com* ⇖*63 rooms* ⌂*In-room: no a/c, Internet, Wi-Fi. In-hotel: restaurant, bar, pools, gym, spa, laundry service, Wi-Fi, parking (paid), no-smoking rooms* ▤*MC, V* ⊘*Closed mid-Apr.–May, Oct., and Nov.* ⦿*BP, MAP.*

NIGHTLIFE & THE ARTS

For some visitors to St. Anton the show, not the snow, is the thing. Most of the bars are in the pedestrian zone.

A popular après-ski spot is the **Bar Kandahar** (⊠*Sporthotel, Dorfstrasse 48* ☎*05446/30260*). With its cellar disco, Gunnar Munthe's **Krazy Kanguruh** (⊠*Moos 113* ☎*05446/2633*) is a favorite gathering spot.

SPORTS & THE OUTDOORS

SKIING   The *Skihaserl*, or ski bunny, as the beginner is called, usually joins a class on St. Anton's good "nursery" slopes, where he or she will have plenty of often-distinguished company. The **Skischule Arlberg** (☎*05446/3411* ⊕*www.skischool-arlberg.com*) here is excellent, considered by some to be the Harvard of ski schools. Once past the Skihaserl stage, skiers go higher in the Arlberg mountains to the superlative runs from the top of the Galzig and the 9,100-foot Valluga above it. Check with your hotel or ski-lift-ticket offices about an **Arlberg Skipass,** which is good on cable cars and lifts in St. Anton and St. Christoph on the Tirol side and on those in Zürs, Lech, Oberlech, and Stuben in Vorarlberg—85 in all. For complete details on St. Anton's skiing facilities, contact the town's **tourist office** (☎*05446/22690* ⊕*www.stantonamarlberg.com*).

ST. CHRISTOPH

2 km (1 mi) west of St. Anton am Arlberg.

EXPLORING

A hospice to care for imperiled travelers stranded by the snows on the pass was founded in what is now St. Christoph as early as the 15th century. Today the snow is what attracts visitors to the area. Although

St. Christoph hasn't the same social cachet as St. Anton, the skiing facilities are precisely the same (and even closer at hand). If you take your skiing seriously and are willing to forgo the high life as too distracting or too expensive, you may find winter sports per se more fun at St. Christoph.

WHERE TO STAY

$$$$ ▣ **Arlberg Hospiz.** This huge pink building re-creates much of the legendary hospital that stood here until a fire destroyed it in the 1950s. Carved-wood paneling and rich Oriental carpets abound. The rooms are luxurious to the extreme; the service is attentive but not obtrusive. The Hospizalm restaurant has earned a reputation for creative cooking: you might be offered cream of lobster or oyster soup, veal or venison, or fish dishes. The wine list is outstanding. **Pros:** plenty of atmosphere; great restaurant. **Cons:** make sure you are booked in the main building instead of a nearby building. ⊠*St. Christoph am Arlberg* ☎*05446/2611* ⊕*www.arlberghospiz.at* ↪*90 rooms* ♧*In-room: no a/c, safe, refrigerator. In-hotel: restaurant, bar, pool, gym, laundry service, Wi-Fi, parking (free), some pets allowed* ☰*AE, DC, MC, V* ☉*Closed May, Oct., and Nov.* ❛☐*BP, MAP.*

ISCHGL & GALTÜR

67 km (42 mi) southeast of St. Christoph.

ESSENTIALS
Visitor Information **Ischgl** (⊠*A-6561* ☎*05444/52660*).

EXPLORING
Ischgl, the largest town in the Paznaun Valley, has become as renowned for its party scene as for its excellent skiing, particularly in the small Fimber Valley to the south, and in summer it's a popular high-altitude health resort. You can get to the 7,500-foot Idalpe via the 4-km-long (2½-mi-long) Silvretta cable-car run. The enchanting Paznaun Valley follows the course of the Trisanna River for more than 40 km (25 mi). The valley runs into the heart of the Blue Silvretta mountains, named for the shimmering ice-blue effect created by the great peaks and glaciers. They are dominated by the Fluchthorn (10,462 feet), at the head of the valley.

Slightly higher up the valley is **Galtür,** the best-known resort in the Paznaun, equally popular as a winter-sports area, a summer resort, and a base for mountain climbing. Although Galtür is a starting point for practiced mountaineers, many of the climbs up the Blue Silvretta are easy and lead to the half-dozen mountain huts belonging to the Alpenverein. Galtür and the Silvretta region inspired Ernest Hemingway's novella *Alpine Idyll*; the author spent the winter of 1925 here, and the town still remembers him.

Following an avalanche of catastrophic proportion on February 23, 1999, that took dozens of lives and destroyed many centuries-old homes and guesthouses, the community of Galtür undertook a massive building project resulting in the **Alpinarium,** which is at once a memorial, museum, conference center, café, indoor climbing hall, library, and, most significantly, a 1,132-foot-long wall built of steel and concrete designed to prevent such an accident from occurring again. On summer Saturdays, 10–4, the *Bauernmarkt* (farmers' market) sets up in front of the Alpinarium, bringing produce, cheese, meat, and specialty products. ⊠*Hauptstrasse 29c* ☎*05443/20000* ⊕*www.alpinarium.at* ⊠*€8* ⊙*Tues.–Sun. 10–6.*

WHERE TO STAY

$$$$ ⌂**Post.** The oldest part of this inn dates back more than 200 years. Seemingly the center of activity in this lively resort town, the Post plies you with Tyrolean charm, attractive rooms, and a recommended restaurant offering many different cuisines. ■TIP→ **The hotel bar is a busy nightspot, so request a room toward the back of the hotel if you're not a late-night person. Pros:** right on the slopes; half board included. **Cons:** small elevators; be prepared for some noise. ⊠*Dorfstrasse 47* ☎*05444/5232* ⊕*www.post-ischgl.at* ↵*83 rooms* ⌂*In-room: no a/c, safe, Internet (some). In-hotel: restaurant, bar, pool, spa, laundry service, Internet* ☰*AE, DC, MC, V* ⏐○⏐*BP, MAP.*

$$$$ ⌂**Trofana Royal.** The Trofana is a luxurious hotel perfectly situated next to the Silvretta cable car. A timeless elegance carries through from the massive lobby to the four unique dining rooms and plushy guest quarters. Room rates include half board, and meals all come from the renowned restaurant, where chef Martin Sieberer delights in a synthesis of haute cuisine and Tyrolean tradition. The wine list is outstanding. **Pros:** great location; exclusive nightclub; après-ski bar. **Cons:** very expensive. ⊠*Ischgl 334* ☎*05444/600* ⊕*www.trofana.at* ↵*82 rooms* ⌂*In-room: no a/c, safe, refrigerator, Internet. In-hotel: restaurant, room service, bar, pool, gym spa, laundry service, parking (free), no-smoking rooms* ☰*AE, DC, MC, V* ⏐○⏐ *MAP.*

$$–$$$ ⌂**Gasthof zum Rössle.** Reputedly the oldest guesthouse in Galtür, the centrally located Gasthof zum Rössle overflows with Tyrolean charm. Guest rooms are given a pleasant pastel color scheme, making them very restful. And speaking of relaxation, the spa–sauna area is particularly nice. The Zirbenstuben restaurant provides a delightful setting for creative dinners featuring fresh local ingredients when possible. There are some excellent, mostly Austrian wines to choose from. **Pros:** plenty of atmosphere; top-notch dining. **Cons:** extra charge for short stays. ⊠*Am Dorfplatz 4* ☎*05443/82320* ⊕*www.roessle.com* ↵*38 rooms* ⌂*In-room: no a/c, safe, refrigerator (some), Wi-Fi. In-hotel: restaurant, bar, pool, spa, parking (free)* ☰*MC, V* ⏐○⏐*MAP.*

Vorarlberg

Updated by
Uli Ehrhardt

SOME SAY VORARLBERG IS AUSTRIA in miniature. Start with the historic state capital Bregenz. At the end of July it becomes the "Summer Capital of Austria" when the Bregenz Festival opens with the Viennese Symphonic Orchestra playing. Thousands flock to see operas and musicals by Giuseppe Verdi or Leonard Bernstein—to name just two—which take place on a huge floating stage with Lake Constance and the Swiss mountains as a backdrop. Next head to the Bregenzerwald—a wide area of dense forests, charming valleys, and lush meadows dotted with thick clusters of red, white, and yellow Alpine flowers—a region that remains unostentatiously beautiful. Music devotees descend on Vorarlberg every summer for its elegant Schubertiade—held in Schwarzenberg and Hohenems. The valley from Bludenz to Feldkirch, Dornbirn, and Bregenz is an economic and industrial powerhouse of Austria, dotted with small and medium-sized factories. Literature buffs come to the village of Tschagguns, where Hemingway spent several winters writing *The Sun Also Rises*. You can also venture into the famous Arlberg ski resorts, where for many, skiing is almost as important as being seen.

Vorarlberg covers an area of less than 1,000 square mi, and is the smallest (with the exception of Vienna) of Austria's federal states. As its name implies, the state lies "before the Arlberg"—that massive range of Alps, the watershed of Europe, mecca of winter sports—and forms the western tip of Austria. Until the tunnel was cut through, the Arlberg was passable only in summer; in winter Vorarlberg was effectively cut off from the rest of the country. The province has much in common with its neighbor, Switzerland. Not only are the dialects similar, but the terrain flows across the border with continuity. Both peoples are descended from the same ancient Germanic tribes that flourished in the 3rd century BC, and both have the same characteristics of thrift, hard work, and a deep-rooted instinct for democracy and independence.

ORIENTATION & PLANNING

GETTING ORIENTED

Bregenz. The Romans built up this sizeable city with a harbor for warships. Today it's used for cruise ships zig-zagging across Lake Constance to Switzerland and Germany.

Through the Bregenzerwald to Bludenz & Feldkirch. Whereas the Bregenzerwald is a charming mountain region southeast of Bregenz, with skiing in winter and hiking in summer, the valley connecting the historic cities Bludenz, Feldkirch, and Dornbirn is now one of the most industrious areas of Austria.

The Arlberg & Montafon Resorts. Tucked away in a valley high in the Arlberg Alps, the mountain villages of Lech and Zürs are havens for high class expensive skiing. On the other end of the spectrum is the Montafon region, a summer and winter resort for the cost-conscious—especially families.

TOP REASONS TO GO

Bernstein in Bregenz. With Swiss mountains on your left, Bregenz behind you, Bavaria to your right, the sun setting over Lake Constance, and the Vienna Philharmonic Orchestra striking up the overture of *West Side Story* on the world's biggest floating stage—this is an unparalled place to see an opera or a musical.

See four countries at once. Take the cable car up Pfänder, the mountain behind Bregenz; the views are incredible.

Dine in a 500-year-old restaurant. In the days of Christopher Columbus the first guests enjoyed Montafon cooking and a good beer at the Löwen in Tschagguns, in the Montafon valley. Today it's a historic house, yet the opposite of a museum—a welcoming Gasthaus with very good food.

Lech. The village of Lech welcome more than 8,000 overnight visitors around Christmas and New Year but it's still a lovely, authentic Austrian Alpine village; Zürs may be higher up the mountains, we think Lech wins any competition with its authentic charm.

Experience top hospitality in a top village. The Gasthof Post is a bit like Lech itself—full of charming understatement. Teatime in overstuffed armchairs for all house guests will prepare you for a delicious dinner. You'll never want to leave.

VORARLBERG PLANNER

WHEN TO GO

Vorarlberg has something to offer visitors in every season. If you're in the province during warm weather, make sure to stop in Bregenz when the city comes to life with the Bregenzer Festspiele (Bregenz Music Festival). Boat excursions to Switzerland and Germany are also a must. History buffs will enjoy the sights in Bregenzand Feldkirch. And sports enthusiasts will love the wealth of hiking, biking, sailing, and fishing that is available around the region. If you travel to Vorarlberg during the winter months, then step into your bindings and head to the slopes.

10

GETTING HERE & AROUND

As in other areas of Austria, having a car makes travel easy, but you can also use the area trains and buses to get around. The Network Vorarlberg ticket, a pass for trains, public buses, and boat trips makes public transport more economical. Passes are available for a day, week, or month. You can choose tickets for regions of various sizes, from a single urban area to the entire Vorarlberg network. The Family 1-day Runabout is a real bargain, and valid for an entire family regardless of size; the Vorarlberg information offices in Bregenz and Vienna have details. A Bodensee-Pass includes the Swiss and German as well as the Austrian lake steamers, all at half price, plus area trains, buses, and cable-car lifts; this pass comes in seven- and 15-day variations.

BY AIR The closest intercontinental airport to Vorarlberg is Zürich Kloten 120 km (75 mi) away. From the airport several Euro City express trains a day make the journey directly to Bregenz in 1½ hours. Munich's airport is 185 km (115 mi) away, and Innsbruck is 200 km (124 mi) from Bregenz.

Austrian Airlines flies from Vienna into St. Gallen/Altenrhein in Switzerland. The other regional airport is Friedrichhafen on the German shore of Lake Constance, 45 minutes from Bregenz, which is served by several airlines.

AIRPORT TRANSFERS In winter a bus leaves the Zürich airport Friday, Saturday, and Sunday several times each day for Zuers and Lech resorts in the Arlberg region. You can book the transfer through Swiss International Airlines.

BY BUS Bus lines operated by the railways and post office connect all the towns and villages not served by train (which includes most of the Bregenzerwald), using vehicles with snow chains when necessary in winter. Even so, some of the highest roads can become impassable for a few hours.

BY CAR A car is the most flexible way of getting about in Vorarlberg, but the roads can be treacherous in winter. Cars are not allowed on some mountain roads in the Arlberg without chains, which you can rent from a number of service stations.

BY FERRY From May to October, passenger ships of the Austrian railroad's Bodensee White Fleet connect Bregenz with Lindau, Friedrichshafen, Meersburg, and Konstanz on the German side of the lake. The Eurailpass and Austrian rail passes are valid on these ships. You must bring your passport.

BY TRAIN The railroads connect the main centers of Vorarlberg remarkably well. The main rail line connecting with Vienna and Innsbruck enters Vorarlberg at Langen, after coming through the Arlberg Tunnel. Both the *Arlberg* and *Orient Express* trains follow this route, which then swings through Bludenz to Feldkirch. There the line splits, the *Arlberg* going south into Liechtenstein and Switzerland, the other branch heading through Dornbirn to Bregenz and on to Lindau in Germany. In addition, the Montafon electric (with occasional steam) rail line runs parallel to the highway from Bludenz southeast to Schruns.

VISITOR INFORMATION

The headquarters for tourist information about Vorarlberg is in Bregenz. There is a branch office in Vienna. Other regional tourist offices (called either Tourismusbüro, Verkehrsverein, or Fremdenverkehrsamt) are located throughout the province using the contact information listed under particular towns.

ESSENTIALS

Air Contact **Swiss International Airline** (⊕ *www.swiss.com*).

Boat Contact **Bodensee White Fleet** (☎ *05574/42868* ⊕ *www.vorarlberg-lines. at*).

Train Contact **ÖBB—Österreichisches Bundesbahn** (Austrian Railway) (☎ *05/1717* ⊕ *www.oebb.at*).

Emergency Services **Ambulance** (☎ *144*). **Fire department** (☎ *122*). **Police** (☎ *133*).

ON THE MENU

Vorarlberq long ago shed its culinary incivility, an image built around simple farm fare like *Kässpätzle*, a filling dish of bite-size noodles smothered in cheese. Today, Vorarlberg's cuisine is as good and varied as any in neighboring Tirol and the rest of Austria—albeit lighter—and is often associated with Swiss gastronomy, from which many of its elements originated. Fresh ingredients from the region's farms, lakes, and forests are the norm, with an emphasis on dairy products from the cows that graze the mountains and meadows of the region. Be sure to try a slab of *Vorarlberg Alpine* from one of the huge rounds, or any of the 30 other varieties of cheese produced at local farms. Cheese is also added to soups and noodle dishes and fried in fritters. Fresh *Egli* (as perch is called here), trout, and whitefish are caught in the waters of Lake Constance and in the surrounding lakes and streams. Fish—fried, broiled, and steamed—appears regularly on restaurant menus throughout Vorarlberg.

Tourist Information (✉ *Bahnhofstrasse 14, Bregenz* ☎ *05574/42525–0* ⊕ *www. vorarlberg.at* ✉ *Tuchlauben 18, Vienna* ☎ *01/535–7890*).

ABOUT THE RESTAURANTS & HOTELS

The gastronomic scene of Austria's westernmost province is as varied as its landscape: first-rate gourmet restaurants, traditional inns, rustic local taverns, as well as international chains and ethnic cuisine are all part of the mix. In small towns throughout the region restaurants are often the dining rooms of country inns, and there are plenty of these. Most restaurants housed in hotels and resorts will be closed in the off-season, usually November and April. In ski season breakfast is typically served early enough so that you can hit the slopes, and dinner early enough for the tired-out to get to bed and rest up for the next day.

Vorarlberg has loads of accommodation options, from local farm-houses where you share chores to ski chalets high on the slopes of the Western Alps to a converted castle-hotel perched above the Bodensee (Lake Constance). In the most famous ski resorts in Vorarlberg, hotel rates in season are often well above the range of our chart. For those on the lookout for savings, tourist offices can usually help lead you to more moderate lodgings in private houses. In some towns, such as Bregenz, summer is the high season, particularly during the Bregenzer Festspiele (Bregenz Music Festival), and may put the establishment into the next-higher price category.

Room rates include taxes and service and almost always breakfast, except in the most expensive hotels, and one other meal. Half-board, as this plan is called, is de rigueur in most lodgings. If requested, most will offer a rate for breakfast buffet only. Most hotels offer in-room phones and TV (some feature satellite or cable programming). Summer prices are often as much as 50% lower than during the ski season.

10

WHAT IT COSTS IN EUROS					
	¢	$	$$	$$$	$$$$
LECH/ZÜRS					
RESTAURANTS	under €10	€10–€16	€17–€22	€23–€28	over €28
HOTELS	under €80	€80–€120	€120–€170	€170–€270	over €270
OTHER TOWNS					
RESTAURANTS	under €7	€7–€12	€13–€17	€18–€22	over €22
HOTELS	under €70	€70–€100	€100–€135	€135–€175	over €175

Restaurant prices are per person for a main course at dinner. Hotel prices are for a standard double room in high season, including taxes and service. Assume that hotels operate on the European Plan (EP, with no meal provided) unless we note that they use the Breakfast Plan (BP), Modified American Plan (MAP, with breakfast and dinner daily, known as halb pension), or Full American Plan (FAP, or voll pension, with three meals a day). Higher prices (inquire when booking) prevail for any meal plans.

BREGENZ

150 km (90 mi) west of Innsbruck, 660 km (409 mi) west of Vienna, 120 km (75 mi) east of Zürich, 193 km (120 mi) southwest of Munich.

Lying along the southeastern shore of the Bodensee (Lake Constance) with the majestic Pfänder as its backdrop, Bregenz is where Vorarlbergers themselves come to make merry, especially in summer. Along the lakeside beach and public pool, cabanas and candy floss lure starched collars to let loose, while nearby an enormous floating stage is the open-air site for performances of grand opera and orchestral works (Verdi, Rimski-Korsakov, Strauss, and Gershwin are just some of the composers who have been featured). Bregenz is the capital of Vorarlberg, and has been the seat of the provincial government since 1819. The upper town has maintained a charming old-world character. The lower city is the vibrant part of town with pedestrian streets, shops, the railway station, restaurants, and offices.

GETTING HERE & AROUND

Fly into Zuerich Kloten airport and take a Euro City Express train directly from the airport to Bregenz Main Station. The trip takes about 1½ hours.

The city of Bregenz runs a very efficient public bus line. (⊠ *Rathausstraße 4 Bregenz* ☎*05574/4100–1833* ⊕*www.stadtwerke-bregenz.at*).

From Insbruck you come through the Arlberg tunnel, from Germany on the autobahn, and from Switzerland on the autobahn via St. Gallen.

Taxis in Bregenz start at about €4, so taking one even a short distance can be expensive. Call to order a radio cab.

From Vienna it takes about 7½ hours, from Munich about 2½.

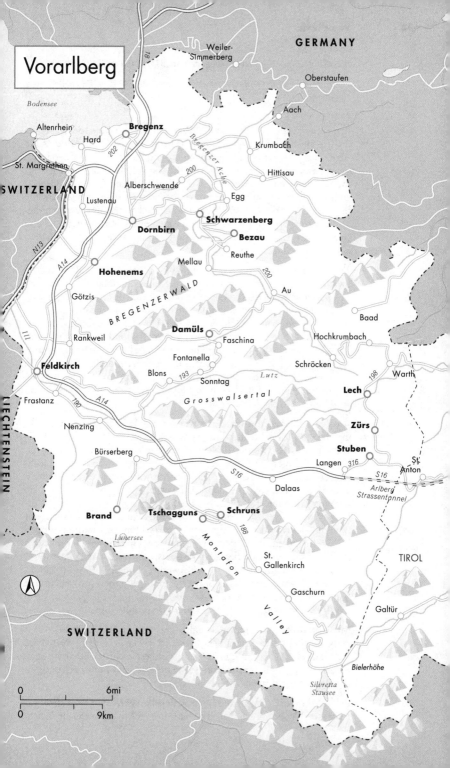

ESSENTIALS

Taxi Companies **City Taxi** (⊠*Bregenz* ☎*05574/65400 or 05574/42222*).

Visitor Information (⊠*Bahnhofstrasse 14, Bregenz* ☎*05574/42525-0* ⊕*www. vorarlberg.at*).

EXPLORING

Fodor'sChoice Bregenz is pleasant at any time of year, but the best time to visit is dur-
★ ing the **Bregenzer Festspiele** (Bregenz Music Festival ⇨*Nightlife & the Arts, below*). Acclaimed artists from around the world perform operas, operettas, and musical comedies on the festival's floating stage, part of the Festspiel- und Kongresshaus (Festival Hall and Congress Center) complex. In front of the stage, the orchestra pit is built on a jetty, while the audience of 6,800 is safely accommodated on the 30-tier amphitheater built on dry land—a unique and memorable setting you are sure to enjoy. Reserve your tickets and hotels in advance, as performances and rooms sell out early.

The lake itself is a prime attraction, with boat trips available to nearby Switzerland and Germany. Don't forget to bring along your passport. The **Bodensee White Fleet** ferries offer several trip options. You can travel to the "flower isle" of Mainau or make a crossing to Konstanz, Germany, with stops at Lindau, Friedrichshafen, and Meersburg. The longest round-trip excursion is the Drei-Länder Rundfahrt, which includes stops in Germany and Switzerland. The ferries have different operating schedules, but most run only in the summer months. The Mainau excursion is the exception, running from May to mid-September. ⊠*Vorarlberg Lines Bodenseeschiffahrt, Seestrasse 4* ☎*05574/42868* ⊕*www.bodenseeschifffahrt.at.*

Fodor'sChoice A cable car takes you up to the **Pfänder,** a 3,460-foot peak overlook-
★ ing the city. It's a breathtaking view—Bregenz, on the shore of Lake
☾ Constance, stretches out for40 mi into the hazy distance below you. On your left lies the Rhine valley, and you can see the hills of Liechtenstein and Switzerland. Just across the water from Bregenz you'll notice the island-city of Lindan in Bavaria, which some insist is also a country, though it's officially called a "Freistaat" (free state). Altogether you can see four countries from the Pfänder—five if you count Bavaria—and almost 240 Alpine peaks. The Pfänder restaurant is open June–mid-September. Children will enjoy a 30-minute circular hike to a small outdoor zoo with deer, Alpine goats, and wild boar. Admission is free. An added attraction is the **Adlerwarte** (☎*0664/905–3040* ≊*€5*), where eagles and other birds of prey demonstrate their prowess in free flight May–September at 11 and 2:30. ☎*05574/42160* ≊*Round-trip €9.40* ☾ *Dec.–Oct., daily 9–7; service on hr and ½ hr.*

Most of Bregenz's important sights can be seen in the course of a walk of about two hours. The town's Neoclassical main **Post Office** (⊠*Seestrasse 5*) was built in 1893 by Viennese architect Friedrich Setz. Because of the marshy conditions, the post office is built on wood pilings to prevent it from sinking.

Behind the post office, the **Nepomuk-Kapelle** (⊠*Kaspar Moosbrugger Platz*), or Nepomuk Chapel, was built in 1757 to serve the city's fishermen and sailors. Today the town's Hungarian community celebrates mass here.

To the right of the Nepomuk Kapelle along Kornmarktstrasse is the **Gasthof Kornmesser,** built in 1720 and a gorgeous example of a Baroque town house.

Just after the alley simply marked THEATER along Kornmarktstrasse you'll reach the **Theater am Kornmarkt,** originally constructed in 1838, when Bregenz was still an important commercial port, as a grain storehouse; in 1954 the granary was converted into a 700-seat theater.

Next door to the Theater am Kornmarkt is the **Landesmuseum** (*Provincial Museum*), housing relics from Brigantium, the Roman administrative city that once stood where Bregenz is today. Gothic and Romanesque ecclesiastical works are also on display in this turn-of-the-20th-century building. ⊠*Kornmarkt 1* ☏*05574/46050* ☒*€2* ☉*Sept.–May, Tues.– Sun. 9–noon and 2–5; June–Aug., daily 9–5.*

Vorarlberg now has its own modern art museum, the **Kunsthaus.** Designed by Swiss architect Peter Zumthor, the steel-and-concrete building shingled in etched-glass panels creates a feeling of space and light. Note the innovative feature of 8-foot openings between each story, which allows sunlight to enter the translucent glass through the ceiling. This marvel of design bathes each gallery in natural light in spite of concrete walls. ⊠*Karl-Tizian-Platz* ☏*05574/485940* ⊕*www. kunsthaus-bregenz.at* ☒*€6* ☉*Tues.–Sun. 10–6, Thurs. 10–9.*

Originally used as a grain warehouse when it was built in 1685, the **Rathaus,** on Rathausgasse, was turned over to the city in 1720. The ornate facade and tower were added to the city hall in 1898.

Next door to the Rathaus is the **Seekapelle** (*Lake Chapel*), topped with an onion dome. The chapel was put up over the graves of a band of Swiss whose 1408 attempt to incorporate Bregenz into Switzerland was defeated.

Behind the Seekapelle is the traditional **Gösser Braugaststätte** (⊠*Anton-Schneider-Strasse 1*). ■TIP→ **This might be just the moment for a cool beer, a cup of coffee, or the daily vegetarian special. Try to get a table in the Zirbenstüble, with its beautifully carved wood-paneled walls and ceiling.**

Off Belrupstrasse, the **Herz-Jesu Kirche** (*Sacred Heart Church*) was built in 1908 in brick Gothic style. The stained-glass windows by Martin Hausle are especially bright and colorful.

Go left from Belrupstrasse onto Maurachgasse. Walking up Maurachgasse, you'll reach the **Stadtsteig** guarding the entrance to the Old City, which bears the emblem of a Celtic-Roman equine goddess (the original is now housed in the Landesmuseum (⇨*above*). Inside the gate are the coats of arms of the dukes of Bregenz and the dukes of Montfort, the latter crest now the Vorarlberg provincial emblem.

Next to the Stadtsteig, explore the interior of the tiny **Martinskirche** (⊠*Martinsplatz*) for its fine 14th-century frescoes.

The **Martinsturm** (⊠*Martinsgasse 3b*) boasts the largest onion dome in Central Europe. The tower (1599–1602) has become a symbol of Bregenz and was the first Baroque construction on Lake Constance; it's closed on Monday from October to April.

Remains of the ancient **city wall** are to the right of the tower on Martinsgasse. The coats of arms of several noble Bregenz families can still be seen on the house standing next to the wall's remains.

Angle on along Martinsgasse to Graf-Wilhelm-Strasse and the brightly shuttered **Altes Rathaus** *(Old City Hall)*. The ornate half-timber construction was completed in 1622.

Behind the Altes Rathaus on Eponastrasse stands the former **Gesellenspital** *(Journeymen's Hospital)*; remnants of a fresco still visible on its wall depict St. Christopher, St. Peter, and a kneeling abbot.

The **Montfortbrunnen** *(fountain)* in the center of Ehreguta Platz is the scene of a ritual washing of wallets and change purses, when carnival jesters clean out their empty pockets and spin tales about the events of the previous year. The fountain honors the minnesinger Hugo von Montfort, who was born in the city in 1357.

The small parallel streets running uphill from Ehreguta Square roughly outline the boundaries of the town in the Middle Ages. Hidden around the corner of the building at the beginning of Georgen-Schilde-Strasse are the **Meissnerstiege** (Meissner steps), named after a local poet, that lead from the Old City to the **parish church of St. Gallus**. At the bottom of the steps, follow Schlossbergstrasse up the hill to the church, which combines Romanesque, Gothic, and Rococo elements. The interior is decorated simply with pastel coloring instead of the usual excessive gilding. Empress Maria Theresa donated the money for the high altarpiece. You'll notice the monarch's features on one of the shepherdesses depicted there.

From the hill outside the church there is a wonderful view of the southwestern wall of the Old City, including the **Beckenturm,** the 16th-century tower once used as a prison and named after bakers imprisoned there for baking rolls that were too skimpy for the town fathers.

The **Künstlerhaus Thurn und Taxis** (⊠*Gallusstrasse 8*) was owned by the princely Thurn und Taxis family until 1915. The building, erected in 1848, now contains a modern gallery. The **Thurn und Taxispark** contains rare trees and plants from around the world.

WHERE TO EAT

¢–$$ ✕**Wirtshaus am See.** This half-timbered house with a gabled roof is right on the shore of Lake Constance, next to the floating stage used for the Bregenz Festival. The menu has the usual Austrian favorites, from schnitzel to *Zwiebelrostbraten* (a skirt steak topped with crispy fried onions), fresh fish, and a worthy wine list. Some dishes from Germany and Switzerland—which you can see without moving from your chair—are also offered. The main attraction here is the spectacular lake view. You can watch the steamers from the nearby harbor go by from the restaurant's extensive outdoor terrace. ⊠*Seepromenade 2* ☎*05574/42210* ⊟*MC, V* ☉*Closed Jan. and Feb.*

$ ✕**Ilge-Weinstube.** This cozy, intimate *Keller* (cellar) is Old Bregenz at its best. The two "Menus of the day" are top quality at a reasonable price, offering either fish or meat. After the midday rush the chef may grant you a visit to his wine cellar, which features wines from some of the top vinyards in Austria. Rustic decor in the basement of a 300-year-old house close to the oldest section of town draws a young crowd; but visitors of any age are always welcome. The atmosphere alone makes the Ilge-Weinstube worth a visit. ⊠*Maurachgasse 6* ☎*05574/43609* ⊟*AE, DC, MC, V* ☉*Closed Mon.*

¢–$ ✕**Gasthof Goldener Hirsch.** Allegedly the oldest tavern in Bregenz and ★ close to the Old City, this rustic restaurant offers delicious traditional fare and drink in lively surroundings. During the oft-repeated Noodle Week, diners can choose from a special menu offering a mouthwatering selection of pasta dishes. In spring you can enjoy "asparagus week" and later in the year the menu focuses on game. Particularly good are the spicy spaghetti in a tomato, onion, bacon, and red pepper sauce, or spinach tagliatelle with grilled turkey in a tomato cream sauce with Gorgonzola gratiné. ⊠*Kirchstrasse 8* ☎*05574/42815* ⊟*AE, DC, MC, V* ☉*Closed Tues. and 2 wks in Sept.*

¢ ✕**Café Götze.** Locals frequent this small, unpretentious café because it's known to have the best pastries in town. The location halfway between the waterfront and the Old City is convenient. ⊠*Kaiserstrasse 9* ☎*05574/44523* ⊟ *No credit cards* ☉*Closed Sun. and Oct. and Nov.*

> **MAID SAVES CITY**
>
> At the bottom of Eponastrasse is Ehregutaplatz, named for the legendary woman who saved Bregenz during the Appenzell War of 1407–09. Ehreguta was a maid who overheard the enemy planning an invasion of Bregenz. Discovered listening at the door, she was warned that she would be killed if she breathed a word to anybody. She decided to tell all to the fire blazing in the kitchen one night, but spoke loud enough for others to overhear and take action to save the city.

10

WHERE TO STAY

$$$$ 🏨**Deuring-Schlössle.** This 400-year-old castle with its Baroque tower ★ has inspired paintings by Turner and Schiele. You will find antiques in many of the public rooms. Guest rooms are tastefully furnished and have polished wood floors and lovely wainscoting. The owner, who is also the chef of the hotel's highly regarded restaurant, offers gourmet cooking classes on request. Specialties include beautifully presented pike-perch on a bed of pumpkin puree with baby asparagus. If you want a blow-out meal in a lovely, romantic setting, this is the place to go. In summer try to get a table in the charming courtyard. **Pros:** a genuine castle, yet modern where needed; excellent kitchen. **Cons:** a bit far from the lower town, where the action is. ⊠*Ehregutaplatz*

4 ☎*05574/47800* ⊕*www.deuring-schloessle.at* ❧*13 rooms* ⚥*In-room: no a/c. In-hotel: restaurant* ▤*AE, DC, MC, V.*

$$$–$$$$ ▥**Schwärzler.** This city hotel atop a green oasis on the edge of town beams with traditional hospitality. It has large, modern rooms and a cozy restaurant, with an elegant space for official dinners and festivities. In summer you can enjoy excellent dishes on the terrace. The menu is a mix of traditional cooking and some international dishes, and the Schwärzler is a member of "Chaine des rôtisseurs," the gourmet club of Vorarlberg. The hotel is only a 15-minute walk from the center of town, but if you'd rather not hoof it, the bus stops right in front. **Pros:** spacious lobby and rooms; very attentive staff. **Cons:** on the edge of town; rooms toward the street are noisy; during the week it's mainly a business hotel. ⊠*Landstrasse 9* ☎*05574/4990* ⊕*www.s-hotels.com* ❧*75 rooms* ⚥*In-hotel: restaurant, room service, bar, gym, spa, pool, bicycles, laundry service, Internet, Wi-Fi, parking (free), some pets allowed, no-smoking rooms* ⊚I*BP.*

$$–$$$ ▥**Weisses Kreuz.** This traditional, family-run, turn-of-the-20th-century house has been renovated with care and charm and is now a Best Western hotel. The location on the edge of the pedestrian zone is central, and the staff is particularly friendly. The rooms are comfortable and modern; those overlooking the private park out back are quieter. The traditional restaurant is a meeting place for the people of Bregenz. A great part of the menu is devoted to regional dishes, and produce from the region is used in the preparation of the dishes wherever possible. **Pros:** it's the traditional center of hospitality in Bregenz; renovated rooms; excellent restaurant; central location. **Cons:** front rooms look out onto a well-traveled street. ⊠*Römerstrasse 5* ☎*05574/4988–0* ⊕*www.bestwestern.com* ❧*44 rooms* ⚥*In-room: no a/c, safe, Internet. In-hotel: restaurant, bar, Internet, bicycles, laundry service, parking (paid), some pets allowed, no-smoking rooms* ▤*AE, DC, MC, V* ⊙*Closed Christmas–mid-Jan.* ⊚I*BP.*

NIGHTLIFE & THE ARTS

Fodor'sChoice   The big cultural event in Bregenz is the **Bregenzer Festspiele** (*Bregenz*
★   *Music Festival* ✉*Box 311* ☎*05574/4070* ⊕*www.bregenzerfestspiele. com*), held mid-July to late August. For information and tickets, contact the festival office. Tickets are also available at the Bregenz tourist office. In the event of rain, the concert performance is moved indoors to the massive Festival Hall and Congress Center adjacent to the floating stage (it can accommodate at least 1,800 of the 6,800 seats usually available for performances on the floating lake stage). Travel and performance packages are available through **Bodensee-Vorarlberg Tourismus** (⊠*Bregenz* ☎*05574/434430* ⊕*www.bodensee-vorarlberg.com*).

The cultural year starts with the **Bregenzer Frühling**, the spring music and dance festival that runs from March to May. Information and tickets are available through the **tourist office** (⊠*Bahnhofstrasse 14* ☎*05574/4959*) in Bregenz.

The **casino** (⊠*Am Symphoniker 3* ☎*05574/45127–0*) is the site of much activity. The house opens at 3 PM. Bring your passport.

Outdoor concerts are held during the summer months in the horseshoe-shape **Music Pavilion** at the end of the promenade on the lake.

SPORTS & THE OUTDOORS

BICYCLING   It's possible to cycle around Lake Constance in two to four days, traveling all the while on well-marked and -maintained paths (don't forget your passport). If this sounds too strenuous, parts of the route can be covered by boat. Rental bikes can be hired at local sports shops, or at the train stations in Bregenz or Feldkirch; the tourist office can provide you with maps and details. Another cycling path, popular with families, follows the Rhine—a 70-km (43-mi) stretch from Bregenz south to Bludenz. Parts of the route are possible by train.

SKIING   Skiers head for the **Pfänder** mountain, in Bregenz's backyard, which has a cable tramway and two drag lifts. The views are stunning from atop the peak, stretching as far as the Black Forest and the Swiss Alps. The **runs** (☎*05572/42160–0* ⊕*www.pfaenderbahn.at*) are closed during the second and third weeks of November.

WATER   With the vast lake at its doorstep, Bregenz offers a variety of water
SPORTS   sports, from swimming to fishing to windsurfing. You can even learn to sail, although a minimum of two weeks is required for a full course at **Segelschule Lochau**. ⊠*Alte Fähre im Yachthafen, Lochau* ☎*05574/52247*.

THROUGH THE BREGENZERWALD TO BLUDENZ & FELDKIRCH

Directly behind Bregenz lies the **Bregenzerwald** (Bregenz Forest), a beautiful area studded with densely wooded highlands, sweeping valleys, and lush meadows radiant with wildflowers in summer, all set against a fabulous backdrop of majestic, towering Alps. As you go along, you come across one village after another with *au*—a term originally used to designated meadows where cows were allowed to graze—in its name (such as Bezau): as such areas developed, names were given to the meadows in which settlements were established. Here you can see the Vorarlbergers as they really are. Secure in their mountains and to a great extent feeling no call to mix with the outside world, Bregenzerwalders have remained true

SAY KÄSE, PLEASE

In the last two decades, cheese making has undergone a magnificent revival in the region. Farmers produce more than 30 varieties of *Käse*—from Emmental to beer cheese, Tilsit to red-wine cheese, and *Bergkäse* (mountain cheese) in dozens of varieties. Look for discreet *KäseStrasse* signs along the road, pointing you toward the region's elite cheese makers, or for the word *Sennerei*, which means Alpine dairy (⊕*www.kaesestrasse.at*).

10

to the habits of their forebears. On religious holidays and at almost all family gatherings in the little villages women wear the handsome, stiffly starched folk dress of their ancestors. On festive occasions the girls wear a golden headdress shaped like a small crown, and married women a black or white pointed cap. The men's costume, in which the cap and the color of various parts of the clothing differ from town to town, is worn by musicians in the local bands—which play traditional marches, polkas, and waltzes, and seem to include nearly everyone.

To reach the Bregenzerwald, travelers can take one of the daily buses that leave Bregenz from the main railway station. There are no train routes servicing the area. By car, leave Bregenz headed south on Route 190; then make a sharp left after crossing the river on a road marked to Wolfurt and Schwarzach. About 21 km (13 mi) farther, at Alberschwende you'll come to Route 200; follow the signs for **Egg,** where you should note the old country houses before heading on to Schwarzenberg.

SCHWARZENBERG

★ *31 km (19 mi) southeast of Bregenz.*

One of the region's most colorful villages is Schwarzenberg. The artist Angelika Kauffmann (1741–1807), who spent most of her life in England and Italy, considered this her real home. Even though she became one of the most renowned female artists of the 18th century, few people in Austria east of the Arlberg mountains knew of her until her picture appeared on a 100 Schilling note issue of the now-extinct Austrian currency. You can see several of her larger works in the Baroque village church, including a painting of the 12 apostles she did at age 16 and an altar painting of the Annunciation from about 1800 (the Landesmuseum in Bregenz has her portrait of the Duke of Wellington).

The Schwarzenberg **Heimatmuseum** has a room dedicated to Angelika Kauffmann. ⊠ *Brand 34* ☎ *05512/2988* 🖾 *€2.50* ⊙ *May–Sept., Tues., Thurs., and Sat. 2–4; in winter by appointment; during Schubertiade, daily 2–4.*

NIGHTLIFE & THE ARTS

Fodor'sChoice Schwarzenberg, along with original site Hohenems, is home to the annual
★ **Schubertiade** (⊠ *Villa Rosenthal, Schweizer Strasse 1* ☎ *05576/72091* ⊕ *www.schubertiade.at*), a small but elegant music festival devoted to Franz Schubert and his circle. *Lieder* lovers come to hear fine musicians offer homage to the great Biedermeier-era composer, as well as works by Brahms, Mozart, Beethoven, and other composers from June through September. Everyone from Vladimir Ashkenazy to Dietrich Fischer-Dieskau has performed here, starring along with members of the Vienna Philharmonic and Vienna Symphony.

BEZAU

★ *4 km (2½ mi) south of Schwarzenberg, 35 km (23 mi) east of Bregenz.*

Stunningly idyllic is the only way to describe this enchanting village snuggled under a mountain range and surrounded by meadows so green they look like Astroturf. According to local legend, Bezau's district hall was built on tall columns and accessible only by ladder. Once the councilors were gathered inside, the ladder would be removed, and not replaced until they came to a decision.

ESSENTIALS

Tourist Information Bezau (✉ *Platz 39* ☎ *05514/2295* ⊕ *www.bezau.at*).

EXPLORING

The **Heimatmuseum,** slightly south of the center, contains exhibits, including local folk costumes, on the town's interesting past. ✉ *Ellenbogen 181* ☎ *05514/2559* 🖅*€2.50* ⊗ *June–Sept., Tues., Thurs., and Sat. 3:30–5:30, Wed. 10–noon; Nov.–May, Tues. 2–3.*

☼ At the **Bregenzerwald Museumsbahn,** visitors can see all that is left of the onetime narrow-gauge railroad that ran from Bregenz to Bezau and was abandoned in 1980. The museum has managed to preserve more than 6 km (almost 4 mi) of track to Schwarzenberg, and runs diesel and steam excursions. ✉ *Langenegg 39* ☎ *0664/466–2330* 🖅*Round-trip by steam €7, by diesel €6* ⊗ *June–early-Oct., 10:30, 1:30, 3:30.*

WHERE TO STAY

$$$ 🖼 **Gasthof Gams and Blütenschloss.** Dating from the 17th century, this
★ friendly house in the center of town offers every comfort. The historic dining room, Gourmetstube—a gem with wood-paneled walls and ceiling—only serves dinner and reservations are advisable. Lunch is served in the hotel's regular dining room. The rooms have an attractive country-rustic decor. The adjacent Blütenschloss (Castle of Flowers) is a decidedly nontraditional wood-and-glass tower. Its 23 "snuggle suites" are designed specifically for honeymooning couples, outfitted with canopy beds, whirlpool, open fireplace, and balcony. **Pros:** warm atmosphere; very good traditional cooking in the Gourmetstube. **Cons:** restaurants are closed Monday and Tuesday. ✉ *Platz 44* ☎ *05514/2220* ⊕ *www.hotel-gams.at* 🛏 *35 rooms, 28 suites* ♿ *In-room: no a/c, Wi-Fi. In-hotel: restaurant, bar, tennis court, pool, gym, Internet* ▭ *MC, V*

SPORTS & THE OUTDOORS

SKIING Bezau has four regular trails for cross-country skiers and one lift that takes downhill skiers up to the 5,300-foot Baumgartenhöhe. This small area is part of the Bregenzerwald Ski Region. A regional pass (the "3 Valley Skipass") gives you access to 135 lifts in Bregenzerwald, Grosses Walsertal, and Lechtal in Tirol, encompassing 337 km (200 mi) of prepared slopes (⇨ *Damüls*).

10

DAMÜLS

14 km (9 mi) south of Bezau, 59 km (37 mi) southeast of Bregenz.

GETTING HERE & AROUND

If you turn right onto Route 193 at Au, you'll be on the way to Damüls—the road is narrow, with a 14% gradient at one point, but when you reach the town you'll agree the climb was worth it. You're at 4,640 feet, the top of the Bregenzerwald.

ESSENTIALS

Tourist Information Damüls (✉ *A-6884* ☎ *05510/6200* ⊕ *www.damuels.at*).

EXPLORING

This is great skiing country in winter; for information on facilities, contact the **Bregenzerwald tourism office** (✉ *Impulszentrum 1135 Egg* ☎ *05512/2365* ⊕ *www.bregenzerwald.at*). There are enough slopes and lifts, and the crowds are generally elsewhere. ■ **TIP→ In summer the area is knee-deep in wildflowers, but don't pick them; it's against the law.** Check the frescoes in the **parish church,** which date from 1490, just after the church was built, but were rediscovered under later plaster only about 40 years ago.

▌ **EN ROUTE**   The **Grosswalsertal** (*Great Walliser Valley*) is extremely scenic. As you start the descent from Damüls heading toward Bludenz along Route 193, look across at the St. Gerold Monastery to your right. After reaching Blons, however, be sure to keep your eyes on the road: it's full of hairpin turns.

FELDKIRCH

33 km (22 mi) southwest of Bregenz.

Feldkirch is Vorarlberg's oldest town, with parts dating from the Middle Ages that contribute greatly to the town's romantic character. Picturesque arcades line the narrow main street, and wrought-iron oriels festoon some of the quainter town houses. Marvelous towers and onion domes top some of the buildings, watched over by an assembly of imposing stone blockhouses, which compose the Schattenburg castle complex just above the town.

A number of luminaries have spent time in Feldkirch. James Joyce stopped for several months en route from Italy to Switzerland, saying later that he formed the basis for *Ulysses* here and that he gathered material for *Finnegan's Wake*. There is a plaque honoring him at the train station, where he spent hours every day observing people and trains for his writing. As a promising student, Sir Arthur Conan Doyle attended the Jesuit boarding school, Stella Matutina, which is now the Provincial Conservatory of Music. He wrote two short stories for the local newspaper, which are stored in the archives. And Thomas Mann used the same boarding school as a setting in *The Magic Mountain*.

ESSENTIALS

Tourist Information **Feldkirch** (✉ *Schlossergasse 8* ☎ *05522/73467* 🖷 *05522/79867*).

EXPLORING

An easy walk around the center of Feldkirch will take you to most of the town's highlights. The center of town is **St. Nicholas Cathedral,** on Domplatz. The light that comes through the stained glass of this church, built in 1478, is beautiful.

From the cathedral, walk toward the river, past the district government offices (once a Jesuit monastery) and the bishop's palace, a block back of Herrengasse, to the **Katzenturm** (literally, "cats' tower"; figuratively, "the clergy"), reconstructed by Emperor Maximilian I. This is the most prominent remnant of the town's fortifications and now holds the 7½-ton town bell.

Down the Hirschgraben, pass the Chur gate, is the **Frauenkirche** *(Church of Our Lady)*, originally dedicated to St. Sebastian in 1473.

Down Montfortgasse you'll find the **Wasserturm** *(water tower)* and the **Diebsturm** (thieves' tower) standing guard over the Schillerstrasse bridge. Wander down Vorstadt to the **Pulverturm** (powder tower) and across to the **Mühlenturm** (mill tower), which contrasts greatly with the modern Leonhardsplatz.

Turning left from the Mühlenturm, you'll find the St. Johann Church (1218) and, behind it, the **market square** (market days Tuesday and Saturday). The square is the site of the annual wine festival during the second week of July. Across the pedestrian zone is Liechtenstein Palace, once the administrative center.

Adjacent to the Liechtenstein Palace is the **Rathaus** of 1493, with frescoes and paneled rooms.

Overlooking Feldkirch, in the Neustadt, is the 12th-century **Schattenburg,** a massive castle that now houses a restaurant and a museum devoted to the decorative arts and armor. Arcades climb up the hill to frame the castle in an intriguing vista. ✉*Burggasse 1* ☎*05522/71982* 💶*€3* ⊙*Jan.–Apr., daily 1–4; May–Oct., daily 9–noon and 1:30–6; Nov. and Dec., on holidays and by request.*

WHERE TO STAY & EAT

$ ✕**Schäfle.** A bit outside the Old City in a neighborhood called *Altenstadt,* this family-run Gasthaus offers atmosphere and food more typical of that in the countryside. The tables are elegantly set, and you can expect such regional fare as schnitzel, beef fillet, or perch from Lake Constance, all served with delicate sauces and a fine touch. They bake their own bread, and serve wine from their own vineyard. When weather permits, request a table in the charming garden. ✉*Naflastrasse 3* ☎*05522/72203–0* ⊟*AE, DC, MC, V* ⊙*Closed Sun.*

$$ 🏨**Alpenrose.** This charming old burgher's house in the center of the ★ Old City has been nicely renovated and offers unusually personal service. The small and tastefully decorated dining room serves tasteful dishes. Fish is a specialty of the chef, and the in-season mushrooms are

a delight. In summer you can enjoy your meals in the small tree-shaded garden in the city's pedestrian zone in front of the house. Rooms are tastefully done in period furnishings. **Pros:** excellent service; very good food; tastefully renovated rooms. **Cons:** danger of tour-bus groups invading the garden and the house. ⊠*Rosengasse 6* ☎*05522/72175* ⊕*www.hotel-alpenrose.net* ⤵*27 rooms* ⚐*In-room: no a/c, Wi-Fi. In-hotel: restaurant, bar, Internet, some pets allowed, no-smoking rooms* ▭*AE, DC, MC, V.*

HOHENEMS

★ *9 km (5½ mi) northeast of Feldkirch, 24 km (15 mi) southwest of Bregenz.*

"The antiquity of Hohenems is so apparent, so forceful, it looms like a presence, a mysterious knight, armored cap-a-pie, visor lowered," observed James Reynolds in his 1956 book *Panorama of Austria.* Hohenems is a town dominated by castles, both ruined (the 12th-century Alt-Ems citadel atop the Schlossberg) and ravishing, especially the Schloss Glopper and the castle of Prince-Archbishop Marcus Sittikus von Hohenems, with its elegantly ornate Rittersaal. Empress Elisabeth of Austria used to stay in this castle toward the end of her tragically shortened life and, in fact, used the title Countess Hohenems when she traveled "anonymously" around the world.

ESSENTIALS

Tourist Information Hohenems (⊠*Schweizerstrasse 10* ☎*5576/42780* ⊕*www.hohenems.at*).

EXPLORING

The **Pfarrkirche** *(parish church),* dedicated to St. Carlo Borromeo and rebuilt in 1797, has a noted painted altarpiece of the Coronation of the Virgin.

In 1617 a decree was signed that welcomed Jews to Hohenems and allowed them to live and work in peace. For the next 300 years a large Jewish community thrived here, but by 1938 fewer than 20 Jews remained. The **Jüdisches Museum** *(Jewish Museum),* housed in the Villa Heimann-Rosenthal, has a large library, as well as photographs and historical documents on display. ⊠*Schweizerstrasse 5* ☎*05576/73989* ⊕*www.jm-hohenems.at* ▭*€5* ⊙*Tues.–Sun. 10–5.*

DORNBIRN

4 km (2½ mi) northeast of Hohenems, 13 km (8 mi) southwest of Bregenz.

Dornbirn, the industrial center of Vorarlberg, is known as the "city of textiles" for its bedding, tablecloths, and undergarment production. The annual Dornbirn Fair, held in early September to tie in with the Bregenz Music Festival, shows a range of goods and technologies, but textiles are especially featured. ■**TIP→ Most of the factories have an outlet where you can buy less expensive quality goods, or seconds.**

WHERE TO STAY & EAT

$$–$$$ ✕**Rotes Haus.** In the center of town on the large "Marktplatz" (market
★   place) sits the historic Red House. The "red" in the name of this 1639
gabled wood building refers to bull's blood, originally used as pigment
for the facade, which is still basically red, with decorative panels. You
may have to wait for a while in the summer before you can sit down at
a table under huge umbrellas on the square. Traditional cuisine—lamb,
game, and fish are on the menu—is served here in a charming series of
small rooms. In season try the mushrooms or any of the other dishes
made of regional produce. ⊠*Marktplatz 13* ☎*05572/31555* ▤*AE,
DC, MC, V* ☼*No lunch Sun.*

$$$–$$$$ ▦ **Four Points Panoramahaus Dornbirn.** The Four Points is a modern busi-
ness hotel ensconced in the upper floors of the steel-and-glass Panora-
mahaus tower, a mile from the autobahn. Rooms are done in cream
and light-wood tones, and all offer sweeping views. As you walk along
the 11th-floor balcony circling the whole building, you can see beyond
the Rhine valley to the Swiss and Austrian Alps. A Sheraton prop-
erty, the hotel offers all the right business services and a well-equipped
spa–fitness center, too. Ask for weekend rates. **Pros:** spacious lobby;
clean lines in modern rooms; sweeping views from all rooms. **Cons:**
lacks "Austrian" charm; a mile from the old town. ⊠*Messestrasse 1*
☎*05572/38880* ⊕*www.4p-sheraton-dornbirn.at* ⇗*106 rooms* ♿*In-
room: safe, Internet. In-hotel: restaurant, bar, pool, gym, spa, bicycles,
laundry service, Internet, Wi-Fi, parking (free), some pets allowed, no-
smoking rooms* ▤*AE, D, DC, MC, V* ⚭*BP.*

$$$–$$$$ ▦ **Martinspark.** This hotel in the very heart of Dornbirn is a functional
fantasy of art and ultramodern architecture. It was the first "Design
Hotel" in Austria and fits into this city, blending its modern design with
the surrounding old historic buildings. The bright and warm rooms
use local wood, tile, and contemporary artwork generously, making
the Martinspark a memorable stay. Most rooms open onto an inte-
rior courtyard or onto a quiet side street. In the restaurant you can
enjoy regional Austrian specialties and international dishes under palm
trees. **Pros:** central location; spacious rooms; very modern style. **Cons:**
restaurant closed Sunday. ⊠*Mozartstrasse 2* ☎*05572/3760* ⊕*www.
martinspark.at* ⇗*98 rooms* ♿*In-hotel: restaurant, bar, laundry ser-
vice, Internet, Wi-Fi, some pets allowed, parking (paid)* ▤*AE, DC,
MC, V* ⚭*BP.*

THE ARLBERG & MONTAFON RESORTS

The Western Alps are a haven for those who love the great outdoors.
It's also a region that provides getaway space and privacy—Ernest
Hemingway came to Schruns to write *The Sun Also Rises*. In spring,
summer, and fall, travelers delight in riding, tennis, swimming, and,
hiking the Montafon Valley, which is dominated by the "Matterhorn
of Austria," the Zimba peak (8,671 feet), and is probably the most
attractive of Vorarlberg's many tourist-frequented valleys. When the
first snowflakes begin to fall, skiers head to the hills to take advantage
of the Arlberg mountain range, the highest in the Lechtal Alps.

Tourist Information **Montafon Valley** (✉ *Montafoner Strasse 21, Schruns* ☎ *05556/72253-0* ⊕ *www.montafon.at*).

BRAND

70 km (43 mi) south of Bregenz.

Since it was first settled by Swiss exiles centuries ago, the lush and beautiful Brand Valley has attracted many travelers interested in visiting the enormous glaciers and one of the largest lakes in the Alps, located near the town. Today Brand is known as a health resort and a winter-sports center. Its hotels lie at the foot of the Scesaplana mountain group (which marks the Swiss border and is the highest range in the Rätikon). There are no rail lines to Brand, so the best way to reach the resort is to take the train to Bludenz and then the bus from there to Brand.

EXPLORING

If you are fond of hiking, you can climb by easy stages along the forest paths without much exertion to the famous glacier lake, the **Lünersee.** In winter the skiing is excellent, and there is a modern chairlift up the Niggenkopf (5,500 feet) to take you up to the finest ski slopes in a few minutes.

Anyone interested in geology should pay a visit to the tiny village chapel, known as the **"trowel stone" chapel,** built of local rock that can be cut into shape quite easily with an ordinary saw. When exposed to the air, the masonry then shrinks slightly and hardens and becomes rather brittle.

WHERE TO STAY

$$$–$$$$ **Sporthotel Beck.** The Beck family runs this sporty, child-friendly hotel in the shadow of the nearby mountains. Rooms are comfortably furnished and light filled and have flower-bedecked balconies that look out over spectacular views. The hotel's restaurant is for house guests only and features classic Austrian fare like schnitzel, but also lighter dishes for those watching their waistlines. Sports enthusiasts will like the myriad activities available in the hotel as well as the great mountain climbing nearby. **Pros:** a wonderful family hotel; children's programs. **Cons:** guests staying only one night will get a room, if available, but the hotel is not set up for them. ✉ *A-6708* ☎ *05559/306-0* ⊕ *www.sporthotel-beck.at* ⤵ *33 rooms, 16 suites* ⌂ *In-room: no a/c, Wi-Fi. In-hotel: restaurant, room service, pool, gym, spa, bicycles, children's programs, (ages 4 and up), Internet, some pets allowed, no-smoking rooms* ▤ *AE, DC, MC, V* ☉ *Closed end of Mar.–mid May, mid-Oct.–mid-Dec.*

$$$ **Hotel Scesaplana.** This family-run hotel is at the end of the Brandner-tal valley—surrounded by the towering mountains and glaciers of the Rätikon region and steps from the Brand ski lift. This is not a special children's hotel, but families are warmly welcome. A variety of pampering options plus sports facilities make staying in fun, too. A half-board option includes breakfast and a champagne bar, organic foods, afternoon snacks, and a dinner buffet. For a gourmet experience à la carte, reserve a table at the Bauernstüberl. **Pros:** modern yet comfort-

able; very spacious lobby; programs for guests. **Cons:** not necessarily a place for those who just want to relax. ⊠*A-6708* ☎*05559/221* ⊕*www.scesaplana.at* ⤳*61 rooms* ⚲*In-hotel: restaurant, room service, bar, tennis courts, pool, gym, spa, Wi-Fi, Internet, parking (free), some pets allowed, no-smoking rooms* ▤*AE, DC, MC, V* ☉*Closed mid-Oct.–mid-Dec.*

SPORTS & THE OUTDOORS

HIKING   From a leisurely stroll to serious mountain trekking, Brand has hiking galore. The most noted trail runs from Brand via Innertal and the Schattenlagant-Alpe to the lower end of the Lünersee. Inquire at the local tourist office for maps.

SKIING   The Brandnertal offers 50 km (31 mi) of groomed ski runs served by eight chairlifts. It's part of the Alpenregion Bludenz, which also includes Klostertal, Grosses Walsertal, Brandnertal, and Walgau. Rental equipment is available. For details on facilities, contact **Tourismus Bludenz** (⊠*Werdenbergesstrasse 42, Bludenz* ☎*05552/62170* ⊕*www.bludenz. at*). The area immediately around the Brandnertal features ski passes good for 1 to 16 days, with rates for adults, children, and senior citizens varying according to season. The Brandnertal encompasses some 14 lifts and 42 km (25 mi) of prepared runs.

SCHRUNS-TSCHAGGUNS

10 km (6 mi) northeast of Brand, 60 km (39 mi) south of Bregenz.

Author Ernest Hemingway spent many winters at the Schruns–Tschagguns skiing area in the Montafon Valley. Today neither of the towns— sited across the Ill River from each other—is as fashionable as the resorts on the Arlberg, but the views over the Ferwall Alps to the east and the mighty Rätikon on the western side of the valley are unsurpassed anywhere in Austria. In winter the powdery snow provides wonderful skiing. Thanks to an integrated system of ski passes and lifts, the Montafon Valley is considered a "ski stadium" by skiers in the know. They love to head for Hochjoch-Zamang—the main peak at **Schruns**—to have lunch on the spectacularly sited sun terrace of the Kapell restaurant. Then it's on to Grabs-Golm over the river in **Tschagguns.** Others prefer the Silvretta-Nova run at Gaschurn and St. Gallenkirch. In summer, the heights are given over to climbers and hikers, the mountain streams to trout fishermen, and the lowlands to tennis players.

10

WHERE TO STAY & EAT

$ ✕**Gasthof Löwen.** Guests started eating here more than 500 years ago, and they have been doing so ever since. The old dining room has wood-paneled walls and ceiling and is the perfect setting in which to enjoy a *Zwiebelrostbraten* (steak with onions) and a good red wine. Unfortunately, the historic tables with the beautiful inlay work are not for sale. Ernest Hemingway certainly enjoyed his stays in "the old inn with the antlers in Tschagguns," as he called it. You can ask the staff if one of the five guest rooms is available. The reception is in the Montafoner

Hof, just across the street, which belongs to the same family. ✉ *Kreuz-gasse 4* ☎*05556/72247* ⊘*Closed mid-June–mid-July.*

$$$$ 🏨**Löwen.** This central hotel looks huge, but inside the country style works well, and the rustic dark-wood exterior is carried over elegantly into the comfortable modern rooms with balconies. The hotel is in the center of a grassy garden platform, which forms a greenbelt around the main building and serves as a roof for the ground-floor pool and restaurants. The excellent Edelweiss restaurant, with its graceful table settings and candlelight, serves regional specialties done with flair. Edel-weiss serves dinner only, but the hotel's other restaurant, Montafoner Stuben, also serves lunch in a relaxed atmosphere at less inflated prices. **Pros:** spacious and luxurious. **Cons:** a bit stiff. ✉*Silvrettastrasse 8* ☎*05556/7141* ⊕*www.loewen-hotel.com* 🛏*85 rooms* ⚘*In-hotel: 4 restaurants, bar, pool, gym* ▤*AE, DC, MC, V* ⊘*Closed mid-Apr.–mid-May and mid-Oct.–mid-Dec.*

$$$$ 🏨**Montafoner Hof.** This cozy hotel in Tschagguns has a very spacious lobby and is a perfect place to relax. The family-management is warm and friendly, welcoming guests and making them feel at home. Ask to meet Armin Tschohl, the owner, who will take guests with a valid hunter's license on a hunt, and can tell you about the best fishing spots in the area. The hotel is also known for its popular restaurant, which features delicious, traditional Austrian cooking. Game is on the menu after a successful hunt. **Pros:** Austrian hospitality at its best; comfort-able atmosphere and wonderful food. **Cons:** after staying here, you will judge any other hotel stay by this standard. ✉*Kreuzgasse 9 Tschag-guns* ☎*05556/7100–0* ⊕*www.montafonerhof.com* 🛏*48 rooms* ⚘*In-room: no a/c, safe, Wi-Fi. In-hotel: restaurant, pool, gym, spa, bicycles, laundry service, Internet, parking (free), some pets allowed, no-smoking rooms* ▤*No credit cards* ⊘*Closed Apr., May, end of Nov.–mid-Dec.*

SPORTS & THE OUTDOORS

FISHING The local mountain streams and rivers are full of fish. Licenses are available; ask the regional tourist office in Bregenz for detailed infor-mation on seasons and locations.

SKIING Schruns is one of the skiing centers of the Montafon region, which also includes the Bartholomäberg, Gargellen, Gaschurn-Partenen, St. Gal-lenkirch/Gortipohl, Silbertal, and Vandans ski areas. They are acces-sible with a Montafon Ski Pass and together have 65 lifts and 208 km (129 mi) of groomed runs. Ski passes are valid for 3 to 14 days or 21 days, with rates for adults, children, and senior citizens varying according to season. Rental equipment is available. For details contact **Montafon Tourism** (✉*Montafonerstrasse 21, Schruns* ☎*05556/722530* ⊕*www.montafon.at*).

STUBEN

38 km (23 mi) northeast of Schruns, 24 km (15 mi) east of Bludenz.

Traveling from Feldkirch to the Arlberg Pass you'll come to the village of Stuben. From December to the end of April, the magnificent skiing, at 4,600 feet, makes Stuben popular among serious skiers willing to forgo the stylish resorts such as Lech just up the road. Stuben has skiing links with St. Anton, Lech, and Zürs. The village is poised right above the 14-km-long Arlberg Tunnel. To get here by public transportion, take the train from either Innsbruck or Feldkirch to Langen am Arlberg and then take a bus on to Stuben.

For information on its skiing facilities contact the **Arlberg region tourist office** (⊠ *Postfach 54, Lech* ☎ *05583/2161–0* ⊕ *www.lech-zuers.at*).

WHERE TO STAY

$–$$ 🖼 **Sporthotel Arlberg.** On the road to the top of the Arlberg Pass, just past the small village of Stuben, you'll notice this inviting hotel and its parking lot on your left. The restaurant is a pleasant place with good food served on a wide terrace or in the spacious dining rooms which boast a view of the slopes on the other side of the valley. Try to get one of the bigger deluxe rooms facing the meadows behind the hotel. **Pros:** excellent location right on the Pass road; good restaurant; inviting guest rooms. **Cons:** no elevator; front rooms are noisy. ⊠ *Arlbergstrasse 50* ☎ *05582/521* 🛏 *18 rooms* ⚬ *In-hotel: restaurant, bar, Wi-Fi, Internet, parking (free), no-smoking rooms* ▤ *MC, V* ⊗ *Closed 3 wks in Nov.*

ZÜRS

13 km (8 mi) north of Stuben, 90 km (56 mi) southeast of Bregenz.

The chosen resort of the rich and fashionable on this side of the Arlberg, Zürs is little more than a collection of large hotels. Perched at 5,600 feet, it's strictly a winter-sports community; when the season is over, the hotels close. But Zürs is more exclusive than nearby Lech and certainly more so than Gstaad or St. Moritz in Switzerland. Full board is required in most hotels, so there are relatively few "public" restaurants in town and little chance to dine around. But the hotel dining rooms are elegant; in some, jacket and tie are de rigueur in the evening. High standards were always part of the history of Zürs—the hotel Zürserhof was built by the aristocratic hotelier Count Tattenbach in the 1920s, and the first ski lift in Austria was constructed here in 1937.

10

ESSENTIALS

Tourist Information Zürs (⊠ *A-6763* ☎ *05583/2245* ⊕ *www.lech-zuers.at*).

WHERE TO STAY

$$$$ 🖼 **Lorünser.** The hospitable elegance of this hotel draws royalty, including Princess Caroline of Monaco and Queen Beatrix of the Netherlands. The Lorünser was one of the first hotels in Zürs, and it continues to improve its quality, though not its size. The local hoteliers have agreed to restrict the growth of their community, and instead focus on raising the standard of quality. Carved ceiling beams, open fireplaces, and attractive accessories create a welcoming reception. Rustic wood is used to good effect in the stylish guest rooms. Prices include half-board and the quality of the kitchen is such that you don't feel like eating anywhere else. **Pros:** hospitable elegance; continued top quality. **Cons:**

closed in summer. ✉ *A-6763* ☎ *05583/2254–0* ⊕ *www.loruenser.at* ➥ *74 rooms* ♿ *In-room: no a/c. In-hotel: restaurant, bar, gym, parking (paid), no-smoking rooms* ☰ *MC, V* ☉ *Closed mid-Apr.–early Dec.*

$$$$ ☖ **Sporthotel Edelweiss.** This 19th-century house has undergone an agreeable face-lift, including the guest rooms, giving the hotel and the guest rooms a colorful, contemporary interior. The Zürserl disco has been *the* place in the evening for the last 30 years. The Edelweiss may not be as fashionable as some of the other hotels, but its restaurant, Chesa (reservations essential), is possibly the best in town, offering fresh fish, game, and other regional standards. Prices include half-board. **Pros:** new guest rooms; excellent restaurant. **Cons:** restaurant is closed Monday. ✉ *A-6763* ☎ *05583/2662* ⊕ *www.edelweiss.net* ➥ *63 rooms, 3 apartments* ♿ *In-hotel: restaurant, bar, gym* ☰ *V* ☉ *Closed mid-Apr.–Nov.*

$$$$ ☖ **Zürserhof.** When celebrities seek privacy, they ensconce themselves
★   here. This world-famous hostelry at the north end of town comprises five of the most luxurious and expensive chalets in the world (prices can top €800 a day with board). You can have your lunch on the sun terrace, weather permitting. Many of the elegant accommodations are spacious apartments or suites with fireplaces; newer ones have Roman baths. The suites can be combined with double rooms for families. At night gentlemen are asked to wear a jacket in all public rooms, and jacket and tie are required at gala evenings. The family-run house has nevertheless managed to preserve a certain intimacy. Prices include full-board. **Pros:** exclusive top luxury; privacy. **Cons:** the price you pay for exclusive top luxury. ✉ *A-6763* ☎ *05583/2513–0* ⊕ *www.zuerserhof. at* ➥ *104 rooms* ♿ *In-hotel: restaurant, room service, bar, tennis court, pool, gym, spa, laundry service, Internet, parking (paid), no-smoking rooms* ☰ *No credit cards* ☉ *Closed mid-Apr.–Nov.*

SPORTS & THE OUTDOORS

SKIING   There are three main lifts: east of Zürs, take the chairlift to Hexenboden (7,600 feet) or the cable car to Trittkopf (7,800 feet), with a restaurant and sun terrace; to the west, a lift takes you to Seekopf (7,000 feet), where there is another restaurant. This mountain often gets huge snowfalls. ■ TIP→ **Skiers need to be particularly aware of avalanche conditions—check with the tourist office or your hotel before you hit the nongroomed slopes.**

LECH

FodorsChoice   *4 km (2½ mi) north of Zürs, 90 km (56 mi) southeast of Bregenz.*
★
Just down (literally) the road from the Zürs resort, Lech is a full-fledged community—which some argue detracts from its fashionableness. But there are more hotels in Lech, better tourist facilities, bigger ski schools, more shops, and more nightlife, with prices nearly as high as those in neighboring Zürs. Zürs has the advantage of altitude, but Lech is a less artificial and very pretty Alpine village, which is perhaps why more members of European royalty check in here. Be sure to check with the hotel of your choice about meal arrangements; some hotels recommend

that you take half-board, which is usually a good deal. You can't get to Zürs or Lech via rail; take the train to Langen am Arlberg station stop, then transfer to a bus.

ESSENTIALS

Tourist Information Lech (⊠ A-6764 ☎ 05583/2161-0 ⊕ www.lech-zuers.at).

WHERE TO STAY

$$$$ Fodor'sChoice ★ ⊞**Gasthof Post.** A *gemütlich* atmosphere enfolds in this blue-shuttered chalet hotel, a member of the prestigious hotel chain Relais & Chateaux (⊕ *www.relaischateaux.com*), with murals, flower boxes, and a wood-paneled interior. The à la carte restaurant Post Stuben (dinner only) is one of the two best in town. Try the medallion of lamb or grilled salmon, and save space

> ## CHAMPAGNE ON THE SLOPES
>
> Accessed by the Trittkopf cable car, at the highest point of the Flexen Pass you'll find the Flexenhäsl (Little Flexen House), perhaps the most exclusive ski hut in the Alps. Where else can skiers order up mouthwatering tidbits such as scampi with garlic butter and *Hirschwürstel* (venison sausage) with fresh horseradish sauce, washed down with a bottle of chilled Dom Pérignon? In the evening join in for piping-hot fondue *chinoise.* There's room for only 20 guests, so call ahead for reservations (☎ 05583–4143).

for one of the outstanding desserts. The restaurant Kutscherstuben serves excellent regional dishes 10–10, but if the weather's nice, try to get a table on the garden terrace. **Pros:** historic and luxurious; antiques artfully displayed throughout the hotel; excellent restaurants. **Cons:** after eating here, it may be difficult to appreciate any other food for days. ⊠ *Dorf 11* ☎ *05583/2206–0* ⊕ *www.postlech.com* ⏎ *40 rooms* △ *In-room: no a/c, safe, Wi-Fi. In-hotel: restaurant, room service, bar, pool, gym, spa, laundry service, Internet, parking (paid), some pets allowed, no-smoking rooms* ▭ *AE, MC, V* ⊙ *Closed May–mid-June, Oct., and Nov.*

$$$$ ⊞**Romantik Hotel Krone.** Across the street from two of the main lifts, this family-managed hotel grew out of a 250-year-old house. It's part of the Romantik Hotels & Restaurants chain, which are all family-owned and tradition-conscious properties that guarantee quality. The adaptations and modernization have not affected the comfort and well-being reflected in the beamed ceilings, tile stoves, and Oriental carpets. The restaurant, one of the town's best, is noted for its game and regional specialties; try the fillet of whitefish on cucumber or the rack of lamb. **Pros:** spacious lobby; excellent staff; delicious cooking. **Cons:** some rooms tend to be noisy, as the hotel is very close to the main street. ⊠ *House 13* ☎ *05583/2551* ⊕ *www.romantikhotelkrone-lech.at* ⏎ *56 rooms* △ *In-room: no a/c, Wi-Fi. In-hotel: restaurant, bar, pool, gym, bicycles, Internet, parking (free), some pets allowed, no-smoking rooms* ▭ *V* ⊙ *Closed mid-Apr.–mid-June, Oct., and Nov.*

$$–$$$$ ⊞**Pfefferkorn's Hotel.** A cozy yet spacious wood-paneled lobby makes you feel welcome as you enter Pfefferkorn's. This warm, wood, Alpine style continues into many of the guest rooms. If have a choice, take a room on a top floor—you'll get an even better view, and you'll hear less from the street as you relax on your balcony. In winter the hotel opens

10

its excellent restaurant, where reservations are advised for dinner. People come to the Pfefferkörndl bar for a snack during the day, and at night it's the *in* place. **Pros:** warm atmosphere; very attentive staff; great location (70 meters from the main lifts). **Cons:** guest rooms near the street on the lower floors can be noisy. ⊠*Dorf 138* ☎*05583/25250* ⊕*www.pfefferkorns.at* 🛏*29 rooms* ♿*In room: no a/c, Internet. In hotel: restaurant, room service, bar, spa, bicycles, laundry service, Wi-Fi, parking (free), no-smoking rooms* ▭*AE, D, MC, V* ⊗*Closed May, June, Oct., and Nov.*

NIGHTLIFE & THE ARTS

Lech is known almost as much for après-ski and nightlife as for the snow and the slopes. Prices vary from place to place, but in general a mixed drink will cost €8–€9.

You can join the snacks-and-drinks crowd as early as 11 AM at the outdoor and famed **Umbrella** (☎*05583/3232*) bar at the Petersboden Sport Hotel at Oberlech. Activity continues at the late-afternoon **tea dance** (☎*05583/2202*) at the Tannbergerhof.

The bar at the **Goldener Berg** (☎*05583/2205*) is usually a hot après-ski spot. The bar in the **Burg** (☎*05583/2291*) hotel in Oberlech features live music most nights. Among the popular places for a mid-evening drink (starting at 9:30) are **Pfefferkörndl** (☎*05583/2525–429*) in the Pfefferkorn's Hotel. The **Krone Bar** in the Krone hotel (⇨ *Where to Stay, above*) opens at 9 PM and goes on until 2 or 3 AM.

SPORTS & THE OUTDOORS

SKIING Lech is linked with Oberlech and Zürs with more than 30 ski lifts and cable cars, all accessed by the regional ski pass, which allows skiers to take in the entire region, including Lech, Oberlech, Zürs, Stuben, St. Christoph, and St. Anton. The area as a whole includes 85 cable cars and lifts (most of them with heated seats!), 260 km (161 mi) of groomed pistes, and 180 km (112 mi) of open slopes. In addition, there is a vast network of cross-country trails.

The ski pistes and open slopes in Lech are spread between 4,757 feet and 9,186 feet above sea level, including the slopes Rüfikopf, Madloch, and Mohnenfluh. Some 400 skiing instructors can help you master the craft here. Snowboarders have their own Fun Park which also has a floodlighted toboggan run and horse-drawn sleigh rides. For complete information on skiing facilities contact the **Lech-Zürs Tourist Office** on the main street in the center of town. (⊠*Postfach 54, Lech* ☎*05583/2161–0* ⊕*www.lech-zuers.at*).

UNDERSTANDING AUSTRIA

POWDER-PERFECT SKIING

Austrian skiing is a fairy tale. Strip away the ski history and the tourist-brochure hype, and it's still a fairy tale. Austria has the same high, treeless bowls and slopes that make skiing all over the Alps so different from skiing in North America, plus something extra—the loveliest mountain villages in Europe. Classic Austrian ski villages look, and feel, like an art director's fantasy of Alpine charm.

It's hard for American skiers who haven't skied in the Alps to imagine the sheer size and scale of Alpine ski resorts, where many individual ski areas are linked together with a common ski pass and a spiderweb network of lifts spanning and connecting different valleys and multiple mountains. To take full advantage of the promise of so much snowy terrain, American skiers should consider hiring a ski-instructor/guide for a day or two. Private instructors are much less expensive in Austria than in the United States, and the upper levels of Austrian ski-school classes are more about guiding than actual teaching.

Another surprise for the American skier in Austria will be the degree to which the entire country seems to embrace skiing (and winter sports in general, including cross-country skiing, snowboarding, and, more recently, snow walking). Skiing is deeply woven into the daily patterns of winter life in the Austrian countryside. A far greater percentage of the population skis than in the United States. In Austria skiing isn't just another sport, it's the national sport. Ski racers are national heroes; the sports pages of Austrian newspapers award ski competitions banner headlines. Winter, Austria, and skiing are virtually synonymous.

PACKAGES, DISCOUNTS & INFORMATION

Your best source for information about Austrian ski vacations and resorts is the **Austrian National Tourist Office** (☎212/944–6880 ⊕*www.austria. info*). It's well connected to stateside tour operators providing ski and vacation packages to Austria, and will be happy to send you all sorts of maps and brochures about Austrian ski regions. Contacting the tourist bureaus at individual resorts for this kind of information is a much slower process. But all of Austria's Alpine resorts do have tourist bureau–central reservation services that can make hotel reservations for you (⇨ *see the addresses and phone numbers for individual resorts, below)*, and most have Web sites offering packages that can be booked directly on the Internet.

Skiing is neither more nor less expensive in the Alps—and in Austria—than in the United States. Some costs, like those for lift tickets, are much lower; others, like those for fine meals, are higher. Some resorts, like Kitzbühel, are very posh indeed, but there are almost always budget alternatives nearby (neighboring ski villages with more modest prices that are nonetheless connected by lifts to the same large ski domain). Some airlines offer all-inclusive air-lodging-skiing packages to many Austrian resorts. ■TIP➔ One of the easiest ways to reach the great resorts of the Vorarlberg and the Tirol is to fly to Munich, then take a short and convenient bus transfer south into the Austrian Alps.

The Austrian ski season typically runs from late November to April, depending on local snow conditions. Areas with glacier skiing are a better bet in dry snow years. A number of these very high glacier locations offer summer and autumn skiing. But summer ski zones are rather small; the real magic of Austrian skiing involves snow-frosted villages and endless slopes. More and more ski areas, including all the major resorts, now have snowmaking machines in case Mother Nature is not cooperating.

Americans can check the Web site of the **Austrian National Tourist Office** (⊕ *www. austria.info*) for very accurate snow reports at all major Austrian resorts.

FAVORITE DESTINATIONS

There are so many choices when it comes to Austrian skiing that you're not going to see it all, and ski it all, in one lifetime. Foreign ski enthusiasts and newcomers to Austrian slopes would do well to focus first on the biggest ski regions of the Arlberg, Tirol, and Land Salzburg. These mega-ski regions showcase what makes Alpine skiing so special: an astonishing variety of slopes and lifts that allows the visitor to ski, day after day, often from one village to the next, without ever repeating a lift or a piste. True, there are many tiny and delightful ski villages in Austria, real discoveries for adventurous skiers, but it makes more sense to sample the feast of a major *Skigebiet* (interconnected ski region, sometimes called a ski arena) first. Here, to get you started, are some of the finest.

The Arlberg

This is a capital of Austrian skiing: a double constellation of ski-resort towns—Zürs, Lech, and Oberlech, in the Vorarlberg; and, just across the Arlberg Pass to the east and thus technically in the Tirol, St. Anton, St. Christoph, and Stuben. These classic Arlberg resorts are interconnected by ski lifts and trails and share more than 260 km (160 mi) of groomed slopes (and limitless off-piste possibilities), 83 ski lifts, snowboard parks, carving areas and permanent race courses and, significantly, a common ski pass.

A skier in **St. Anton**, where Hannes Schneider started the first real ski school, can feel like a character out of a 1930s Luis Trenker ski film: from enjoying Jaeger tea after skiing to dinner at the Post Hotel. Neighboring **St. Christoph** is a spartan resort for skiing purists, a handful of handsome hotels lost in a sea of white,

high above timberline, and the permanent home of the Austrian National Ski School's training and certification courses.

The pièce de résistance of Arlberg skiing is the all-day round-trip, on skis, from Zürs to Lech, Oberlech, and back. This ski epic starts with a 5-km (3-mi) off-piste run from the Madloch down to Zug and ends, late in the afternoon, many lifts and many thousands of vertical feet later, high on the opposite side of Zürs, swinging down the slopes of the Trittkopf.

VISITOR INFORMATION

Lech (✉ *Tourismusverband Lech* ☎ 05583/2161–0 ⊕ *www.lech-zuers.at*). St. Anton (✉ *Tourismusverband St. Anton am Arlberg* ☎ 05446/22690 ⊕ *www.stantonamarlberg.com*).

The Tirol/Innsbruck

The Tirol is really the heart of Austrian skiing—about a third of all Austrian ski resorts are found in this province. After St. Anton and the Arlberg, **Kitzbühel**, in the heart of the Tirol, is Austria's best-known ski destination, and although not as exclusive as Lech or Zürs, certainly one of Austria's most elegant. "Kitz" is picture-perfect and posh—all medieval cobbled streets, wrought-iron signs, and candles flickering in the windows of charming restaurants.

The "SkiWelt Wilder Kaiser—Brixental" (91 lifts serving 279 km of slopes) **is the largest interconnected skiing area of Austria** and covers the all the following towns: Brixen im Thale, Ellmau, Going, Hopfgarten, Itter, Kelchsau, Scheffau, Söll, and Westendorf. Here, a brand-new conveyor-belt system together with a drag lift transports skiers from the end of one slope to a new valley lift station. A common pass lets you access all the lifts.

The Kitzbühler Alpen region covers 54 lifts serving 167 km (103 mi) of groomed slopes—the most celebrated of which is the Hahnenkamm, the course for Europe's toughest downhill race. Deep-snow enthusiasts will gravitate to the

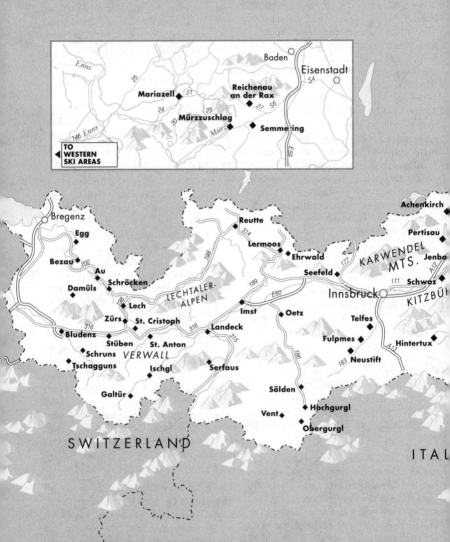

Ski
Areas

Enns

25

Baden

Eisenstadt

S4

Mariazell

21

Reichenau
an der Rax

27

S6

24

Mürzzuschlag

23

Mürz

Semmering

146 Enns

E59

TO
WESTERN
SKI AREAS

Bregenz

Egg

Reutte

314

Achenkirch

Lermoos

Pertisau

Bezau

200

Ehrwald

177

KARWENDEL

Jenba

Au

Schröcken

Seefeld

MTS.

A12

Damüls

LECHTALER-
ALPEN

189

171

Schwaz

36

Lech

E60

Innsbruck

KITZBÜ

Zürs

St. Cristoph

Imst

Oetz

Telfes

Bludenz

316

316

Landeck

Fulpmes

Hintertux

Stüben

St. Anton

315

A13

Schruns

VERWALL

Ischgl

Serfaus

186

183

Neustift

Tschagguns

Galtür

Sölden

Vent

Hochgurgl

SWITZERLAND

Obergurgl

ITAL

ungroomed slopes of the Schwarzkogel. You can "fly" between the slopes of Kitzbühel, Pass Thurn, Jochberg, Kirchberg on one of the longest, most spectacular cable-car systems in the world, which means you never have to leave the slopes to ski all the area pistes.

In high season, if you want to enjoy the chic atmosphere of Kitz, ski all the celebrated pistes of the Kitzbüheler Ski Safari, and avoid high-end prices, consider staying in the Brixen Valley in neighboring **Kirchberg.** But if you must be where the action is, with a little looking around you'll find accommodations in all price ranges in Kitzbühel itself.

For an altogether different sort of ski vacation, especially for mixed groups of skiers and nonskiers, consider staying in downtown **Innsbruck** and making day trips to the six ski areas of Olympia Ski World Innsbruck. Innsbruck has twice hosted the winter Olympics, and boasts a stunning collection of medium-size ski areas with grand views: Seegrube-Nordpark, Patscherkofel, Glungezer, Schlick 2000, Stubaier Gletscher, and especially Axamer-Lizum. Year-round skiing is possible on the Stubaier Gletscher, at the upper end of the spectacular Stubai Valley.

In ever-increasing numbers, skiers are attracted by the excellent snow conditions and après-ski nightlife of **Ischgl,** in the Paznaun (Valley) southwest of Innsbruck, and not far from better-known St. Anton. Although it's not as chic as Kitz or St. Anton, skiers and snowboarders are drawn to Ischgl and neighboring resorts **Galtur** and **Kappl** by the 265 km (165 mi) of groomed slopes and 67 lifts found here. It is even possible to ski from Ischgl into the village of Samnaun, Switzerland, for some duty-free shopping, before hopping the impressive double-decker *Pendlebahn* back into Austria.

No tour of Austria's finest ski areas would be complete without a look into the Ötz

Valley, particularly **Sölden,** the valley's premier resort, and one of the best, most au courant all-round resorts in Austria. While not so well-known to Americans, Sölden has excellent snow conditions, due to its three superbly developed 10,000-foot mountains, known as the "Big 3." State-of-the-art mountain railways (34 ski lifts and gondolas holding a capacity of 68,000 persons per hour) guarantee ultimate skiing fun without lift lines. The wide variety of 151 km ski runs and modern snowmaking machines guarantee good skiing, and the Aqua Dome, a grandiose new spa facility, ensures relief for your tired muscles.

A favorite Austrian Skigebiet has to be the **Zillertal,** just south and east of Innsbruck. Almost unknown to American skiers, there are 10 different ski areas, strung like pearls up the long Ziller Valley, culminating in the Tux Glacier at the very top (a popular summer-skiing site, too). Mayerhofen, a pretty town full of painted buildings halfway up the Zillertal, is a perfect base for skiing the whole valley. The Zillertal super ski pass includes efficient bus and train transportation up and down the valley from one ski area to the next, and lets you ski 639 km (397 mi) of groomed slopes and use 167 lifts.

VISITOR INFORMATION

Innsbruck (☎ *0512/59850* ⊕ *www.tiscover. com/innsbruck).* **Ischgl** (☎ *050990/100* ⊕ *www.ischgl.com).* **Kitzbühel** (☎ *05356/777* ⊕ *www.kitzbuehel.com).* **Mayrhofen** (☎ *05285/6760* ⊕ *www.mayrhofen.com).* **Sölden/Ötztal Arena** (☎ *057200/200* ⊕ *www.soelden.com).* **Söll** (☎ *Snow phone: 05333/400* ⊕ *www.skiwelt.at).* **Zillertal** (☎ *05282/2281* ⊕ *www.zell.at).*

Salzburg

Farther east, in the province of Salzburg, there are also a number of stunning integrated ski regions. Despite its grandiose name, the **Europa-Sportregion** is only a grouping together of two—splendid—ski resorts, Kaprun and Zell am See. The skier population here comes from all across Europe, and the large number of British and Scandinavian skiers guarantees that Americans without a word of German will feel at home. Zell am See, a lakeside village, sits beneath the Schmittenhöhe, a wide mountain served by 25 ski lifts and known for its long runs. A few miles away, the village of Kaprun lies under the 10,509-foot Kitzsteinhorn peak, and its glacier skiing makes a winter vacation here very "snow safe." (This is also a major summer-skiing location.)

The **Gasteiner Tal** (Gastein Valley) is the place to combine skiing and spa vacationing. Bad Gastein and neighboring Bad Hofgastein are better known to Americans for their luxurious thermal and mineral baths. But their ski slopes, linked with those of Grossarl in the next valley over, comprise a beautiful and rather large ski region. Accommodations range from luxury hotels—Bad Gastein has a distinctly chichi reputation—to traditional Alpine farmhouses. The Gasteiner Tal and nearby Grossarl together offer 44 ski lifts serving 201 km (124 mi) of groomed slopes.

The slopes of **Saalbach Hinterglemm,** linked with nearby Leogang, are not particularly steep or difficult, but this is a beautifully integrated ski offering with 200 km (120 mi) of groomed pistes and more than 70 lifts, one of which, the Schattbergbahn, is said to be the largest cable car in Austria. It's a good choice for long, aesthetic, intermediate ski runs.

The **Salzburger Sportwelt** is Austria's largest interlinked skiing area. One ski pass is valid for eight resorts with a total of 276 ski lifts and 865 km of runs in the Salzburger Land reaching over to Styria. It includes Flachau, Wagrain, St. Johann-Alpendorf, Radstadt, Altenmarkt-Zauchensee, Kleinarl, Eben, and Filzmoos. These resorts may never have been featured in American ski magazines, which invariably stick with the big

names like St. Anton and Kitz, but this ski region is well worth a visit.

VISITOR INFORMATION
Europa-Sportregion (☎06542/770 ⊕www.zellamsee-kaprun.com). **Gasteiner Tal** (☎06432/3393 ⊕www.gastein.at). **Saalbach Hinterglemm** (☎06541/6800–68 ⊕www.saalbach.com). **Salzburger Sportwelt** (☎06457/2929 ⊕www.salzburgersportwelt.at).

Styria
The mountains tend to become lower and the snow conditions less certain as you travel east in the Austrian Alps, so it makes sense for American skiers to concentrate on the more westerly ski destinations.

One exception is in Styria, the **Dachstein-Tauren Region.** Here the Dachstein Glacier offers a bonus of high-altitude snow. Nine separate villages—Schladming, Rohrmoos-Untertal, Pichl, Haus im Ennstal, Aich-Assach, Pruggern, Gröbming, Mitterberg, and Ramsau am Dachstein—share a common pass that gives access to 109 lifts, serving 223 km of groomed slopes above the wide Enns River valley. Free ski buses run throughout the entire region daily during the season. Schladming's so-called "Four Mountain Ski Link" connects the four largest Styrian skiing mountains allowing you to ski nonstop from Hauser-Kaibling via Planai and Hochwurzen to Reiteralm. The "Planai Golden Jet" is a cable car with 87 cabins, capable of transporting 2,400 people per hour up the mountain. There's also an abundance of groomed cross-country trails.

VISITOR INFORMATION
Ramsau am Dachstein (☎3687/81833 ⊕www.ramsau.com). **Schladming** (☎3687/23310 ⊕www.schladming-rohrmoos.com).

—Lito Tejada-Flores, Updated by Diane Naar-Elphee

AUSTRIA AT A GLANCE

FAST FACTS

Capital: Vienna

National anthem: "Land der Berge, Land am Strome" ("Land of Mountains, Land on the River")

Type of government: Federal republic

Administrative divisions: Nine states

Independence: 1156 (from Bavaria)

Constitution: 1920; revised 1929, reinstated 1945

Legal system: Civil law system with Roman law origin; judicial review of legislative acts by the Constitutional Court; separate administrative and civil/penal supreme courts

Suffrage: 18 years of age; universal; compulsory for presidential elections

Legislature: Bicameral Federal Assembly consists of Federal Council (62 members; members represent each of the states on the basis of population, but with each state having at least three representatives; members serve a five- or six-year term) and the National Council (183 seats; members elected by direct popular vote to serve four-year terms)

Population: 8.2 million

Median age: Female 42, male 39.8

Life expectancy: Female 82, male 76

Infant mortality rate: 4.6 deaths per 1,000 live births

Literacy: 98%

Language: German (official nationwide), Slovene (official in Carinthia), Croatian (official in Burgenland), Hungarian (official in Burgenland)

Ethnic groups: Austrian 91%, former Yugoslavs 4% (includes Croatians, Slovenes, Serbs, and Bosnians), Turks 1.6%, German 0.9%, other or unspecified 2.4%

Religion: Roman Catholic 74%; other 17%; Protestant 5%; Muslim 4%

GEOGRAPHY & ENVIRONMENT

Land area: 82,444 square km (31,832 square mi)

Terrain: Steep Alps in the west and south; mostly flat along the eastern and northern borders; at the crossroads of central Europe with many easily traversable Alpine passes and valleys

Natural resources: Antimony, coal, copper, graphite, hydropower, iron ore, lignite, magnesite, natural gas, oil, salt, timber, tungsten, uranium, zinc

Natural hazards: Avalanches, earthquakes, landslides

Environmental issues: Forest degradation caused by air and soil pollution; soil pollution results from the use of agricultural chemicals; air pollution results from emissions by coal- and oil-fired power stations and industrial plants and from trucks transiting Austria between northern and southern Europe

ECONOMY

Currency: Euro

Exchange rate: 0.79 EUR

GDP: $293.4 billion (2005 est.)

Inflation: 2%

Unemployment: 5.2%

Work force: 4.3 million; services 67%; industry and crafts 29%; agriculture and forestry 4%

Major industries: Chemicals, communications equipment, construction, food, lumber and wood processing, machinery, paper and paperboard, vehicles and parts, tourism

Agricultural products: Cattle, dairy products, fruit, grains, lumber, pigs, potatoes, poultry, sugar beets, wine

Exports: $122.5 billion

Major export products: Chemicals, foodstuffs, iron and steel, machinery and equipment, metal goods, motor vehicles and parts, paper and paperboard, textiles

Export partners: Germany 31.5%; Italy 9.3%; Switzerland 5.4%; U.S. 4.9%; U.K. 4.9%; France 4.7%; Hungary 4.3%
Imports: $118.8 billion
Major import products: Chemicals, foodstuffs, machinery and equipment, metal goods, motor vehicles, oil and oil products
Import partners: Germany 42.6%; Italy 6.6%; Hungary 5.1%; Switzerland 4.8%; Netherlands 4.4%

Who could deny that our Austria is richer than any other country? As the saying goes: "We have money like manure."
–Franz Grillparzer

POLITICAL CLIMATE

Austria has been moving to the right in recent years. After three decades of social-democratic governments, political battles have centered on which parties belong in the ruling right-wing coalition, with reactionary politicians garnering enough support to create a stir. Austria has long been one of the most developed and self-sufficient nations, so its entry into the EU has been a prickly one. Inside its borders, pension and health-care reform as well as lower taxes and unemployment form the boilerplate of the debate.

DID YOU KNOW?

■ **The Vienna Staatsoper, the venue of many of the world's most famous musical performances, is the site of the world's longest round of applause.** For 90 minutes and 101 curtain calls, an Austrian crowd applauded Placido Domingo for his performance in *Othello* in 1991.

■ **Austria recycles around 80% of its glass products, second only to Switzerland with 91%.**

■ **Austria has the most organically farmed land of any nation.** An estimated 10% of the land is farmed without chemically formulated fertilizers, growth stimulants, antibiotics, or pesticides. It's also considered to be nearly self-sufficient in terms of food production.

■ **The Alps take up three-fourths of Austria.**

■ **Though almost nine-tenths of Austria's people are of Germanic origin, the nation has received almost 2 million refugees since 1945.** About 300,000 of Austria's workforce are now foreign laborers.

CHRONOLOGY

ca. 800 BC Celts move into Danube Valley.

ca. 100 BC Earliest fortresses set up at Vindobona, now the inner city of Vienna. Roman legions, and Roman civilization, advance to Danube. Carnuntum (near Petronell, east of Vienna) is established about 30 years later as a provincial capital.

AD 180 Emperor Marcus Aurelius dies at Vindobona. Other Roman settlements include Juvavum (Salzburg) and Valdidena (Innsbruck).

ca. 400–700 The Danube Valley is the crossing ground for successive waves of barbarian invaders. Era of the events of the Nibelung saga, written down circa 1100.

ca. 700 Christian bishop established at Salzburg; conversion of pagan tribes begins.

791–99 Charlemagne, king of the Franks, conquers territory now known as Austria.

800 Pope Leo III crowns Charlemagne Emperor of the West.

ca. 800–900 Invasion of Magyars; they eventually settle along the Danube.

962 Pope John XII crowns Otto the Great, of Germany, emperor of the Holy Roman Empire, constituting the eastern portion of Charlemagne's realm. Neither holy, nor Roman, nor an empire, this confederation continued until 1806.

THE HOUSE OF BABENBERG

976 Otto II confers the eastern province of the Reich—Österreich, or Austria—upon the margrave Leopold of Babenberg.

1095–1136 Reign of Leopold III, later canonized and declared patron saint of Austria.

1156 Austria becomes a duchy. Duke Heinrich II makes Vienna his capital, building a palace in Am Hof.

1192 Leopold V imprisons King Richard the Lion-Hearted of England, who is on his way back from a crusade. Parts of Vienna and several town walls, particularly Wiener Neustadt, south of Vienna, are later built with the ransom money.

THE HOUSE OF HABSBURG

1273 Rudolf of Habsburg in Switzerland is chosen duke by the electors of the Rhine; his family rules for 640 years.

1282 Habsburgs absorb the land of Austria.

1365 University of Vienna founded.

1496 Maximilian's son, Philip, marries Juana of Castile and Aragon, daughter of Ferdinand and Isabella of Spain.

1519   Death of Maximilian; his grandson, Charles I of Spain, inherits Austria, Burgundy, and the Netherlands; he is elected Holy Roman Emperor as Charles V.

1521   Charles V divides his realm with his brother Ferdinand, who becomes archduke of Austria and the first Habsburg to live in the Hofburg in Vienna.

1529   Turks lay siege to Vienna.

1556   Charles V abdicates; Ferdinand becomes Holy Roman Emperor. A Catholic with many Protestant subjects, he negotiates the Peace of Augsburg, which preserves a truce between the Catholic and Protestant states of his realm until 1618.

1618–48 Thirty Years' War begins as a religious dispute but becomes a dynastic struggle between Habsburgs and Bourbons, fought on German soil by non-Germans. The Peace of Westphalia, 1648, gives Austria no new territory and reestablishes the religious deadlock of the Peace of Augsburg.

1683   Turks besiege Vienna; are routed by combined forces of Emperor Leopold I, the duke of Lorraine, and King Jan Sobieski of Poland. By 1699, armies led by Prince Eugene of Savoy drive the Turks east and south, doubling the area of Habsburg lands. The Turkish legacy: a gold crescent and a sack of coffee beans; Vienna's coffeehouses open for business.

1740   Last male Habsburg, Charles VI, dies; succession of his daughter Maria Theresa leads to attack on the Habsburg dominions; long-term rivalry between Austria and Prussia begins.

1740–80 Reign of Maria Theresa, a golden age, when young Mozart entertains at Schönbrunn Palace and Haydn and Gluck establish Vienna as a musical mecca. Fundamental reforms modernize the Austrian monarchy.

1780–90 Reign of Maria Theresa's son Joseph II, who continues her liberalizing tendencies by freeing the serfs and reforming the Church. Her daughter, Marie Antoinette, has other problems.

1806   Napoléon forces Emperor Franz II to abdicate, and the Holy Roman Empire is no more; Franz is retitled emperor of Austria and rules until 1835.

1814–15 The Congress of Vienna defines post-Napoleonic Europe; Austria's Prince Metternich (who had arranged the marriage between Napoléon and Franz II's daughter Marie Louise) gains territory and power.

1815–48 Rise of nationalism threatens Austrian Empire; as chief minister, Metternich represses liberal and national movements with censorship, secret police, and force.

1848   Revolutions throughout Europe, including Budapest, Prague, Vienna; Emperor Ferdinand I abdicates in favor of his 18-year-old nephew

Franz Josef. Under his personal rule (lasting until 1916), national and liberal movements are thwarted.

1856–90   Modern Vienna is created and much of the medieval city torn down; the Waltz Kings, Johann Strauss father and son, dominate popular music. Sigmund Freud (1856–1939) begins his research on the human psyche in Vienna. By 1900 artistic movements include the Secession and Expressionism.

1866   Bismarck's Prussia defeats Austria in a seven-week war, fatally weakening Austria's position among the German states.

1867   In response to Hungarian clamor for national recognition, the Ausgleich, or compromise, creates the dual monarchy of Austria-Hungary with two parliaments and one monarch.

1889   Franz Josef's only son, Rudolf, dies mysteriously in an apparent suicide pact with his young mistress, Baroness Marie Vetsera.

1898   Empress Elisabeth is murdered in Geneva by an anarchist.

1914   June 28: Archduke Franz Ferdinand, nephew and heir of Franz Josef, is assassinated by a Serbian terrorist at Sarajevo in Bosnia-Herzegovina. By August 4, Europe is at war: Germany and Austria-Hungary versus Russia, France, and Britain.

1916   Death of Franz Josef.

THE REPUBLIC

1918   End of World War I; collapse of Austria-Hungary. Emperor Karl I resigns; Republic of Austria is carved out of Habsburg crown lands, while nation-states of the empire declare autonomy. Kept afloat by loans from the League of Nations, Austria adjusts to its new role with difficulty. Culturally it continues to flourish: Arnold Schoenberg's 12-tone scale recasts musical expression, while the Vienna Circle redefines philosophy.

1934   Dollfuss suppresses the Socialists and creates a one-party state; later in the year he is assassinated by Nazis. His successor, Kurt von Schuschnigg, attempts to accommodate Hitler.

1938   Anschluss: Hitler occupies Austria without resistance.

1945   Austria, postwar, is divided into four zones of occupation by the Allies; free elections are held.

1955   Signing of the Austrian State Treaty officially ends the occupation. Austria declares itself "perpetually" neutral.

1989   Austria becomes the first destination for waves of Eastern European emigrants as the borders are opened.

1990   Austria applies for membership in the European Union.

1999   Spearheaded by Jörg Haider, the anti-immigration and extremist Freedom Party is admitted to Austria's national cabinet, setting the government on a collision course with fellow members of the European Union, who subsequently issue economic and political sanctions against Austria.

2002 The Austrian government is in full upheaval. The status of the ÖVP coalition as the leading party in power is in doubt, with the SPÖ party coming to the fore. The leaders of the Freedom Party resign because of differences with Jörg Haider, who in the September elections becomes head of this party again, only to back down from taking over the leadership. Happily, the launch of euro notes and coins continues to be a tremendous success in Austria.

2004 Elfriede Jelinek wins the Nobel Prize for Literature, confirming her status as one of Austria's most important and controversial cultural figures. Her novels deal with sexual violence and oppression and right-wing extremism. After years of friction with the government, her plays are once again performed in her homeland. The revered and respected president of Austria, Dr. Thomas Klestil, dies of heart failure just days before his second four-year term expires in July. He is replaced by Dr. Heinz Fischer, a prominent member of the Socialist Party, who is elected in April. Pope John Paul II beatifies the last Austrian emperor, Karl I, who was against fighting in World War I. And Austria's most famous export since Mozart, Arnold Schwarzenegger, completes his first year as governor of California.

WORDS & PHRASES

Austrian German is not entirely the same as the German spoken in Germany. Several food names are different, as well as a few basic phrases.

Umlauts have no similar sound in English. An ä is pronounced as "eh." An äu or eu is pronounced as "oy". An ö is pronounced by making your lips like an "O" while trying to say "E" and a ü is pronounced by making your lips like a "U" and trying to say "E".

Consonants are pronounced as follows:
CH is like a hard H, almost like a soft clearing of the throat.
J is pronounced as Y.
Rs are rolled.
ß, which is written "ss" in this book, is pronouced as double S.
S is pronounced as Z.
V is pronounced as F.
W is pronounced as V.
Z is pronounced as TS.

An asterisk (*) denotes common usage in Austria.

	ENGLISH	GERMAN	PRONUNCIATION
BASICS			
	Yes/no	Ja/nein	yah/nine
	Please	Bitte	**bit**-uh
	May I?	Darf ich?	darf isch?
	Thank you (very much)	Danke (vielen Dank)	**dahn**-kuh (**fee**-len dahnk)
	You're welcome	Bitte, gern geschehen	**bit**-uh, gairn ge**shay**-un
	Excuse me	Entschuldigen Sie	ent-**shool**-di-gen zee
	What? (What did you say?)	Wie, bitte?	vee, **bit**-uh?
	Can you tell me?	Können Sie mir sagen?	kunnen zee meer **sah**-gen?
	Do you know _____?	Wissen Sie _____?	**viss**-en zee
	I'm sorry	Es tut mir leid.	es toot meer lite
	Good day	Guten Tag	**goo**-ten tahk
	Goodbye	Auf Wiedersehen	owf **vee**-der-zane
	Good morning	Guten Morgen	**goo**-ten **mor**-gen
	Good evening	Guten Abend	**goo**-ten **ah**-bend
	Good night	Gute Nacht	**goo**-tuh nahkt

ENGLISH	GERMAN	PRONUNCIATION
Mr./Mrs.	Herr/Frau	hair/frow
Miss	Fräulein	**froy**-line
Pleased to meet you	Sehr erfreut.	zair air-**froyt**
How are you?	Wie geht es Ihnen?	vee **gate** es **ee**-nen?
Very well, thanks.	Sehr gut, danke.	sair goot, **dahn**-kuh
And you?	Und Ihnen?	oont **ee**-nen?
Hi!	*Servus!	**sair**-voos

DAYS OF THE WEEK

Sunday	Sonntag	**zohn**-tahk
Monday	Montag	**moan**-tahk
Tuesday	Dienstag	**deens**-tahk
Wednesday	Mittwoch	**mitt**-voak
Thursday	Donnerstag	**doe**-ners-tahk
Friday	Freitag	**fry**-tahk
Saturday	Samstag	**zahm**-stahk

USEFUL PHRASES

Do you speak English?	Sprechen Sie Englisch?	**shprek**-hun zee **eng**-glisch?
I don't speak German.	Ich spreche kein Deutsch.	isch **shprek**-uh kine doych
Please speak slowly.	Bitte sprechen Sie langsam.	bit-uh **shprek**-en zee **lahng**-zahm
I don't understand	Ich verstehe nicht	isch fair-**shtay**-uh nicht
I understand	Ich verstehe	isch fair-**shtay**-uh
I don't know	Ich weiss nicht	isch vice nicht
Excuse me/sorry	Entschuldigen Sie	ent-**shool**-di-gen zee
I am American/British	Ich bin Amerikaner(in)/ Engländer(in)	isch bin a-mer-i-**kahn**-er(in)/**eng**-len-der(in)
What is your name?	Wie heissen Sie?	vee **high**-sen zee
My name is . . .	ich heiße . . .	isch **high**-suh
What time is it?	Wieviel Uhr ist es?	**vee**-feel oor ist es
	*Wie spät ist es?	**vee** shpate ist es

ENGLISH	GERMAN	PRONUNCIATION
It is one, two, three . . . o'clock.	Es ist ein, zwei, drei . . . Uhr.	es ist ine, tsvy, dry . . . oor
Yes, please/	Ja, bitte/	yah **bi**-tuh/
No, thank you	Nein, danke	**nine** dahng-kuh
How?	Wie?	vee
When?	Wann? (as conjunction, als)	vahn (ahls)
This/next week	Diese/nächste Woche	**dee**-zuh/**nehks**-tuh **vo**-kuh
This/next year	Dieses/nächstes Jahr	**dee**-zuz/**nehks**-tuhs yahr
Yesterday/today/ tomorrow	Gestern/heute/morgen	**geh**-stern/**hoy**-tuh/ **mor**-gen
This morning/ afternoon	Heute morgen/ nachmittag	**hoy**-tuh **mor**-gen/ **nahk**-mit-tahk
Tonight	Heute Nacht	**hoy**-tuh nahkt
What is it?	Was ist es?	**vahss** ist es
Why?	Warum?	vah-**rum**
Who/whom?	Wer/wen?	vair/vehn
Who is it?	Wer ist da?	vair ist dah
I'd like to have . . .	Ich hätte gerne . . .	isch **het**-uh gairn
a room	ein Zimmer	ine **tsim**-er
the key	den Schlüssel	den **shluh**-sul
a newspaper	eine Zeitung	i-nuh **tsy**-toong
a stamp	eine Briefmarke	i-nuh **breef**-mark-uh
a map	eine Karte	i-nuh **cart**-uh
I'd like to buy . . .	ich möchte . . . kaufen	isch **merhk**-tuh **cow**-fen
cigarettes	Zigaretten	tzig-ah-**ret**-ten
How much is it?	Wieviel kostet das?	**vee**-feel **cost**-et dahss?
It's expensive/ cheap	Es ist teuer/billig	es ist **toy**-uh/**bill**-ig
A little/a lot	ein wenig/sehr	ine **vay**-nig/zair
More/less	mehr/weniger	mair/**vay**-nig-er
Enough/too much/too little	genug/zuviel/zu wenig	geh-**noog**/tsoo-**feel**/tsoo **vay**-nig

ENGLISH	GERMAN	PRONUNCIATION
I am ill/sick	Ich bin krank	isch bin krahnk
I need . . .	Ich brauche . . .	isch **brow**-khuh
a doctor	einen Arzt	I-nen artst
the police	die Polizei	dee po-lee-**tsai**
help	Hilfe	**hilf**-uh
Fire!	Feuer!	**foy**-er
Caution/Look out!	Achtung!/Vorsicht!	**ahk**-tung/**for**-zicht
Is this bus/train/subway going to...?	Fährt dieser Bus/dieser Zug/diese U-Bahn nach...?	fayrt **deez**-er buhs/ **deez**-er tsook/**deez**-uh oo-bahn nahk...
Where is...	Wo ist...	**vo** ist
the train station?	der Bahnhof?	dare **bahn**-hof
the subway station?	die U-Bahn-Station?	dee **oo**-bahn-**staht**-sion
the bus stop?	die Bushaltestelle?	dee **booss**-hahlt-uh-**shtel**-uh
the airport?	der Flugplatz?	dare **floog**-plats
	*der Flughafen	dare **floog**-hafen
the hospital?	das Krankenhaus?	dahs **krahnk**-en- house
the elevator?	der Aufzug?	dare **owf**-tsoog
the telephone?	das Telefon?	dahs te-le-**fone**
the rest room?	die Toilette?	dee twah-**let**-uh
open/closed	offen/geschlossen	**off**-en/ge-**schloss**-en
left/right	links/rechts	links/recktz
straight ahead	geradeaus	geh-**rah**-day-owws
is it near/far?	ist es in der Nähe/ist es weit?	ist es in dare **nay**-uh? ist es vite?

MENU GUIDE

ENGLISH	GERMAN
Entrées	Hauptspeisen
Homemade	Hausgemacht
Lunch	Mittagsessen
Dinner	Abendessen

ENGLISH	GERMAN
Dessert	Nachspeisen
At your choice	Önach Wahl
Soup of the day	Tagessuppe
Appetizers	Vorspeisen

BREAKFAST

Bread	Brot
Butter	Butter
Eggs	Eier
Hot	Heiss
Cold	Kalt
Caffeine-free coffee	Café Hag
Jam	Marmelade
Milk	Milch
Juice	Saft
Bacon	Speck
Lemon	Zitrone
Sugar	Zucker

SOUPS

Stew	Eintopf
Goulash soup	Gulaschsuppe
Chicken soup	Hühnersuppe
Potato soup	Kartoffelsuppe
Liver dumpling soup	Leberknödelsuppe
Onion soup	Zwiebelsuppe

FISH AND SEAFOOD

Trout	Forelle
Prawns	Garnele
Halibut	Heilbutt
Lobster	Hummer
Crab	Krabbe
Salmon	Lachs

ENGLISH	GERMAN
Squid	Tintenfisch
Tuna	Thunfisch
Turbot	Steinbutt

MEATS

Veal	Kalb
Lamb	Lamm
Beef	Rindfleisch
Pork	Schwein

GAME AND POULTRY

Duck	Ente
Pheasant	Fasan
Goose	Gans
Chicken	Hühner
Rabbit	Kaninchen
Venison	Reh
Turkey	Truthahn
Quail	Wachtel

VEGETABLES AND SIDE DISHES

Red cabbage	Rotkraut
Cauliflower	Karfiol
Beans	Bohnen
Button mushrooms	Champignons
Peas	Erbsen
Cucumber	Gurke
Cabbage	Kohl
Lettuce	Blattsalat
Potatoes	Kartoffeln
Dumplings	Knödel
French fries	Pommes frites

FRUITS

Apple	Apfel

ENGLISH	GERMAN
Orange	Orangen
Apricot	Marillen
Blueberry	Heidelbeere
Strawberry	Erdbeere
Raspberry	Himbeere
Cherry	Kirsche
Cranberry	Preiselbeere
Grapes	Trauben
Pear	Birne
Peach	Pfirsich

DESSERTS

Cheese	Käse
Crepes	Palatschinken
Soufflé	Auflauf
Ice cream	Eis
Cake	Torte

DRINKS

Tap water	Leitungswasser
With/without water	Mit/ohne wasser
Straight	Pur
Non-alcoholic	Alkoholfrei
A large/small dark beer	Ein Krügel/Seidel Dunkles
A large/small light beer	Ein Krügel/Seidel Helles
Draft beer	Vom Fass
Sparkling wine	Sekt
White wine	Weisswein
Red wine	Rotwein
Wine with mineral water	Gespritz

CONVERSIONS

DISTANCE

KILOMETERS/MILES

To change kilometers (km) to miles (mi), multiply km by .621. To change mi to km, multiply mi by 1.61.

km to mi		mi to km	
1 =	.62	1 = 1.6	
2 =	1.2	2 = 3.2	
3 =	1.9	3 = 4.8	
4 =	2.5	4 = 6.4	
5 =	3.1	5 = 8.1	
6 =	3.7	6 = 9.7	
7 =	4.3	7 = 11.3	
8 =	5.0	8 = 12.9	

METERS/FEET

To change meters (m) to feet (ft), multiply m by 3.28. To change ft to m, multiply ft by .305.

m to ft		ft to m	
1 =	3.3	1 =	.30
2 =	6.6	2 =	.61
3 =	9.8	3 =	.92
4 =	13.1	4 =	1.2
5 =	16.4	5 =	1.5
6 =	19.7	6 =	1.8
7 =	23.0	7 =	2.1
8 =	26.2	8 =	2.4

TEMPERATURE

METRIC CONVERSIONS

To change centigrade or Celsius (C) to Fahrenheit (F), multiply C by 1.8 and add 32. To change F to C, subtract 32 from F and multiply by .555.

°F	°C
0	-17.8
10	-12.2
20	-6.7
30	-1.1
32	0
40	+4.4
50	10.0
60	15.5
70	21.1
80	26.6
90	32.2
98.6	37.0
100	37.7

WEIGHT

KILOGRAMS/POUNDS

To change kilograms (kg) to pounds (lb), multiply kg by 2.20. To change lb to kg, multiply lb by .455.

kg to lb		lb to kg	
1 =	2.2	1 =	.45
2 =	4.4	2 =	.91
3 =	6.6	3 =	1.4
4 =	8.8	4 =	1.8
5 =	11.0	5 =	2.3
6 =	13.2	6 =	2.7
7 =	15.4	7 =	3.2
8 =	17.6	8 =	3.6

GRAMS/OUNCES

To change grams (g) to ounces (oz), multiply g by .035. To change oz to g, multiply oz by 28.4.

g to oz		oz to g	
1 =	.04	1 =	28
2 =	.07	2 =	57
3 =	.11	3 =	85
4 =	.14	4 =	114
5 =	.18	5 =	142
6 =	.21	6 =	170
7 =	.25	7 =	199
8 =	.28	8 =	227

LIQUID VOLUME

LITERS/U.S. GALLONS

To change liters (L) to U.S. gallons (gal), multiply L by .264. To change U.S. gal to L, multiply gal by 3.79.

L to gal		gal to L	
1 =	.26	1 =	3.8
2 =	.53	2 =	7.6
3 =	.79	3 =	11.4
4 =	1.1	4 =	15.2
5 =	1.3	5 =	19.0
6 =	1.6	6 =	22.7
7 =	1.8	7 =	26.5
8 =	2.1	8 =	30.3

CLOTHING SIZE

WOMEN'S CLOTHING

US	UK	EUR
4	6	34
6	8	36
8	10	38
10	12	40
12	14	42

WOMEN'S SHOES

US	UK	EUR
5	3	36
6	4	37
7	5	38
8	6	39
9	7	40

MEN'S SUITS

US	UK	EUR
34	34	44
36	36	46
38	38	48
40	40	50
42	42	52
44	44	54
46	46	56

MEN'S SHIRTS

US	UK	EUR
14½	14½	37
15	15	38
15½	15½	39
16	16	41
16½	16½	42
17	17	43
17½	17½	44

MEN'S SHOES

US	UK	EUR
7	6	39½
8	7	41
9	8	42
10	9	43
11	10	44½
12	11	46

Travel Smart Austria

WORD OF MOUTH

"When I'm in Vienna, I get either a weekly ticket for mass transit or the 8 ride strip ticket. Depends on how much you plan to use mass transit v. your own two feet (or taxis). Many of the sights within central Vienna can be reached on foot from your hotel."

—BTilke

GETTING HERE & AROUND

∎ BY AIR

Flying time from New York to Vienna is 8 hours; it's 9 hours from Washington, D.C., and 2 hours from London.

Airlines & Airports Airline and Airport Links.com (⊕ *www.airlineandairportlinks.com*) has links to many of the world's airlines and airports.

Airline Security Issues Transportation Security Administration (⊕ www.tsa.gov) has answers for almost every question that might come up.

AIRPORTS

Austria's major air gateway is Vienna's **Schwechat Airport,** about 12 mi southeast of the city. **Salzburg Airport** is Austria's second-largest airport, about 2½ mi west of the center. Just south of Graz, in Thalerhof, is the **Graz Airport.** Two other airports you might consider, depending on where in Austria you intend to travel, are Bratislava's **M. R. Stefanik** international airport in neighboring Slovakia, and **Munich's airport,** not far from Salzburg. Bratislava is about 60 kms (36 mi) east of Vienna and is the hub for RyanAir and Sky Europe, two budget carriers with low-cost connections to several European cities. Frequent buses can take you from Bratislava airport to central Vienna in about an hour. Consider Munich if your primary destination is western Austria, Salzburg, or Innsbruck.

Airport Information Graz Airport (GRZ) (☎0316/2902–0). **M. R. Stefanik Airport (Bratislava, BTS)** (☎00421–2–3303–3353 from outside of Slovakia). **Munich Airport International (MUC)** (☎0049–89–97500 from outside Germany). **Salzburg Airport (SZG)** (☎0662/8580). **Schwechat Airport (Vienna, VIE)** (⊕ www.viennaairport.com ☎01/7007–0).

GROUND TRANSPORTATION & TRANSFERS

The City Airport Train (CAT) provides service from Schwechat to downtown Vienna for €8 (single ticket); the trip takes about 16 minutes. Travel into the city on the local S-Bahn takes about 25 minutes and costs €4.50. City bus No. 2 runs every 10 minutes between Salzburg's main railway station and the airport; transfers cost €2. A local bus runs from Graz Jakominiplatz to the airport every hour and costs €1.80 for the 10-minute ride. The Vienna Airport Web site has information for all ground transfers

Ground Transportation Contacts CAT (⊕ www.cityairporttrain.com//langen/). **S-bahn** (⊕www.schnellbahn-wien.at/english/index.htm or www.oebb.at). **General** (⊕ www.viennaairport.com). **Vienna bus** (⊕ www.wienerlinien.at).

FLIGHTS

Austria is easy to reach from the United States. Austrian Airlines, Austria's national carrier, flies nonstop to Vienna from the U.S., departing from New York's JFK airport and Washington Dulles. From Canada, Austrian flies direct from Toronto. Austrian Airlines is a member of the Star Alliance, and is partnered with United in the United States, meaning usually good connections from cities serviced by United. Once in Vienna, Austrian Airlines has an excellent network of internal flights linking the capital with major regional cities like Salzburg and Graz. It's also possible to travel from North America with major U.S. carriers—such as American, Northwest, and United—but you'll be routed to a major

European hub, such as London, Amsterdam, or Frankfurt, to change planes for Vienna. Be sure to leave plenty of time between connections (two hours is ideal), as these hubs tend to be enormous and getting from your arrival gate to your new departure point will inevitably take some time. Travelers from North America should note, too, that many international carriers offer service to Vienna after stopovers at major European airports.

In addition to the major international carriers, a new breed of European budget airlines, including RyanAir and Sky Europe, has expanded greatly in recent years, offering low-cost flights from major cities around the Continent. Although these airlines are not normally ideal for connecting with transatlantic flights because of the hassle of changing airports, they provide an extremely low-cost way of getting around for travel within Europe. In 2004, former Formula I champion Niki Lauda teamed up with budget carrier Air Berlin for FlyNiki, a low-cost airline with travel between Vienna, Graz, Linz, Innsbruck, and major hubs in Europe, Asia, Africa, the Caribbean, the U.S., and Canada (⊕*www.flyniki.com*).

Within Austria, Austrian Airlines and its subsidiary **Austrian Arrows** offer service from Vienna to Linz and Innsbruck; they also provide routes to and from points outside Austria.

Airline Contacts American Airlines (☎800/433-7300 ⊕www.aa.com). **Austrian Airlines** (☎800/843-0002, 01/051-789 within Austria ⊕www.aua.com). **British Airways** (☎800/247-9297, 0844/493-0787 within Great Britain, 01/7956-7567 within Austria). **Lufthansa** (☎800/645-3880, 0810/1025-8080 within Austria ⊕www.lufthansa.com). **Northwest Airlines** (☎800/225-2525 ⊕www.nwa.com). **Swiss** (☎0810/810-840 within Austria ⊕www.swiss.com). **United Airlines** (☎800/864-8331 for U.S. reservations, 800/538-2929 for international reservations ⊕www.united.com).

Smaller Airlines Fly Niki (☎0820/737-800 within Austria for €0.12/minute ⊕www.flyniki.com). **Air Berlin** (☎0820/737-800 within Austria for €0.12/minute ⊕www.airberlin.com). **Ryanair** (⊕www.ryanair.com). **SkyEurope** (⊕www.skyeurope.com).

▌BY BUS

Austria has an extensive national network of buses run by the national postal and railroad services. Where Austrian trains don't go, buses do, and you'll find the railroad and post-office buses (bright yellow for easy recognition) in even remote regions carrying passengers as well as mail. You can get tickets on the bus, and in the off-season there is no problem getting a seat; on routes to favored ski areas, though, reservations are essential during holiday periods. Bookings can be handled at the ticket office (there's one in most towns with bus service) or by travel agents. In most communities bus routes begin and end at or near the railroad station, making transfers easy. Increasingly, coordination of bus service with railroads means that many of the discounts and special tickets available for trains apply to buses as well. There are private bus companies in Austria, too. Buses in Austria run like clockwork, typically departing and arriving on time. Most operators on the information lines below speak English.

Bus Information Columbus (☎01/534-110). **Blaguss Reisen** (☎01/5018-0150). **Post und Bahn** (☎01/711-01). **Dr. Richard** (☎01/33100-0).

▌BY CAR

Carefully weigh the pros and cons of car travel before choosing to rent. If your plans are to see Vienna and one or two other urban destinations, you're better off saving yourself the hassles and added expense by taking the train. Bear in mind that in addition to the not inconsiderable cost of renting, you'll have to pay for gasoline (which remains stubbornly high at more than twice the cost as in the U.S.) and frequent tolls. In addition you'll find yourself having to deal with bumper-to-bumper traffic on most of the trunk roads connecting the major cities. Added to that is the constant headache of finding a place to park. Central Vienna is completely restricted and the situation is not much better in the smaller cities.

On the other hand, if you have the time and your plan is a more leisurely tour of the country, including back roads and off-the-beaten-track destinations, then car rental is certainly an option. You'll have more freedom and be able to reach places where public transportation is scarce.

Vienna is 300 km (187 mi) east of Salzburg, 200 km (125 mi) north of Graz. Main routes leading into the city are the A1 Westautobahn from Germany, Salzburg, and Linz and the A2 Südautobahn from Graz and points south.

GASOLINE

Gasoline and diesel are readily available, but on Sunday, stations in the more out-of-the-way areas may be closed. Stations carry only unleaded (*bleifrei*) gas, both regular and premium (super), and diesel. If you're in the mountains in winter with a diesel, and there is a cold snap (with temperatures threatening to drop below -4°F [-20°C]), add a few liters of gasoline to your diesel, about 1:4 parts, to prevent it from freezing. Gasoline prices are the same throughout the country, slightly lower at discount and self-service stations. Expect to pay about €1.30 per liter for regular gasoline and slightly less for diesel. If you are driving to Italy, fill up before crossing the border, because gas in Italy is even more expensive.

RENTING A CAR

Rates in Vienna begin at about €77 per day and €84 per weekend for an economy car with manual transmission and unlimited mileage. This includes a 21% tax on car rentals. Rates are more expensive in winter months, when a surcharge for winter tires may be added. Renting a car may be cheaper in Germany, but make sure the rental agency knows you are driving into Austria and that the car is equipped with the *Autobahnvignette,* an autobahn sticker for Austria. Get your sticker, also known as a Pickerl, before driving to Austria (⇨ *Rules of the Road, below*). When renting an RV be sure to compare prices and reserve early. It's cheaper to arrange your rental car from the U.S., but be sure to get a confirmation of your quoted rate in writing.

The age requirement for renting a car in Austria is generally 19, and you must have had a valid driver's license for one year. There is no extra charge to drive over the border into Italy, Switzerland, or Germany, but there may be some restrictions for taking a rental into Slovakia, Slovenia, Hungary, the Czech Republic, or Poland. If you're planning on traveling east, it's best to let the agency know beforehand.

In Austria your own driver's license is acceptable. An International Driver's Permit (IDP) ($15), while not strictly necessary, is a good idea; these international permits are universally recognized, and having one in your wallet may save you a problem with the local authorities. Check the AAA Web site for more info.

ROAD CONDITIONS

Roads in Austria are excellent and well maintained—perhaps a bit too well maintained, judging by the frequently encountered construction zones on the autobahns. Secondary roads may be narrow and winding. Remember that in winter you will need snow tires and often chains, even on well-traveled roads. It's wise to check with the automobile clubs for weather conditions, since mountain roads are often blocked, and ice and fog are hazards.

Car Rental Resources

LOCAL AGENCIES		
Denzel Drive Erdberg Center/U-Bahn (U3), A-1110, Vienna	01/740–200	www.denzel.at
Autoverleih Buchbinder Schlachthaus-gasse 38, A-1030, Vienna	01/717–500, with offices throughout Austria	www.europcar.co.at
MAJOR AGENCIES		
Alamo	800/462–5266	www.alamo.com
Avis	800/230–4898	www.avis.com
Budget	800/331–1212	www.budget.com
Hertz	800/654–3131	www.hertz.com
National Car Rental	800/227–7368	www.nationalcar.com

ROADSIDE EMERGENCIES

If you break down along the autobahn, a small arrow on the guardrail will direct you to the nearest emergency (orange-color) phone that exist along all highways. Austria also has two automobile clubs, ÖAMTC and ARBÖ, both of which operate motorist service patrols. Both clubs charge nonmembers for emergency service.

Emergency Services **ARBÖ** (☎123). **ÖAMTC** (☎120). No area or other code is needed for either number.

RULES OF THE ROAD

Tourists from EU countries may bring their own cars into Austria with no documentation other than the normal registration papers and their regular driver's license. A Green Card, the international certificate of insurance, is recommended for EU drivers and compulsory for others. All cars must carry a first-aid kit (including rubber gloves), a red warning triangle, and a yellow neon jacket to use in case of accident or breakdown. These are available at gas stations along the road, or at any automotive supply store or large hardware store.

The minimum driving age in Austria is 18, and children under 12 must ride in the back seat; smaller children require a restraining seat. Note that all passengers must use seat belts.

Drive on the right side of the road in Austria. Unmarked crossings, particularly in residential areas, are common, so exercise caution at intersections. Trams always have the right of way. No turns are allowed on red.

Drinking and driving: the maximum blood-alcohol content allowed is 0.5 parts per thousand, which in real terms means very little to drink. Remember when driving in Europe that the police can stop you anywhere at any time for no particular reason.

Unless otherwise marked, the speed limit on autobahns is 130 kph (80 mph), although this is not always strictly enforced. If you're pulled over for speeding, though, fines are payable on the spot, and can be heavy. On other highways and roads the limit is 100 kph (62 mph), 80 kph (49 mph) for RVs or cars pulling a trailer weighing more than 750 kilos (about 1,650 lbs). In built-up areas a 50-kph (31-mph) limit applies and is likely to be taken seriously. In some towns special 30-kph (20-mph) limits apply. More and more towns have radar cameras to catch speeders. Remember that insurance does not necessarily pay if it can be proved you were going above the limit when involved in an accident.

■ TIP➜ **If you're going to travel Austria's highways, make absolutely sure your car** is equipped with the *Autobahnvignette*, a little sticker with a highway icon and the Austrian eagle, or with a calendar marked with an M or a W. This sticker, sometimes also called a Pickerl, allows use of the autobahn. It costs €73.80 for a year and is available at gas stations, tobacconists, and automobile-club outlets in neighboring countries or near the border. Rental cars should already have them. You can also purchase a two-month vignette for €22.20, or a 10-day one for €7.70. Prices are for vehicles up to 3.5 tons and RVs. For motorcycles it is €29.50 for one year, €11.10 for two months, and €4.40 for 10 days. If you are caught without a sticker you may be subjected to extremely high fines. Get your Pickerl before driving to Austria from another country. Besides the Pickerl, if you are planning to drive around a lot, budget in a great deal of toll money: for example, the tunnels on the A10 autobahn cost around €10, the Grossglockner Pass road will cost about €30 per car—less after 6 PM. Driving up some especially beautiful valleys, such as the Kaunertal in Tirol, or up to the Tauplitzalm in Styria, also costs money—around €20 per car for the Kaunertal.

▌ BY SHIP

For leisurely travel between Vienna and Linz, or eastward across the border into Slovakia or Hungary, consider taking a Danube boat. **DDSG Blue Danube Schifffahrt** offers a diverse selection of pleasant cruises, including trips to Melk Abbey and Dürnstein in the Wachau, a grand tour of Vienna's architectural sights from the river, and a dinner cruise, featuring Johann Strauss waltzes as background music. **Brandner Schifffart** offers the same kind of cruises between Krems and Melk, in the heart of the Danube Valley.

Most of the immaculate white-painted craft carry about 1,000 passengers each on their three decks. As soon as you get on board, give the steward a good tip for a deck chair and ask him or her to place it where you will get the best views. Be sure

to book cabins in advance. Day trips are also possible on the Danube. You can use boats to move from one riverside community to the next, and along some sections, notably the Wachau, the only way to cross the river is to use the little shuttles (in the Wachau, these are special motorless boats that use the current to cross).

For the cruises up and down the Danube, the DDSG Blue Danube Steamship Company departs and arrives at Reichsbrücke near Vienna's Mexikoplatz. To reach the Reichsbrücke stop, you walk two blocks from the Vorgartenstrasse stop on the U1 subway toward the river. The DDSG stop is on the right side of the Reichsbrücke bridge. There is no pier number, but you board at Handelskai 265. Boat trips from Vienna to the Wachau are on Sunday only from May to September. The price is about €20.50 one-way and €27 round-trip. There are other daily cruises within the Wachau, such as from Melk to Krems. Other cruises, to Budapest for instance, operate from April to early November. The Web site has dozens of options and time-tables in English. For cruises from Krems to Melk, contact Brandner Schifffahrt. *For more information,* ⇨*see the "Danube River Cruises" box in Chapter 4.*

Cruise Lines **Brandner Schifffahrt** (☎07433/2590–21 ⊕www.brandner. at). **DDSG/Blue Danube Schifffahrt** (☎01/588-8044-0 ⊕www.ddsg-blue-danube. at).

▌ BY TRAIN

Austrian train service is excellent: it's fast and, for Western Europe, relatively inexpensive, particularly if you take advantage of discount fares. Trains on the mountainous routes are slow, but no slower than driving, and the scenery is gorgeous. Many of the remote rail routes will give you a look at traditional Austria, complete with Alpine cabins tacked onto mountainsides and a backdrop of snow-capped peaks.

Austrian Federal Railways trains are identifiable by the letters that precede the train number on the timetables and posters. The IC (InterCity) or EC (EuroCity) trains are fastest, and a supplement of about €5 is included in the price of the ticket. EN trains have sleeping facilities. The EC trains usually have a dining car with fairly good food. The trains originating in Budapest have good Hungarian cooking. Otherwise there is usually a fellow with a cart serving snacks and hot and cold drinks. Most trains are equipped with a card telephone in or near the restaurant car.

The difference between *erste Klasse* (first class), and *zweite Klasse* (second class) on Austrian trains is mainly a matter of space. First- and second-class sleepers and couchettes (six to a compartment) are available on international runs, as well as on long trips within Austria. Women traveling alone may book special compartments on night trains or long-distance rides (ask for a *Damenabteil*). If you have a car but would rather watch the scenery than the traffic, you can put your car on a train in Vienna and accompany it to Salzburg, Innsbruck, Feldkirch, or Villach: you relax in a compartment or sleeper for the trip, and the car is unloaded when you arrive.

Allow yourself plenty of time to purchase your ticket before boarding the train—if you purchase your ticket on board, you must pay a surcharge, which is around €3 or more, depending on how far you're going. All tickets are valid without supplement on D (express), E (*Eilzug*; semifast), and local trains. For information, call *05/1717* from anywhere in Austria. Unless you speak German fairly well, it's a good idea to have your hotel call for you. You may also ask for an operator who speaks English. You can reserve a seat for €3 up until four hours before departure. Be sure to do this on the mainline trains (Vienna–Innsbruck, Salzburg–

Klagenfurt, Vienna–Graz, for example) at peak holiday times.

For train schedules from the Austrian rail service, the ÖBB, ask at your hotel, stop in at the train station and look for large posters labeled ABFAHRT (departures) and ANKUNFT (arrivals), or log on to their Web site. In the Abfahrt listing you'll find the departure time in the main left-hand block of the listing and, under the train name, details of where it stops en route and the time of each arrival. There is also information about connecting trains and buses, with departure details. Workdays are symbolized by two crossed hammers, which means that the same schedule might not apply on weekends or holidays. A little rocking horse sign means that a special playpen has been set up for children in the train.

There's a wide choice of rail routes to Austria, but check services first; long-distance passenger service across the continent is undergoing considerable reduction. There is regular service from London's Waterloo station to Vienna via Brussels and points south and east. An alternative is to travel via Paris, where you can change to board an overnight train to Salzburg and Vienna. Be sure to leave plenty of time between connections to change stations. First- and second-class sleepers and second-class couchettes are available as far as Innsbruck.

Information **ÖBB (Österreichische Bundesbahnen)** (⊕ www.oebb.at).

ESSENTIALS

■ ACCOMMODATIONS

You can live like a king in a real castle in Austria or get by on a modest budget. Starting at the lower end, you can find a room in a private house or on a farm, or dormitory space in a youth hostel. Next up the line come the simpler pensions, many of them identified as a *Frühstückspensionen* (bed-and-breakfasts). Then come *Gasthäuser,* the simpler country inns. Fancier pensions in cities can often cost as much as hotels; the difference lies in the services they offer. Most pensions, for example, do not staff the front desk around the clock. Among the hotels, you can find accommodations ranging from the most modest, with a shower and toilet down the hall, to the most elegant, with every possible amenity. Increasingly, more and more hotels in the lower to middle price range are including breakfast with the basic room charge, but check when booking. Room rates for hotels in the rural countryside can often include breakfast and one other meal (in rare cases, all three meals are included).

Lodgings in Austria are generally rated from one to five stars, depending mainly on the facilities offered and the price of accommodation rather than on more subjective attributes like charm and location. In general, five-star properties are top of the line, with every conceivable amenity and priced accordingly. The distinctions get blurrier the further down the rating chain you go. There may be little difference between a two- and three-star property except perhaps the price. In practice, don't rely heavily on the star system, and always try to see the hotel and room before you book. That's said, lodging standards are generally very good, and even in one- and two-star properties you can usually be guaranteed a clean room and a private bath.

These German words might come in handy when booking a room: air-conditioning (*Klimaanlage*); private bath (Privatbad); bathtub (*Badewanne*); shower (*Dusche*); double bed (*Doppelbett*); twin beds (*Einzelbetten*).

All hotels listed in this guide have private bath unless otherwise noted. Lodging price categories from ¢ to $$$$ are defined in the Where to Stay sections of the Vienna and Salzburg chapters and in the opening pages of each regional chapter.

Most hotels and other lodgings require you to give your credit-card details before they will confirm your reservation. If you don't feel comfortable e-mailing this information, ask if you can fax it (some places even prefer faxes). However you book, get confirmation in writing and have a copy of it handy when you check in.

Be sure you understand the hotel's cancellation policy. Some places allow you to cancel without any kind of penalty— even if you prepaid to secure a discounted rate—if you cancel at least 24 hours in advance. Others require you to cancel a week in advance or penalize you the cost of one night. Small inns and B&Bs are most likely to require you to cancel far in advance. Most hotels allow children under a certain age to stay in their parents' room at no extra charge, but others

Online Booking Resources

Barclay International Group	516/364–0064 or 800/845–6636	www.barclayweb.com
Drawbridge to Europe	541/482–7778 or 888/268–1148	www.drawbridgetoeurope.com
Interhome	800/882–6864	www.interhome.us
Villas & Apartments Abroad	212/213–6435	www.vaanyc.com
Villas International	415/499–9490 or 800/221–2260	www.villasintl.com

charge for them as extra adults; find out the cutoff age for discounts.

■TIP➜ Assume that hotels operate on the European Plan (EP, no meals) unless we specify that they use the Breakfast Plan (BP, with full breakfast), Continental Plan (CP, continental breakfast), Full American Plan (FAP, all meals), or Modified American Plan (MAP, breakfast and dinner), or are all-inclusive (AI, all meals and most activities).

Contacts. Vienna Tourist Information's hotel assistance service (☎01/24-555 ⊕www.wien.info.).

APARTMENT & HOUSE RENTALS

Rentals are an important part of the accommodations mix in Austria, with one-, two- or four-week rentals becoming increasing popular. Most of the rental properties are owned privately by individuals, and often the main rental organizers are simply the local tourist offices. For rental apartments in Vienna, check out ⊕*www.apartment.at* or ⊕*www.netland.at/wien/*.

CASTLES

Schlosshotels und Herrenhäuser in Österreich, or "Castle Hotels and Mansions in Austria," is an association of castles and palaces that have been converted into hotels. The quality of the accommodation varies with the property, but many have been beautifully restored and can be a memorable alternative to standard hotels. The Web site is in English and has plenty of photos. The association also links a scattering of castles in the Czech Republic, Hungary, Slovenia, Croatia, and Italy.

Information Schlosshotels und Herrenhäuser in Österreich (☎0662/8306–8141 ⊕www.schlosshotels.co.at).

FARM VACATIONS
⇨*See Eco Tours in Guided Tours below.*

HOME EXCHANGES
With a direct home exchange you stay in someone else's home while they stay in yours. Some outfits also deal with vacation homes, so you're not actually staying in someone's full-time residence, just their vacant weekend place.

Exchange Clubs Home Exchange. com (☎800/877-8723 ⊕*www.home exchange.com*); $99.95 for a first-time 1-year online listing. HomeLink International (☎800/638-3841 ⊕*www.homelink.org*); $110 for a 1-year membership. Intervac U.S. (☎800/756-4663 ⊕*www.intervacus.com*); $95 for membership.

Austria has more than 100 government-sponsored youth hostels, for which you need an HI membership card. Inexpensively priced, these hostels are run by the Österreichischer Jugendherbergsverband and are popular with the back-pack crowd, so be sure to reserve in advance.

Information Hostelling International— USA (☎301/495-1240 ⊕*www.hiusa.org*). Österreichischer Jugendherbergsverband (☎01/533-53-53 ⊕*www.oejhv.or.at*).

■ COMMUNICATIONS

INTERNET

Better hotels in Austria have worked hard to upgrade their Internet offerings and most of them will offer some form of Internet access for jacking in your laptop, either via a LAN line or Wi-Fi. Occasionally these services are offered free of charge; usually you have to pay a surcharge. Before you leave home, contact your Internet service provider to get the local access number in Austria. Hotels that don't offer Internet access in the rooms will usually have a computer somewhere in their business center or lobby available for guests to check e-mail. Outside of hotels there some, but not many, Internet cafés (ask at your hotel). The standard rate is about €2 an hour. A good number of cafés offer Wi-Fi to customers. The charge for this is usually around €2 an hour.

Contacts Cybercafés (⊕ *www.cybercafes.com*) lists more than 4,000 Internet cafés worldwide.

PHONES

The good news is that you can now make a direct-dial telephone call from virtually any point on earth. The bad news? You can't always do so cheaply. Calling from a hotel is almost always the most expensive option; hotels usually add huge surcharges to all calls, particularly international ones. In some countries you can phone from call centers or even the post office. Calling cards usually keep costs to a minimum, but only if you purchase them locally. And then there are mobile phones, which are sometimes more prevalent—particularly in the developing world—than land lines; as expensive as mobile phone calls can be, they are still usually a much cheaper option than calling from your hotel.

When calling Austria, the country code is 43. When dialing an Austrian number from abroad, drop the initial 0 from the local Austrian area code. For instance, the full number to dial for the Hotel Sacher in Vienna from America is 011 (international dial code)—43 (Austria's country code)—1 (Vienna's full city code is 01, but drop the 0)—and 514–560 (the hotel number). All numbers given in this guide include the city or town area code.

CALLING WITHIN AUSTRIA

As the number of cell phones has risen in Austria, the number of coin-operated pay telephones has dwindled. If you're lucky enough to find one, it may be out of order or available only for emergency calls. But if you find one that works, a local call costs €0.20 for the first minute and €0.14 per minute. Most pay phones have instructions in English.

When placing a long-distance call to a destination within Austria, dial the local area codes with the initial zero (for instance, 0662 for Salzburg). Note that calls within Austria are one-third cheaper between 6 PM and 8 AM on weekdays and from 1 PM on Saturday to 8 AM on Monday.

For information concerning numbers within the EU and neighboring countries, dial *118–877*; for information outside Europe, dial *0900/118–877*. Most operators speak some English; if yours doesn't, you'll most likely be passed along to one who does.

CALLING OUTSIDE AUSTRIA

It costs more to telephone *from* Austria than it does to telephone *to* Austria. Calls from post offices are usually the least expensive way to go, and you can get helpful assistance in placing a long-distance call; in large cities these centers at main post offices are open around the clock. To use a post office phone you first go to the counter to be directed to a certain telephone cabin; after your call you return to the counter and pay your bill. Faxes can be sent from post offices and received as well, but neither service is very cheap.

To make a collect call—you can't do this from pay phones—dial the operator and ask for an *R-Gespräch* (pronounced air-ga-*shprayk*). Most operators speak Eng-

Local Do's & Taboos

CUSTOMS OF THE COUNTRY

Austrians are keen observers of social niceties, and there are strongly embedded cultural norms for guiding behavior in all sorts of public interactions, ranging from buying a piece of meat at the butcher's (be extremely polite) to offering your seat on the metro to an elderly or disabled person. In general, always err of the side of extreme politeness and deference (particularly to age).

GREETINGS

Greetings are an important part of day-to-day interaction with strangers. On entering a shop, for example, it's customary to say *Grüss Gott* or *Guten Tag*, "good day," to the shopkeeper as if he or she were an old friend. Don't forget to say a hearty *Auf Wiedersehen*, good-bye, on leaving. Austrians do like their academic titles. PhDs go as "Frau/Herr Doktor"; those who have earned M.A.s or M.S.s are addressed as "Frau/Herr Magister."

OUT ON THE TOWN

In restaurants it's not uncommon to have to share a table with strangers—particularly in crowded places at meal times. You're not expected to make conversation across the table, but you should at least offer a tip-of-the-hat *Grüss Gott* when sitting down and a farewell *Auf Wiedersehen* on leaving. When your neighbor's food arrives, turn and wish him or her *Mahlzeit*, literally "meal time," the Austrian-German equivalent of "Bon Appetit." When it comes to table manners, there are a few departures from standard American practice (beyond how one holds a knife and fork). Toothpicks are sometimes found on restaurant tables, and it is normal to see people clean their teeth after a meal, discreetly covering their mouth with their free hand. Austria is a dog-loving society, and you will often find dogs accompanying their masters to restaurants.

If you have the pleasure of being invited to someone's home for a meal, it's customary to bring a small gift, like a bouquet of flowers or a nice bottle of wine.

Austrians tend to be far more comfortable with public nudity than Americans. Women routinely remove their tops on public beaches and sauna facilities at hotels and resorts with saunas are usually used in the buff by both sexes and the towel is optional.

LANGUAGE

German is the official language in Austria. One of the best ways to avoid being an Ugly American is to learn a little of the local language. In larger cities and most resort areas you will usually have no problem finding people who speak English; hotel employees in particular speak it reasonably well, and many young Austrians speak it at least passably. However, travelers do report that they often find themselves in stores, restaurants, and railway and bus stations where it's hard to find someone who speaks English—so it's best to have some native phrases up your sleeve. Note that all public announcements on trams, subways, and buses are in German. Train announcements are usually given in English as well, but if you have any questions, try to get answers before boarding.

lish; if yours doesn't, you'll be passed to one who does.

The country code for the United States is 1.

U.S. Phone Access Codes from Austria **AT&T Direct** (☎0–800–200–288, 800/435–0812 for other areas). **AT&T Direct** (☎0–800–200–288). **MCI Verizon Worldwide Access** (☎ 0–800–999–762).

CALLING CARDS

If you plan to make calls from pay phones, a Telecom Austria calling card is a convenience. You can buy calling cards with a credit of €10 or €15 at any post office or Telecom Austria shop, and they can be used at any public phone booth. Insert the card, punch in your access code, and dial the number; the cost of the call is automatically deducted from the card—note that the "credits" displayed is not usually the amount of money left on the card, but a different sort of counter. A few public phones in the cities also take American Express, Diners Club, MasterCard, and Visa credit cards.

MOBILE PHONES

In Austria a cell phone is called a *Handy*.

If you have a multiband phone (some countries use different frequencies from what's used in the United States) and your service provider uses the world-standard GSM network (as do T-Mobile, Cingular, and Verizon), you can probably use your phone abroad. Roaming fees can be steep, however: 99¢ a minute is considered reasonable. And overseas you normally pay the toll charges for incoming calls. It's almost always cheaper to send a text message than to make a call, since text messages have a very low set fee (often less than 5¢).

If you just want to make local calls, consider buying a new SIM card (note that your provider may have to unlock your phone for you to use a different SIM card) and a prepaid service plan in the destination. You'll then have a local num-

ber and can make local calls at local rates. If your trip is extensive, you could also simply buy a new cell phone in your destination, as the initial cost will be offset over time.

■TIP→ If you travel internationally frequently, save one of your old mobile phones or buy a cheap one on the Internet; ask your cell phone company to unlock it for you, and take it with you as a travel phone, buying a new SIM card with pay-as-you-go service in each destination.

If you want to use your own mobile phone in Austria, first find out if it's compatible with the European 1800 GSM standard (usually this is the case with a "tri-band" telephone, but be sure to ask specifically). Once in Austria, stop by a mobile phone store, usually identifiable by the word "Handy" in the name, and purchase a prepaid SIM card (make sure your existing SIM card is unlocked). Prepaid cards start at around €20–€30. Local mobile calls are then billed at about €0.15 to €0.20 a minute. If you don't have a phone, but want to use one here, look into buying a used phone. Rates are reasonable. Buy the prepaid card in the same way you would as if you were bringing in your own phone.

When dialing an Austrian "Handy" from abroad (generally 0676, 0699, or 0664), dial 00–43, then the number without the 0.

Contacts Cellular Abroad (☎800/287–5072 ⊕www.cellularabroad.com) rents and sells GMS phones and sells SIM cards that work in many countries. **Mobal** (☎888/888–9162 ⊕www.mobalrental.com) rents mobiles and sells GSM phones (starting at $49) that will operate in 140 countries. Per-call rates vary throughout the world. **Planet Fone** (☎888/988–4777 ⊕www.planetfone.com) rents cell phones, but the per-minute rates are expensive.

▌ EATING OUT

When dining out, you'll get the best value at simpler restaurants. Most post menus with prices outside. If you begin with the Würstelstand (sausage vendor) on the street, the next category would be the Imbiss-Stube, for simple, quick snacks. Many meat stores serve soups and a daily special at noon; a blackboard menu will be posted outside. A number of cafés also offer lunch, but watch the prices; some can turn out to be more expensive than restaurants. Gasthäuser are simple restaurants or country inns. Austrian hotels have some of the best restaurants in the country, often with outstanding chefs. In the past few years the restaurants along the autobahns, especially the chain Rosenberger, have developed into very good places to eat (besides being, in many cases, architecturally interesting). Some Austrian chain restaurants offer excellent value for the money, such as the schnitzel chains Wienerwald and Schnitzelhaus and the excellent seafood chain Nordsee. You can also grab a quick sandwich made from wide variety of scrumptious whole wheat breads at bakery chains such as Anker, Felber, and Mann. With migration from Turkey and Northern Africa on the rise, thousands of small kebab restaurants have set up shop all over Austria, offering both Middle Eastern fare and sometimes pizza at a reasonable rate.

▌TIP→ **In all restaurants be aware that the basket of bread put on your table isn't free.** Most of the older-style Viennese restaurants charge €0.70–€1.25 for each roll that is eaten, but more and more establishments are beginning to charge a per-person cover charge—anywhere from €1.50 to €4—which includes all the bread you want, plus usually an herb spread and butter. Tap water (*Leitungswasser*) in Austria comes straight from the Alps and is some of the purest in the world. Be aware, however, that a few restaurants in touristy areas are beginning to charge for tap water.

Austrians are manic about food quality and using agricultural techniques that are in harmony with the environment. The country has the largest number of organic farms in Europe, as well as some of the most stringent food-quality standards. An increasing number of restaurants use food and produce from local farmers, ensuring the freshest ingredients for their guests.

MEALS & MEALTIMES

Besides the normal three meals—*Frühstück* (breakfast), *Mittagessen* (lunch), and *Abendessen* (dinner)—Austrians sometimes throw in a few snacks in between, or forego one meal for a snack. The day begins with an early continental breakfast of rolls and coffee. *Gabelfrühstück,* normally served a little later in the morning, is a slightly more substantial breakfast with eggs or cold meat. A main meal is usually served between noon and 2, and an afternoon *Jause* (coffee with cake) is taken at teatime. Unless you are dining out, a light supper ends the day, usually between 6 and 9, but tending toward the later hour. Many restaurant kitchens close in the afternoon, but some post a notice saying *durchgehend warme Küche,* meaning that hot food is available even between regular mealtimes. In Vienna some restaurants go on serving until 1 and 2 AM, a tiny number also through the night. The rest of Austria is more conservative.

Unless otherwise noted, the restaurants listed in this guide are open daily for lunch and dinner.

PAYING

Restaurant price categories from ¢ to $$$$ are defined in the Where to Eat sections of the Vienna and Salzburg chapters and in the opening pages of each regional chapter.

For guidelines on tipping ⇨ see Tipping below.

RESERVATIONS & DRESS

Regardless of where you are, it's a good idea to make a reservation if you can. In some places it's expected. We only mention reservations specifically when they are essential (there's no other way you'll ever get a table) or when they are not accepted. For popular restaurants, book as far ahead as you can (often 30 days), and reconfirm as soon as you arrive. (Large parties should always call ahead to check the reservations policy.) We mention dress only when men are required to wear a jacket or a jacket and tie.

WINES, BEER & SPIRITS

Austrian wines range from unpretentious *heurigen* whites to world-class varietals. Look for the light, fruity white *grüner veltliner*, intensely fragrant golden *traminer*, full-bodied red *blaufränkisch*, and the lighter red *zweigelt*. Sparkling wine is called *sekt*, some of the best coming from the Kamptal region northwest of Vienna. Some of the best sweet dessert wines in the world (Spätlesen) come from Burgenland. Austrian beer rivals that of Germany for quality. Each area has its own brewery and local beer that people are loyal to. A specialty unique to Austria is the dark, sweet Dunkles beer. Look for Kaiser Doppelmalz in Vienna. Schnapps is an after-dinner tradition in Austria; many restaurants offer several varieties to choose from.

▌ ELECTRICITY

The electrical current in Austria is 220 volts, 50 cycles alternating current (AC); wall outlets take Continental-type plugs, with two round prongs.

Consider making a small investment in a universal adapter, which has several types of plugs in one lightweight, compact unit. Most laptops and mobile phone chargers are dual voltage (i.e., they operate equally well on 110 and 220 volts), so require only an adapter. These days the same is true of small appliances such as hair dryers. Always check labels and manufacturer instructions to be sure. Don't use 110-volt outlets marked FOR SHAVERS ONLY for high-wattage appliances such as hair-dryers.

Contacts **Steve Kropla's Help for World Traveler's** (⊕ www.kropla.com) has information on electrical and telephone plugs around the world. **Walkabout Travel Gear** (⊕ www. walkabouttravelgear.com) has a good coverage of electricity under "adapters."

▌ EMERGENCIES

On the street, some German phrases that may be needed in an emergency are: *Hilfe!* (Help!), *Notfall* (emergency), *Rettungswagen* (ambulance), *Feuerwehr* (fire department), *Polizei* (police), *Arzt* (doctor), and *Krankenhaus* (hospital).

Foreign Embassies **Embassy of the United States** (✉ Boltzmanngasse 16, 9th District, Vienna ☎ 31339–0). **Consulate of the U.S./ Passport Division** (✉ Gartenbaupromenade 2–4 , 1st District, Vienna ☎ 31339–7580).

General Emergency Contacts **Ambulance** (☎ 144). **Fire** (☎ 122). **Police** (☎ 133).

▌ HEALTH

Travel in Austria poses no specific or unusual health risks. The tap water is generally safe to drink. If in doubt, buy bottled water—available everywhere. The only potential risk worth mentioning is tick-bite encephalitis, which is only a danger if you're planning to do extensive cycling or hiking in the back country.

OVER-THE-COUNTER REMEDIES

You must buy over-the-counter remedies in an *Apotheke,* and most personnel speak enough English to understand what you need. Try using the generic name for a drug, rather than its brand name. You may find over-the-counter remedies for headaches and colds less effective than those sold in the U.S. Austrians are firm believers in natural remedies, such as homeopathic medicines and herbal teas.

SHOTS & MEDICATIONS

No special shots are required before visiting Austria, but if you will be cycling or hiking through the eastern or southeastern parts of the country, get inoculated against encephalitis; it can be carried by ticks.

Health Warnings **National Centers for Disease Control & Prevention** (CDC ☎877/394–8747 international travelers' health line ⊕www.cdc.gov/travel). **World Health Organization** WHO (⊕www.who.int).

Contact **Transportation Security Administration** (TSA ⊕www.tsa.gov).

▎HOURS OF OPERATION

In most cities banks are open weekdays 8–3, Thursday until 5:30 PM. Lunch hour is from 12:30 to 1:30. All banks are closed on Saturday, but you can change money at various locations (such as American Express offices on Saturday morning and major railroad stations around the clock), and changing machines are also found here and there in the larger cities.

Gas stations on the major autobahns are open 24 hours a day, but in smaller towns and villages you can expect them to close early in the evening and on Sunday. You can usually count on at least one station to stay open on Sunday and holidays in most medium-size towns, and buying gas in larger cities is usually not a problem.

Pharmacies (called *Apotheken* in German) are usually open from 9 to 6, with a midday break between noon and 2. In each area of the city one pharmacy stays open 24 hours; if a pharmacy is closed, a sign on the door will tell you the address of the nearest one that is open. Call *01/1550* for names and addresses (in German) of the pharmacies open that night.

HOLIDAYS

All banks and shops are closed on national holidays: New Year's Day; Jan. 6, Epiphany; Easter Sunday and Monday; May 1, May Day; Ascension Day (6th Thursday after Easter); Pentecost Sunday and Monday; Corpus Christi; Aug. 15, Assumption; Oct. 26, National Holiday; Nov. 1, All Saints' Day; Dec. 8, Immaculate Conception; Dec. 25–26, Christmas. Museums are open on most holidays, but are closed on Good Friday, on Dec. 24 and 25, and New Year's Day. Banks and offices are closed on Dec. 8, but most shops are open.

▎MAIL

All mail goes by air, so there's no supplement on letters or postcards. Within Europe a letter or postcard of up to 20 grams (about ¾ ounce) costs €0.65. To the United States or Canada, a letter of up to 20 grams takes postage of €1.40. If in doubt, mail your letters from a post office and have the weight checked. The Austrian post office also adheres strictly to a size standard; if your letter or card is outside the norm, you'll have to pay a surcharge. Postcards via airmail to the United States or Canada need €1.40. Always place an airmail sticker on your letters or cards. Shipping packages from Austria to destinations outside the country can get expensive.

You can also have mail held at any Austrian post office; letters should be marked *Poste Restante* or *Postlagernd*. You will be asked for identification when you collect mail.

SHIPPING PACKAGES

For overnight services, Federal Express, DHL, and UPS service Austria; check with your hotel concierge for the nearest address and telephone number.

▌ MONEY

ATMS & BANKS

Your own bank will probably charge a fee for using ATMs abroad; the foreign bank you use may also charge a fee. Nevertheless, you'll usually get a better rate of exchange at an ATM than you will at a currency-exchange office or even when changing money in a bank. And extracting funds as you need them is a safer option than carrying around a large amount of cash.

▌**TIP**→ PIN numbers with more than four digits are not recognized at ATMs in many countries. If yours has five or more, remember to change it before you leave.

Called *Bankomats* and fairly common throughout Austria, ATMs are one of the easiest ways to get euros. Cirrus and Plus locations are easily found throughout large city centers, and even in small towns. Look for branches of one of the larger banks, including Bank Austria, Raiffeisen, BAWAG, or Erste Bank. These are all likely to have a bank machine attached somewhere nearby. If you have trouble finding one, ask your hotel concierge. Note, too, that you may have better luck with ATMs if you're using a credit card or debit card that is also a Visa or MasterCard rather than just your bank card.

ATM Locations Cirrus (☎800/424–7787). Plus (☎800/843–7587).

CREDIT CARDS

Throughout this guide, the following abbreviations are used: **AE**, American Express; **DC**, Diners Club; **D**, Disover; **MC**, MasterCard; and **V**, Visa.

It's a good idea to inform your credit-card company before you travel, especially if you're going abroad and don't travel internationally very often. Otherwise, the credit card company might put a hold on your card owing to unusual activity—not a good thing halfway through your trip. Record all your credit-card numbers—as well as the phone numbers to call if your cards are lost or stolen—in a safe place, so you're prepared should something go wrong. Both MasterCard and Visa have general numbers you can call (collect if you're abroad) if your card is lost, but you're better off calling the number of your issuing bank, since MasterCard and Visa usually just transfer you to your bank; your bank's number is usually printed on your card.

If you plan to use your credit card for cash advances, you'll need to apply for a PIN at least two weeks before your trip. Although it's usually cheaper (and safer) to use a credit card abroad for large purchases (so you can cancel payments or be reimbursed if there's a problem), note that some credit-card companies *and* the banks that issue them add substantial percentages to all foreign transactions, whether they're in a foreign currency or not. Check on these fees before leaving home, so there won't be any surprises when you get the bill.

▌**TIP**→ Before you charge something, ask the merchant whether or not he or she plans to do a dynamic currency conversion (DCC). In such a transaction the credit-card *processor* (shop, restaurant, or hotel, not Visa or MasterCard) converts the currency and charges you in dollars. In most cases you'll pay the merchant a 3% fee for this service in addition to any credit-card company and issuing-bank foreign-transaction surcharges.

Dynamic currency conversion programs are becoming increasingly widespread. Merchants who participate in them are supposed to ask whether you want to be charged in dollars or the local currency, but they don't always do so. And even if they do offer you a choice, they may well avoid mentioning the surcharges. The good news is that you *do* have a choice. And if this practice really gets your goat, you can avoid it entirely thanks to American Express; with its cards DCC simply isn't an option.

Reporting Lost Cards **American Express** (☎800/992-3404 in U.S., 336/393-1111 collect from abroad ⊕www.americanexpress. com). **Diners Club** (☎800/234-6377 in U.S., 303/799-1504 collect from abroad ⊕www. dinersclub.com). **Discover** (☎800/347-2683 in U.S., 801/902-3100 collect from abroad ⊕www.discovercard.com). **MasterCard** (☎800/627-8372 in U.S., 636/722-7111 collect from abroad ⊕www.mastercard.com). **Visa** (☎800/847-2911 in U.S., 800/200-288 collect from Austria ⊕www.visa.com).

CURRENCY & EXCHANGE

As it is a member of the European Union (EU), Austria's unit of currency is the euro. Under the euro system there are eight coins: 1 and 2 euros, plus 1, 2, 5, 10, 20, and 50 euro cent, or cents of the euro. All coins have one side that has the value of the euro on it and the other side with a country's own national symbol. There are seven banknotes: 5, 10, 20, 50, 100, 200, and 500 euros. Banknotes are the same for all EU countries.

At this writing (fall 2008), the euro had strengthened against the U.S. dollar, and one euro was worth about 1.41 U.S. dollars.

Although fees charged for ATM transactions may be higher abroad than at home, Cirrus and Plus exchange rates are excellent, because they are based on wholesale rates offered only by major banks. Otherwise, the most favorable rates are through a bank. You won't do as well at exchange booths in airports or rail and bus stations, in hotels, in restaurants, or in stores, although you may find their hours more convenient than at a bank.

■TIP➔ **Even if a currency-exchange booth has a sign promising no commission, rest assured that there's some kind of huge, hidden fee. (Oh . . . that's right. The sign didn't**

say no *fee.*) **And as for rates, you're almost always better off getting foreign currency at an ATM or exchanging money at a bank.**

Contacts **American Express** (☎888/412-6945 in U.S., 0800/232-340 collect in Austria to add value or speak to customer service ⊕www.americanexpress.com).

Currency Conversion **Google** (⊕www. google.com) does currency conversion. Just type in the amount you want to convert and an explanation of how you want it converted (e.g., "14 Swiss francs in dollars"), and then voilà. **Oanda.com** (⊕www.oanda.com) also allows you to print out a handy table with the current day's conversion rates. **XE.com** (⊕www.xe.com) is a good currency conversion Web site.

▌PACKING

Austrians, particularly the Viennese, are dapper dressers. Packing "musts" include at least one nice shirt and sport coat for men and a casual but stylish shirt and skirt combination for women. These will see you through nearly any occasion, from a decent dinner out on the town to a night at the opera. Note that Austrians dress nicely for the opera and the theater. Men should bring a nicer pair of dress shoes than might otherwise be on the packing list, since this is a wardrobe staple that the locals pay particular attention to. As a general rule of thumb, the more expensive the shoes, the more respect you're likely to get. High on the list, too, would be comfortable walking or hiking shoes. Austria is a walking country, in cities and mountains alike. And since an evening outside at a Heurige (wine garden) may be on your agenda, be sure to take a sweater or light wrap; evenings tend to get cool even in the summer. Music lovers might consider toting those rarely used opera glasses; the cheaper seats, understandably, are usually far from the action (and standby tickets will have you craning your neck at the back).

If you are heading into the mountains, bring sunscreen, even in winter. Sunglasses are a must as well—make sure that they prevent lateral rays. Boots that rise above the ankle and have sturdy soles are best for hiking. Consider packing a small folding umbrella for the odd deluge, or a waterproof windbreaker. Mosquitoes can become quite a bother in summer around the lakes and along the rivers, especially the Danube. Bring or buy some good insect repellent.

SHIPPING LUGGAGE AHEAD

Imagine globetrotting with only a carry-on in tow. Shipping your luggage in advance via an air-freight service is a great way to cut down on backaches, hassles, and stress—especially if your packing list includes strollers, car-seats, etc. There are some things to be aware of, though. First, research carry-on restrictions; if you absolutely need something that isn't practical to ship and isn't allowed in carry-ons, this strategy isn't for you. Second, plan to send your bags several days in advance to U.S. destinations and as much as two weeks in advance to some international destinations. Third, plan to spend some money: it will cost least $100 to send a small piece of luggage, a golf bag, or a pair of skis to a domestic destination, much more to places overseas. Some people use Federal Express to ship their bags, but this can cost even more than air-freight services. All these services insure your bag (for most, the limit is $1,000, but you should verify that amount); you can, however, purchase additional insurance for about $1 per $100 of value.

Contacts **Luggage Concierge** (☎800/288–9818 ⊕www.luggageconcierge. com). **Luggage Free** (☎800/361–6871 ⊕www.luggagefree.com).

▌PASSPORTS & VISAS

U.S. citizens need only a valid passport to enter Austria for stays of up to three months.

▌TIP➔ Before your trip, make two copies of your passport's data page (one for some-

one at home and another for you to carry separately). Or scan the page and e-mail it to someone at home and/or yourself.

▌RESTROOMS

Vienna has a scattering of public toilets that are suitably clean and cost about €0.50 to use. Metro stations invariably have decent public facilities. Public toilets are less common outside the big cities, but you can usually use the facilities of hotels and restaurants without too much fuss. It's courteous to purchase something in a bar or restaurant beforehand, but this is rarely a problem and nothing that can't usually be resolved with a smile and a *Danke*. Gas stations along highways usually have restrooms attached, and these are generally open to the public whether you purchase gas or not. Cleanliness standards vary, but are usually on the acceptable side.

Find a Loo The Bathroom Diaries (⊕www. thebathroomdiaries.com) is flush with unsanitized info on restrooms the world over—each one located, reviewed, and rated.

▌SAFETY

Austrians are remarkably honest in their everyday dealings, and Vienna, given its size, is a refreshingly safe and secure city. That said, be sure to watch your purses and wallets in crowded spaces like subways and trams, and to take the standard precautions when walking at night along empty streets. The number of pickpocketing incidents has increased over the years. Be particularly careful if you're traveling with a bicycle. Here, as everywhere else, bikes routinely go missing. Always lock your bike firmly.

▌TIP➔ Distribute your cash, credit cards, IDs, and other valuables between a deep front pocket, an inside jacket or vest pocket, and a hidden money pouch. Don't reach for the money pouch once you're in public.

TAXES

The Value Added Tax (V.A.T.) in Austria is 20% generally, but this is reduced to 10% on food and clothing. If you are planning to take your purchases with you when you leave Austria (export them), you can get a refund. Wine and spirits are heavily taxed—nearly half of the sale price goes to taxes. For every contract signed in Austria (for example, car-rental agreements), you pay an extra 1% tax to the government, so tax on a rental car is 21%.

When making a purchase, ask for a V.A.T. refund form and find out whether the merchant gives refunds—not all stores do, nor are they required to. Have the form stamped like any customs form by customs officials when you leave the country or, if you're visiting several European Union countries, when you leave the EU. After you're through passport control, take the form to a refund-service counter for an on-the-spot refund (which is usually the quickest and easiest option), or mail it to the address on the form (or the envelope with it) after you arrive home. You receive the total refund stated on the form, but the processing time can be long, especially if you request a credit-card adjustment.

Global Refund is a Europe-wide service with 225,000 affiliated stores and more than 700 refund counters at major airports and border crossings. Its refund form, called a Tax Free Check, is the most common across the European continent. The service issues refunds in the form of cash, check, or credit-card adjustment.

V.A.T. Refunds Global Refund (⊕www. globalrefund.com).

TIME

The time difference between New York and Austria is 6 hours (so when it's 1 PM in New York, it's 7 PM in Vienna). The time difference between London and Vienna is 1 hour; between Sydney and Vienna, 14 hours; and between Auckland and Vienna, 13 hours.

Time Zones ⊕www.timeanddate.com/worldclock.

TIPPING

Although virtually all hotels and restaurants include service charges in their rates, tipping is still customary, but at a level lower than in the United States. In very small country inns such tips are not expected but are appreciated. In family-run establishments, tips are generally not given to immediate family members, only to employees. Tip the hotel concierge only for special services or in response to special requests. Maids normally get no tip unless your stay is a week or more or service has been special. Big tips are not usual in Austrian restaurants, since 10% has already been included in the prices.

TOURS

Guided tours are a good option when you don't want to do it all yourself. You travel along with a group (sometimes large, sometimes small), stay in prebooked hotels, eat with your fellow travelers (the cost of meals sometimes included in the price of your tour, sometimes not), and follow a schedule. But not all guided tours are an if-it's-Tuesday-this-must-be-Belgium experience. A knowledgeable guide can take you places that you might never discover on your own, and you may be pushed to see more than you would have otherwise. Tours aren't for everyone, but they can be just the thing for trips to places where making travel arrangements is difficult or time-consuming (particularly when you don't speak the language). Whenever you book a guided tour, find out what's included and what isn't. A "land-only" tour includes all your travel (by bus, in most cases) in the destination, but not necessarily your flights to and from or even within it. Also, in most cases prices in tour brochures don't include fees and taxes. And remember that you'll be expected to tip your guide (in cash) at the end of the tour.

Among companies that sell tours to Austria, the following are nationally known, have a proven reputation, and offer plenty of options. The classifications used below represent different price categories, and you'll probably encounter these terms when talking to a travel agent or tour operator. The key difference is usually in accommodations. Note that each company doesn't schedule tours to Austria every year; check by calling.

Super-Deluxe Abercrombie & Kent (☎800/554–7016 ⊕www.abercrombiekent.com). **Travcoa** (☎ 866/591–0070 ⊕ www.travcoa.com). Deluxe **Globus** (☎ 866/755–8581 ⊕ www.globusjourneys.com). **Maupintour** (☎800/255–4266 ⊕www.maupintour.com). **Tauck Tours** (☎ 800/788–7885 ⊕ www.tauck.com).

First-Class Brendan Tours (☎800/421–8446 ⊕www.brendanvacations.com). **Collette Tours** (☎800/340–5158 ⊕www.collette vacations.com). **DER Travel Services** (☎ 800/782–2424 ⊕www.der.com). **Gadabout Tours** (☎800/952–5068 ⊕www.gadabout tours.com). **Trafalgar Tours** (☎866/544–4434 ⊕www.trafalgartours.com).

Budget Cosmos (☎ 800/276–1241 ⊕www.cosmos.com). **Trafalgar Tours** (see above).

SPECIAL-INTEREST TOURS

BIKING

The Austrian national tourist information Web site ⊕*www.austria.info* includes excellent sections on hotels that welcome cyclists, as well as some of the better-known tours and routes.

You can no longer rent a bike at train stations in Austria. The cost of renting a bike (21-gear) from a local agency is around €30 a day. Tourist offices have details (in German), including maps and hints for trip planning and mealtime and overnight stops that cater especially to cyclists. Ask for the booklet "Radtouren in Österreich" or go to the Web site ⊕ www.radtouren.at. There's also a brochure in English: "Biking Austria—On the Trail of Mozart" that provides details in English

on the cycle route through the High Tauern mountains in Salzburg Province and neighboring regions in Bavaria (⊕*www.mozartradweg.com*).

■TIP→ **Most airlines accommodate bikes as luggage, provided they're dismantled and boxed.**

Contacts **Austria Radreisen** (☎07712/5511–0 ⊕www.austria-radreisen.at). **Backroads** (☎800/462–2848 ⊕www.backroads.com). **Butterfield & Robinson** (☎ 866/551–9090 from the U.S. and ☎ 800678–1477 from other countries ⊕www.butterfield.com). **Euro-Bike Tours** (☎800/321–6060 from the U.S. and ☎815/758–8851 from other countries ⊕www.eurobike.com). **Mountain Bike Hotels** (☎0810/101818 ⊕www.austria.info). **Pedal Power** (☎01/729-7234 ⊕ www.pedalpower.at). **VBT (Vermont Biking Tours)** (☎800/245–3868 ⊕ www.vbt.com) offers a spectacular Salzburg Sojourn tour.

CHRISTMAS/NEW YEAR'S

Contacts **Annemarie Victory Organization** (☎212/486–0353 ⊕*www.annemarievictory.com*) is known for its spectacular "New Year's Eve Ball in Vienna" excursion. Annemarie Victory also organizes a "Christmas in Salzburg" trip, with rooms at the Goldener Hirsch and a side trip to the Silent Night Chapel in Oberndorf. Smolka Tours (⇨*see Barge/River Cruises, above*) has also conducted festive holiday-season tours that included concerts, gala balls, and the famous Christmas Markets of Vienna and Salzburg.

ECO TOURS

Austria is a popular vacation spot for those who want to experience nature—many rural hotels offer idyllic bases for hiking in the mountains or lake areas. The concept of the *Urlaub am Bauernhof* (farm vacation), where families can stay on a working farm and children can help take care of farm animals, is increasingly popular throughout Austria. There are numerous outfitters that can provide information on basic as well as specialty farms, such as organic farms or farms for children, for the disabled, or for horse-back riders.

Contacts **Landidyll-Hotels in Österreich** (⊕www.landidyll.at)—unfortunately the Web site is in German only, but there are plenty of photos to show what the accommodations look like. **Austrian Tourist Board** (⊕www.austria.info).

Information on Farm Vacations **Farmhouse Holidays in Austria** (⊕www.farmholidays. com)—based in Salzburg, with an English language Web site and online booking. **Kärnten/ Landesverband Urlaub auf dem Bauernhof** (⊕www.urlaubambauernhof.com)—based in Carinthia and with English language Web site. **Oberösterreich/Das Land vor den Alpen** (Upper Austria ☎050/69–02–1248 ⊕www.upperaustria.farmholidays.com)— farm vacations in Upper Austria, English Web site. **Salzburg/Das Land der Tradition** (☎0662/870–571–248 ⊕www.salzburg. farmholidays.com). **Tirol/Das Land der Berge** (☎05/9292–1172 ⊕www.bauernhof.cc).

HIKING & MOUNTAIN CLIMBING

With more than 50,000 km (about 35,000 mi) of well-maintained mountain paths through Europe's largest reserve of unspoiled landscape, the country is a hiker's paradise. Three long-distance routes traverse Austria, including the E-6 from the Baltic, cutting across mid-Austria via the Wachau valley region of the Danube and on to the Adriatic. Wherever you are in Austria, you will find shorter hiking trails requiring varying degrees of ability. Routes are well marked, and maps are readily available from bookstores, the Österreichische Alpenverein/ÖAV, and the automobile clubs.

If you're a newcomer to mountain climbing or want to improve your skill, schools in Salzburg province will take you on. Ask the ÖAV for addresses. All organize courses and guided tours for beginners as well as for more advanced climbers.

Tourist offices have details on hiking holidays; serious climbers can write directly to Österreichischer Alpenverein/ÖAV (Austrian Alpine Club) for more information.

Membership in the club (€48.50, about $68.3) will give you a 30%–50% reduction from the regular fees for overnights in the 275 mountain refuges it operates in Austria and for huts operated by other mountain organizations in Europe. Membership also includes accident insurance for vacations of up to six weeks. Senior citizen memberships have a reduced price.

Contacts **Alpine Adventure Trails Tours** (☎888/478–4004 ⊕www.swisshiking. com). **Mountain Travel-Sobek** (☎ 888/831–7526 or 510/594–6000 ⊕www. mtsobek.com). **Österreichischer Alpenverein** (☎0512/59547 ⊕www.alpenverein.at).

▮ RESOURCES

ONLINE TRAVEL TOOLS

All About Austria For Austria, here are some top Web sites: **train information** (⊕www.oebb. at) (select English from the drop-down menu) and **Austria. At Last!** (⊕www.austria.info). "**About Austria**" (⊕www.aboutaustria.org) is a nice general overview of facts and figures.

All About Salzburg For basic information: **Salzburg** (⊕www.salzburg.info).

All About Vienna For basic information: **Vienna** (⊕www.wien.info). Here are some other top Web sites for Vienna: **Wien Online** (⊕www. magwien.gv.at)—the city government's official Web site; **Wienerzeitung** (⊕www.wienerzei tung.at)—a newspaper site with English translation; **Die Presse** (⊕www.diepresse.at)—German only, but the Web site of the city's leading serious newspaper; **Die Falter** (⊕www.falter. at)—unfortunately also mostly in German, but with excellent movie and restaurant reviews and comprehensive coverage of the city's "alternative" scene; **Time Out Vienna** (⊕www.timeout. com/vienna/index.html); **Jirsa Tickets Wien** (⊕www.viennaticket.at/english)—for prebooking event tickets online; and **MuseumsQuartier** (⊕www.mqw.at)—for the scoop on what's happening in Vienna's trendy museum quarter.

VISITOR INFORMATION

Austrian National Tourist Office (☎212/944–6880 ⊕www.austria.info).

INDEX

NOTES

NOTES

NOTES

NOTES

NOTES

NOTES

NOTES

NOTES